Sexual Disorders

Sexual Disorders

TREATMENT, THEORY, AND RESEARCH

C. David Tollison

and

Henry E. Adams

GARDNER PRESS, INC.
New York

The case histories presented in this book represent
compilations of different patients seen by the
authors. Any identifying description resembling
any person, living or dead, is purely accidental.

Gardner Press, Inc.
19 Union Square West
New York 10003

Library of Congress Cataloging in Publication Data

Tollison, C   David, 1949–
    Sexual disorders.

    Bibliography: p.
    Includes indexes.
    1. Sexual disorders. I. Adams, Henry E., 1931–
joint author. II. Title. [DNLM: 1. Sex deviation.
2. Sex disorders. WM611 T651s]
RC556.T64   616.8'583   79-20853
ISBN 0-89876-029-1

Printed in the United States of America

This book is dedicated to our patients.

CONTENTS

PREFACE

This book is designed to introduce students and professionals to an applied approach in the assessment and treatment of sexual deviations and dysfunctions. The orientation of the book is behavioral, although contrasting psychoanalytic and psychodynamic approaches are presented. The book is divided into three major sections: (1) foundations of sexual behavior; (2) sexual dysfunctions; and (3) sexual deviations. A prevailing emphasis throughout is attention to the components of specific sexual deviations and dysfunctions, etiology and maintenance, assessment, and treatment. Numerous case histories are dispersed throughout the text to illustrate the etiology of such disorders as well as assessment and treatment techniques employed in actual clinical practice.

While there are a number of texts which discuss sexual dysfunctions, this book is unique in a number of important ways. First, it represents, to our knowledge, the only attempt to discuss treatment, theory, and research of sexual dysfunctions *and deviations.* With attention to both sexual deviations and dysfunctions, this approach represents the only applied reference source of this type available to students and practitioners. Second, it discusses not only the psychological treatment of sexual disorders but chemotherapy and surgical interventions in specific sexual disorders as well. As a result, we believe that the text will be of particular interest to both psychologists and physicians. Third, this text targets the reading toward those students and practitioners who demand specificity in the actual mechanics of assessment and treatment of sexual disorders. The area of sex and behavioral sex therapy is certainly one of the most popular areas in psychology today, yet interested individuals are often forced to resort to various and scattered journal articles in an effort to learn how most effectively to treat disorders of a sexual nature. A distinct effort was made in the preparation of this text to develop a comprehensive yet easy to read book that presents, in a logical and concise fashion, the components of sexually deviant and dysfunctional behaviors and specific techniques of assessment and treatment. Finally, our text represents the only attempt thus far to formulate and outline behavioral etiological theories for specific sexual disorders. As such, we believe that the text will also serve as a valuable reference text for both researchers and clinicians.

C.D.T.
H.E.A.

ACKNOWLEDGMENTS

Many individuals have contributed to this book and we are pleased to acknowledge their assistance. Several students evaluated preliminary drafts of portions of the manuscript, including Betsy Lamson, Bob Moss, and Tracy Potts Carson. Dr. Mary Baine extensively edited and contributed constructive comments regarding style and presentation for which we are most grateful. Joan Hoffman, Debbie Spivey, and Peg Bryant greatly facilitated the preparation of the book by their unflagging and uncomplaining efforts in typing various portions of the manuscript.

While working with patients in distress, we have often seen the unfortunate effects of the absense of a spouse due to work-related commitments. Writing this book in addition to our daily responsibilities of patient care and study has often kept us away from our homes. We are indebted to our wives and children for their tolerance of our absenses and for their support throughout.

C.D.T.
H.E.A.

INTRODUCTION

Of all the biological drives, sex is the one with which our society seems most preoccupied. On the one hand, society attempts a careful governing of sexual expression and behavior through legal and social contingencies, rules, and expectations; yet, on the other, it allows a vast exploitation of the power of sex. At the same time as many forms of sexuality are condemned as illicit, such mass-communications media as the motion picture industry, the publishing industry, and the advertising industry are allowed to utilize quite effectively the powerful influences of sexuality. While the resulting conflict has produced some of the world's great literature as well as some of its most famous philosophical and psychological speculation, it has also produced a great amount of anxiety and human suffering. One may safely conjecture that all too many people have been led to question with the poet:

Why were we crucified into sex?
Why were we not left rounded off, and finished in ourselves.
As we began . . . so perfectly alone?
(D.H. Lawrence, "Tortoise Shout")

Our society is presently engaged in a widespread questioning of traditional sexual mores. More and more we are coming to realize that the preferences which govern sexual behavior, and the expressions and activities which constitute it vary widely from individual to individual and from culture to culture. Gradually, sometimes all too gradually, we are beginning to challenge the male and female "Archie Bunkers" who look upon sexual behavior that differs from their own as intolerable, lewd, perverted, or at best inappropriate. The imposition of puritanical sexual standards on others is being questioned. Many sexual patterns once considered "perverse" or "immoral" are being examined anew; some are even being redefined as desirable. Sexual myths are being explored and we are beginning to see that an orgasmically dysfunctional woman may need more than "a real man" to bring her to orgasm, that women respond differently from men in sexual relationships, that impotent males are not "just faggots," that homosexuals are not "some kind of weird perverts," and that oral-genital sex may not be "disgusting." We are discovering through research and

xix

more open attitudes that the vast majority of men and women, both single and married, masturbate frequently and that approximately 50 percent of women prefer masturbation or other noncoital forms of stimulation to intercourse and respond more intensely to them. We now know that, within the upper socioeconomic classes, oral-genital contact is commonly practiced and that the "missionary" or man-on-top position is not the most popular position for sexual intercourse outside the United States. Many people now consider homosexuality a permissible alternative to heterosexual relationships and are organizing in an attempt to reverse the legal sanctions imposed against homosexuality (Davison, 1976). Wife-swapping, group sex, and premarital and extramarital relationships are considered by some to be the route to honest and open interpersonal relationships. As the noted sex researchers Kinsey, Pomeroy, and Martin (1948) reported, "In spite of society's efforts over the years to suppress all but marital sexual relationships, a considerable portion of all the sexual acts in which the human animal engages still fall into the category which the culture rates as perverse" (p.28).

The recent re-examination of human sexuality and sexual patterns once considered perverse or psychologically classified as deviant has effected major changes in attitudes among mental health personnel. Some theories of sexual behavior now begin with the assumption that there are no "normal" and "abnormal" sexual behaviors and that these labels often represent nothing more than the way in which society views certain behaviors (Ullmann & Krasner, 1969; Davison, 1976). We must remember, of course, that the inclusion or exclusion of any sexual disorder or psychiatric entity in the *Diagnostic and Statistical Manual of Mental Disorders, Second Edition* (DSM II), the major diagnostic classification manual of the American Psychiatric Association, is determined largely by majority opinion. While physicians can recognize and agree that a certain condition such as a perforated ulcer is a physical disorder, mental health personnel do not find their task as simple because they often deal with behaviors and cognitions. Thus the behavioral clinician cannot simply x-ray a patient in order to diagnose a sexual disorder or dysfunction. The fact of the matter is that the classification of a certain behavior as normal or abnormal depends largely on societal influences. Thus, organized homosexual lobby groups were successful in influencing the APA to vote homosexuality out of the sexual deviance classification. Homosexuality hasn't changed, society has.

Although what is considered abnormal varies from individual to individual and from society to society, certain sexual behaviors are almost universally considered abnormal or inappropriate and are often termed *sexually deviant* behaviors. Societies vary little in classifying pedophilia, necrophilia, and certain fetishes as deviant. These modes of sexual expression are generally termed deviant because of what society considers to be an inappropriate object or method of sexual gratification. On the other hand, certain other sexual behaviors also considered undesirable by society are associated more with sexual performance than with the object or method of gratification. These behaviors are generally termed *sexual dysfunctions* and include such problems as impotence in the male and orgasmic dysfunctions in the female. For the most part, however, labels such as sexually deviant, dysfunctional, and even sexual disorder serve little purpose other than structuring our discussion of certain sexual behaviors. As Kinsey and his colleagues have noted, "The prominence given to classification of behavior as normal or abnormal, and the long list of special terms used for classifying such behavior, usually represent moralistic classifications rather than any scientific attempt to discover the origin of such behavior, or to determine their real social significance" (Kinsey, Pomeroy, Martin, & Gebhard, 1953, pp. 645–646). Or, as Thomas Szasz states more succinctly, "Perversion . . .[is] sexual practice disapproved by the speaker" (1974, p. 12).

REFERENCES

Davison, G. C. Homosexuality: The ethical challenge. *Journal of Consulting and Clinical Psychology,* 1976, 44, 157–162.

Kinsey, A. C., Pomeroy, W. B., & Martin, C. E. *Sexual behavior in the human male.* Philadelphia: W. B. Saunders, 1948.

Kinsey, A. C., Pomeroy, W. B., Martin, C. E., & Gebhard, P. H. *Sexual behavior in the human female.* Philadelphia: W. B. Saunders, 1953.

Szasz, T. S. *The mythology of mental illness* (3rd ed.). New York: Harper & Row, 1974.

Ullmann, L. P., & Krasner, L. *A psychological approach to abnormal behavior.* Englewood Cliffs, N. J.: Prentice-Hall, 1969.

CHAPTER 1

The Components
of Sexual Behavior

Human sexuality is a complex biological and psychological phenomenon which controls or subtly influences a variety of human behaviors. Our sexuality influences not only our sexual practices, but also our mannerisms, dress, speech characteristics, mode of interpersonal interaction, and numerous other behavior patterns. One method of attempting to understand the complex phenomenon of human sexuality is to organize it in terms of distinct but related components (Barlow, 1974). The major component of sexuality is sexual arousal, which is concerned with the biological and psychological nature of the sexual response. Other components include gender role, heterosocial, and heterosexual behaviors. In this chapter we will discuss these components of sexual behavior in order to illustrate in the remainder of the book how they interact to determine or influence sexual orientation and adjustment.

SEXUAL AROUSAL

Sexual arousal describes a number of psychological and physiological states in response to erotic stimuli, varying from mild excitement to a generalized state of physiological hyperactivity preceding and accompanying orgasm. Somewhat different but complementary physiological changes occur in both sexes during sexual arousal. As Kaplan (1974) has noted, these changes are not limited to the genital area. On the contrary, sexual stimulation and arousal elicit neurological, vascular, muscular, and hormonal reactions which affect the functioning of the entire body.

Penile erection is recognized as the most accurate measurement of male sexual arousal (Abel, Barlow, Blanchard, & Mavissakalian, 1975), and the degree of the erection is considered proportional to the degree of stimulation, whether this stimulation be internal (fantasy) or external (Freund, Langevin, Cibiri, & Zajac, 1973). Sex researchers generally agree on the validity and reliability of penile tumescence as an arousal index

1

(Bancroft, 1971; Zuckerman, 1971); on penile erection as the major physiological and psychological response in sexual arousal (Masters & Johnson, 1966); and on penile circumference change as a response specific to sexual arousal (Barlow, Becker, Leitenberg, & Agras, 1970). Obviously, penile erection is a necessary precursor to any consummatory sexual behavior. Galvanic skin response, heart rate, and other physiological indices which have been employed as measures of sexual arousal (Solyom & Beck, 1967) may be elicited by emotional states not correlated with sexual arousal (Lacey, Bateman, & Van Lehn, 1953; Montague & Coles, 1966), whereas penile erection during the waking state seems to occur infrequently in the absence of sexual arousal (Barlow et al., 1970). Bartlett (1956), as well as Masters and Johnson (1966), reported increased heart rate, respiration, and blood pressure during sexual activity such as masturbation and coitus, but did not find these reported responses during inactive sexual arousal. On the other hand, Wenger, Averill, and Smith (1968) employed 16 male participants to determine peripheral autonomic responses to reading pornographic literature. They found that the responses of these individuals to sexual and nonsexual literature showed significant differences only in blood pressure and skin conductance; respiration rate, basal temperature, heart rate, and finger pulse volume were not different. Bancroft and Matthews (1971), in a study with 10 males, measured penile erection, electrodermal response, heart rate, and forearm blood flow to sexual and nonsexual stimuli, and found a differential response only with penile erection.

Less information is available about the sexual arousal of females because of the difficulties in physiologically measuring female arousal, and also the fact that until recently societal and cultural norms discouraged sexual experimentation with females. However, recent research has suggested that vaginal blood volume and pressure pulse can reliably differentiate stages of sexual arousal in females, and that this may be a response similar to penile erection in males (Geer, Morokoff, & Greenwood, 1974). A brief review of the anatomical and physiological aspects of sexual arousal in men and women may clarify the mechanisms of these responses.

Anatomy of the Genitalia

The male genitalia consist, in part, of the *testes* and *penis*. The testes produce sperm, which later mixes with prostatic fluid to form *semen*. Semen is a thick, white, milky alkalkine fluid that consists of various chemical substances including citric acid, calcium, cholesterol, protein, and various enzymes and acids. The substance of semen, or ejaculate, varies from male to male and even within the same individual at different times. The testes, while responsive to gentle massage, are very sensitive and can be injured easily, causing waves of nausea and pain.

The penis is composed primarily of spongy erectile tissue that becomes engorged with blood to produce an erection. Erection is lost when blood leaves the penis faster through the veins than it flows in through the arteries. The *glans* is the smooth head of the penis which contains the urethral opening for urinating and ejaculating. The glans of the penis is the most sexually sensitive and excitable part of a man's body (McCary, 1973). The *corona* is the ridge adjoining the back edge of the glans at the juncture of the glans and penile shaft. The corona consists of a number of nerve endings and becomes highly sensitive to sexual stimulation during arousal. The *penile shaft* is covered with thin loose skin that stretches as the penis becomes erect. Encompassing the glans is a section of penile shaft skin, the *prepuce*, which is partially removed during circumcision.

The female genitalia are made up of both internal and external organs. The internal organs serve the primary function of reproduction, and consist of four-fifths of the *vagina*. The external organs are collectively termed the *vulva* and consist specifically of the *mons veneris, labia majora, labia minora, clitoris, vestibule,* and the outer one-fifth of the vagina. We shall discuss here only those organs whose partial function involves sexual stimulation and excitment.

The vagina serves as the muscular receptive tube for the penis during intercourse. The internal four-fifths of the vagina extends vertically upward in a standing woman, and measures approximately 3 inches long on the front wall and 3.5 inches on the back wall; however, the vagina extends its length during sexual arousal. During sexual excitement small beads of lubrication appear on the walls of the vagina, and occasionally the puboccygeus muscles surrounding the vagina will spontaneously contract, forcing the lubricant out of the vagina in a spurting fashion. This occasional spurting of vaginal lubricant, together with vaginal muscle contractions during orgasm may be responsible for the mistaken notion that the female ejaculates during sexual intercourse much like a male. The vagina contains few nerve endings, yet vaginal penetration is reported to play a major role in the enjoyment and satisfaction of sexual activities for many women. McCary (1973) claims that vaginal penetration may provide more psychological than physiological pleasure to a woman during intercourse.

The mons veneris consists of layers of fatty tissue covering the pubic bone. Nerve endings located in the mons veneris can produce sexual arousal when stimulated by the pressure and weight of a sexual partner or a similar stimulus. The labia minora are located within the lips of the labia majora, and are highly sensitive to sexual stimulation. The lips of the labia minora join at the top of the vaginal orifice to form the prepuce which encloses the clitoris. The clitoris, like the penis, is composed of spongy erectile tissue which becomes engorged with blood during sexual excitement and is the most sexually excitable area of a woman's body. The clitoris is located at the top of the vestibule and is covered, except for the glans, by the labia minora. During intercourse the clitoris is stimulated by pulling and tugging of the labia minor as the penis moves in and out of the vagina, or by pressure and friction against the clitoris by the man's pubic bone. Masters and Johnson (1966) claim that during masturbation most females tend to stimulate the side of the clitoris rather than stimulate it directly. The vestibule is located with the labia minora and encircles the vaginal orifice. This area is highly sensitive to sexual stimulation. Located on either side of the vaginal orifice are the *Bartholin's glands*, which secrete a small amount of lubricating fluid around the vaginal orifice during sexual arousal.

Various nongenital areas of the body are also sensitive to sexual stimulation. The inner and outer regions of the thighs, abdomen, buttocks, and the breasts, particularly the nipples, have numerous free nerve endings. Other areas such as the earlobes, neck, mouth, and tongue are highly sensitive to sexual stimulation (McCary, 1973).

Development of Sexual Differentiation

Sexual differentiation of males and females begins at conception when the female receives two X-chromosomes and the male an X and a Y chromosome. These events initiate but do not determine sexual morphology. With the exception of the gonads, the development of male and female sex structures during fetal ontogeny is dependent upon the presence or absence of testicular hormones. Under the influence of these sexual hormones the gonads begin to function early in the prenatal period and produce male hormones (androgens). In males these hormones circulating in the blood stream at critical periods sensitize target tissue. The internal duct system is influenced so that the vas deferens and seminal vesicles develop, and the differentiation of the fallopian tubes and uterus is suppressed. At a slightly later time the external morphology becomes a penis and scrotum rather than clitoris, labia majora, and a vagina. On the other hand, if the gonads become ovaries, only small amounts of hormones are released during the fetal life, the result being an absence of the testicular hormones and the consequent development of the female anatomy. This initial process is relatively complete by the third prenatal month, although gradual development continues until pubescence when, with the sudden increase of sexual hormones, the individual develops secondary sex characteristics and the differentiation between the sexes becomes more exaggerated.

Physiological Mechanisms of Arousal

Penile erection results from stimulation of the parasympathetic division of the autonomic nervous system. Neural impulses which pass through the nervi erigentes from the sacral portion of the spinal column to the penis dilate the arteries and constrict the veins of the penis (to a lesser degree), allowing arterial blood to flow under high pressure into the erectile tissue of the penis. This erectile tissue dilates greatly when arterial blood flows into it so that the penis becomes hard and elongated.

When flaccid, the adult penis averages from 2.5 to 4 inches in length, is slightly over 1 inch in diameter, and is about 3.5 inches in circumference (Masters & Johnson, 1970). The size of the flaccid penis varies considerably from man to man. When erect, the penis averages around 5.5 to 6.5 inches in length, about 1.5 inches in diameter, and about 4.5 inches in circumference. The size of the erect penis also varies between individuals, although less so than the flaccid penis (Masters & Johnson, 1970).

The physiology of female sexual arousal is similar. Located around the introitus and extending into the clitoris is erectile tissue which also is controlled by the parasympathetic nerves that pass through the nervi erigentes from the sacral plexus to the external genitalia. In the early phases of sexual arousal, the parasympathetic impulses dilate the arteries to the erectile tissues and allow rapid blood flow into the tissue. Parasympathetic impulses also pass to the Bartholin's glands located beneath the labia minora to cause secretion of mucus immediately inside the introitus. This mucus, along with large quantities of mucus secreted by the vaginal mucosa itself, is responsible for appropriate lubrication before and during sexual intercourse.

Psychological Arousal

The idea that there are marked differences in susceptibility to sexual arousal in men and women has little scientific basis. Research has demonstrated that female sexual arousal is as intense as that of males. Evidence also suggests that there is little difference in the degree to which men and women respond to sexually arousing stimuli. McCary (1973) claims that while women may respond in a slightly different manner and to slightly different stimuli than men, both sexes are equally aroused by sexual literature, films, and fantasies. Osborne and Pollack (1977) have presented evidence to suggest that women may become more sexually aroused to "soft core" sexual literature than to explicit "hard core" erotic literature. Their results indicated that while both types of erotic literature produced sexual arousal as measured by the vaginal photoplethysmograph (this instrument will be discussed in Chapter 2), soft core literature produced more physiologic and subjective sexual arousal.

While knowledge of the anatomy and physiology of male and female sexual arousal is necessary to understand the arousal component of sexual behavior, such knowledge does not reveal the complete story. Given the similarities in anatomical and physiological sexual functioning, why do some men or women become sexually aroused to females while others are aroused to males? Both homosexual and heterosexual males or females respond sexually in the same anatomical and physiological manner, but differ distinctly in what kind of sexual stimuli set the anatomical and physiological mechanisms in motion. To understand these individual differences in the ways that sexual arousal can be elicited requires a knowledge of learning principles and how they interact with biological processes.

Sexual arousal and behavior have a physiological bases in that physical stimulation of the genitals is innately pleasurable and orgasm intensely so; however, patterns of behavior associated with sexual arousal and gratification are largely the result of conditioning and learning which begin almost at birth. Nothing in the undifferentiated sexual potentialities of an infant guarantees that the final result will be a heterosexual arousal pattern. Individuals may develop a very wide variety of patterns of sexual preferences and behaviors. Whether an adult views himself or herself as male or female, is sexually aroused to members of the same or the opposite sex, prefers tall or short partners, prefers brief or extended periods of foreplay, is sexually aroused to feet or breasts is a function of learning history. Learning experience largely determines sexual arousal, practices, preferences, and expression. While many experiences influence the unique behavior of a given individual, many authorities consider masturbation and sexual arousal as major factors in the conditioning of stimuli eliciting a sexual response, at least in males (McGuire, Carlisle, & Young, 1965).

Masturbation and Sexual Arousal

It is safe to say that most individuals have engaged in masturbation. Various studies have reported that 92-100 per cent of men and 58-85 per cent of women have masturbated at some point in thier lives (Dearborn, 1967; Kinsey, Pomeroy, & Martin, 1948; Kinsey, Pomeroy, Martin, & Gebhard, 1953). It is also probably safe to assume that the vast majority of those individuals who masturbate do so without considering the effects of masturbation on the shaping and the strengthening of their "personal" pattern of sexual arousal. More about this effect later, but first let us see how the practice of masturbation, which once was condemned by our society has become a more acceptable mode of sexual activity.

Our earliest accounts of society's condemnation of masturbation can be traced to a unique interpretation of the Bible and to the practice of early medicine. In 1758 a physician named Tissot wrote a book entitled *Onania, or a Treatise Upon the Disorders Produced by Masturbation*, which claimed that masturbation was the cause of most of the physical, emotional, and spiritual problems that plague mortal man (and woman). This text had a powerful effect upon both the public and medicine, and later resulted in doctors' attempts to detect those unfortunate souls who committed such acts. Physicians employed various diagnostic tests to distinguish the masturbators from the nonmasturbators. If a woman was easily angered, acted shy or timid in the presence of her husband or parents, and had a tendency to lie, the physician was not fooled: he had discovered a masturbator. In males, the inability to love anyone, a downcast appearance, easy blushing, and a lack of emotion were acceptable diagnostic signs of a masturbator.

Although many myths recount the dangers of masturbation to both body and mind, none of them have any proven scientific value (Johnson, 1968). Even today some athletic coaches warn that masturbation and sexual intercourse will weaken a man and should therefore be avoided before athletic contests! Masturbation does not weaken an individual, nor does it lead to insanity, blindness, moral depravity, or "hair on the palms of the hands." There is also no such thing as "excessive masturbation," for the body will simply refuse to respond when a state of sexual cessation occurs.

Masturbation may, however, have an effect on the patterning of sexual arousal. Some behavior therapists believe that the sexual stimuli employed in masturbation will acquire through the reinforcement of orgasm a positive valence (McGuire, et al., 1965). In simple terms, a common sexual thought or fantasy employed during masturbation will become conditioned (strengthened) through repeated reinforcement (orgasm) until a pattern of sexual arousal to that stimuli is established (Rachman & Hodgson, 1968). For example, a young male may masturbate to a picture of a tall, large-breasted nude female found in one of his father's "men's magazines." Through repeated masturbation and orgasm he establishes a pattern of sexual arousal to tall women with large breasts. It should now be obvious why some men jokingly refer to themselves as "leg men," "rear men," or "breast men," while others are aroused to stimuli such as other males, children, articles of clothing, or even activities such as violence. In males, and perhaps females, masturbation plays a crucial role in the development, patterning, and expression of sexual arousal.

GENDER ROLE BEHAVIOR AND SEXUAL IDENTIFICATION

Another major component of sexual behavior is *gender role behavior*, that is, the enactment of behaviors labeled as masculine or feminine. Sexual identity is the acceptance of one's biological gender and is distinct from gender role behavior. For example, a woman may identify herself as belonging to the female gender, yet exhibit behaviors traditionally characteristic of males. Gender role behaviors and sexual identity are not always positively correlated.

The development of appropriate gender role behavior is the result of the developmental learning process which begins at birth. Traditionally male infants are dressed in blue and female infants in pink. The learning process continues into early childhood when boys may be given guns and footballs as toys while girls get dolls, and after that into early adulthood, when males are encouraged to engage in sports and become doctors, while girls are influenced to be cheerleaders and become nurses.

Modeling is another important component of teaching a child gender role behaviors. Children model their behaviors from the behaviors of their same-sex parent as well as from those of other adults and learn, over a period of time, those behaviors traditionally associated with and expected from members of their sex. These deeply ingrained ideas of typical masculine or feminine behavior may later become a problem in sexual therapy. For instance, in the treatment of female sexual dysfunctions, the woman is often requested to take a more active role in the sexual relationship and assume a female-superior position during intercourse. If the man and the woman have been conditioned to perceive this type of "aggressiveness" as atypical of traditional male-female sexual interaction, enthusiastic adherence to the treatment program may be threatened.

A percentage of patients, particularly those with certain patterns of deviant arousal, may exhibit variance in gender role behavior. These individuals may exhibit behaviors more appropriate to the opposite sex. This inappropriate gender role behavior is most commonly exhibited in the effeminate homosexual and transsexual. The case of a 21-year-old homosexual male who requested treatment to change his sexual orientation illustrates this point. During the initial interview, the patient sat with his buttocks resting tightly against the back of his chair, and his legs crossed one knee on the other. His voice was high-pitched, and he spoke with a slight lisp. Throughout the conversation he made exaggerated motor and facial gestures. He wore several rings on each hand, and continually toyed with his fingernails and rings throughout the interview. It was discovered during the interview that his father had died when the patient was an infant, and he was raised by his mother, an aunt, and four older sisters. When he was a child he would entertain himself by playing dolls with his sisters and allow them to dress him up as a girl by applying his mother's facial make up. His mother and his aunt would then reinforce him for playing with his sisters, and for not leaving the house to venture down the street where the neighborhood boys played each day. When he began school his classmates called him sissy, so that he began to withdraw further from contact with males and thus further decreased his opportunities to model male gender role behaviors.

Closely associated with those patients who exhibit behaviors of the opposite sex are those who verbalize a preference for the role of the opposite sex. When opposite-sex behavior is completely adopted and the patient consistently thinks, feels, and behaves in an opposite-sex role, this mistaken gender identity is termed *transsexualism* (Green & Money, 1969). These patients often request surgery to reassign their sex. Male transsexuals, for example, often describe themselves as being a female "trapped in a male body." These patients often describe themselves as feeling more comfortable in the opposite-sex gender role, and should not be confused with the transvestite who experiences sexual pleasure from cross-dressing.

Some evidence suggests that problems of gender role may manifest themselves in early childhood. Normal boys will occasionally display behaviors that are socially assigned to girls. Conversely, girls will occasionally behave as tomboys. This exploration and flexibility is, obviously, part of the normal socialization process. Rekers (1977) states that on rare occasions, however, behavior that may have begun as curiosity-induced exploration of sex-role stereotypes becomes a persistent pattern. One such example is the boy who rejects the male role and insists that he is a girl or wishes to become a girl.

Rekers (1977) distinguishes four types of childhood gender disturbance: (1) excessive femininity in boys; (2) excessive masculinity in boys; (3) excessive femininity in girls; and (4) excessive masculinity in girls. Of these four potential types of gender disturbance in children, research deals almost exclusively with the case of the extremely feminine boy. This state of the literature is, in part, a function of the finding that problems of gender dysfunction and sexual deviations occur more frequently in males than in females (Green & Money, 1969; Kinsey et al., 1948; Money & Ehrhardt, 1972; Stoller, 1969) and the relatively greater concern by American parents over feminine sex-role behavior in their sons (Rekers, 1977).

Rosen, Rekers, and Friar (1977) have differentiated two basic syndromes: gender behavior disturbance; and cross-gender identification in physically normal boys who display feminine behavior. The boy with gender behavior disturbance has adopted feminine behaviors to a greater or lesser degree, but does not show an identification with the opposite gender. This syndrome involves cross-gender clothing preferences, actual or imagined use of cosmetic articles, feminine gestures and mannerisms, feminine voice inflection, predominantly feminine speech content, and aversion to masculine sex-typed activities. These behaviors are coupled with a preference for girl playmates, feminine activities, and female roles in play. On the other hand, the boy with cross-gender identification not only behaves in a feminine way, but truly wishes, fantasizes, or believes that he is a girl (Greenson, 1966; Stoller, 1964, 1965). This identification is evidenced in his verbal statements about his desire or preference to be a girl or mother, to bear children and breast feed infants, and to have his penis removed (Rekers, 1972, 1977; Rekers & Lovaas, 1974).

There are, unfortunately, no published studies that report the base rate for gender disturbances in the general population of boys. There are only limited longitudinal data to indicate, for example, what percentage of feminine boys spontaneously outgrow gender disturbance, what percentage grow up to become adult transsexuals, what percentage develop into homosexual transvestites, and what percentage become adult male homosexuals.

HETEROSOCIAL BEHAVIOR

In clinical practice many patients may have adequate sexual arousal patterns as well as the necessary behavioral repertoire to engage in the genital aspects of sex. However, these patients may be unable to engage in the type of social behavior necessary for meeting, dating, and relating to persons of the opposite sex (Barlow, 1977). When patients exhibit these inabilities they are considered to be demonstrating a deficiency in *heterosocial skills*. We shall limit our discussion to heterosocial behaviors associated with sexual behavior since a discussion of all heterosocial behaviors would be beyond the scope of this book.

The components of heterosocial behavior may be divided into social behaviors necessary to initiate relationships with the opposite sex; social and interpersonal behaviors preceding sexual behavior; and behaviors required to maintain heterosocial relationships. A skills deficit in one or more of these areas often results in such complaints as, "I just can't seem to get any dates"; or "I get dates, but they never call back again"; or even, "I just don't have many friends of the opposite sex."

Initiating Heterosocial Behavior

Lack of social skills necessary to initiate relationships with the opposite sex is the most commonly observed type of heterosocial deficit. The types of behaviors required to initiate such relationships are numerous, but we will discuss five general categories. The first category may be defined as the ability to ask *open-ended* questions (Arkowitz, Lichtenstein, McGovern, & Hines, 1975). For example, James is introduced to Kathy at a university party for incoming freshmen. James says, "So you're going to be attending school here, huh?" Kathy replies, "Yes." James then searches desperately for another question, and asks, "Have you bought your season football tickets yet?" Kathy responds, "No, I don't like football." Giving up, James excuses himself and leaves.

If James had been skilled in the art of asking open-ended questions, the entire conversation might have been different. Open-ended questions call for more than a "yes-no" type of response. Asking open-ended questions facilitates a smooth flowing conversation and is an essential part of initiating conversation with the same or opposite sex (Twentyman & McFall, 1975).

A second important category is the art of the *extended conversation* (Glasgow & Arkowitz, 1975). Extended conversation is closely related to open-ended questions in that both are techniques for soliciting participation of both parties in the conversation and serve to keep the conversation flowing. Extended conversation may best be thought of as one participant's taking the statement of another participant and responding to it in such a way as to extend or prolong the conversation within the same topic area. For example, Gregg and Caroline meet at a real estate convention, and sit down at a bar to have a drink. Gregg says, "This is my first trip to New York. Wow! It's even bigger than I thought." Caroline has many potential responses to this statement, including "Yeah!" or "It sure is." But instead she elects to extend the conversation by responding, "In a city this big there are so many things to see and do. Last night my girlfriend and I went to a taping of the Merv Griffin show." Gregg, in turn, extends the conversation even further by adding, "I went to the Merv Griffin show last year when he was taping in Miami. I especially enjoyed his band that played when he broke for commercials." Caroline then picks up the topic of music and bands and carries the conversation further.

Extended conversations serve a useful function not only in keeping the conversation flowing, but also by demonstrating an interest in the topic of conversation and in the conversational participant and by serving as an avenue for *self-disclosure* (McDonald, Lindquist, Kramer, McGrath, & Rhyne, 1975). Self-disclosure is an important component in developing close social relationships as well as contributing substance to conversation (Jourard, 1971). Appropriate self-disclosure enables the conversational partners to get to know each other amid what some consider the superficialities of initial conversation. Individuals who adamantly refuse to discuss themselves under any circumstances, preferring to maintain complete privacy, or individuals who tell intimate personal details of their lives in initial interactions are both unlikely to establish or maintain friendships. One example of the tell all conversationalist is George, who met Barbara on a blind date arranged by a mutual friend. Barbara asked, "Have you lived in Los Angeles all of your life?" George inappropriately responded,

No, I moved here with my first wife about four years ago. We moved here so that she could finish college at UCLA. When she left me for one of her professors, I decided to move back to Kansas, but I met this topless dancer, and before long I was married. The four men she was living with were selling dope so I went in with them for fast money. That's how I ended up in jail. When I got out of jail, I said to myself, "What the hell, why not stay here in Los Angeles!" How about you, have you lived here long?

Although this fictitious illustration may be somewhat extreme, it does illustrate that telling all is as inappropriate as telling nothing.

A fourth component of initiating relationships is appropriate *eye contact* (Arkowitz et al., 1975). Maintaining appropriate eye contact during a conversation enables a person to appear interested in what the other has to say. The old adage, "He can't be trusted because he has shifty eyes," has, in fact, an element of truth. Appropriate eye contact during a conversation does add an element of sincerity and confidence to the interaction (Goldberg, Kiesler, & Collins, 1969). If you want an illustration of this fact, the next time you are at a party or in a situation in which you are to meet a number of people, observe the eye-contact behavior of those you meet. You will, no doubt, see that some are quite skilled at it, while others have difficulty in maintaining appropriate eye contact. Now take the experiment one step further and note your initial impression of those who maintain eye contact and those who do not. Chances are that your initial impression of those maintaining eye contact will generally be more favorable.

The final component of initiating relationships with the opposite sex is *appropriate physical appearance* (Berscheid & Walter, 1974). Curran and Lippold (1975) claim that physical appearance is one of the most powerful determinants of heterosocial attraction. For example, Joan was introduced to Mark at a student newspaper party. Although she was initially attracted to him, she soon noticed that he alternated between leaning against the wall and shifting his weight from one leg to the other. He also stood with his shoulders slumped, and his entire appearance gave the impression that standing was taking all his energy. Joan noticed what she could only interpret as Mark's discomfort, and suggested they sit down. Upon sitting, however, Mark slumped far down into the sofa and propped his feet up on the coffee table. Sitting in such a position he was unable to drink properly and proceeded to spill his drink on his shirt, an event that prompted Joan to go in search of other company. While Mark thought he was giving the impression of being "cool," Joan got the distinct impression that he was crude and totally uninterested in her or their conversation.

Social Behaviors
Preceding Sexual Behavior

A major component of heterosocial behavior is social and interpersonal behaviors preceding sexual behavior (Barlow, 1974). These behaviors are more nebulous in nature than those behaviors required to initiate a relationship with the opposite sex, and have not been investigated as extensively. Three major types of presexual and interpersonal behaviors are *self-disclosure, rewardingness,* and *ingratiation.*

Self-disclosure may be used not only to help initiate a relationship, but also to add substance, depth, and interest to the ensuing relationship (Curran, 1975). Those social and interpersonal behaviors preceding sexual behavior may be more commonly conceptualized as "developmental," "courting," or simply "getting to know each other" behaviors. Self-disclosure within this context allows the sharing of knowledge and places the relationship on a more personal basis. The knowledge thus gained and shared may serve to reinforce and strengthen the attraction between the partners, or to decrease the feelings of commonality and attraction (Jourard, 1971). Either way, self-disclosure serves a very important informative function. The degree and the structure of self-disclosure during presexual behaviors is somewhat different from self-disclosure used during initiating a relationship. George's inappropriate use of self-disclosure in initiating a friendship was cited above. The following example illustrates the appropriate use of self-disclosure within the context of behaviors preceding sexual activity.

Roy and Clara met at an Audubon Society meeting, and have been dating once or twice a week for the past five weeks. Both enjoy the company of the other, and together they spent many hours attending sports events, movies, and simply walking through a park located near Clara's home. On several occasions when Roy walked Clara to her door, she invited him inside for a drink, which he always refused. After one of these occasions, Roy said, "Thank you, I wouldn't care for a drink, but I would like to come in and talk to you about something."

Once inside, he said, "The reason that I've always refused a drink when you offered it is simple, I had a drinking problem about five years ago, but with lots of determination, hard work, and the help of some doctors, I've managed to control it. It's been over five years now since I've had a drink, and to be honest with you, I'm just a little scared to have one now after what I've been through. I hope you understand.

Clara responded, "Of course I understand, and I appreciate your sharing this with me. Actually, I really don't even care for the taste of alcohol and only drink it socially because it seems everyone else does. How about if I fixed us both a cup of coffee, and let's watch the late movie on television?

Roy's confession would be considered an inappropriate self-disclosure during the initial stages of a relationship, but it serves an appropriate and useful function in behaviors preceding sexual or courting behavior. Roy's self-disclosure gives Clara some understanding of his actions. Also, the fact that Clara followed Roy's self-disclosure with one of her own facilitated communication and should reinforce even more self-disclosure on Roy's part.

A second component of behaviors preceding actual sexual behavior is *rewardingness* (Freedman, Carlsmith, & Sears, 1974). Potential relationships between two persons begin with initiation behaviors, but we seldom continue to develop relationships with persons whom we do not like. It follows, then, that people like others who reward them or who are associated with pleasant experiences (Banks, 1976). The effects of rewardingness can be explained in terms of simple learning principles. If someone reinforces us or we share a rewarding experience with that person, the positive aspects of the experience are associated or linked with the other person.

How rewardingness is employed in those social and interpersonal behaviors preceding sexual behavior is obvious if we can conceive of behaviors preceding sexual behavior as developmental or courting behaviors: rewardingness facilitates the *development* of the relationship. The ability to reward someone creates a positive cognitive set in that person's mind, and that set in turn facilitates the developing relationship by allowing us to associate positive reinforcement with the individual.

A final component of those behaviors generally labeled social and interpersonal behaviors preceding sexual behavior is *ingratiation* (Barron & Byrne, 1977). Ingratiation, in fact, may be considered a type of rewardingness in that we have a tendency to like or be attracted to a person who says nice things about us or to us. Be aware, however, that we distinguish between saying something nice about an individual and behaving in an ingratiating manner. While it is nice to receive favorable comments from others, occasionally even when we suspect the person's motives (Byrne, Rasche & Kelley, 1974), when the praise is inaccurate or exaggerated, when a person has something to gain from us, or when we are in a superior position, we may tend to perceive this behavior as ingratiating rather than honest. In general, flattery is not as effective as an honest compliment. Under some circumstances it may even cause dislike, presumably because we feel that flatterers are dishonest and are trying to take advantage of us. In other words, although we generally tend to like someone who says nice things, the effect is not as strong when the compliments are perceived as mere ingratiation.

Maintaining Heterosocial Behavior

A final major component of heterosocial behavior is those behaviors required to maintain intimate, heterosocial relationships. Of these behaviors, *predictability* and *familiarity* are important factors. When a relationship is established firmly enough so that we say we are "maintaining" it, we usually replace the "I" and "you" with the more endearing "us" and "we." We may assume that relationships have the best chance of enduring or being maintained when the participants need and can predict what each other has to offer (Freedman et al., 1974). In other words, if a person's preferred activities are known, it may be possible to predict the ways in which his or her relationships will develop. Whenever an activity providing one member of a pair with maximal pleasure also provides the other with maximal satisfaction, the relationship should succeed.

However, a very important additional element must be considered, which is that whether or not two people find an exclusive relationship satisfying and worth the time and effort of being maintained depends not only on their payoffs within that relationship, but also on the payoffs available in competing relationships. An outside partnership that would provide higher overall reward and fulfillment for the same expenditure is always a threat to any relationship. For example, a man may enjoy the tenderness and love given him by a woman, but if the same tenderness and love can be given him by another woman who happens to be wealthy and more attractive, the relationship may become threatened. By the same token, mutually dissatisfying relationships often persist for a long time simply because the partners in the relationship are not aware of alternative relationships that offer higher payoffs. One well-known example of someone who scrapped a marital relationship in favor of others that offered higher payoffs is Henry VIII of England. He had a habit of disposing of his wife whenever he became aware of the charms of another woman. Another more contemporary illustration is what has been called the "graduate student marriage syndrome." Here a graduate student regards the payoffs of a working spouse as satisfactory for maintaining the relationship while in school, but after graduation perceives a higher payoff with another partner.

Thus, people tend to move toward exchanges that are maximally satisfying to all participants. If this were the entire story, however, all relationships would be satisfying. Obviously, a look at friends and acquaintances who have gone through breakups or divorces should convince you that this is certainly not the case. Consider, for example, a situation in which you are crazy about football, find watching basketball okay if there is nothing better to do, and absolutely despise baseball. Your friend, on the other hand, loves to watch and attend baseball games, is somewhat neutral about basketball, but loathes football games because of the violence. If you as partners have established a pattern of predictability concerning each other's likes, dislikes, and behaviors, then a compromise situation in which you attend basketball games might represent the highest payoff for both of you. However, both of you would find the situation rather unsatisfactory because it is not maximally fulfilling for either of you. Thus, in attempting to maximize your pleasure, you probably would not maintain the relationship, but would seek out other partners, at least for purposes of attending sporting events.

Presumably, the more you see someone else, the more you learn about the person, and the better you can predict how the person will behave in a variety of situations. When you know fairly well how another will act or react to what you do, you're less likely to do something to annoy the other person, and vice versa. Each learns how to act to make the interaction free of unpleasantness, and therefore does not cause unpleasantness intentionally. Of course, couples can still annoy each other, but generally they avoid conflict through predictability, which, in turn, facilitates the maintenance of the relationship.

Familiarity is an important variable in heterosocial relationships (Freedman et al., 1974). Familiarity is, in fact, closely related to predictability in that familiarity facilitates accurate prediction which, in turn, enables individuals to avoid unpleasant or unsatisfying interactions and behaviors. The positive effects of familiarity have been demonstrated by Zajonc (1968), who showed subjects a series of pictures of people's faces. Some of the faces were shown only once or twice while others were shown as many as 20 or 25 times. Afterward, the subjects were asked individually how much they liked each face and how they thought they would like the person pictured. The more the subjects had seen the face, the more they liked the face, and the more they predicted they would like the person.

A number of investigators (*e.g.*, Burgess & Sales, 1971) have offered an explanation of the familiarity effect in terms of reinforcement principles. These investigators argue that in all of the studies performed so far, the stimuli were presented in a predominantly positive situation, so that the familiarity effect could be due merely to a greater number of positive reinforcements for those stimuli that were presented more often. Although the simplicity of this explanation is appealing, Freedman et al. (1974) claim that there is little reason to accept it at the present time. Freedman states that it is hard to see why these situations were particularly positive. Watching a long series of words or faces doesn't seem to be an especially pleasant or positive way to spend an afternoon.

HETEROSEXUAL BEHAVIOR

The final major component of human sexual behavior is *heterosexual behavior*. Heterosexual behavior is heavily influenced by other components of sexual behavior. For example, our pattern of sexual arousal influences our physiological and psychological ability to be "turned on" to an individual; gender role behavior influences how other individuals perceive us; and heterosocial behavior determines whether the relationship will endure and permit the possibility of sexual behavior.

The nature of the sexual act and attitudes concerning sexual behavior in our society make heterosexual behavior the most difficult component of sexual behavior to investigate. Due to the private nature of the sexual act, we must often rely on an individual's verbal report. Unfortunately, an individual's verbal report is heavily influenced by his/her expertise and knowledge in this area, as well as by willingness to disclose information accurately. Directly observing aspects of heterosexual behaviors for research and clinical purposes is a procedure which has been used by Masters and Johnson (1970) and others but, in most cases, it remains a questionable procedure (LoPiccolo, 1977). These problems will be further discussed in Chapter 2. However, it must be emphasized that heterosexual behavior involves a complex sequence of behaviors starting with the initiation of sexual activity or seduction, and, most often, terminating with coitus. Some aspects of this sequence have been well documented while other aspects have not.

The first element of heterosexual behavior is *seduction*. Investigators have found that many subhuman species engage in specific ritualistic behaviors in an attempt to attract and secure a sexual partner (Ford & Beach, 1951). Humans engage in a variety of mating or seduction behaviors that are influenced by cultural and social norms and expectations; however, there are certain common elements of seduction behavior, particularly within a given society. The fact that seduction is a complex social skill is documented by the many how to books on seduction and so-called "marriage manuals."

During seduction and sexual activities, individuals are likely to engage in traditional masculine and feminine behavioral roles. In our society males typically take the role of sexual aggressor, while females typically play a more passive role, although this role behavior is changing. Cultural mores and societal customs also dictate what we view as seduction behavior. The traditional American theme, for example, is a candlelight dinner with accompanying wine and soft music, considered by many to be the optimal environment and atmosphere for seduction.

The common elements of seduction behaviors exhibited during the candlelight dinner are also observed in most attempts to initiate sexual behavior. Seduction is usually attempted in a psychologically and physically private or semiprivate place. The setting or location of the seduction attempt is often crucial. One patient, for example, reported being frustrated and perplexed over his inability to seduce a female plant worker in the back of the factory warehouse. It turned out that the patient had never entertained the female worker socially. His only contact with her and the resulting seduction attempts occurred each day in the warehouse after the couple had shared lunch, which the female worker had prepared. It is true that the back of the warehouse did represent a somewhat physically private location, but successful seduction is not easy amidst boxes of freight with the noises of engines and trucks in the background.

Other elements of seduction are *affection* and *physical contact*. Physical contact may be more affectionate than sexual in the early stages of the relationship. Take the candlelight dinner in a restaurant as a convenient illustration. Phil and Marla are dining at a small, dimly lit restuarant. Phil maximizes physical contact with Marla by holding her hand as they sip their wine. As they go on to and leave the dance floor, he guides her with a gentle hand on her back. While dancing Phil holds Marla in a gentle, yet secure manner and maintains eye contact throughout their conversation. Driving home after dinner, he alternates between holding her hand and gently resting his arm around her shoulders. Affectionate physical contact which facilitates seduction is, like most behaviors, learned. Expertise in a learned behavior, whether it be riding a bicycle, hitting a baseball, or seducing a sexual partner, is gained through practice or modeling.

If seduction is successful, positive reinforcement should occur. Examples of verbal positive reinforcement are compliments, such as, "You really look nice tonight. I especially like your hair," or by self-disclosure statements expressing feelings, desires, and affection. Nonverbal positive reinforcement consists of eye contact, attentiveness, and physical contact. Phrases found in many romantic novels, such as "they gazed longingly into each other's eyes" are nothing more than dramatized descriptions of nonverbal positive reinforcement.

Aphrodisiacs have often been inaccurately viewed as an alternative to skilled seduction behavior, or as a method of overcoming a lack of sexual interest on the part of the prospective partner. Aphrodisiacs, that is, substances that increase sexual desire, have been dreamed of by humans for centuries. Certain foods have long been thought to have sexually stimulating properties. The newness or the rarity of a particular food (such as the potato when it first appeared in England) often arouses the hope that it will be a sexual stimulant. The shape of some foods, particularly those resembling sexual organs, leads to a belief, termed the "doctrine of signatures," that certain foods contain erotic properties which, when the foods are ingested, manifest themselves in increased sexual desire and performance (McCary, 1973). Foods frequently believed to be aphrodisiacs include oysters, peanuts, clams, celery, raw hog's testicles ("mountain oysters"), raw bull's testicles ("prairie oysters"), Italian foods, and even powdered rhinoceros horn. McCary (1973) notes that it is not difficult to recognize how the term "horny" came into popularity as meaning strong sexual desire.

Various drugs also carry the connotation of being sexual stimulants.

The most popular of these drugs, cantharides or "Spanish Fly," is derived from the powdered remains of a Southern European beetle. When the powder is ingested, acute irritation of the genitourinary tract occurs with accompanying dilation of the associated blood vessels. Irritation of the vaginal walls and penile erection may also occur, but with no increase in sexual desire. Excessive dosage of this drug may produce violent illness and death (MacDougald, 1961).

Other drugs such as opium, morphine, marijuana, and alcohol have been claimed to have aphrodisiac properties. Investigations have revealed, however, that few if any of these drugs have an aphrodisiac effect on the individual (MacDougald, 1961). This finding may disappoint those who scheme to spike their partner's drink with Spanish Fly or hope to get their partners intoxicated as a way to seduce them. Alcohol, in fact, is a general depressant which effects behavior in a specific sequence. First, alcohol depresses the brain centers which govern fear, thereby reducing anxiety and producing disinhibition. As the level of consumption increases, alcohol depresses cortical activity and impairs the cognitive functions. At high consumption levels, alcohol produces a loss of consciousness and irregularly descending paralysis in the manner of sedatives, hypnotics, and anesthetics (Kaplan, 1974). Since the anxiety-reducing effects of alcohol appear before the central nervous system depressant effects, consumption of small levels of alcohol may release inhibitions sufficiently to result in a temporary increase in sexual desire. However, as Shakespeare (*Macbeth*, Act II, Scene 3) so accurately stated, "It [alcohol] provokes the desire, but it takes away the performance." The simple fact is that individuals interested in seduction and heterosexual skills will probably fare better by using basic seduction skills rather than relying on so called aphrodisiacs.

Sexual Foreplay

In the later stages of seduction and early stage of coitus, sexual arousal is enhanced by sexual foreplay. Sexual foreplay may be defined as behaviors which increase pleasure and heighten sexual arousal in both partners prior to intercourse. Foreplay usually initiates the excitement phase and carries over into the plateau phase of the sexual response cycle.

Techniques of sexual foreplay vary greatly but often include activities such as kissing, caressing, genital manipulation, and oral-genital contact. Through verbal and physical sexual pleasuring, couples learn those techniques which are particularly arousing to their partner, and the probability of mutual sexual satisfaction is facilitated. Individuals skilled in heterosexual foreplay recognize and attend to psychological, anatomical, and physiological differences in sexual arousal and functioning between the sexes and pattern their techniques of foreplay accordingly.

Knowledge of Sexual Functioning: Sexual Response Cycle

In order to understand heterosexual skills, we need to understand the sexual response cycle. One female patient, for instance, reported depression and feelings of inadequate self-worth. When she was asked to be more specific, she said that each time she had intercourse her partner would reach orgasm only once. Although some of her male partners would, after a short rest, initiate further sexual activity, every partner she had ever experienced had had only one orgasm without stopping for a rest. Since she claimed she was capable of multiple orgasms, she concluded her male partners must not care for her since they stopped at one. A short sex-education lecture concentrating on differences in the male and female sexual response cycle convinced the patient that her depression and feelings of inadequate self-worth were the result of sexual ignorance.

At present our knowledge of the sexual response cycle is largely derived from the work of Masters and Johnson (1970). They have identified in their research four distinct phases of the sexual response cycle.

The *excitement phase* is the initial stage of the sexual response cycle. Any form of sexual stimulation, be it physical or psychological, can initiate the excitement phase. This phase can be extended by stopping and subsequent resumption, or can be stopped completely by withdrawing the sexual stimulus. Physiological changes associated with the excitement phase include increased muscular tension (myotonia) and an engorgement of the blood vessels (vasocongestion), which causes the surrounding tissue to swell, especially in the genital area. Another physiological change, the maculopapular sex flush, appears in about three-fourths of sexually stimulated women and in about one-fourth of sexually stimulated men, although it may not appear in men until the plateau stage. It normally begins in the stomach region and at the throat and neck and spreads quickly to the breast. As a rule, the intensity of the flush is in direct proportion to the intensity of the stimulation received. Finally, as sexual tension builds, corresponding increases occur in heart rate and blood pressure.

During the *plateau phase,* sexual tension increases and physiological changes are intensified. If sexual stimulation is withdrawn during this period, orgasm will not occur, and sexual tensions will decrease gradually over a prolonged period of time. Increased muscular tension is the most marked bodily response in both sexes during this period, but it is perhaps more pronounced in the male. Both voluntary and involuntary muscles are involved

TABLE 1-1

Reactions of Sex Organs During the Sexual Response Cycle

Male	*Female*
Excitement Phase	
1. Penile erection (within 3–8 seconds)	1. Vaginal lubrication (within 10–30 seconds)
2. Partial testicular elevation and size increase	2. Expansion of inner ⅔ of vagina
Plateau Phase	
1. Increase in penile circumference and testicular tumescence	1. Orgasmic platform in outer ⅓ of vagina
2. Full testicular elevation (orgasm inevitable)	2. Full expansion of ⅔ of vagina
3. Purple hue on corona of penis	3. "Sex skin" discoloration of minor labia
4. Mucoid secretion from Cowper's gland	4. Mucoid secretion from Bartholin's gland
	5. Withdrawal of clitoris
Orgasmic Phase	
1. Ejaculation	1. Pelvic response
2. Relaxation of external bladder sphincter	2. Minimal relaxation of external cervical opening
3. Contractions of penile urethra at 0.8 second intervals for 3–4 contractions	3. Contraction of orgasmic platform at 0.8 second intervals for 5–12 contractions
4. Anal sphincter contractions (2–4 contractions)	4. External rectal contractions (2–4 contractions)
	5. External urethral sphincter contractions (2–3 contractions)
Resolution Phase	
1. Refractory period with rapid loss of pelvic vasocongestion	1. Ready return to orgasm with retarded loss of pelvic vasocongestion
2. Loss of penile erection in primary (rapid) and secondary (slow) stages	2. Loss of "sex skin" color and orgasmic platform in primary (rapid) stage
	3. Remainder of pelvic vasocongestion as secondary stage.

Source: Katchadourian, H. A., Lunde, D. T. *Fundamentals of Human Sexuality.* New York: Holt, Rinehart & Winston, 1972. Reprinted with permission of Holt, Rinehart & Winston.

in strong contractions of the face, neck, and abdomen. As the plateau phase increases, the heart rate increases, sometimes to more than twice the usual rate, and during the latter part of this phase a marked elevation of

TABLE 1-2

General Body Reactions During the Sexual Response Cycle

Male	*Female*

Excitement Phase

1. Nipple erection (30%)	1. Nipple erection (consistent)
	2. Sex-tension flush (25%)

Plateau Phase

1. Sex-tension flush (25%)	1. Sex-tension flush (75%)
2. Generalized skeletal-muscle tension	2. Generalized skeletal-muscle tension
3. Hyperventilation and tachycardia	3. Hyperventilation and tachycardia

Orgasmic Phase

1. Muscle contractions, hyperventilation, and tachycardia	1. Muscle contractions, hyperventilation, and tachycardia

Resolution Phase

1. Sweating, hyperventilation, and tachycardia	1. Sweating, hyperventilation, and tachycardia

Source: Katchadourian, H. A., & Lunde, *Fundamentals of Human Sexuality*. New York: Holt, Rinehart & Winston, 1972. Reprinted with permission of Holt, Rinehart & Winston.

blood pressure occurs. Hyperventilation may also begin during the plateau phase.

The *orgasmic phase* consists of those few seconds when the sexual tension evidenced by muscular spasms and engorgement of blood vessels reaches its maximum and is discharged in the orgasm. If there has been a sex flush, the intensity of the flush during the orgasmic phase is proportionate to the intensity of the orgasm. Breathing during this time is at least twice as fast as normal and is directly correlated with the duration and intensity of the orgasm. Blood pressure may elevate by a third or more, and heart rate commonly increases to between 110 and 180 beats per minute.

The final phase of sexual response is known as *resolution* and involves a fairly rapid loss of the vasocongestion which characterized the previous phases. Blood pressure and heart rate begin a gradual return to normal levels, as does the respiratory rate.

Immediately after orgasm the male experiences a *refractory* period during which he cannot be stimulated to another orgasm. The duration of this period varies, but for several minutes after orgasm further stimulation is experienced as unpleasant and for some men even painful. An important distinction between the sexes is thus evident, for the female does not necessarily experience a refractory period. While some women prefer a single orgasm followed by a resolution period, other women prefer multiple orgasms without the interruption of a refractory period. Thus, while the man typically finds genital stimulation after orgasm neutral or unpleasant, the woman may find it very desirable and may experience a chain of orgasms.

Although an understanding of the sexual response cycle tells us much about the physiology of orgasm, it tells us nothing about the parameters or norms of sexual behavior. A major problem for clinicians working with sexual disorders is that there are no norms for sexual behavior. This makes determining if a particular type or degree of sexual behavior is normal or abnormal difficult. For example, suppose that a male regularly performs intercourse at a nonstop, fast-pace rate for 20 minutes without ejaculating. Should he be considered a sexual athlete and the envy of his male friends, or should he be considered as suffering from retarded ejaculation? What if he lasts for 30 minutes, or even 40 minutes? At what point should the distinction between adequate and appropriate ejaculatory control and retarded ejaculation be drawn? Consider the female who goes bra-less, and wears see-through blouses and the most revealing of string bikinis. Where does the adherence to fashion stop and exhibitionism begin? Unfortunately, we have no identifiable and universally agreed-upon norms for sexual behavior so that it is hard to categorize these behaviors as normal or not.

Sexual Intercourse

The final element of heterosexual skills is a knowledge of the variety and function of sexual intercourse techniques. The number of potential intercourse positions that two people can adopt is nearly limitless. A couple's preference for one or more positions should come after practice and experimentation and through honest communication of their preferences and satisfaction.

Contrary to the belief of some, there is no one position that is more "normal" than others. The man-on-top or "missionary" position may be a common intercourse position, but it should be adopted by a couple for no other reason than that it is mutually satisfying and enjoyable for both partners. Indeed, continued experimentation with and adoptions of new and preferred positions add spice to the sexual act and prevent it from becoming monotonous. In clinical practice we have found that it is not unusual to hear both male and female patients condemning their partner's lack of initiation and experimentation. Individuals who exhibit this sexual passivity often excuse their behavior as due to particular religious doctrine, habit, boredom, or inhibition. Sexual intercourse, however, should be a time of enjoyment and interest. Experimentation with positions serves to facilitate the excitement and pleasure of the sexual act.

Like most of our conceptualizations of abnormal and normal behavior, coital positions are popularized and thus "normalized" by societal and cultural beliefs. McCary (1973) speaks of four common positions while Kaplin (1974) discusses three. For our purposes, five common coital positions will be briefly discussed.

The face-to-face, male-superior position is common in our society, but does not have the popularity in other cultures and countries that it does in the United States.

Penetration is easily achieved in the face-to-face, male-superior position. The woman, lying on her back, spreads her legs and thus allows the man to cradle himself between her legs while resting his body weight on his knees and elbows. The man is thus responsible for the majority of the couple's bodily movements, although the woman may vary the position of her legs by pressing her knees to her shoulders or wrapping her legs around her partner in an attempt to maximize clitoral contact and stimulation. The male can assist in clitoral stimulation by either keeping penile pressure on the upper part of the woman's vulva, or by situating his body weight in such a way as to free a hand for added digital stimulation.

The second coital position is termed *face-to-face, female-superior.* The man, lying on his back, keeps his legs together, or slightly parted, allowing the woman to sit astride him with her hands either forward resting on the man's shoulders, or behind her resting on the man's knees. The man may vary this position somewhat by raising his bent knees so that the woman may rest her buttocks against his thighs as she sits astride him.

This position allows the woman to control the tempo of bodily movement and degree of penetration. This position also allows more direct clitoral pressure and friction and allows the male to free his hands for further stimulation of the woman. This position is however less stimulating to the male because his body is less active, and may therefore result either in inability to ejaculate or loss of erection. As a result of decreased stimulation and potentially delayed ejaculation, this position is often employed with cases of premature ejaculation.

A third position for sexual intercourse is the *side-to-back position.* In this position the woman lies on her back and pulls the bent knee of one leg to her chest. This allows the man, lying on his side at a 45° angle to the woman, to scissor the woman's extended leg between his and make penetration. The position has the advantage of allowing maximum bodily movement by both partners and freedom of both partners' hands for added mutual stimulation. The side-to-back position is also less physically strenuous and is ideal for extended periods of coitus.

In the *face-to-face, side position,* both partners lie on their sides facing each other. Like the side-to-back position, this position allows freedom of bodily movement to both partners. The advantages of this position are that neither partner is supporting the weight of the other and less physical exertion is required. The face-to-face, side position is thus often employed when periods of intercourse are extensive, when one partner is fatigued, or when one partner is considerably taller than the other.

The final position of sexual intercourse we shall discuss is termed the *rear-entry position*. There are numerous variations of the rear-entry position. The woman may sit astride the man with her back to him, she may lie on her stomach with the man between her legs in a superior position, or she may assume a position on her knees and hands (or elbows) and allow the man to make vaginal penetration from behind. Some of the advantages of this position are that it allows a degree of freedom in bodily movement to both partners, and allows the male to free his hands for added stimulation to the woman's breasts or clitoral area. In addition, the man often finds the sensation of the woman's buttocks against his genital and stomach areas an added stimulation.

One major factor that facilitates or limits a couple's choice of a particular coital position is their feelings about the psychological implications of that position (McCary, 1973). Some men may feel too controlled and passive with the woman in a superior position. Conversely, some women may desire a feeling of being "dominated," which is lacking in the female-superior positions. Again, we refer to powerful societal influences that socialize many individuals into traditional sex roles. Given the willingness of both partners to experiment with varied coital positions and activities, the only factor that should influence the adoption or rejection of a particular position should be the pleasure and enjoyment the partners experience.

CHAPTER 2

Clinical Assessment
of Sexual Behavior

The basic requirement for the development of scientific knowledge is measurement. Before a phenomenon can be understood, it must be observed, described, and evaluated in some objective fashion in order to permit other individuals to replicate the researcher's observations and agree with or correct claims. This basic requirement is not simple, it requires an objective (data) language which allows consensual agreement on terms, clear definitions of phenomena, careful reporting or measurement of events, and meaningful and cautious interpretation of the significance of these events. The problem is compounded for those who work with human behavior by many philosophical, legal, and personal objections to this sort of scientific inquiry. Obviously, these objections are particularly stringent in the area of human sexuality. No other area of human behavior is as threatening—but at the same time as fascinating—to the public as sexual behavior. For this reason, research and clinical activities requiring assessment of sexual behavior must observe both the canons of science and the public's codes for appropriateness. Unfortunately, with sexual behavior, research and clinical procedures which the scientific community would consider ethical sometimes conflict with the moral values or even the legal restrictions of society. These conflicts will be obvious throughout this book and will be discussed where appropriate.

In this chapter we shall first discuss traditional (psychodynamic, psychoanalytic) assessment and compare these techniques with the behavioral approach. Next, since a clinical assessment of sexual behavior begins with an initial interview that allows the clinician to devise or plan an assessment strategy for a particular individual, we shall discuss the initial clinical interview which focuses on sexual behavior. And finally, we will cover assessment of the various components of sexual behavior as measured by the three channels of information: self-report, behavioral observation, and physiological indices.

26

PSYCHODYNAMIC AND BEHAVIORAL ASSESSMENT

The assessment of sexual behavior may be conducted in a number of ways. Throughout this text we will present behavioral formulations of assessment and treatment as well as brief descriptions of psychodynamic and/or psychoanalytic conceptualizations. In this way the reader may readily contrast two opposing but popular orientations. For example, although both behavioral and traditional (psychodynamic, analytic, or trait) assessment procedures attempt to produce reliable, valid, and useful data, the methods they employ are quite different because of the differing nature of their assumptions about the causes of human behavior (Table 2-1).

According to dynamic or analytic theories, problem behaviors such as sexual disorders are surface manifestations or symptoms of deeply-seated conflicts or fears (somewhat different assumptions are made by trait theorists). Because these conflicts are assumed to be unconscious, assessment techniques are for the most part projective tests which attempt to tap unconscious processes. Psychological intervention (psychotherapy) seeks to bring unconscious conflicts to consciousness through insight: the desired result is either the elimination of the pathogenic portions and the strengthening of the healthy portions of the personality, or a complete restructuring and reintegration of the entire personality. Unfortunately, the relation-

TABLE 2-1

A Comparison of Traditional and Behavioral Assessment Strategies

	Behavioral Assessment	*Traditional Assessment*
Assumptions		
1. Personality	Behavior (f) environment	Behavior (f) underlying causes
2. "Test" interpretation	Behavior as sample	Behavior as sign
3. Situations sampled	Varied and specific	Limited and Ambiguous
Primary Functions	Descriptive in behavioral-analytic terms	Descriptive in psychodynamic terms
	Treatment selection	Diagnostic labeling
	Treatment evaluation	
Practical Aspects		
1. Relation to treatment	Direct	Indirect
2. Time of assessment	Continuous with treatment	Prior to treatment

Source: Adapted from Ciminero, A. R. Behavioral assessment: An overview. In Ciminero, Calhoun, and Adams (Eds.), *Handbook of Behavioral Assessment*. New York: John Wiley and Sons, 1977. Reprinted with permission of John Wiley and Sons.

ship between psychodynamic or trait assessment and treatment is indirect. Assessment should lead to the recommendation of a particular treatment procedure, but all too often, as Stuart (1970) has shown, the diagnosis resulting from traditional methods of assessment does not influence modification or treatment procedures. Regardless of the behavior involved, traditional psychotherapists use their own brands of treatment, most all of which focus on insight produced through talk therapy, which may be some form of analysis (Freudian, Jungian, Alderian, or whatever), nondirective counseling, reality therapy, primal scream, or other similar methods.

Behavioral theorists, on the other hand, see maladaptive or distressing behaviors themselves as the problem. Once the deviant behavior is modified, the problem is eliminated and the patient is "cured." In essence, the behavior therapist agrees with Johnson (1964) as to what the therapist must do in order to help the patient:

> What the therapist has to do . . . is to get the person not to tell him what he *is* or what he *has,* but what he does, and the conditions under which he *does* it. When he stops talking about the *type* of person he is, what his outstanding *traits are,* and what type of disorder he *has*—when he stops making these subject-predicate statements, and begins to use actional terms to describe his behavior and his circumstances—both he and the therapist begin to see what specifically may be done in order to change both the behavior and the circumstances. (p. 220)

Because behavior therapy focuses on changing or modifying overt behaviors rather than producing insight and effecting personality reorganization, behavioral assessment demands precise descriptions of the behaviors in question. In addition, behavior therapy views overt behavior as a learned response to a given set of circumstances which thus requires a description of the conditions in which the problem behavior occurs and the consequences it has for the patient. Treatment then centers around changing or eliminating the behavior and substituting another behavior pattern which will bring the individual more pleasure and less distress. As Mischel (1968) summarizes,

> Behavior assessments seek behavioral referents for the client's complaints; thereafter they identify the precise conditions that seem to be maintaining or influencing the problem so that appropriate rearrangements can be designed to achieve more advantageous outcomes.

In behavior therapy, assessment is the first step in developing and/or selecting a treatment program. This relationship between assessment and modification will be illustrated throughout this book. Assessment is also necessary for evaluation of the effects of the treatment plan (Ciminero, 1977). Because accurate assessment demands continuous monitoring of

the problem behavior, behavioral assessment requires operational definitions of observable behaviors, and eschews inferences and assumptions
about underlying psychological processes and unconscious conflicts or
motivation.

Let us consider a hypothetical example. Frank was divorced two years
ago, and for four years has suffered from impotence. His six-year marriage
had been difficult from the start. His wife had engaged in a series of extramarital affairs with little or no attempt at discretion. When angry with
Frank, she would boast of the sexual prowess of her lovers and accuse
Frank of continually poor sexual performance. In his final two years of
marriage, Frank was impotent with his wife, a situation which resulted in
increased abuse until divorce terminated the relationship. He has since
dated a variety of women, but the result is always the same: failure to
achieve and maintain an erection. After each failure, he offers excuses to
his partner such as being overly tired or having had too much to drink, and
immediately begins to search for a new partner.

In dynamic terms, Frank's inability to achieve and maintain an erection might be viewed as a symptom of an unconscious fear that sexual activity is dangerous (castration anxiety). The physical inhibition of the sexual response is thus seen as a defense against the threatening impulse. Or
more specifically, with a Freudian model, anxiety over sexual expression
might be seen as a result of the Oedipal conflict. As Fenichel (1945)
explains,

> In the simplest and most typical cases, evidence is based on a persistence of an
> unconscious sensual statement to the mother. Superficially no sexual at-
> tachment is completely attractive because the partner is never the mother; in a
> deeper layer every sexual attachment has to be prohibited, because every
> partner represents the mother. (p. 170)

In other words, Frank's inability to perform sexual intercourse with
his wife and others is viewed as a symptom of underlying personality problems. Assessment of the problem would thus involve instruments such as
the Rorschach and other projective tests, which would, through Frank's
interpretation of neutral stimuli such as inkblots, reveal to the therapist the
nature of Frank's unconscious process. The purpose of therapy would then
be to bring Frank to the realization and understanding of his underlying
conflicts.

In behavioral terms, Frank's problems would be interpreted as the result of a period of stress associated with intense anxieties over sexual performance. Frank's anxiety-provoking marital environment did not
stimulate and/or reinforce appropriate sexual behavior. Instead, tensions
associated with the sexual and social components of the marriage served to
condition Frank to experience anxiety in sexual situations, which suppressed

his sexual arousal. In this model, traditional assessment techniques would not be helpful since no assumptions are made about unconscious or underlying processes or conflicts. On the contrary, assessment procedures which accurately describe the situations that elicit anxiety and inadequate sexual performance are necessary. Tests which reveal intense castration anxiety and an unconscious sensual attachment to the mother do not help the behavior therapist. What the behavior therapist requires before formulating a treatment strategy is assessment in terms of a definable, measurable behavior: the inability to achieve and maintain erection during heterosexual activity. Later, this assessment should also provide an objective basis for evaluation of the success of the treatment program.

The first conceptualization of Frank's behavior is based upon the notion that underlying psychological disturbances, much like a diseased appendix, must be removed before the patient will improve and the symptoms disappear. This "medical model" has enjoyed a popularity based on its success in treating physical disease, in which symptoms such as pain, fever, and the like may indeed indicate some underlying problem such as viral or bacterial invasion. The second conceptualization, the behavior model, is based upon learning theory and other scientific principles of psychology. The behavior therapist does not necessarily agree that underlying pathogenic personality disturbances must be altered or even that they exist.

Since many sexual responses are specific, identifiable behaviors that can be systematically recorded or observed, sexual disorders are very amenable to behavioral assessment and treatment. Recent advances and progress in physiological techniques of sexual assessment such as the penile strain gauge and the vaginal photoplethysmograph provide accurate physiological data about arousal patterns and sexual responsiveness. Clearly, these and other relatively recent successful advances in behavioral assessment and treatment of sexual disorders are helping free the entire area of sexual functioning from questionable traditional assessments by emphasizing more empirical objective approaches.

THE INITIAL CLINICAL INTERVIEW

The initial step in sexual assessment is a clinical interview which yields information about the individual's problems and allows planning of the assessment procedure. Generally, behavior therapists focus on the most objective description of presenting complaints, their development, and their maintenance. Various outlines for obtaining the individual's subjective report with sexual cases are available. Masters and Johnson (1970), for example, outline specific questions to be asked during an interview and a specific sequence in which to ask the questions. Generally, the interview should include: (1) a brief report of the presenting complaints as perceived by the patient; (2) information about the patient's marriage or present and past sexual relationships; (3) events and influences from childhood to the present that pertain to the problem; (4) perception of self; and (5) sensitivity to sensory stimuli of touch, vision, audition, and olfaction which contribute to sexual arousal or repugnance. It is true that an organized, structured interview outline is often conducive to obtaining an accurate and detailed analysis of the problem, especially for the inexperienced therapist who may be somewhat uneasy asking questions about sexual behavior; however, we feel that adherence to a rigidly defined, structured outline often turns the therapist into a question asking machine, and eliminates the spontaneity and natural conversational flow that should exist in the doctor-patient interaction. Peterson (1968), presents the following outline as a general guide for use in a behavioral interview:

1. Definition of problem behavior

    a. Nature of the problem as defined by patient (as I understand it, you came here because . . . . Discuss reasons for contact as stated by referral agency or other source of information).
    b. I would like you to tell me more about this. What is the problem as you see it? (Probe as needed to determine patient's view of the problem behavior, i.e., what the patient is doing, or failing to do, which the patient or somebody else defines as a problem).

2. Severity of the problem

    a. How serious a problem is this as far as you are concerned? (Probe to determine perceived severity of problem.)
    b. How often do you . . . (exhibit problem behavior, if a disorder of commission, or have occasion to exhibit desired behavior, if a problem of omission. The goal is to obtain information regarding frequency of response).

3. Generality of the problem

    a. Duration (how long has this been going on?)
    b. Extent (under what conditions does this problem usually occur?) Probe to determine situations in which problem behavior occurs (e.g., do you feel that way at work? How about at home?)

4. Determination of problem behavior

    a. Conditions that intensify problem behavior (now I want you to think about the times when . . . the problem is worse. What sort of things are going on then?)
    b. Conditions that alleviate the problem behavior (what about the times when . . . the problem gets better? What sort of things are going on then?)

c. Perceived origins (what do you think is causing the problem?)
d. Specific antecedent (think back to the last time the problem occurred. What was going on at that time?)
e. Specific consequences (what happened after the problem behavior occurred?)

    1. Social consequences (what did significant others identified do?)
    2. Personal consequences (how did that make you feel?)
    3. Suggested changes (you have thought about this problem. What do you think might be done to improve the situation?)
    4. Suggested leads for further inquiry (What else do you think I should find out about to help you with this problem?)   (pp. 121–122)

Peterson's outline identifies the problem behavior and the conditions surrounding its occurrence. Other behavioral interview outlines emphasize the A-B-Cs (antecedents, behavior, and consequences) paradigm of behavior on the SORC (stimulus, organism, response, and consequence) model of behavior (Goldfried & Sprafkin, 1974). Whatever model is used, however, a common theme in all behavioral interview outlines is the identification of the problem *behavior,* in sharp contrast to most traditional interviews which probe for clues to conflicts, fears, and other unconscious causes of behavior. The behavior therapist should thus collect a clear description of the specific sexual problem; information concerning onset, course and duration of the behavior; a statement of how the patient feels about the problem and how he or she has tried to cope with the problem; and an indication of what effect the problem has had on the patient's life. Recently, LoPiccolo and Heiman (1978) have developed a good outline of the type of historical and current information needed which can be integrated into the behavioral interview.

In any assessment, a critical factor is the communication between the clinician and the patient. In a clinical interview, language is the primary source of communication; therefore, the type of language the clinician uses should be tailored to the comprehension and comfort of the patient. For example, the following excerpts were extracted from different clinical interviews. The first excerpt is from an interview with a 37-year-old attorney who complained of premature ejaculation:

Patient: I've had this problem ever since we've been married, five years now. During intercourse, I maintain my erection for approximately 5–10 seconds and ejaculate. Nothing that I try seems to help.

Doctor: What happens after you ejaculate? Do you in some way attend to your wife's sexual needs?

Patient: This has happened so often that it has developed into a pattern. After I ejaculate, I perform cunnilingus on my wife. Most of the time she has little trouble achieving orgasm this way, although I'm sure she would prefer that she have an orgasm during intercourse.

The next excerpt is taken from an interview with a 20-year-old factory worker who had dropped out of school in the eighth grade. This patient also complained of premature ejaculation:

> *Patient:* I've had this a long time, Doc. I guess ever since I was a kid. I think it started when I first started screwing.
>
> *Doctor:* What happens when you screw now?
>
> *Patient:* Terrible. About the time I get it in good it's all over. I mean, I don't even get going good before I get my rocks off.
>
> *Doctor:* How does your wife feel about this?
>
> *Patient:* She doesn't like it at all, but she puts up with it. I mean, about the time I get her hot, I'm through.
>
> *Doctor:* Do you take care of her then, oral-sex, go down on her?
>
> *Patient:* Yeah, I go down on her till she gets her rocks off, but she says it ain't the same as screwing.

Notice the similarities in the two interviews, both in the questions asked by the clinician and the responses given by the patients. Also notice the variation in language employed as the clinician alters interviewing style to suit the comprehension and comfort of the patient. An ability to be flexible in the style of language employed during the interview will facilitate communication and verbal report information.

The collection of clinical interview data is greatly facilitated by a demonstration of sensitivity to the patient's problem and by the nature of the clinician's conversation. Bernstein, Bernstein, and Dana (1974) presented a list of five conditions for effective interviewing that are especially relevant to interviewing patients with a sexual difficulty: (1) attentiveness, generated when the interviewer talks neither too much nor too little, but shows interest and encourages the patient's self-expression; (2) rapport, an indication of genuine interest in the patient's problem demonstrated by courtesy and respect, which in turn fosters the patient's ease and confidence; (3) freedom from interruption, encouraging the first two conditions by keeping consultation time exclusively for the patient, and by keeping telephone and other interruptions to a minimum if they cannot be totally excluded); (4) psychological privacy, a condition different from geographical privacy, and defined as the therapist's attitude of undivided interest in and concern for the patient; (5) emotional objectivity, a quality essential to every therapist that primarily involves control of subjective feelings which the therapist may experience in interaction with the patient. It is not to be equated with coldness or attempts to hide or control all spontaneous reactions, but with the mature acceptance of the patient. Adherence to these conditions for interviewing and the ability to be accepting and at ease with sexual material will assist in putting the patient at ease and, in turn, will enhance the quality and quantity of information obtained in the interview.

The therapist should attempt to investigate a patient's sexual behavior and functioning in a manner similar to that in which he or she would investigate the patient's past medical history or current financial situation. If the patient should have difficulty in answering questions regarding sexual behavior, the therapist should simply inform the patient that they will come back to the topic later in the interview. At some later time in the interview the therapist should inform the patient that a detailed history of all important aspects of his or her life, including sexual behavior and functioning, is important in order to discover how he or she might best be helped. Although experience will soon enable the therapist to discuss sexual material in a routine manner, two obvious but often forgotten points should be kept in mind. First, the patient probably is not as experienced in discussing sexual material as the therapist is. Second, the patient considers the sexual material under discussion in a clinical interview as personal in that it concerns his or her own sexual behavior. Discussion of the patient's sexual behavior should therefore be conducted in an atmosphere of acceptance and support.

In many cases, treatment of sexual disorders involves a couple. While some clinicians such as Schumacher and Lloyd (1976) recommend that the couple be initially interviewed together, we do not feel this is a wise procedure since the couple who can be completely frank with one another about their current and past sexual behavior is rare. This procedure can cause marital difficulties and/or result in misinformation that outweighs any advantages the joint interview might offer. We recommend that the individual with the sexual problem be interviewed first with the assurance of confidentiality. At the end of the interview the patient should be asked what information can be discussed with the spouse. The spouse should then be interviewed with the same assurances. Finally, both parties should be interviewed together in such a way that their wishes concerning privileged information are respected. This procedure often yields three different stories and gives the clinician a great deal of information about both the sexual problem and the marital situation.

Two other points are also important to remember in conducting initial interviews with couples. First, it is important to recognize that in most cases the sexual problem is *not* always a mutual responsibility of the couple and is not always caused by the relationship. It is doubtful that the disorder is present only in that specific relationship. However, if it is, the problem is with the marriage or the relationship, and that problem should be the focus of the clinical intervention. To assume, however, that one spouse is responsible for the other's pedophilia is asinine. Second, it should be remembered that spouses assisting mates in obtaining professional help for a problem may rightfully resent being considered a "patient" unless they request or agree to such status. In sexual cases the assistance of a spouse is usually required. Alienating a spouse by automatically assuming he or she has a problem too and treating him or her as a patient should be carefully avoided. One of the quickest ways to alienate a spouse is to require him or her to submit to unnecessary clinical procedures which can be viewed as an invasion of privacy.

In general, the clinical interview should be a method of generating initial hypotheses about the disorder, which can then be confirmed or discarded as further information is collected through additional interviews and other assessment procedures. Thus, at the end of the initial interview the clinician should have some tentative hypotheses about the case which should be discussed openly with the patient. The patient is entitled to know what the problem may be and what the recommended assessment or treatment procedures are. It is both wise and ethical to discuss fully the recommended assessment and/or treatment procedures, and to obtain written agreement from the patient for further investigation or treatment. When the assessment is completed, all diagnoses, hypotheses about how the behavior developed, alternative methods for dealing with the problem, probability of successful intervention, cost, and similar information should be discussed with the patient in depth. Such a discussion allows the patient to evaluate the information and make decisions including seeking other professional opinions or not entering a treatment program. Giving the patient a few days to come to a decision is usually wise.

MEDICAL CONSIDERATIONS

One area that is often overlooked in both traditional and behavioral assessment is the medical-psychosocial history of the patient. Assessment emphasizing sexual development and early patterns of sexual behavior often add much to the conceptualization of the sexual problem. A complete medical history is obligatory.

Schumacher and Lloyd (1976) provide a detailed discussion of the importance of physiological-medical data in the assessment of sexual disorders. As these authors suggest, a complete medical history should include details of all serious illnesses and a thorough dietary history. Poor eating habits can often contribute to feelings of fatique and general dysphoria. Included in the dietary history should be the level of alcohol consumption. Excessive alcohol consumption can often impair sexual funcioning in men and women. A list of medications that the patient has taken or is presently taking should also be compiled. Medications that alter autonomic nerve transmission can also alter sexual functioning. Some of these compounds include agents that elevate mood, such as the tricyclic drugs and monoamine oxidase inhibitors; tranquilizers; some antihypertensive agents such as methyl dopa; and anticholinergic agents.

Estrogen, given to men for treatment of carcinoma of the prostrate, can markedly decrease sexual drive; so can cyproterone acetate, which is sometimes used in Europe for treatment of dangerous sexual offenders, and progestational agents which have been used in the United States for the same purpose. Women using an oral contraceptive sometimes experience decreased sexual drive. This decrease is often related to the type of gestagen in the contraceptive, and can often be eliminated by changing to a different ratio of estrogen and progesterone.

Some investigations have reported that heavy tobacco intake can decrease potency in the male, or that smoking marijuana can enhance sexual feelings. These studies are at the moment scientifically unsupported. It is known, however, that the use of narcotics can decrease sexual functioning.

After a complete and systematic assessment, and before the onset of treatment, a complete physical examination by a physician is essential. The physical should include thorough laboratory analysis; a complete blood count and urinalysis; a biochemical screen (estimates of electrolytes and tests for hepatic and renal function); analysis of plasma cholesterol and triglyceride levels; and indices of thyroid function. Men suffering from impotence are sometimes found to have significant hypertension, arteriosclerotic heart disease with cardiac failure, hyperthyroidism, Parkinsonism, prostatic hypertrophy, small and underdeveloped secondary sexual structures, hydrocele, varicocele, and Peyronie's disease. Women reporting problems of orgasmic dysfunction have sometimes been found to have significant hypertension, small and underdeveloped secondary sexual structures, a prolapsed uterus, painful vaginal or perineal scars, vaginal mucosal atrophy, and imperforated hymen. Laboratory tests have often discovered elevated triglyceride levels and decreased hepatic and renal function in sexually dysfunctional men and women. If a problem is due to a disease process or abnormality, it should be diagnosed and treated as such by a physician. For both clinical psychologists and psychiatrists a good working relationship with a primary-care physician based on mutual respect for each other's abilities and recognition of each other's limitations is certainly in the best interest of the clinician, physician, and patient alike. Only after we have eliminated an organic etiology and/or maintenance of a sexual disorder may we assume that the disorder lies in the domain of the clinical psychologist or the psychiatrist, and proceed with treatment.

ASSESSMENT METHODS

When feasible, assessment of sexual functions should include subjective reports, behavioral observations, and physiological indices. As we will see in the remainder of this chapter, this ideal is not always realizable for a variety of reasons. However, any agreement or discrepancy among the three channels of report is a source of valuable information which can play a direct role in evaluation and modification of sexual disorders.

Obviously, the ideal assessment situation would involve direct, continuous monitoring of all three channels of report in the individual's natural environment, where the problems occur. However, this is seldom possible, and the clinician is normally required to develop analog or contrived situations for assessment and treatment purposes. The contrived situation should contain as many aspects of the natural environment as possible. Unfortunately, contrived situations are usually highly artificial, at best. For example, some sex therapists do observe and record couples engaging in overt sexual behaviors, including intercourse (Hartman & Fithian, 1972; Serber & Keith, 1974). This procedure is certainly questionable, since it raises problems of subject reactivity, patient privacy, the doctor-patient relationship, and other ethical, moral and scientific issues. Consequently, the clinician is usually required to devise strategies which measure earlier components in the sequence of the various sexual acts which indicate sexual arousal. However, the reliability and validity of these analogs must be constantly monitored to insure they are yielding information concerning the individual's actual behavior in the natural environment (Barlow, 1977).

ASSESSMENT OF SEXUAL AROUSAL

Physiological Indices

Physiological measurement of human sexual arousal was popularized, in part, by the work of Masters and Johnson (1966). Both Bartlett (1956) and Masters and Johnson found that such nongenital measures as increased blood pressure, heart rate, respiration, skin conductance, and pupillary dilation correlate with *active* sexual behavior such as masturbation and coitus. The majority of sexually dysfunctional individuals, however, have problems of sexual arousal with *precede* the act of sexual intercourse. Thus, physiological data collected in assessment must also be pertinent to the arousal phase in the chain of sexual responses. The physiological responses most frequently employed in the investigation of male sexual arousal fall into five categories: (1) *electrodermal responses;* (2) *cardiovascular responses;* (3) *respiratory responses;* (4) *pupillary responses;* and (5) *penile erection.* For any of these physiological responses to be useful and valid as measures of sexual arousal, it must be demonstrated that the response is specific to sexual arousal.

Electrodermal Responses. A number of studies have been conducted to determine the specificity and thus the accuracy and validity of the electrodermal responses as indicators of sexual arousal. Results have not been as encouraging as the work of Masters and Johnson might lead us to believe.

Solyom and Beck (1967) investigated electrodermal responses in three fetishists and one homosexual while these men were viewing pictures of fetish objects and a seminude male, respectively. Pictures of seminude females and geometric designs were used as control stimuli. The electrodermal reactions measured were (1) fall in skin resistance (galvanic skin response); (2) latency of GSR; (3) latency of maximum fall in skin resistance; (4) recovery time to regain prestimulus GSR level; (5) change in skin resistance over one-minute intervals; and (6) the number of spontaneous GSR fluctuations over each of the one-minute intervals. Of the six reactions measured, only the amplitude of the GSR, recovery time, and change in basal skin resistance showed any appreciable variation from picture to picture.

Wenger et al. (1968) employed 16 male participants in researching 10 various peripheral autonomic responses to reading pornographic literature. Slides of sexually relevant and sexually neutral literature were alternately presented to each participant while various peripheral autonomic responses were monitored. The most sensitive index of sexual arousal was skin conductance.

Romano (1969) employed 39 male participants in researching electrodermal response to: (1) a film depicting explicit heterosexual intercourse, (2) filmed scenes from a World War II Nazi concentration camp including corpses, and (3) neutral slides. Both of the films resulted in significant GSR activity relative to the control stimuli. Although changes in skin conductance were greater with the sexual film, the difference was not significant. It is interesting to note that although the participants reported that the film depicting the concentration camp aroused unpleasant feelings and the sexual film aroused pleasant feelings, GSR activity did not differentiate these reactions. Similar results were obtained by Roessler and Collins (1968), who investigated GSR response with a group of male participants viewing films of sexual relevance and a piano recital.

In a similar study, Barlow, Leitenberg, and Agras (1969) reported on the electrodermal reactions of a male homosexual and male pedophiliac when a covert noxious stimulus (imagining nausea and vomiting) was associated with sexual fantasy. Electrodermal reactions were measured as the change in log conductance over baseline, acquisition, extinction, and reacquisition. Results indicated that with the pedophiliac, a drop in conductance occurred during acquisition followed by a rise during extinction followed by another drop during reacquisition. For the homosexual, a drop in conductance occurred during acquisition and did not recover during extinction although subjective reports of homosexual impulses increased during the extinction phase.

As these studies indicate, electrodermal reactions appear to measure general arousal levels and may be elicited by general emotional states not correlated with sexual arousal. Thus, these reactions do not discriminate between sexual arousal and nonsexual arousal, a deficiency with severely limits the validity and utility of electrodermal responses as a measure of sexual arousal (Montague & Coles, 1966).

Cardiovascular Responses. Studies of cardiovascular responses have been no more promising than those measuring electrodermal responses. Bernick, Kling, and Borowitz (1968) used 11 heterosexual males in an investigation of cardiovascular response to erotic movies (one heterosexual and one homosexual in content) and an Alfred Hitchcock film. Baseline data were obtained using an adaptation period and a series of sexually neutral photographic slides which preceded and followed each of the stimulus movies. Mean heart rates were calculated for the 4-minute slide periods and the 16 minutes of each film. Mean changes were +7 beats per minute (bpm) during the heterosexual film, +6 bpm during the homosexual film, and +4 bpm during the suspense film. Significant increases were obtained for the heterosexual and suspense films, but not for the homosexual film. None of the differences between films was significant.

In an unpublished study Corman (1968) employed 10 males in an investigation of eight autonomic variables including heart rate. Reaction was measured in response to a sound stimulus, control slides, slides of nude females, and a sexual movie. Results indicated that heart rate did not increase significantly between the control slides and the slides of nude females; however, the sexual movie did significantly increase heart rate by a mean five beats per minute during the most arousing scene. Moreover, both systolic and diastolic blood pressure showed significant increases when subjects moved from the control slides to the nude slides and also from the nude slides to the movie. The blood pressure response to the film was significantly greater than the response to the slides of nudes or the sound stimulus.

Utilizing the same erotic film as Corman and instituting a negatively arousing film of a German concentration camp, Romano (1969), however, obtained different results. He found that the negatively arousing film also resulted in significant increases in blood pressure, and that the differences in the effect in blood pressure between the films were not significant. Furthermore, Romano's study did not confirm the heart rate increases to the erotic movie reported by Corman.

The results of these experiments indicate that sexually arousing stimuli do not appear to produce consistent increases in heart rate, face temperature, or finger pulse volume. Although blood pressure appears to show a more graded reaction to increasingly arousing stimuli, lack of discriminative validity obviates the utility of this measure.

Respiratory Responses. Use of respiratory changes as a measure of male sexual arousal have also been disappointing. Corman (1968), whose investigation we described above, discovered no significant changes in respiration rate or variability when participants viewed a sexual movie or slides of nudes. Koegler and Kline (1965) also found no differences in respiration rate when participants viewed sexual or stressful movies. Wenger et al. (1968) discovered no differences in respiration rate when participants read neutral control and sexually relevant literature. More recently, Bancroft and Mathews (1971) investigated six physiological responses, one of which was respiration rate, to visual stimuli and fantasy in a study employing 10 heterosexual males. Results indicated that respiration rate did not discriminate between sexually relevant and sexually neutral stimuli.

Pupillary Responses. Investigations of pupillary responses have also failed to yield a reliable and valid measure of sexual arousal. Hess, Seltzer, and Shlien (1965) investigated the pupillary responses of a group of five homosexuals and five heterosexuals to slides of nude males, nude females, and works of nonerotic art. Results indicated that all five heterosexuals showed a higher degree of pupil dilation to the female nudes than to the male nudes. Four of the five homosexuals showed a higher degree of dilation to the slides of male nudes than to the female nudes. Results also indicated, however, that three of the homosexuals also dilated to the nude female slides, and that two of the heterosexuals dilated to the nude male slides.

Scott, Wells, Wood, and Morgan (1967) utilized five homosexual and five heterosexual participants in the investigation of pupillary responses to pictures of clothed males, clothed females, nude males, nude females, and control picture of grey rectangles. Results indicated that two of the five participants in each group dilated more in response to the pictures of males than to those of females. Differences between groups were not significant. A second investigation involved the pupillary responses of a group of 10 males and 10 females to the sound of a pistol shot, pictures of seminude females, and pictures of seminude males. Again, no significant differences in responses were demonstrated.

Nunnally, Knot, Duchnowski, and Parker (1968) studied the pupillary responses of 30 male volunteers to a series of four slides depicting a female undressing. The first slide showed the female fully dressed; the other three slides depicted the female in various states of undress. Results indicated that the sexual slides produced a significant dilation increase as compared with control slides, and that a significant dilation was recorded in movement from the first slide (fully clothed) to the second slide (partial-ly clothed). Unfortuntely, however, no further significant increases oc-curred during the strip-tease progression.

Chapman, Chapman, and Brelje (1969) also investigated pupillary dilation, plus another important aspect of scientific inquiry, investigator influence. Control slides of numbers and landscapes and sexually relevant slides of clothed, seminude, and nude males and females were shown to 51 male volunteers. Two investigators were used: one was a young undergrad-uate male who handled the investigation in a "light" manner; the other in-vestigator was an older male graduate student who handled the investiga-tion in a "formal" manner. Results indicated that changes to stimuli were significant with the informal-investigator group and not significant with the formal-investigator group.

As these studies show, the evidence for pupillary response as a mea-sure of male sexual arousal is disappointing. Pupillary dilation occurs to sounds of gun shots, pictures of beautiful faces, and explicit male and fe-male nude photographs. Lack of response specificity thus eliminates pupil-lary response as a valid and reliable assessment measure of sexual arousal.

Penile Erection Responses. The most accurate measurement of male sexual arousal in both psychological and medical research has been penile erection (Abel et al., 1975; Barr, Raphael, & Hennessey, 1974; Freund, 1963, 1967; Freund et al., 1973). Zuckerman (1971), as well as Craighead, Kazdin, and Mahoney (1976), have claimed that the measurement of penile erection is the most valid, objective assessment of male sexual arousal known.

Several investigators, beginning with Freund (1957), have described techniques for measuring penile erection utilizing various types of penile transducers (Bancroft, Jones, & Pullan, 1966; Barlow et al., 1970; McCon-aghy, 1967). The devices employed are of two distinct types: (1) volumetric and (2) circumferential. Freund, Sedlacek, and Knob (1970) described a technique in which the penis is inserted into a glass cylinder. As penile tumescence displaces air in the cylinder, a measure of the volume of dis-placed air is recorded. Bancroft et al. (1966) described a mercury filled elastic tube that measures penile circumference change, and Barlow et al. (1970) described a strain gauge that involves a metal clip to surround the penis and detect circumference change.

Exactly which type of apparatus is preferable is still a subject of de-bate. McConaghy (1974) compared the volumetric and circumferential de-vices, and claimed that while the circumferential measurement devices were less expensive, less cumbersome, and more durable, volumetric de-vices are more sensitive and record smaller penile changes. Barlow (1977), however, concluded that more data are needed before a final evaluation can be made. He did admit, however, that while both devices are capable of

Figure 2-1. Mercury Strain Gauge.

detecting low levels of arousal of which even the subject is not aware, volumetric devices are more accurate when extremely low arousal level recordings are necessary.

Although the research evidence supports penile erection as the most systematic, valid, and reliable measure of male sexual arousal, this measure does have some obvious deficiencies. One such deficiency is the ability to suppress penile erections. Laws and Rubin (1969) and Hensen and Rubin (1971) presented erotic films to groups of participants and had them verbalize the content of each film as their penile responses were being monitored. When instructed to do so, these participants were able to suppress, to a degree, their level of penile erection.

Barlow (1977) has reviewed the literature with more encouraging results. For example, Freund (1967) found that only one of 27 pedophiliacs was able to physiologically represent himself as exclusively heterosexual for adult women. Several other pedophiliacs were able to fake typical heterosexual arousal patterns, but only one was able to avoid demonstrating pedophiliac arousal patterns. It should also be noted that although participants were able to suppress erections in the Hensen and Rubin (1971) investigation, measurable erectile responses were still demonstrated even under instructions to suppress arousal. Nevertheless, it is critical that the clinician/researcher be aware that the patient/subject can distort his erectile response.

In order to accurately assess male sexual arousal, several methodological issues in the assessment procedure should be considered. First, the nature of the sexual stimuli employed is vitally important: what kinds of stimuli are used and how explicit they are. Frequently, the literature reports the use of *Playboy*-type slides or pictures. Until recently, these were the most readily available sexual material. However, any adult book store or even the neighborhood news shop offers more explicit adult publications now, and these sources should be considered when choosing sexual stimuli.

Another important factor is the type of sexual stimulus used: magazines, slides, written descriptions, tape recordings, motion pictures, or videotapes. In some of his earlier work, Freund (1963) described a method of determining the sexual orientation of male subjects by continuously recording changes in penile volume while the subjects viewed still photographs of nude male and female children, adolescents, and adults. Freund's use of still photographs as sexual stimuli, however, did not take into consideration the erotic effect of movement and behavior. McConaghy (1967) measured penile circumference change to moving pictures of male and female nudes with two separate groups of homosexual and heterosexual males. Twenty-two homosexual and 11 heterosexual males viewed film clips of both adult males and females removing articles of clothing, showering, toweling off, and similar activities. Each film clip was then followed by the presentation of a nude same-sex photograph. This procedure seemed more effective than slides in producing sexual arousal and differentiating between sexual orientations. Similar results were obtained by Barr and McConaghy (1971) with an increased sample size of 60 first-year-male university students and 44 male patients who had presented themselves for treatment of homosexual impulses.

Various stimulus modalities, including fantasies (Marks & Gelder, 1967; McGuire & Valance, 1964), literature (Evans, 1968; Thorpe, Schmidt, Brown, & Castell, 1964), movies (Herman, Barlow, & Agras, 1971; McConaghy, 1967, 1969), and slides or pictures (Davison, 1968; Feldman & MacCulloch, 1971; Thorpe, Schmidt, & Castell, 1963) can be used to assess sexual arousal. Abel et al. (1975) studied the erectile tumescence response, as measured by a penile strain gauge, of 20 male homosexuals presented sexually relevant and nonsexual videotapes, slides or pictures, and audio-

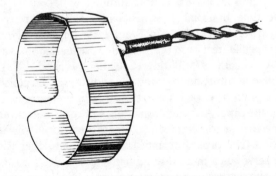

Figure 2-2. Penile Strain Gauge.

tapes. Their results confirmed previous findings in that of the three stimulus modalities investigated, videotapes generated the highest level of arousal, audiotapes the lowest arousal level, and slides an intermediate level. Tollison, Adams, and Tollison (1977) compared the erectile responses, as measured by a strain gauge, of three groups of homosexual, bisexual, and heterosexual males presented both homosexual and heterosexual slides and films. Their results indicated significant differentiation of arousal patterns and supported Abel et al.'s (1975) claim of the increased arousal potential of sexual films.

As the results of the above studies have shown, to facilitate the effectiveness of the arousal stimulus, one should employ a variety of sexual stimuli. Moreover, the assumption that what is arousing to the clinician will also be arousing to the patient is certainly not valid. The available stimuli should be presented to the patient before the sexual assessment in order that he may choose those that are the most arousing to him. One should also keep at a minimum the number of erotic stimuli employed in order to prevent habituation and a decrease in measured arousal.

A review of the literature further shows that a number of reported investigations do not mention an adaptation period as part of the experimental procedure. To avoid including the effects of shock, surprise, and similar reactions as data of sexual arousal, one should allow a 15-20 minute adaptation period in the experimentl procedure for the individual to habituate to the assessment environment.

To facilitate maximum arousal to the sexual stimuli, the clinician should attempt to control for the period since the patient's last orgasm. Of course, strict control of this variable is practically impossible, but the individual can be requested to avoid orgasm for an appropriate time before the sexual assessment. This time-span should be long enough to guard against distortion of the sexual response by the effects of a recent orgasm.

In any assessment procedure, standardization is required, particularly when the individual's response to various stimuli is to be compared with his response at a later time. In sexual assessment with males, some researchers (Barr & McConaghy, 1971; Barr et al., 1974; Freund, 1963; McConaghy, 1967) have used the level of penile erection at the onset of the sexual stimulus as a baseline, while others (Abel et al., 1975; Barlow et al., 1970; Freund, 1973) have considered the stable-over-time, nonerection, flaccid state at the conclusion of an appropriate adaptation period prior to the stimulus presentation as an appropriate baseline measure. Although consistency of measurement from session to session is the vital factor, certain advantages are associated with the use of the latter method. This procedure appears to accentuate response specificity, and therefore serves as a more discriminative evaluative measure of sexual arousal. It may be that the latter procedure also more reliably records graded erectile responses to a range of sexual stimuli. However, additional research is needed before this claim can be made.

TABLE 2-2

Steps in a Physiological Sexual Assessment

1. Explain assessment procedure to patient, answer all questions, and obtain written approval at the end of the clinical interview.

2. Have patient select several sexual stimuli deemed arousing and attractive by him/her from a collection of erotic stimuli.

3. Calibrate polygraph and explain to patient the proper placement of the strain gauge on the penile shaft midway between the glans and scrotum or vaginal probe approximately 1 inch into the vagina.

4. Place the patient in a private chamber and have him/her fit the plethysmograph and determine if they have followed instructions.

5. Allow orientation and habituation to the laboratory (approximately 15-20 minutes).

6. Have the patient masturbate to just short of orgasm. Measurement of this penile/vaginal response is considered 100% arousal.

7. Allow complete penile detumescence or decreased vaginal vasocongestion to original baseline level.

8. Presentation of the first sexual stimulus (approximately 3-5 minutes).

9. Presentation of first neutral stimulus until penile detumescence/vaginal vasocongestion approaches baseline.

10. Presentation of second sexual stimulus followed by second neutral stimulus, and so on.

11. Inform the patient that the assessment is completed and that he/she should remove the plethysmograph and dress himself/herself.

12. Debriefing.

Physiological Assessment of Female Sexual Arousal. Measurement of sexual arousal in women has, in the past, been hindered by the lack of reliable method of assessing responses in female genital structure, as well as by ethical considerations of privacy and confidentiality. In their early research, Masters and Johnson (1966) reported that one of the principle physiological responses during female sexual arousal is genital vaso-congestion. Later, Shapiro, Cohen, DiBianco, and Rosen (1968), and Cohen and Shapiro (1970) reported the construction of an isothermal relative blood-flow meter which measured vaginal blood flow. This device consisted of two thermisters held at equal distance from the anterior midline of a diaphragm ring. With this measuring device they detected increases in vaginal blood flow in response to sexual fantasy, and no changes in vaginal blood flow in response to fantasy-produced feelings of fear, embarrassment, or anger. Although a significant development in the measurement of physiological correlates of female sexual arousal, the isothermal blood flow meter had the disadvantage of requiring individual diaphragm fittings for every female.

Geer and his colleagues (Geer, 1975; Geer et al., 1974; Sintchak & Geer, 1975) avoided the problem of individual fittings in their development of a vaginal photoplethysmograph. Using the principle of photoplethysmography (Brown, 1967), Sintchak and Geer (1975) introduced a clear acrylic probe 0.5 inches in diameter and 1.75 inches in length which contained an incandescent light source mounted on one end of the probe and a Selenium photo cell detector mounted on the side (Figure 2-3). When the probe is inserted approximately one inch into the vagina, the light source illuminates the tissue of the vaginal wall, while the photoelectric transducer detects changes in the optical density of the tissue which result from changes in blood flow in the tissue. The less light reflected, the more vasocongestion and, presumably, the more arousal. According to Brown (1967), the output due to blood from a photoplethysmograph may be partitioned into two components: (1) the residual component which represents the relatively constant amount of blood in the tissue; and (2) the variable component due to changes induced by the pressure pulse wave, called *blood-volume pulse*. Direct coupling input circuitry (DC) from a photoplethysmograph to an amplifier displays both components simultaneously, thus recording changes in blood volume. AC coup-

Figure 2-3. Vaginal Photoplethysmograph.

ling with a time constant and greater amplification produces a blood-volume-pulse recording only.

Hoon, Wincze, and Hoon (1967) validated the vaginal photoplethysmograph as a measure of vaginal vasocongestion by presenting subjects with control, dysphoric, and erotic videotapes while measuring changes in blood volume level. Subjects were six sexually experienced women. Vaginal blood volume increased significantly during the erotic videotape, but showed no significant changes during the control or dysphoric videotapes. In addition to validating a measure of a physiological correlate of sexual arousal in the female, these data also demonstrated specificity of vaginal vasocongestion in response to sexual stimuli, a specificity not demonstrated with other autonomic measures (Hoon et al., 1976).

Verbal Report

Verbal or self-report is information provided by an individual or members of the individual's environment regarding the individual's behavior (Craighead et al., 1976). For example, one may ask, "What is your level of sexual arousal to females (males)?" or "Are you interacting with females and what is the nature of the interaction?" Given the private and sensitive nature of sexual behavior in our society, and the problems inherent in the behavioral measurement of sexual activity, verbal report measures of sexual functioning were the major assessment tools available to the clinician for many years. With the development of reliable physiological measures some clinicians and researchers now tend to discount verbal report of sexual activity. However, as Barlow (1977) indicates, to ignore verbal report is inappropriate, because verbal report is itself a type of behavior and is as important as other behavioral or physiological measures.

Self-Report Inventories. Self-report information may be obtained by use of questionnaires that attempt to assess patterns of sexual arousal or sexual attitudes. Common procedures are either the comparison of repeated measures on these devices over time, or the comparison of an individual with a standardized group.

In the past, traditional scales such as responses to the Rorschach or the masculine-feminine scale of the Minnesota Multiphasic Personality Inventory (MMPI) have provided vague measures of sexual arousal. Much of the variance in these scales is, however, determined by factors other than sexual arousal. Feldman (1966), for example, indicates that highly educated males tend to score in a more "feminine" range on the MMPI because less educated males score rather low on cultural interests. Schumacher and Lloyd (1976) analyzed MMPI data on 302 patients with sexual difficulties, and did not find the data predictive of specific distress, intensity of distress, or treatment outcome. Additional application of traditional psychodiagnostic tests is found in the work of Hartman and Fithian (1972), who administered a battery of tests including the MMPI, the Taylor-Johnson Temperament Analysis, The Draw-a-Person Test, and the Luscher Color Test to measure sexual arousal. However, they have not as yet published a systematic, definitive evaluation of their data.

More specific verbal-report measures have been employed in the assessment of sexual arousal. Feldman, MacCulloch, Mellor, and Pinschoff's (1966) Sexual Orientation Method (SOM) was designed to measure shifts in heterosexual and homosexual arousal patterns during treatment of males. Psychometric research on this scale (Feldman & MacCulloch, 1971) has demonstrated that the scale is internally consistent, and that test/retest reliability is satisfactory. Barlow (1977), however, claims that the scale suffers from the authors' early inclination to arbitrarily label a patient as improved or cured after a small change on the scale, and that the scale is difficult to score.

Other investigators have attempted to include the assessment of anxiety in sexual activity. Harbinson, Graham, Quinn, McAllister, and Woodward (1974) revamped the original SOM to include scales indicating anxiety in sexual behavior, while Obler (1973) developed a Sexual Anxiety Scale (SAS) intended to assess cognitively experienced social and sexual anxiety. Obler's scale contains 22 items which range from anxiety experienced during nonsexual contact with a member of the opposite sex to that experienced during vaginal penetration. The author claims that the scale is both reliable and valid.

Hoon, Hoon, and Wincze (1976) have developed an inventory scale designed to measure female sexual arousal. The SAI (Sexual Arousal Inventory) consists of 28 items describing erotic experiences which the patient rates along a 7-point scale of arousal. The advantages of this scale, according to its authors, are that (1) it is easy to administer and score; (2) it may be used for single, married or lesbian women; and (3) at present it appears to be the only scale specially applicable to women.

Another type of verbal-report device is the card-sorting technique devised by Barlow et al., (1969). In this technique various sexual scenes depicting the patient's experiences or fantasies are typed on cards with each card depicting one scene. Barlow, Reynolds, and Agras (1973) cite the following example of one scene in a 24-year-old pedophiliac's card sort: "You are alone in a room with a very sexy looking 10-year-old girl with long blonde hair." As often as desired, the patient takes the cards and sorts them into one of five envelopes labeled 0-4. The patient is instructed that the numbered envelopes represent a hierarchy of sexual arousal with 0 representing no arousal and 4 representing very strong arousal. The authors admit that the card-sorting technique is highly individualized, and therefore has not been subjected to psychometric evaluation.

While some investigators have attempted to measure arousal and sexual anxiety, others have concentrated on the development of sexual experience scales (Brady & Levitt, 1965; Zuckerman, 1971). Podell and Perkins (1957), for example, constructed a 15-item questionnaire that sampled heterosexual behaviors ranging from "embrace" to "oral contact with female genitalia." These scales are constructed on the assumptions that sexual activity is hierarchical, and that subjects would not be expected to experience items higher on the scale until they first had experienced lower items. Bentler (1968) developed a similar scale of heterosexual experience for females which was intended to assess change in sexual behavior during therapy.

LoPiccolo and Steger (1978) have devised and standardized an instrument called the Sexual Interaction Inventory designed to measure individuals' sexual functioning and satisfaction with themselves and their sexual partners. This inventory is particularly useful with sexually dysfunctional couples, but can be adapted for use with a variety of sexual disorders. The inventory appears to have adequate reliability, and is capable of discriminating between individuals with sexual dysfunctions and sexually satisfied normals, as well as detecting progress or success of sexual treatment. The items, scales, and an illustrative example are shown in Tables 2-3, 2-4, and Figure 2-4.

Self-Monitoring Procedures. A type of verbal report of sexual arousal is *behavioral recording* or *self-monitoring*. Self-monitoring procedures require the individual to record the occurrences of a specified behavior as well as the events that precede and follow the behavior. The frequency of the behavior and the recording of antecedent and consequent events that may influence the behavior provide some of the basic information for behavioral assessment (Ciminero, Nelson, & Lipinski, 1977). For example, a patient in treatment for voyeurism might be asked to keep a daily record of all sexual urges. He might be asked to specify the nature of each sexual urge (*e.g.*, voyeuristic or coital) as well as the antecedents and consequences of each urge (*e.g.*, "I saw this beautiful woman leaving the theatre so I followed her home and later peeped through her window to watch her undress").

Herman & Prewitt (1974) provide detailed behavioral self-monitoring records that the patient can use to record all instances of sexual activity, all instances of masturbation and the fantasies employed during masturbation, and the sexual fantasies occurring independently of sexual activity and masturbation. These give the therapist baseline data, as well as comparative data on which to evaluate the effects of treatment. The authors claim that the records are constructed so that the person may carry them conveniently, and are coded so that recording is as simple as placing a mark in the appropriate column.

TABLE 2-3

Sexual Interaction Inventory Item List

1.   The male seeing the female when she is nude.

2.   The female seeing the male when he is nude.

3.   The male and female kissing for one minute continuously.

4.   The male giving the female a body massage, not touching her breasts or genitals.

5.   The female giving the male a body massage, not touching his genitals.

6.   The female carressing the female's breasts with his hands.

7.   The male caressing the female's breasts with his mouth (lips or tongue).

8.   The male caressing the female's genital with his hands.

9.   The male caressing the female's genitals with his hands until she reaches orgasm (Climax).

10. The female caressing the male's genitals with her hands.

11. The female caressing the male's genitals with her hands until he ejaculates (has a climax).

12. The male caressing the female's genitals with his mouth (lips or tongue).

13. The male caressing the female's genitals with his mouth until she reaches orgasm (climax).

14. The female caressing the male's genitals with her mouth (lips or tongue).

15. The female caressing the male's genitals with her mouth until he ejaculates (has a climax).

16. The male and female having intercourse.

17. The male and female having intercourse with both of them having an orgasm (climax).

Source: Adapted from LoPiccolo, J., & Steger, J. C. The Sexual Interaction Inventory. In J. LoPiccolo & L. LoPiccolo (Eds.), *Handbook of Sex Therapy.* New York: Plenum Press, 1978. Reprinted with permission of Plenum Press.

Self-monitoring techniques should be a mandatory component of assessment and treatment of sexual cases. An example of this procedure is shown in Table 2-5. The patient is given a supply of forms and instructed that a separate form should be used for each sexual encounter. However, the purpose of this self-monitoring is not for cross-patient comparison, but for collection of baseline data and the examination of changes over time in a given patient.

Another use of self-monitoring occurs during a sexual assessment. For example, during a sexual assessment individuals may be shown neutral and erotic stimuli and requested to estimate their percentage of erection, percentage of sexual arousal, and similar responses, which can then be correlated with their physiologically measured arousal. These records allow a

TABLE 2-4

Sample page of the Sexual Interaction Inventory

The male carressing the female's breasts with his mouth (lips or tongue). When you and your mate engage in sexual behavior, does this particular activity usually occur? How often would you like this activity to occur?

1. Currently occurs:

1. _____ Never
2. _____ Rarely (10% of the time)
3. _____ Occasionally (25% of the time)
4. _____ Fairly often (50 % of the time)
5. _____ Usually (75% of the time)
6. _____ Always

2. I would like it to occur:

1. _____ Never
2. Rarely (10% of the time)
3. _____ Occasionally (25% of the time)
4. _____ Fairly often (50% of the time)
5. _____ Usually (75% of the time)
6. _____ Always

How pleasant do you currently find this activity to be? How pleasant do you think your mate finds this activity to be?

3. I find this activity:

1. _____ Extremely unpleasant
2. _____ Moderately unpleasant
3. _____ Slightly unpleasant
4. _____ Slightly pleasant
5. _____ Moderately pleasant
6. _____ Extremely pleasant

4. I think my mate finds this activity:

1. _____ Extremely unpleasant
2. _____ Moderately unpleasant
3. _____ Slightly unpleasant
4. _____ Slightly pleasant
5. _____ Moderately pleasant
6. _____ Extremely pleasant

Source: LoPiccolo, J., & Steger, J. C. The sexual interaction inventory. In J. LoPiccolo & L. Lo Piccolo (Eds.), *Handbook of sex therapy.* New York: Plenum Press, 1978. Reprinted with permission of Plenum Press.

moment-to-moment determination of the congruence of verbal report and physiological indices.

Verbal report measures have a very serious flaw, however, which is response bias. The most commonly discussed bias is social desirability (Goldfried & Sprafkin, 1974). In other words, the patient may conceivably give what he or she feels to be a socially acceptable answer rather than a truthful one. In a sexual assessment, for example, a male patient may report high sexual arousal to a series of heterosexual stimuli when, in fact, his physiologically measured erectile response indicates little or no tumescence. He thus distorts his "perceived failure" in a self-reported estimate of high arousal in order to appear more socially acceptable. Other contingencies such as legal threats imposed against the homosexual and the exhibitionist may also serve to distort verbal reports. Taken alone, as it often is by the more traditionally-oriented clinician, verbal report may be a poor assessment technique. The value of verbal report lies in its use as a single component within a multidimensional assessment procedure.

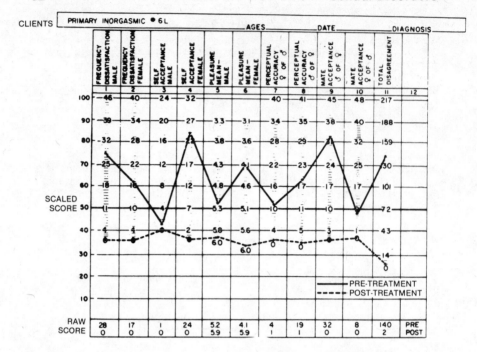

CLIENTS | PRIMARY INORGASMIC ● 6 L | AGES_____ DATE_____ DIAGNOSIS_____

Figure 2-4. Pre- and posttreatment profiles in a case of primary orgasmic dysfunction. [**Source:** The sexual interaction inventory. In J. LoPiccolo & L. LoPiccolo (Eds.), *Handbook of Sex Therapy.* New York: Plenum Press, 1978. Reproduced by permission of Plenum Press.]

Behavioral Observations

Because of the private nature of sexual functioning in our society, assessment of sexual arousal utilizing direct behavioral observation is generally considered questionable. Masters and Johnson (1970), however, observed several hundred couples involved in sexual activity, and the data obtained from these observations have been of monumental importance in the field of human sexuality and sexual therapy. In contrast to this type of observation, some therapists reportedly engage in quasi-sexual or direct sexual contact with the patient under the pretext of sexual assessment and therapy. For example, one form of questionable therapist-patient sexual contact is the "sexological exam" (Hartman & Fithian, 1972). In this procedure each nude patient is sexually stimulated by an opposite-sex therapist and may undergo breast and genital manipulation. Proponents of the exam claim its purpose is to determine sexual response and demonstrate the response to the patient. Ethical, moral, and scientific problems in regard to the exam as well as the possibilities for its abuse by therapists are obvious.

TABLE 2-5

Behavioral Recording Form

Date _____

Time	Place	Partner	Antecedents	Cognitive Arousal	Percent of Erection at Highest Point	Consequence
11 P.M.	Her apartment	Girl I met at a bar on Peachtree Street	I was at a bar when I saw this girl and I asked her to dance. After we had danced and talked about an hour she asked if I wanted to go to her apartment for a drink. I kept wondering what I was going to do if she wanted to have sex and I couldn't get an erection.	Yes, she had me turned on becuase she was so good looking.	About 30% I tried to get inside her before it went down but it was no use.	I told her that I had overworked this week and was just too tired and that it had never happened to me before. She was nice about it and acted like she believed me but I think she suspected my problem. I told her I had to leave and go home to bed because I had to be at work early.

Another technique for the direct observational assessment of sexual arousal is the use of sexual surrogates. Masters and Johnson pioneered this technique, using carefully screened and trained surrogates under close supervision in cases in which a man lacked a sexual partner. While at first glance the use of surrogates with partners lacking a sexual partner seems a logical approach, some have termed this practice "thinly veiled prostitution" (Holden, 1974), and claim that providing surrogates to married men with wives who are unwilling to enter therapy with their husbands is at best questionable, even if other problematic issues involved in such cases are ignored (Apfelbaum, 1976). Perhaps more disturbing is the current trend for sexual surrogates to move toward becoming independent therapists and to operate without professional supervision (LoPiccolo, 1977).

ASSESSMENT OF GENDER SPECIFIC BEHAVIORS

The most recently investigated and probably the least understood of the four major components of sexual behavior is gender role behavior. Barlow (1977) defines deviation of gender role as "some degree of incongruence between one's biological and genetic sex and the behavior accompanying that sex as defined by a given culture" (p. 494). Although the formal assessment of gender role behavior is not necessary with every patient, it is our experience that most transsexuals, some transvestites and homosexuals, and a smaller percentage of patients with heterosocial skills deficiencies behave atypically enough to draw attention to themselves or to sabotage their efforts at successful heterosexual interactions.

Our culture is quite familiar with the concepts of masculine and feminine behaviors, yet a pervasive ambiguity associated with these labels has thwarted attempts to operationally define these behaviors. For example, consider the woman who goes to graduate school, obtains an advanced graduate degree, takes a teaching position at a major university, and then publishes and works hard to achieve recognition and promotion. Many people would see nothing atypical about her successful behavior, yet others might consider it masculine. The lack of agreement as to what constitutes masculine and feminine behaviors and whether these behaviors are even desirable has slowed the development of techniques to assess gender role behavior. At this time only limited information from verbal report and behavioral observation is available to assess gender behavior. Physiological assessment of gender role behavior has, to date, been almost nonexistent, although some recent evidence does suggest that gender role behavior may be biochemically influenced (Yalom, Green, & Fisk, 1973). This finding will undoubtedly be further investigated in the future.

Verbal Report

One of the earliest attempts to assess gender role behavior was the Masculine-Feminine (M-F) test devised by Terman and Miles (1936). This test was very traditional in orientation; it required that the patient answer various questions and also complete exercises, including the Rorschach. Variations of this early test include the masculine-feminine scale of the MMPI and the femininity scale of the California Psychological Inventory (Gough, 1952). Barlow (1977) claims, however, that scales of this type have proven useless in assessing gender role behavior because of the vagueness and cultural-temporal relativity of the questions. For example, the California Psychological Inventory asks the question, "I would like to be a soldier," and requires an affirmative answer to indicate masculinity.

In opposition to such vague masculine-feminine assessment techniques, Freund, Nagler, Langevin, Zajac, and Steiner (1974) devised a 19-item scale designed to assess gender role behavior. Of the 19 items, 12 are applicable to all males, while the remaining 7 are applicable only to homosexual and transsexual males. This scale is heavily weighted toward sampling developmental behavior as an indicator of present gender role behavior. For example:

Between the ages of 13 and 16, did you wish you had been born a girl instead of a boy

(a) often
(b) occasionally
(c) never

Since the age of 17, have you put on women's underwear or clothing

(a) once a month or more for at least a year
(b) (less often, but) several times a year for at least a year
(c) very seldom did this since age 17
(d) never did this since age 17

The authors have provided norms of different group scores on the masculine-feminine continuum which may be compared to an individual's scores. The authors also report that the scale has satisfactory psychometrical properties with a broad spectrum of subjects.

A second instrument for assessing gender role behavior is the body-image scale developed by Lindgren and Pauly (1975). Although this scale is designed to assess gender role behavior in general, it is specifically constructed to assess and evaluate transsexuals. The body-image scale, as the name implies, supposedly assesses a subject's satisfaction with the physical appearance of his different body parts. Barlow et al. (1973) report that transsexuals are typically dissatisfied with their physical appearance, especially in the genital area. As mentioned in Chapter 1, the transsexual often describes himself as a "woman trapped inside a man's body" and requests surgery to change his sexual gender. It stands to reason that a transsexual would find his masculine body features incongruent with his preferred gender role and identification. Barlow et al. (1973) note that the assessment of a transsexual's satisfaction with his bodily appearance is useful whether one is treating the transsexual by surgical means or by modifying gender role behavior.

Another verbal-report scale of gender role behavior is the sex role inventory (Bem, 1974). The sex role inventory attempts to assess inclination for the masculine or feminine sex role by asking subjects to choose items that best describe themselves. Feminine items include such descriptions as "cheerful" and "affectionate" while masculine descriptive items include "aggressive" and "ambitious." Bem considers masculinity and femininity as two separate and distinct entities and believes it is possible to categorize individuals as either masculine, feminine, or androgynous, a category which represents the positive aspects of both sex roles. Although this scale has proven to be psychometrically sound, it has been tested only with nonclinical populations and is not designed to measure the degree of gender role deviation. Barlow (1977), however, claims that the scale has been used in his laboratory and has provided useful information regarding sex role preferences with transsexuals and other individuals with gender role variation.

Behavioral Observations

The assessment of gender role behavior through observation of overt behavior is accomplished largely with the use of behavioral checklists and coding systems. Two different types of checklists have been developed, one for children and the other for adults.

Behavioral assessment of children's gender role behavior has been reported in both contrived and naturalistic settings. Rekers (1977) claims that most of the work of developmental psychologists in assessing sex-typed play in children is suspect because (1) many techniques assess only the child's initial choice of a toy or pictorial representation of a toy rather than continuous play over a period of time (*e.g.,* Sutton-Smith, Rosenberg, & Morgan, 1963); (2) many tests of sex-typed behavior require that an adult be present for the administration of the experimental task (*e.g.,* Rabban, 1970) and thus pose a stimulus-specific condition; and (3) many tests employ projection with little psychometric support data.

Rekers (1977) has devised a method of assessing children's sex-typed play within the clinical setting which (1) employs stimuli related to significant differences in the sex-typed play behavior of normal boys and girls; (2) provides data through the use of repeated dependent measures over time; (3) does not require the presence of a male or female experimenter; and (4) can be administered to children from ages 3 to 8 years. The procedure requires the continuous time-sample recording from behind a one-way mirror of individual children's play with sex-typed toys.

Investigations (Rekers & Yates, 1976), utilizing this procedure with "gender disturbed" and normal boys have found that a boy's sex-typed behavior varies in the presence of the mother, the father, a male clinical psychologist, and a female clinical psychologist. The data suggest that only if the child is playing alone with sex-typed toys will the recording checklist accurately assess gender role disturbances.

Rekers and his colleagues have identified certain physical mannerisms that they claim reliably distinguish between normal male and female children as well as between normal males and gender-disturbed males. Rekers, Amaro-Plotkin, and Low (1977) investigatged the various physical mannerisms among different age groups and found that limp wrist (flexing the wrist towards the palmar surface of the forearm and/or upper arm while the elbow is either flexed or extended), flutters (a rapid succession of up and down movements of the forearm and/or upper arm while the wrist remains relaxed), and flexed elbow (walking or standing with the arms held such that the angle between the forearm and upper arm is approximately between 1° and 135°) significantly discriminated between sexes and between groups of normal and gender-disturbed boys. These data are important, for, although both clinicians and the general public have labeled as "effeminate" certain behavioral mannerisms in boys, no data previously existed on the type and occurrence of mannerisms that accurately differentiate normal boys from girls and gender-disturbed children.

Assessment of sex role behavior in the naturalistic environment has also been the target of much of the effort of Rekers and his colleagues. Rekers records the gender-disturbed child's masculine and feminine behaviors outside the clinic by teaching parents and behavioral observers a time-sampling procedure using daily behavioral checklists in the child's natural environment (Rekers, 1972; Rekers, Yates, Willis, Rosen & Taubman, 1976; Rekers & Varni, 1977). In addition, the parents provide a detailed behavioral history of the child's gender development on the Rekers Behavioral Checklist of Childhood Gender Problems (Rekers, 1972).

Other instruments used to assess gender role behavior and the degree of gender role disturbance include the Child Behavior and Attitude Questionnaire and the Child Game Participation Questionnaire (based on research of normal and gender-disturbed boys reported in Bates & Bentler,

1973; Bates, Bentler & Thompson, 1973). Scores from these instruments provide a quantitative measure of the degree of effeminate behavior as compared to the standardization grouping of normal boys and girls ages 4 through 10 years.

The second major type of behavioral checklists are those designed to assess gender role behavior in adults. Although research in this area of assessment is limited, Schatzberg, Westfall, Blumetti, and Birk (1975) recently introduced a quantitative rating scale for effeminacy in males that appears promising. The checklist is based upon the authors' observations that variation in gender role is often a component of many sexual deviations. They thus devised a 67-item checklist that attempts to break down gender role behavior into discreet behavioral units, the presence of absence of which could be recorded simply by checking the appropriate yes/no block. The checklist was devised to record overt behaviors such as gait (Does he move sinuously?), mouth movement (Does he purse his lips when he speaks?), and speech (Does he speak in soft tones?). It was initially tested on a nonpatient population of homosexual and heterosexual males, each of whom was seen during a 15-minute interview session. Results indicated that although 17 of the 67 items were not scored for any of the 32 subjects in the investigation, correlational scores of two raters were sufficiently high (0.94). Interrater agreement, however, was rather low at 0.54, probably due, in part, to the inability of the raters to score the subject's behavior until after the completion of the interview. In a discussion of the checklist, Barlow (1977) indicates that the range of its effectiveness is rather small, in that of the 67 items, 17 items were never scored for any subject and that the authors consider a score of between five and nine as indicating mildly effeminate behavior. The checklist is, however, the first of its type, and the results of its initial use are such that further investigation is warranted.

Barlow et al. (1973) have approached the assessment of gender role behavior by directly assessing the motor behaviors of sitting, standing, and walking. They assessed the motor performance of a group of males and females according to those modes of sitting, standing, and walking specific to traditional male and female gender role behavior. For example, females tend to sit with their lower back and buttocks close to the back of a hard-backed chair and cross their legs with one knee resting on the other. On the other hand, males tend to sit with the lower back and buttocks away from the back of a chair and cross their legs with one ankle resting on the opposite knee. Interrater agreement was 100 percent for sitting, 97.4 percent for standing, and 92.5 percent for walking. Barlow (1977) has claimed that the checklist demonstrates that females have a much greater variety of behaviors while sitting, standing, and walking than do males, who exhibit a very narrow range of characteristically masculine behaviors. Transsexual

TABLE 2-6

Masculine and Feminine Gender Role Behaviors

Gender Role Behavior	Masculine	Feminine
Sitting		
buttocks: position from back of chair	distant	close
legs uncrossed, knees	apart	close
legs crossed	foot on knee	knee on knee
arm movement from	shoulder	elbow
fingers	together and straight	relaxed
wrist action	firm	limp
Standing		
feet apart	greater than 3 inches	less than 3 inches
arm movement from	shoulder	elbow
hand motion	minimal or in pocket	greater than 4 movements per minute
wrist action	firm	limp
Walking		
strides	long	short
hip "swish"	absent	present
arm movement from	shoulder	elbow
wrist action	firm	limp
arm-to-trunk relationship	free and swinging	close and nonswinging

Source: Barlow, D. H., Reynolds, J., & Agras, W. S. Gender identity in a transsexual. *Archives of General Psychiatry,* 1973, *28,* 569-579. Reprinted with permission of the American Medical Association.

males, however, scored consistently more feminine than the female sample employed in the initial investigation, a finding which raises the question of the differences in these motor behaviors between females and effeminate males.

Assessment of gender role behavior begins with videotaping (or observing) the patient while he/she sits, stands, and walks and afterward insturcting him/her to act as masculine (or feminine, depending on the goal of gender role behaviors) as possible while he/she again sits, stands and walks. The videotape is then rated by trained raters as to the presence or absence of the previously described gender role behaviors per unit of time. Barlow (1977) has claimed that raters can be easily trained and that the total observation time of a trained rater is under 30 seconds. The masculine-feminine checklist is somewhat limited, however, in that it deals only with gender-specific motor behavior and does not assess interactional components of sexual behavior.

ASSESSMENT OF HETEROSOCIAL SKILLS

One is certainly not hard pressed to see the relevancy and importance of the assessment of heterosocial skills, especially with the patient who reports sexual difficulties. We recognize and admire those individuals who seem to meet and mix successfully and effortlessly with persons of the opposite sex. We call these individuals "cool," and envy their good fortune in interacting regularly with such a variety of opposite sex partners. But what is it about these heterosocially successful individuals that differentiates them from those who inappropriately and awkwardly interact with members of the opposite sex? Obviously, if an individual is deficient in heterosocial skills or has never learned those skills necessary for successful heterosocial behavior, we can hardly expect competence in heterosocial interactions. Even if the individual is heterosexually sophisticated in that he/she possesses the sexual knowledge and expertise required for successful sexual behavior, he/she may still be unable to meet, date, and successfully relate to persons of the opposite sex (Barlow, 1977).

The importance of adequate heterosocial skills has been recognized by clinicians of various theoretical persuasions as germaine to successful heterosexual functioning. For example, believing that homosexuality was the result of fear or avoidance of the opposite sex, nonbehavioral clinicians have attempted to instruct and encourage heterosocial skills in their patients for some time (Barlow, 1977). These early attempts to teach appropriate heterosocial functioning have relied heavily on unstructured attempts to improve socializing through therapeutic milieus or group therapy. The behavioral approach to heterosocial skills, on the other hand, requires a precise analysis of the verbal and nonverbal components of adequate social skills (Hersen & Eisler, 1976).

Most research on assessment of heterosocial skills has involved analogue studies of college students. This is not surprising, since most psychological research is conducted within the university setting, and college students represent a convenient population pool for the psychological academician. These studies typically involve students presumed to be deficient in heterosocial skills when their self-reports show minimal dating. Two somewhat different theoretical positions have been postulated to account for this low frequency of dating. The first of these approaches sees maladaptive heterosocial functioning as a result of conditioned anxiety which inhibits expression of normal feeling and the performance of adaptive heterosocial skills (Borkovec, Stone, O'Brien, & Kaloupek, 1974; Wolpe & Lazarus, 1966). The second approach views low-frequency dating as a function of the patient's having never acquired adaptive heterosocial skills (Twentyman & McFall, 1975). These somewhat contrasting approaches to etiology are also reflected in a choice of assessment techniques. Assuming that maladaptive heterosocial skills are a result of conditioned anxiety, Borkovec et al (1974) utilized self-report measures of anxiety and subjective awareness of internal autonomic cues as assessment techniques. They also recorded behavioral measures of their subjects' speech dysfluencies during vocalizations, and physiological recordings of heart rate before and after social interactions.

Twentyman and McFall (1975), however, assumed that maladaptive heterosocial functioning is a result of the patient's having never learned the appropriate skills, and employed a social-skills educational training program for shy males. Self-report and physiological indices of anxiety, as well as behavioral measures of the subjects' frequency and duration of his interactions with females, were obtained pre- and posttraining. Their data indicate that subjects who received social skills training significantly increased their frequency and duration of heterosocial interaction as compared to the no-treatment control group.

From a clinical standpoint, assessment of both social anxiety and knowledge or requisite social skills is important. Behavioral techniques for the assessment of heterosocial skills have primarily emphasized verbal report and direct observation of behavior. Although a limited amount of research employing physiological responses has been conducted, these results remain inconclusive.

Verbal Report

Assessment of heterosocial functioning via verbal report has directed itself primarily toward the measurement of social anxiety. Information on social anxiety may be elicited in three different ways: (1) *paper and pencil inventories;* (2) *clinical interviews;* and (3) *self-monitoring techniques.*

The first of these, paper and pencil inventories, has been employed extensively in the assessment of heterosocial skills. Believing that social anxiety has two distinct components—fear of receiving negative evaluation from others, and negative affect and discomfort in social situations—Watson and Friend (1969) developed a scale termed the Fear of Negative Evaluation Scale (FNE), a 30-item scale consisting of statements to which the patient responds True/False. Examples of the items are: "I am usually worried about what kind of impression I make"; and "I react very little when other people disapprove of me."

Watson and Friend (1969) also attended to the second component of heterosocial anxiety, negative affect and discomfort in social situations, by developing the Social Anxiety and Distress Scale (SAD). This 28-item scale also consists of items that the patient answers True/False. Examples of the items include, "I try to avoid talking to people unless I know them well," and "I feel relaxed even in unfamiliar situations." The authors report adequate reliability and consistency for both scales, although the reliability of the SAD has been questioned (Hersen & Bellack, 1977).

Twentyman and McFall (1975) devised a verbal-report scale to assess heterosocial avoidance. The Survey of Heterosexual Interactions (SHI) is a 20-item scale that presumably assesses a male's ability to interact effectively with females in social situations. The authors collected a variety of verbal-report, behavioral, and physiological measures from groups of subjects previously classified as heterosocially shy or confident on the basis of dating frequency and SHI scores. Significant differences were found between shy and confident subjects on all three measures. The SHI thus appears to be a promising assessment device, but should be subjected to psychometric analysis and standardization for both male and female populations (Hersen & Bellack, 1976).

The Situation Questionnaire (SQ) developed by Rehm and Marston (1968) assesses heterosocial anxiety and discomfort in males. The questionnaire consists of 30 situations for which the patient must indicate the degree of anxiety he would experience if he were in that situation; for example, telephoning a girl to conduct a social conversation, or dancing with a girl on a date. While Rehm and Marston (1968) do not explicitly report on the reliability and validity of the questionnaire, they do report significantly greater decreases in SQ scores for subjects exposed to treatment than for those in a no-treatment control group. While the SQ appears promising, further psychometric analysis is required before wide range use of the scale can be recommended.

The second mode of verbal report for heterosocial assessment is the clinical interview. Much has been said about the importance of the clinical interview in assessing behavior by verbal report earlier in this chapter. Therefore, at this point, we simply remind the reader that while information obtained in a clinical interview should be supported by data from the other two response channels whenever possible, the focus of behavioral assessment is on behavior and interview data are behavior.

The final mode of assessing heterosocial behavior by verbal report is self-recording. Generally, self-recording techniques require the patient to record instances of heterosocial interactions and the antecedent and the consequent events associated with these interactions. For instance, Table 2-7 is an example of a self-recording form we used with a 21-year-old college male who presented low-frequency dating and heterosocial anxiety.

The recording form divides the behavior of interest into the heterosocial interaction, the length of the interaction, the antecedent events that precipitated the interaction, and the consequences of the interaction. A separate form is used daily, and the patient is encouraged to record each heterosocial interaction. The information obtained throughout treatment

TABLE 2-7

Daily Heterosocial Recording Form

Name: Tommy Shy
Date: Tuesday, March 10

Partner	Time	Antecedent	Consequence
1. Girl in history class	30 sec.	She asked to borrow my notes.	I gave her my notes for overnight study.
2. Girl who lives next door	9 min.	I went over to ask her to the movies.	She already had date.
3. Girl in my chemistry class	26 min.	I met her in cafeteria and had lunch with her. Also asked her out for Friday night.	She accepted.
4. Roommate's girlfriend	30 sec.	I asked her to get me a date sometime.	She said she didn't know anyone that I would like.

gives the therapist assessment information as to the frequency of heterosocial contacts, as well as baseline data to evaluate the effects of treatment.

Arkowitz et al. (1975) devised a self-recording technique they call the Peer Rating Inventory. This requires patients to provide the names of peers who could evaluate their dating behavior and skill. Results indicated that peer ratings and self-recording information were adequately correlated. High-frequency daters were viewed as more highly skilled and comfortable in heterosocial situations, and were reported to date more frequently than those subjects who identified themselves as low-frequency daters.

Obviously, the majority of verbal-report techniques for assessing heterosocial skills have been developed for male patients only. However, Glasgow and Arkowitz (1975) have recently begun to investigate heterosocial behavior in females.

Behavioral Observations

Heterosocial skills may also be measured by assessing specific behaviors that presumably comprise heterosocial skills, and by assessing situations in which these target behaviors have been observed (Hersen & Bellack, 1977). Assessment has typically involved either role playing or *in vivo* heterosocial interactions. Unfortunately, most of this work has been of limited usefulness for clinical purposes.

Arkowitz et al. (1975) attempted to develop precise behavioral measures that would specifically define heterosocial competence in college males by having groups of high- and low-frequency daters interact with a female in an attempt to get to know her better. The behavioral components measured were talk time, number of silences, number of verbal reinforcements, number of head nods, number of smiles, time gazing at partner, and measures of prosocial speech content. Results indicated that of the seven behavioral measures, only the number of conversational silences significantly differentiated the high- and low-frequency daters.

In contrast to results obtained by Arkowitz and his colleagues, Twentyman and McFall (1975) discovered a number of consistent behavioral differences between high- and low-frequency daters. The authors devised a Forced Interaction Test in which subjects were instructed to interact with a female confederate as if they had recently met her in class and wanted to know her better. Ratings of the subjects resulted in low-frequency daters being rated lower in skill.than high-frequency daters, and higher in specific anxiety as well as over-all anxiety. Reliability measures ranged from 0.40 to 0.68.

Rehm and Marston (1968) developed the Situation Test (ST) to assess heterosocial skills across 10 specific situations. Each situation is read over an intercom to the subject. A female confederate then reads a line of dialogue appropriate to the specific situation. The subject must respond to the confederate's dialogue as if he were actually in the situation; his responses are taped and subsequently rated. An example of those situations assessed is the following: you are on a date and have just come out of a theater after seeing a movie. You ask your date what she would like to do, since it is still early, and she replies, "Oh, I don't know. It's up to you." Adequate psychometric qualities of the ST have been reported by the authors.

Barlow, Abel, Blanchard, Bristow, and Young (1977) developed a behavioral checklist of three heterosocial behaviors that supposedly differentiate heterosocially successful males from socially incompetent males with sexual problems. High school and college males judged socially attractive by a panel of popular female students in their respective schools were videotaped interacting with female research assistants. Patients who reported sexually deviant behaviors and were judged heterosocially inadequate were also videotaped interacting with the same research assistants. The following categories of behavior proved adequate to differentiate the heterosocially competent and incompetent males:

I   VOICE
    sufficiently loud, without breathy overtones
    lower in pitch than female role player's

no excessive inflection

no dramatic affect

II   FORM OF CONVERSATION

introduces, initiates conversation

responds at least once to female's vocalizations

allows no pauses five seconds or longer in conversation

comments reflect interest in female

III AFFECT

facial expression appropriate to conversation's content

eye contact occurs five seconds per 30 seconds of conversation

laughter is without giggling or high pitch

In favor of the scale, Barlow et al. (1977) have claimed that responses can be reliably scored by trained raters and that the scale is psychometrically sound. Also, assessment within the natural environment utilizing this scale would require only a change of location for the raters.

ASSESSMENT OF HETEROSEXUAL BEHAVIOR

Heterosexual behavior refers to those behaviors that are specifically sexual in nature, yet are heavily influenced by each of the three other components of sexual behavior. Obviously, adaptive and successful sexual behavior is a result of the degree and direction of sexual arousal; the gender behavior that one exhibits to society and especially to potential sexual partners; and the skill with which one meets and interacts with members of the opposite sex. Heterosexual skill, on the other hand, is an evaluative label that refers to the level of success and expertise in heterosexual behavior that the individual demonstrates.

Assessment of heterosexual skills is important in determining if the patient has the required knowledge and skills necessary for successful sexual behavior. An individual may have adequate and appropriate heterosexual arousal, project typically appropriate gender behaviors, and be skilled in the art of initiating and maintaining heterosocial relationships, yet may lack the sexual knowledge and skills required for adequate heterosexual functioning.

Contrary to the belief of many, skilled sexual behavior is not simply a matter of "doing what comes naturally." Sexual behavior, and especially *skilled* sexual behavior, is learned over a period of trials and is subject to the same laws of learning as other types of behavior. If the reader, confident in the knowledge of his or her sexual expertise, doubts this assertion, a moment's meditation on the details of his or her first sexual experience should banish any doubts.

The private nature of the sexual act makes heterosexual skills one of the more difficult behaviors to measure. Obviously, the clinician cannot send a team of trained behavioral raters to the patient's home to record systematically the patient's sexual behavior. Nor is it possible to assess a patient's sexual skills physiologically. Therefore we must rely largely on verbal report for the assessment of heterosexual skills, although behavioral observation by a spouse or other partner can be useful if this option is available.

Verbal Report

Assessment of heterosexual skills by means of verbal report is conducted primarily during the clinical interview. The major goals of the interview should be assessment of the critical areas of heterosexual functioning. We are not attempting to present sexual behavior as a mechanical routine. Certainly, the feelings that a couple share influence their perception of the sexual experience and therefore their perception of each other's sexual skills. These feelings of closeness and sharing are not only intangible and varying, but unique to a particular couple. Assessment efforts should, therefore, be directed toward the more behavioral and general aspects of sexual functioning.

The sexual history is important in determining where and how the patient first learned and applied sexual skills. The patient should indicate at what age he/she began dating, and provide information as to the patterns of early and later dating behavior. The therapist should question the patient about his/her early sexual experiences, the sexual partners in these early sexual experiences (prostitutes, friends, and the like), and the results of these experiences. Information should also be obtained about the characteristics of partners and heterosexual behaviors the patient prefers, and whether any unusual instances have occurred during the sexual experiences (for example, embarrassment during sexual play, or ridicule from a sexual partner). Exploring any sexual fantasies that the patient may entertain during sexual activity is also helpful. Additional information may be obtained by asking patients how they would characterize their heterosexual skills and why.

Assessment of heterosexual skills also requires assessment of the patient's knowledge of the functioning of the sexual anatomy. Areas of assessment should include the patient's knowledge of sexual responses, knowledge of the male and female genital anatomy, and techniques for sexual arousal. A short questionnaire of this type is shown in Table 2-8.

The therapist should also question the patient to ascertain his/her knowledge of the sexual response cycle. For example, a heterosexually skilled individual might be expected to know that the male experiences a re-

TABLE 2-8
Sexual Knowledge Questionnaire

1. What part of the female anatomy is the most responsive to sexual stimulation? (Clitoris)
2. Do most women prefer direct or indirection stimulation of the clitoris? (Indirect)
3. Is there a difference in excitability between the circumcised and uncircumcised penis? (No)
4. Is the male capable of mutiple orgams within a short time span like some women? (Generally, no)
5. Are the testes of most males sensitive to sexual stimulation? (Yes)
6. What is the most sexually sensitive part of the male penis? (Glans or head)
7. Does the vagina contain an abundance of sexually sensitive nerve endings? (No)
8. Has the practice of swallowing semen during oral-genital sex been proven to be harmful to one's physical health? (No)
9. Does the female ejaculate during sexual intercourse? (No)
10. Is the male anatomically responsive to sexual stimulation immediately after orgasm? (No) Females? (Generally, yes)
11. Does penis size influence the probability and magnitude of the female's physiological orgasm? (Generally, no; if any influence it is primarily through expectancy)
12. What is the length of time required for males and females to reach orgasm during intercourse? (Variable, although females, as a rule, require more time than males)
13. Does the size of the clitoris have any relationship to a woman's sexual responsiveness or drive? (No)
14. Is breast size related in any way to the degree of a woman's sexual drive? (No)
15. Is the intensity of female orgasm a direct reflection on the strength of uterine contractions? (No)
16. Is a man's balding condition a good indicator of his sex drive? (No)
17. Is masturbation physically harmful to males or females? (No)
18. Is it possible for a woman to become pregnant having never engaged in intercourse? (Infrequent, but yes)
19. Is a man standing six feet tall more likely to have a larger penis than a man 5'6" tall? (Not necessarily)
20. Is a man's biological sex drive stronger than a woman's? (Not necessarily)
21. Are sexual fantasies normal during intercourse? (Yes)
22. Is it true that women prefer a passive role during sex play in contrast to male's masculine aggressiveness? (Variable with individual differences)
23. Do most men enjoy sex more than women? (Not necessarily)
24. Is penile width more important than penile length? (Not necessarily)
25. Are women less bothered by sexual abstinence than men? (Not necessarily)

fractory period after orgasm in which he cannot be stimulated to another orgasm while the female does not experience a refractory period. Assessment of a patient's knowledge of the sexual response cycle occasionally uncovers areas of sexual misunderstanding and ignorance that may often be corrected with a simple short sexual education lecture by the therapist.

The unfortunate effects of an inadequate knowledge of genital functioning are demonstrated by a depressed male patient who complained of, among other things, an inability to satisfy women sexually. When his knowledge of sexual functioning was assessed, it was learned that the patient was unaware that women, in contrast to men, do not ejaculate during orgasm. Although he reported that many of his sexual partners had demonstrated hyperventilation, tachycardia, increased muscular tension, and vaginal contractions during intercourse, some even voluntarily commenting on the magnitude of their orgasms, he felt they were simply staging a demonstration to protect his "male ego." He reasoned that since males ejaculate when they are sexually satisfied, females must also. The fact that his experiences showed that females do not ejaculate proved to him that his partners were not experiencing orgasm and that, therefore, he was unable to satisfy women sexually.

The final area of assessment of heterosexual skills is knowledge of sexual arousal techniques. Preferences in techniques of sexual arousal are highly individualized. Some individuals enjoy long periods of mutual kissing and caressing before intercourse, while others prefer brief periods of foreplay, desiring instead to proceed with intercourse.

Many individuals consider the time each partner engages in sexual arousal of the other as one of the more enjoyable experiences in sexual activity. Certainly, sexual arousal behavior is pleasurable in itself and should not be considered as preliminaries that must be endured in order to "get to the good stuff." McCary (1973) presents an excellent discussion of techniques of sexual arousal which can be used in assessing an individual's heterosexual skills.

Behavioral Observations

Assessment of heterosexual skills by means of behavioral observation is usually limited to questioning the individual's sexual partner. In the absence of a willing sexual partner, however, some therapists have utilized sexual surrogates. Observational data should include an assessment of the individual's skills from sexual foreplay through intercourse and should focus on specific indices.

ETHICAL CONCERNS

While the context of any clinical assessment and especially the assessment of sexual dysfunctions and deviancies, the question of ethics and competency must be addressed. These should be critical concerns for the legitimate clinician, for a number of "sex clinics" exist which have no professional status. The clinical psychologist or psychiatrist who treats sexual dysfunctions and deviancies should recognize that competency within this area of specialization does not come simply with an earned doctorate and the completion of a clinical psychology training program or a residency in psychiatry. Skills in sexual assessment and treatment should be studied and developed under structured and supervised practice. Maintaining high professional and ethical standards provides protection for both the patient and the clinician and is essential, given the number of quacks and exploiters practicing sex therapy. Most states are seeking ways to pass statues to limit and control who may practice "psychotherapy"; in the meantime, it is up to the legitimate clinician to insure his or her own competence and ethical practice. A staunch behaviorist might even agree that given the latitude that exists in the laws of most states governing who may practice psychotherapy, it is easier to get a license to practice sex therapy than to become sexually dysfunctional or deviant. After all, a maladaptive sexual response must be learned, while a license to practice sex therapy requires hardly any learning at all!

CHAPTER 3

Modification of
Sexual Behavior

Recently, the practice of sex therapy has enjoyed a surge in popularity among professional clinicians, so that today a number of clinical psychologists and psychiatrists restrict their clinical practice solely to the treatment of sexual problems. This interest is undoubtedly due to more liberal and accepting attitudes toward sexual behavior, the realization that people not only enjoy sex but have the right to seek professional assistance to further enhance or modify their sexuality, and the development of adequate sexual treatment techniques. These new behavioral techniques appear to fulfill Chapman's (1968) requirements of "intelligent and efficient and rapid management."

This chapter will present an overview of some of the modification techniques commonly employed in the behavioral treatment of sexual dysfunctions and deviations. More detailed discussions of various treatment procedures will be presented in subsequent chapters focusing on treatment modalities for specific sexual disorders. It should be kept in mind that the choice of a treatment technique (or combination of techniques) is logically the result of a comprehensive, systematic behavioral assessment, and that intervention strategies should be implemented only after a case has been thoroughly investigated. Some sexual problems require little more than a brief educational discussion between the therapist and patient. Modification of other sexual disorders may require an exhaustive armamentarium of behavioral techniques. In our own clinical practice we adhere to the following procedure:

1. Initial clinical interview and case history.

2. Further assessment of specific sexual and related problem behaviors. This includes a complete physical examination by a competent primary-care physician.

3. Case formulation. Initial hypotheses concerning the development of the problem behavior and why it continues to occur.

4. Selection and/or development of specific treatment plans. Ideally,

several alternatives are desirable to allow the patient a choice of treatment techniques.

5. Presentation of the formulation and treatment plans to the patient. At this time, all information is made available to the individual: discussion of fees, length of treatment, probability of success, qualifications and experience of the therapist, alternative procedures and therapists, answers to all questions posed by the patient. The individual should be allowed several days to make a decision or consult other specialists.

6. Implementation of treatment procedure. We suggest that a written contract describing the treatment plan be signed by both therapist and patient. Continuous monitoring of the patient's progress to determine if the treatment procedures are effective or require revising is mandatory.

The presentation of treatment techniques in this chapter will be consistent with the recognition of independent but related components of sexual behavior: sexual arousal, gender role behavior, heterosocial behavior, and heterosexual behavior. For example, techniques to modify decreased or deviant sexual arousal will be discussed under the major section of sexual arousal. Although some overlap will occur across components (for example, relaxation training may be a component of techniques to modify sexual arousal and heterosexual behavior), we will attempt to clarify how and when these techniques are normally employed.

MODIFYING SEXUAL AROUSAL

Elimination of Deviant Arousal

The major procedures used to decrease inappropriate sexual arousal are collectively termed *aversion therapy*. Probably no other contemporary treatment techniques have generated as much controversy. In fact, among clinical psychologists and psychiatrists the topic of aversion therapy surely has surpassed religion and politics as a conversational topic guaranteed to elicit heated debate. In one recent two-hour case conference for graduate students in clinical psychology, for instance, the question arose of how a male homosexual who requested a change of sexual orientation might be treated. The graduate students were so divided over the issue of aversion therapy that a four-hour debate ensued, marked by name-calling, questioning of various students' family origins and sexual orientations and periodic threats of physical violence. A similar situation occurred once when a group of staff psychiatrists requested an evaluation of potential behavioral techniques available to treat a male pedophile. When electrical aversion was mentioned as one potential treatment, the distinguished group, who casually and frequently employed electroconvulsive therapy, called the technique brutal and barbaric.

Aversion therapy is typically employed in the treatment of behavioral disorders in which the patient's behavior is undesirable but self-reinforcing (Rachman & Teasdale, 1969). It is not surprising that so-called "sexual deviations" have been popular target behaviors for aversion therapy. For example, a homosexual may experience discontent and a genuine desire to alter his sexual orientation. At the same time, however, his homosexual behavior is reinforcing via orgasm, companionship, and affiliation. Aversion therapy is employed in an attempt to associate aversive experiences as a consequence of homosexual behavior. The development of such an association should be followed by a cessation of the target behavior. It is important to note, however, that aversion therapy is designed to eliminate an undesired response and does not insure the development of alternative behaviors. We emphasize the fact that altering an undesirable sexual response is not enough. An appropriate alternative means of gratifying the sexual urge must be developed. Thus, the purpose of aversion therapy is twofold: elimination of deviant sexual arousal in conjunction with training of a satisfactory alternative (and preferably incompatible) form of sexual arousal and behavior.

Types and Nature of Aversion Therapies

A variety of aversive stimuli have been reported in the literature including chemical, olfactory, electrical, cognitive, and shame. Feldman (1966), in his review of the literature on aversion therapy for sexual deviations found that most studies used pictures or fantasies of the erotic but unsocial object (or person), and paired these erotic stimuli with aversive stimulation.

Chemical Aversion. Chemical aversion therapy involves the administering of a pharmacological agent to produce an aversive physical state. Generally, an emetic or nausea-producing drug is the agent of choice. A study by Morganstern, Pierce, and Linford-Rees (1965) will serve as an example of chemical aversive therapy. These researchers treated 13 transvestites by administering apomorphine injections and requiring the patients to engage in cross dressing during the onset of nausea. Each patient received 39 sessions at a rate of three sessions per day. Results indicated that 7 of the 13 patients ceased cross dressing completely, while the other 6 showed improvement but periodic relapses. A detailed follow-up ranging from eight months to four years later produced three interesting points. First, most of the patients stated that the formerly exciting clothing had lost its sexual appeal. Second, no symptom substitution was observed. Third, the relapses which had occurred tended to be episodic and could be related to specific events in the patient's life (*e.g.*, sexual deprivation during wife's pregnancy). Raymond (1956) earlier treated a fetishist by introducing an emetic drug every two hours for one week and reported cessation of deviant sexual behavior.

A number of problems are inherent in the use of chemical aversion therapy. First, chemical aversion techniques are complicated by individual differences and reactivity to various nausea-producing drugs, as well as by the requirement that medically-trained personnel administer the drug. Individuals differ in the speed and extent of their physiological reaction to drugs; therefore precise control over the extent and duration of the aversive stimulus is impossible. Second, the complicated and unpleasant nature of chemical aversion techniques also limits the number of aversion sessions that can be administered to an individual. Thus, the pairing of the conditioned and unconditioned stimuli may be weak because of few associations. Third, some evidence suggests that chemical aversion increases aggressiveness and hostility in patients (Morganstern & Pierce, 1963). While these difficulties require solutions, many clinicians agree that the potential dangerous side effects of drug inducement alone are sufficient to discontinue chemical aversion.

Olfactory Aversion. In olfactory aversion therapy an odiferous chemical replaces the nausea-producing agent employed in chemical aversion. For example, Levin, Barry, Gambaro, Wolfinsohn, and Smith (1977) used olfactory aversion in the treatment of pedophilic behavior. In this study covert sensitization was combined with valeric acid so that aversive imagery was accompanied by exposure to the odiferous chemical. The vial was uncorked just before the patient imagined nausea and was covered immediately preceding cessation of the aversive imagery. The results indicated a significant decrease in the patient's sexual response to young girls while sexual arousal to mature women increased. Follow-ups conducted at 2.5, 4.5, and 10 months showed the therapeutic effects to be maintained over time.

Maletzky (1977) reports the use of olfactory aversion in the treatment of 12 exhibitionists. In this study patients used imagery and photographs of exhibitionistic activities to become sexually aroused, at which point a noxious odor was administered. The original treatment consisted of 10 to 12 bimonthly sessions combined with 15 to 25 tri-weekly sessions at home using the noxious odor and tape recordings describing exhibitionistic activities. At one year follow-up, only four of the exhibitionists showed deviant sexual arousal, which was eliminated through aversive booster sessions.

Electrical Aversion. In electrical or faradic aversion, electrical shock serves as the aversive stimulus. A study by Feldman and MacCulloch (1965) is a good example of an aversion procedure for homosexual behavior. A male patient arranged a series of slides picturing semi-clothed and unclothed males and females in a hierarchy of attractiveness. The patient then chose a level of electrical shock which he considered "very unpleasant." At this point the patient was shown the slide of the least attractive male and told he could turn off the slide by pressing a switch whenever he no longer found it to be sexually attractive. Electrical shock was administered to the patient's forearms eight seconds after the onset of the male slide. If the patient did not switch off the slide at this point, the shock intensity was increased until he did so. Shock was terminated when the patient removed the male slide. After a few pairings of shock and the male slide, the patient was placed on a predetermined schedule of shock, that is, only a certain proportion of male slides produced shock after eight seconds. Female slides, beginning with the most attractive, were then presented upon termination of the male slide. The therapist determined when the female slide was to be terminated, and, of course, shock was never paired with the female slide. The rationale behind this procedure, termed aversion relief, was to associate the female stimulus with the relief of anxiety and the male stimulus with the onset of aversion and anxiety.

Forgione (1976) reported the use of electrical aversion in the treatment of two males with court histories of nonviolent child molesting. It is interesting to note in this study that the patients were required to engage in their deviant behavior with life-sized mannequins of children. These interactions were photographed and later used in electrical aversion. The author claimed that the procedure was effective in alleviating the pedophilic behavior.

Marshall (1973) employed electrical aversion in the treatment of two fetishists, two rapists, two homosexual pedophiliacs, two heterosexual pedophiliacs, one mixed pedophiliac, and three homosexuals. Treatment consisted of classical conditioning with relevant deviant fantasies and slides paired with shock which was preceded by the command, "Stop." Six trials with continuous shock were followed by six trials with 75 percent shock, then six trials with 50 percent shock for 27 sessions. The results indicated successful elimination of the deviant sexual arousal in 11 of 12 subjects. Follow-up from 3 to 16 months on eight of the subjects indicated one pedophiliac had engaged in deviant behavior on one occasion, and one homosexual had relapsed completely.

Electrical aversion, unlike chemical and olfactory aversion, enables the therapist to precisely control the intensity, extent, and duration of aversive stimulation. Individual differences in reactivity to unpleasant stimulation are controlled by allowing the patient to choose the level of stimulation he judges to be just about the paint threshold. Increased therapeutic control, administration by nonmedically trained personnel, and the less complex technique, which allows frequent treatment sessions, are all reasons that favor the use of electrical aversion techniques. We should emphasize, however, that aversion techniques should not be used with patients who have cardiovascular difficulties.

 Covert Sensitization. Covert sensitization, or aversive imagery, is considered by many as a form of aversion therapy less unpleasant than chemical, olfactory, or electrical stimulation. Rachman and Teasdale (1969) report that Gold and Neufeld (1965), in the development of covert sensitization, "did a Wolpe" with aversion therapy. In other words, they substituted an imaginal event for an external physical event in a way similar to Wolpe's development of systematic desensitization (to be discussed later in this chapter).

 Although covert sensitization has yet to be conclusively demonstrated as an effective treatment technique, a body of research is developing that suggests the usefulness of this treatment procedure. Gold and Neufeld (1965) employed covert sensitization in the successful elimination of homosexual behavior in a 16-year-old boy convicted of homosexual soliciting. Davison (1968) treated a case of sadistic fantasy with a combination of counterconditioning and covert sensitization; Hayes, Brownell, and Barlow (1978) reported the successful elimination of a fetish in a 14-year-old male; and Cautela (1967) claimed the effective treatment of a homosexual male. Cautela (1967), in an enthusiastic discussion of covert sensitization, emphasizes the importance of instructing the patient to practice this technique at home. His clinical observation is that the effectiveness of covert sensitization is facilitated when the technique is employed with a highly motivated patient who is above average in intelligence and possesses an ability to vividly imagine aversive scenes (*i.e.,* color, shape and form). We have effectively used covert sensitization in the modification of homosexual and fetish behavior, but have also encountered failures with the technique.

 A study by Harbert, Barlow, Hersen, and Austin (1974) will illustrate the use of covert sensitization. The patient was a 52-year-old male convicted of incestuous behavior. The patient had a 12-year history of incestuous behavior consisting primarily of kissing, fondling, and mutual masturbation with his 17-year-old daughter. This individual was first trained in deep muscle relaxation, followed by covert sensitization sessions in which he was to imagine being discovered by his wife, his father-in-law, or his family priest while engaging in incestuous behavior. For example, one of the scenes presented was:

You are alone with your daughter in your trailer. You get the feeling that you want to caress your daughter's breasts. So you put your arm around her, insert your hand in her blouse and begin to caress her breasts. Unexpectedly the door to the trailer opens and in walks your wife with Father X (the family priest). Your daughter immediately jumps up and runs to the door. Your wife follows her. You are left alone with Father X. He is looking at you as if to ask for some explanation of what he has just seen. You think of what Father X must be thinking as he stands there staring at you. You are very embarrassed you want to say something, but you can't seem to find the right words. You realize that Father X can no longer respect you as he once did. Father X finally says, "I don't understand this; this is not like you." You begin to cry. You realize that you may have lost the love and respect of both Father X and your wife, which are very important to you. Father X asks, "Do you realize what this has done to your daughter?" You think about this and you hear your daughter crying; she is hysterical. You feel like you want to run, but you can't. You are miserable and disgusted with yourself. You don't know if you will ever regain the love and respect of your wife and Father X. (p. 82)

Covert sensitization treatment consisted of 150 pairings over a period of 15 days. The subject was discharged from the hospital and then seen for follow-up with booster sessions at intervals of two weeks, one month, two months, three months, and six months. These follow-up results indicated no deviant sexual arousal at the end of training, although a slight indication of deviant arousal appeared at three months follow-up.

Shame Aversion. Shame aversion consists of having a patient who is embarrassed by his/her deviant sexual behavior engage in the act in front of a number of observers. The act is continued for 15 to 35 minutes in as similar a way as possible to the sexual behavior that occurs in the natural environment. Serber (1971) reports using shame aversion in the treatment of eight patients including cases of transvestism, voyeurism, exhibitionism, pedophilia, and frotteurism, all of at least 10 years duration. The results of this investigation indicate that five patients remained free of their deviant sexual behavior at six months follow-up.

An additional example of the successful use of shame aversion is the case of a 23-year-old transvestite who for 10 years enjoyed dressing two or three times each week in his mother's undergarments. He would terminate each cross dressing session by masturbating in either his bedroom or bathroom. The patient was required to engage in cross dressing while being photographed. He was initially reluctant, claiming he was too embarrassed and ashamed to be observed while cross dressing. When he did engage in cross dressing, he became markedly anxious, flushed, felt weak, and had to sit down several times. He was also unable to become sexually excited and reported that the photographic session had completely "turned him off" as well as changed his entire feelings about cross dressing (Serber, 1971).

Conclusions

It would appear from the available research that electrical aversion is presently the treatment of choice for eliminating deviant sexual arousal, since, unlike chemical and olfactory aversion, it enables the therapist to precisely control the intensity, extent, and duration of aversive stimulation. In addition, individual differences in reactivity to unpleasant stimulation are controlled by allowing the patient to choose the level of stimulation he/she judges to be just above the pain threshold. While shame aversion and particularly covert sensitization procedures appear highly promising, and in fact have proven clinically effective with several of our patients, additional controlled investigations are needed utilizing these techniques with patients presenting a variety of sexually deviant behavior.

Ethical Considerations in the Use of Aversion Therapy

Aversion treatment techniques are useful in many therapeutic situations. However, these techniques are subject to the possibility of abuse and therefore involve a number of ethical considerations, which fall into several major categories.

The first consideration relating to aversion therapy is whether the technique works. While one of the most outspoken critics of aversive techniques is Skinner (1948, 1953), most behavioral scientists who have systematically investigated aversion as a therapeutic technique have concluded that, when administered correctly, aversion is successful in the modification of human behavior (Azrin & Holtz, 1966; Baer, 1971; Forgione, 1976). Even those who take a less positive attitude admit that aversion therapy has been very promising in areas where other therapeutic techniques have failed (Rachman & Teasdale, 1969). Krapfl (1975) points out that the demand for accountability in our society will continue to increase, and that accountability should be defined in terms of patients, not solely in terms of other professionals in the field. Consequently, an important consideration in a decision for or against the use of aversion therapy is how successful it is for specific behavior disorders. Although the efficacy of aversive therapy has been demonstrated, researchers and clinicians should continue to investigate less painful, less discomforting techniques to achieve the desired behavioral changes. Many clinicians have suggested the use of cognitive aversion or covert sensitization as an alternative to physically aversive techniques, since they are less aversive than chemical, olfactory, and electrical techniques (Brownell & Barlow, 1976; Hayes et al., 1978).

Although techniques using painful or uncomfortable stimulation are successful, aversive stimulation produces discomfort to the patient which other effective therapies may not. Even if aversion therapy is less painful or damaging than other therapies such as electroconvulsive therapy and surgery, Rachman and Teasdale (1969) have stated,

> We doubt that a patient who is about to undergo an unpleasant form of treatment derives much comfort from being reminded that there are other experiences which are even more unpleasant. (p. 316)

An even more disturbing problem is that aversive therapeutic techniques are easy to abuse and can be used for punitive reasons that are objectionable, unethical, and contrary to the traditions of the helping disciplines.

All therapeutic techniques should be performed in a manner that assures maximal effectiveness and rapid results. This consideration is especially important when one is using techniques that produce pain and discomfort. Consequently, the variables that affect the efficacy of aversion must be carefully considered in each case. For example, with punishment techniques, low or intermediate levels of intensity often produce adaptation; in those cases, the frequency and/or the intensity of the stimulus would have to be increased to even greater proportions before behavioral suppression is achieved (Azrin & Holtz, 1966). Thus, it may be more humane as well as more effective to use a relatively high level of intensity at the beginning of treatment. The timing relationship between response and negative stimulation is also an important variable. The closer the aversive stimulus follows the undesired response the more effective the suppression of the response. Further, the therapist should also insure that escape from contact with the aversive stimulus is not possible, since this will reduce the effectiveness of the procedure. Delivering an aversive stimulus for each response is more effective than any other schedule. Another important variable is the motiviation the patient has to perform the undesirable behavior. The lower the motivation, the greater will be the effect of the aversive stimulus. The motivation to engage in the deviant behavior can also be decreased by reinforcing an alternative, competing response. Programming contingent reinforcing consequences for alternative responses insures that aversive stimulation will not have to be used as frequently or for as long a period of time.

Another consideration in the selection of aversion rather than alternative treatment techniques must be time. If a patient's behavior is unlawful, such as rape or pedophilia, and the therapist uses a treatment procedure that requires an extended period of time, the possibility of the patient's committing a crime increases. Given this situation, the usually rapid results produced by aversion therapy may make it preferable to another therapeutic procedure which requires a longer period of time to be effective.

The patient should always be given a detailed description of the proposed aversive treatment plan and an appraisal of the chances of success. The therapist should refrain from attempting to persuade or coerce the patient into accepting aversive treatment. Rachman and Teasdale (1969) note that there are many kinds of coercion, such as making a prisoner's release or parole contingent upon his/her agreeing to undergo aversion therapy. Using aversion therapy without giving the patient an opportunity to refuse treatment is also coercion, and must be avoided. One precaution against the possibility of coercion is to require a waiting period of a week from the time the aversive technique is explained to the patient until the patient makes a final decision.

Therapeutic aversive techniques can be used ethically as long as there is concern for the welfare of the patient involved. In recommending aversive therapy to a patient, the therapist should consider four critical factors: (1) the amount of pain or discomfort the patient will experience; (2) the benefits to be achieved by the technique; (3) the speed at which the technique will achieve its goal; and (4) the feasibility of other therapeutic procedures. Aversive techniques themselves are not unethical, nor should they be simply because they are aversive. As a matter of fact, many therapeutic procedures including psychotherapy may cause distress to the patient. What is important is that appropriate measures should be taken to protect the patient (Begelman, 1971). In using any psychological technique, the therapist should take into account these considerations and use the techniques that produce the greatest change in behavior with the least amount of pain and discomfort.

ENHANCING HETEROSEXUAL AROUSAL

The major goals of behavioral treatment of deviant sexual arousal are suppression or elimination of inappropriate arousal patterns and teaching or enhancing appropriate sexual arousal. Most behavioral researchers agree that successful suppression of a deviant sexual arousal pattern also requires development of an alternative mode of gratifying the sexual drive. It is presently unclear whether suppression of deviant arousal increases appropriate arousal; however, it is agreed that enhancement of appropriate sexual arousal should not be left to chance.

What constitutes an appropriate pattern of sexual arousal is a topic of current debate among mental health professionals, various social and political organizations, as well as many other members of our society. The traditional model of heterosexual arousal and behavior as "normal" has recently come under attack by various gay rights advocates who have been successful in influencing the American Psychiatric Association to eliminate homosexuality from the deviant sexual orientation classification. Opposition forces to the gay rights movement who question the appropriateness of a homosexual orientation also exist. The bulk of research dealing with arousal modification emphasizes a heterosexual orientation, but the treatment techniques to be described may be employed, with obvious modifications, to enhance either a heterosexual or homosexual arousal pattern.

We have elected to organize the presentation of those techniques used to enhance sexual arousal by differentiating between direct and indirect attempts to modify arousal patterns. Direct methods include techniques developed specifically for producing or facilitating heterosexual arousal (aversion relief, pairing techniques, and pubococcygeal muscle exercise). Indirect methods include techniques that address behaviors such as anxiety which are assumed to inhibit sexual arousal (assertiveness training and systematic desensitization).

Aversion Relief

Aversion relief is a treatment technique frequently associated with aversion therapy, yet differing in that it involves pairing a heterosexual stimulus with relief from the aversive stimulus. In other words, heterosexual stimuli become associated with the relief of noxious stimulation, a condition which, over time, becomes a positive reinforcer.

Thorpe et al. (1964) pioneered the use of aversion relief in the treatment of sexual deviations. Three homosexuals, one transvestite, and one fetishist were presented a number of words which served as a stimulus for deviant sexual experiences. As the patients read each stimulus word, they received an electrical shock. The number of words in each presentation series varied, but the last word presented in each series described "normal" sexual behavior (for example, "heterosexual") and signified the termination of the aversive session. As might be expected, the presentation of the word "heterosexual" soon became associated with relief. Following treatment, all patients reported increased heterosexual interest although the authors did not assess this interest and did not attempt a follow-up. Thorpe et al. (1964) speculated that the aversion relief technique worked by either inhibiting heterosexual anxiety or positively reinforcing heterosexual approach behavior.

Barlow (1974) reported that in the numerous case studies since this pioneering effort the heterosexual "relief" stimulus has taken two forms: verbal, usually words or phrases associated with heterosexual interest, such as "intercourse" (Gaupp, Stern, & Ratliff, 1971); or pictorial, such as slides or films of nude females (Larson, 1970). The majority of cases subjected to this procedure report incrèases in heterosexual interest and responsiveness.

Barlow (1974) reviewed the use of aversion relief techniques and reported that a procedure developed by Feldman and MacCulloch (1965) is perhaps the most popular aversion relief procedure, having been utilized in over 150 reported cases. This procedure, described in a previous section, involved the presentation of slides of nude males to homosexual patients. Sexual arousal to the deviant stimuli resulted in electrical shock whose termination coincided with the presentation of "relief" slides of nude females. Feldman and MacCulloch claim that the goal of aversion relief therapy is the reduction of heterosexual anxiety and suggest that it is therefore an indirect method of increasing heterosexual arousal.

McConaghy (1969) compared the effects of electrical aversion therapy containing an aversion relief paradigm with chemical aversion therapy which did not contain a procedure to increase or reinforce heterosexual behavior. Subjective reports of heterosexual interest from two groups of homosexuals two weeks after treatment, however, revealed no differences in the two treatment modalities.

In one of the few studies designed to measure heterosexual interest continually by means of an objective valid measurement device (penile plethysmography), Abel, Levis, and Clancy (1970) administered aversion therapy to five nonhomosexual deviates by shocking verbalization of the deviant acts at varying points during the verbalizations. Upon completion of the initial series of verbalizations and shocks, the subjects verbalized heterosexual behavior which was associated with aversion relief. The results one week after treatment indicated that heterosexual arousal had decreased somewhat. An eight-week follow-up indicated that heterosexual arousal had increased back to the original baseline but no further. These results obviously do not support the effectiveness of aversion relief techniques as a treatment modality. In fact, there appears to be little, if any, evidence that aversion relief techniques reduce heterosexual anxiety or increase heterosexual interests. This finding has led Barlow (1974) to wonder why, in the empirical field of behavior therapy, a treatment technique is reported in over 150 cases and continues to be employed clinically when little evidence exists to demonstrate its effectiveness.

Pairing

Pairing is the term commonly used to refer to a collection of techniques in which elicited sexual arousal is paired with heterosexual stimuli in an attempt to increase heterosexual arousal. When masturbation is employed to produce sexual arousal, the procedure has been termed orgasmic reconditioning or masturbatory conditioning.

These techniques are based on the hypothesis that sexual arousal patterns are learned through association (Binet, 1888; Dollard & Miller, 1950). More recent clinical research also documents the effectiveness of pairing techniques. Lovingbond (1963) and Wood and Obrist (1968) conditioned autonomic responses associated with sexual arousal to previously neutral stimuli by means of repeated pairings with sexual arousal. McConaghy (1970) paired sexual slides with geometrical configurations to produce penile circumference changes to the configurations in 10 heterosexuals and 15 homosexual subjects. Rachman (1966) paired a slide of a woman's boot with slides of nude females, an association which resulted in penile circumference increases to the slide of the boot in three heterosexual subjects. Rachman and Hodgson (1968) later replicated these findings with five additional subjects.

Other investigators utilized hormone injections to facilitate sexual arousal. Freund (1967) pioneered this procedure in a series of male homosexuals. Aversion therapy was first employed to eliminate deviant sexual arousal and was followed by the injection of 10 mg. of testosterone proprinate. Approximately seven hours following the hormone injection, pictures and slides of nude and seminude women were presented to the subjects. The results of 47 cases indicated that a "heterosexual adjustment" had occurred in over 40 per cent of the patients. However, after a three-year follow-up this figure had dropped to approximately 25 per cent.

Several other investigators have reported pairing sexual arousal produced by masturbation with heterosexual stimuli in the treatment of homosexuality (Annon, 1971; Marquis, 1970), sadomasochism (Davison, 1968; Marquis, 1970; Mees, 1966), voyeurism (Jackson, 1969), and heterosexual pedophilia (Annon, 1971). In the majority of cases the patient is encouraged to use deviant sexual fantasies to attain erection and approach orgasm in masturbation. At the instant of orgasm, however, the patient is to switch to heterosexual fantasies. If arousal is lost, he is briefly to switch back to the deviant fantasy and then return again to heterosexual fantasies. Over successive occasions of masturbation, the time of the switch from deviant to heterosexual fantasies is gradually moved backward from the point of orgasm until the patient is finally using exclusive heterosexual fantasies during the entire masturbatory session. The procedure also involves fading, a procedure to be discussed in the next section.

Unfortunately, the efficacy of masturbation training has yet to be conclusively determined and in only a few cases has the procedure been investigated as the lone therapeutic technique (Jackson, 1960). While further research is needed, masturbation training does appear promising as a method of altering sexual preference and arousal.

Fading

Fading, an operant technique, was derived from the work on errorless discrimination (Terrance, 1966), and concentrates on introducing or "fading in" heterosexual stimuli during periods of sexual arousal in an effort to change stimulus control of sexual responsiveness (Barlow & Agras, 1973). In the Barlow and Agras procedure, one male and one female slide were superimposed on one another. Through the use of an adjustable transformer, a decrease in the brightness of the male slide resulted in a simultaneous increase in the brightness of the female slide. During treatment the female stimulus was faded in, contingent on the subject's maintaining 75 per cent of a full erection as measured by a strain gauge device, through a series of 20 steps ranging from 100 per cent male brightness to 100 per cent female brightness. The technique was investigated in three controlled, single case experiments with homosexuals. A reversal experimental design was also utilized which consisted of fading, then a control procedure during which fading was reversed or stopped, and then a return to fading.

The first homosexual completed the fading procedure and became sexually aroused to the female slide alone in six sessions. This arousal generalized to female slides in separate measurement sessions and to reports of behavior. In a control phase, when fading was reversed, heterosexual arousal and reports of behavior dropped considerably. When the female slide was faded in once more, heterosexual arousal increased. Homosexual responsiveness remained high throughout the experiment.

In the second experiment heterosexual arousal rose during the initial fading, continued rising, but then dropped sharply during a control phase in which fading was stopped at the halfway point and the slides were shown separately, and rose once again when fading was reintroduced. Again, homosexual arousal remained high but dropped sharply after termination, *without* therapeutic attempts to accomplish this goal, at follow-ups of one and three months. This experimental procedure and its result were replicated with a third homosexual. Although these experiments suggest that a fading procedure is effective in instigating new patterns of sexual arousal, clinical assessments following treatment indicated that the first two subjects needed training in heterosocial skills to implement their newly acquired arousal (Barlow, 1974).

The rationale for fading is that heterosexual and deviant sexual arousal can be paired to produce an increase in heterosexual arousal. Clinically, this implies that, first, the increase in heterosexual arousal should be obtained before the deviant arousal is extinguished. If extinction of deviant arousal is effected concurrently with fading, as it often is, the procedure may be ineffective. Second, if fading is used as a singular treatment technique, as in masturbation training, it is possible that an individual may become sexually aroused to both deviant and heterosexual stimuli as does the bisexual person, if that sexual orientation truly exists. In any case, the various parameters, implications, and techniques of fading are in need of additional scientific exploration.

Shaping

Direct selective positive reinforcement, or shaping, to increase heterosexual arousal has been used by Quinn, Harbinson, and McAllister (1970) and Harbinson, Quinn, and McAllister (1970) in the treatment of two cases of homosexuality. These investigators attempted to increase penile response to heterosexual stimuli using the following procedure. The patients were initially treated with aversion therapy in an attempt to eliminate their deviant sexual arousal. Next, after a lengthy period of dehydration, the patients were positively reinforced with a drink of lime juice for longer and more elaborate heterosexual fantasies and/or penile circumference increases to slides and pictures of nude females. Penile responses increased over the course of treatment as did the heterosexual score on an attitude scale. The results also indicated a decline in the homosexual score on the attitude scale over pretreatment values. No report of environmental sexual behavior was given.

The use of direct shaping of sexual responses by contingency reinforcement is a technique with much promise. However, the results of the Quinn, Harbinson, and McAllister research have largely been ignored. Further exploration of this technique is needed because of the many advantages shaping has in comparison to similar techniques.

Exposure

Exposure is a technique whereby the individual is exposed to explicit heterosexual erotic stimuli in an effort to elicit sexual arousal. For example, Herman and his colleagues (Herman, 1971; Herman, Barlow, & Agras, 1971) employed a procedure which exposed sexual deviants to movies of nude females. This technique was experimentally analyzed in three single cases with two homosexuals and a pedophiliac. The procedure involved an 8-mm. movie of a nude, seductive female shown daily to the patients for 10 minutes. During the control phase a movie of a nude, seductive male was presented. A third phase consisted of a return to the female exposure condition. In all subjects, exposure to the female film increased heterosexual arousal. During the homosexual film, heterosexual arousal dropped for all subjects and rose once again when the heterosexual film was reintroduced. All subjects verbally reported generalization to fantasies and behavior outside of treatment. Homosexual arousal had earlier been decreased in one subject through aversion therapy. In other subjects homosexual arousal did not decrease during treatment. Follow-ups from three months to one year revealed that two subjects had difficulty in heterosexual relations, despite continued arousal, due to deficient social skills.

Although the experimental analysis isolates exposure as responsible for changes in patterns of sexual arousal, the mechanism of action is not clear (Barlow, 1974). This process may be similar to flooding, and result in a decrease in heterosexual anxiety rather than a direct increase in heterosexual arousal. Another possibility is that it provides the subjects with new fantasy material which is then associated with sexual arousal outside treatment (Barlow, 1974), one of several rationales also used to explain video desensitization to be discussed later in this chapter.

Pubococcygeal Muscle Exercises

Interest in the problem of physiological efficiencies of the vaginal musculature began in the 1940s with Arnold Kegel's work. He treated urinary stress incontinence, secondary to weakness of the supporting musculature of the pelvic organs (Kegel, 1948, 1952, 1956). The sexual aspects of "Kegel's exercises" were first reported as an accidental finding in the treatment of a woman suffering from a frequent loss of urine (Kegel, 1952). A physical examination revealed not only poor condition of the vaginal muscle but also the patient's inability to contract the muscle. Kegel's exercise program was successful in treating her urinary condition, and the patient also reported a dramatic improvement in her sex life. Further investigation showed that although both the woman and her husband had previously wanted to engage in more sexual activity, intercourse had not been enjoyable for the woman. Following retraining of the pubococcygeal muscle the couple had intercourse several times each week and the woman was able to achieve orgasm, which previously she had not been able to do. Kegel (1952) made the following generalization from his clinical population of several thousand women treated:

> Wherever the perivaginal musculature is well developed . . . sexual complaints are few or transient. On the other hand, in women with a thin, weak,

pubococcygeus muscle. . .expressions of indifference or dissatisfaction regarding sexual activity were frequently encountered. When a more careful history was taken, the symptoms revealed a definite pattern. . . .In the patient's own words: "I just don't feel anything," or "I don't like the feeling," or "The feeling is disagreeable." . . . Following restoration of the pubococcygeus muscle, numerous patients incidentally volunteered the information: "I can feel more sexually"; and some experienced orgasm for the first time. (p. 112)

The pubococcygeus muscle gets its name from its attachment—the pubic bone in front (under the pubic hair region) and the coccyz or tailbone in back (Kline-Graber & Graber, 1978). Since both of these bones are immobile, the pubococcygeus gets no exercise during the course of the day as most other muscles in the body do, except in two situations: when it is consciously contracted, and involuntarily during orgasm.

Exercises designed to facilitate control of the pubococcygeus muscle are normally done during urination. The woman sits on the toilet with her legs separated and forearms resting on her thighs in an effort to relax the abdominal muscles by supporting the upper bodyweight. The patient next begins to allow urine to flow but only about one teaspoons and then volunatrily cuts off the flow of urine. When the flow is completely stopped, she repeats the cycle. The muscular exercises are then continued until the bladder is completely emptied.

Many popular magazine articles and books have advocated using "Kegel's exercises." Unfortunately, as yet we have very little scientific data to support these recommendations; however, this technique does deserve further clinical research evaluation.

Sensate Focus

Sensate focus, as described originally by Masters and Johnson (1970), is a technique designed to increase sexual arousal and responsiveness. Sensate focus, which has been primarily employed in the treatment of sexual dysfunctions, is a technique of graded sexual exposures in which the patient participates with a sexual partner. As this approach has been well described elsewhere (Masters & Johnson, 1970), it will not be discussed in detail here. Briefly, the couple is forbidden to engage in any sexual activity until instructed. They are then given, each week, a "homework" assignment to increase their repertoire of sexual behaviors. In the first week, for example, only kissing, hugging, and body massage may be allowed. This assignment enables the patient to learn enjoyment of sexual pleasures, without worrying about further sexual behavior. In following weeks, other sexual behaviors are gradually added including breast and genital touching, stimulation of the penis in a "teasing" manner, simultaneous masturbation, penile insertion with no movement, mutual genital manipulation, to orgasm, and finally intercourse. The partners must comply with the instructions of the therapist, although a couple will often find that the initial stages of sensate focus create no difficulties, and, as a result, are tempted to proceed to more advanced levels of activity.

Conclusions

With the exception of aversion relief, techniques designed to enhance heterosexual arousal have had little controlled investigation. Variations of aversion relief procedures have been reported in over 150 studies with little evidence that these techniques reduce heterosexual anxiety or increase heterosexual arousal. On the other hand, data on pubococcygeal muscle exercises, fading, and pairing appear promising, but only a few investigations of these techniques have been reported. Shaping of increased heterosexual arousal appears particularly promising, yet the early research of Quinn et al. (1970) and Harbinson et al. (1970) has largely been ignored. Perhaps the best known of the techniques designed to increase heterosexual arousal is sensate focus. The publicity given the work of Masters and Johnson means that sensate focus techniques are widely known and utilized; however, this procedure also suffers from a lack of reliable research to document its efficacy. Despite this lack of investigation and documentation, in our clinical practice we have found both masturbation training and sensate focus to be useful and effective treatment techniques for enhancing heterosexual arousal.

ELIMINATING INHIBITIONS OF
HETEROSEXUAL AROUSAL

Indirect treatment techniques generally address anxiety and other target behaviors assumed to be associated with the inhibition of heterosexual arousal and functioning. In this section we will discuss five such treatment modalities: imaginal desensitization, video desensitization, *in-vivo* desensitization, assertive training, and behavioral rehearsal.

Imaginal Desensitization

In contrast to *in-vivo* desensitization, which involves instructing the patient through "real life" anxiety-producing situations, imaginal or classical systematic desensitization, as developed by Wolpe (1958), employs the cognitive process of imagery as the critical focus of attention. The goal of desensitization is the elimination of negative emotions in the sexual situation which inhibit sexual arousal. Normally, a hierarchy of anxiety-provoking or phobic scenes is compiled by the therapist and the patient working together. Wolpe (1958) has stressed the importance of minimal distance between scenes with very careful development of the hierarchy so that each scene elicits only slightly more anxiety than the scene before. The patient is next instructed in relaxation techniques which may be achieved via hypnosis, subanesthetic doses of methohexital sodium (Brevital), or muscular relaxation training. Each scene, beginning with the least anxiety-provoking, is then described to the patient in sufficient detail for the patient to vividly picture the scene, preferably in the kinds of words that are familiar and comfortable to the individual. If the patient experiences feelings of anxiety at any point during the hierarchical presentation, he signifies this fact to the therapist, who immediately instructs the patient to eliminate the image and regain deep muscular relaxation. Repeated presentation of anxiety-eliciting imaginal scenes during which the patient engages in a response directly contrasting an anxiety response (relaxation) supposedly "neutralizes" the anxiety-eliciting properties of the scene and generalizes to actual behavior.

Husted (1975) provides a heterosexual behavior hierarchy for females that will serve as an illustration of imaginal desensitization (Table 3-1). He claims that the major ingredient in the successful psychological treatment of sexual dysfunctions is desensitization. However, Kockett, Dittmar, and Nusselt (1975) compared the effects of imaginal desensitization, medication and general advice, and a no-treatment control in the treatment of erectile impotence. The therapeutic effect was investigated on three levels—behavioral, subjective, and physiological—with a total of 24 patients. The results indicated that imaginal desensitization as a singular treatment method had only a limited therapeutic effect as measured by each of the three response channels. The authors claim that this result was not surprising, since imaginal desensitization is a technique for dealing with anxiety-related problems alone; during the behavioral analysis of the patients it became clear that there were a great number of other factors in addition to anxiety that appeared to maintain the disorder. Some of these factors were identified as social anxiety, anxiety about the level of performance, unrealistic sexual standards, limited range of sexual behaviors, and negative attitudes toward sex. The authors altered the treatment strategy by incorporating sex education lectures in addition to imaginal desensitization in the treatment of the 12 patients who had originally shown no improvement. Of the 12 patients, the authors report 8 as successfully treated, 3 showing no change, and 1 relapsing shortly after treatment was com-

TABLE 3-1

Imaginal Desensitization Hierarchy

Item

1. You are dancing with your husband/boyfriend while fully clothed.
2. You are sitting on your husband's lap, fully clothed.
3. He kisses your cheeks and forehead tenderly.
4. He kisses and caresses your face and hair.
5. You are home alone with him and he gives you a warm, suggestive look or comment.
6. He kisses you in a warm, suggestive way on your lips.
7. He caresses your shoulders and back (vice versa).
8. He caresses your buttocks and thighs (v.v.).
9. He French-kisses you, with tongue contact.
10. You embrace and hug while clothed, and are aware of your partner's desire for sexual relations.
11. You caress your partner's genitals while you are clothed.
12. He caresses your breasts while you are clothed.
13. He caresses your genital area while you are clothed.
14. You are lying in bed clothed, are hugging and cuddling, and are aware of your partner's erection and desire for intercourse.
15. You are lying in bed unclothed, hugging and holding your partner prior to his arousal, and aware of the feeling of his body against yours, and of his desire for sex.
16. You are lying in bed unclothed, hugging him, and aware of his erection as you feel his body against yours.
17. He caresses your breasts while you are naked.
18. He orally stimulates your breasts and nipples.
19. You are lying in bed unclothed, and he runs his hands over your nude body (v.v.).
20. You caress your partner's genitals while he is nude, prior to his arousal.
21. You caress his genitals, while is nude, and he has an erection.
22. He manually stimulates your clitoral area.
23. He inserts his finger into your vagina during foreplay.
24. He penetrates you for the initiation of intercourse, with you in the superior position.
25. You encompass his penis in your vagina while in the female-superior position, and begin slow pelvic movements.
26. You are engaged in active sexual intercourse.
27. You are engaged in sexual intercourse, using a new position.
28. You are having sexual intercourse in the living room or some other location.
29. Your husband is stimulating your genitals with his lips and tongue.
30. You are stimulating your husband's genitals with your lips and tongue.

Source: Husted, J. R. Desensitization procedures in dealing with female sexual dysfunction. *The Counseling Psychologist*, 1975, *5*, 30–37. Reprinted with permission of the American Psychological Association, Division 17.

pleted. This study demonstrates the necessity of a multimodal behavioral treatment package as well as a systematic and comprehensive behavioral assessment of each case.

The most systematic attempt to evaluate the efficacy of imaginal desensitization in treating sexual deviation was conducted by Bancroft (1970), who treated two groups of homosexuals, each group consisting of 15 subjects. The first group was treated with systematic desensitization using imagination to heterosexual themes, while the second group was treated with electrical aversion therapy. Measures of behavioral change were considered to be the subject's verbal report of homosexual or hetero-sexual behavior and the physiological assessment of sexual arousal by means of penile plethysmography. At the conclusion of treatment and at six months' follow-up, no changes between groups were noted. When changes from the beginning of treatment to the follow-up are examined within groups, however, both treatments appear to have increased hetero-sexual arousal (as measured by penile circumference change) immediately after treatment, with aversion increasing heterosexual arousal slightly but not significantly more than systematic desensitization. Only aversion significantly reduced homosexual arousal immediately after treatment.

Bancroft then divided the groups into improved and unimproved, on the basis of their verbal reports of behavior at six months' follow-up, and noted that during treatment reduction of homosexual arousal was evidenced in both the improved and unimproved groups, but that significant increases in heterosexual arousal were noted only in the improved group. These results again indicate that suppression of deviant arousal is not sufficient for change in sexual orientation unless heterosexual arousal is enhanced, a finding verified by Adams and Sturgis (1978). If an alternate means of sexual gratification is not provided, relapse will occur.

Video Desensitization

The major differences between exposure, as previously described, and video desensitization are the goals and theoretical assumptions of the tech-niques. Exposure to high-intensity sexual stimuli is believed to enhance arousal to erotic heterosexual stimuli. In addition, exposure may also reduce sexual anxiety (Herman et al., 1971). An example is provided by Sayner and Durrell (1975), who attempted to enhance sexual functioning by having couples sit through hours of pornographic movies.

Video desensitization is a technique in which the patient is visually presented a hierarchy of sexual scenes. The technique is based largely on research in which slides and movies depicting models engaging in feared or phobic behavior proved effective in reducing anxiety (Bandura, Blanchard, & Ritter, 1969; Bandura & Menlove, 1969). In other words, an individual can learn to perform an activity similar to that done by another individual whom he/she has observed. Bandura (1971) maintains that modeling or vicarious learning produces three major effects: (1) observers may acquire new behavior patterns not previously existing within their behavioral repertoiries; (2) an observers' behavior may be either inhibited or disinhibited as a result of viewing a model's behavior; and (3) the expressions of already existing responses may be facilitated by watching a model being rewarded for these responses.

Caird and Wincze (1977) report that the format of video desensitization—relaxation training and hierarchy construction—follows the same format as that described in imaginational desensitization. Each item on the hierarchy is presented by way of a four-minute video cassette. Specific scenes are chosen from a library of 140 films produced and filmed by the authors, ranging from a couple standing in a living room talking through nude intercourse. The patient is instructed to view each film while imagining the same-sex actor as him/herself and the opposite-sex actor as his/her partner. Once a particular scene has been viewed completely without anxiety, the next scene on the hierarchy is shown. Wincze and Caird (1973) compared the relative effectiveness of imaginal desensitization and video desensitization to an untreated control condition in the treatment of 21 females complaining of sexual frigidity. Both treatment groups showed significant decreases in heterosexual anxiety immediately after treatment. However, in follow-up, the authors claim the video-treated group showed more overall positive changes than the group exposed to standard desensitization procedures. Similar results were obtained by Caird and Wincze (1974) in the successful attitude change and improved sexual performance of 9 of 10 women treated for heterosexual anxiety. Follow-up data as long as 18 months later substantiated the effectiveness of this procedure.

In a variation of video desensitization, More (1973) described using videotapes and films of research couples engaging in various heterosexual behaviors which the patient is requested to perform. More stresses the importance of showing the patient the videotapes *after* the patient has engaged in the behavior on his/her own so as not to induce "performance anxiety." On the other hand, Renick (1973) reports using similar procedures except that he suggests showing the patient the videotapes of research couples *before* the patient has engaged in a particular sexual behavior so as to provide a possible "model" for him/her. Both researchers report equal success, and only systematic research will be able to evaluate which procedure might be most effective for what particular patient with what presenting problem (Annon & Robinson, 1978).

Serber (1974) reports the use of videotapes in a somewhat different fashion. Couples are given homework assignments of specific sexual activities along with instructions on how to use a videotape recorder. The couple then makes a videotape recording of their homework assignment, and subsequently brings the tape with them to their interviews with the therapist, during which the couple and the therapist view the tape and mutually discuss what they observe. Then discussions are followed by feedback and further directions from the therapist. While Serber reports the success of this technique in the treatment of sexually dysfunctional couples, the procedure is, at best, questionable. The potential for abuse is obvious.

Video desensitization is an interesting and potentially promising treatment technique; however, research is needed to replicate the effectiveness claimed by early investigators. Obviously, few clinicians involved in the private practice of sex therapy have the time or equipment required to produce and film a wide variety of sexual behaviors.

In-Vivo Desensitization

In-vivo desensitization is a procedure whereby the clinician and patient construct a hierarchy of anxiety-related situations which the patient is to carry through with a consenting partner. In the treatment of sexual dysfunctions and deviations, *in-vivo* desensitization is an extremely effective treatment tool because it does not rely on generalization of treatment effects to real life situations. In addition, communication and effective interpersonal behaviors may also be facilitated by techniques which require intimate and mutual participation by both partners. Many clinicians and researchers have documented the effectiveness in *in-vivo* desensitization. In an early study, Cooper (1963) successfully treated a fetishist by chemical aversion and by instructing the patient to lie in bed naked with his wife until he felt comfortable. Next, he was instructed to attempt small steps progressively leading to sexual intercourse, but only when he felt no anxiety when engaging in the previous step. Gray (1970) employed a similar procedure in conjunction with covert sensitization for treatment of a homosexual. Successful *in-vivo* desensitization in the absence of aversion therapy has been reported by numerous other researchers, including DiScipio (1968) with a homosexual, and Wickramasekera (1968) with an exhibitionist.

Obviously, *in-vivo* desensitization is similar to sensate focus; it differs in that the primary goal of *in-vivo* desensitization is the elimination of anxiety in the sexual situation as well as the increase of heterosexual arousal. When combined with some of the exercises of sensate focus, *in-vivo* desensitization is a very powerful treatment technique.

Social Retraining

Social retraining procedures are those treatment techniques also called assertive training and behavioral rehearsal, a special form of role playing.

In each of these techniques new social skills are taught to those patients who, because of avoidance or behavioral deficiencies, are unable to function effectively in heterosocial and heterosexual situations (Barlow, 1974). Numerous cases of both sexual deviation (Edwards, 1972; Stevenson & Wolfe, 1960) and sexual dysfunctions (Wolpe, 1973; Yulis, 1976) have been successfully treated with assertive training, particularly in conjunction with other techniques. Patients are usually taught nonsexual assertion that presumably enables them to be more successful in heterosocial situations, and in turn leads to successful heterosexual relations. Many of these investigations dealing with sexual deviations report that deviant sexual arousal disappears once heterosexual behavior is established. For example, Cautela and Wisocki (1969) reported a treatment program of aversion therapy and behavioral rehearsals with a female co-therapist to teach adaptive social and assertive behavior to six homosexuals who verbally reported increases in heterosexual arousal. An example of the use of a prepared script in the assertive-behavioral rehearsal treatment of impotence, as described by Lazarus (1978), is shown in Table 3-2.

It is important to distinguish between assertive and aggressive behaviors since some individuals erroneously equate these two (Table 3-3). Assertive behavior lies on a continuum between nonassertive behavior on one end and aggressive behavior on the other. For example, nonassertive individuals allow others to choose for them; aggressive individuals choose for others; and assertive individuals choose for themselves. Assertive training is geared toward teaching individuals behaviors that are personally satisfying and that enhance the probabilities of obtaining reinforcement from interpersonal relations and the social milieu. It should be noted that assertive training can also be used to help people express positive feelings like love and affection, and generally to offer praise and approval, as well as to disclose negative emotions.

The establishment of effective social behavior would seem to be a necessary precursor of sexual behavior (Barlow, 1974). This hypothesis is similar to the assumptions of Salter (1961) and Ellis (1959) who treated homosexuality by avoiding attention to homosexual behavior. Instead the patient was taught to be more assertive and reinforced for appropriate heterosocial and heterosexual behavior.

Conclusions

Techniques designed to eliminate inhibitions of heterosexual arousal are considered indirect treatment techniques, since generally they address anxiety and other target behaviors associated with the inhibition of heterosexual arousal and functioning. As a result, these techniques are most often included as a singular component in a multicomponent treatment program. There is a growing body of research documenting their efficacy.

TABLE 3-2

Use of a Prepared Script in Behavioral Rehearsal

A twenty-four-year-old lawyer, after 6½ months of marriage, was perplexed and distressed by his partial impotence. He was sexually adequate some of the time but was generally inclined to obtain only a semierection. His case history indicated that his domineering mother had taught him to fear and revere women, and that he was therefore unwilling, if not unable to challenge or upbraid his wife on any terms whatsoever. Finally inquiry revealed that he had accumulated considerable resentment toward his wife but felt, paradoxically, that giving vent to his feelings would be unmanly. Therapeutic attention was accordingly directed at his absurd and irrational attitudes; which led him to regard women as objects rather than as people. These topics were covered during the course of three interviews.

The patient was then required to memorize a carefully worded speech that he and the therapist composed together:

"Grace, I have something very important and very serious to discuss with you. It concerns you, me, our marriage, and life in general. I want you please to hear me out without interrupting me. I've spent a hell of a lot of time mulling over these points, and finally I think I've straightened out my ideas, and I want very much to share them with you.

"Let me put it as clearly as possible. I was raised by my mother to bottle up my feelings, especially in relation to women. In thinking over this attitude, I now realize that this is crazy and even dishonest. I feel, for instance, that if I resent the fact that you turn to your father for advice in matters about which I have more knowledge than he, I ought to express my resentment instead of hiding it from you. I feel that when you order me about and treat me like a child, I ought to tell you how I really feel about it instead of acting like an obedient puppy dog. And most important of all, when you go ahead and make plans for me without consulting me, and especially when you yell at me in front of your parents, maybe I should quit acting as if I didn't mind and let you know how strongly I really react inside.

"What I am getting at is simply that in spite of my love and affection for you, I would really rather be unmarried than be a henpecked husband like my father."

This little monologue was rehearsed several times during a one-hour session until playbacks on a tape recorder convinced the therapist that the clinet was ready to confront his wife and that he could do so in a forthright and sincere manner. His wife's most probable reactions to the various accusations and insinuations also received careful consideration. Rehearsal techniques were used in preparing the patient to cope with tears, interruptions, denials, counterallegations, etc. His assignment was then put into effect. The patient reported that his wife "heard me out without interruption . . . seemed a little upset, but agreed that I should not withhold or conceal my feelings, I felt incredibly close to her and that night we had very good sex."

The patient was seen once every two or three weeks to reinforce his newfound assertiveness. He also had a successful confrontation with his mother and reported therapeutic gains that extended beyond his original marital and sexual impasse.

Source: Lazarus, A. A. Overcoming sexual inadequacy. In A. Lazarus (Ed.), *Behavior therapy and beyond.* New York: McGraw-Hill, 1971. Reprinted with permission of McGraw-Hill.

For example, the establishment of effective social skills through social retraining techniques has been documented as a necessary precursor to appropriate sexual behavior (Barlow, 1977). Imaginal desensitization to reduce heterosexual anxiety and phobic symptomatology has been favorably reported in the treatment of a number of various cases (Husted, 1975). Video desensitization, in which photographic slides and movies serve the role of the verbally described scenes used in imaginal desensitization, appears promising, but there is a lack of controlled research. There is also significant expense involved in collecting appropriate stimuli. Finally, an increasing amount of data indicate that *in-vivo* desensitization is a powerful treatment technique for eliminating the inhibition of heterosexual arousal. This is probably because *in-vivo* desensitization does not rely on generalization of treatment effects to real-life situations. In our clinical practice we have found social retraining and *in-vivo* desensitization to be useful and effective treatment components when included in a multicomponent treatment program.

GENDER ROLE BEHAVIOR

A matter often overlooked in the treatment of deviant sexual behavior is the presence of opposite-sex role behaviors. Although the development of gender role behavior has always been a topic of some interest (Brown,

TABLE 3-3

Differences in Nonassertive, Assertive, and Aggressive Behaviors

Nonassertive Behavior	Assertive Behavior	Aggressive Behavior
Actor		
Self-denying	Self-enhancing	Self-enhancing at expense of another
Inhibited	Expressive	Expressive
Does not achieve desired goal	May achieve desired goal	Achieves desired goal by hurting others
Allows others to choose for him	Chooses for self	Chooses for others
Hurt, anxious	Feels good about self	Depreciates others
Acted Upon		
Guilty or angry	Self-enhancing	Self-denying
Depreciates actor	Expressive	Hurt, defensive, humiliated
Achieves desired goal at actor's expense	May achieve desired goal	Does not achieve desired goal

Source: Alberti, R. E. & Emmons, M. L. *Your perfect right: A guide to assertive behavior* (3rd ed.). San Luis Obispo, Calif.: Impact Publishers, 1978. Reprinted with permission of Impact Publishers.

1958), its relationship to deviant sexual behavior has seldom been examined. The transsexual patient, whose deviant gender role behavior is so complete that he or she requests sex reassignment surgery, presents the most striking example of opposite sex role behavior. Few patients encountered in clinical practice will demonstrate such a complete predominance of opposite-sex identification and behavior. Nevertheless, some degree of gender role deviation and opposite-sex behavior is present in many patients. Recently, Freund, Nagler, Langevin, Zajac, and Steiner (1974) reported that gender role deviation for homosexuals lies on a continuum from masculine to feminine. In other words, some homosexuals have masculine gender role behaviors which overlap with those of normals, while others exhibit feminine gender role behaviors which overlap with behaviors of transsexuals, while the vast majority of homosexuals fall somewhere between. Clinical evidence indicates that the same may be said for transvestites, who dress in clothing of the opposite sex for sexual pleasure only. The stereotype of the limp-wristed, hip-swishing fag is therefore just that.

The presence of gender role deviation correlates negatively with treatment of deviant sexual arousal (Barlow, 1974). Gelder and Marks (1969) observed that unlike "simple" transvestites who responded well to aversion therapy, transvestites with opposite-sex role interests did poorly. The one patient who fit Stoller's (1974) definition of a true transsexual did not improve at all. Bieber, Bieber, Dain, Dince, Drellich, Grand, Frundlach, Kremer, Wilber, and Bieber (1963) also noted that homosexuals with gender role problems in childhood responded more poorly to psychoanalytic interventions than did those without such problems. Barlow (1974) has claimed that these results suggest that modification of deviant gender role behavior is necessary in the treatment of such cases.

Modeling

Barlow (1974, 1977) has developed a behavioral checklist of gender-specific motor behaviors which represents one of the few attempts to deal with deviant gender role behaviors within a behavioral framework. As previously discussed in Chapter 2, four characteristics of sitting, walking, and standing were differentiated as typically masculine and feminine behaviors. For example, one of the behavioral components characteristic of sitting in males is crossing the legs with one ankle resting on the opposite knee. The feminine counterpart is sitting with legs crossed closely together with one knee on top of the other. Barlow et al. (1973) employed modeling and videotape feedback in treating the gender role behavior of a 17-year-old transsexual, and analyzed the effects of the treatment modalities in a multiple-baseline design in which the modification of only one category of behavior was attempted while measures of all three categories were collected (See Figure 3-1). After successful completion of the first category, modification of the second category was attempted, and so on.

In the experimental treatment phase, daily measures of masculine and feminine components of sitting, standing, and walking were taken by a rater who was not aware of changes in the treatment program as the patient came into the waiting room before each session. A 30-minute session was held daily. After five days of baseline procedures in which no treatment was given, modification of sitting behavior was begun. In each session the components of appropriate gender behaviors were broken down and taught step-by-step. Each behavior was modeled by a male therapist and then attempted by the patient. Praise for success and verbal feedback of errors was administered. The last trial of the day was videotaped and shown at the beginning of the following session. When the patient was sitting appropriately in the session and reported feeling comfortable, treatment was begun on walking.

Pretreatment measurement showed the patient's motor behavior was almost exclusively feminine with only an occasional instance of masculine behavior. During treatment he learned to behave in a more masculine

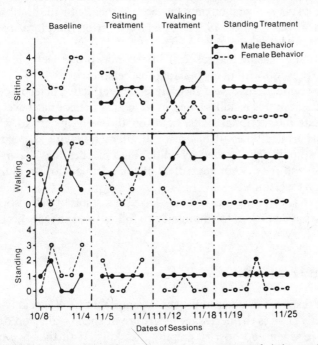

Figure 3-1. Masculine and feminine behavioral components of sitting, walking, and standing during therapeutic attempts to increase masculine behavior in each of three categories. (**Source:** Barlow, D. H., Reynolds, E. H., and Agras, W. S. Gender identity change in a transsexual. *Archives of General Psychiatry*, 1973, *28*, 569-579. Reproduced with the permission of the American Medical Association.)

manner while sitting, standing, and walking. The experimental design demonstrated that the treatment was responsible for these changes, since female sitting and walking behaviors did not change appreciably until treated. That is, treatment of sitting produced changes in that category, but not in walking behavior; the latter, in turn, improved when treatment was administered directly to walking. Rekers and Varni (1977) used similar modeling and feedback techniques to modify deviant gender role behaviors in children.

We are not offering this case as a way to treat transsexuals, since first we would need systematic replication of its effects with a number of transsexuals. The study does, however, suggest the importance of modifying sex role behaviors that are gender inappropriate in the treatment of sexual deviations. We have found modeling and videotape feedback of appropriate gender role behavior to be an effective and useful clinical procedure.

HETEROSOCIAL BEHAVIOR

Failure in dating or heterosocial interactions may lead to a high degree of social anxiety. Social anxiety has been associated with homosexuality (Feldman & MacCulloch, 1971), sexual dysfunction (Bandura, 1969), and various "mental disorders" (Argyle, 1967). Hence, techniques that are effective in decreasing heterosocial anxiety may prove useful in the treatment and prevention of many maladaptive behaviors.

As previously discussed in Chapter 2, ineffective heterosocial skills may be the result of a skills deficit in which the patient has never learned appropriate interactional skills, or of conditioned anxiety in which the previously neutral cues of heterosocial interactions are associated with aversive stimuli. The anxiety conditioning episodes may be *in-vivo* or vicarious, and may occur regardless of the adequacy of an individual's behavioral repertoire.

Curran (1977) examines in detail the current status of heterosocial skills techniques and much of the discussion to follow is taken from his excellent review.

Response Practice

The response practice approach assumes that heterosocially-anxious individuals possess the necessary repertoire of social skills and only need practice in when and how to employ the skills. It further assumes that exposure to heterosocial encounters will lead to appropriate utilization of social skills and a decrease in social anxiety.

Martinson and Zerface (1970) were the first investigators to examine the therapeutic effect of practice dating on subsequent dating behavior and comfort. They randomly assigned 24 male subjects to either a five-week individual counseling program, a delayed treatment control, or a practice dating program. The practice dating program consisted of semistructured, arranged interactions with female volunteers. All subjects included in this study had not dated in the previous month and had identified themselves as fearful of dating situations. The practice dating program was reported as significantly more effective than either the counseling program or the control group in reducing a specific dating fear, and significantly more effective than the delayed control in increasing dating frequency. No significant differences between groups were found on a test of general manifest anxiety.

Christensen and Arkowitz (1974) studied the effectiveness of a practice dating program that included a feedback exchange from dating partners. A total of 14 males and 14 females volunteered for a program that was advertised as aiming to increase dating comfort, skill, and frequency. No screening procedures were employed, and the data indicated that the subjects were not particularly low frequency daters. Once each week for a six-week period each subject was matched with an opposite-sex subject for a practice date. Following each date, the subjects completed a feedback form that required them to state aspects of their partner that they liked and did not like. These forms were mailed to the experimenters, who forwarded them to the dating partner subjects. The subjects in the dating practice program reported a significant decrease in anxiety on the Social Avoidance and Distress Scale (Watson & Friend, 1969) and the S-R Inventory of Anxiousness (Endler, Hunt, & Rosenstein, 1962) after treatment. Significant increases in heterosocial interactions were also reported, as well as decreases in anxiety and increases in skill on actual dates.

Practice dating with feedback and practice dating without feedback were compared in a study by Christensen, Arkowitz, and Anderson (1975). As in the previous study, no screening of volunteers for the program occurred, although the data indicated they were dating at a considerably lower frequency than in the previous study. The 30 male and female volunteers were assigned to the various groups that were then equated on the basis of the Social Avoidance and Distress Scale (Watson & Friend, 1969) and the S-R Inventory of Anxious (Endler et al., 1962). No other premeasures were taken, although treatment effectiveness was assessed at posttreatment by a variety of self-report, behavioral, and physiological measures. The results indicated that both treatment groups were significantly different from the control group on the self-report composite anxiety measure, in frequency and range of dating and casual interactions, and with regard to number of silences, speech latency, and pulse rate in the behavioral situation. However, no significant differences appeared between groups on the observer's and partner's ratings of anxiety and skill in the behavioral situation. A three-month follow-up consisting solely of self-report measures was conducted with the subjects in the treatment groups but not with the control group. Significant prefollow-up decreases in anxiety and increases in skill were reported on some of the measures.

Curran (1977) comments on the investigations presented thus far by calling for better designed research evaluating the effectiveness of practice dating. Because this approach requires only the use of a clerk to match subjects, it is less costly than those programs that require a clinical psychologist or psychiatrist. If the effects of practice dating can be replicated, practice dating groups can be used as a less expensive therapy control group (Paul, 1969) in designs evaluating other types of treatment programs. The exchange of information and *in-vivo* exposure experienced in practice dating may indeed prove therapeutic. However, there is always some danger that the exposure may become simply another failure experience and lead to an increase in anxiety (Curran, 1977). As Curran suggests,

> Perhaps instead of randomly matching program members, the subjects could be matched with a surrogate date trained in techniques to elicit pleasant interchanges. The training of surrogate partners would, of course, increase the effort (cost) of such a program. (p. 145)

Self-Reinforcement

Rehm and Marston (1968) felt that the anxiety males experienced in heterosocial situations was not the result of an inadequate behavioral repertoire. They reasoned that if the could increase the approach behavior of heterosocially anxious males toward females and teach them to self-reinforce such attempts, a decrease in anxiety and positive changes in self-concept would result. The investigators assigned 24 male university students to one of three groups: (a) self-reinforcement; (b) nonspecific therapy control (nondirective counseling); or (c) contact control, in which the subjects were requested to think about their problem and its solution but no suggestions were given. The self-reinforcement subjects were asked to work up systematically a hierarchy of *in-vivo* heterosocial interactions, evaluate their performance using individualized goals, and reward themselves with a self-approval for each situation. The criterion for participation in the study was solely the subjects' self-report of discomfort in dating situations. Treatment consisted of 30 minutes of individual sessions per week for five weeks. Assessment was conducted pre- and posttreatment and at a 7–9 month follow-up. The assessment battery consisted of self-report global measures of anxiety, self-report, and behavioral measures derived from the Situation Test, and an indirect measure of transfer (frequency of dates). The Situation Test consisted of 10 social situations presented orally on tape. A male voice described a situation, and a female voice read the dialogue. Various ratings and frequency counts were conducted on the response of the subjects to the situations.

Results of the investigation indicated that the self-reinforcement group demonstrated significant decreases in anxiety for most of the self-report measures as compared to the nonspecific and contact control groups. Very few significant differences were found between the groups on measures derived from the Situation Test. No differences between groups were found for observers' ratings of anxiety, adequacy of response, likability, overt anxiety signs, or latency. The self-reinforcement group did show a significant decrease in self-reported anxiety, an increase in the total number of words spoken on the Situation Test, and an increase in number of dates over baseline when compared to the other two groups. Curran (1977) summarizes the results of the study favoring the self-reinforcement group over the control groups by indicating that significant differences were noted in self-report measures only. None of the behavioral ratings or specific behavioral measures (except for the number of words at posttest) showed any significant differences between groups. Thus, it appears that self-reinforcement led to a decrease in self-reported anxiety, but did not produce behavioral changes as measured by the assessment instruments.

Response Acquisition

A number of investigations have examined the effectiveness of such behavioral techniques as modeling, behavioral rehearsal, self-observation, and the like, in the treatment of heterosocial difficulties. The assumption underlying the treatment procedures employed in these investigations is that maladaptive heterosocial functioning is due to defective behavioral repertoires. Deficiencies in effective heterosocial skills lead to aversive consequences that produce reactive anxiety (Kanfer & Phillips, 1970) and avoidance of heterosocial interactions (Curran & Gilber, 1975). As previously mentioned, this treatment model follows a response acquisition approach (Bandura, 1969), and assumes that the acquisition of an effective behavioral repertoire leads to effective heterosocial interactions and a decrease in anxiety.

McGovern, Arkowitz, and Gilmore (1975) compared the effectiveness of three behavioral training programs for dating-inhibited males. The subjects were recruited from students completing the Social Activity Questionnaire (Arkowitz et al., 1975). Criteria for subject selection were as follows: (1) less than three dates in the previous month and/or less than seven dates in the previous six months; (2) subject's self-report that his social skills could use some improvement; (3) subject's self-report of anxiety in social situations; and (4) subject's self-reported desire to date more frequently. Thirty-four males were assigned to either a waiting list control group, a discussion group, or to one of two types of behavioral rehearsal groups. In an effort to facilitate treatment effectiveness, female assistants were assigned to each group, and each participating subject was required to read a dating manual. In the discussion group the material in the manual was presented, and the female assistants elicited concerns from the subjects, gave feedback, and suggested alternative strategies. In the behavioral rehearsal group, male subjects rehearsed situations presented in the manual with the female assistants, and received feedback.

Assessment techniques consisted of a battery of self-report questionnaires conducted pre- and posttreatment. Significant differences between groups were found for two self-report measures—the Survey of Heterosexual Interactions (Twentyman & McFall, 1975), and a self-rating form for anxiety and skill. All three treatment groups were significantly different from the control group on the Survey of Heterosexual Interactions, and the discussion and behavioral rehearsal groups were superior to the control group on the self-rating form. No significant differences were noted between groups on the Social Avoidance and Distress Scale (Watson & Friend, 1969), the Fear of Negative Evaluation Scale (Watson & Friend, 1969), or the S-R Inventory of Anxiousness (Endler et al., 1962).

McGovern et al.'s (1975) investigation would appear to indicate that heterosocial group discussion that focuses on dating problems and strategy may be an effective treatment technique for dating problems. Surprisingly, the addition of the behavioral rehearsal component to the discussion group did not lead to any increment in therapeutic outcome. However, several methodological flaws in experimental design make conclusions drawn from this investigation somewhat tentative (Curran, 1977).

Melnick (1973) investigated the incremental effectiveness of various behavioral techniques in the modification of minimal dating behavior. The selection criteria for subject participation consisted of reported feelings of dating discomfort, expressed interest in modifying feelings toward dating, and a dating frequency of less than twice a week. The 59 subjects were randomly assigned to one of four treatment groups or to one of two control groups. The control groups consisted of a minimal contact and nonspecific therapy control (insight-oriented individual therapy). Treatment group procedures consisted of (1) vicarious learning; (2) vicarious learning and participant modeling; (3) vicarious learning plus participant modeling plus self-observation (via videotape); and (4) vicarious learning plus participant modeling plus self-observation plus therapist reinforcement.

Pre- and postassessment consisted of the Adjective Check List (Gough & Heilbrum, 1965) and two behavioral assessment tasks. The behavioral situations consisted of a videotape presentation of the Situation Test (Rehm & Marston, 1968) and a four-minute interaction with a female confederate. Because of the small number of subjects in each group, Melnick chose to combine groups so that the two control groups, the two groups not receiving self-observation feedback, and the two groups receiving self-observation feedback could be compared. On the behavioral task requiring interaction with a female, the two self-observation groups were rated significantly superior to the two control groups with regard to appropriateness, assertiveness, pleasantness, and decrease in anxiety; and significantly superior to the other two treatment groups on assertion and decrease in anxiety. On the Situation Test, the two self-observation groups were rated significantly higher than the other two treatment groups with regard to pre-post differences on the appropriateness and assertion dimension. No differences between groups were found with regard to speech latency and disturbances on the Situation Test, on the Adjective Check List, or with regard to dating frequency during treatment.

Melnick (1973) concluded that participant modeling plus self-observation (via videotape) was an effective technique in inducing behavioral change, whereas participant modeling alone was not. However, Curran (1977) notes several methodological flaws in Melnick's study that make interpretation of the data somewhat hazardous.

In a series of three studies, Curran and his colleagues (Curran, 1975; Curran & Gilbert, 1975; Curran, Gilbert, & Little, 1976) evaluated the effectiveeness of a replication training program (Kanfer & Phillips, 1970) for alleviating heterosocial anxiety. The program consisted of presentation of information, modeling, behavioral rehearsal, coaching, video and group feedback, and *in-vivo* assignments. The skills presented were the giving and receiving of compliments, nonverbal methods of communication, assertion training, feeling talk, handling periods of silence, training in planning and asking for dates, ways of enhancing physical attractiveness, and approaches to problems of physical intimacy. Curran (1977) claims that the first study was essentially a pilot study in which students were recruited via advertisement and asked to report for a screening interview. Nineteen males and three females who completed the study appeared to be heterosocially anxious (upper one-third of the distribution on norms obtained from the Situation Questionnaire), and to have experienced a minimal dating history (three of the subjects had never had a date). The male subjects were randomly assigned to either the replication skills-training program, a systematic desensitization condition, an attention placebo control (relaxation training only), or a waiting list control. All females were assigned to the replication condition.

Pre- and postassessment consisted of both self-report (Situation Questionnaire and the interpersonal items on the Fear Survey Schedule)

and behavioral ratings of anxiety and skill from a simulated dating interaction. The results indicated significant interaction effects for the anxiety
and skills rating, with the Situation Questionnaire approaching significance. Analysis also indicated that both the skills-training and systematic
desensitization groups demonstrated significant within-groups changes
over time for both behavioral ratings, with neither control group experiencing significant changes.

The next study undertaken (Curran & Gilbert, 1975) assessed the
effectiveness of the skills-training program at a six-month follow-up and
obtained an indirect measure of transfer (frequency of actual dates). The
students selected for participation were in the upper one-third of the distribution on the Situation Questionnaire and on the interpersonal items on
the Fear Survey Schedule. Curran (1977) indicates that they also appeared
to be minimal daters, with over 50 per cent having not dated in the seven-
eight weeks prior to the study. Twenty-one males and 14 females were
randomly assigned to either the replication skills-training program, a
systematic desensitization training program, or a waiting list control
group. Assessment was conducted pre- and posttreatment and at a six-
month follow-up. In addition to the assessment instruments employed in
the previous investigation, state anxiety measures were completed by the
subjects after the simulated dating interaction.

Results of the study indicated that both the replication training group
and the systematic desensitization group demonstrated significant decreases on both the self-report and behavioral anxiety indicators at both
posttest and follow-up periods, and did not differ significantly from each
other. The replication training group was significantly different on the
skills rating from the waiting list control group at posttest, and significantly different from both the waiting control and systematic desensitization group at the six-month follow-up. Both treatment groups demonstrated significant increases in dating frequency during and after treatment
when compared to equivalent time periods prior to treatment.

Curran et al. (1976) completed this series of investigations by
comparing the effectiveness of the replication of the skills training program
to a sensitivity training procedure. The criteria for subject selection was
essentially that employed in the previous two studies. The 21 males and 2
females were assigned to either a sensitivity training program or a
replication training program. Curran (1977) states that the lack of female
subjects necessitated the group procedures. Assessment was conducted
pre- and posttreatment and was similar to previous studies, with some
additional measures of trait and state anxiety employed.

Results indicated no significant differences between the sensitivity
and replication training procedures on a self-report measure of social anxiety. However, the replication program demonstrated, in general, signi-

ficant treatment effectiveness on more specific measures of heterosocial dating anxiety, including both self-report and behavioral measures, as well as an indirect measure of transfer (dating frequency).

Curran (1977) claims that the three investigations taken as a whole support the effectiveness of the response acquisition model as a comprehensive treatment procedure for heterosocial anxiety. The groups that received the replication skills-training program appeared superior to various control groups at posttest and at a long-term follow-up. The major weaknesses of these investigations are that they lack physiological indicators of anxiety, a direct measure of transfer, and validity data on some of the assessment instruments (Curran, 1977).

The clinical implications of these studies are seriously limited by the use of a college student population. In addition, dating skills represent only one component of heterosocial behavior. Both further research, and the development of more comprehensive treatment techniques for heterosocial skills deficits are currently needed.

Conclusions

Modification of ineffective heterosocial behavior may be targeted in any one of three different ways: (1) *Response Practice* makes the assumption that the patient possesses the necessary repertoire of social skills and only needs practice in when and how to employ the skills; (2) *Self-Reinforcement* also assumes that the heterosocially anxious patient possesses adequate social skills and needs to be reinforced for approach behavior; (3) *Response Acquisition* assumes that the socially anxious patient has a defective behavioral repertoire and that he/she is deficient in appropriate social skills and thereby must acquire effective social skills before social anxiety is reduced. In our clinical experience the majority of patients experiencing heterosocial anxiety simply have not learned or have not had the opportunity to learn effective heterosocial behavior. Response acquisition techniques such as modeling and behavioral rehearsal appear to be reasonably effective methods of instructing and practicing effective social skills. However, research in the area of ineffective heterosocial behavior does suffer from the almost exclusive use of college students as subjects.

HETEROSEXUAL BEHAVIOR

Deficient heterosexual skills and/or avoidance of heterosexual behaviors frequently results from a patient's exaggerated fear of heterosexual activities, ignorance and inexperience in heterosexual behaviors, and/or lack of heterosexual arousal. The distinction between a heterosexual phobia, the lack of heterosexual arousal, and sexual inexperience is critical, and has obvious ramifications for treatment. The woman who experiences severe anxiety and repulsion at the sight of a penis should hardly be treated in the same manner as a man who is totally inexperienced and ignorant of effective seduction and sexual techniques, or as a patient who experiences a lack of heterosexual arousal. Once again we emphasize the importance of a thorough assessment in delineating these conditions.

Treatment techniques designed to modify lack of heterosexual arousal and heterosexual phobias have previously been described. In this section, therefore, we shall limit our discussion to the modification of heterosexual ignorance and inexperience emphasizing the role of the therapist, the sexual couple, and, in the absence of a consenting sexual partner, the sexual surrogate.

Heterosexual Inexperience and Ignorance

Occasionally, a comprehensive behavioral assessment of an individual or couple presenting themselves for sexual therapy will reveal a serious lack of sexual education and/or experience. For example, research has documented that many lower socioeconomic class females do not experience orgasm during intercourse partly as a result of the prevailing attitude among these couples that sex is an activity to be initiated and enjoyed primarily by the male. Another example is that of a 24-year-old male patient, who as a 15-year-old virgin, visited a prostitute. She laughted at and severely criticized his fumbling and unrefined techniques of lovemaking. Severely humiliated by this experience, he never again dated or attempted any type of sexual play, either heterosexual or homosexual. To avoid becoming sexually aroused, the patient would go to elaborate means to resist temptation, preferring to deny himself any sexual expression.

The role of the therapist confronted with these types of behaviors may be described as that of sexual educator, counselor, and permission-giver. Often, behavior change can come as a result of the patient's learning the anatomy and physiology of the genitals, or by an attitude change as a result of the therapist, as an authority figure, granting permission, coaching, or labeling as "normal" preferred sexual activities or cognitions. The couple who believes something is "wrong" with the male because he is incapable of multiple orgasms; the couple who believes that sexually compatible partners *always* orgasm simultaneously; the male who avoids heterosexual activities because of his lack of knowledge of seduction techniques; the woman who is upset because she occasionally has a sexual thought about someone other than her husband–all are expressing fears and concerns associated with sexual inexperience and ignorance. The therapist need not al-

ways involve himself with complex cases of sexual dysfunction and deviation in order to justify his existence and training as a clinical psychologist
or psychiatrist. Occasionally, as Kolvin (1967) indicates, sexual education,
counseling, and reassurance alone may generate behavior change.

Educational Aids

Direct advice, guidance, information, reassurance, and instruction
may suffice to overcome the milder, simpler, and more transient cases of
sexual problems, yet it is often helpful to prescribe nontechnical but au-
thoritative literature as well (Ellis, 1958; Kronhausen & Kronhausen, 1965;
McCary, 1973). Various marriage manuals and sexual how-to books also
exist, but the therapist should exercise caution in recommending these
texts.

Sexual Surrogates

Countless patients who have no partners seek help for their sexual difficulties. An overriding problem associated with treating a patient without
a partner is the need for a sexual partner who can share the patient's concern for treatment success, cooperate in the physical application of sexual
activities assigned in therapy, and exemplify different levels of opposite-sex
response (Reckless & Geiger, 1975). The facilitating treatment effects of *in-
vivo* exercises as compared to covert procedures have previously been noted. In clinical practice it is not uncommon to meet the patient who has already recognized the logical facilitating effects of a sexual partner, and reports numerous visits to prostitutes in search of assistance. Prostitutes,
however, have rarely proven helpful with the patients we have seen, and indeed, patients often complain of increased anxiety during such sexual contacts.

In an attempt to meet the needs of the patient who is experiencing
sexual difficulties and has no cooperative partner, some therapists and
clinics have experimented with sexual group therapy in which persons without partners participate. Normally, the procedures include the showing of
erotic films and some erotic stimulation between the participants. Heavy
emphasis may be placed on masturbation (Kaplan, 1974). Other techniques include nudity and massage between the patient and therapist
(Hartman & Fithian, 1971), and "body-work therapy" in which an opposite-sexed therapist engages in sexual activity with the patient (Williams,
1976). As might be expected, no systematic evaluation of such methods is
available.

The idea that sexual problems which do not have their genesis in hostile and maladaptive marital interactions are nevertheless amenable to con-

joint treatment was originally supported by Masters and Johnson (1970) with the use of surrogate sexual partners. These investigators found that when no other sexual partner is available to the patient, the use of a cooperative and skilled surrogate partner who had no prior association with the patient was as effective as the participation of marital partners in the conjoint treatment of sexual difficulties. A number of sex therapists and clinics offer surrogate partners for the treatment of male patients who have none. Some women who are employed as surrogates may be prostitutes by profession, but many are not, and are often involved in other professions. One recent announcement of a two-day lecture series on human sexuality, held in a major southeastern city listed three of the eight invited speakers as social workers and part-time sexual surrogates. Many surrogates are, in fact, housewives who consider their participation a way to make extra money providing a needed service. Most therapists who utilize surrogates prefer women who are not prostitutes by profession since they are more likely to be sensitive to the therapeutic subtleties (Caird & Wincze, 1977).

The utilization of sexual surrogates has raised many eyebrows and is certainly a serious ethical concern but is, nonetheless, standard practice with some therapists and clinics. Opponents of the practice argue that it is nothing more than prostitution weakly disguised as a therapeutic technique, and as a result is susceptible to misuse and may involve damaging consequences (Holden, 1974). Proponents defend the practice as being in the best interest of the sexually troubled patient who has no sexual partner, and claim the surrogates are carefully screened and educated in appropriate behavior—for example, in how to discourage the patient's emotional attachment to the surrogate. In the final analysis, the decision for or against the use of sexual surrogates should be based on the therapist's personal value system and also on the basis of legality. The therapist who uses surrogates should be aware that, although there seems to be no ruling in regard to the practice, law enforcement officers may interpret the practice as prostitution. Given the potential damage and the consequences should patient, surrogate, and therapist be arrested, it is wise to consider the matter carefully before deciding in favor of this practice.

CHAPTER 4

Sexual Dysfunctions
in Males

Sexual dysfunctions may be considered as impaired or ineffective sexual performance. In contrast to sexual deviation, which implies a variation in sexual orientation, aim, mode, or object from some generally accepted norm, dysfunctional sexual behavior is defined as failure to engage in effective sexual behavior, and is considered by many to be one of the more frustrating and potentially damaging problems an individual or couple may face. Certainly, the importance of effective sexual functioning as both a reproductive and recreational activity means that a sexually dysfunctional individual is cast into a societal and sexual role of nonconformity. In contrast to some behaviors, individual efforts to modify sexually dysfunctional behavior generally make matters worse. Anxiety created by rumination over one's problem, or concentrated efforts to "try a little harder" produce an atmosphere of frustration that not only may have a detrimental effect on an individual's sexual functioning but also may strain a couple's marriage or relationship.

There are similarities and differences in male and female sexual dysfunctions. Two of the three behaviors comprising male sexual dysfunction have physiological and conceptual counterparts in female sexual dysfunctional behavior. Retarded ejaculation and impotence in the male are the counterparts of orgasmic dysfunction and general sexual dysfunction in the female. Also similar are the causal factors in the development of dysfunctional behaviors. It is generally agreed that anxiety, puritanical rearing, physical and/or psychological trauma, habituation to a sexual partner, misinformation, and ignorance of sexual functioning are frequently associated with both male and female sexual dysfunctions (Kaplan, 1974). In addition, severe emotional disorders such as schizophrenia and depression often result in sexual dysfunctions. In clinical practice it is common to identify at least one or more of these events in most patients presenting sexually dysfunctional behavior.

On the other hand, a major difference between male and female sexual dysfunctions is that men, unlike women, cannot fake sexual performance. Inability to achieve and maintain an erection, and penile detumescence as a result of premature ejaculation are obvious to a sexual partner. Of the

three sexual dysfunctions commonly thought specific to males, only retarded ejaculation is less than blatantly obvious. Women with difficulties
of general sexual dysfunction and orgasmic dysfunction can fake effective
sexual response, if they desire, and often the male is none the wiser. Of the
sexually dysfunctional behaviors specific to women, only vaginismus is
easily detectable by the male. Men and women may also differ in the degree
of importance they attach to sexual intercourse. While some women are
content with affection and close physical contact, including foreplay without engaging in intercourse, men are much more likely to be concerned
with intercourse and orgasm (Caird & Wincze, 1977). This attitude further
exacerbates the frustration and anxiety of the male faced with a problem of
sexual dysfunction.

The types of male sexual dysfunction commonly encountered in clinical practice include premature ejaculation, retarded ejaculation, and
impotence or erectile dysfunction.

PREMATURE EJACULATION

Ejaculation is a reflexive action activated and controlled by the lumbar area of the spinal cord. It is mediated by the sympathetic nervous system and cannot be terminated once activated (Reckless & Geiger, 1975).
Premature ejaculation is commonly defined as ejaculation prior to coital
penetration or shortly after intromission. For example, Abelson (1974) defines premature ejaculation as "the male ejaculation just prior to, at the
time of, or too soon after penetration not allowing his partner to achieve
gratification in at least 50% of the intercourse experiences" (p. 83). Other attempts to define premature ejaculation in terms of time, number of
thrusts before ejaculation, or the percentage of coital experiences in which
ejaculation occurs before the woman's orgasm have not proven as useful as
those which define it as the absence of voluntary control over the ejaculatory reflex (Kaplan, 1974). While most men experience occasional premature ejaculation at some point in their lives, loss of ejaculatory control is
not considered a serious problem unless it becomes common behavior. In
its most acute form, involuntary ejaculation takes place without the presence of a sexual partner, perhaps while the individual is reading or viewing
erotic stimuli; this should not be confused with nocturnal emission or wet
dreams, which normally involve such masturbatory behavior as rubbing
the erect penis against the mattress during sleep. It has been reported that
persistent premature ejaculation may result in secondary impotence in the
male and/or orgasmic dysfunction in his partner (Lowe & Mikulus, 1975).

Cultural and social variables dictate to a large degree whether an individual perceives premature ejaculation as a problem. Individuals from
lower socioeconomic classes who experience premature ejaculation may

not consider the dysfunction as severe as do individuals from upper socio-economic classes (Kerchoff, 1974). This perception appears to be a function of the sensitivity to the needs and desires of the sexual partner, observed more frequently in educated and informed individuals. Kerchoff (1974) indicates:

> In the lower classes, coitus is viewed primarily as a male activity, something many women feel they must simply "put up with." There is little indication that women should desire and enjoy sexual relations, even after marriage. Rainwater (1960) reports that in his sample of working class married couples: ". . . both husbands and wives feel that sexual gratification for the wife is much less important, so that, consciously at least, wives seem generally content if intercourse results in the husband's pleasure, even if not in their own. These couples see sex as primarily a male activity in initiation, interest, frequency of desire, and consistent gratification." Kinsey (Kinsey, Pomeroy, & Martin, 1948) too has pointed out that: "At lower educational levels, it is usual for the male to try to achieve an orgasm as soon as possible after effecting genital union." (p. 210)

When intercourse is oriented only toward male sexual gratification, premature ejaculation may not be considered a serious problem unless ejaculation occurs before vaginal penetration. In fact, some women may view rapid ejaculation as desirable since it frees them from extended periods of unenjoyable sexual activity (Masters & Johnson, 1970).

The dearth of reliable statistical estimations regarding the incidence of premature ejaculation may be a function of cultural and sociological factors. However, most authorities agree that premature ejaculation is the most common of the male sexual dysfunctions (Johnson, 1968; Masters & Johnson, 1970).

Research and Theory: Physiological Factors

Theoretical explanations emphasizing physiological factors as determinants of premature ejaculation often have a common theme of penile hypersensitivity. These theories typically offer little explanation for the development of this penile hypersensitivity in terms of genetic, disease, or learned processes. It must be admitted that penile hypersensitivity obviously explains this disorder, since hypersensitivity of the penis to stimulation should result in rapid ejaculation. If this is the case, however, techniques to decrease penile stimulation should remedy the situation. In fact, wearing multiple condoms, distraction techniques such as replaying the most recent Super Bowl football game in imagination during intercourse, and other homespun remedies are often attempted long before therapeutic intervention is instigated. Another attempt to remedy the problem, the "hands-off" technique, involves the man's concentrating solely upon sex- ually arousing the woman. The woman plays a passive role, avoiding con- tact with the man's penis; she signals when she is sufficiently aroused. At this point the man hurriedly attempts penetration, but most often, he in- voluntarily ejaculates. Masters and Johnson (1970) claim that it is usually the female partner who instigates therapeutic intervention and then only after a number of years of unsuccessful home remedies have been attempt- ed. Presently, there is no evidence that decreasing the intensity of penile stimulation will obviate the problem of premature ejaculation (Kaplan, 1974; Masters & Johnson, 1970). These techniques may postpone intense sexual arousal temporarily but do not teach ejaculatory control. In these cases, once sexual arousal is sufficient, reflex ejaculation will result.

There are data suggesting that in rare instances premature ejacula- tion may be the result of physical abnormalities, with various degenerative neurological dysfunctions, local genital disease, and some surgical proced- ures as suspected causal agents (Figure 4-1).

Research and Theory: Psychological Factors

Various theoretical models have been proposed to explain premature ejaculation. Unfortunately, most of these theories have little supporting data for their claims. In an effort to present contrasting etiological posi- tions, we shall briefly describe the psychoanalytic theory of premature ejaculation, and follow it with a discussion of the behavioral formulation.

Psychoanalytic Formulations. Psychoanalytic theory conceptualizes premature ejaculation as the result of intense sadistic feelings toward wo- men (London, 1957). This unconscious hatred of women has its develop- ment during the urethral erotic phase of psychosexual development and manifests itself in defiling, soiling, and denying pleasure to the woman. Kaplan (1974) reviewed the psychoanalytic literature and found three ma- jor factors assumed to be important in this disorder. First, the premature ejaculator harbors an ambivalence toward women. Second, the emotional immaturity that characterizes individuals with premature ejaculation pre- vents their adaptive coping with this ambivalence. Third, these uncon- scious ambivalent feelings find symbolic expression in the ejaculatory dys- function which serves a dual purpose of causing disappointment and pain to the woman (mother), as well as maintaining the inherent conflict in a repressed state, thus preventing the intrusion of the conflict into conscious- ness. The psychoanalytic formulation therefore views premature ejacula- tion as an unconscious attempt to punish the female by means of rapid ejaculation.

Behavioral Formulations. Behavioral explanations view involuntary

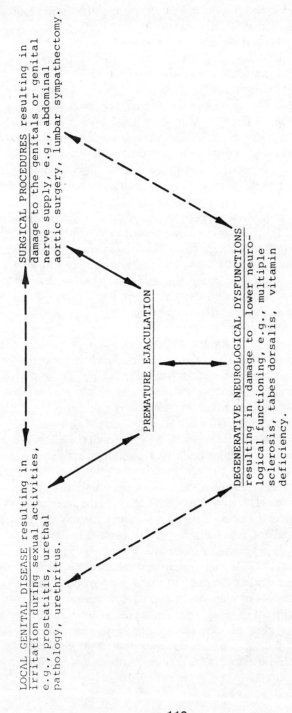

Figure 4-1. Physiological factors influencing premature ejaculation. Local genital disease, various surgical procedures, and certain degenerative neurological dysfunctions or any combination of these factors may result in premature ejaculation.

ejaculation as a learned response. Two major hypotheses are represented in the behavioral literature: (1) premature ejaculation is acquired as a function of conditions requiring rapid ejaculation, the result being inadequate control of the ejaculatory response; and (2) premature ejaculation is a function of anxiety conditioned to the sexual situation.

Masters and Johnson (1970) developed a theory of inadequate ejaculatory control after interviewing and collecting the sexual histories of numerous patients. They found that young men generally report their early sexual experiences as taking place in locations which called for ejaculatory expediency, like the back seats of parked automobiles. Teenagers and young adults occasionally depend on a technique called "dry humping" to reach orgasm. This technique involves the male rubbing his erect penis against the female's vulva while both partners are clothed and may, over time, condition ejaculation to foreplay prior to intercourse. Older men often report early sexual experiences involving prostitutes during which sexual intercourse is generally characterized by encouragement to ejaculate rapidly. Masters and Johnson (1970) also found that some males who suffer from premature ejaculation used interruption of coitus as a method of contraception at some point in their lives. A common theme in all of these experiences is learning a rapid ejaculatory response.

Wolpe (1973) examined the role of anxiety in the development of premature ejaculation and concluded that since ejaculation is mediated by the sympathetic branch of the autonomic nervous system, anxiety (which is also sympathetically mediated) facilitates ejaculation. Thus, according to Wolpe, anxiety may result in premature ejaculation. Cooper's (1968, 1969) research also suggests that, in some cases anxiety may be involved in the development of premature ejaculation.

Anxiety, in fact, may be a common factor in all male sexual dysfunctions. In other words, a major etiological similarity between male sexual dysfunctions may be that anxiety precipitates premature ejaculation in some individuals, delayed ejaculation in others, and impotence in others, depending, in part, on an individual's particular response to anxiety. Individual differences or response stereotypy to anxiety may be a function of both physiological and past learning history variables. Certainly, performance anxiety ("Will I ejaculate too soon?" "Can I ejaculate?" or "Can I maintain an erection?") is common in all three conditions, and is usually precipitated by an incident characteristic of these disorders. If the dysfunctional incident results in rumination and worry over possible future failures, the recurrence of dysfunctional sexual behavior is likely to be a self-fulfilling prophesy. Further clinical evidence for this hypothesis is that it is not unusual for a patient to report incidents of all three disorders—premature ejaculation, retarded ejaculation, and impotence—on different occasions.

Kaplan (1974), on the other hand, believes that anxiety is not a major causal agent in the genesis of premature ejaculation, but rather plays an indirect role. If the level of anxiety is such that it prevents the man from focusing on the sensations prior to orgasm, it may prohibit him from learning to control his ejaculatory reflex.

At present, the relationship between anxiety and premature ejaculation has not been conclusively established. Cooper's (1969) research suggests that the relationship is probably complex: anxiety may be a causal factor in some cases but not in others.

CASE HISTORY 4-1

A 24-year-old man and his wife came for treatment of the husband's premature ejaculation which had plagued the couple throughout their two years of marriage. The couple, not having attempted sexual intercourse before marriage, agreed that the difficulty first became evident during the honeymoon. At that time it was dismissed as a result of both partners' fatigue and anxiety. It was several weeks afterward that the wife first became seriously concerned over her husband's inability to maintain vaginal insertion for more than 15 to 20 seconds without ejaculating. Over the next two years the wife made several attempts to discuss the problem with her husband, but each attempt only made the husband angry and refuse to talk. At one point in the marriage the husband attempted intercourse with a woman he knew at work, the result being not only repeated involuntary ejaculation but also a three-week marital separation when his wife learned of his infidelity. The husband claimed he engaged in the shortlived affair in an attempt to discover if his ejaculatory dysfunction was specific to sexual activity with his wife, and explained, "I had to know if it was really my problem or if it had something to do with her." The couple decided to terminate the marital separation on the condition that the husband seek professional help for his problem. The couple presented their difficulty to their family physician, who referred the couple for psychological intervention.

A detailed history of the husband's prior sexual experiences and functioning revealed the following data:

1. His first three coital experiences involved him and three of his friends in intercourse with a willing female. He reported that each took his turn amid the cheering and rowdy encouragement of the others.

2. Soon afterward he began a steady high-school romance with a girl who allowed sex play short of intercourse. A typical evening involved periods of passionate kissing, unbuttoning her blouse and fondling her breasts through her bra, and terminated by her masturbating him to orgasm. He reported that after approximately two months their sex play had gradually shifted to his lying between her legs and rubbing his penis against her vulva until he ejaculated. This relationship lasted approximately five months, during which sexual activity occurred on the average of twice per week.

3. As a senior in high school, he and several friends would occasionally visit the home of an older woman known for her willingness and expertise in oral sex. He re-

ported that on five or six occasions he and several friends would visit her home late at night, usually after an evening of heavy drinking, and engage the woman in oral sex. Again, this activity would occur in the presence of a group.

4. After graduation from high school he met and began dating a woman for whom he cared a great deal. Since he and the woman lived with their respective parents, opportunities for relaxed and private sexual activity were severely limited. This necessitated their engaging in sexual intercourse, which they did regularly, in the awkward and cramped confines of his automobile. He reported that he first became aware of his premature ejaculation at this time, but attributed it to the awkwardness of the situation and fear of being observed.

5. Following this relationship he reported several coital experiences with a variety of partners, each of which resulted in rapid and involuntary ejaculation.

The behavioral conceptualization of the patient's premature ejaculatory response focuses on the anxiety and patterning of rapid ejaculation. Fear of being discovered and/or engaging in sexual activity in a crowd does not usually facilitate the learning of adequate ejaculatory control. The continued practice of techniques emphasizing rapid ejaculation probably strengthens the response of premature ejaculation.

Modification of Premature Ejaculation

A number of techniques have been used in an effort to modify premature ejaculation. Individuals who believe that premature ejaculation is the result of penile hypersensitivity frequently suggest various penile anesthetics, usually ointments and creams, such as Nupercainal. Nonprescription creams with names like "Prolong," "Last-a-While," and "Sta-Hard," are readily available and evidently popular. Others have treated premature ejaculation by recommending wearing one or more condoms. The major difficulty with these techniques is that, while they may reduce penile sensitivity, they do not teach the patient voluntary ejaculatory control. When a sufficient level of sexual arousal is reached, the patient ejaculates regardless of the anesthetic.

Psychotherapy. The goal of psychoanalytic treatment of premature ejaculation is generally to uncover or bring into consciousness various unresolved unconscious oedipal conflicts (Fenichel, 1945). Analysts believe that if this goal is reached the patient's sadistic feelings toward women will also vanish and premature ejaculation will cease to be a problem. Psychoanalytic treatment techniques designed to accomplish this objective include dream interpretation, free association, and interpretation of transference.

There has been no systematic evaluation of the success of psychoanalysis in the treatment of premature ejaculation. Kaplan (1974), however, claims that the results are disappointing and that even when the difficulty is eliminated, this happens only after years of analysis. If the patient is treated two to five times per week for several years, as Kaplan claims, the cost to the patient is monumental. Given an average cost of psychotherapy between 50 to 60 dollars per hour, an individual could invest between $15,000 to $20,000, so that psychoanalytic treatment of premature ejaculation can be extremely expensive, if it works at all.

Other clinicians, especially those who enjoy transactional analysis and focus on the dyadic relationship, have treated premature ejaculation by focusing on the marital relationship (Walen, Hauserman, & Lavin, 1977). This therapy assumes that premature ejaculation is a function of a maladaptive marital relationship. Premature ejaculation may certainly create frustration and strain in a marital or sexual relationship, but it is doubtful that a marital relationship in any large measure causes premature ejaculation. Kaplan (1974), in fact, claims that marital therapy may improve a couple's relationship but has little effect on their sexual functioning. There is little evidence for the therapeutic effects of marital therapy in the treatment of premature ejaculation; however, cooperation of partners facilitates a variety of treatment approaches, and the marriage may benefit from the inclusion of marital therapy within a treatment program designed to address the problem of involuntary ejaculation.

Chemotherapy. Pharmacological treatment of premature ejaculation has been suggested by a variety of clinicians. Lazarus (1971) and Wolpe claim that antipsychotics (*e.g.,* Mellaril), depressants (*e.g.,* barbiturates), antidepressants (*e.g.,* MAO-inhibitors), and tranquilizers (*e.g.,* Valium) are useful in the treatment of this disorder. *The International Drug Rx Newsletter* (1966), in fact, suggests the following procedure for management of premature ejaculation:

> Depending on the dose administered, a unique pharmacological action of the phenothiazine, thioridazine (Mellaril-Sandoz), is retardation or inhibition of ejaculation. To relieve premature ejaculation prescribe 25 mg., two to four times daily (occasionally a higher dose may be required). Some men respond immediately; others only after taking the drug up to two months. After two months of symptomatic relief, reduce dosage by one-half for another month. If relief is maintained for this month, thioridazine should be discontinued. If premature ejaculation recurs, a second course of thioridazine therapy, with the same or slightly higher dosage, for two or three months, often produces lasting relief. (p. 21)

Unfortunately, medication that impairs the autonomic nervous system occasionally can produce unwanted side effects (Kaplan, 1974). In addition, these drugs often take weeks and even months to become effective, and the effects are usually temporary.

Behavior Therapy. The behavioral treatment of premature ejaculation attempts to control anxiety by relaxation techniques and systematic desensitization, and/or to teach control of the ejaculatory response. Although relaxation techniques and systematic desensitization have not been utilized extensively in the treatment of premature ejaculation, some evidence suggests the effectiveness of these treatment techniques (Ince, 1973; Obler, 1973). We shall discuss both approaches.

The utilization of relaxation training and systematic desensitization is designed to lessen anxiety and sympathetic arousal during sexual intercourse. Generally, this procedure involves the clinician's instructing the patient in relaxation techniques (Jacobsen, 1939) for two or three sessions, and requesting that he practice the exercises once or twice daily. After successful relaxation is achieved, the clinician and the patient collaborate on the construction of a sexual hierarchy. Care should be taken in the construction of the hierarchy to see that the initial scenes have minimal anxiety-arousing effect, and that small successive steps characterize the hierarchial progression. The effectiveness of systematic desensitization as a treatment technique is severely reduced if the space between the steps in the hierarchy span too great a distance and create gaps in the intended gradual approximation of the hierarchy. An example of a systematic desensitization hierarchy employed in the treatment of a 36-year-old married male who experienced premature ejaculation in approximately 50 percent of his coital attempts is presented in Table 4-1.

After the patient is assisted in relaxation exercises and is completely relaxed, the lowest item on the hierarchy is presented. The patient is instructed to imagine the scene as vividly as possible and to indicate to the clinician if he should feel any anxiety. Each scene is presented 30 to 60 seconds, and if the patient demonstrates no signal of anxiety, the next item is presented. If any anxiety response is given, the therapist instructs the patient to eliminate the thought from his mind and to clear his mind of the anxiety-provoking scene. Relaxation exercises are then begun again until the patient is once again completely relaxed and the anxiety-provoking item is repeated. This procedure is repeated until the entire hierarchy can be presented with no anxiety response given by the patient.

An interesting variation of the above-described procedure was employed by Ince (1973) in the treatment of a 22-year-old male who experienced premature ejaculation on each attempt at intercourse. Ince first utilized relaxation exercises followed by systematic desensitization to reduce the patient's sexual anxiety. During the second week of therapy the patient was trained in thought stoppage. The patient was asked to visualize sexual relations with his female partner and, when he cognitively reached the brink of ejaculating, to indicate this by raising his hand. The therapist then shouted "Stop." Following three such trials the patient's visualizations

TABLE 4-1

Systematic Desensitization Hierarchy for Premature Ejaculation

1. You are sitting in your living room watching television with your wife. While she is concentrating on the TV you look at her wearing your favorite night-gown and her hair pulled up the way you like it and become sexually aroused.

2. You get up from your chair and walk over to sit beside her on the sofa. As you reach for her hand she pulls you to her and kisses you passionately.

3. You respond to her kisses by slipping your hand under her gown and fondle her breasts as you hold her tightly.

4. She encourages you with her soft pleasurable moans as you gently begin to manually massage her genital area.

5. She breaks from your kisses, stands, and drops her gown to the floor. You stare at her naked body and feel your erection straining against your pants.

6. You stand up from the sofa and walk together into the bedroom where she begins to undress you.

7. As she undresses you, you begin to wonder whether you will be able to control your ejaculation tonight.

8. You both get into bed and begin to kiss and fondle each others genitals as you feel the excitement building in your penis.

9. You perform oral sex on your wife in an attempt to heighten her arousal as much as possible. You find it difficult to concentrate on pleasuring her for thinking about how much you hope that tonight you will be able to control your ejaculation.

10. As you move on her body and begin kissing her breasts she reaches down to fondle your erect penis. After a moment of this you feel as if you are going to ejaculate and move her hand quickly before you orgasm.

11. As you continue kissing and caressing your wife and waiting for the feeling of ejaculation to subside, you realize that you won't be able to hold your ejaculation tonight.

12. You position yourself between your wife's legs, make penetration and begin thrusting. Suddenly, you again feel an ejaculation coming on. As you fight for control, you ejaculate into your wife some 30 seconds after penetration.

13. As you begin your regular routine of attempting to orally satisfy your wife, you feel embarrassed and wonder what your wife must be thinking of you.

stopped on hearing the cue word. He was then directed to shout "Stop" while envisioning the same scene and later instructed only to think the word "Stop." The patient was instructed to think the word "Stop" when he experienced the sensation of an approaching orgasm during intercourse until his partner reached orgasm. Following treatment the patient reported satisfaction in his sexual relationship and no further need to employ the technique.

Caird and Wincze (1977) claim that while there are data on the efficacy of systematic desensitization, *in-vivo* treatment or direct training in the control of premature ejaculation is more rapid and effective and is the treatment of choice. *In-vivo* treatment should start with a session of honest communication among the clinician, the patient, and the patient's sexual partner. The clinician should explain to the couple that the chances for successful treatment are excellent, but contingent upon several important factors. First, the clinician emphasizes that the couple must abide by the instructions and should not under any circumstances proceed to more advanced treatment stages without instructions from the clinician. Second, the clinician should insure that both the patient and his partner are strongly committed to the treatment program. Since this procedure places the woman in the role of "giver" and the man in the role of "receiver" of pleasure, at least in the initial stages, methods by which the patient can satisfy his partner's sexual needs during treatment should be explored. Although the patient is prohibited from engaging in intercourse during the initial stages of treatment, he may employ oral, manual, or mechanical means to sexually satisfy his partner. Finally, the clinician should explain that the treatment procedure is based on successive approximations toward a goal and consequently requires strict adherence to the treatment program. This includes carrying out of homework assignments and avoiding the cancellation of therapy appointments. Usually appointments are scheduled twice weekly for a total of 4-6 weeks.

Many treatment programs have been sabotaged by the clinician's failure to emphasize the importance of these treatment criteria. If the couple rushes through the treatment steps or fails to perform the steps properly, the treatment program may fail. The couple thus sees no change in the patient's problems and may blame the clinician and/or the program for the failure.

Once the preliminary discussion has been concluded, the couple is instructed to engage in limited sexual foreplay to the point where the male is sexually aroused. If the woman appears to be uncomfortable or unsure of herself in the sexual situation, sensate focus which involves various nondemand, nongenital pleasuring exercises may be recommended as a starting point for the couple. Most couples, however, can ignore sensate focus and proceed directly to genital stimulation by the woman. This involves the partners disrobing and the woman caressing and manipulating the male's genitals with her hands or mouth. If the couple prefers manual stimulation, the man should lie on his back and the woman should find a comfortable position for pleasuring. Masters and Johnson (1970) recommend that she rest her back against the headboard of the bed while the man lies with his head toward the foot of the bed and his legs over hers. The couple is instructed that this should be a time of silence during which the woman excites and manipulates while the man lies passively and focuses his attention on the sensations he is experiencing. In this way genital stimulation becomes a biofeedback technique in which the male learns to discriminate the sensations preceding ejaculation.

When the man feels as though he is approaching ejaculation, he signals his partner who employs either the Semans Start-Stop Technique (Semans, 1956) or the Masters and Johnson Squeeze Technique (Masters & Johnson, 1970). The start-stop technique simply involves the woman halting contact with the genitals until the urge to ejaculate diminishes. She then resumes genital stimulation as before. The number of pauses required to sustain stimulation and delay ejaculation rapidly decreases over successive occasions with this procedure until the male soon gains the capacity for penile stimulation of great duration without any pauses at all. The underlying mechanism in the Semans procedure may be Guthrie's "crowding the threshold" process for extinguishing stimulus-response connections. In the case of premature ejaculation the connection is between minimal stimulation and ejaculation. According to Guthrie, such extinction is produced by gradually exposing the subject to progressively more intense and more prolonged stimulation, while always keeping the intensity and duration of the stimulus just below the threshold for elicitaton of the response (Guthrie, 1952).

The squeeze technique involves the woman encircling the tip of the penis with her hand (Figure 4-2). The thumb is placed against the frenulum located on the underside of the penis while the index and second fingers are placed on either side of the coronal ridge located on the upper side of the penis. The clinician should demonstrate the proper grip to the woman by using an anatomical model or an explicit picture to make sure that the woman has a thorough understanding of the technique. When the man signals his premonitory orgasmic sensations to the woman, she simply applies the squeeze technique to the penis. Rather strong pressure should be applied to the penis for 3-5 seconds and should be terminated with a sudden release. When the sensations of pending ejaculation diminish (usually within 20-30 seconds) the woman should again begin genital stimulation. The clinician should instruct the patient that at no time should he attempt voluntarily to control his ejaculation, but should simply rely on either the start-stop or squeeze technique to diminish his desire for ejaculation. The couple should be instructed to repeat the ascending and descending ejaculatory exercises 3-4 times each session before allowing ejaculation. If the squeeze technique is used, the couple should be warned to release the squeeze immediately if the patient ejaculates as a result of not stopping stimulation early enough. Ejaculation when the urethra is held closed, can, in rare instances, produce retrograde ejaculation with concomitant risk of physiological problems in the bladder, prostate, or seminal vesicles.

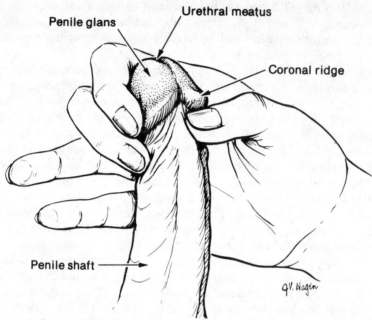

Figure 4-2. Demonstration of the "Squeeze Technique." (Source: Masters, W. H., & Johnson, V.E. *Human sexual inadequacy.* Boston: Little, Brown Company, 1970.)

If the couple reports no problems as a result of the initial stages of treatment, another dimension is added. The woman continues genital stimulation sessions as before, but adds a lubricant such as Vasoline or K-Y jelly to the penis. The addition of a lubricant produces penile sensations that more closely resemble those experienced during intravaginal penetration. The woman continues the schedule of bringing the man to the brink of ejaculation before applying the squeeze technique; she then repeats the procedure 3-4 times before allowing him to ejaculate.

If this step is satisfactorily completed, then the couple is instructed to replace genital stimulation sessions with intercourse using the female superior position. In the female superior position the man lies on his back while the woman sits across him. The couple should begin by assuming the female superior position, at which time the woman guides the penis into her vagina remaining as motionless as possible. The couple should not begin thrusting at this time but lie motionless to give the man time to adjust to penetration. It is important that the clinician emphasize to the couple that the squeeze technique remains an integral part of treatment and should be employed throughout this stage of treatment as needed to halt ejaculation. When the man feels comfortable and in no danger of ejaculation the woman should begin intercourse by slowly lifting her body on and off the man's. The female superior position enables the man to place his hands on the woman's hips to control the tempo of intercourse. If the man should signal the sensation of oncoming orgasm, the woman should dislodge herself from his penis and apply the squeeze technique. After the sensation of ejaculation has diminished, she should again insert the penis and begin intercourse. The male should not be allowed to ejaculate until the start-stop or squeeze technique has been applied 3-4 times or until the woman has experienced orgasm. The couple should be instructed to practice female superior intercourse every other day for 8-10 days.

By this time the male should be demonstrating increased voluntary control of ejaculation. Detailed discussion of both partners' feelings about the procedure and appropriate modifications if needed should be a part of each office visit. If progress is sufficient, lateral or side-by-side intercourse should be initiated with use of the start-stop or squeeze technique as needed. If success is maintained, the final step is the male superior intercourse position, again using the start-stop or squeeze technique as needed. Kaplan (1974) reports that many of her patients use the lateral coital position as a matter of choice even after several successful male superior intercourse experiences are reported. At this point choice of intercourse positions or techniques is left to the couple. We suggest that the couple continue to practice the squeeze technique routinely once every 7-10 days, and encourage them to report for a follow-up visit three months after termination to insure the continued effects of treatment.

Another less known technique which reportedly enhances the effectiveness of the pause procedures is reported by LoPiccolo (1978). Since contraction of the scrotum and elevation of the testicles occurs during high arousal and orgasm (Masters & Johnson, 1966), LoPiccolo reports that pulling down on the scortum and testes seems to work like the squeeze technique to reduce sexual arousal and the urge to ejaculate. Definitive data on this technique are presently lacking.

Reports on the success of behavioral treatment of premature ejaculation are excellent. Kaplan (1974) claims that premature ejaculation is almost always amenable to treatment with ejaculatory control achieved in the female superior and lateral coital positions within 2-4 weeks. Masters and Johnson (1970) report a treatment success rate of 98 percent with a two-week intensive training program. Semans (1956) reports a 100 percent success rate with an average patient contact of 3.2 hours.

CASE HISTORY 4-2

A 31-year-old oral surgeon and his 29-year-old wife were referred for treatment of his premature ejaculation. During the clinical interview it was discovered that rapid ejaculation first became a problem for the patient when he and his wife began dating while in college. Due to the apparent difficulty the wife had never experienced orgasm during intercourse with her husband, but did report that she was now orgasmic during masturbation and oral stimulation by her husband. Both partners appeared committed to following the treatment program and agreed to undergo a physical examination by the referring physician before beginning treatment.

Treatment began by instructing the couple in genital stimulation. Both partners appeared cooperative and asked many questions; for instance, if a particular nightgown that the husband considered "extremely sexy" could be substituted for the wife's nudity during genital stimulation exercises. A brief discussion revealed that the request was made not because of the husband's aversion to his wife's nudity, nor because the wife was reluctant to appear nude in front of her husband; thus approval was given. It was suggested that the couple begin genital stimulation exercises that evening and practice the exercises every other day until their next appointment the following week.

The couple arrived for their next appointment pleased to report that the exercises had gone well and were considered enjoyable by both partners. The wife reported that by the fourth session she was able to stimulate her husband for two minutes before he signaled premonitory sensations of ejaculation. The partners considered this a success, since previous attempts by the wife to stimulate the husband had resulted in his ejaculation within 30 seconds. The couple, pleased and even more committed to treatment, were warned not to let their early success and enthusiasm override their commitment to the structured timetable of treatment. We next instructed the couple to continue with genital stimulation exercises, but to add a lubricant during the exercises. The importance of utilizing the squeeze technique was again emphasized.

The couple reported for their next appointment with continued enthusiasm and further success. The addition of a lubricant to the stimulation exercises had had little effect in hastening the husband's sensations of oncoming ejaculation, but it did increase pleasure. The husband was now routinely able to continue the exercises for over six minutes before ejaculatory sensations. At one point during the week the couple met for lunch, and when they got back to the husband's office, they locked the door and engaged in a 40-minute stimulation exercise on the office sofa. The couple also used our suggestions regarding the wife's sexual release. After one genital stimulation exercise the husband removed the wife's gown and gave her a complete body massage with the lubricant (the couple preferred warm body oil), which resulted in the wife's orgasm. We next instructed the couple to advance to intercourse in the female superior position.

A week later the couple returned for their regularly scheduled office visit and reported that the husband was experiencing difficulty in maintaining an erection during intercourse. Questioning revealed that achieving and maintaining an erection was not a problem during sexual foreplay, but occurred specific to penetration. Further questioning revealed that the husband was experiencing significant anxiety and concern over the possibility of premature ejaculation during intercourse. The husband complained that the initial stages of treatment had progressed well, and that his wife was so encouraged and enthusiastic that he now feared failure to control his ejaculation during intercourse. Several sessions of relaxation training and systematic desensitization were indicated to eliminate the performance anxiety the husband associated with intercourse. Three desensitization sessions were conducted during the next week before the husband could imagine a hierarchy of scenes involving vaginal penetration and intercourse without experiencing anxiety. At this point the couple was instructed to reinstitute intercourse in the female superior position.

The following week the couple reported their homework exercises as successful. The squeeze technique was employed frequently during the first attempt at intercourse, but later attempts required infrequent utilization. The wife also experienced her first coital orgasm with her husband during one of the sessions, and the second two days later. We verbally reinforced the couple for adhering to the treatment procedure and instructed them to begin intercourse in the lateral coital position.

The couple returned in two weeks with glowing and enthusiastic reports of their present sexual compatibility and functioning. Both partners agreed that the husband was presently controlling his ejaculatory response with little, if any, reliance upon the squeeze technique, and the wife was experiencing regular coital orgasms. The couple also admitted that they had broken the training rules for the first time by engaging in intercourse on an average of twice a day, and had employed a variety of coital positions. Since the couple agreed during the initial interview they were not interested in the male superior coital position due to their differences in height—he was 6'2'' and she was 5'—the two week successful lateral coital exercises represented the completion of active treatment. The couple was instructed to employ the squeeze technique several times every 7-10 days and were asked to report for a follow-up visit in three months. At three months' follow-up the couple reported continued success with no instances of premature ejaculation.

RETARDED EJACULATION

Retarded ejaculation is also called ejaculatory incompetence (Masters & Johnson, 1970), ejaculatory impotence (Cooper, 1968), and delayed orgasm. Usually there is no problem in the individual's ability to become sexually aroused and achieve an erection, but there is difficulty in ejaculating intravaginally. Kaplan (1974) defines retarded ejaculation as a specific inhibition of the ejaculatory reflex, and notes the biphasic nature of the problem wherein erectile functioning remains intact while ejaculation is selectively impaired. The inability to ejaculate intravaginally contrasts sharply with premature ejaculation, but the frustration may be equally severe. In fact, some individuals report embarrassment so great that they fake orgasm and later masturbate without their partner's knowledge.

Retarded ejaculatory dysfunction can be primary or secondary in nature. In the primary form the inability to ejaculate is evidenced from the initial coital experience. Kaplan (1974) claims that the majority of these patients have little difficulty ejaculating extravaginally by masturbation or oral-genital sex. Secondary retarded ejaculation is characterized by a period of effective sexual functioning until the onset of the dysfunction. Occassionally the specific event associated with the onset of sexual dysfunction cannot be identified, but in many cases events such as fear of pregnancy, being discovered during forbidden sexual intercourse, or being unable to concentrate as a result of group sex may be identified as precipitating factors in the onset of this problem. Being intoxicated during intercourse can also cause or initiate this problem.

Retarded ejaculation varies in severity. In its mildest form, inhibited ejaculation may be associated with a specific anxiety-eliciting situation or partner (Kaplan, 1974). For example, a male may function effectively with his wife but experience dysfunction when he engages in extramarital affairs or vice versa. In most of these cases, individuals rarely seek professional help.

Cases that are encountered by the clinician include the more severe instances in which the patient is never able to reach intravaginal orgasm. These individuals often report marathon sessions of intercourse lasting an hour or more which result in physical exhaustion and sore and aching genitals for the woman. Most of these individuals can, however, ejaculate during oral sex and manual stimulation by their partner. Others, however, are inhibited if their partner merely touches their genitals.

Occasionally, retarded ejaculation is complicated by reactive impotence. Anxiety over sexual performance may be manifested by impotence and retarded ejaculation and may, on occasion, result in sufficient anxiety so that erectile dysfunction is manifested. This obviously has important implications for treatment, and should be investigated during the sexual assessment. Masters and Johnson (1970) recommend that the patient's impotence be the initial focus of treatment with attention to retarded ejaculation once potency is restored. Kaplan (1974), however, claims that reactive impotence as a result of retarded ejaculation is normally specific to demand situations in which the patient feels he is expected to have intercourse. Generally, failure to achieve an erection does not occur in nondemand genital stimulation exercises which constitute the initial treatment stages as they do in the treatment of premature ejaculation.

Priapism (continuous erection) is a condition occasionally confused with retarded ejaculation. Priapism, however, is a pathologic erection unassociated with sexual arousal, and results from damage of the valvelike structures in the corpus cavernosum, abnormal stimulation of the efferent nerves, blood dyscrasia, infection, or lesions of the spinal cord (Reckless & Geiger, 1975). A defect in the mechanism that releases blood from the corpus cavernosum results in ischemia, which further results in fibrosis.

The incidence of retarded ejaculation is unknown. Masters and Johnson (1970) report on only 17 cases out of 510 couples treated in their extensive experience. Friedman (1973) could not find a single paper in the literature devoted solely to the topic of retarded ejaculation, although a few have since appeared (Newell, 1976). Kaplan (1974), however, claims a significant number of individuals requested treatment of retarded ejaculation at her Cornell University Clinic. Since this dysfunction may not be blatantly obvious to the female partner, some males may be reluctant to seek treatment.

Research and Theory: Physiological Factors

An organic causal factor for retarded ejaculation is rarely encountered, yet the possibility of a physiological basis for the dysfunction should not be disregarded simply because it is infrequent. Diseases that impair lower neurological apparatus may potentially result in retarded ejaculation (Figure 4-3). Tabes dorsalis, spina bifida, amyotrophic lateral sclerosis, springomylia, multiple sclerosis, malnutrition, and vitamin deficiency may result in ejaculatory dysfunction as a result of interference with periperal nerves or spinal cord reflex centers that subserve the sexual response (Gardner, 1975). Kaplan (1974) claims that neurological diseases that impair the tactile sensory perception of the penis, the autonomic nervous outflow, or the ejaculatory reflex centers in the spinal cord may also result in retarded ejaculation.

Various surgical procedures are occasionally associated with ejaculatory dysfunction. Abdominal aortic surgery, especially to the testicular aortic arteries which supply the blood flow to the genitals, often results in retarded ejaculation. Evidence exists that lumbar excision of a portion of the sympathetic division of the autonomic nervous system (lumbar sympathectomy), and rhizotomies which involve the severing of a portion of the ventral or dorsal root of the spinal nerve to ameliorate severe pain may precipitate retarded ejaculation.

The use of certain medications frequently prescribed for treatment of psychotic and hypertensive conditions are thought to block the autonomic adrenergic nerves and thus periodically cause ejaculatory dysfunction. Phentolamine, ergot alkaloids, halo-alkylamines, guanethidine, methyldopa (Aldomet), and Rauwolfia alkaloids supposedly may impair ejaculation because of their autonomic adrenergic nerve blockage. Tranquilizing

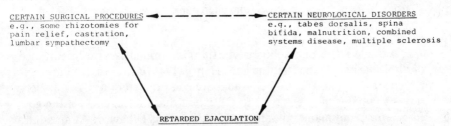

CERTAIN SURGICAL PROCEDURES ◄ — — — — — — — ► CERTAIN NEUROLOGICAL DISORDERS
e.g., some rhizotomies for   e.g., tabes dorsalis, spina
pain relief, castration,   bifida, malnutrition, combined
lumbar sympathectomy   systems disease, multiple sclerosis

RETARDED EJACULATION

Figure 4-3. Physiological factors influencing retarded ejaculation. Certain surgical procedures as well as various neurological disorders or a combination of both of these factors may result in retarded ejaculation.

drugs, especially phenothiazines, as well as alcohol, can also result in retarded ejaculation by blocking the sympathetic ejaculatory response.

Research and Theory: Psychological Factors

Theoretical models proposed to explain retarded ejaculation are scarce.
As previously mentioned, through 1973, Friedman (1973) could not find a
single paper in the literature devoted exclusively to retarded ejaculation.
Although a few investigations have appeared in the literature within recent
years, there are very few systematic and reliable data.

Psychoanalytic Formulations. The psychoanalytic conceptualization
of retarded ejaculation views the dysfunction as a variant of impotence,
since little distinction is made between the two in analytic thinking (Fenichel, 1945). Retarded ejaculation is thus described as the result of the fear of
physical injury, such as castration, and the conflict that exists as the man
seeks the pleasure of an activity which he fears will do him physical harm.
In other words, the patient desires the pleasurable act of intercourse but
unconsciously fears castration if he should deposit his semen into a vagina
(representative of his mother). The neurotic solution to this dilemma is to
engage in intercourse short of ejaculation (London, 1957). In this way the
individual can partially fulfill his desire for sexual pleasure while protecting himself against retribution for ejaculating.

Friedman (1973) offers a slight variant of this analytic conceptualization by postulating that retarded ejaculation is the result of a "success phobia." Success phobia can be thought of as a person's attempt and desire for
success until success is near, at which time he terminates his strivings in fear
that the success be associated with some undesired retaliation.

> The patient with success phobia has to maintain a good erection to por-
> tray that which he really lacks, a conviction of strength. However, in the dem-
> onstration of strength with his penis he is willing to go only so far, but no
> further and stops just short of the culmination of success, ejaculation. This
> control is exercised at the very last point compatible with safety. Thus through
> his symptoms the patient with retarded ejaculation saves his life, preserves his
> penis, and supposedly emerges from intercourse a man. (Friedman, 1973, p.
> 63)

A final variant of psychoanalytic thinking emphasizes the importance
of "holding back" and "letting go." Henry (1948) claims that children experience anxiety and fear of being abandoned by their mother. This anxiety
serves to inhibit their behavior to the extent that they avoid "letting go"
completely, and maintain apprehensive, cautious behavior. As an adult,
the man projects his unconscious infantile fear of being abandoned to his

primary adult love object (wife). If he ejaculates or "lets go," he runs the risk of abandonment. He thus defends against this unconscious fear by "holding back" or retarded ejaculation.

Behavioral Formulations. There is general agreement among behavior therapists that retarded ejaculation is the result of anxiety associated with sexual activities, but unfortunately there are few data to support this assumption (LoPiccolo, Stewart, & Watkins, 1972). Anxiety may develop as a result of an obvious traumatic experience or more slowly through the socialization process (Figure 4-4). An overt psychological trauma might be being discovered by a policeman while engaging in sexual intercourse in some supposedly secluded place. An example of covert trauma would be severe guilt felt as a result of a strict, puritanical religious upbringing that prohibits premarital sex. In many cases both factors are present; the moralistic history may predispose the individual to sexual dysfunction if a traumatic event should occur. Obviously, however, everyone who experiences psychological trauma in a sexual situation does not exhibit retarded ejaculation. Further data are needed before we will be able to accurately describe, predict, and modify this behavior.

CASE HISTORY 4-3

B. M., a twenty-four-year-old, engaged, postgraduate student, referred himself to the Behavior Therapy Unit with the complaint of never having been able to ejaculate intravaginally satisfactorily since his first attempt at coitus six years previously. Although able to achieve and maintain an erection sufficient for intercourse, both before and during intercourse he would have doubts about his ability to perform, and at the same time become anxious about the possibility that he might impregnate his partner. As a result, even though he was able to maintain his erection

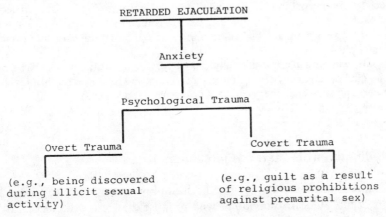

Figure 4-4. Behavioral etiological hierarchy.

intravaginally for several minutes, he would gradually lose it and eventually withdraw without ejaculation. This understandably left him and his partner disappointed and frustrated.

Since the age of fourteen he had masturbated regularly an average of three times a week with no premature emissions. He dated infrequently during his high school years, the extent of his sexual activity being kissing and light petting. Since the onset of his sexual difficulty, he had retained a normal desire for intercourse as evidenced by his use of fantasies of women during masturbation.

Six years before his coming to the clinic, while a freshman in college, he had taken a girl friend to a motel after a dance with the intention of having intercourse (his first attempt). The girl expressed fear of becoming pregnant even though she had had a hysterectomy, and he became apprehensive about this possibility. He attained a firm erection, but in attempting penetration, aimed inaccurately, the result being both an increase in his anxiety and premature ejaculation. Thereafter, he became reluctant to have intercourse, and even though he dated off and on, did not try intercourse again until four years later when he became engaged for the first time.

He attempted intercourse with his first fiancee a total of seven times, but each experience ended with partial loss of erection and withdrawal without ejaculation. His first engagement lasted thirteen months and ended because of sexual dysfunction. After a three-month period, he became engaged a second time. Four months later he came for treatment. With his second fiancee he had attempted intercourse a total of thirteen times. On three occasions he was able to ejaculate intravaginally, but with much apprehension and anxiety. On eight occasions he had suffered partial loss of erection, and on two occasions lost his erection before penetration. He was clearly on a path toward secondary impotence (Masters & Johnson, 1970) when he came for treatment. His fiancee was understanding and eager to cooperate, and he was highly motivated for treatment.

His initial clinical evaluation and psychological testings (Fear Survey Schedule, Eysenck Personality Inventory, SPAT Self-Analysis Form, and MMPI) revealed a somewhat shy, passive, and introspective young man who suffered from a lack of confidence in his sexual performance. He was well adjusted in his occupational and social environment, and there was no evidence of any overt interpersonal anxiety or of phobic or obsessional symptoms. His acquaintances perceived him as a warm and sensitive person, and he had been able to establish several close interpersonal contacts.

He was born in a Jewish family, who were not religiously devout. His past history did not reveal any significant neurotic symptoms, and he described his childhood as a happy one. There had been no discussions dealing with sexual matters at home. (Razani, 1972, pp. 65–67)

Modification of Retarded Ejaculation

A variety of techniques have been employed in an effort to modify retarded ejaculation. Individuals who propose that retarded ejaculation is the result of insufficient sexual arousal (Hogan, 1978) frequently suggest "love vacations" involving a weekend trip away from the anxieties and frustrations of home and work. Others suggest sexy lingerie for the female partner, and explicit erotic films and literature in an effort to increase sexual arousal. The major difficulty with these techniques is that most males who experience retarded ejaculation do not demonstrate diminished sexual arousal. The vast majority, in fact, claim that they desire sexual intercourse and ejaculation.

Psychotherapy. The goal of psychoanalytic treatment of retarded ejaculation is to resolve the unconscious fears of abandonment and intrapsychic conflict supposedly maintaining the behavior (London, 1957). The patient is encouraged to free his inner psychic feelings responsible for the marital conflict influencing the dysfunction. The analyst employs free association, dream analysis, and interpretation of the transference that supposedly exists between the patient and the wife (who is unconsciously perceived as the mother), as well as between the patient and the analyst (Fenichel, 1945). The resolution of deep-seated unconscious conflicts between the desire for intercourse and fear of castration will supposedly culminate in the patient's effective sexual functioning.

As with premature ejaculation, no systematic investigation of the success of psychoanalysis is available; however, there appears to be little evidence that insight serves as a catalyst for effective behavior change (Kilmann & Auerbach, 1979).

Chemotherapy. The pharmacological treatment of retarded ejaculation is generally targeted on the reduction of anxiety or depression. Believing that anxiety is at the core of retarded ejaculation, some physicians prescribe various muscle relaxers in an attempt to alleviate the dysfunction. We have noted a number of referred patients taking minor tranquilizers such as Valium, Librium, or Tranxene. Other physicians prefer to address the dysfunction from the point of view of depression, and prescribe various antidepressants such as Elavil and Tofranil.

Occasionally the patient will attempt to treat himself, and employ various drugs including hallucinogens and amyl nitrite in an attempt to heighten sexual sensitivity and achieve intravaginal ejaculation. Marijuana and LSD appear to be two common hallucinogens encountered in clinical practice. Amyl nitrite, considered by some to heighten and intensify erotic sensations, is "popped" at the peak of sexual arousal in an attempt to increase orgasmic sensation. Investigative data on the ability of these drugs to heighten sexual excitement are scarce and often contradictory. It is known, however, that amyl nitrite is potentially dangerous. Coronary occlusions can occur and can result in death.

Behavior Therapy. Presently there are two major behavioral approaches toward the modification of retarded ejaculation. The first attempts to modify the patient's sexual anxiety through the use of progressive muscular relaxation and systematic desensitization. The second approach attempts to shape intravaginal ejaculation through successive approximations *in-vivo*.

The muscular relaxation-systematic desensitization treatment of retarded ejaculation closely resembles the application of this procedure in the treatment of premature ejaculation. The patient is instructed in muscular relaxation exercises to be practiced at home while the clinician and the patient conjointly construct a hierarchy of anxiety-provoking scenes, an example of which may be seen in Table 4-2. Treatment consists of the presentation of anxiety-provoking scenes while the patient is as relaxed as possible. The goal of treatment is to gradually defuse the anxiety-arousing components of the hierarchical scenes by pairing each scene with a relaxation response.

If the patient is married or has a willing sexual partner, we prefer to treat retarded ejaculation by emphasizing *in-vivo* desensitization or shaping. As previously noted, it is generally agreed that *in-vivo* training more closely approximates real life sexual situations, and therefore avoids many of the potential problems of imaginal desensitization (such as generalization).

In the behavioral treatment of retarded ejaculation, no one *in-vivo* treatment program can be uniformly constructed and universally applied to every patient. The level of sexual functioning in retarded ejaculation varies considerably, probably more than in any other male sexual dysfunction. For example, two men may both be unable to ejaculate intravaginally, yet experience no ejaculatory difficulty during masturbation. However, one may be able to ejaculate when masturbated by a female while the other can ejaculate only when self-stimulated. Treatment programs should be tailored to the needs of the individual, and often challenge the ability of the best clinicians. For purposes of illustration we shall assume effective sexual functioning with the exception of the ability to ejaculate intravaginally.

The first step in treatment is attention to the same treatment precautions recommended in the treatment of premature ejaculation: (1) the entire formulation and treatment procedure should be carefully explained to the couple in detail; (2) both partners should express a willingness to participate; and (3) the clinician should emphasize the importance of adhering to the treatment timetable and schedule. After the satisfactory completion of this step the couple can be given their first homework exercise.

The first stage of active treatment is nondemand pleasuring. The couple is instructed to engage in masturbation of the male emphasizing, however, that ejaculation is prohibited during this initial treatment stage. The couple should assume a comfortable position during this exercise and focus attention on the sexual pleasuring of the male. The couple is instructed to practice this exercise every other night for a week. The clinician should emphasize that ejaculation is *not* allowed during this stage, and should also

TABLE 4-2

Systematic Desensitization Hierarchy for Retarded Ejaculation

1. You and your wife have turned out the lights and are lying in bed talking before going to sleep.

2. As you continue talking she places her head on your shoulder and you pull her closer to you.

3. You feel very close to her at this moment as you begin to kiss her.

4. She places her arms around your neck and pulls you to her breasts.

5. You feel your penis becoming erect as you continue kissing and begin to fondle her breasts.

6. She responds warmly to your caresses by rubbing your inner thigh.

7. You now feel your penis becoming hard and elongated as you manually stimulate her genitals.

8. She slides her hands around the waistband of your pajama bottoms and gently lowers them freeing your erect penis.

9. You reach to the bedside table and take out the electric vibrator you know gives her pleasure and begin to stimulate her genitals as she massages your penis.

10. She moves her body to you and presses your penis against her stomach while whispering how much she wants you.

11. You remove her gown and position yourself between her legs.

12. As your penis penetrates her vagina you experience very pleasurable sexual sensations.

13. You both begin thrusting, gradually at first, enjoying the sensations of intercourse.

14. As you continue thrusting you notice your wife increasing the tempo of thrusting as she nears orgasm.

15. As you meet the tempo of your wife's thrusting she reaches orgasm while holding you tightly.

16. You continue thrusting and feel the sensations of approaching climax.

17. You speed the tempo of thrusting as your wife meets every thrust.

18. You feel your muscles tensing as you continue thrusting while your wife verbally encourages you toward ejaculation.

19. Your muscles tighten and you feel a wave of sensations radiating through your body as you ejaculate into your wife's vagina.

inform the couple that the woman's sexual needs may be attended to throughout treatment at the couple's discretion (excluding intercourse). This step is designed to extinguish any anxiety present in the sexual situation.

The next step of treatment is similar to the first, only the male is allowed to ejaculate. The man is instructed to focus his attention exclusively on sexual sensations during the masturbation exercises. The clinician may also suggest the use of sexual fantasy, magazines, or films if the male reports a facilitating effect from these stimuli. Instructions to engage in these exercises in a relaxed manner without setting ejaculation as a goal but merely allowing orgasm if the male is sufficiently stimulated should be emphasized in this session.

The third stage of treatment involves the man's first penile contact with the vagina. The couple is instructed to assume a comfortable, position—say, lateral—and engage in normal masturbation exercises. However, just prior to orgasm the penis is inserted into the vagina. The woman should assume the responsibility for penile insertion to avoid any potential increase in anxiety as the man searches for the vaginal opening. If the man should find it impossible to ejaculate intravaginally, the penis should be withdrawn and restimulated.

The next stage of treatment is a continuation of the previous stage with penile insertion taking place for increasing periods of time before ejaculation. In other words, instead of inserting the penis into the vagina just prior to ejaculation, penile insertion should occur before the premonitory sensations of ejaculation.

Once the man is repeatedly successful in penile insertion before ejaculation the couple is instructed in intercourse with combined genital and mannual stimulation. This involves the couple's assuming the male superior intercourse position with the woman positioning her hand under her buttocks. In this way the woman may place the thumb and index finger on the sides of the penis and add increased manual stimulation to the vaginal intercourse. Thus, the man benefits from both vaginal and manual stimulation during sexual intercourse. If the man prefers, the woman may gently massage the testicles during intercourse as an alternative to manual penile stimulation.

The final stage of treatment is fading of the manual-vaginal stimulation technique. This is accomplished by instructing the wife to gradually decrease the amount of manual stimulation as long as the man maintains his ability to ejaculate intravaginally. The clinician should conduct a series of monthly follow-ups for approximately six months after termination of treatment. Little research data exist on the long-term effectiveness of treatment. Masters and Johnson (1970) report an 83–84 percent success rate with 17 patients in a five-year follow-up investigation. Kaplan (1974) volunteers no follow-up statistics but does admit to treatment successes and failures in her practice. Cooper (1969) reports a success rate of 85 percent in seven cases treated.

CASE HISTORY 4-4

The couple consisted of a 40-year-old teacher and his 35-year-old wife referred by the husband's psychiatrist for treatment of retarded ejaculation. The couple reported the onset of the dysfunction some four years before, when the husband learned of his wife's infidelity with her employer. The couple began marital therapy with a clinical psychologist at that time and later with a psychiatrist. Both partners agreed that the marriage suffered from no problems at the present time other than the husband's retarded ejaculation. The couple appeared committed to the treatment program as it was explained and seemed anxious to begin. A detailed assessment of the couple's current sexual functioning revealed the frequency of intercourse to be approximately twice per week. During lovemaking, the couple would engage in mutual genital stimulation and intercourse until the wife was orgasmic at which time she would orally stimulate the husband to climax. The couple reported the husband's ability to ejaculate only as a result of masturbation or oral sex.

The couple was first instructed in nondemand pleasuring excluding ejaculation. Both partners were instructed to make this exercise as sexually stimulating as possible by prolonging each session as long as the husband wished. Body oil was suggested for added stimulation if the husband desired.

The couple returned the following week reporting that the three practice sessions had gone well and were considered enjoyable. They appeared much more at ease in the clinical setting and maintained their desire to continue treatment. The partners were instructed to continue the masturbation exercises and to allow the husband to ejaculate if he desired. In an effort to prevent increased sexual anxiety it was emphasized that ejaculation should not be considered the *goal* of this treatment stage.

Midway through the following week a call was received from the couple claiming that the husband's sexual arousal was decreasing. We investigated the complaint further and determined that rather than ejaculating, the husband was now experiencing only partial erections. Since the couple had previously expressed enjoyment in viewing sexual 8-mm. films in their home, we suggested the husband facilitate his sexual arousal by viewing sexual films while the wife masturbated him.

Several days later the couple returned for their scheduled office visit, and reported that the addition of sexual films had proved beneficial in restoring the husband's full potency and in ejaculatory success. The remainder of treatment was uneventful and followed the course of the case previously discussed of retarded ejaculation. The husband successfully progressed to making vaginal insertion at the point prior to ejaculation and progressively increased the length of time between penile insertion and ejaculation. We instructed the wife in the technique and positioning for manual-vaginal stimulation which she enjoyed successfully, gradually extinguishing manual stimulation over a four-week period. At the termination of treatment the couple reported the wife remaining orgasmic and the husband ejaculating intravaginally. Monthly office visits for a seven-month follow-up period resulted in no relapse of retarded ejaculation. The couple reported being more secure and happy in their marriage than at any previous time.

IMPOTENCE

Impotence, or erectile dysfunction, is a term used to describe a male's inability to achieve and maintain an erection sufficient for intercourse in the majority of sexual contacts. Impotence is a common male dysfunction and may result in severe psychological damage to the individual. With our society's emphasis on sexual performance, the impotent male often experiences severe humiliation and frustration. He also faces the possibility of marital difficulty; some wives respond angrily to the dysfunction, while others often report feelings of sexual and personal rejection. Of the three male sexual dysfunctions discussed in this chapter, we agree with others (Cooper, 1971; Kaplan, 1974) in considering impotence the most clinically common and potentially damaging dysfunction in terms of both personal humiliation and marital discord. One patient, for instance, reported going through, in a period of 15 years, two wives, close to 100 women, over 20 doctors of varying specialties, and a small fortune in search of a "cure."

Impotence (Latin for "without power") varies somewhat among individuals. Some men experience firm erections during sexual foreplays but experience detumescence upon penetration. Others have no erectile difficulty during oral sex but lose their erection when attempting intercourse. Some men experience nothing more than a partial erection during sexual activity, while others achieve firm erections with one woman and are impotent with another. The central theme expressed in these cases is sexual arousal, a desire for intercourse, and fear that they will be unable to achieve and/or maintain an erection (performance anxiety). These conditions are thought by many clinicians to practically insure erectile dysfunction.

In the assessment of impotence a distinction must be made between organic and psychogenic etiology. *Organic impotence* is due to physiological and chemical causes and is seldom encountered in clinical practice (although the possibility always exists). Organic impotence may be related to anatomical difficulties in genital structure, various central nervous system dysfunctions, certain diseases, medications, and surgical procedures, as well as some brain and spinal cord injuries, and excessive use of alcohol and drug abuse. *Psychogenic impotence* results from psychological causes and is by far the most frequent type of impotence encountered in clinical practice. Reports vary, but generally show that 90 percent of all impotence is psychogenic in origin. Morning erections are generally considered a reasonable indication that impotence is psychogenic in etiology, although physiological assessment of nocturnal penile tumescence represents a more objective and comprehensive index. Karacan (1977) explains that nocturnal penile tumescence evaluations are conducted over a period of three consecutive nights in a sleep laboratory designed to measure penile erection, eye movement, and EEG. Psychogenic impotence is most frequently characterized as the result of inhibition of cephalic impulses that act on the neural center of the spinal cord controlling erection (Reckless & Geiger, 1975). The catalyst for this inhibitory response is assumed by many to be anxiety associated with sexual performance and activities (Caird & Wincze, 1977; Walen et al., 1977).

Impotence may also be categorized as primary or secondary in nature. Primary impotence is suspected when the patient reports never having been able to achieve and maintain an erection whether in heterosexual, homosexual or self-administered stimulation (Walen et al., 1977). Secondary impotence may be defined as at least one successful coital experience with erectile dysfunction in 25 percent or more current attempts at sexual intercourse. It is generally agreed that secondary impotence is more commonly encountered in clinical practice and is more amenable to psychological treatment (Cooper, 1971; Kaplan, 1974). The majority of our patients with complaints of impotence claim their first and subsequent coital experiences were successful until the onset of the dysfunction.

It is important to remember that infrequent episodes of erectile failure do not mean an individual is impotent. McCary (1973), in fact, claims that the vast majority of men have experienced episodic bouts of impotence. Statistics on the frequency of occurrence of impotence suggest a gradual increase with age: 0.5 percent under 25 years of age, 2 percent at 35, 10 percent at 55, and 50 percent at 75 (Greenblatt, Jungck, & Blum, 1972). Other evidence, however (Sviland, 1975), suggests that there is little physiological explanation for declining potency in advanced age. The statistical data may represent the self-fulfilling prophecy of a society that appears to expect declining potency in advanced age.

Research and Theory: Physiological Factors

Walen et al. (1977) suggest 17 potential physiological causes of impotence that should be investigated before a psychological etiology is assumed: (1) diabetes; (2) prostatitis; (3) lumbar disc disease; (4) circulatory disturbances, such as Leriche's syndrome; (5) surgical sympathectomy involving the lumbar ganglion; (6) brain and spinal cord injuries or tumors; (7) trauma to the perineal nerves; (8) endocrine disorders; (9) severe systemic disease; (10) sickle cell disease in the Negro; (11) drug abuse, particularly alcohol and heroin; (12) chronic barbiturate intoxication; (13) chronic use of anticholinergic agents; (14) use of tranquilizers, including phenothiazines and MAO inhibitors; (15) use of sympathetic blocking agents such as drugs employed in the treatment of hypertension, such as Aldomet; (16) radical or perineal prostatectomy; and (17) aging, although Kinsey et al. (1949) reported only 30 percent of men at age 70 were impotent.

Kaplan (1974) emphasizes a comprehensive collection of potential medical illnesses that may influence erectile functioning by grouping the disorders under five general categories: (1) systemic diseases; (2) endocrine disorders; (3) local genital diseases; (4) surgical conditions, and (5) vascular diseases. Figure 4-5 presents a sample of physical factors which may af-

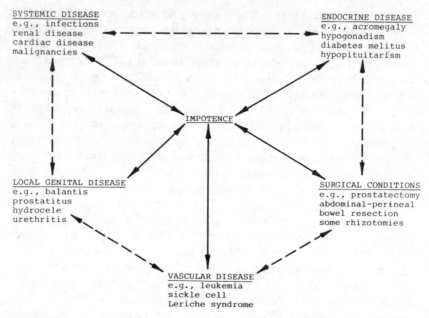

Figure 4-5. Physiological factors influencing the etiology of impotence. Although the physical etiology of impotence is rare, any single or combination of physical conditions is evidenced as a potential causal agent.

fect erectile functioning, and shows that the potential physical causes of impotence are quite numerous and varied.

As previously stated, however, psychogenic impotence represents the most prevalent type of erectile dysfunction, and Amelar (1971) claims that if the patient can achieve an erection in some situations, for instance, masturbation or in the morning upon waking, but not others, such as sexual intercourse, the dysfunction is psychogenic and not organic in nature. However, a routine medical examination by a primary care physician for all patients referred for sexual treatment is advised.

Various types of drugs can also result in impotence, as Table 4-3 indicates. The addicting drugs result in chronic depression in the central nervous system and thus decrease the sexual drive (Reckless & Geiger, 1975). Tranquilizers and antidepressant drugs may result in impotence in a variety of ways, depending on the chemical composition of the drug. Chlorpromazine (Thorazine) may inhibit erectile ability by adrenergic blocking of the hypogastric plexus of the thoracolumbar sympathetic system (Reckless & Geiger, 1975). Antidepressants such as imipramine (Tofranil) and amitriptyline (Elavil) can result in impotence by interfering with cholinergically medicated systems, and potentiate the sympathomimetic amines, especially norepinephrine, increasing sympathetic action (Simpson, Blane, & Amoso, 1965). The monoamineoxidase (MAO) inhibitors (Parnate) have direct sympathomimetic effects. Several antihypertensives are also known to occasionally produce impotence as a side effect, although the method of the action is not clear (Reckless & Geiger, 1975).

Research and Theory: Psychological Factors

A number of psychological reasons have been said to cause impotence, ranging from excessive masturbation to the wrath of an uncharitable God. Among the explanations advanced include fear of impregnating the female; sexual abstinence as a result of religious beliefs; strain and fatigue; latent homosexual conflicts; fear of venereal disease; marital discord; anxiety; seductive maternal behavior; early traumatic sexual experiences; and severe parental restrictiveness (Walen et al., 1977).

Psychoanalytic Formulations. The psychoanalytic conceptualization of impotence is based upon the notion that unresolved oedipal fixations with associated feelings of guilt and fear result in unconscious intrapsychic conflicts responsible for the dysfunction (Kaplan, 1974). The oedipal complex, of course, is characterized by the young boy's wish to possess his mother and destroy his father, who is viewed as the primary rival for his mother's affection. The child's wish results in guilt, and in fear of the fathers retaliation by means of castration. If the oedipal conflict is not resolved, the adult male will unconsciously associate sexual arousal with the infantile fear of castration as a result of his incestuous desire for his mother. Impotence is thus viewed as a neurotic defense against the intrusion of unacceptable anxiety resulting from the oedipal conflict (Allen, 1962).

Behavioral Formulations. Most behavior therapists assume that

TABLE 4-3

Drugs That May Lead to Impotence

Drugs of addiction	Barbiturates, morphine, heroin, cocaine, alcohol, amphetamine, and bromide
Tranquilizers and antidepressants	Chlordiazepoxide, chlorprothixene, imipramine, certain phenothiazines, such as chlorpromaxine and thioridazine, and drugs of the monoamine-oxidase inhibitors
Drugs of the vascular system	Reserpine, nicotine, digitalis, guanethidine, and methantheline

Source: Reckless, J., & Geiger, N. Impotence as a practical problem. In H. F. Dowling (Ed.), *Disease-a-month*. Chicago: Year Book Medical Publishers, 1975. Reprinted with permission of Year Book Medical Publishers.

impotence is the result of performance anxiety (Friedman, 1968; Obler, 1973). Masters and Johnson (1970) and Kaplan (1974) believe that anxiety over sexual performance is the most important immediate cause of sexual dysfunction, since it can turn a single sexual failure, no matter what the original cause, into a chronic sexual problem. Performance concerns have two components: (1) the affective component, or "performance anxiety"; and (2) the cognitive component, which Masters and Johnson (1970) call "spectatoring." In other words, instead of being an active participant engulfed in the sexual experience, the male constantly monitors and checks his sexual functioning and performance, thus becoming a "spectator" rather than an "participant." Continued evaluation of the occurrence and degree of penile erection prohibits the spontaneity and natural flow of lovemaking. Performance anxiety and spectatoring have been noted in cases of impotence by many clinicians (Annon, 1976; Kockett et al., 1975).

In a typical case of impotence, the onset of the disorder is precipitated by a failure to achieve an erection during a sexual contact. This failure may be caused by overindulgence in drugs such as alcohol; sexual intercourse in situations or circumstances which elicit anxiety, depression, or other emotion conditions; or a sexual partner who is not sexually arousing. For example, it is not unusual for a man who has been married for a number of years to become habituated to the same sexual partner, particularly if he does not have an active fantasy, and, as a result, become insufficiently aroused to maintain an erection. However, an incidental erectile failure does not mean that the individual will develop impotence. The situation which seems frequently to dictate the development of this disorder arises when the erectile failure results in anticipation of another failure. This anticipatory anxiety usually occurs in males who are puritanical and/or concerned with their masculinity. The male may, as a result of one failure, rush into another sexual encounter in order to reassure himself that he has not lost his potency. Unfortunately, his obsessive concern with his ability to maintain an erection may inhibit sexual arousal and cause a further failure which initiates the cycle of performance anxiety, cognitive ruminating ("Can I get it up?" or "Can I keep it up?"), and inhibited sexual arousal. Often if a partial erection is achieved, the individual will try vaginal penetration immediately. Doing so, however, may cause further problems if the erection is not sufficient for penetration, if the female is not sufficiently lubricated to allow penetration, or if the erection is lost on penetration because of insufficient sexual arousal. A variation on this theme occurs when an individual is, explicitly or implicitly, criticized for sexual performance or inadequate penile dimensions, or harbors misconceptions concerning sexual performance (Table 4-4). These criticisms and misconceptions may elicit the same cycle of performance anxiety. After a number of failures, the male may begin to avoid sexual intercourse and experience anxiety in situations when sexual intercourse is a possibility. This type of psychogenic impotence has all the characteristics of a phobic disorder or a conditioned avoidance response. It is worth noting that the same course of events occurs in homosexual males with problems of impotence.

CASE HISTORY 4-5

The patient was a 41-year-old factory worker referred by a clinical psychologist colleague for treatment of impotence. A clinical history of the patient's sexual functioning revealed a six-year history of the dysfunction. The patient was married for 13 years and divorced two years prior to seeking treatment.

The patient described his marriage as "rocky" from the start. Frequent and violent arguments between the couple would often result in the wife's threatening to leave or even murder the patient during his sleep. During one violent episode the wife attacked the patient with a knife and produced a wound which required more

TABLE 4-4

Misconceptions Frequently Noted in Cases of Impotence

Masculine notions

1. It is the function of the male to satisfy the female partner.
2. A real man can achieve an erection rapidly under any circumstances, even in a casual male-female encounter.
3. The size and firmness of the erection are necessary determinants of the female partner's satisfaction, and any deficit in either automatically causes failure in sexual intercourse.
4. The number of ejaculations of which a man will be capable during his lifetime is limited, and excessive masturbation can exhaust a man's potential by his early middle age.

On occasion, women may reinforce their partner's sense of inadequacy because of their own value systems and attitudes, which often are based on the following:

Feminine notions

1. It is a man's duty to be available for sex and to manage to give his partner orgasm in intercourse.
2. A man's failure to achieve an erection indicates not only a diminution of affection for his partner but in all probability his involvement with another woman.
3. A man should know instinctively how to please a woman despite the fact that during sexual activity her pleasure in different kinds of caresses may change from moment to moment.

Source: Reckless, J., & Geiger, N. Impotence as a practical problem. In H. F. Dowling (Eds.), *Disease-a-month.* Chicago: Year Book Medical Publishers, 1975. Reprinted with permission of Year Book Medical Publishers.

than a dozen stitches to mend. Another argument cuminated in the patient's awakening one morning with his head pressed against the barrel of a pistol and his angry wife tightly gripping the trigger. The patient, a strapping six-foot, 210 pound man, appeared no match for his 112 pound wife.

The wife left the patient at one point in their marriage and remained gone for over five months. Upon returning she refused to disclose where she had been,' yet the patient helped move her back into the home. The couple continued fighting, and the patient soon learned that his wife was involved in an extramarital affair. When confronted, his wife readily admitted her involvement, informed him of five additional men she had been romantically involved with, announced her intention of having sex with anyone she desired, and pointed the patient toward the door. The patient declined to leave, however, and the relationship continued.

The patient reported the onset of impotence at this time. The patient's first and subsequent sexual failures were met with the wife's outrage and accusations against the patient's manhood. Subsequent arguments were characterized by the wife's detailed verbalization of her current lover's techniques, penile dimensions, and virility. Four years from the initial episode of impotence the patient deserted his wife and filed for divorce.

Upon terminating the marriage the patient entered into a series of unsuccessful attempts at sexual intercourse with a variety of women. Romantically involved with a woman whom he wished to marry and who was sympathetic to his dysfunction, the patient actively sought professional attention.

Modification of Impotence

Due to the severe potential psychological and marital effects of impotence, a number of approaches have been tried to remedy this disorder. In the fifteenth century impotence was attributed to curses, witchcraft, sorcery, and the like, and modifications required forgiveness of the gods. More recently excessive masturbation and sexual activity have been blamed, so that periods of abstinence were prescribed to restore potency. We now know that impotence may result from a number of physiological and psychological circumstances. In this section we will discuss psychotherapy, medical therapy, chemotherapy, and behavior therapy as means of correcting this disorder.

Psychotherapy. Psychoanalytic treatment of impotence attempts to uncover the deeply rooted unconscious oedipal conflicts believed to be maintaining the neurotic defense of impotence (Friedman, 1973). Dream analysis, interpretation of transference, and free association enable the clinician and the patient to gain insight into the dynamics of the psychic disturbance. Once the patient gains sufficient insight to enable resolution of the oedipal conflict, the dysfunction should disappear. If it does not, the patient's resistance is blamed for resulting in insufficient insight to effect behavior change (Fenichel, 1945). It is difficult or impossible to comment on the efficacy of analytic treatment; most of the claims made for it are based on single or a few case studies, or merely stated as theoretical assertions without supporting data. Obler (1973) and Cooper (1971) refute the necessity and effectiveness of long-term insight psychotherapy.

Medical Therapy. Surgery is occasionally attempted in the treatment of impotence. Surgical procedures most commonly employed include the sectioning and tightening of the perineal muscles and revascularization of the penis. In addition, remarkable progress has been made in the past two decades in the field of surgical implants for impotent men. Earlier types were "constant erection" or "semirigid," with the use of bone; then came the more flexible Small-Carrion silicone implants (Schuster, 1976). While these devices are not difficult to insert, they do require wearing a truss to conceal the permanent erection (Merrill & Swanson, 1976). Although prosthetic implants do not produce ejaculation, they do facilitate intromission with a flaccid penis, and the polyethylene implants covered with soft tissue appear to be well tolerated (Morales, Ducrez, Delgado, & Whitehead, 1973). These approaches are most applicable to cases of primary impotence or where other techniques have failed.

Chemotherapy. There has recently been a revival of drug therapy for impotence with, it seems, mixed results. Although hormones have been used for many years to treat impotence, if they are prescribed when impotence is not due to hormone deficiency, they can increase libido without improving performance and thus worsen the patient's plight (Reckless & Geiger, 1975). Hormone treatment increases the risk of atherosclerosis, coronary thrombosis, and cancer of the prostate (Reckless & Geiger, 1975), and is felt by many physicians to be contraindicated in cases other than those involving definite endocrinopathy. Sobotka (1969), however, reports significant improvement in a series of controlled and uncontrolled studies on over 4,000 patients using Afrodex (combination of methyltestosterone, yohimbine, and nux vomica). Miller (1968) and Sobotka (1969) attest to the importance of psychological factors in drug therapy, since patients also demonstrated significant improvement on placebo, and maintained potency for a prolonged period of time after the drug was discontinued.

Vitamin therapy and nutritional supplements are also occasionally employed in the treatment of impotence, especially when hepatic dysfunction due to long-term alcohol abuse and nutritional deficiency is thought to be a causal factor. Greenblatt et al. (1972) claim that the liver's inability to inactivate estrogen results in an estrogen-androgen imbalance which may cause both impotence and gynecomastia (breast enlargement) in the male. Vitamin and nutritional therapy is part of an impotence treatment program offered by numerous chiropractors (Langley, 1979).

Behavior Therapy. Wolpe (1958) was the first to formalize the behavioral treatment of impotence by recognizing that since erection is mediated by the parasympathetic nervous system, the state of sympathetic arousal associated with anxiety inhibits erection. Wolpe therefore employed systematic desensitization as a treatment technique for impotence. Other researchers quickly followed suit and contributed to the documented efficacy of this technique (Friedman, 1968; Jones & Park, 1972; Kockett et al., 1975). Other researchers attempted to improve, shape, and polish the behavioral treatment of impotence by investigating novel approaches and treatment techniques, as noted by Walen et al. (1977), and including: (1) techniques to increase the sexual drive, including orgasmic reconditioning and abstinence; (2) sexual education and correction of misconceptions; (3) assertive training to assist the patient in expressing his desires and assuming a less subservient role; (4) desensitization to neutralize any phobic component of sexual activity; and (5) distraction training or thought-stopping to eliminate the patient's tendency to spectatorate rather than participate in lovemaking. Garfield, McBrearty, and Dichter (1969) and Lobitz and LoPiccolo (1973) have presented comprehensive treatment packages which combine a number of these behavioral treatment techniques. Masters and Johnson (1970), while not specifically labeling their approach behavioral, developed a treatment approach very similar to behavioral techniques. Caird and Wincze (1977) claim the majority of behavioral treatment programs for impotence now include three general components:

1. *Reeducation:* Many behavior therapists emphasize the importance of open and honest communication in an effective sexual relationship. Communication skills as well as instructions in sexual technique and anatomical functioning are often important prerequisites to successful behavioral treatment.

2. *Redirection of Sexual Behavior:* One of the critical treatment goals of behavior therapy is the redirection of the impotent patient's concentration from self-monitoring of penile erection to pleasuring the sexual partner. Emphasis is placed on redirecting the patient from the role of sexual spectator to sexual participant.

3. *Graded Sexual Exposure.* The majority of behavioral treatment programs present a hierarchy of sexual behaviors to the patient. Performance anxiety, believed responsible for the dysfunction, is neutralized by means of graded sexual exposure to the anxiety-provoking stimuli. This may be accomplished through imagery as in systematic desensitization, or through gradual and repeated *in-vivo* desensitization practice with a sexual partner.

The first step in the behavioral treatment of impotence involves a session of honest and open communication in which the clinician emphasizes that the ability to achieve an erection is greatly diminished when the patient is anxious or distressed over the inability to erect. The couple is informed that the treatment program requires the patient be "selfish," in that treatment is directed toward the erotic pleasuring and reduction of anxiety in the male. Manual and oral stimulation of the woman is permitted if desired, although intercourse is prohibited. The patient is instructed to concentrate solely upon his sexual fantasies and sensations and to refrain from masturbation or other forms of sexual release. These instructions are intended to reduce performance anxiety and increase sexual arousal in the male.

Treatment is frequently facilitated by teaching progressive muscular relaxation to the male with the sexual partner present. This procedure can then be used as a method of controlling anxiety in the sexual situation, and may be administered by the female partner. Further, systematic desensitization with an individually constructed hierarchy for each particular case enhances the probability of success. Each item on the hierarchy (usually the steps in foreplay) is presented in imagination and is then practiced at home by the couple. In some severe cases the initial hierarchical steps may be kissing and caressing which later progress to undressing each other. The couple can then begin with nude nongenital touching and caressing followed by genital touching and exploring. Both partners are instructed that erection is *not* a concern in this stage. It should be emphasized that this is a time reserved for relaxed mutual exploring of the partner's body, and should not involve concerns or monitoring of erection or ejaculation. If penile erection should occur, the couple is not to attempt coitus or prevent the erection from subsiding. The patient is warned that just as one erection occurs, others will also occur, and no concern should be given to an erection that does not maintain itself, a technique Masters and Johnson (1970) term the "teasing technique."

When the couple reports being comfortable in genital caressing they are given permission to attempt penetration. McCary (1973) states that it is critical to emphasize that attempted penetration should come only as a result of the couple's comfort and desire, and should not be heavily emphasized by the clinician lest he re-establish performance anxiety. The couple should leave the clinician's office understanding that penetration is now *permissible*, not mandatory. The couple is instructed to initiate intercourse in the female superior position. The woman should be responsible for inserting the penis, and should remain as motionless as possible to give the man time to adapt to the sensation of intromission. If the penis detumefies, the woman should dismount and restimulate. As the male becomes comfortable and confident of his erection he is instructed to begin coital thrusting. On occasion, however, we have used "paradoxical intention" in an effort to control reinstituting performance anxiety. The couple is instructed *not* to initiate thrusting. They usually fail to follow the deceiving instruction.

Kaplan (1974) claims the treatment of secondary impotence has an excellent prognosis, especially if it involves a willing, cooperative sexual partner. Masters and Johnson (1970) claim a 60 per cent success rate with primary impotence, with no reports of relapse in a five-year follow-up; and a 74 per cent success rate with secondary impotence, with an 11 per cent relapse rate. Kaplan postulates that relapse may occur if the patient experiences a great amount of stress in his life. We have found a willing, cooperative sexual partner to be a major criterion for successful treatment.

CASE HISTORY 4-6

The patient was a 33-year-old musician who complained of impotence of eight months' duration. The patient reported a history of effective sexual functioning with his first two wives, and related that the onset of impotence coincided with his latest honeymoon. The patient was sexually functional with his current wife during courtship and reported that his first erectile failure occured the night of his wedding. During the course of the initial interview it was determined that the wife was both sexually active and demanding. Volunteering information that she had participated in three pornographic movies, and had had a short-lived career as a topless dancer, the wife openly threatened to leave the patient if the dysfunction was not corrected.

We explained the treatment procedure to the couple and emphasized that the chances of successful treatment were greatly facilitated by the cooperation of a willing and patient female. Our attempt to explain that we did not feel the couple's present relationship would be conducive to effective treatment was interrupted by the wife's exclamation that she was totally and adamantly opposed to involving herself in treatment. Saying she did not need "a damn shrink" telling her what to do, and claiming that it was not her problem, the wife suggested the patient solicit the sexual assistance of a female companion who was waiting for the couple in an adjoining room. Before we could quiet the wife, she was out the door and returned with a woman introduced to us as the wife's best friend and a frequent sexual partner of the patient. Detailed investigation into this unusual situation revealed that the friend lived with the couple and openly engaged in sexual activity with the patient with the wife's knowledge, approval and frequent participation. The trio reported the patient's impotence with the friend as well, and all parties agreed that the friend and patient would make a much more willing treatment team. Despite this highly unusual situation, we agreed to proceed with treatment.

The wife was instructed to leave the house when the couple practiced the treatment exercises, to avoid making any sexual demands on the patient, and to wait in the adjoining room during each office visit. The couple was instructed in nongenital touching progressing to genital caressing leading to intercourse as previously described. The couple later reported the wife as very cooperative in following the instructions, and said that she periodically showed an interest in the patient's progress.

Upon termination of treatment the trio reported the patient's effective sexual functioning with the friend and periodic dysfunctioning with the wife. We then suggested an abbreviated treatment program involving the wife and husband which was agreed to by both partners. Four month follow-up revealed effective sexual functioning with both the surrogate-friend and the wife.

SPECIFIC SEXUAL PHOBIAS AND AVERSIONS

The practicing clinical psychologist or psychiatrist may infrequently encounter a patient whose complaints of premature ejaculation or, more commonly, impotence may be due to a sexual phobia or aversion to some specific component of sexual activity. Fear of the female genitalia and aversion to feminine genital odor represent common complaints. Just as a flight phobic is often caught between his love for travel and his fear of flying, the sexual phobic is often caught between his desire for effective sexual functioning and his phobic response to an aspect of sexual activity. One patient, for example, reported that, as a teenager, his face was pressed into the genitals of a prostitute by a group of drunken friends who had previously taken turns ejaculating into her vagina. The patient later reported an ability to achieve and maintain an erection until he either touched or viewed his partner's vagina, at which time he became impotent.

The behavioral treatment of sexual phobias and aversions generally consists of systematic desensitization to the anxiety-provoking stimulus or *in-vivo* desensitization in which the patient is encouraged to gradually practice touching, viewing and smelling the female genitalia (Bass, 1974; Garfield et al., 1969). If the patient is phobic to the sight of the female genitalia and has no cooperative sexual partner, repeated presentation of pornographic movies and magazines may also be employed in the desensitization effort.

CHAPTER 5

Sexual Dysfunctions in Females

At present our society seems to be undergoing a sexual revolution in which attitudes toward sex are becoming more liberal, and previously prohibited pursuits such as pre- and extra-marital sex and homosexuality are becoming more acceptable. An important aspect of contemporary thinking is that enjoyment of sexual activity by females is now acceptable, expected, and often demanded. The myths, prejudices, and double standards of sexual conduct which have so often hindered the healthy expression of female sexual behavior are clearly being abandoned, partly as a result of the women's movement, which has rejected "Kinder, Kuche, Kirche" (children, kitchen, church) as the one role for the ideal woman (Lydon, 1971). Today few women remain content to consider sex their wifely duty with little thought to their own pleasure. Instead, they are demanding increased attention to and alleviation of impaired sexual functioning. The development of adequate treatment techniques for female sexual dysfunctions has lagged behind those for male dysfunctions, however; this is partly because many researchers have been hesitant to subject women to sexual experimentation and investigation, and also because, with the exception of vaginismus, female dysfunctions are less obvious than male dysfunctions. Women, if they wish, may fake adequate sexual functioning, pleasure, and orgasm whereas, because of differences in genital anatomy and physiology, males are not afforded this choice. Only recently have treatment techniques for female sexual dysfunctions developed to the level of efficacy that exists for treating male dysfunctions.

Sexual dysfunctions can occur in any of the stages of appetite, excitement, orgasm, and resolution (American Psychiatric Association, 1978). If an individual is uninterested in or does not desire sexual activity, usually reflected by little or no sexual fantasy, then a disorder of sexual appetite can be postulated. Since there is wide variation in sexual interest and appetite among individuals, this behavior would be diagnosed by the

Diagnostic and Stastical Manual III (DSM III) as a psychosexual dysfunction with inhibited desire only if the individual is dissatisfied and no other sexual dysfunction is present. Disorders of sexual excitement and orgasm are frequently encountered in clinical practice. Disorders of resolution associated with a sense of well-being and general relaxation are rare, but do occur. This chapter will discuss the female sexual dysfunctions previously termed general sexual dysfunction (frigidity), orgasmic dysfunction, vaginismus, and dyspareunia.

GENERAL SEXUAL DYSFUNCTION (FRIGIDITY)

General sexual dysfunction, termed psychosexual dysfunction with inhibited sexual excitement in the DSM III, refers to a lack of response to sexual stimulation, failure to find pleasure in sexual activities, lack of erotic feelings, and reports of anxiety, disgust, anger, or other negative emotions toward all sexual activity (Walen et al., 1977). Subjectively, the woman may report an essential absence of positive sexual feelings and negative emotions at the initiation of sexual activity. On the physiological level, the woman may not lubricate, evidence no expansion of the vagina, and show no formation of the orgasmic platform. On the behavioral level the woman may demonstrate an avoidance of sexual situations. This disorder may be considered a disturbance of the vasocongestive or excitement phase of the sexual response cycle.

The term *frigidity* previously used to describe this disorder is somewhat ambiguous and connotes different meaning to different individuals. It is not uncommon to hear a man call any woman who refuses an offer of sexual activity "frigid." We shall use the term "general sexual dysfunction," which is descriptive and less insulting.

In contrast to men, women exhibit far more variation in their psychological reactions to their inability to respond to erotic stimulation (Kaplan, 1974). Erectile dysfunction is frequently a psychological disaster for the male. Women, however, appear to respond to general sexual dysfunction in a range of behaviors from anxiety and distress to casual acceptance of their dysfunction, associated with avoidance of sexual activity. Different psychological reactions to sexual problems are, to a great extent, the result of socialization and cultural determinants. In almost every society the man is expected to be sexually active and to perform effectively. The man who, for whatever reason, cannot fulfill his cultural role as an active sexual performer is considered abnormal. Women, on the other hand, are not generally subjected to the same performance pressures as men, and in many cultures are not expected to be sexually responsive.

A clinically useful distinction in general sexual dysfunction is between primary, secondary, and situational dysfunctions. Utilizing the same descriptive criteria employed in the description of male dysfunctions, we can define primary general sexual dysfunction for women as no experience of erotic pleasure with any partner in any situation. The woman who suffers from secondary sexual dysfunction has a history of sexual response to stimulation during an earlier time in her life which has become inhibited. Some of these women report sexual arousal as a result of petting before marriage and the loss of sexual responsiveness after marriage when coitus became the objective of most sexual encounters (Kaplan, 1974). In situational general sexual dysfunction, the individual who is sexually responsive in specific situations or with certain partners is unresponsive in other situations or with other partners. Thus, a woman may reject the thought of sexual contact with her husband as aversive, yet become instantly aroused at the thought of coitus with another man. Whether this type of difficulty is indeed a sexual disorder is questionable.

Precise information on the incidence of general sexual dysfunction is not available because, until recently, most researchers combined this dysfunction with that of orgasmic dysfunction (Walen et al., 1977). Undoubtedly, this problem is rather common, and, because of increased publicity in the scientific and public media, is being brought to the attention of clinicians with increasing frequency.

Research and Theory: Physiological Factors

Masters and Johnson (1970) claim that gynecological examinations of all female patients in their treatment program revealed only a small percentage of general sexual dysfunction cases could be associated with physical disease. In light of gender differences in anatomical and physiological structure and functioning between the sexes, one might logically assume that the female sexual response is less vulnerable to physical factors than the sexual response of males. For example, impotence may be the earliest sign of diabetes in a male, yet a female's sexual response is usually not affected until this disease is far advance (Kaplan, 1974).

Although the vast majority of general sexual dysfunction cases are psychological in etiology, the therapist should be aware that this disorder may occur as a result of specific physical causes (Figure 5-1). Transient inhibition of sexual excitement is common during or after pregnancy, lactation, loss of virginity, and most physical illnesses that produce general malaise (Lazarus, 1971). Local factors such as vaginitis due to trichomonas, monilia, specific or nonspecific infections, and pelvic pathology, such as pelvic inflammatory disease and endometriosis, should be ruled out by careful medical examination (Greenblatt, et al., 1972). Hastings (1966)

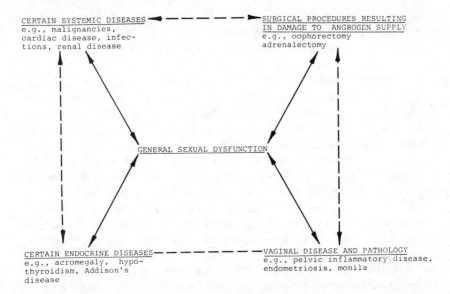

Figure 5-1. Physiological factors influencing general sexual dysfunction. Certain systemic diseases, surgical procedures resulting in damage to androgen supplies, certain endocrine diseases, vaginal disease and pathology or any combination of these factors may result in general sexual dysfunction.

claims a physical etiology may be ruled out if general sexual dysfunction occurs in some circumstances and situations or with some partners, but does not occur at other times.

Various drugs, chemicals, and toxins have been reported to decrease libido and may result in general sexual dysfunction. These include anti-androgens (adrenal steroids, aldactazide); sedatives (narcotics, alcohol, and barbiturates); and some antipsychotic drugs (butyrophenones).

Research and Theory: Psychological Factors

A list of psychological factors that may potentially result in inhibited sexual excitement would be extensive. Several factors, however, have been identified by various researchers as commonly associated with general sexual dysfunction. In broad neurophysiological terms, sexual arousal is a function of the autonomic nervous system, and clitoral enlargement and vaginal distension are predominantly parasympathetic functions. On the other hand, the sympathetic division exerts an inhibitory effect on sexual arousal. Therefore, doubt, fear, guilt, shame, conflict, embarrassment, tension, disgust, irritation, resentment, grief, hostility toward the sexual partner, and most other "negative emotional reactions" will tend to diminish or extinguish sexual enjoyment (Lazarus, 1971). Furthermore, if these reactions are associated with a puritanical and moralistic upbringing, the potential for inhibited sexual excitement is facilitated.

The sexual unresponsiveness of many women can be directly attributed to lack of adequate sexual stimulation. Thus, the husband may play an important contributory role in the dysfunction. Annon (1971) has pointed out a number of errors made by the male which can inhibit arousal in women, including: (1) carelessness in grooming; (2) preoccupation with work; (3) insistence on sexual practices that are unacceptable to the woman; (4) homosexuality; (5) maintenance of a double standard, so that active sexuality by the woman causes him to view her as a "bad girl"; (6) male guilt over sex, which may lead him to place blame on the woman and cause her to feel guilty about tempting him; and (7) fear of sex or women which may result in impotence, premature ejaculation, and subtle or violent cruelty.

Poor communications between sexual partners is also likely to facilitate female sexual inhibition. Lovemaking is often largely under the man's control, and he may erroneously initiate intercourse on the basis of the cues provided by his own state of sexual arousal and his perception of his partner's sexual readiness. The woman is also partially responsible for inadequate stimulation if she does not accept the responsibility for accurate communication; that is, if she assumes that her partner is aware of her stage of arousal, when, in fact, her physiological readiness is internal (Walen et al., 1977).

Psychoanalytic Formulations. Psychoanalytic theory postulates two specific causes of female sexual inhibitions: (1) the oedipal conflict, and (2) penis envy.

In analytic terms, "Oedipus complex" means a characteristic grouping of instinctual aims, object relations, and fears which are believed to be universally found at the height of the phallic phase of psychosexual development (Kaplan, 1974). This period is characterized by the young girl's wish for sexual union with her father and the death or elimination of the mother. Conflict arises from the desired possession of the father and guilt over the death wish for the mother. The young girl fears that her continued incestuous desire for the father will result in the loss of her mother's love. If the child is unable to resolve this conflict by identifying with the mother, by suppressing it, or by renouncing her sexual wishes toward the father and marrying a man who possesses some of the father's desirable qualities, she is likely to become sexually neurotic.

Penis envy is another hypothetical psychoanalytic construct used to explain the origin of frigidity (Fenichel, 1945). Penis envy may be defined as the inferiority, envy, guilt, and rage experienced by the young girl who, in the phallic stage of psychosexual development, realizes that she has been denied a penis. Kaplan (1974) lists three outcomes of childhood penis envy:

1. The mentally healthy woman has resolved her penis envy and is able to accept her femininity with a minimum of conflict and envy. She assumes an inferior, passive role in society, expressing this sexually by a preference for vaginal orgasms and a repudiation of clitoral eroticism.

2. Other women may attempt a "flight from womanhood" by developing a neurotically driven, competitive, aggressive personality. She thus attempts to deny her absence of a penis by adopting those behaviors traditionally associated with males. This type of intense penis envy may lead to homosexuality.

3. Other women reject this type of masculine behavior as a coping mechanism, and elect seductive and feminine behavior. This behavior is also neurotic, however, for at the same time these women harbor deep-seated, intense hatred of men, which leads them to act in a castrating manner once the male's attention has been gained.

Psychoanalytic theory thus postulates that women who are unable to resolve their penis envy are likely to suffer from sexual dysfunctions in later life. General sexual dysfunction may be the result of the woman's unconsciously equating sexual pleasure in marriage with incestuous sexual pleasure involving the father. This equation results in uncomfortable internal conflict which cannot be tolerated; Consequently, sexual responsiveness and pleasure are denied.

Behavioral Formulations. Many therapists believe that general sexual dysfunction often has its origin in the learning and conditioning of negative emotional reactions associated with sexual activities, as a result of psychological and/or physical trauma, as well as early learning experiences that are similar to those in the development of a phobia. As Lazarus (1971) states:

> The sexual drive and its expression are often likened to the hunger drive and its ramifications. Despite obvious differences between so-called hunger pangs and a sexual appetite, both are stimulated by complex control and peripheral physiological processes, and both show wide individual differences in taste and appeal which, in turn, are a function of past experiences and cultural conditioning. The crude and hurried ingestion of an ill-prepared meal and the gourmet's epicurean delights occupy vastly different psychological planes. And so it is with sex where the flimsy division between ardor and obscenity can transform passion into an assault. The sexual anorexia of many a frigid female may be traced to formative encounters with insensitive men who provided crudeness and vulgarity in place of tenderness and consideration. (pp. 21–22)

Physical trauma, such as occurs in rape, and severe pain during an initial or early sexual encounter may also be causal factors in the development of general sexual dysfunction. If a woman's initial or early sexual experience is characterized by inadequate arousal and pain as a result of the fumbling and disruptive antics of her lover, or as a result of rape, the sexual experience is unlikely to be positively reinforcing.

Caird and Wincze (1977) claim that the etiology of general sexual dysfunction may be anxiety associated with sexual activities caused by the young girl's observing and perhaps misinterpreting sex between her parents. Much of a child's learning develops via observation; and as any parent who smokes and then observes his child puffing away on a stick or pencil in imitation will confess, we cannot program the child to learn only the right things via observation and disregard the wrong. Unfortunately, neither can we be assured that what the child observed is being accurately perceived. Sexual intercourse may be a prime example of "what appears to be, is not." The sexually unsophisticated child may observe and perceive the motor and verbal responses of her parents engulfed in the passion of oncoming orgasm as actions typical of fear and pain. Instead of perceiving the act as mutual pleasuring, she may perceive her father attempting to inflict harm and her mother's behavior as evidence of pain. This feeling is magnified when the father *is* actually hurting his wife, when he is forcing himself on her, and when she is responding with tears. Learning about sex from this type of observation has all the effects of learning through modeling, and it is no wonder that young girls introduced to sex in this manner later develop distorted notions about marriage and sex.

What these developmental factors have in common is the conditioning of anxiety and sexual activity. General sexual dysfunction may therefore be thought of as severe anxiety associated with the imitation of sexual behavior.

CASE HISTORY 5-1

The patient was a 28-year-old single female graduate student referred to us by a former patient. The woman, who described herself as very active in the feminist movement, requested treatment for her inhibited sexual excitement.

The patient reported her rearing as "very traditional." She reported that, as far back as she could remember, her mother had warned her against the perils of relationships with men, claiming that "the only thing men want from women is sex." A sexual history revealed that the patient's first sexual experience occurred during her junior year in high school, and involved intercourse in the back seat of an automobile. She recalled that the sexual experience of both her and her youthful partner resulted in inadequate lubrication and extremely painful coitus. She said the experience left her feeling guilty, and convinced her that her mother's evaluation of male motivation was correct.

Subsequent sexual experiences were characterized by anxiety, fear of pregnancy, absence of sexual arousal, and guilt. The patient reported that she began doubting her ability to experience any degree of satisfaction and desire for sexual activities, and later began actively avoiding dating situations in which sexual contact was a possibility. This pattern of sexual avoidance continued until, at the time of the initial interview, the patient reported even the thought of sexual activity resulted in extreme anxiety and distress.

Modification of General Sexual Dysfunction

Some years ago inhibited sexual excitement was thought to be normal behavior for all proper and refined women, and enjoyment of sexual activities was reserved exclusively for the male. Because of these prevailing social norms it has been only in the past decade or so that general sexual dysfunction has come to the attention of clinicians. Today, four major types of intervention strategies are employed in its treatment: (1) psychoanalysis; (2) marital therapy; (3) chemotherapy; and (4) behavior therapy.

Psychoanalysis. As already noted, psychoanalytic theory postulates that failure to resolve the oedipal conflict and penis envy are the two major causes of adult neuroticism which manifests itself in sexual problems (London & Caprio, 1950). Analytic therapy therefore attempts to give the patient insight into her emotional conflicts. Resolving the incestuous desire for the father and accepting her worth as a woman, even though she has no penis, is thought to neutralize the neurotic hold these conflicts may have on a woman, and thus free her to accept her femaleness and effectively function sexually (London & Caprio, 1950). Psychoanalytic therapy, however, has not proven uniformly successful in the treatment of general sexual dysfunction (Kaplan, 1974).

Marital Therapy. Marital therapy, primarily employed by social workers, marriage counselors, ministers, and psychologists trained in schools of education, views general sexual dysfunction as a result of a dysfunctional marital relationship. Frequently, the goal of marital therapy is to change the sexual system in which the sexually inhibited woman functions by creating a nondemanding, relaxed, and sensuous ambience that permits the natural unfolding of the sexual response during love making (Kaplan, 1974). The couple is encouraged to communicate openly about their sexual feelings and wishes and thus foster such ambience. While it is true that, on occasion, general sexual dysfunctional behavior may be situationally specific in that a woman may exhibit sexual behavior with her husband while sexually desiring another male, the dysfunction may also be exhibited by unmarried women or many generalize to all males. Marital therapy has not proven significantly successful in the treatment of general sexual dysfunction (Walen et al., 1977).

Chemotherapy. A variety of drugs, particularly the hormones, have been employed in the treatment of general sexual dysfunction. Birth control pills (either combining or sequencing estrogen and progesterone) have been documented as both facilitating and inhibiting sexual desire (Greenblatt et al., 1972). Greenblatt et al. (1972) claim that in those cases reporting increased sexual desire and responsiveness the effect is assumed to be a function of removal of the fear of pregnancy. The administration of androgen has been shown to produce a rapid and dramatic increase in libido; however, the patient must be carefully monitored for early signs of virilization. Minor tranquilizers have been used in an effort to control sexual anxiety. Antidepressants have also been prescribed for those patients with an associated depression, since limitation of sexual interest is a common counterpart of depression (Paykel & Weissman, 1972).

Behavior Therapy. Behavioral treatments for general sexual dysfunction encompass a broad range of very specific modification procedures designed to decrease the patient's anxiety and increase erotic responsiveness. Included are systematic desensitization; assertive training; muscular relaxation exercises; pubococcygeal muscle exercises; and on occasion, and most prominently, *in-vivo* desensitization by means of graduated sexual assignments. As Masters and Johnson (1970) have suggested, treatments of general sexual dysfunction should focus on teaching four basic points: (1) male and female sexual anatomy; (2) the fact that sex in marriage is an aspect of sharing; (3) the development of a mutually stimulative sexual pattern adapted to the individuals involved; and (4) the necessity of gentleness, sensitivity, and technical effectiveness on the part of the male.

Masters and Johnson (1970), as well as Kaplan (1974), have claimed that the treatment of general sexual dysfunction involves sensate focus and nondemand pleasuring. These investigators also have reported general sexual dysfunction as the most difficult to treat of the sexual dysfunctions specific to females. Perhaps this difficulty is the result of these researchers' disregard of the anxiety component inherent in the initiation of sexual activity. In other words, sensate focus and nondemand pleasuring may be too high on the desensitization hierarchy to neutralize anxiety associated with the mere initiation of sexual contact. Imaginal desensitization with an individualized hierarchy of sexual initiation scenes should sufficiently neutralize the anxiety associated with sexual initiation behaviors, and facilitate the effectiveness of sexual behaviors higher on the anxiety hierarchy, such as senate focus and nondemand pleasuring.

Various therapists have successfully used imaginal desensitization as an initial treatment component in general sexual dysfunction (Wolpe, 1973). Relaxation may be induced by a variety of techniques, including progressive muscular relaxation or subanesthetic administration of methohexital sodium (Brevital). Once the patient is relaxed, she is exposed to a sequence of graded sexual stimuli as described in Chapter 3.

Variations of the basic systematic desensitization procedure include the participation of the husband or sexual partner in the desensitization process. The couple is instructed to refrain from sexual activity until instructed, and the man is taught to administer muscular relaxation exercises and the hierarchy items to the woman (Bentler, 1968). Whalen et al. (1977) claim that with the active involvement of both partners, open communication may be facilitated, generalization may be enhanced, and the husband may feel less like an outsider, left to speculate about the therapy.

If the patient is unable to express her desires, choices, or resentment to her husband, assertive training may be considered a viable treatment modality (Goldstein, 1971). It is not uncommon for a woman exhibiting general sexual dysfunction to express feelings of being "used" or "overly controlled" by her husband. Yet the woman may not express her feelings because of rigid and unrealistic ideas of the wife's role in marriage. Increasing the patient's comfort and skills in expressing her feelings directly and effectively by modeling and behavioral rehearsal may be augmented by counseling sessions with the husband aimed at teaching and explaining his wife's needs and rights for independence and autonomy.

There is widespread belief in and some research documenting the therapeutic effects of vaginal muscular exercises in the treatment of inhibited sexual excitement as well as orgasmic dysfunction (Kegel, 1956). The treatment involves instructing the patient to repeatedly contract, and thereby strengthen, the pubococcygeus muscle which surrounds and is attached to the vaginal walls. A simple way of instructing the patient is to have her imagine that she is cutting off a stream of urine by tightly contracting her vaginal muscles. This treatment technique requires more systematic and evaluative research before it can be incorporated into a behavioral treatment program. It may be, however, that awareness of the muscle's contractibility will enhance sexual excitement in some women.

Once anxiety or other negative emotions have been neutralized, the next major step in treatment is the enhancement of sexual arousal and responsiveness. In pursuit of this goal, *in-vivo* desensitization is the treatment of choice.

Depending on the degree of severity of the patient's dysfunction, the therapist may initiate this treatment with sensate focus or nondemand pleasuring. Nondemand pleasuring begins with the therapist's insistence that the couple refrain from intercourse and that the husband not threaten the wife with his sexual arousal (Chapman, 1968). Instead, the couple limit their erotic activity to touching and caressing each other's bodies with no coital intent. The wife is commonly instructed to explore the husband's body first before the husband takes his turn in exploring hers. Kaplan (1974) claims that this order will help counteract any guilt the wife may experience as a result of receiving sexual attention, and enable her to concentrate on the erotic sensations evoked by the husband's caresses without being distracted by such guilt feelings. The therapist should emphasize that the responsibility of the giver is to pleasure and to attend to the personal pleasures of touching. The responsbibility of the receiver is only to prevent the giver from touching in an uncomfortable or irritating manner. It is extremely important that the patient not be tense or anxious as the couple progresses through the hierarchy of sexual behaviors. The importance of progressive muscular exercises as taught during imaginal desensitization should be emphasized. The husband should administer the relaxation exercises to the woman before the initiation of sensate focus exercises. If the woman should feel anxious at any point during sensate focus, the couple should stop and reinstruct relaxation exercises.

Often the couple may report rather dramatic results simply as a result of sensate focus exercise. The woman, freed from the pressures of providing coital "service" to her husband, may report sexual arousal and pleasure for the first time. The therapist next instructs the couple in nondemand genital stimulation.

Genital stimulation involves nondemand genital and breast caressing while avoiding an orgasm-oriented type of stimulation. The therapist should be certain the couple's knowledge of sexual anatomy is adequate before instructing the couple in this exercise. Masters and Johnson (1970) have recommended a specific position for this phase of treatment. They suggest that the man rest his back against the headboard of the bed with his legs spread, allowing the wife to sit between them with her back against his chest (Figure 5-2). This position allows the male easy access to the breasts and vagina, removes the often uncomfortable spectator aspect, and is usually comfortable for both partners.

Walen et al. (1977) suggest that the woman place her hand over the man's in order to gently but effectively communicate her desire for specific stimulation. If genital stimulation proves too arousing to her husband, the patient may elect to bring him to orgasm, manually or orally, but not before the completion of nondemand gential stimulation exercises. Once the therapist is convinced that both partners are comfortable and the woman is receiving some erotic return for the couple's exercise expenditure, the next exercise is initiated.

The next step in the treatment is nondemand coitus. This exercise involves sensate focus and genital stimulation until the woman reaches a sufficient level of sexual arousal whereupon *she* initiates sexual intercourse. Many therapists suggest that thrusting be slow and exploratory at first rather than forceful and orgasm-oriented. This suggestion is, of course, in keeping with the nondemand ambience that characterizes these exercises. Kaplan (1974) instructs her patients to experiment with contracting the pubococcygeal muscles during this stage.

Nondemand coitus is generally attempted in the female superior position. This position allows the woman a greater degree of freedom to experi-

Figure 5-2. Nondemand stimulation of the female genitals. (**Source:** Kaplan, H. S. *The new sex therapy.* New York: Brunner/Mazel, 1974.)

ment and to control the depth of penile intromission and the pace of thrusting. The couple is instructed to disengage several times during coitus, to lie in each other's arms and engage in nondemand genital stimulation. Should detumescence or ejaculation occur the couple should not be alarmed but simply continue with nondemand pleasuring until the husband again achieves an erection. A final variant of nondemand coitus is to switch from female superior to the lateral coital position, which Masters and Johnson (1970) recommend for its comfort and tendency to enhance ejaculatory control. Throughout sensate focus, genital stimulation, and nondemand coitus the patient is encouraged to engage in any sexual fantasy she finds arousing and to maintain her relaxation. If anxiety or tension is encountered at a particular step in the sequence it is important to return to a lower step in the hierarchy before proceeding. Once the couple has progressed to the point of orgasm via intercourse, the fantasy material may be reconditioned, so that, just before orgasm, the patient is instructed to switch to visualizing the partner in sexual activity (Walen et al., 1977).

Kaplan (1974) summarizes the advantages of nondemand, pleasure-oriented treatment techniques as follows: (1) because the woman is relieved of the pressure to produce a sexual response, these exercises are not likely to mobilize her anxiety over sexual contact and thus prevent her from experiencing unimpeded erotic enjoyment; and (2) the therapeutic effectiveness of these exercises derives in large part from the fact that they are specifically structured to evoke sexual excitement in the woman in hopes of facilitating sexual enjoyment and desire. In addition, anxiety or other negative emotions are extinguished. The exercises are intended not only to arouse the man sexually, as has been her past experience, but also to provide primary stimulation for *her* sexual enjoyment.

Success rates for *in-vivo* desensitization treatment of inhibited sexual excitement are excellent: Chapman (1968) and Masters and Johnson (1970) report success in 80 per cent of patients treated. We have also found this dysfunction highly responsive to behavioral intervention, with imaginal desensitization and *in-vivo* desensitization the primary treatments of choice. Chapman (1968) claims that a poor response or total failure is invariably accompanied by haphazard or complete disregard of the instructions to abstain from intercourse. Thus, the woman's sexual anxieties and disdain for sexual activity may be maintained by disregard of the nondemand nature of the exercises, and a failure to counteract her anxiety associated with the initiation of sexual activity. Chapman claims this is typical of the "immature male" who poses the greatest deterrent to successful treatment of general sexual dysfunction by reciprocal inhibition.

In an effort to avoid this problem, Lobitz and LoPiccolo (1973) developed a program designed to enable the therapist to carefully monitor the couple's adherence to the exercise program while collecting valuable behavioral data. This program involves the couple's completing a daily record form on each day that sexual activity takes place. The self-report form rates the duration of the sexual activity, each partner's pleasure and degree of sexual arousal, and subjective evaluations and comments concerning the sexual activity. Motivation to complete the form is ensured by a large monetary deposit consisting of prepayment for the complete course of therapy plus an equal amount as a penalty deposit. The couple is presented a contract during the initial stages of therapy which outlines the requirements regulating the couple's forfeiture of portions of the deposit money. The requirements include: (1) keeping appointments; (2) turning in completed daily monitoring forms to the therapist; and (3) avoiding any sexual behaviors which have not been discussed and approved by the therapist. The penalty deposit is divided into five equal portions, one of which is forfeited each time the couple breaks one of the contract rules. Thus, the fifth violation represents loss of the entire deposit while the sixth violation results in termination of the couple from treatment. Lobitz and LoPiccolo (1973) report the success of this program by attesting to the low rate of violations; an average of 0.7 violations with a maximum of 3 in 19 couples treated.

CASE HISTORY 5-2

The couple consisted of a 22-year-old woman and her 29-year-old husband referred by the couple's family physician because of the wife's severe aversion to sexual activity. The couple met while both were working for a government agency and had been married five months prior to seeking treatment.

A sexual history of the couple revealed that both were virgins at the time of their marriage. Both partners described their wedding night as disasterous, the woman anxious and extremely uncomfortable and the husband fumbling and unsure of himself. The patient described this first sexual encounter as disappointing and reported severe pain during intercourse. She reported her husband initiated sexual activity 6 or 7 times afterward, with each encounter creating more disgust and revulsion toward coitus than the time before. Finally she was unable to tolerate further sexual activity, and became uncontrollably emotional during foreplay, begging her husband to not force her to have sex with him again.

The patient reported extreme disappointment with the sexual act, claiming "it was nothing like I had thought it would be." She claimed that her aversion was magnififed by her husband's ineffective technique of kissing and genital stimulation for 2-3 minutes, after which he attempted penetration. Unable to muster the courage to complain of the ineffective technique to her husband, she simply endured the pain, disappointment, and frustration as long as she could. The patient also reported that she was a "habitual masturbator," engaging in this practice 1 to 3 times per day and feeling guilty because her husband was unaware. She denied any masturbatory fantasy, claiming the practice was purely a "mechanical act." She characterized her feelings toward sexual contact with her husband as "nauseating," but very much desired to enjoy marital intercourse.

The treatment program was explained to the couple, who enthusiastically agreed to cooperate. The therapists instructed the couple to halt all sexual contacts until instructed. The patient was privately instructed to halt her masturbatory practices until given permission.

Due to the patient's severe anxiety regarding the initiation of sexual contact, imaginal systematic desensitization to sexual activity with her husband was begun first. The patient cooperated with the therapists in constructing a hierarchy of sexual initiation behaviors; walking through the park with her husband's arm around her was the low item on the hierarchy, and nude intercourse on the living room floor was the highest anxiety-provoking item. The patient was seen twice weekly for four weeks. After that the husband, who had been taught the mechanics of muscular relaxation exercises and systematic desensitization, assumed the responsibility of assisting his wife through the desensitization hierarchy twice a week. This schedule of two office visits with exercises of systematic desensitization combined with two desensitization practices involving the husband and wife was continued an additional two weeks. At this time the patient was able to imagine each item on the hierarchy with no report of anxiety at the thought of sexual contact.

The next three office visits were devoted to assertive training in an attempt to teach the patient appropriate and effective ways of communicating her sexual desires to her husband. Both therapists, as well as a knowledgeable secretary often recruited for such duties, actively engaged in modeling, role playing, and behavioral rehearsal of appropriate assertive responses until the patient reported feeling comfortable exhibiting these behaviors. We also took advantage of this opportunity to counsel and education the husband in more appropriate and effective heterosexual skills.

The next step in treatment involved sensate focus or nondemand pleasuring. A discussion of the mechanics of sensate focus resulted in the agreement between both partners that the wife would be the primary pleasure receiver but would manually masturbate the husband to orgasm at the conclusion of each session. At this time the couple's schedule of office visits was reduced from twice per week to once every other week.

In two weeks the couple returned and reported successful completion of sensate focus exercises. The patient admitted a slight sensation of awkwardness and anxiety during the first and second attempts which were soon replaced with graded feelings of sexual arousal and desire. The couple reported a tremendous desire and temptation to engage in genital stimulation of the wife, but had resisted after a 30-minute discussion devoted to "trying to talk each other out of going further than we were supposed to." Both partners were praised for their strict adherence to the treatment plan and were reinforced by instructions to begin genital and breast stimulation.

The couple returned for their next schedule visit with enthusiastic reports of the couple's enjoyment of genital and breast stimulation and a desire to proceed to nondemand coitus. The wife reported her recently developed assertive skills had enabled her to make appropriate suggestions as to the pace and location of her husband's genital stimulation, and that she had informed him of her masturbation practices and received praise for her efforts to achieve a more effective sexual relationship. The couple was instructed in nondemand coitus and requested to return in two weeks.

The couple telephoned several days after the last office visit to report that the wife was again experiencing increased anxiety and disgust in association with sexual activity. An office appointment was scheduled for both partners the following day, but the wife did not keep the date. The husband reported that treatment was progressing well until the couple attempted nondemand coitus during which the wife became somewhat anxious and asked to reschedule the exercises the following evening. The next evening the wife voiced objections, but due to the husband's insistence proceeded with intercourse. Several minutes after penetration, however, the wife became extremely agitated, hysterically crying and screaming for the husband to leave her alone. It was explained to the husband that we had undoubtedly failed to completely desensitize his wife to coital contact, but that we could not reinstitute desensitization techniques unless the wife desired such intervention. We encouraged the husband to discuss the situation with his wife and to contact us with a decision. Several days later the wife telephoned us to request continuation of treatment. We carefully discussed alternative options with the woman, and convinced that she desired to continue in therapy, reinstituted imaginal systematic desensitization to sexual foreplay and intercourse. Eleven additional sessions of systematic desensitization were followed by six sessions of sensate focus before we judged that she was ready to again attempt nondemand coitus. The couple was scheduled to return for an office visit in two weeks and instructed to contact us if any problems were encountered during the homework assignment.

At the next office visit the wife reported increased sexual excitement as well as her first three orgasms via intercourse. Both partners verbalized satisfaction with their new level of sexual functioning. Three- and six-month followups revealed that the couple was effectively functioning and enjoying their sexual activities together.

ORGASMIC DYSFUNCTION

Orgasmic dysfunction may be defined as a sexual disorder in which the female is either unable to experience orgasm or experiences difficulty in reaching orgasm even though a strong sex drive may be present (Craighead et al., 1976). The DSM III classifies orgasmic dysfunction as psychosexual dysfunction with inhibited sexual orgasm. In this regard orgasmic dysfunction is similar to retarded ejaculation in the male. Physiologically, the orgasmically dysfunctional woman, unlike the woman suffering from general sexual dysfunction, may lubricate copiously and evidence vaginal swelling. She may enjoy sexual foreplay and experience strong sexual arousal over the sensation of penile penetration. Behaviorally she may anticipate and actively engage in sexual activities. In other words, the orgasmic dysfunctional woman exhibits no significant inhibition of the vasocongestive and excitement components of the sexual response cycle. Kaplan (1974), as well as DSM III, claim that the disorder is, in fact, specific to the orgasmic phase of the sexual response cycle.

Various researchers have classified subtypes or broad categories of orgasmic dysfunctions. Masters and Johnson (1970) describe three subtypes: (1) *masturbatory* dysfunction, in which the woman may achieve orgasm during intercourse but not by manual stimulation by herself or her partner; (2) *coital* dysfunction in which orgasm can be reached only by means other than coitus; and (3) *random* dysfunction in which the woman on rare occasions experiences orgasm but generally exhibits little sexual arousal. Kaplan (1974) categorizes orgasmic dysfunctions into *absolute* and *situational*. Absolute dysfunction is defined as the inability to experience orgasm under any set of circumstances; situational dysfunction is defined as the ability to experience orgasm under specific circumstances only, *e.g.,* masturbation but not intercourse. The usage of these classifications may vary with individual therapists, but in general, a distinction is also made between *primary* and *secondary* orgasmic dysfunction. Primary dysfunction is the failure of a woman ever to have experienced an orgasm by any means; secondary dysfunction refers to those cases in which a woman experiences the dysfunction after a period of effective sexual functioning.

Various researchers have discussed a number of variables that affect a woman's ability to experience orgasm. Although the sexual drive is generally thought to be biological in nature, its expression in orgasm requires practice or experience before it develops fully (McCary, 1973). Most researchers consider marriage to reflect sexual practice (or conditioning), and consequently most data have been drawn from married women. This research demonstrates variability in reported incidence rates.

Brown (1966) reported that 60–70 percent of married women usually or always experience orgasm; approximately 25 percent experience occasional orgasm; and 5–15 percent rarely or never achieve orgasm. Kaplan (1974) estimated that although 90 percent of all women are capable of experiencing orgasm by some means, less than half these women do so without the aid of additional clitoral stimulation.

Gebhard (1966) reported a positive correlation between the number of years a woman was married and the probability of experiencing orgasm (Table 5-1). As may be noted, however, the differences are not great. The women who did not experience orgasm have been married an average of seven years, while the women who were almost always orgasmic have been married an average of 8.8 years. The same trend was noted among the marriages that ended in separation or divorce.

Kinsey et al. (1953) demonstrated that a relationship exists between a woman's premarital orgasmic experience and her later marital responsiveness. Women who experienced orgasm (whether it be through masturbation, dreams, intercourse, petting, or homosexual relationships) before marriage were far more likely to be orgasmic after marriage than women who had not experienced orgasm. Kinsey claims that during the first year of marriage:

> Of those with premarital orgasmic experience, only 19% failed to reach orgasm with coitus, while 45–47% reached orgasm on nearly all coital occasions. Of those who had never experienced orgasm prior to marriage, 44%—nearly half—continued to fail; only 25% achieved orgasm on nearly all coital occasions. (p. 121)

These data suggest that orgasm before marriage is a good predictor of the ability to achieve orgasm postmaritally (Caird & Wincze, 1977). Kinsey

TABLE 5-1

Female Orgasm Rate and Duration of Marriage

Percent of coitus resulting	Intact Marriages		Broken Marriages	
	Median years duration	Cases	Median years duration	Cases
0–	7.0	74	4.9	76
1–9	7.0	54	5.0	36
10–39	7.6	87	5.5	46
40–59	8.5	119	6.3	32
60–89	8.3	168	5.3	30
90–100	8.8	524	7.6	94

Source: Gebhard, P. H. Factors in marital orgasm. In J. LoPiccole & L. LoPiccolo (Eds.), *Handbook of sex therapy.* New York: Plenum Press, 1978. Reprinted with permission of Plenum Press.

did not find any significant differences in the postmarital orgasmic responsiveness of women whose premarital orgasmic experiences were via coitus or other types of stimulation.

If premarital coital orgasm was achieved at least 25 times, only 3–8% failed to achieve it postmaritally, and 50–57% were regularly responsive. If no premarital coital orgasm was achieved, 38–56% continued to fail postmaritally, and only 17–29% were regularly responsive. (p. 122)

Kinsey et al. (1953) quite rightly point out that these relationships may be more complex than they first appear. From a statistical point of view, there exists a positive relationship between premarital orgasmic experience and postmarital orgasm frequency. However, this certainly does not suggest that premarital sexual experience is an assurance of effective sexual functioning during marriage.

Gebhard (1966) analyzed data from interviews conducted by the Institute of Sex Research to look specifically at correlations among duration of foreplay, length of intromission, and orgasm. The data show that only a small percentage of women who consistently reach orgasm fall in the category of couples who employ brief foreplay (Table 5-2). Many more of these women engage in foreplay lasting 15-20 minutes or longer. A similar set of correlations was found with respect to duration of intromission. Women who consistently reached orgasm usually engaged in intercourse of longer duration than women who reached orgasm less frequently.

Women's reactions to their inability to experience orgasm vary greatly. Some women recognize and adapt to their dysfunction with little, if any, overt consequences. Often, these women will deny the importance of orgasm and claim enjoyment of the nonsexual aspects of lovemaking, like kissing and caressing. Occasionally these women simulate coital orgasm because they are too embarrassed to admit to their partner that they are unable to achieve orgasm. Other women do not adapt to their orgasmic inability as well. Often these women become frustrated after repeated attempts to achieve orgasm during intercourse, and harbor hostile and angry feelings toward their partner. Finally, some women's understandable distress over their inability to achieve orgasm, in combination with their anticipation of failure during each sexual encounter eventually results in inhibited sexual desire.

Research and Theory: Physiological Factors

An organic etiology of orgasmic dysfunction is rarely encountered, yet care should be exercised to require a gynecological examination of all patients before treatment. Diseases that impair lower neurological appara-

TABLE 5-2

**Female Orgasm Rate and Duration of
Precoital Foreplay in Intact Marriages**

Percent of coitus resulting in orgasm	*Average Duration of Foreplay in Minutes*			
	0	*1-10*	*15-20*	*21 plus*
	Percent			
0	(2 cases)	3.9	7.6	7.7
1–39	(1 case)	19.5	12.6	7.7
40–89	(1 case)	34.6	28.9	25.6
90–100	(2 cases)	41.9	50.6	58.9
Cases	6	179	79	78

Source: Gebhard, P. H. Factors in marital orgasm. In J. LoPiccole & L. LoPiccole (Eds.). *Handbook of sex therapy. New York: Plenum Press, 1978. Reprinted with permission of Plenum Press.*

tus may potentially result in orgasmic dysfunction (Figure 5-3). Spina bifida, amytrophic lateral sclerosis, and trauma or surgery of the sacral or lumbar cord may cause orgasmic dysfunction as a result of the interference with peripheral nerves or spinal cord reflect centers that subserve the sexual response (Gardner, 1975).

Various surgical procedures are occasionally associated with orgasmic dysfunction. Scarring from episiotomy, obstetrical trauma, and complications from a hysterectomy are occasional causal factors.

Genital disease such as clitoral adhesions, tight clitoral hood, and pubococcygeal muscle weaknesses or fibrosis may result in orgasmic dysfunction, although these disorders should be detectable during a pelvic examination.

The use of various drugs, such as ergot alkaloids and methyldopa, that are frequently prescribed for treatment of psychotic and hypertensive conditions are periodically reported to result in orgasmic dysfunction.

Research and Theory: Psychological Factors

For years clinicians and researchers considered general sexual dysfunction and orgasmic dysfunction as a single psychological entity. Inhibition of orgasmic release was long thought to be simply an extension of inhibited sexual arousal. Although contemporary research has delineated inhibited sexual arousal and inhibited orgasm as separate and independent dysfunctions, traditional psychological thinking maintains a number of common causal factors.

Psychoanalytic Formulations. The major emphasis of analytic thinking is that inhibition of a woman's orgasm may be the result of acquired symbolic meaning (Fenichel, 1945). Thus a woman may symbolically perceive the intense release of orgasm as total acceptance of her husband, when, in fact, she accepts him only conditionally. Inhibitions of orgasm may also occur because the intensity of orgasmic release is frightening to the woman (Friedman, 1973). If this is the case, women who demand and require a sense of control of situations and their lives would be unable to tolerate the vulnerability and lack of control characteristic of intense orgasmic release. Kaplan (1974) cites as other factors that may inhibit orgasm: the patient's ambivalence about her commitment to the relationship; fear of being abandoned; guilt about sexuality; hostility toward her mate; and fear of asserting her independence. The defense mechanisms of holding back or over-control are thus crucial concepts in her analytic psychological thinking about the pathogenesis of orgasmic dysfunction.

Behavioral Formulations. Behavioral formulations of orgasmic dysfunction frequently emphasize a variety of cogent developmental factors, including religious prohibitions; negative emotional reactions to the sexual partner; habituation to the sexual partner; and technical inadequacies of the sexual partner.

Anxiety may also play a role in the development and/or maintenance of inhibited orgasm, although the specific role of anxiety is unclear. Kaplan (1974) maintains that the excitement and orgasmic phases of the sexual

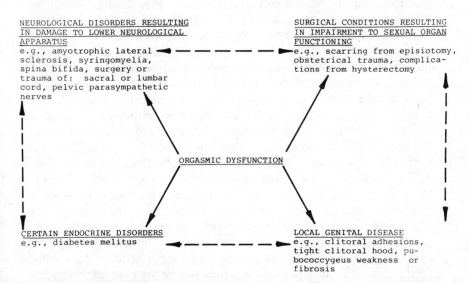

Figure 5-3. Physiological factors influencing orgasmic dysfunction. Certain neurological disorders, surgical conditions, endocrine disorders, and local genital disease or any combination of these factors may result in orgasmic dysfunction.

response cycle are largely independent. The excitement phase is mediated by the parasympathetic nervous system, and the orgasmic phase mediated by the sympathetic nervous system; one phase may be inhibited without the other's being affected. Hogan (1978), however, claims that anxiety plays an indirect role in orgasmic dysfunction by inhibiting the excitement phase of sexual response to the degree that the individual is unable to become sufficiently aroused to reach orgasm. Hogan's (1978) claim has support from numerous researches (Lazarus, 1971; Masters & Johnson, 1970; Zeiss, Rosen & Zeiss, 1977) who describe cases of orgasmic dysfunction in which anxiety appears to be involved. In fact, in at least 8 of the 17 cases of impaired orgasm reported by Masters and Johnson (1970), anxiety appears to be involved in the development and/or maintenance of the disorder. If these researchers are correct, Kaplan's (1974) claim of the independent biphasic nature of the sexual response must be rejected. However, it should again be noted that many clinicians have confused general sexual dysfunction and orgasmic dysfunction. In general sexual dysfunction, negative emotions are associated with the initiation of sexual activity. In orgasmic dysfunction, anxiety is not associated with the initiation of sexual activities but rather with orgasm. Contrary to the behavior of a woman with general dysfunction, women with orgasmic dysfunction frequently take an active and eager role in sexual activities, experiencing negative emotions only with their inability to experience orgasm.

It may be that anxiety plays a role in the maintenance of orgasmic dysfunction when the individual sees orgasm as a goal during intercourse. When orgasm is not reached, the individual experiences performance anxiety and begins to play the role of spectator, cognitively observing and monitoring her body for signs of approaching orgasm, rather than playing the role of participant. Many orgasmically dysfunctional women report that they desire to be multiply orgasmic, and that they exert substantial physical and cognitive energy toward this goal. Kaplan (1974) describes the monitoring and spectatoring role of the orgasmic dysfunctional woman as an impediment to sexual abandonment. The ability to put aside all cognition, and to abandon to erotic feelings, thus divorcing the sexual response from rigid conscious control, is imperative for effective and satisfying sexual functioning. A man's abandonment is often impaired by his excessive concern with the ability to perform sexually; a woman's abandonment is more often inhibited by her excessive concern with reaching orgasm. Thus, while the development of inhibited orgasm may result from such factors as negative emotional reactions to the sexual partner, technical inadequacies of the sexual partner, and religious prohibitions, performance anxiety and spectatoring may also be important modulating factors. At present, research has failed to differentiate anxiety as a consequence or cause of orgasmic dysfunction.

Other research has suggested that, on occasion, impaired orgasm may be conditioned as a result of premature ejaculation in the male partner (Lazarus, 1971). If a woman is repeatedly aroused and halted in her attempts to achieve orgasm because of the male's premature ejaculation, the strength of the conditioning process may, over time, effect her sexual functioning as well.

CASE HISTORY 5-3

The patient was a 29-year-old divorced social worker referred by her psychiatrist. The patient's presenting complaint was the inability to achieve orgasm during intercourse, although orgasm was no problem during masturbation. She reported having never climaxed during intercourse, although she had been married for five years. She characterized herself as sexually active while married, as well as before and after her marriage. The patient reported a strong sex drive and enjoyment of sexual activities. She characterized her present sexual behavior as one of enjoying intercourse but feeling sexually frustrated over her inability to achieve orgasm. She masturbated after her partner had departed or gone to sleep.

A sexual history revealed that the patient first remembered masturbating at the age of 12 and had continued until the present on an average of 3-4 times per week. When the patient was 15 years old she was discovered masturbating by her mother, who became quite upset and reprimanded her for "acting in such a lewd and unspeakable way." She reported feeling extremely guilty afterward, wondering if her mother had informed her father, and for several months would lie in bed and manipulate herself to just short of orgasm, thinking that it was somehow "less wrong" if she did not orgasm.

When the patient was 16 she began dating a boy from her school. Although she was not permitted to leave the house on a date, she was permitted to have the boy visit her home one or two evenings a week. The patient described a typical visit as one in which she and her boyfriend listened to records in the living room and "kissed on the sofa for one, sometimes two hours straight" while her parents remained in the adjoining room. She admitted become extremely aroused during these sessions, but would not allow her boyfriend to "get very far" for fear of being discovered by her parents. Each one of these dates would end with the patient's walking the boy to the front door, where they were hidden and felt less in danger of being seen, and allowing him to manipulate her genitals under her dress while she masturbated him to orgasm. The patient remembered feeling highly aroused during these activites and somewhat frustrated because her boyfriend was privileged to enjoy orgasm while she was denied this pleasure.

The patient was 19 years old when she experienced her first coital activity with a male she had been dating for several months. She described the episode as something less than expected. Coitus occurred in the back seat of her boyfriend's automobile while they were at a drive-in movie. She was unable to achieve orgasm during this initial coital experience, and because of her fear of losing her boyfriend to a rival female, she allowed this activity to continue on a regular weekly basis for over a year, never once experiencing orgasmic relief during intercourse.

The patient's history of orgasmic inability continued through her five-year marriage. She was wed at the age of 21 to a very considerate man who tried with a series of techniques to help her experience orgasm. She reported her husband perceived her orgasmic dysfunction as a manifestation of his sexual failure. The result was that she anticipated failure but desperately tried to achieve orgasm during each coital experience.

Since the termination of her marriage the patient reported a series of coital experiences, each characterized by intense sexual arousal but the inability to achieve orgasm. "It's like slowly climbing a high mountain," she explained, "only to get within reaching distance of the mountain top and being unable to pull yourself over the top, no matter how hard you struggle."

Modification of Orgasmic Dysfunction

Numerous techniques have been used in an effort to modify orgasmic dysfunction. These include dynamic psychotherapy, marital therapy, chemotherapy, psychoanalysis, and behavior therapy.

Dynamic Psychotherapy. Dynamic psychotherapy is geared toward assisting the patient to accept her sexuality and to recognize and accept her repressed hostile feelings, frequently associated with the perception of being mistreated (Kaplan, 1974). Establishment of a supportive, empathetic doctor-patient relationship is thought to facilitate an environment of mutual trust in which the patient feels comfortable in exploring her feelings. The elimination of neurotic intrapsychic defense mechanisms which inhibit the patient's sexual response in such a way as to prohibit orgasmic release is generally considered to be the aim of dynamic psychotherapy (Sherfey, 1966).

Marital Therapy. Marital therapy approaches the treatment of orgasmic dysfunction from a marital-interaction point of view. Recognizing that a dysfunctional marital relationship may potentiate disregard and inconsideration of each partner's needs and desires, the marriage counselor may attempt to construct more effective patterns of communication and interaction between the partners. There is little doubt that disruptive marital interactions generally do not foster consideration and concern for sexual desires and pleasure, but it is unlikely that a more congenial marriage will result in the elimination of orgasmic dysfunction in the majority of cases. In fact, we have found in only a very small number of cases that orgasmic dysfunction could be directly related to a disruptive marriage.

Chemotherapy. Chemotherapy may be prescribed as an adjunct to psychotherapy, or as an independent treatment technique by some clinicians who maintain that anxiety and/or depression are important factors in orgasmic dysfunction. We have seen a number of referred patients who have been given various minor tranquilizers or tricyclic antidepressant administration. However, there appears to be little evidence for the efficacy of chemotherapy in the treatment of orgasmic dysfunction (Lazarus, 1971).

Psychoanalysis. Since most analysts do not make a distinction between general sexual dysfunction (inhibited sexual excitement) and orgasmic dysfunction (inhibited sexual orgasm), the psychoanalytic treatment of orgasmic dysfunction is similar to that of general sexual dysfunction, that is, resolution of the woman's penis envy and oedipal conflicts (Friedman, 1973). Dream interpretation, free association, and interpretation of transference are used to direct the patient toward developing insight into her maladaptive intrapsychic process. Sufficient insight supposedly eliminates the orgasmic conflict and results in the patient's acceptance of her womanhood.

Freud's distinction between vaginal and clitoral orgasms is the theoretical basis on which the pathology is explained. The normal woman is thought to move from a "juvenile" clitoral orgasm to a "mature" vaginal orgasm. A desire for clitoral stimulation and the failure to make the transition from clitoral to vaginal orgasm is considered a measure of neurosis (Fenichel, 1945). In light of Masters and Johnson's (1970) findings that clitoral stimulation is a major component of most all orgasms, this theoretical distinction between clitoral and vaginal orgasms is not as clear as it once was.

Behavior Therapy. Behavior therapy for orgasmic dysfunction involves techniques to: (1) heighten sexual arousal so that the woman is approaching the orgasmic level when coitus commences; (2) enhance the woman's awareness of and pleasure in her vaginal sensations; (3) maximize clitoral stimulation; (4) rehearse the verbal and motor responses frequently associated with orgasm; and (5) enhance the sexual skills of the sexual partner.

LoPiccolo (1978) describes a treatment program for orgasmically inhibited women that involves four major components. First, for the primary orgasmic dysfunctional woman who has never experienced an orgasm, a program of masturbation training gradually directs the woman to self-induced orgasms. Kohlenberg (1974) claims that the rationale for the use of masturbation training rests on the facts that (1) the training is directly related to the sexual problem; (2) it is likely to be more successful in inducing orgasm than coitus; (3) it enables the patient to experience the sensations that precede and accompany orgasm so that she may eventually communicate these to her partner; and (4) the exercise may be less anxiety producing than stimulation by the sexual partner since it is completely under the control of the patient.

In prescribing masturbation training LoPiccolo and Lobitz (1972) describe a nine-step program. In step one the woman visually examines her genitals with the aid of a hand mirror and diagrams (Figure 5-4). At this

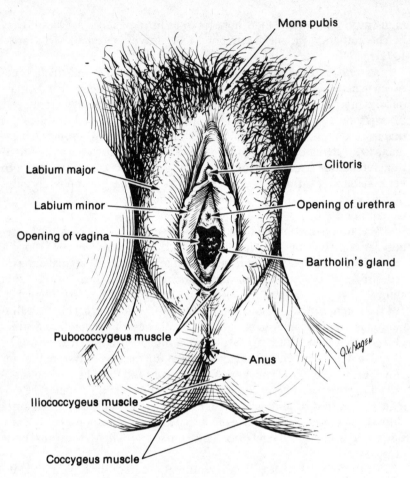

Figure 5-4. Muscles and genital organs located on the pelvic floor.

time she is also started on a program of pubococcygeal muscle exercises (Kegel, 1952) in an effort to enhance her orgasmic potential through increasing the strength and vascularity of the pelvic masculature.

In steps two and three the woman engages in tactile exploration of her genitals in an effort to locate pleasure-sensitive areas. In steps four and five the woman is encouraged to intensely stimulate these areas while using erotic fantasies or explicit literature and photos to enhance sexual arousal. These instructions to examine her genitals, concentrate on sexual fantasies or erotic stimuli, and masturbate may evoke anxiety in patients who have been taught from childhood to regard masturbation and sexual thoughts as dangerous and sinful. It is not uncommon in clinical practice to encounter a patient who, as an adult, continues to harbor childhood fears that masturbation will cause insanity, blindness, or the growth of hair on the palms of the hands. These inhibitory attitudes must obviously be dealt with in the therapeutic session. We have attempted to re-educate and desensitize women who have masturbatory inhibitions by having them view several short (8–12 minute) films of women masturbating. These films demonstrate different masturbatory techniques and indicate that masturbation to orgasm may be experienced without harm to those who practice it. Lehman (1974) suggests showing the patient a series of slides of women masturbating and allowing the woman to ask questions; Walen et al. (1977) recommend reading material describing how other women regard and engage in masturbation. (One such book is *For Yourself, the Fulfillment of Female Sexuality,* by L. G. Barach, New York: Doubleday, 1975.)

If the woman has not experienced orgasm by step five, vibrator stimulation is suggested in step six (LoPiccolo & Lobitz, 1972). Various clinicians, as well as patients, suggest a two-speed, hand-held model with a scalp massager attachment. The patient is instructed to apply a lubricant to the genital area, and place the vibrator on the mons pubis, near the clitoris, where it is held in a passive manner while the patient uses erotic imagery or literature to heighten her arousal. Lobitz and LoPiccolo (1973) claim that the most resistant case found in the literature required three weeks of daily 45-minute stimulation sessions to produce orgasm. Typically, patients report approaching orgasm; feeling tense, uncomfortable and uncertain; and slowly building back to preorgasmic sensations, only to experience a repetition of the same sequence of responses. The therapist should reassure and encourage the patient who experiences difficulty achieving orgasm, and make sure that she is not trying too hard, and viewing orgasm as a goal that must be attained by means of a struggle.

Steps seven through nine involve LoPiccolo's second major component of treatment for orgasmic dysfunction: skill training for the husband. In step seven he observes his wife's masturbation to learn what is effective for her. In step eight he learns to manipulate her to orgasm, and in step nine this manipulation is paired with coitus (LoPiccolo & Lobitz, 1972). In addition, various components of sensate focus exercises are employed, beginning with nondemand body massage and progressing through kissing and hugging, breast stimulation, genital stimulation, penile insertion, and slow thrusting.

LoPiccolo's third major component of treatment of orgasmic dysfunction involves disinhibition of arousal. A number of nonorgasmic women may be inhibited from reaching orgasm by fear of loss of control, or embarrassment about displaying intense sexual arousal and pleasure in the presence of their husbands (LoPiccolo & Lobitz, 1972). These women may be able to achieve high levels of sexual arousal and orgasm through masturbation when alone but not in the presence of their sexual partner. In such cases the patient is instructed to repeatedly role-play a grossly exaggerated orgasm with violent convulsions, screaming, and other extreme behavior. Repeated role play of exaggerated orgasm during the couple's prescribed homework assignments usually turns the initial fear and embarrassment into amusement and eventually into boredom (Lobitz & LoPiccolo, 1973).

The fourth component of treatment of orgasmic dysfunction involves instructing the woman in certain behaviors that, if performed during high sexual arousal, will often facilitate the orgasmic response (LoPiccolo, 1978). These behaviors tend to occur involuntarily during intense orgasm (Singer & Singer, 1972) and, when performed voluntarily, may initiate orgasm. These behaviors include pelvic thrusting, pointing the toes, tensing the thigh muscles, holding the breath, pushing down with the diaphram, contracting the vaginal musculature, and throwing the head back to displace the glottis (LoPiccolo, 1978).

According to LoPiccolo, the components of treatment described above seem to be most effective in cases of primary orgasmic dysfunction. Secondary orgasmic dysfunction frequently does not require such an extensive therapeutic regimen. If a systematic and comprehensive behavioral asessment indicates that orgasmic dysfunction is the result of a distressed interpersonal relationship, treatment should be targeted both toward the sexual problem and the distressed relationship (Synder, LoPiccolo, & LoPiccolo, 1975). If secondary orgasmic dysfunction is not a result of a distressed relationship, nondemand sensate focus exercises combined with techniques to heighten sexual arousal are often effective. Kaplan (1974) claims that arousal can frequently be heightened by the use of teasing, interrupted, nondemand coital techniques. The couple is instructed to engage in foreplay until the wife is highly aroused, at which time penile insertion occurs followed by the male thrusting in a slow, teasing manner. After a brief period has elapsed, the male withdraws his penis and again engages in sexual foreplay. After a few moments of this, he again penetrates the woman's vagina and the teasing, slow thrusting begins again. Variations of this technique include instructing the male to leave his penis inserted at all times and vary periods of slow penile thrusting with periods of manual clitoral stimulation.

CASE HISTORY 5-4

The couple consisted of a 36-year-old housewife and her 35-year-old husband who were referred by the couple's family physician for treatment of the wife's orgasmic dysfunction. A history of the couple revealed that they had been married for 14 years and had two children. The couple reported a contented marriage with the exception of the wife's inability to achieve orgasm. The wife claimed that she and her husband had experimented with intercourse before marriage, when she was nonorgasmic; but they felt this was due to being somewhat uncomfortable and anxious. After marriage the wife continued to be nonorgasmic, but concealed this from her husband by faking orgasms for approximately five years. The patient explained that she deceived her husband because she felt he would think something was wrong with her. The couple had read about masturbation training, and the wife reported trying to masturbate to orgasm several times but giving up in frustration. She also reported that although she anticipated failure each time the couple engaged in sexual intercourse, she tried "so hard to climax that I end up crying because I feel like I'm going to go crazy."

The decision was made to begin treatment with masturbation training. It was explained to the patient that although she had attempted masturbation before without orgasmic success, we felt that instructions and guidelines in regard to masturbatory techniques might prove effective. Instructions were given to the patient to pick a time for self-pleasuring when she could be assured there would be no interruptions from her husband or children, and when she was in no rush. We emphasized that the exercises were intended to be self-pleasuring, and that she should make every effort to make it enjoyable. Instructions were given for the three-stage masturbation training exercises: visual exploration, tactual stimulation, and genital stimulation. The couple were told to cease coitus until instructed to resume, and were scheduled for a return visit in two weeks. Instruction to cease coitus eliminates the performance anxiety and the obsession with orgasm which often maintains the problem.

When the couple returned for their second appointment, the wife reported comfort, enjoyment, and sexual arousal as a result of the masturbation exercises, but no success in having an orgasm. We reassured the couple that orgasm could not be rushed, and suggested that she continue genital stimulation exercises for another two weeks. Since the woman had previously reported that she regularly enjoyed *PLAYGIRL* magazine and found pictures of males arousing, we recommended that she incorporate viewing the pictures of nude males into her exercises. Permission was also given to the wife to manually or orally masturbate the husband when both partners desired. In the final quarter hour the therapists gave the somewhat discouraged patient a pep talk to motivate her to continue the exercises.

The wife returned in two weeks and again reported enjoyment and sexual arousal as a result of masturbation, but no success in achieving orgasm. At this point we decided to reassess the woman's knowledge of masturbatory techniques by showing her a 20-minute masturbation training film. Although a variety of masturbatory techniques were demonstrated and subsequently discussed, the patient decided to purchase a battery-operated vibrator for self-pleasuring. It was again emphasized that she should not consider orgasm a goal to be strived for, but should concentrate on enjoyment and pleasuring. We reassured her that orgasm would result as a consequence of heightened sexual arousal and masturbatory practice. The couple was scheduled to return in two weeks.

The next two weeks brought a success. The patient enthusiastically reported achieving her first orgasm three days after her last office visit. She reported her success to her husband, who praised her and encouraged her to continue the training. Since that time she had achieved seven orgasms and claimed that each was achieved earlier than the one before. Since she was now achieving orgasm with little effort, we instructed the couple to begin gradually shifting the responsibility of manual genital stimulation to the husband. The patient was instructed to communicate her desires and to guide her husband's movements.

The couple returned for their next visit and reported no therapeutic setbacks. The patient experienced orgasm on each attempt, and the husband soon took complete control of genital stimulation. The couple also confessed that during one session as they both lay nude and on their sides facing each other, the patient placed the husband's erect penis between her legs so that her clitoris was pressed down against the husband's penis. This resulted in a brief period of frantic thrusting by both partners and mutual orgasm. Both partners eagerly requested permission to attempt coitus. The couple was instructed in the female superior coital position and clitoral stimulation techniques available in this position, and were asked to return in two weeks.

The couple returned reporting that clitoral stimulation techniques were not needed since the patient achieved orgasm at the first as well as each subsequent coital attempt. Both partners expressed elation over their present sexual functioning and claimed no difficulties at all. We emphasized it was unlikely that orgasm would be achieved on every coital attempt, and that neither partner should be concerned when the patient was unable to climax. Followup at three months post-treatment indicated a continuation of therapeutic gains.

VAGINISMUS

Vaginismus is an intense and frequently painful involuntary spasm of the muscles surrounding the vaginal opening, the major muscle being the bulbocavernosus. Physiologically, vaginismus arises anteriorly, covering the outer aspects of the bulb of vestibule and Bartholin's gland (see Figure 5-4). Posteriorly, it occurs in the perineal body whenever the insertion of an object into the vagina is attempted. Vaginismus may be superficial or deep; the former characteristically occurs at the entrance to the vagina due to spasm of the bulbocavernosus and the levator ani muscles. Levator spasm is also called posterior vaginismus. Perineal vaginismus occurs as a result of sustained contraction of the perineal musculature. Contrary to what some believe, vaginismus is not restricted solely to penile penetration. The woman may be phobic to vaginal penetration by a finger, a tampon, or gynecologic examinations, as well as to coitus. Since the vaginal introitus shuts tightly, pelvic examination must often be conducted under anesthesia. As might be expected, vaginismus may be associated with unconsummated marriage, occasionally of several years' duration. The dysfunction may also be associated with general sexual dysfunction and orgasmic dysfunction. The importance of a complete and systematic behavioral assessment cannot be overemphasized, for in these cases of association, vaginismus should be considered a separate dysfunction and the initial focus of treatment.

Vaginismus must also be differentiated from simple avoidance of coitus and from physical conditions that can obstruct vaginal entry. The diagnosis of vaginismus can of course be made from the verbal report of the patient or the sexual partment; however confirmation of the dysfunction can only be made by pelvic examination. The therapist should keep in mind that an occasional patient may tolerate a gynecological examination well, yet still exhibit vaginismus in the coital situation. Others may tolerate a pelvic examination in the presence of the physician and nurse, yet exhibit vaginismus in the same situation if the husband is present. Since the sexual partner may be the phobic stimulus in such cases, it is often useful to have the husband present during the vaginal examination.

Because vaginismus makes intercourse impossible or extremely painful, the dysfunction is seldom tolerated as nonchalantly as orgasmic dysfunction. In addition to the physical pain experienced on penile penetration, the woman is likely to report feeling abnormal, embarrassed, humuliated, and frustrated. Recurrent failures at coitus may result in depression, feelings of inadequate self-worth, and fears of being rejected and abandoned by her partner.

Kaplan (1974) claims that it is not surprising that, in time, many vaginistic women attempt to avoid confrontation with the inability to engage in coitus by avoiding all sexual encounters. Since attempts at vaginal penetration produce anxiety and pain and these feelings abate only when such efforts cease and the perceived "danger" of penetration is eliminated, it is understandable that such avoidance behavior may reinforce the dysfunction. Many therapists agree that this phobic avoidance behavior, combined with the intense anxiety commonly reported, represents the major hurdle to the success of treatment.

The man's reaction to his partner's vaginismus may vary, but is likely to be significant. He may perceive the dysfunction as his partner's purposeful rejection of sexual activity or of him as a lover, and become frustrated, angry, and resentful. One patient reported to us that her husband had become so angry that he unsuccessfully attempted to forcefully penetrate her while holding her down on the bed. On the other hand, he may perceive the dysfunction as evidence of his abilities as a lover and become withdrawn and inhibited himself. Certainly performance anxiety and secondary impotence are not uncommon sequellae of the dysfunction.

Precise information on the incidence of vaginismus is not available. While some clinicians describe the dysfunction as relatively rare (Kaplan, 1974), others report the incidence rate as higher than commonly believed (Ellison, 1972). Ellison (1972) investigated 130 cases of vaginismus and reported the occurrence in all socioeconomic classes.

Research and Theory: Physiological Factors

Any pathology of the genital organs which results in painful vaginal entry or coitus has the potential for later development of a vaginismic response (Figure 5–5). Among those physical factors related to painful intercourse are: endometriosis; relaxation of the supporting uterine ligaments; rigid hymen; hemmorrhoids; painful hymenal tags; stenosis of the vagina; pelvic tumors; pelvic inflammatory disease; senile atrophy of the vagina; childbirth pathologies; and urethral caruncle. Kaplan (1974) claims that while most of these physical conditions do not actually involve the vaginal inlet, the fact that they may cause pain on penetration and intercourse provides the negative contingencies under which the pathological conditioned vaginismic response may be acquired.

Research and Theory: Psychological Factors

Traditionally the psychodynamic etiology of vaginismus has been postulated to be the woman's neurotic defense against overt or psychological trauma. Traumatic factors frequently mentioned include rape, traumatic loss of virginity, painful intercourse, ignorance, and sexual misinformation. Guilt reactions may result from strict religious rearing, marital incompatibility, fear of pregnancy, or a reaction to the recurrent impotence or premature ejaculation of the sexual partner.

Psychoanalytic Formulations. Psychoanalytic theory regards vaginismus as a conversion or hysterical sympton—the symbolic expression of a specific unconscious intrapsychic conflict (Sherfey, 1966). A theme common in most variations of psychoanalytic theory is the patient's unconscious envy and hatred of men. Hatred toward males is considered to be a retaliatory defense against men, who, having a penis, are responsible for

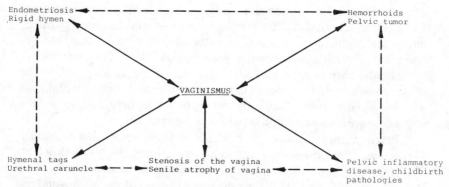

Figure 5-5. Physiological factors influencing vaginismus. Certain physiological factors or any combination of these factors may result in vaginismus.

denying women the pleasure of having a penis. Penis envy and concomitant hatred of men are thought to lead to the development of the vaginismic response. Vaginismus is thus merely the physical expression of the woman's unconscious desire to frustrate the man's sexual expression or, more specifically, of her wish to "castrate" him in revenge for her own "castration" (Kaplan, 1974). There is little evidence, however, to support this psychoanalytic hypothesis of vaginismus (Friedman, 1973); it has certainly not been confirmed by our clinical experience.

Behavioral Formulations. Behavior therapists generally agree that vaginismus is a response acquired by classical conditioning, in which the unconditioned stimulus is real or imagined (Walen et al., 1977). The vaginal response is then maintained on an avoidance basis; the woman's distress in the phobic situation is relieved only when vaginal penetration is made impossible. Vaginismus has obvious repercussive effects on the husband, and performance anxiety, secondary impotence, premature ejaculation, and marital discord are frequently associated with its occurrence.

Vaginismus may often be traced back to pelvic pathology. Dyspareunia, as a result of pelvic pathology, may result in consequent avoidance of painful sexual intercourse. The necessity for ruling out local pathology before initiating treatment is obvious. Other events that may be considered potentially anxiety provoking or painful include early traumatic events such as rape; traumatic loss of virginity; guilt and strict religious rearing; and sexual ignorance or misinformation. Fuchs, Hoch, Paldi, Abramovici, Brandes, Timor-Tritsch, and Kleinhaus (1973), in fact, claim that vaginismus may develop if the sexual ignorance and inexperience of a couple cause them to mistake the anus or urethra for the vaginal opening. Current causative factors may include marital discord, fear of pregnancy, or a conditioned response to the repeated premature ejaculation of the sexual partner. Whatever the aversive or anxiety-provoking event, the principle of conditioning may function to associate vaginal penetration and anxiety in such a way as to make avoidance of vaginal penetration anxiety-reducing and thereby reinforcing. It makes little difference whether the causal events be recent or remote, real or fantasized; the essential etiological element within the behavioral conceptualization of vaginismus is the association of anxiety or other noxious stimuli with vaginal penetration.

CASE HISTORY 5-5

The patient was a 21-year-old undergraduate female referred by a community mental health clinic for treatment of vaginismus. Her dysfunction had prevented her from engaging in any sexual activity involving vaginal penetration though she had been living with her boyfriend for over a year. The patient expressed great concern over her dysfunction in light of the couple's planned marriage and her desire to have children. Sexual activity between the couple currently involved mutual mas-

turbation and oral sex. The patient claimed to be highly responsive to sexual foreplay, and orgasmic during clitoral masturbation and oral sex. A gynecological examination revealed no local pelvic pathology.

A systematic behavioral assessment revealed that the dysfunction appeared to
be a very specific, discrete problem, apparently unrelated to any other source of
conflict or interpersonal difficulties. The patient could remember no physically or
psychologically painful experiences associated with sexual activity, no reported an-
tagonism or hostility toward her boyfriend, appeared to exhibit no significant psychopathology, and reported no guilt or anxiety about her sexual activities, which she
regarded as normal and desirable.

After another appointment had been scheduled and the patient was preparing
to leave, she admitted, ''There is one thing that I guess I kinda forgot to tell you that
you might need to know, but you can never tell my boyfriend!'' The patient then admitted that when she was a freshman, she and another girl became very close. Both
girls were far from home and somewhat lonely, and they spent most afternoons and
evenings together talking and listening to records in the patient's room. She reported that, over time, the two became sexually involved in sessions of mutual masturbation on a somewhat regular schedule. She characterized this homosexual activity
as extremely pleasureable, but felt guilty and ashamed at times. She maintained that
her masturbatory fantasies were of heterosexual activities and that she continued
dating various males throughout this time.

During one masturbatory session, her girlfriend's fingernail abraded the patient's vagina, which later became extremely painful and infected, requiring several
visits to a physician for treatment. The guilt and anxiety she was already experiencing combined with the painful vaginal infection were considered grounds for terminating the relationship. The patient claimed that for several weeks she did little
more than feel guilty, worry, and feel lonely. She soon resumed the homosexual relationship, only to have it end in trauma and pain again. During a mutual masturbation session in which the patient's girlfriend was masturbating her with a plastic
dildo, a classmate walked unexpectedly through the unlocked door and discovered
the couple. The patient reported the discovery startled her girlfriend who, when
jumping from the bed, accidentally jammed the dildo with her knee far into the patient's vagina. She reported feeling horrible and excruciating pain. For several days
she experienced vaginal bleeding until she sought medical attention. Since that experience the patient reported a vaginismic reflex each time an attempt is made to penetrate her vagina.

Modification of Vaginismus

Years ago, when proper women were not expected to voluntarily engage in pleasurable sexual activity (Sherfey, 1966), vaginismus was not
considered the severe problem that it is today. In fact, what better proof of
a woman's virtue could there be than that a physical assault was required
for vaginal penetration! We now know that vaginismus may result from a
number of physiological and psychological circumstances. In this section

we will discuss psychoanalysis, medical therapy, and behavior therapy as means of correcting this disorder.

Psychoanalysis. Psychoanalysis attempts to foster the patient's awareness of her repressed and unconscious penis envy and concomitant hostility toward men (Fenichel, 1945). Free association and dream interpretation are used to enable the analyst to delve into the patient's unconscious and explore the etiology of the patient's hatred of men. Believing that the vaginismic response is merely a physical symptom of deep underlying psychopathology, the analyst attempts to bring into conscious resolution the unconscious inadequacies and retaliatory unresolved hatred of men which is responsible for the neurotic disease process (London & Caprio, 1950). The therapy is directed toward the transference of repressed and hostile impulses onto the therapist so that the patient may achieve insight into the irrationality of her neurotic behavior.

Medical Therapy. If local pathology is the catalyst for the conditioned vaginismus reflex, its amelioration is, obviously, an essential prerequisite to the successful treatment of vaginismus. In the past the recommended method for the medical treatment of intractable vaginismus was surgery to enlarge the introitus by means of an adequate perineotomy, with or without division of the perineal muscles. Anatomically speaking this surgical procedure was an instant success in that it enlarged the vaginal orifice sufficently to allow penile penetration. However, eliminating the physical cause of painful intercourse does not guarantee that the vaginismic reflex will neutralize. Frequently medical correction of pelvic pathology is not sufficient to extinguish the vaginismic response. Moreover, a perineotomy may enlarge the vaginal opening so that neither partner is able to generate genital friction during coitus. General surgery itself frequently compounds the trauma suffered by the already frightened woman so as to adversely affect the patient's sexual responsiveness. Kaplan (1974, page 145) illustrates this iatrogenic effect in the following excerpt from a case history:

> In the course of the couple's initial interview, the wife reported that she had had a perineotomy (and that the operation had required 75 stitches) for treatment of vaginismus six years earlier. Prior to surgery she had been unable to have intercourse, but was sexually responsive and multiorgasmic on clitoral stimulation. Surgery was successful in that it enabled her to have intercourse. However, she was no longer able to achieve orgasm, and over the years, had experienced a progressive loss of interest in any sexual activity, including the non-coital stimulation she had previously enjoyed. (p. 415)

Clinicians who elect to treat vaginismus by chemotherapy of anxiety frequently prescribe Valium and other smooth muscle action minor tranquilizers. While minor tranquilizers may prove beneficial in reducing the general anxiety of some patients during the initial stages of treatment, their efficacy as a singular treatment modality has yet to be demonstrated.

Behavior Therapy. There is general agreement in the behavioral literature that the treatment of vaginismus requires two basic elements: (1) reduction of the phobic elements so that the patient is made less anxious
about the treatment and the results of treatment; and (2) *in-vivo* extinction
of the spastic vaginal response. Occasionally it may be necessary to implement these treatment procedures sequentially, but more commonly they
are programmed concurrently. The combined therapeutic goal of behavioral treatment is to enable the patient to repeatedly and progressively
experience dilation of the vagina and allow vaginal penetration while in a
relaxed state.

The patient's fear and apprehension and her consequent phobic avoidance of vaginal penetration may represent a major stumbling block to successful treatment. As a result, elimination of the patient's phobic avoidance of vaginal penetration should be the first objective of treatment. While
Kaplan (1974) claims that she rarely finds it necessary to use more than encouragement and reassurance to neutralize the phobic element, we have
not found this to be true. The vaginismic patients we have treated exhibited
a severe phobic response to vaginal penetration and thus required definitive behavioral treatment. Kaplan (1974) claims:

> ... reassurance, support, some rapid interpretation of the unconscious com-
> ponents of the patient's fears and, above all, confronting the patient with the
> fact that if she can't insert something in her vagina she can't be cured usually
> reduce the intensity of her fears sufficiently so that she is able to proceed with
> vaginal dilation exercises. (p. 421)

The patient is thus forewarned by Kaplan to expect and accept the fact
that she will experience some transient anxiety and discomfort during
treatment and, in contrast to her avoidance behavior, is expected to attend
to and tolerate any unpleasantness that she may experience.

The first stage of behavioral therapy involves reducing the patient's
anxiety regarding vaginal penetration sufficiently to enable her to proceed
later with vaginal dilation exercises. To this end Wolpe (1973) suggests systematic desensitization in which the patient is relaxed and then gradually
presented with imagery of rods being inserted into her vagina until the
images no longer result in anxiety. The lowest anxiety-evoking item on the
hierarchy may be the penetration of a wire-thin rod. Over time, the length
of insertion, the width of the rod, and finally movement of the rod are gradually increased until the patient can imagine penile-sized rods inserted into
her vagina with no experienced anxiety. Variations in the constructed hier-
archies may also be employed. Some therapists prefer to use scenes depicting penile penetration of the vagina. Thus, the patient may first imagine lying in bed nude; then, when she can tolerate this fantasy without anxiety,

she may imagine her nude husband approaching her, achieving an erection, and finally penetrating her.

Variations of systematic desensitization have also been utilized (Kaplan, 1974). In contrast to systematic desensitization procedures which involve the gradual presentation of increasingly threatening imagery, imaginal flooding, for example, involves having the patient imagine the most anxiety-producing and threatening image possible. Repeated exposure to this high-anxiety stimulus may neutralize the patient's conditioned fears. Thus, when imaginal flooding is employed in the treatment of vaginismus, the patient may be asked to imagine being forcefully penetrated and ripped apart by her husband's penis and suffering severe pain as a result. Therapists advocating this procedure might explain that once the patient is able to tolerate this fantasy without experiencing anxiety, she should be able to tolerate coitus.

Masters and Johnson (1970) claim that an initial step toward the reduction of the patient's anxiety may be a pelvic examination of the vaginismic wife in the presence of and with the participation of the husband. The spastic vaginal reflex is thereby experienced within a medical context, and as a result may be perceived in a more relaxed manner. Another advantage of the conjoint pelvic examination procedure, as explained by Kaplan (1974), is that it dramatically demonstrates the nature of the closed vagina to both partners, and may help dispel the mystery which surrounds this dysfunction.

Once the phobic anxiety of vaginal penetration has been neutralized, treatment is focused on the extinction of the conditioned vaginal response. The most common technique employed is vaginal insertion of catheters of graduated dimensions. The composition of the catheters may be rubber, glass, or wax and should always be inserted with the aid of a lubricant. The catheter used for the patient's first dilation exercise is normally wire-thin. When this dilator is tolerated with no pain, the next size is introduced; the last catheter in the series has the circumference of an erect penis. In addition, many therapists advise the patient to retain the dilator intravaginally overnight or to go about her daily activities with the catheter inserted in order to facilitate the deconditioning process.

The treatment sequence begins with the patient, or the couple, depending on the patient's preference, inserting the smallest catheter until it can be accommodated comfortably. The catheter is then rotated laterally within the vagina and later used to gently stretch the vaginal walls. When this exercise can be tolerated with little or no pain, the size of the dilators is gradually increased. Walen et al. (1977) suggest that vaginal relaxation may be facilitated by instructing the patient to practice alternating voluntary tensing and relaxing of the vaginal musculature in a way similar to "bearing down" in childbirth. When the largest catheter can be inserted at will and the patient experiences no discomfort as a result, coitus is suggested with the restrictions that the patient be responsible for guiding the penis into the vagina, and that the husband is to refrain from active, orgasm-oriented thrusting during the initial attempts at penetration.

Controversy presently exists over whether the husband should be actively involved in treatment from the onset, or if not, at what point his involvement should begin. Some therapists feel that since the dysfunction affects both partners the husband should involve himself at the onset of treatment, inserting the catheters while the wife communicates her feelings (Masters & Johnson, 1970). Other therapists, however, caution against involving the husband too early in treatment since his presence may engender increased anxiety (Ellison, 1972).

Various applications of these behavioral principles have produced one of the highest success rates with any of the sexual dysfunctions. Masters and Johnson (1970), for example, reported a 100 percent success rate with their intensive two-week therapy program and claim no relapses on a five-year followup. Kaplan (1974) also reports similar success rates in her less intensive treatment program. She reports that, on the average, the vaginismic response was extinguished within seven days, using 4–8 sessions of catheter exercises; penile penetration was accomplished in 3–14 weeks. Fuchs et al. (1973) reported a 100 percent success rate with 31 patients. No followup data were reported.

CASE HISTORY 5-6

The patient was a 24-year-old secretary. She and her 24-year-old husband had been referred by the wife's neurologist. The couple had been married for 1.5 years and had yet to experience intercourse. The farthest the patient had been able to proceed with coitus was to allow partial penetration of the vaginal opening for a brief period of time. Even this, however, was deemed intolerable and resulted in acute pain. Repeated attempts at coitus during the first two months of marriage had failed. The patient reported engaging in sexual foreplay for extended periods of time with no anxiety and claimed participation in oral sex, both actively and passively, with no difficulties. However, as soon as her husband attempted vaginal penetration her pelvic muscles would go into spasm, making penetration impossible. In desperation the patient consulted a gynecologist who diagnosed an intact hymen which was surgically excised. The effect of surgery on her sexual functioning was unnoticeable; she continued experiencing severe pain whenever her husband attempted penile insertion. If the husband's attempts at penetration persisted, she would end up crying and screaming that her vagina was too small, despite repeated assurances from several gynecologists to the contrary, until he finally abandoned the attempt in frustration.

Since the patient did not appear to be phobic to the sexual situation, and the vaginismic response was felt to be a specific and discrete dysfunction, the decision was made to begin treatment with dilation training. Several catheters of graduated circumference were given to the patient who was instructed in the mechanics of the exercises. At the end of the third week of treatment it was apparent that no success was being achieved. The patient was still unable to tolerate vaginal penetration of any of the dilators other than the smallest. It also appeared that the patient's motivation left much to be desired. Frequently she reported "forgetting" to perform the exercises even though her husband reminded her daily.

The decision was thus made to eliminate vaginal dilation exercises and begin systematic desensitization in an effort to neutralize the anxiety that was maintaining her avoidance behavior. The therapists and patient conjointly constructed a desensitization hierarchy. The lowest anxiety-producing item was her husband's manual stimulation of her external genitalia, and the highest item was penile penetration of her vagina. The 19-item hierarchy required seven desensitization sessions before the patient could imagine each scene in a relaxed, nonanxiety state.

Dilation exercises were once again recommended in an effort to extinguish the conditional vaginal response. In contrast to the initial attempt at dilation training the patient made remarkable progress. Seven sessions of catheter penetration were required to enable the patient to intravaginally tolerate the largest catheter with no pain or discomfort.

The couple's initial attempts at intercourse proved unsuccessful. The patient could offer no explanation, but claimed that when penile penetration was attempted her vaginal muscles reflexed spastically. After an additional two sessions of systematic desensitization the couple's next attempt at coitus was successful. Three- and five-month follow-ups revealed that the couple was continuing to function effectively with no reccurrence of the dysfunction.

DYSPAREUNIA

Dyspareunia, or painful intercourse, may be perceived as a momentary sharp pain of varying intensity, intermittent painful twinges, repeated intense discomfort, and/or an aching sensation (Abarbanel, 1978). Combinations of these sensations may occur before, during, or after coitus. With coital discomfort, anxiety replaces sexual enjoyment, and, as noted above, may eventually result in vaginismus. Complaints of occasional pain during intercourse are fairly common among women, but persistent dyspareunia was very uncommon among the cases reported by Masters and Johnson (1970) and was usually the result of an anatomical or physiological disorder.

Research and Theory: Physiological Factors

Coital discomfort may occur during precoital foreplay, as the penis penetrates the vagina, while the penis is located in the midvagina, during deep penetration with thrusting, during orgasm, or during postcoital resolution.

Dyspareunia during precoital foreplay may be associated with dis-

eases and disorders of the external genitalia (Table 5-3) and/or physiological disorders of the areas surrounding the vaginal introitus (Table 5-
4). Active skin diseases and chronic vulvovaginitis associated with the external genitalia, as well as lack of lubrication and urethritis associated with
the introitus may result in genital discomfort during sexual foreplay.

Genital pain as the penis penetrates the vagina may be the result of disease and disorders of the areas surrounding the vaginal introitus (Table 5-
4). Lack of lubrication resulting in a friction burn may leave the labia minora sore for several days. Painful scars at the vaginal opening, frequently
the result of genital surgery for a repair of a rectocele or an episiotomy,
may also result in dyspareunia (Abarbanel, 1978).

Coital discomfort while the penis is located in the midvagina may be
associated with diseases and disorders of the areas about the vaginal tract
and adjacent viscera (Table 5-5). Common causes of this disorder are
urethritis, trigonitis, and cystitis, although anorectal disorders such as
cryptitis and internal hemorrhoids may occasionally play a casual role.

Dyspareunia during deep penetration and thrusting is occasionally the
result of diseases and disorders of the cervix, uterus, and adjacent viscera
(Table 5-6). Common causal factors include pelvic congestion syndrome
with varicosities of the broad ligament, endometriosis involving the utero-
sacral ligaments and the lower of the broad ligaments, residue of a previous
pelvic inflammatory disease, and prolapsed ovary (Abarbanel, 1978).

If pain is experienced during orgasm it is commonly felt in the lower
back, deep pelvis, or lower abdomen (Abarbanel, 1978). Orgasmic pain
may result from varicosities of the broad ligament, endometriosis, and scars
on the vaginal vault or abdominal wall.

Postcoital pain is infrequent, although diseases and disorders of adnexae
and broad ligaments are considered causal factors on occasion (Table 5-7).
Since orgasm involves the abdominal muscles, these muscles may, on occasion, go into spasm, particularly if a vertical midline scar is present.

Research and Theory: Psychological Factors

While most instances of persistent dyspareunia are the result of physiological disorders, psychological factors may, on occasion, play a casual
role. Probably the most common factors involved in the disorder are insufficient foreplay and inadequate precoital techniques; these may contribute
to a lack of sexual arousal in the female and result in insufficient lubrication for comfortable coitus. Repeated coital discomfort may, over time,
result in an active avoidance of sexual acticity, or in vaginismus.

Situational factors may also play a role in dyspareunia. For example,
anxiety that children may wander into the bedroom, or hostility and ill feelings toward the sexual partner may create a response of anxiety, fear, and
tension resulting in decreased sexual arousal and lubrication, as well as

TABLE 5-3

**Diseases and Disorders of External Genitalia
That May Result in Dyspareunia**

Site	Diseases and Disorders of External Genitalia
Labia majora	1. Skin lesions—may be local or local manifestatation of a generalized skin disease or of various constitutional diseases, especially diabetes mellitus. May also represent drug reactions, allergy. 2. Local irritants—clothing, medication, excessive local sprays, nylon underwear. 3. Venereal diseases—chancroid, granuloma inguinale, lymphopathia venereum, chancre, herpes progenitalis. 4. Hidradenoma 5. Varicosities 6. Carcinoma—especially postradiation dermatitis. 7. Congenital and developmental anomalies are very rare.
Labia minora	1. Local irritants clothing, medications. 2. Infections—local or from vaginitis. 3. Trauma—(a) from lack of coital lubrication. 　　　(b) from oral—genital action—too vigorous insucking, biting, unshaven chin of male. 4. Varicosities—especially in pregnancy. 5. Synechiae—rare in adult, usually results from poor hygiene. 6. Postradiation
Clitoris	1. Synechiae—of frenulum (prepuce). 2. Balanitis—rare. 3. Improper hygiene—very common. 4. Hypertrophy—rare. 5. Inept or excessive stimulation—common
Posterior commissure (Below and caudad to fossa navicularis)	1. Hypertrophied—rare. 2. May rise high enough up to block introitus when woman spreads drawn-up thighs. 3. Easily traumatized—if high. 4. Local irritants
Perineal body	1. Chronic irritation—most common from repeated attacks of herpes progenitalis of fossa navicularis (relatively rare.) 2. Iatrogenic—after vaginal surgery.
Fossa navicularis (fourchette) Area between hymen and frenulum labiorum pudendi (posterior commissure) (Actually posterior aspect of area just before vaginal opening).	1. Congenital—very rare. 2. Developmental—very rare. 3. Infections—(a) primary—herpes progenitalis. 　　　(b) secondary—to vulvovaginitis of monilia or trichomoniasis: systemic diseases. 4. Postoperative—vaginal repair—painful scar. 5. Postpartum—episiotomy—painful scar. 6. Traumatic—(a) injury—lack of precoital lubrication. 7. Chronic irritation 8. Postradiation

Source: Abarbanel, A. R. Diagnosis and treatment of coital discomfort. In J. LoPiccolo & L. LoPiccolo (Eds.). *Handbook of sex therapy*. New York: Plenum Press, 1978. Reprinted with permission of Plenum Press.

TABLE 5-4

Diseases and Disorders of Areas Surrounding
Vaginal Introitus That May result in Dyspareunia

Site	Disease and Disorder
Hymen	1. Congenital and developmental (a) Imperforate (b) Cribiform (c) Bipartite (d) Absent—associated with absent vagina 2. Hymeneal scars (a) After rupture at first coitus (b) After episiotomy repair (c) After posterior vaginal repair (d) May be secondary to repeated attacks of herpes provaginalis. (e) Posttrauma—postirradiation
Urethra	1. Urethral caruncle 2. Urethritis. (a) Primary (b) Secondary to prolonged cunnilungus 3. Urethral diverticulum 4. Scar tissue—secondary to anterior vaginal repair
Anorectal area	1. Fissures 2. External hemorrhoids 3. Cryptitis 4. Postoperative—scars 5. Ischiorectal abscess 6. Pinworms
Perineal body and levator ani muscles	1. Vaginismus (a) Psychosomatic—primary or secondary (b) Secondary to (1) hymeneal scars (2) chronic herpes provaginalis 2. Chronic vulvovaginitis 3. Postoperative scars 4. Endometriosis
Vaginal opening (Introitus)	1. Marked regression (a) Postmenopausal (b) Postradiation 2. Congenital and developmental anomalies 3. Inadequate precoital lubrication
Symphysis pubis	1. Subluxation in pregnancy 2. Postfracture
Skene's and Bartholin glands	1. Acute infection 2. Cysts rarely unless large

Source: Abarbanel, A. R. Diagnosis and treatment of coital discomfort. In J. LoPiccolo & L. LoPiccolo (Eds.). *Handbook of sex therapy.* New York: Plenum Press. 1978. Reprinted with permission of Plenum Press.

TABLE 5-5

Diseases and Disorders of Areas About Vaginal Tract and Adjacent Viscera That May Result in Dyspareunia

Site	Disease and Disorder
Vagina	1. Congenital (a) Absence (b) Mid-canal stenosis (c) Gartner's cyst (d) Dermoid cyst 2. Postoperative (a) Narrowing (b) Scars—including vault (c) Shortening (d) Stenosis—(especially after transexual operation) 3. Infections (a) Monilia (b) Trichomoniasis (c) Mixed 4. Postmenopausal regression 5. Postradiation 6. Endometriosis 7. Postpartum—scarring of fornices—cervical tears 8. Disproportion—excessive penile size 9. Coccydynia
Urethra and bladder	1. Infections—urethritis, cystitis, trigonitis 2. Urethral caruncle 3. Urethral diverticulum 4. Scar tissue—after vaginal surgery 5. Postradiation
Anorectal area	1. Internal hemorrhoids 2. Cryptitis 3. Diverticulitis 4. Marked constipation 5. Postradiation 6. Pinworms 7. Coccydynia

Source: Abarbanel, A. R. Diagnosis and treatment of coital discomfort. In J. LoPiccolo & L. LoPiccolo (Eds.). *Handbook of sex therapy.* New York: Plenum Press, 1978. Reprinted with permission of Plenum Press.

tightening of the vaginal musculature. Ignorance of the anatomy and physiology of the sexual response and the life cycle may also serve to perpetuate anxiety and coital discomfort; for example, fears of sexual activity during pregnancy or fears about becoming pregnant. Another situational factor may be physical or mental fatigue which may be sufficiently strong to inhibit sexual arousal and adequate vaginal lubrication.

TABLE 5-6

**Diseases and Disorders of Cervix, Uterus, and
Adjacent Viscera That May Result in Dyspareunia**

Site	Disease and Disorder
Cervix	1. Infection especially with: (a) lymphangitis of uterosacral ligaments (b) parametritis 2. Hypertrophy
Fornices	1. Scars after difficult delivery 2. Varicosities of broad ligament 3. Metastatic tumors
Uterosacral ligaments	1. Endometriosis 2. Post-P.I.D. 3. Lymphangitis 4. Adnexal tumors
Uterus	1. Adenomyosis 2. Fixed retroversion
Lumbosacral area, obturator and psoas muscles	1. Usually follows trauma— Muscles become tender and spastic Obturator neuritis
Low back, hips	1. Any disease or disorder that produces discomfort, pain, or aching on motion or in certain positions: Congenital and developmental Posttrauma Arthritides

Source: Abarbanel, A. R. Diagnosis and treatment of coital discomfort. In J. LoPiccolo & L. LoPiccolo (Eds.). *Handbook of sex therapy.* New York: Plenum Press, 1978. Reprinted with permission of Plenum Press.

TABLE 5-7

**Diseases and Disorders of Adnexae and Broad
Ligaments That May Result in Dyspareunia**

Site	Disease and Disorder
Broad ligaments and adnexae	1. Varicosities 2. P.I.D.[a] with residual adhesions 3. Prolapsed ovary in cul-de-sac 4. Endometriosis 5. Postoperative scar tissue at vault or in cul-de-sac

[a]P.I.D., pelvic inflammatory disease.

Source: Abarbanel, A. R. Diagnosis and treatment of coital discomfort. In J. LoPiccolo & L. LoPiccolo (Eds.). *Handbook of sex therapy.* New York: Plenum Press, 1978. Reprinted with permission of Plenum Press.

CHAPTER 6

Homosexuality

The word *homosexuality* is derived from the Greek root "homo," meaning sameness. Homosexuality thus means that two individuals of the same sex are involved in sexual activity. The term therefore, applies to women as well as men, although female homosexuality is more often called *lesbianism,* because the classic Greek poet Sappo described sexual relations between women on the island of Lesbos. More specifically, homosexuality is defined as an erotic preference for same-sex persons when a choice of sexual partners is available. Note the phrase a *preference for sexual partners;* this definition says nothing about the *type* of sexual activity. Homosexual activity may occur for a number of reasons: as a result of restricted choice of sexual partners; as a means of satisfying curiosity; as a religious ritual in some cultures; and as foreplay for arousal purposes in group sex; as well as in other similar episodic ways. Infrequent homosexual experience is common in both sexes. This does not mean that everyone who has engaged in a homosexual act is, in fact, homosexual or has a homosexual orientation; as we said above, homosexuality is based on a preference for a same-sexed partner who consistently arouses in fantasy and in sexual situations. This definition is meaningful since it includes cognitive and physiological indices as well as overt behavior. It is highly probable that individuals are able to engage in nonpreferred sexual activity through the use of preferred sexual fantasies. Consequently a definition of homosexuality which is based upon sexual preference, overt behaviors, and physiological indices is both accurate and useful.

MALE HOMOSEXUALITY

The following is taken from one of our interviews.

Jim and Frank have been living together as lovers for two years. Jim is 26, and Frank is 25; they live in a large southern city. Jim is a college student in marketing, and Frank currently works as a salesman.

Jim was reared in a Roman Catholic family and attended parochial schools. His father deserted the family when Jim was 2 years old. His mother remarried when he was 11; though he is fond of his stepfather, he feels that he has never had a real father. When questioned why he believed he was homosexual, he replied that he felt the cause was his lack of a father during his early formative years.

After graduating from high school, Jim joined the Peace Corps and served in Mexico. His first sexual experience was with a Mexican prostitute, and although he felt fairly positive about the physical aspect of this experience, he also felt something was missing emotionally. He had his first homosexual experience at the age of 22 with a male friend.

Frank also grew up in a Roman Catholic family and attended parochial schools. He has also gotten along well with both his parents and his two siblings, and he recalls his childhood as uneventful. He had his first homosexual experience at the age of 17 with a male he met at a social function. He reports engaging in sexual activities with approximately six females before deciding on an exclusively homosexual lifestyle. Before meeting Jim, he had had sex with about 16 other men.

Both Jim and Frank maintain that their relationship will last and that they are very much in love with each other. Their relationship is exclusive; that is, they have an agreement that they will be faithful to each other and that neither will have sex with anyone else.

One of the significant facts about homosexuality is that it exists throughout the entire social spectrum; that is, in all categories of age, occupation, social class, education, and interests. Nonetheless, misconceptions concerning homosexuality abound, one of the more common being that homosexuals manifest qualities of the opposite sex to a striking degree. D. H. Lawrence (1923) railed against homosexuals as "flat-chested, crop-headed, chemicalized women of indeterminate sex and wimbly-wambly young men of sex still more indeterminate" (p. 110). The male homosexual is thought of as an effeminate, limp-wristed lisper who works as a hairdresser or interior decorator. The female homosexual is often conceptualized as a butch, cigar-smoker who drives a truck. Effeminate male and masculine female homosexuals, however, are a distinct minority, and though they may occasionally work in the jobs noted, their range of occupations are similar to those of society at large. The misconceptions surrounding homosexuality have gotten out of control when Kiell (1976) relates that:

> Every college student studying the American novel knows that the relationship between Huck Finn and Nigger Jim, between Ishmael and Queequeq, Robinson Crusoe and Friday, and Chingachgook and Natty Bumpo forms one long daisy chain of failed queers while the principle occupation of our national literature has been disguised by obsessive homosexuality. (p. 222)

As a Way of Life

In discussing homosexuality, there are two important considerations: whether a person is a primary or secondary homosexual; and whether a person is a covert or overt homosexual. Primary homosexuality is defined as no prior heterosexual experiences; secondary homosexuality is defined as one or more heterosexual experiences. Covert male homosexuals may be married, may be parents, and may resemble heterosexual individuals so much so that they are largely indistinguishable from the general population. These men frequently lead double lives by restricting their homosexual behavior to times when they are away from home, not unlike other men who participate in extramarital heterosexual behavior.

Overt homosexuals represent a smaller percentage of homosexuals and are characterized by an open and occasionally blatant homosexual lifestyle. These men frequently rely upon the homosexual community for gratification of their social and sexual needs. They tend to defy the heterosexual world in such a way as to deny fear of retribution for their life-style. Obviously, overt and covert homosexuals often are at odds with each other. Overt homosexuals tend to consider covert homosexuals hypocrites; while covert men shun blatant homosexuals to protect themselves.

Male homosexuals generally have short-term relationships, although some commitments may be durable and very intense (Gagnon & Simon, 1973). This fact, whatever the explanation, has an important bearing on the life-style of the male homosexual. Since most homosexual relationships tend to be short-lived, obviously male homosexuals must frequently search for new partners, and many homosexuals go "cruising" in search of "tricks" or "pickups." Practically every city has its known homosexual meeting places or hangouts, which may be parks, men's rooms, "gay bars" or "gay clubs." Some homosexual men prefer elegant environments with all the gentility and accoutrements of the idealized heterosexual romance: however, the gay bar is a popular and significant avenue of identification and expression for many homosexual persons.

The gay bar is not the only place in which male homosexuals may seek sexual contacts. Called "tea rooms" in the argot of the homosexual subculture, public restrooms are accessible to those who wish to engage in anonymous sexual encounters. In his book *Numbers,* John Rechy (1963) describes these impersonal sexual contacts.

Johnny enters a movie whose marquee lights proclaim that it is open all night and has a balcony. Johnny knows—just as anyone who has hung out in gay bars knows—what that means. The haunting shadows in the dark . . . the frantic moving in and out of the toilet. (pp. 39–40)

Johnny enters and climbs to the balcony when suddenly the mood lifts. Instantly it's converted to euphoria. He's like someone reacting to a powerful stimulant—like an alcoholic returning to his liquor, an addict to his drug: spuriously renewed, as if the storm that raged is over but within the calm the devestation remains. (p. 74)

As he prowls the balcony, allowing himself to be seen, wanting those on the top rows to hope he'll make himself available, he plays a sadistic, teasing game, sprawling on his seat in a casual, sexually inviting pose until he is approached, permitting the stranger a liberty but then abruptly rejecting him.

Another prowler takes the man's place, and still another until he permits a young man to fellate him. Others have witnessed the scene—a scene not rare but common even in such a balcony, where the groping is usually done as an end in itself or as an invitation for completion in the restroom. Now, as if Johnny's sexual release has made them restless, there's a silent moving among those others—as if they're playing a game of musical chairs without music. (p. 82)

Important as life around gay bars, theaters, and the like is for many homosexuals, such behavior is not unique to them. Female prostitutes and heterosexuals of both sexes looking for quickies or one-night stands operate in much the same manner. The prospective partner is spotted; subtle and less subtle cues are exchanged; the couple may then have a drink or two, become progressively more intimate, and leave together or arrange to meet somewhere. The female prostitute who cruises heterosexual X-rated theaters offering to masturbate or fellate male patrons as they watch the movie is becoming more common, especially in larger cities.

For those ignorant of homosexual ways, it is difficult to understand their interactions and relationships; but what happens is just like what happens in a comparable situation between a man and a woman. Homosexuals, like heterosexuals, may be shy and inhibited or forward and aggressive. Witty homosexuals tell witty jokes, and uncouth homosexuals tell vulgar jokes; some are subtle in their approaches, others clumsy; some would never engage in sex in a darkened theater, while others, given a chance, would engage in homosexual sex on the fifty-yard line during halftime at the Super Bowl while Howard Cosell described the action.

Even more mystifying to many people is what homosexuals actually do when they are together. The answer is that they, like most heterosexuals, do what is physically possible with, of course, the exception of vaginal intercourse. Kissing and petting are usual preliminaries, followed by mutual genital stimulation. The two main behaviors leading to orgasm are oral-genital contact (singly or mutually), and, less frequently, anal intercourse. With practice and the use of lubricants, the anus can readily admit an erect penis and even considerably larger objects with little or no discomfort. There is no homosexual act that cannot be performed by a heterosexual couple. Any emergency room physician knows the frequency with which homosexuals and heterosexuals, have foreign objects removed from their bowels which have somehow become lodged there. What characterizes the behavior as homosexual is not the behavior itself, but the fact that the participants are of the same sex.

Homosexuals claim that anal intercourse is just as real and satisfying as is vaginal intercourse. Many heterosexual couples, in fact, incorporate anal intercourse into their lovemaking routine although it may be done for variety's sake rather than routine. Many prostitutes claim that a willingness to specialize in anal sex means that a woman can increase her business and charge larger fees. Whatever its rewards, anal intercourse also carries some of the penalties as does vaginal intercourese. Venereal disease, for instance, is readily transmitted in this way, and promiscuous homosexuals have some of the highest rates of such disease in the country. In addition, many medical authorities claim that repeated anal intercourse results in hemorrhoids and possible intestinal trauma (Walen et al., 1977).

Some feel that it is important to determine whether the homosexual engages in the active or passive role during sexual activities. The individual who inserts the penis is considered the active, dominant partner and the other the passive or feminine one. Such distinctions are generally not useful, and in oral-genital contact they are quite meaningless (Katchadourian & Lunde, 1972). In practice only a small minority of male homosexuals demonstrate a definite preference for one role over the other. Most investigators agree that the majority of male homosexuals practice all forms of sexual activity and vary their roles depending upon their wish for variety. Some professionals, however, attempt to link active and passive roles to character traits and histories of psychosexual development.

Many organizations exist to counteract what homosexuals consider society's distorted view of their life. Perhaps the best known is the Mattachine Society (named after medieval court jesters who were fearlessly outspoken), a national organization with chapters in various major cities and a predominately, but not exclusively, homosexual membership. The stated purpose of the Mattachine Society is to promote fair and equal treatment for homosexuals and to protest the oppression and abuse directed against homosexuals. The Mattachine Society conducts meetings, arranges lectures, and issues several publications, including the *Homosexual Citizen* and *Mattachine Newsletter*. Other organizations, such as the Gay Liberation Front and the Gay Activist Alliance are more outspoken and attivist than the Mattachines.

Statistics

The largest survey of homosexual behavior to date was conducted by Kinsey et al. (1948). In order to aid the description of homosexual behavior, Kinsey developed a simple heterosexual-homosexual rating scale which ranged from 0 (exclusively heterosexual) to 6 (exclusively homosexual); see Figure 6-1. Kinsey's investigation found that 37 percent of the total male population surveyed reported at least incidental homosexual experience to the point of orgasm between adolescence and old age. Twenty-five percent reported more than incidental homosexual experience or reactions for at least three years between the ages of 16 and 55 years; 18 percent reported at least as much homosexual as heterosexual behavior in their histories for at least three years between the ages of 16 and 66 years; 10 percent were more or less exclusively homosexual for a period of three years between the ages

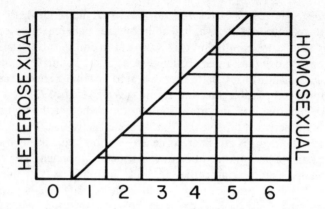

0. Individuals are rated as 0's if they make no physical responses which result in erotic arousal or orgasm, and make no psychic responses to individuals of their own sex. Their sociosexual contacts and responses are exclusively with individuals of the opposite sex.

1. Individuals are rated 1's if they have only incidental homosexual contacts which have involved physical or psychic response, or incidental psychic responses without physical contact. The great preponderance of their sociosexual experience and reactions is directed toward individuals of the opposite sex. Such homosexual experiences as these individuals have may occur only a single time or two, or at least infrequently in comparison to the amount of their heterosexual experience. Their homosexual experiences never involve as specific psychic reactions as they make to heterosexual stimuli. Sometimes the homosexual activities in which they engage may be inspired by curiosity, or may be more or less forced upon them by other individuals, perhaps when they are asleep or when they are drunk, or under some other peculiar circumstance.

2. Individuals are rated 2's if they have more than incidental homosexual experience, and/or if they respond rather definitely to homosexual stimuli. Their heterosexual experiences and/or reactions still surpass their homosexual experiences and/or reactions. These individuals may have only a small amount of

of 16 and 55 years; and finally, 4 percent of the males surveyed were exclusively homosexual throughout their lives after the onset of adolescence, and a further 4 percent were exclusively homosexual for at least three years between the ages of 16 and 55 years.

Roesler and Diescher (1972) reported that over 50 percent of homosexual males sampled claimed the onset of homosexual fantasy and contact appeared around the ages of 14–16 years and usually involved friends of the same age. In this sample the median number of homosexual contacts was 50, while the modal number of contacts per week was 2.5. It should be noted, however, that 73 percent of the respondents in Roesler and Diesher's study were overt homosexuals who were functioning members of a homosexual community.

(Figure 6-1 continued)

homosexual experience or they may have a considerable amount of it, but in every case it is surpassed by the amount of heterosexual experience that they have within the same period of time. They usually recognize their quite specific arousal by homosexual stimuli, but their responses to the opposite sex are still stronger. A few of these individuals may even have all of their overt experience in the homosexual, but their psychic reactions to persons of the opposite sex indicate that they are still predominately heterosexual. This latter situation is most often found among younger males who have not yet ventured to have actual intercourse with girls, while their orientation is definitely heterosexual. On the other hand, there are some males who should be rated as 2's because of their strong reactions to individuals of their own sex, even though they have never had overt relations with them.

3. Individuals who are rated 3's stand midway on the heterosexual-homosexual scale. They are about equally homosexual and heterosexual in their overt experience and/or their psychic reactions. In general, they accept and equally enjoy both types of contacts, and have no strong preferences for one or the other. Some persons are rated 3's, even though they may have a larger amount of experience of one sort, because they respond psychically to partners of both sexes, and it is only a matter of circumstance that brings them into more frequent contact with one of the sexes. Such a situation is not unusual among single males, for male contacts are often more available to them than female contacts. Married males, on the other hand, find it simpler to secure a sexual outlet through intercourse with their wives, even though some of them may be as interested in males as they are females.

4. Individuals are rated 4's if they have more overt activity and/or psychic reactions in the homosexual, while still maintaining a fair amount of heterosexual activity and/or responding rather definitely to heterosexual stimuli.

5. Individuals are rated 5's if they are almost entirely homosexual in their overt activities and/or reactions. They do have incidental experience with the opposite sex and sometimes react psychically to individuals of the opposite sex.

6. Individuals are rated 6's if they are exclusively homosexual, both in regard to their overt experience and in regard to their psychic reactions.

Figure 6-1. Kinsey Heterosexual-Homosexual Rating Scale. (**Source:** Kinsey, A. C., Pomeroy, W. B., & Martin, C. E. *Sexual behavior in the human male.* Philadelphia: Saunders, 1948. Reprinted with permission.)

FEMALE HOMOSEXUALITY

The following is taken from one of our interviews:

Joanne and Lynn have been living together in an arrangement they consider marriage for three years. Joanne is 31 and Lynn is 25. Joanne is originally from a large northeastern city, and Lynn is from a medium-sized southern city.

Joanne was reared by her parents and attended public schools. Her father is a dentist and her mother a housewife. She has two older sisters, both of whom are married. She described her childhood as uneventful.

After graduating from high school, Joanne married her school sweetheart. Her first sexual experience was on her honeymoon; she described it as being neither enjoyable nor aversive. The marriage became troubled after the first year and resulted in divorce some two years later. She had her first homosexual experience at the age of 24 with a woman she met at work. When asked why she thought she was gay, she said she felt it was because the oppressive nature of her former husband, as well as men in general, forced her into a more satisfying homosexual lifestyle.

Lynn was reared by her mother and older sister. Her father had died when she was 10. She maintains a close relationships with her family, but admits that they do not understand her lifestyle. She realized she was gay when she was in high school but tried to date several men in an effort to conform to what her family wanted. She had her first homosexual experience at the age of 17 with an older girl from her neighborhood. She has never had intercourse with a man, but admits having sexual relations with approximately seven different women before meeting Joanne.

Joanne and Lynn claim that the greatest problem in their relationship is coping with the scorn of others about their homosexual orientations. Joanne feels that the greatest joy in their relationship is having someone to love and understand her. Lynn agrees and adds that the security of their relationship is important.

With astonishing regularity the published literature on female homosexuality bewails the dearth of data concerning this behavior. Socarides (1962) stated that, for a variety of reasons, overt female homosexuality is a relatively neglected clinical entity in contrast to male homosexuality. Abbott and Love (1972) state that "the lesbian is one of the least known member of our culture. Less is known about her—and less accurately—than the Newfoundland dog." (p. 13).

The majority of lesbians, are indistinguishable from the general population. Despite some differences, much of what we have said about male homosexuals also applies to females. Many of the differences between the life styles of female and male homosexuals simply reflect role expectations for men and women in general. Other distinctions are less specific: lesbians appear to form more lasting relationships, operate in less differential subcultures, and are generally far less often detected and harassed (Hedblom, 1973).

As a Way of Life

There are far fewer gay bars and known meeting places for female homosexuals, and those that do exist present an environment and atmosphere much different from those catering primarily to gay males. Female homosexuals seldom visit a gay bar in search of a quick pickup. Lesbians far more frequently patronize gay bars in pairs to socialize, drink, and dance, just the way straight women go in pairs to heterosexual bars.

There is a much greater tendency among lesbians to pair off and to live as couples in relatively stable relationships (Katchadourian & Lunde, 1972). Such relationships are often termed "marriages," and may involve the exchange of wedding rings. Typical masculine and feminine roles are usually somewhat more clearly defined in lesbian relationships, and one partner usually takes on the role as "head of the family" with protective responsibilities. The "butch" and "femme" couple represent these roles most clearly. The butch or "bull dyke" is, in a sense, the counterpart of the male queen. She may wear masculine pants and shirts, cut her hair short, and even work in a predominately male occupation. Nonetheless, despite her aggressiveness and masculine appearance and manner, she may still be viewed in the straight world as simply a "masculine woman," because our society is not as apt to suspect or to identify lesbians as effeminate males (Roesler & Diescher, 1972). The femme member of the couple is typically feminine in dress, mannerisms, and general appearance. She is the more passive member of the couple, and is more likely to be involved in a traditionally feminine occupation than is the butch.

While some lesbian couples do tend to preserve particular roles in lovemaking, the distinction between butch and femme often becomes less than distinct. Contrary to many popular lesbian stag movies, homosexual females rarely use a penis substitute for sexual gratification (Hedblom, 1973). Inserting an object into the vagina also appears to be a rare masturbatory activity of adult heterosexually-oriented females. These types of activities are usually reserved for movies and "live shows" directed toward a heterosexual male audience. Incidentally, though it is not uncommon for prostitutes and call girls to be lesbians, they sell their services mainly to men rather than to women.

A more common type of lesbian relationship involves two girls who live together in a close and mutually dependent relationship but not as butch or femme. Often both are employed, and may be schoolteachers, models, clerks, professional women, and the like. Unlike males in a similar situation, these women may live together for years without arousing the suspicions of their neighbors or families. Consequently, they are subject to relatively little harassment or social pressure, except for an occasional well-meaning friend or relative who insists on arranging heterosexual dates and outings for them. Needless to say, female friends may live together without being lesbians.

Sexual activity between lesbians may consist of kissing, caressing, fondling and oral stimulation of the breasts, mutual masturbation, and oral-genital contacts. *Tribadism* is an exclusively lesbian but not particularly common practice in which the genitals are mutually stimulated as one woman lies on top of the other and simulates coitus.

Many lesbians with heterosexual experience state that orgasms achieved via homosexual activities are incomparably more satisfying (Katchadourian & Lunde, 1972). Athanasiou, Shaver, and Travis (1970), in fact, reported that lesbians are more likely than heterosexual women to reach orgasm and are twice as likely to be multiorgasmic. One possible explanation is that lesbians have a natural advantage over male partners, with unclear and misdirected notions of female anatomy and sexual functioning.

Lesbian organizations are both more recent and less prominent than their male counterparts. One of the better known is the Daughters of Bilitis, founded in 1956. This organization derives its name from a book of prose poems by Pieere Louys (1894) supposedly a translation from the Greek of Sappho's love poems to a courtesan named Bilitis. The objectives and functions of this organization are comparable to those of male homosexual organizations although lesbians claim they are fighting a double social disadvantage, since they are both female and homosexual. Changes similar to those affecting male homosexuals are also currently affecting lesbians. Liberation efforts among lesbians, however, appear to be primarily concerned with the protection of women's rights in general, rather than of lesbians' rights in particular.

Statistics

Kinsey et al. (1953) estimated that 28 percent of females had indulged in some form of homosexual behavior by the age of 45. Thirteen to 20 percent had done so to the point of orgasm. Hedblom (1973) reported that 42 percent of his sample had their first homosexual fantasies between the ages of 11 and 15 years; estimates of the age of onset of homosexual activity appears to occur somewhat later in life as compared to male homosexuals. Further comparison of male and female homosexuals suggests that females have fewer partners than do males. Two studies report finding a mean of 3.7 partners for lesbians (Kenyon, 1968; Loney, 1973), while Hedblom (1973) reported that 80 percent of his sample had engaged in sexual activities with fewer than eight women. Heterosexual activity among female homosexuals is more common than it is with male homosexuals. Hedblom (1973) reported that 58 percent of his sample had engaged in heterosexual intercourse.

Studies of gender preference among homosexual women provide contradictory evidence. Loney (1973) reported that no homosexual women in his sample claimed they would like to have been born male as compared to 20-30 percent of heterosexual women. On the other hand, Kenyon (1968) found that 42 percent of homosexual women in his sample reported a preference for masculine-type dress, compared to 2 percent of heterosexual women; and 29 percent of the homosexual women reported feeling "fully feminine" compared to 97 percent of heterosexual women. Kenyon (1968) also found a positive family history of homosexuality in 24 percent of his lesbian sample compared to 2 percent of control subjects; and that 80 percent of the homosexual sample reported engaging in masturbation, compared to 41 percent of the heterosexual sample.

TYPES OF HOMOSEXUAL BEHAVIOR

Various attempts have been made to categorize male and female homosexual behavior. Although no universally accepted taxonomy is currently available, Coleman (1972), in an attempt to better understand the range and patterns of homosexual behavior, categorized homosexuality into six different types:

1. The *blatant* homosexual describes the individuals who fit the popular stereotype of the effeminate, limp-wristed male and the butch female. Also included in this category are what Coleman calls the "leather boys," who advertise their sado-masochistic homosexuality by wearing leather jackets, chains, and often boots.

2. The *desperate* homosexual denotes those homosexuals who hang around public restrooms (tea-rooms) or steam baths. These homosexuals are unable to or prefer not to establish and sustain a serious homosexual relationship. Humphrey (1970), in a study of tea-room homosexual behavior, found that 54 percent of the patrons were married. The anonymity and the short-lived nature of such contacts conceal their homosexuality from their spouses. Humphrey cites the case of a highly successful businessman who visited tea-rooms almost daily:

> I guess you might say I'm pretty highly sexed (he chuckled a little), but I really don't think that's why I go to tea rooms. That's really not sex. Sex is something I have with my wife in bed. It's not as if I were committing adultery by getting my rocks off—or going down on some guy—in a tea room. I get a kick out of it. Some of my friends go out for handball. I'd rather cruise the park. Does that sound perverse to you? (p. 19)

3. The *secret* homosexual describes those individuals who are often married and attempt to conceal their homosexual behavior from their spouse, employer, and friends. Through years of practice they are extremely skilled at camouflage and passing as straights. They do not frequent tea rooms and gay bars, and protect their double life to the utmost. The secret homosexual will often have only one partner. Living in continual fear and anxiety over detection often takes its toll on the lives of these individuals.

4. The *adjusted* homosexual refers to those individuals who accept their homosexuality, locate in a homosexual community, or are active in

homosexual organizations. These individuals may be thought of as having come out of the closet. Many of these individuals attempt to form stable homosexual relationships and even enter into marriages. Stable homosexual relationships, especially among men, however, are rare. Most often these individuals tend to form fragile, short-lived relationships lasting less than a year.

5. The *situational* homosexual describes those individuals who, because of a particular situation, engage in homosexual behavior without a deep commitment. Many heterosexual individuals may engage in homosexual activities while in prison, institutions, or situations in which opportunities for heterosexual activities are unavailable. In fact, we may question the inclusion of such behavior as homosexual, since by definition there is no free choice of a sexual partner.

Some prisoners act as homosexual prostitutes, engaging in this type of behavior for economic advantage. Davis (1968) has stated that homosexual rapes are also a part of prison and institutional behavior. This behavior may take place in police vans, detention centers, and cells; with men, it typically involves anal intercourse. Homosexual prison rape may be perpetrated by an individual or gang of men or women who do not consider themselves homosexual but who are attempting to assert dominance and authority. Part of one female patient's initiation into a popular sorority at a well known women's college involved being held down and stripped, after which senior sorority sisters forced a broom handle in and out of her vagina. This act was supposedly carried out all in fun, to assert the senior members' dominance over the freshman recruit; the sorority sisters were perplexed when the target of this "fun" became extremely emotional and depressed.

6. The homosexual *prostitute* refers to those individuals who, most often, do not consider themselves homosexual, but who sell their sexual services to homosexual partners. Males more often than females are likely to engage in homosexual prostitution; sometimes a student will sell his sexual services to get money to pay for his education. These prostitutes rarely continue in this type of behavior if they become financially secure. The homosexual act becomes an economic venture to them, so they find it possible to maintain their sense of male identity.

BISEXUALITY: FACT OR FANCY?

The term *bisexual* is often mistakenly applied to homosexuals. Bisexuality describes individuals who engage in both homosexual and heterosexual behavior, and who claim a permanent need and desire for relations with both sexes. Because of their dual orientations and desire to enjoy the best of both worlds, they are frequently called "AC–DC." Their stated bipolar orientation and behavior puts them in the middle range of Kinsey's Homosexual-Heterosexual scale (see Figure 6-1).

Some researchers claim that bisexuals are merely homosexuals attempting to rationalize their activities. For example, Tollison et al. (1977) investigated male homosexual, bisexual, and heterosexual arousal to both homosexual and heterosexual stimuli. Ten subjects in each group of homosexual, bisexual, and heterosexual males individually viewed the following stimuli: (1) an explicit homosexual film consisting of two males embracing as they removed each other's clothes, caressing, and performing oral-genital sex; (2) an explicit heterosexual film consisting of a male and female embracing as they removed each other's clothes, caressing, and performing coitus; (3) a slide each of both nude male and female models; and (4) neutral stimuli consisting of films and slides of landscapes. A penile strain gauge physiologically assessed each subject's level of penile erection to the various stimuli. In addition, subjects were requested to estimate their highest level of penile erection to each stimulus in percentages of 100 percent erect.

The results of the investigation indicated that homosexuals were physiologically aroused to homosexual stimuli, while heterosexuals were physiologically aroused to heterosexual stimuli. The penile responses of bisexuals to the various stimuli could not be significantly distinguished from those of the homosexual group: high arousal to homosexual stimuli and minimal arousal to heterosexual stimuli. Estimates of penile erection levels revealed similar results for the homosexual and heterosexual groups, each estimating significantly higher penile erections when viewing stimuli of their stated sexual orientation. The bisexual group, however, estimated approximately equal levels of penile erection to both homosexual and heterosexual stimuli, although physiological assessment did not substantiate their estimations.

In terms of physiologic arousal, this study does not support the existence of male bisexuality as distinct from homosexuality or as a separate sexual orientation in males. Penile erectile responses of the homosexual and bisexual groups to homosexual and heterosexual stimuli were indistinguishable. Subjects who verbally reported themselves as bisexual, who expressed no gender preference in sexual partners, and whose sexual history as well as scores on the Kinsey Homosexual-Heterosexual scale (see Figure 6-1) were congruent with their stated orientation, were not significantly differentiated from homosexual subjects' erectile responses to various sexual stimuli (Figure 6-2). Heterosexual subjects' responses were, however, significantly different from both homosexual and bisexual groups. Thus, penile erectile changes to male and female nudes and films provided a valid measure of the stated sexual orientation of both the homosexual and heterosexual groups, but not of the bisexual group.

These results raise some important questions concerning issues of sex-

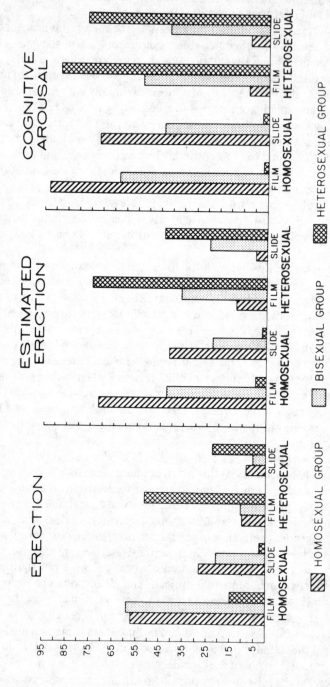

Figure 6-2. Physiologically measured erection, estimated erection, and cognitive arousal to sexual stimuli by groups of homosexual, bisexual, and heterosexual males. (**Source:** Tollison, C. D., Adams, H. E., & Tollison, J. W. *Physiological measurement of sexual arousal in homosexual, bisexual, and heterosexual males.* Unpublished manuscript, University of Georgia, 1977.)

ual orientation. Again we refer to the question of whether sexual orientations should be defined by sexual activities or sexual preferences. One reason that individuals may claim to be bisexual is that they adhere to the first definition. In other words they assume they are bisexual because they participate in both homosexual and heterosexual behavior. If this is so, verbally reported bisexuality would be predicted from attribution theory (Shavers, 1975). The discrepancy between actual erections and verbal reports in the bisexual group, combined with their drastic overestimation of penile erection to heterosexual stimuli, may also be an attempt at cognitive balance (Festinger, 1957). Dissonance may be created by an individual's homosexual behavior and his inability to accept his homosexual orientation. Reduction of dissonance may take place if the individual considers himself bisexual rather than homosexual; a classification that is perhaps less threatening and is, in fact, viewed as positive in some intellectual and scholarly communities. He therefore denies his primary homosexuality and engages in sexual activity with both sexes. Our clinical experience has been that bisexuals are able to achieve and maintain penile erection in heterosexual relationships through the use of homosexual fantasy. Participation in sexual activity with both sexes thus allows the bisexual to perceive himself as more normal than the homosexual.

ISSUES IN HOMOSEXUALITY

For years various individuals and groups have questioned whether homosexuality is normal or abnormal behavior. Many professionals have long considered homosexuals to be emotionally disturbed or ill (Bieber, 1973). This judgment has been based both on theoretical grounds and clinical experience. These clinicians view homosexuals as having suffered from stunted psychosexual development; they may consider homosexuals to be unhappy, immature, and neurotic, unable to achieve satisfying sex lives, and unable to have the rewards of mature heterosexual relationships, parenthood, and family life (Katchadourian & Lunde, 1972).

Other professionals do not consider homosexuality as abnormal behavior or homosexuals as disturbed (Silverstein, 1972). They point out that homosexuality has occurred throughout history in virtually all countries, as well as in animal species other than man. Silverstein (1972) claims that pathology is inherent not in the homosexual person but in our society, which harasses and scorns homosexual orientations.

Many of the issues surrounding homosexuality have recently been discussed by Davison (1974, 1976) and by Sturgis and Adams (1978). These authors have debated a number of issues including whether homosexuality is normal or abnormal, whether social prejudice is the primary agent in homosexual distress, whether effective sexual reorientation programs reinforce societal prejudices about homosexuality, and whether sexual preferences are equivalent to sexual values. They have concluded with opposing proposals for therapy with homosexuals. This debate of pertinent issues in homosexuality deserves review.

Davison (1976), addressing the normality-abnormality issue of homosexuality, maintains that before we can conclude that etiological factors in an individual's life are pathological, the behavior pattern which instigates such a search must first be labeled abnormal. In other words, before medical and psychological clinicians should concern themselves with a search for causes and cure for homosexuality, they must first have conclusive evidence that homosexuality is, in fact, abnormal. Sturgis and Adams (1978), however, maintain that the abnormality of homosexuality or any other behavior is irrelevant as a prerequisite for psychological intervention. Many individuals who seek the aid of clinical psychologists or psychiatrists are normally functioning individuals who experience difficulties in some aspect of their lives. These authors suggest that psychological intervention is warranted when an individual's behavior pattern results in discomfort and distress to the individual. To respond differently to homosexuality than to other problems in living is to react to social and political pressure, rather than to the basic issue of the right of the individual to seek treatment.

The political power of organized gay liberation groups is seen in the fact that the American Psychiatric Association responded to their lobbying by excluding homosexuality from the sexual deviation classification in the taxonomy of psychiatric conditions (DSM II). In the DSM III (1978), homosexuality is not labeled as a mental disorder unless the individual has strong negative feelings toward his/her homosexual arousal. When such feelings are present the individual is diagnosed as an ego-dystonic homosexual. However, the normality or abnormality of homosexuality (or anything else) cannot be proven or disproven by pressure or by votes of any group, no matter how prestigious. The abnormality of homosexual behavior, like the classification of any behavior pattern, is an issue to be resolved empirically by scientific methods (Adams, Doster, & Calhoun, 1977).

Davison (1976) further claims that social prejudice against the homosexual is a major cause of personal distress to the gay individual. He notes that society does not attribute problems to heterosexuals on the basis of their sexual orientation. Silverstein (1972) elaborates on this point:

> To suggest that a person comes voluntarily to change his sexual orientation is to ignore the powerful environmental stress, oppression if you will, that has been telling him for years that he should change. To grow up in a family where the word "homosexual" was whispered, to play in a playground and hear the words "faggot" and "queer," to go to church and hear of "sin" and then to

college and hear of "illness," and finally to the counseling center that promises to "cure," is hardly to create an environment of freedom and voluntary choice. (p. 4)

Sturgis and Adams (1978), while noting that these observations may be valid, claim that presently no data base exists for such a statement, other than opinion. Further, it is obvious that society frequently employs pressure tactics in an attempt to change most behaviors that deviate from normative behavior patterns, including behaviors labeled as mental disorders. It could be just as easily claimed that distress to an individual with a hand-washing ritual is the result of societal oppression. Sturgis and Adams question Davison's (1976) contention that emphasis should be placed on modifying the attitudes of society rather than the sexual reorientation of the individual. They believe that efforts should be made to educate the public concerning factual issues related to homosexuality; however, Sturgis and Adams also believe that clinical psychologists and medical scientists should refrain from using nonfactual personal opinions or social propaganda in lieu of empirical evidence as a basis for influencing the public, particularly if these opinions are represented, implicitly or explicitly, as scientific facts.

Begelman (1975) and Davison (1976) maintain that the very existence of treatment programs for homosexuality constitutes a significant causal element in reinforcing the doctrine that homosexuality is undesirable. Sturgis and Adams (1978) note that the logic of this claim is questionable. Does penicillin cause negative public attitudes toward venereal disease? Does systematic desensitization cause negative public attitudes toward phobias? It is more logical to assume that treatment programs are a consequence rather than a cause of negative public opinion.

Davison's (1976) argument that homosexuals seek change of orientation treatment primarily because of social pressures seems to assume that the sexual preferences of individuals determine their values concerning sexual behavior. However, numerous examples in the literature suggest that many individuals experience annoyance and/or shame concerning patterns of sexual gratification, but are unable to bring the patterns under self-control (Kohlenberg, 1974). Sturgis and Adams (1978) maintain that Davison's argument ignores these data, and neglects the possibility that there are homosexuals who wish to alter their sexual preference to be congruent with their values, rather than change their value system.

Finally, Davison (1976) and Silverstein (1972) propose that all individuals with homosexual preferences be treated by desensitizing them to their guilt about homosexual preference and lifestyles. This proposal, however, allows the patient no greater freedom of choice than a proposal that all homosexuals should be subjected to sexual reorientation treatment regardless of their personal preference. Sturgis and Adams (1978), in fact, maintain that such a standardized procedure appears to be a return to the state of affairs in which it was not possible to tailor treatment procedures to the particular needs or desires of an individual, and that it eliminates the patient's freedom of choice concerning treatment procedures. They argue that one distinctive characteristic of behavior therapy is that behavioral procedures are appropriate for altering a variety of behaviors, normal or abnormal. Any *a priori* decision to use only specific techniques for a specific problem behavior eliminates one advantage of behavior therapy, which is that it allows the clinician to select treatment procedures appropriate to the individual case. Bieber (1973), as a matter of fact, has distinguished psychoanalysis and behavior therapy on this very basis.

These issues are difficult problems, ones for which there may be no real solutions. In the final analysis, the decision to offer or refuse to offer sexual reorientation therapy to any homosexual patient must be made by each clinician. Clinicians should consult with their patients and give them an unbiased evaluation of the issue, discuss alternative possibilities, and then allow the patient to make the final choice.

RESEARCH AND THEORY: PHYSIOLOGICAL AND CHEMICAL FACTORS

During the early part of this century, many therapists believed that homosexuality had a biological basis through direct genetic inheritance. This view was popularized in an investigation made by Kallman (1953) of a group of 85 pairs of male fraternal and identical twins in which one member was known to be homosexual. Of the fraternal twin pairs studied, both members were discovered to be homosexual in less than half the cases. Of the identical twin pairs studied, however, both members in every pair were discovered to be homosexual. The results of this study support the view that homosexuality is very largely genetically determined. Kallman's own view, however, was more cautious, supporting instead a genetic-environmental interaction. In fact, a year later, Kallman (1953) considered the 100 percent concordance obtained between identical twins in his earlier study to be a "statistical artifact."

Numerous criticisms of Kallman's (1953) study can be made. The identical twins were all reared together, and thus shared not only common genes but also a common environment; therefore environmental factors might explain the results. Furthermore, nonidentical twins are not genetically unrelated; they share, on the average, half their genes. Hence, if homosexuality were genetic, one would expect a moderate degree of concordance for them. Other investigators have failed to replicate Kallman's findings (Heston & Shields, 1968), and today the genetic-inheritance theory of homosexual genesis is largely discounted.

The possibility that endocrine imbalance contributes significantly to homosexual behavior has been another attractive hypothesis. Various researchers have explored whether the testosterone (male hormone) levels of male homosexuals differ from those of male heterosexuals. There are considerable studies in the animal literature on the effects of variations in adult behavior due to the level and type of gonadal hormones present in the newborn mammal. However, a series of early studies on humans failed to find any differences between homosexual and heterosexual males in testosterone levels (Glass, Deuel, & Wright, 1940). While techniques for measuring hormone levels were not very accurate in the 1940s, more recent studies using highly sophisticated measurement techniques still fail to find any hormonal difference between adult male homosexuals and heterosexuals (Rose, 1975). Although it is agreed that testosterone plays a crucial role in the development of secondary sex characteristics in males, such as growth of facial hair, deepening of the voice, and the enlargement of the testes for the manufacture of sperm, the data available do not support the idea of hormonal differences in primary sex characteristics and behavior.

Another speculation is that homosexuality develops as a result of an exposure to inappropriate hormones during the prenatal period. Evidence shows that exposure to inappropriate hormones during fetal development can lead a genetic female to have male genitals or a genetic male to have female genitals (Money & Ehrhardt, 1972). It has been suggested that a similar process might account for homosexuality, but no evidence in support of this hypothesis has been produced. If homosexuality did result from prenatal hormone exposure, it would be reasonable to expect the inappropriate hormone doses also to have some anatomical effect. There is considerable evidence, however, that homosexuals do not differ anatomically from heterosexuals (Wolff, 1971).

The present lack of conclusive physiological and chemical evidence does not mean that none will be forthcoming. Many researchers remain convinced (as Freud was) that a genetic or hormonal predisposition toward homosexuality does exist, and that life experiences of the individual serve either to reinforce or extinguish it. A related concept is that of *infantile bisexuality;* this hypothesis states that elements of both masculinity and feminity are present at birth, and that the balance between them is determined by genetic and hormonal factors.

RESEARCH AND THEORY:
PSYCHOLOGICAL FACTORS

A considerable number of psychological hypotheses have been advanced to explain the development and maintenance of homosexuality as the result of an interplay of numerous complex causal factors (Walen et al.,

210 Sexual Disorders

1977). Much of the literature, however, also suggests that early learning plays a critical role in the etiology of homosexuality.

Psychoanalytic Formulations

According to Freud (1910), the newborn infant is polymorphously perverse; that is, the infant's sexuality is totally undifferentiated and is therefore directed toward all sorts of objects, both appropriate and inappropriate. As the child matures into an adult, sexuality is increasingly directed toward members of the opposite sex. Therefore, according to Freud, homosexuals are fixated at an immature state of psychosexual development.

1. *The autoerotic phase of development partially persists and objects cathexis is partially accomplished, but on a narcissistic level.* As a consequence, the individual seeks a love object representing himself, who therefore necessarily has to possess the same genitalia. The individual is thus sexually involved with himself and his own genitalia in the form of another individual who symbolizes himself (Fenichel, 1945).

2. *Mental attitudes that exist during the phallic phase.* At this stage, sexual impulses formerly expressed through other zones and instincts now become organized, so that the penis becomes the principal organ of discharge and pleasure (London & Caprio, 1950). The boy begins to place enormous value on the male organ as the chief executor of sexual function. As a result of earlier experiences with deprivation of other sources of pleasure, an unconscious fear of the loss of the prized organ develops during this phallic phase. When the male child discovers the absence of the penis in the female, this knowledge confirms the fear that the penis can be lost or removed. Females are consequently avoided to prevent the arousal of castration anxiety, and are devalued because of their lack of narcissistically overvalued male genitalia (Fenichel, 1945).

3. *Difficulties associated with the Oedipus phase.* A second type of castration anxiety fostering homosexuality is associated with unconscious incestuous feelings for the mother, later transferred to all women. The castration anxiety in this context derives from fear of retaliation for wishes to castrate the father who is perceived as a sexual rival for the mother (Fenichel, 1945).

Many analysts believe that sexual practices in the homosexual relationship symbolize regressions to developmental fixation points. For instance, if there is an anal fixation, the individual may identify with his mother and then attempt to play the mother's role through the symbolic equation of the anus with the vagina. On the other hand, if there is stronger identification with the father, the homosexual may subject other males to passive roles in sexual activities, roles that symbolically transform these men into females and at the same time covertly expresses hostility toward them as males (London & Caprio, 1950). Homosexuality, therefore, becomes one way of coping with rivalry with the father while at the same time gratifying sexual wishes.

Bieber (1962) investigated the families of 106 male homosexuals and 100 male heterosexuals, all of whom were in psychoanalysis, and reported that the families of homosexuals were characterized by a dominant mother and a weak or passive father. The mother was both overly protective and overly intimate. Bieber thus originated the concept of the "homoseductive mother" as an explanation of male homosexuality. The structure of the homosexual's family, according to Bieber, has a twofold effect: the man as an adult fears heterosexual activity both because of his mother's jealous possessiveness, and because her seductiveness produced heterosexual anxiety. Bieber (1976) also described the homosexual's relationship with his father as seriously disturbed. The fathers were described as detached or openly hostile; thus the son matured into adulthood hating and fearing his father, yet deeply desiring the father's love and affection.

Wolff (1971) conducted a similar program of research on the development of lesbianism. She studied over 100 nonpatient lesbians, comparing them with a control group of heterosexual women matched for family, profession, background, and social class. The most prominent family characteristics among lesbian women which were seldom seen in heterosexual women's families were a rejecting or indifferent mother and a distant or absent father. Wolff hypothesized that lesbianism therefore results from the girl's receiving inadequate love from the mother; as a result, she continues to seek the missing love in other women. Secondarily, because her father was distant or absent, she may have never learned to relate to men.

Behavioral Formulations

The most generally accepted attempt to formulate a behavioral theory about the development of homosexual behavior in males was made by McGuire et al. (1965) and Gagnon and Simon (1973). The basis of their theory, which is similar to the work of Masters and Johnson (1979), is the important role of sexual arousal and masturbation in shaping sexual behavior. These researchers argue that ejaculation or orgasm resulting from masturbation is the critical reinforcing event for conditioning stimuli accompanying or preceding masturbation. Thus, sexual preference for same-sex partners, as opposed to opposite-sex partners, may be determined by the nature of the initial sexual experience, which may or may not include orgasm. If it is regarded as positive, the experience is then used in fantasy as a method of eliciting sexual arousal as well as in masturbation. Thus, the learning experience involves an early sexual encounter intensified by fantasy and maintained and reinforced through cognitive rehearsal and masturbatory orgasm. If a second similar sexual encounter is experienced, the conditioning process is further strengthened and intensified. It is thought that various predisposing factors, such as inappropriate gender identification, inadequate heterosocial/sexual relationships, aversion to heterosexual stimuli for example, and so on, serve to facilitate the likelihood of homosexual conditioning in males.

Societal norms may also play an important role in the development of female homosexuality. Gagnon and Simon (1973) claim that while most males begin to masturbate and seek to actively explore sexual activities during early adolescence, this period is for most females a profoundly nonsexual period, both in the sense of sexual fantasy and overt sexual activity. Thus, while the sexual orientation and patterns of sexual behavior in males are being determined through masturbation and sexual experimentation, the female is learning patterns of behavior that are only indirectly related to sexual orientation. Gagnon and Simon (1973) claim that this is the result of the fact that society permits opportunities for the young male to learn and perform sexual activities which are not provided the early adolescent female. Consequently, the young girl's attention is centered on indirect sexual activities through stimuli such as romantic novels and movies in which sexual elements are presented in the context of legitimizing emotional circumstances, as, for instance, a couple deeply in love. Gagnon and Simon (1973) therefore claim that while sexual orientation in the male may result from early sexual experiences and masturbatory fantasies, the development of female homosexuality is more likely to result from strong emotional ties between two women that precede sexual activity.

CASE HISTORY 6-1

The patient was a 22-year-old single male who came into treatment for his depression and unhappiness over his homosexual orientation. The patient had previously lived with several male sexual partners for varying lengths of time, but when he contacted us was living with his mother and father and attending graduate school.

A sexual history revealed that the patient's initial sexual experience occurred at the age of 13 years when, after a school club social at the home of a male teacher, he was seduced by the adult. The patient reported that he had few friends and was quite naive concerning sexuality during this time, and that he became very strongly attracted to the teacher who demonstrated masturbation techniques for him. The patient's relationship with his teacher lasted approximately six months and was characterized by mutual masturbation, fellatio, and anal intercourse. The patient reported that during this time he began masturbating daily to homosexual fantasies and explicit homosexual magazines given to him by the teacher.

When the patient was approximately 15 years old he became involved in a homosexual relationship with an older youth he met working a part-time job after school. This relationship involved the patient's fellating the older youth and allowing the partner to engage in anal intercourse with him. The patient reported that the older youth was clearly the dominant partner in the relationship, and that he refused to fellate, masturbate, or assist the patient in reaching orgasm in any way. The patient would, therefore, masturbate himself to orgasm after serving as a sexual partner for the older youth.

When the patient was a freshman in college he became active in a campus homosexual organization and became sexually involved with a number of males. By his senior year in college he was an elected officer in the organization. He claimed he was not happy with his sexual orientation, and desired treatment to alter his sexual preference.

This case history emphasizes the role of postive sexual experiences in shaping homosexual orientation. Behavior therapists also pay attention to the important role of negative sexual experiences in the development of a particular pattern of sexual behavior. If heterosexual activity takes place under aversive or negative conditions, one might expect an alternative sexual expression to emerge.

CASE HISTORY 6-2

The patient was an attractive 20-year-old female referred after an attempted suicide. The patient reported that she had become progressively more depressed as a result of her homosexual orientation until she took an overdose of Tofranil. During the sexual history the patient reported the following story.

By the age of 15 the patient was physically mature and popular with male classmates; but she had resisted all forms of sexual activity. Finally, afraid that further resistance to the sexual advances of an older college male would mark the end of their relationship, she engaged in sexual intercourse with the youth. Her boyfriend, totally unskilled in sexual activities himself, fumbled roughly and painfully through a short period of foreplay. Determined to go through with what she had thought would be a pleasurable experience, she said nothing and allowed him to undress her in the backseat of his automobile. After she has naked, he quickly undressed from the waist down, mounted, and made some forceful thrusts. The combination of her virginity, improper lubrication, and his crude and rough technique made her cry out in pain. After five or six painful thrusts, he ejaculated, got off her, and dressed. Disgusted and nauseated from the painful experience, she vomited, then wept until he took her home.

The next week was spent in ruminating about her first sexual experience; she felt disgusted and bitter. At this time, her parents made a trip out of town and hired a recently widowed female to stay with the patient. The two women became friends almost immediately. Late the first night the conversation between the women turned to the topic of sex. The patient carefully questioned the older woman about heterosexual intercourse, and then, breaking into tears, blurted out the entire story of her recent sexual adventure. The woman spent the next hour holding the patient and comforting her. The close physical contact and warm reassurance provided by the woman eased much of the distress. Later that night the patient participated in her second sexual experience. This time, however, instead of a painful, hurried, frustrating, and disgusting experience, she enjoyed a session of long, luxurious, gentle lovemaking with her female friend. The patient soon quit dating and heterosocial activities altogether, preferring instead to spend her evenings with her new companion or masturbating to the fantasy of their last homosexual activity.

Thus far we have considered homosexual behavior that results from early sexual experiences, either positive or negative, which are then strengthened and maintained through repeated homosexual contacts and masturbatory orgasm. This formulation does not, however, explain why a functioning heterosexual individual may change his/her preference for sexual partners at some later point in life.

Feldman and MacCulloch (1971) proposed a theory to explain this type of phenomenon. They suggested that some individuals may encounter both pleasant homosexual experiences and unpleasant heterosexual experiences. If such a combination of experiences occurs to individuals who have a tendency to incubate unpleasant experiences, the outcome is likely to be a gradual shifting, through the process of a reduction in cognitive dissonance, from a heterosexual orientation to a homosexual orientation.

Another explanation may be that these individuals were homosexual in orientation all the while but were sexually active with both males and females. It has been proposed that homosexuals are often capable of achieving an erection and engaging in heterosexual intercourse. This performance, however, may be due to the fact that they fantasize during it that they are engaging in anal intercourse with a male (Craighead et al., 1976; Tollison et al., 1977). The female homosexual does not have to worry about an obvious sexual dysfunction when engaging in heterosexual activity; all she has to do is fake effective heterosexual functioning.

Eysenck and Rachman (1966) states that no one etiological theory of homosexuality has yet emerged as better than any other. A useful research strategy might be to begin a prospective long-term behavioral study as soon after conception as possible. Such a study could relate maternal prenatal circulating hormonal levels to the development of postnatal sexual and sex-linked behaviors; it might also look at the sociosexual experiences of both sexes of developing infants and attempt to relate the development and direction of sexual interests over several years to the form and outcome of such behavioral experiences. The first set of data would be concerned with the development of the primary type of homosexual, the second set with the secondary type. Other useful studies might relate both these areas of research to the social setting of the developing child and adolescent, and particularly to the nature of the reinforcements provided by parents and other significant persons for the display of sexual and sex-typed behaviors—that is, behaviors considered appropriate or inappropriate by society in general for the morphological sex.

MODIFICATION OF HOMOSEXUAL BEHAVIOR

Many clinicians who treat homosexuals define treatment success as altering a homosexual orientation to a heterosexual one. This yardstick of success gives us few cures. Katchadourian and Lunde (1972) reported several reasons for the poor success rate in the traditional psychotherapeutic treatment of homosexuality.

First, many homosexuals do not consider themselves abnormal or sick and do not seek treatment. When they do come to clinical psychologists or psychiatrists for problems of anxiety or depression, they may pay lip service to the need to resolve their "sexual problems" without any real intention of changing their orientation. What they want is relief of their symptoms. Whether or not such distress is inherent in homosexuality or results from the pressures experienced as a member of an illegal minority are open questions. Certainly a number of homosexuals develop difficulties such as depression and anxiety for the same reasons that heterosexuals do (Green, 1972).

A small number of homosexuals are arrested and forced to undergo treatment by court order, either in state institutions or as a condition of probation. These individuals are normally not forced directly by the court to undergo treatment, but they are frequently encouraged to do so by their lawyers on the basis of "either undergo treatment or go to jail." These individuals are seldom motivated to change their sexual orientation; what they will do occasionally is to play along in order to satisfy the law.

Traditional psychotherapeutic techniques do not usually change sexual orientation because these procedures can neither break the chain of reinforcing behaviors nor substitute an alternate repertoire of appropriate heterosexual behaviors and skills. Psychotherapeutic attempts are based on gaining insight into the idea that some children for various reasons do not outgrow and repress these infantile tendencies. But insight or knowledge does not necessarily alter behavior.

Chemotherapy

In the 1940s when sex hormones were first synthesized there was much interest taken in possible relationships between hormonal levels in blood and urine and sexual orientation. Recently, however, hormones have been shown to have only limited value in the treatment of homosexuals; they have never been shown to change the direction of a patient's sexual orientation, only the strength of his/her sexual urge and desire. Androgen is an enhancer of the sex drive for both sexes; consequently it may possibly increase homosexual behavior. Estrogen functionally lowers the sex drive and may decrease sexual initiation and activity; however, usefulness in treating male homosexuality is limited by its side effects of breast growth and related secondary sexual characteristic changes.

Psychoanalysis

To the psychoanalyst, homosexuality is considered psychopathological (Bieber, 1962). It is inevitable, therefore, that a great deal of attention has been given to the treatment of homosexuality.

Jones (1964) quotes Freud on the prognosis for treatment of homosexuality by psychoanalysis: "In a certain number of cases we succeed . . . in the majority of cases it is no longer possible . . . the result of our treatment cannot be predicted." (p. 22) Rubenstein (1958) agrees that analysis can help in a fair number of cases, often beyond the original expectation, yet the prognosis in general is poor. Mintz (1966) studied 10 male homosexuals who voluntarily entered psychoanalysis and remained in therapy for a total of two or more years. Results indicated that three of the subjects reportedly showed "satisfactory heterosexual adjustment," three subjects "hope to achieve satisfactory heterosexual adjustment," and four subjects showed no progress. The author does not define, however, what is meant by "satisfactory heterosexual adjustment."

Group Therapy

Modification of homosexual behavior has also been attempted by various group therapies. Mintz (1966), in fact, claims that group therapy has important advantages over one-to-one psychotherapeutic modalities in that it promotes (1) dissolution of rationalization about homosexuality; (2) development of a stronger sense of personal identity through contact with women and heterosexual men; (3) emergence of unconscious anxieties related to heterosexual drives; and (4) corrective emotional experiences which often result in enhanced self-esteem.

Hadden (1966), in a study of the treatment of male homosexuals in group therapy, expressed a belief that if therapists themselves adopted a less pessimistic attitude toward homosexuality and viewed it simply as a pattern of maladaption, greater numbers of homosexual individuals might be helped. In this study, private weekly sessions of approximately 1–1.5 hours were conducted with groups of four to eight patients. Groups were categorized in terms of age, intellectual level, economic background, and motivation for treatment. According to the experimenter, of 32 patients, 12 "have progressed to an exclusively heterosexual pattern of adjustment and have shown marked improvement in, or disappearance of, other neurotic traits" (p. 22). The lack of experimental control and the fact that the author admits the groups are "open-ended" in that they continue indefinitely tend to vitiate the experimental results.

Behavior Therapy

Homosexuality is not a unidimensional phenomenon; thus the goal of sexual reorientation procedures is not merely the elimination of homosexual preferences. In an appropriate modification procedure there should also be a program to teach adaptive forms of sexual behavior. As previously mentioned, Barlow (1974) has indicated that there may be four components to deviant sexual behavior. First, the arousal pattern itself may be directed toward inappropriate objects and/or may be excessive and maladaptive for the individual. In addition, the deviant arousal may also be accompanied by deficits in heterosexual arousal, heterosocial skills, and/or deviations in gender role behavior. The presence of deviant sexual arousal may or may not be accompanied by deficits in the other three areas of sexual behavior. Only a comprehensive and systematic assessment of each case will allow the clinician to determine this.

After a comprehensive sexual assessment to determine the deficiencies and excesses of each behavioral component, a treatment strategy based upon objective evidence should be offered to the patient. A knowledge of the critical components of behavior techniques for reorientation which have been employed with homosexual behavior in the past should allow clinicians better to utilize the data that have been collected within this area.

The first step in the behavioral treatment of homosexuality is extinction of the deviant sexual arousal. As previously noted, aversion therapy has been the most commonly employed behavioral treatment for eliminating homosexual behavior (Wilson & Davison, 1974).

The most complete description of a methodology of aversion therapy with homosexuals has been described by Feldman and MacCulloch (1971) who refer to the procedure as *anticipatory avoidance*. Larson (1970) and Tanner (1975) reported the successful use of this procedure. Tanner (1975) also compared homosexual patients receiving electrical aversion booster sessions with homosexual patients who were treated in an avoidance training paradigm but did not receive booster sessions. Self-report measures, physiological data, and behavioral recordings were used to assess treatment progress. The results indicated that the treatment was successful in modifying erectile responses, preferred sex object, sexual fantasies, frequency of homosexual and heterosexual behaviors, and patterns of socializing. No significant improvement was noted in the treatment-plus-booster-sessions group relative to the treatment-only group.

Covert sensitization has also been employed in the treatment of homosexual behavior. Covert sensitization involves an imagined noxious event paired with an imaginal approach behavior. Cautela (1967) reported using the following scenes with homosexual patients:

> I want you to imagine you are in a room with X. He is completely naked. As you approach him you notice he has sores and scabs all over his body, with some kind of fluid oozing from them. A terrible foul stench comes from his body. The odor is so strong it makes you sick. You can feel food particles coming up in your throat. You cannot help yourself and you vomit all over the place, all over the floor, on your hands and clothes. And now that makes you even sicker and you vomit again and again all over everything. You turn away and you start to feel better. You try to get out of the room, but the door seems to be locked. The smell is still strong as you try desperately to get out of the room. You kick at the door frantically until it finally opens and you run out into the nice clean air. It smells wonderful. You go home and shower and you feel so clean.

Maletzky and George (1973) employed a variation of covert sensitization using scenes of vomiting, nausea, contact with feces, urine, or insects, and vile odors, combined with the actual (not imagined) smell of valeric acid. As each scene progressed and the patient escaped from the imagined homosexual behavior, the odor was removed and suggestions of calm were presented. This investigation was unique in the measurement devices used: (1) self-recordings of the frequency of homosexual and heterosexual covert and overt behaviors; (2) an observer's (friend, wife, parent) recordings of the frequency of suspicions of homosexual behavior; and (3) a homosexual approach to the patient by a "solicitor" employed by the experimenters at the end of treatment and a 12-month followup. The authors claimed that 9 or 10 patients were treated successfully.

Since the most important predictor of successful treatment of homosexual behavior is a history of heterosexual experience (Feldman & MacCulloch, 1971), the clinician should gather a detailed history of prior heterosexual fantasy, arousal, and activity. If the patient has virtually no history of heterosexual experiences (primary homosexuality), the components of the deficit should be explored. Frequently, a phobic element of avoidance is present which may relate, for example, to fear of rejection or fear of female genitalia. For such patients, systematic desensitization may be necessary. Huff (1970) reported a hierarchy used successfully to reduce heterosexual anxiety (Table 6-1).

The purpose of systematic desensitization is to reduce the negative valence of approaches to the opposite sex, but it must be emphasized that although this may be an important and necessary treatment component, it is certainly not sufficient. Systematic desensitization is often critical in eliminating inhibitions of heterosexual arousal, but serves only as a prerequisite to enhancing heterosexual arousal.

The clinician may choose among a number of techniques which enhance heterosexual arousal. The selection of a particular procedure should be predicated on the availability of special equipment and the data obtained in the sexual assessment. Treatment choices include classical conditioning, operant techniques, and aversion relief.

In the *classical conditioning* model, the goal of treatment is to increase heterosexual arousal by repeatedly pairing an unconditioned stimulus (UCS) with a neutral stimulus until it, too, is capable of eliciting a similar response (Walen et al., 1977). The neutral stimulus is normally a picture, movie, or fantasy of a female which is paired with another visual stimulus evocative of arousal (Rachman & Hodgson, 1968), arousal short of orgasm (Rachman, 1966), or masturbation or orgasm (Davison, 1968). In many of these studies the pictures or fantasies to which the patient masturbates are progressively sequenced to approximate the desired sexual behavior.

TABLE 6-1

Anxiety Hierarchy to Intimacy with Women

16 Girl moves while penis inserted
15 Places penis in vagina
14 Girl touches penis
13 Nude, lying on top of girl
12 Nude, lying beside girl
11 Touching girl's mons, pubic hair
10 Feeling girl's legs and thighs
 9 Fondling girl's breasts
 8 Kissing girl on lips
 7 Kissing girl on forehead
 6 Looking into girl's eyes, tilting head up
 5 Hugging a girl
 4 Putting arms around girl
 3 Holding hands with a girl
 2 Having a conversation with a girl alone
 1 Having conversation with several girls

Source: Huff, F. W. The desensitization of a homosexual. *Behavior Research and Therapy*, 1970, *8*, 99-102. Reprinted with permission of Pergamon Press.

Freeman and Mayer (1975) reported an interesting classical conditioning paradigm which involved pairing heterosexual pictures with homosexual slides and masturbation activities. Homosexual arousal was first eliminated by means of electrical aversion which, of course, was not administered during presentation of heterosexual slides. Self-monitoring and penile responsivity were considered as dependent measures. Results indicated that seven of nine subjects maintained an exclusive heterosexual orientation for 18 months following treatment, and all subjects did so for one year. Of particular importance in this study was the fact that all six "primary" homosexuals achieved a heterosexual orientation for a year, and four of the six maintained the preference at 18-month followup.

Operant technique such as shaping and fading are often used to gradually enhance penile erections to heterosexual stimuli. As in classical conditioning paradigms, operant techniques require that the patient exhibit arousal first to homosexual stimuli which is then gradually transferred to heterosexual stimuli.

Shaping with feedback has been used to gradually establish penile erection to heterosexual stimuli (Herman & Prewitt, 1974; Quinn et al., 1970). Quinn et al. employed an operant shaping procedure to increase penile responsiveness to heterosexual stimuli in the treatment of a 28-year-old male homosexual. Of particular interest in this case was that previous treatment with anticipatory avoidance conditioning and systematic desensitization had been unsuccessful with the patient. The subject was deprived of liquids for a period of time; subsequently, increased episodes of sexual arousal to heterosexual stimuli were reinforced with sips of iced lime. Results revealed increased heterosexual interest and arousal although there were no changes in homosexual patterns.

Fading in images of heterosexual stimuli superimposed upon pictures of homosexual stimuli is a technique commonly employed to promote heterosexual arousal (Barlow & Agras, 1973; McCrady, 1973). Barlow and Agras employed a fading procedure with one primary and two secondary homosexuals. A slide of a nude female was superimposed on the slide of a nude male. As long as the patient maintained at least a 75 percent erection, as measured by a strain gauge, the brightness of the female slide was gradually increased. The results indicated that heterosexual arousal increased in all three patients while homosexual arousal was unchanged. No change in sexual practices was reported.

McCrady (1973) demonstrated that a reverse order of the fading procedure can also be employed. He began by projecting a female slide which gradually faded out as a superimposed male slide was faded in. During the course of treatment, measured erections occurred earlier in the fading sequence. McCrady (1973) maintained that the reverse fading procedure was more useful than that of Barlow and Argas since the patient did not need to begin by achieving an erection, and less expensive equipment was needed since precise penile circumferential measures were not essential.

Aversion relief therapy involves pairing a heterosexual stimulus with relief from a noxious stimulus, thereby producing a decrease in the avoidance of the heterosexual stimulus. Heterosexual relief stimuli have been pictorial, such as slides of nude females (Larson, 1970), or verbal, such as words or phrases (Gaupp et al., 1971).

Bancroft (1969) administered electrical shock contingent upon penile arousal to homosexual fantasies and slides with a group of ten homosexual subjects. As a variation, three subjects were administered shock contingent upon penile arousal resulting from homosexual fantasy alone. An aversion relief paradigm resulted in a reduction of homosexual interest in five of the subjects and reductions in homosexual behavior in four subjects at followup. This success was accompanied by increases in both heterosexual interest and behavior in seven and four individuals, respectively. One-third of the subjects showed significant and lasting improvements at the one-year followup, while 50 percent exhibited a diminished interest in homosexual activity.

An important goal in the treatment of homosexual behavior is the extinction of deviant sexual arousal and enhancement of heterosexual arousal; the long-term goal of behavioral sexual reorientation techniques is an adequate and appropriate heterosexual adjustment outside the clinic or office. In other words, while sexual arousal is an important component of sexual reorientation therapy, so too are appropriate gender role behaviors, heterosocial skills, and heterosexual skills. As noted, assessment and intervention of all four major components of sexual behavior are essential in successful sexual reorientation therapy (Barlow, 1977). Techniques to modify inadequate or inappropriate gender role behavior, heterosocial, and heterosexual skills have been discussed above in Chapter 3.

Conclusions

In clinical practice the multicomponent treatment techniques for sexual reorientation are recommended, particularly when a systematic and thorough behavioral assessment indicates deficiencies in more than one area of behavior. In our clinical experience both electrical aversion and covert sensitization seem to be effective procedures in eliminating deviant sexual arousal, although on occasion we have found it necessary to follow covert sensitization with several sessions of electrical aversion in order to completely eliminate the unwanted arousal pattern. Perhaps this piggybacking of treatment techniques may be unneccessary with assisted covert sensitization procedures in which powerful noxious odors are paired with verbally described scenes including nausea (Maletzky, 1974, 1977). The enhancement of heterosexual arousal may be attempted through a number of techniques, although we have found a combination of exposure and masturbation training to be useful. In fact, it is frequently helpful to supply the patient with heterosexual masturbatory stimuli such as magazines or books, to assist in masturbation training. Occasionally the enhancement of heterosexual arousal in a homosexual patient is inhibited because anxiety associated with heterosexuality may reach phobic proportions. We have noted that a number of male homosexuals in treatment find female breasts repulsive, particularly large breasts. Systematic desensitization to the physical characteristics of the opposite sex followed by *in-vivo* desensitization should prove effective in eliminating these inhibitions of arousal.

Primary homosexuals and a number of secondary homosexuals frequently demonstrate deficits in heterosocial skills which may impair their ability to meet and interact with opposite-sexed partners. As a consequence, many homosexual patients need training in heterosocial skills in order to set the stage for potential heterosexual involvement. We have found response practice with a variety of opposite-sexed partners and videotaped role playing to be effective teaching techniques. Finally, the cooperation and assistance of a opposite-sexed partner is obviously invaluable in the successful reorientation of homosexual patients.

CASE HISTORY 6-3

The patient was a 22-year-old male undergraduate senior referred by the patient's family physician. During the initial interview the patient reported his homosexual preference and requested treatment to change his sexual orientation. A lengthy sexual history revealed that the patient's first sexual experience (homosexual in nature) occurred at the age of 13. This early experience was followed by a series of homosexual encounters with a variety of partners. During high school and college he occasionally dated various females in an effort to conceal his homosexual orientation, but these heterosexual activities never involved sexual or romantic contact. The patient was involved in a steady homosexual relationship during his last two years of high school and first year of college with a male who lived in a nearby city. This relationship was described as purely sexual in nature. The partners met at a motel once or twice each week to engage in secret sexual activities. The patient reported feeling disgusted with himself during this time and was constantly concerned with different ways he might control his homosexual preference. He reported driving over a hundred miles once or twice each month during his college career to a city to purchase explicit homosexual magazines and to attend X-rated gay movies. He was invariably approached by other patrons at the movie and would end up engaging in sexual activities in the darkened theater, an automobile, or a motel room.

The patient's heterosexual history involved four attempts at coitus, two of which were marginally successful. During his sophomore year at college he dated a "sexually aggressive" female several times in an effort to conceal his homosexual orientation. On the second date the female initiated sexual activity which lead to the patient's unsuccessful attempt at intercourse. Several days later the female again initiated sexual activity, and the patient discovered he could achieve and maintain an erection sufficient for penetration and coitus through homosexual fantasy. Although he was unable to ejaculate, he was successful in maintaining an erection in this manner on two occasions. His fourth and final attempt at heterosexual intercourse was unsuccessful even with homosexual fantasy. The patient reported little or no pleasure from his heterosexual experiences.

The patient reported at the time of the initial interview that he was presently dating a woman whom he cared for a great deal. This relationship had existed for approximately five months prior to his seeking treatment, but the patient had not allowed the relationship to progress further than kissing and fondling her breasts. Although he received little sexual satisfaction from these activities, he felt it was "expected" of him, and he did enjoy her company.

We informed the patient that he should reconsider his decision to change his sexual orientation for two weeks; then if he was still interested then he should call again. He was encouraged to contact a local chapter of Gay Lib to discuss the situation; however, he refused because he was afraid they would not keep it confidential. Exactly two weeks later the patient called to schedule an appointment. Another lengthy interview satisfied us that the patient was sincere in his desire to alter his sexual preference and was aware of the consequences of such action. An appointment for a sexual assessment was scheduled for the following week. The patient was instructed to begin monitoring and charting his sexual urges, both homosexual and heterosexual. We advised the patient of the assessment procedure and answered all his questions.

After the patient had agreed to the assessment he was taken to a private sound-resistant, temperature-controlled laboratory equipped with a standard hospital bed, Kodak movie screen, and an intercom system. The patient was given instructions on how to place the penile strain gauge midway between the scrotum and glans; and left alone to place it and make himself comfortable in bed. We informed the patient via intercom that his penile responses would be monitored on a polygraph for 15–20 minutes while he got used to the environment. After this adaptation period the patient was asked to masturbate himself to a point just short of ejaculation, a point that, measured on the polygraph, was considered a 100 percent erection. When the patient told us he had successfully completed this task, he was allowed to rest so that his penile response could return to baseline. A minimum of three minutes of stable penile baseline response was monitored before the presentation of the sexual stimuli. The order of presentation employed was to alternate homosexual stimuli (films, slides, and literature) and heterosexual stimuli (films, slides, and literature). Each sexual stimulus was presented for four minutes; neutral stimuli were presented between every two sexual stimuli to allow detumescence and rest. For example, a typical order of presentation was:

1. Four minute slide of nude female
2. Neutral slide until detumescence was stable for four minutes
3. Four minute homosexual film
4. Neutral film until detumescence was stable for four minutes
5. Four minute presentation of heterosexual literature

6. Neutral film until detumescence was stable for four minutes
7. Four minute slide of nude males
8. Neutral slide until detumescence was stable for four minutes
9. Four minute presentation of homosexual literature
10. Neutral literature presentation until detumescence was stable for four minutes
11. Four minutes heterosexual film

Upon termination of each sexual stimulus the patient was requested to estimate his percentage of erection and his estimate of the percentage of cognitive arousal to the preceding stimulus. This allowed us to compare the patient's percentage of erection with his estimated percentage of erection, as well as to compare the estimated percentage of cognitive arousal with measured percentage of erection.

Assessment of sexual preference revealed a homosexual orientation. The patient's penile response was approximately 70–80 percent erect during the homosexual film, 60–65 percent erect in response to the homosexual slide, and 60–70 percent erect in response to the homosexual literature. This compared to the patient's penile response of approximately 10–20 percent erect to the heterosexual film, 0–10 percent to the heterosexual slide, and 5–10 percent erect to the heterosexual literature.

Twelve sessions of electrical aversion relief were administered to the patient over a four-week period. The patient was instructed to cease all sexual activity during this time, including masturbation. Each session involved the patient's viewing homosexual magazines and films while penile responses were monitored via a strain gauge. The administration of electrical aversion was varied throughout each session so that the patient was unsure when he would receive the shock. The administration of shock was followed immediately by the presentation of heterosexual stimuli in an effort to associate heterosexual stimuli with the relief from shock. The homosexual and heterosexual stimuli used were changed each session in order to prevent the patients habituating to the sexual stimuli.

By the end of the eighth treatment session, penile response and self-report assessment revealed little sexual arousal to homosexual stimuli. We next instituted masturbation training and instructed the patient to masturbate to heterosexual material and fantasy. A variety of heterosexual stimuli were made available to the patient to assist in masturbation training, including heterosexually oriented magazines, books, and films.

The patient was successful in gradually fading in heterosexual stimuli into his masturbatory fantasies. During this time he reported only occasional homosexual urges. Monitoring and charting of sexual urges six weeks into treatment revealed a drastic change in the number of homosexual and heterosexual urges. Heterosexual urges were numerous; homosexual urges were infrequent. A second sexual assessment was conducted seven weeks into treatment. The physiological indices of penile response supported the patient's self-reported cessation of homosexual urges.

Behavior change was targeted primarily toward change of sexual orientation, increased heterosocial skills, and increased heterosexual arousal, since the patient exhibited no inappropriate gender behaviors and demonstrated no anxiety and/or fear of women. Assessment of heterosocial skills revealed a slight deficit which was quickly modified via interactional skills training.

The patient followed with several reports of successful heterosexual coitus with his steady girlfriend. Three-month followup revealed a continuation of treatment gains and increased heterosexual arousal and desire. Six-month followup revealed that the patient's steady relationship had broken off. However, the patient was dating several different women and had engaged in sexual activity with two females with no reported difficulty. The patient reported being pleased with his life. He was looking forward to graduation, and claimed he had experienced no further homosexual urges or behaviors.

CASE HISTORY 6-4

The patient was a 35-year-old male referred by his minister. During the initial interview the patient reported his homosexual orientation and admitted having been arrested several months before for homosexual solicitation; he had been sentenced to three months probation. He claimed that he had been unhappy for several years with his sexual orientation and that his recent arrest had no bearing on his desire to alter his sexual preference. The patient also reported that he had never had a long-term homosexual relationship with any male, preferring instead impersonal sexual activity with partners contacted at bars and parties. He had his first homosexual experience at the age of 15, followed by a series of one-night homosexual affairs. He reported his first heterosexual experience at the age of 23 with a woman he later married. Sexual activity between the couple was described as approximately once per month with homosexual fantasies enabling the patient to achieve and maintain an erection sufficient for intercourse. The two-year marriage ended in divorce soon after the patient admitted his homosexual orientation to the suspicious wife. At the time of the initial interview the patient estimated his frequency of homosexual activity at approximately twice weekly. The patient was encouraged to reconsider his request for reorientation for two weeks, and to contact a local Gay Lib chapter for counseling; he agreed he would call us in two weeks with his decision.

Several weeks later the patient informed our office that he remained firm in his decision to reorient his sexual preference. He was therefore requested to begin charting his daily sexual urges and advised to halt all sexual behavior until instructed differently. A physiological assessment was conducted which substantiated the patient's homosexual orientation. The assessment also identified as particularly arousing those stimuli depicting or describing anal intercourse with a male. Assessment of heterosocial skills indicated significant deficits in interactional style, initiation behavior, and conversational content.

Treatment was first aimed at the elimination of deviant sexual arousal. Covert sensitization describing scenes such as "being defecated upon while attempting anal penetration," and "contracting genitourinary infections as a result of anal intercourse as well as veneral disease of the mouth as a result of fellatio" were presented to the patient a total of 46 times during a three-week period. The scenes were altered periodically to avoid his habituating to the descriptions. A physiological assessment conducted at this point indicated only slight sexual arousal to homosexual stimuli (average 10 percent of full erection), and a moderate increase in arousal to heterosexual stimuli although the enhancement of heterosexual arousal had not been specifically attempted. We next introduced masturbation training in which the patient was requested to masturbate only to heterosexual material and fantasy; we also started instruction in heterosocial skills. Skills training consisted of modeling and response practice with female secretaries and students in clinical training. Each practice session was videotaped and replayed to the patient at the end of the session for review and critique. As the patient became more proficient in heterosocial skills we encouraged him to begin initiating conversations with women outside the clinic. During the next several weeks the patient reported increased heterosexual arousal (verified by a third physiological assessment), and continuation of heterosocial interaction practice; however, he had had no success in achieving a date. We feared that prolonged sexual abstinence, combined with a discouraging lack of success in meeting and dating women might lead the patient to resort to a homosexual encounter; we therefore reinstated heterosocial skills training on a more intensive basis. Two weeks later the patient was able to get a date, and was soon dating several different girls. Not long afterward he reported successful and pleasurable sexual activity with one of them and three and six months followups indicated a continuation of treatment gains.

EFFICACY OF BEHAVIORAL REORIENTATION PROCEDURES

Between the first use of behavioral techniques to modify sexual preference in 1960 and 1976, 13 group studies and 24 case studies (Table 6-2) have been conducted designed to alter one or more characteristics of sexual preference in over 350 homosexuals (Adams & Sturgis, 1977). These studies differ considerably in the degree to which the experimenter attempted to control for extraneous variables. Only 54 percent of the group studies and 46 percent of the case studies included some control variables. In general, those studies that employed an uncontrolled design indicate that changes in sexual orientation did occur; however, there is no way to isolate the active treatment ingredient, or even determine that the treatment techniques were indeed responsible for the behavior change. Unfortunately, even the controlled single case and group studies noted in this literature are characterized by a lack of experimental rigor and appropriate controls.

Adams and Sturgis compared the results of behavioral treatment procedures with homosexuals and found that 72 percent of patients in the group studies and 85 percent of patients in single case studies showed significant improvement in at least one homosexual target behavior. The current status of sexual reorientation procedures as clinical techniques for modifying sexual preference is not overwhelmingly positive; nonetheless, there are indications that, as the level of sophistication of the conceptualizations and treatment procedures rises, more significant results are achieved. In particular, the reduction of homosexual arousal and behavior is not seen as only one component of an effective treatment program. Multicomponent treatment techniques are recommended for clinical practice, particularly when the patient has obvious deficiencies in more than one area of behavior. Such techniques should increase the likelihood that, when therapeutic gains are made, the patient will be able to maintain them.

TABLE 6-2

Summary of Experimental Findings in Sexual Reorientation Literature

Variable	Uncontrolled group		Controlled group		Uncontrolled single case		Controlled single case		Total	
	n	%	*n*	%	*n*	%	*n*	%	*n*	%
Studies	6		7		13		11		37	
Assessment										
Self-report	6	100	5	71	8	62	6	55	25	68
Physiological	2	33	5	71	2	15	7	64	16	43
Behavioral	4	67	5	71	8	62	9	82	26	70
Targeted behavior										
Homosexual arousal	6	100	7	100	10	72	7	64	30	81
Heterosexual arousal	6	100	7	100	11	85	8	73	32	86
Social skill	0	0	0	0	2	15	3	27	5	14
Two or more targeted	6	100	7	100	7	54	5	45	35	68
Three or more targeted	0	0	0	0	1	8	1	9	2	5
Follow-up										
Average (mo.)	18.5		16.5		10.6		14.4			
Percentage followed up		100		50		36		58		
Subjects	124		179		23		24		350	
Primary	*		*		8	35	≤11		*	
Secondary	*		*		15	65	≥13		*	
Coital	*		*		10	43	≥8	36	*	
Outcome										
Homosexual urge	62	50	≥61	34	18	78	14	58	155	44
Homosexual behavior	52	42	≥33	18	17	74	13	54	115	33
Heterosexual urge	68	55	≥47	26	16	70	17	71	148	42
Heterosexual behavior	61	50	≥14	8	15	65	11	46	101	29
Coitus	46	37	≥5	3	13	57	6	25	70	20
No change	45	36	39	22	2	9	5	21	91	26
Improved	79	64	111	62	21	91	19	79	259	74

*Unable to determine from data presented.

Source: Adams, H. E., & Sturgis, E. T. Status of behavioral reorientation techniques in the modification of homosexuality: A review. *Psychological Bulletin*, 1977, *84*, 1185. Reprinted with permission of the America! Psychological Association.

CHAPTER 7

Voyeurism
and Exhibitionism

Voyeurism and exhibitionism are paraphilias which involve deviations of sexual activity. These orders have two major characteristics. First, sexual gratification is displaced to early components in the chain of sexual responses. "Looking" and "showing" are not unusual, and are part of the sequence of behaviors leading to heterosexual and homosexual coitus. In voyeurism and exhibitionism, however, observing and exposing become focal rather than peripheral activities. Thus, the difference between "normal" and "deviant" is more quantitative than qualitative. Second, both voyeurs and exhibitionists typically avoid sexual partners who voluntarily participate, and prefer instead noncontact sexual activities with nonconsenting partners.

Clinical and research data on voyeurism and exhibitionism remain scarce, but several facts about both behaviors have been observed. The first of these is that both these behaviors are restricted to males. Few cases of female voyeurs or exhibitionists have been reported. The second is that voyeurs and exhibitionists frequently display deficits in heterosocial skills. The third is that masturbation is the crucial element in the sexual activity and plays an important role in the development and maintenance of the deviant behavior. We will describe voyeurism and exhibitionism separately, but since treatment conditions are similar, only one treatment section will be presented.

VOYEURISM

Only the very naive would be surprised to hear that men are usually sexually aroused at the sight of nude or seminude females. As the eleventh-century legend of Lady Godiva and Peeping Tom the Tailor attests, watching females has been a pastime for many years, and for American males it probably ranks equal with sports as an entertainment. In our culture many forms of viewing the nude or seminude female are socially acceptable, or at least marginally so. Men's magazines, topless bars, burlesque shows, and the like may still raise a few conservative eyebrows, but beauty contests continue to thrive; squads of briefly-clad cheerleaders rival the quarterback for the fans' attention in sports arenas all over the country; and braless women or those wearing string bikinis capture the attention of the average male.

Such watching behavior is sometimes referred to as "voyeuristic," but it does not usually constitute a sexual deviation. Indeed, few deny that seeing plays a major role in normal sexual development and enjoyment. As Freud (1905) explained:

> Visual impressions remain the most frequent pathway along which libidinal excitation is aroused; indeed natural selection counts upon the accessibility of this pathway—when it encourages the development of beauty in the sexual object. The progressive concealment of the body which goes along with civilization keeps sexual curiosity awake. (p. 196)

Seeing becomes voyeurism and a sexual deviation (and often a criminal act as well) when it is *preferred* to coitus, when the party being observed does not consent to the observation, and/or when the voyeur risks serious consequences if detected.

Generally speaking, his willingness to run risks is what distinguishes the voyeur from the average girl-watcher. In pursuit of what he prefers to see, a voyeur may cling to narrow window ledges, scale high fences, run from neighbors and police who discover him, or sit patiently for hours. In fact, some clinicians think that the element of risk or danger is sexually exciting to many voyeurs. This desire to take a chance may well explain why voyeurs are generally not attracted to nudists camps, burlesque shows, or other environments in which observing nude bodies is accepted. In such environments most voyeurs do not become sexually aroused. The voyeur wants to see what he is somehow forbidden to see, and must thus wait for an opportunity to peek secretly (Sagarin, 1973).

The following is taken from our files:

Typical of the voyeur's willingness to take risks and wait patiently for a view is a 27-year-old man who was caught spying on women and couples in a small motel. A clerk on the evening shift, he said he took this job in order to put his carefully laid out plan into operation. When alone in the motel office he would use a straightened paper clip to bore holes in the walls separating the motel office from three adjoining guest rooms. He took as long as a month to bore each hole with this primitive tool, being careful that it was small enough not to be detectable. Once his three peep holes were completed he assigned attractive women and couples to these rooms and watched them. When he was finally apprehended he had engaged in the behavior for almost a year, often patiently waiting for hours for a view and running to the different walls to check the view in each of the rooms. When he could see a woman undress or was lucky enough to watch a couple having intercourse, he would masturbate while viewing the arousing scene.

It is our opinion that men who dial a woman, breathe deeply, masturbate, and say nothing while hoping she will talk exhibit characteristics and behaviors similar to voyeurs.

Characteristics of Voyeurs

Convicted voyeurs are almost invariably males; this behavior has been estimated to occur at 9:1 male-female ratio (McCary, 1973). Women may admit to being crotch watchers, but they seldom go to great lengths to peep; it is usually the clothed male crotch that excites fantasy and imagery in these women. Women, as a rule, are not as fascinated or aroused by the sight of male nudity as males are by the sight of female nudity. The women's magazine *Playgirl* features centerfolds of a nude male, and some authorities believe that may be sufficient to satisfy curiosity in women who are not exposed to the volume of erotic viewing available in the men's magazines. Others believe, however, that there may be more female voyeurs than arrest and conviction records indicate. A man out for a walk who stops to view the nude figure of a woman in a window across the street may be arrested for voyeurism. However, if a man undresses in an open window and a woman stops to look, the man might very well be arrested for exhibitionism. Police and court records may thus be skewed.

Convicted voyeurs tend to be men, 26 years of age. The average age at first conviction is 23.8 years (Katchadourian & Lunde, 1972). Two-thirds of them are unmarried; one-fourth are married; and the remainder either divorced, widowed, or separated. Few voyeurs show evidence of serious psychopathology, and alcohol and drugs are infrequently involved in their behavior; only 16 percent of the sample taken by Gebhard, Gagnon, Pomeroy, and Christenson (1965) were intoxicated at the time of the offense, and none was under the influence of drugs. Gebhard et al. also found that voyeurs, as a group, attempt their first coitus at a significantly later age than do most other males.

As far as intelligence, occupational choice, and family backgrounds are concerned, voyeurs tend to be heterogeneous. They are, however, more likely to be the youngest children in their families (Delora & Warren, 1977). The single most common characteristic of this group is a history of grossly deficient (both in quantity and in quality) heterosexual relationships. Many voyeurs report fear and anxiety over forming an appropriate heterosexual relationship, as well as a compelling desire to seek sexual arousal through peeping. They then satisfy their sexual excitement through mas-

turbation, which allows them to continue to avoid social and sexual interaction with females.

Of those voyeurs who are married, many are only minimally aroused
and are perhaps made impotent by the sight of their nude wives. Frequently
these individuals report engaging in voyeurism, becoming sexually aroused,
and hurrying home to their spouses for intercourse. Others report imagining their latest or favorite voyeuristic scene in order to achieve and maintain an erection sufficient for intercourse.

Nature of the Act

The typical voyeur is not interested in peeping at a woman he knows
well. It is extremely rare to hear of a voyeur peeping at a girl friend, relative, or spouse. Katchadourian and Lunde (1972), in fact, claim that 95
percent of voyeuristic behavior is centered on strangers. This is not just a
precaution against being recognized; it is a preference for the novelty and
forbidden quality of seeing a stranger (Gebhard et al., 1965).

Not only does the voyeur prefer strangers, he usually takes a great care
that the object of his attention does not see him. Most voyeurs are reported
to the police by passersby or neighbors rather than by the victim. Contrary
to popular belief, however, peepers are not always harmless individuals. A
small percentage commit rape, burglary, or physical violence. Rape is
more common among habitual than occasional voyeurs. Most voyeurs locate themselves in dark areas for protection and try to peep into dwellings.
Those who enter dwellings in order to peep are more likely to attempt rape,
just as those who are detected and cornered are more likely to attempt physical violence in an effort to escape (Gebhard et al., 1965). It is not clear,
however, whether the voyeur who enters a dwelling to peep and consequently attempts rape is primarily a voyeur who attempts rape secondary to
peeping, or, is in fact primarily a rapist who peeps as a prerequisite to physical attack. Our clinical experience leads us to believe that the latter hy-
pthosis is probably correct.

Reaction of the Victim

One female patient as part of her report of her social history told us of
once seeing a neighborhood male peeping at her through the bedroom
window as she undressed. Partly out of anger and partly as a joke, she decided that "if he wanted a show, he was going to get one," and paraded
around the room naked for half an hour or so, occasionally cupping her
breasts in a sensuous pose or lightly masturbating. After a while she

strolled to the window, called the peeper's name, and invited him into her home. Terrified, the voyeur ran and after that strictly avoided her as long as she lived in the neighborhood.

In contrast to her boldness, most women are usually frightened when they discover that they are the object of a voyeur's attention, and resentful of the invasion of their privacy. Legal processes designed to protect privacy may do more harm to the voyeur than is perhaps warranted by his behavior; as Chesser (1971) points out:

> A typical example is that of a clergyman, age forty-six, who was caught spying on a nudist colony through binoculars . . . . He was a married man with two teenage daughters and even if the incident had been kept a close family secret the shame he felt was unbearable . . . . In despair he attempted suicide. It might have been kinder to let him succeed. He left the Church and found employent in an East End hotel, but although he made heroic efforts to live down the scandal, his family relationships were irretrievably ruined. (p. 226)

Research and Theory: Physiological Factors

Sexual arousal and the enjoyment felt when observing the nude or seminude body of an opposite-sexed person is usually considered normal, as in foreplay prior to intercourse and in viewing pornographic stimuli. Only when a person obtains primary sexual satisfaction by compulsively and repetitively observing others, often at great risk, is voyeurism considered a sexual deviation (APA, DSM III). With this distinction in mind, it is not difficult to understand why there have been so few attempts made to explain the development of voyeurism on the basis of organic etiology. Solomon and Patch (1974), in fact, claim that only in very rare instances is voyeurism associated with organic brain disease, as in senility or episodes of temporal lobe epilepsy.

Research and Theory: Psychological Factors

Psychological factors have long been suspected as causal agents in most cases of voyeurism. Freud (1905) outlined a psychological formulation for this behavior that remains popular even today.

Psychoanalytic Formulations. According to psychoanalytic theory, normal sexual development proceeds through the oral, the anal, and the phallic phases before adult sexuality emerges in the genital phase. During each of these three phases there are certain pleasurable activities which later become subordinated to genital excitement and gratification and contribute to it. Among these are kissing, fondling, exhibiting, looking, and the like. In abnormal sexual development, however, one or several infantile interests or actions become the chief source or sources of adult sexual satisfaction (Brenner, 1973). In voyeurism, it is the preference for looking that persists, and the individual is said to be fixated at the phallic stage of development.

Explanations for this fixation are various. One is unresolved Oedipal conflict. Perhaps the patient unconsciously desires to have intercourse with his mother, but due to socialization and the development of his ego he regards such a desire as grossly unacceptable. Since, according to analytic theory, all women represent the mother, the patient's conscious repulsion at the thought of sexual relations with his mother generalizes to all women. Still desiring sexual fulfillment, however, he resorts to a form of noncontact sexual excitement which poses no threat to the ego. Or perhaps the patient has severe fears of castration. In his mind an unconscious connection may exist between the mouth with its dangerous teeth and the vagina. He may therefore fear that inserting his penis into the vagina will result in its being bitten off. Thus, he resorts to a noncontact and therefore safe form of sexual gratification (Fenichel, 1945). Still another explanation is that the patient has a recurrent desire to reassure himself that women do not have penises and that that organ is his exclusive possession by virture of his manhood (Fenichel, 1945). Whatever the explanation, however, the overt behavior of peeping is attributed to unconscious fears and/or conflicts which the patient must resolve before his symptom will disappear and he can begin to engage in adult sexual activities.

A variant psychoanalytic theory postulates voyeurism as a function of a poor self-concept. Coleman (1972) states that if a youth with sexual curiosity feels shy and inadequate in his relations with the opposite sex, he may accept the substitute of peeping. In this way he satisfies his curiosity and to some extent meets his sexual needs without the trauma of actually approaching a female. He thus avoids the failure and lowered self-concept that such an encounter might cause. Moreover, peeping makes voyeurs able to compensate for their feelings of inferiority in regard to females because it gives them feelings of power and superiority over the females they review. These compensatory feelings relieve the fears of inferiority and worthlessness only temporarily, however, and the voyeur must continually repeat the act.

Behavioral Formulations. Compared to normal sexual functioning, voyeurism represents a behavior deficit. For most individuals sexual behavior may be conceptualized as a continuum ranging from precoital sexual arousal behaviors through intercourse. Behaviors such as kissing, caressing, genital manipulation, and viewing the nude body of the sexual partner are usually considered to facilitate sexual arousal. Whereas most individuals consider viewing a component in the chain of sexual arousal behaviors leading to intercourse, the voyeur typically obtains his *primary* source of sexual gratification from viewing without consent. Although the voyeur may masturbate during or following peeping or may even regularly engage in intercourse, the act or fantasy of peeping is the primary sexual stimulus for the voyeur.

Behavioral formulations of voyeuristic behavior are built upon the foundations of learning, conditioning, and the reinforcing nature of orgasm. Learning may take place by way of purposeful intent, as with the male who carefully plans his voyeuristic act; curiosity, as with the male who peeps on a female primarily out of sexual curiosity; or accident, as with the male who by chance views a female unclothed. In any case, the association of sexual arousal with the act of clandestine viewing sets the stage for the development, maintenance, and preference for voyeuristic behavior. We must emphasize, however, that the mere association of peeping and sexual arousal is not sufficient to result in voyeuristic preferences. This association simply serves as a potential sexual behavior that, influenced by various positive and negative variables, may be strengthened and developed into a pattern of sexual preference.

If a voyeuristic sight is positive in that it proves sexually arousing and the male masturbates while peeping or later while recalling the act in fantasy, the association is strengthened. Repeated voyeuristic behaviors and continued masturbation to the fantasy of peeping serve to generalize and further strengthen the association of sexual arousal and peeping.

The association of sexual arousal and peeping may also result from negative factors. Frequently, voyeurs report feeling guilty about sexual activity as a result of puritanical rearing. In other cases, there's a history of poor heterosocial and/or heterosexual relationships, a phobia of females, or inadequate heterosocial skills. If these individuals experience an accidental or planned voyeuristic incident, such negative factors may potentiate the association of peeping and sexual arousal. For those individuals who experience guilt in the sexual situation or who possess a deficient repertoire of heterosocial skills, voyeurism provides a mode of sexual satisfaction that is enjoyable (via sexual arousal and masturbation) and does not subject them to the threat of attempting heterosocial and heterosexual interactions.

CASE HISTORY 7-1

The patient was a 25-year-old salesman whose work required that he spend most evenings out of town. After he has checked into a motel and had dinner, he often found himself with little to do. On these occasions he would drive around residential neighborhoods for hours searching for a "good safe place" from which to peep. Normally, the patient would attempt to locate a residence which was situated a good distance from other homes, near which he could park his car to make a quick getaway if necessary. After locating such a residence he would quietly make his way to the home and peep in different windows to determine who lived in the home and where the bedroom was located. The patient reported that over a period of time he had located several homes in various cities he visited regularly which had become favorites because of the safety they afforded, and because of the view he was frequently able to see. One of his favorite locations was a residence in which he had peeped three different times on a young married couple having intercourse. Another favorite was the residence of a single middle-aged woman who "always undressed in the bedroom" and "always left her curtains open." The patient would hide for hours waiting to peep. If he were fortunate to "get a good view," he would masturbate while peeping. More often than not, however, he would be unsuccessful in viewing an erotic scene although he reported occasionally becoming sexually excited and masturbating while simply hiding and waiting.

The patient's sexual history revealed that as a 12-year-old boy he had, out of sexual curiosity, climbed a tree to view his older sister taking a bath. The patient claimed that he experienced an erection while viewing his nude sister. Pressing his penis against the tree limb across which he was lying, he experienced his first masturbatory orgasm. Ignorant of masturbation but desiring to repeat the pleasurable sensations, he soon discovered that rubbing his erect penis against the bed sheets while fantasizing his nude sister would produce the desired sensations. He later reported peeping on his sister and mother a variety of times and masturbating on an average of four to six times weekly to this fantasy.

When the patient was 14 years old he and several school friends began peeping on various female classmates. The group, calling themselves the "Tom Cats," would gather each weekend evening and go peeping on different girls. When successful in viewing a nude classmate, they would relay the particulars of the act and the anatomical details of the female to other male classmates who were often amazed at the heroics and good fortune of the club members. The patient reported that he would return home after each voyeuristic venture and masturbate.

The patient also claimed that when he was a senior in high school, he worked part-time in a local department store. Soon after his employment he discovered if he climbed on ceiling supports in the stockroom, he could peep through a ventilation vent into one of the dressing rooms. This provided him with a variety of voyeuristic scenes to which he could masturbate while hidden from view. The patient reported he had never been discovered peeping. He had dated only minimally, and had never experienced heterosexual contact and activities.

Voyeurs will frequently go to great lengths and take monumental chances in order to engage in peeping. One example of this strong motivation to peep is offered by a young man referred by the police. The youth had been peeping for several years, most recently around several women's dormitories on a university campus. One evening he was discovered by the police who chased after him. The voyeur, thirty years younger and in better physical condition than the officers, left them behind as he raced into the darkness. As luck would have it, as he fled down an alley behind a women's dormitory he noticed a nude female form through a window. He stopped, retraced his steps, and stood masturbating outside the window until the police arrived and arrested him.

Another example of the lengths that some voyeurs will go to to satisfy their sexual preference is illustrated in the following case history.

CASE HISTORY 7-2

The patient was a 38-year-old laborer who had recently been apprehended by the police for voyeurism, although charges were subsequently dropped. The patient reported a history of peeping since the age of 10 when he frequently spied on his female cousins as they bathed. As a teenager he regularly prowled the neighborhood peeping into windows in hopes of discovering a nude woman. After completing high school the patient attempted intercourse with several women but was unable to achieve an erection. Impotence, however, was not a problem in masturbation, which he reportedly engaged in almost daily to a fantasy of peeping.

When the patient was approximately 22 years old he began to visit a prostitute who would undress and masturbate in her bedroom while the patient pretended to hide in the living room and peep through the keyhole. After five or ten minutes of this activity, the patient would achieve an erection, enter the room, and have intercourse with the woman. The patient reported visiting the prostitute approximately twice monthly for nearly three years.

When the patient was 27 years old he met and married his wife. The couple engaged in premarital intercourse at various times during the year of courtship preceding their marriage. The patient reported, however, that he continued his voyeuristic activities during this time, the fantasy of which he used to achieve and maintain an erection for intercourse. The patient admitted to five or six instances of impotence during this period, although he claimed his partner did not appear to be concerned.

At the time of the interview the patient had been married for approximately 11 years. During this time he had continued peeping one or two times weekly. The patient reported that over time he had become increasingly impotent with his wife except on those occasions when he successfully peeped at an erotic scene and hurried home for intercourse while the image was fresh in his mind.

Approximately three years before coming for treatment the patient confessed his sexual behavior and preference to his wife. This confession, coupled with his increasing impotence and her own frustration, led to the wife's taking an active role in providing voyeuristic scenes that would sexually arouse and satisfy the patient. The couple began by having the wife invite female friends and neighbors over for a social visit. During the course of the visit the wife would begin to talk about a new dress or swimsuit that she had purchased, and suggest that the visitor try the garment on in an adjoining room where the patient would be hidden in a closet and become sexually aroused while peeping on the unsuspecting woman. These activities soon progressed to the point where the wife was engaging in sexual activities with female prostitutes while the patient peeped from the closet. Later, the couple placed ads in swingers' magazines for married couples interested in sexual activities with a "lonely housewife." When couples who had answered the ad came to the house, the patient would hide in the closet and peep while his wife and the couple engaged in three-way sexual activities. When the couple left, the patient, fully aroused, would have intercourse with his wife. However, after several of these arranged visits the patient discontinued the practice because, although he became aroused watching the couple engage in sexual activities, he got very depressed watching his wife engage in coitus with another man.

EXHIBITIONISM

Exhibitionism may be defined as the exposure of the sexual organs to the opposite sex in situations in which exposure is socially defined as inappropriate, and is carried out, at least, in part, for the purpose of sexual arousal and gratification (Delora & Warren, 1977). This definition rules out instances in which the exposure is seen as appropriate, such as during petting and coitus and in nudist camps. It also differs somewhat from the more general usage of the word "exhibitionist" to denote anyone who enjoys showing off his or her body and being admired and desired for his physical attractiveness. There are many people, both men and women, who frequent nude beaches, public beaches, or even cocktail lounges whose manner of dress (or undress) serves to call attention to the sexual attractiveness of their bodies. This sort of exhibitioning is distinguished from illegal exhibitionism by its motivation and its appropriateness; that is, it is motivated by a desire to appear fashionable and attract the attention of potential sex partners, and it is done in a manner that society considers reasonably appropriate for the situation. In these respects, it differs from true exhibitionism, in which the genital exposure is highly inappropriate—as on a public street or in a subway—and the motive is the arousal and, in some cases, the orgasm that results from the exposure.

Exhibitionism is almost exclusively a male disorder; few cases of female exhibitionism have been reported in the literature (Evans, 1970). Women have socially acceptable outlets for exposing their bodies as stripteasers or nude models, but apparently this behavior rarely if ever leads to their own sexual arousal. In a study of the background and motivation of striptease artists, Skipper and McCaghy (1969) reported that strippers come from varied backgrounds and stripped primarily for economic gain rather than sexual pleasure. As one stripper reported to us,

I've been in this business now close to three years but I still remember the first night I stripped, boy was I nervous! It's just a job, no different from other jobs really, only the money is better. There's nothing glamorous or that exciting about it really. You just go through your show taking off your clothes three times nightly. I rarely even think about what I'm doing. Usually I'm thinking about what time I get off work or deciding what groceries to buy the next morning while shopping. It's just a job, really. I mean it's nice to occasionally look out at the audience and see them admiring you; every woman enjoys that. Also, tell me where I could make this kind of money doing something else? You sure can't make it being a teacher or nurse or something like that.

Characteristics of Exhibitionists

Generally, exhibitionists may be classified into three types: (1) the simple exhibitionist who usually exposes without an erection and who is not menacing to his victim; (2) the public masturbator, who uses active fantasy in which the victim approaches and offers sexual service; and (3) the assaultive exhibitionist who uses aggressive fantasies and strives for a reaction of shock or terror from his victim; he may be more disturbed (Hackett, 1971).

The exhibitionist is frequently described as a timid, sexually inhibited, and fundamentally righteous man. Hackett (1971) estimates that compared to the average male, exhibitionists have a history of fewer heterosexual contacts and, if married, a lower number of coital attempts per week. As a rule, exhibitionists are thought to be quiet, submissive people who do not want to harm anyone (Delora & Warren, 1977).

Convicted exhibitionists are fairly young, the average age at first conviction being 30 years (Delora & Warren, 1977). Most begin exhibiting around the onset of puberty, experiencing peak periods between 15 and 30 years of age (Evans, 1970). Less than one-third are married, and many are judged to have difficulties relating to members of the opposite sex (Gebhard et al., 1965). Most are judged emotionally immature. One study evaluates 63 percent as severely emotionally disturbed (Ellis & Brancale, 1956); but most investigators think that this estimate is far too high.

Nature of the Act

The vast majority of exposures occur in public and semipublic places—in the street, in parks, in buildings, in subways, and in parked cars. The behavior is most prevalent in the spring and summer months, presumably because of the presence of more provacative stimuli and greater opportunity (Evans, 1970).

The act itself is quite variable, ranging from exposure of the flaccid penis without sexual satisfaction to exposure of the erect penis, often accompanied by masturbation and intense sexual satisfaction. Moreover, the nature of the act can vary with the same individual according to circumstances and intensity of the sexual urge. Hirning (1947) described the exhibitionist act as compulsive neurotic behavior. In some cases, it is described as an "uncontrollable urge" which overcomes the individual. Some exhibitionists describe the inception of the act as an "attack" preceded by feelings of sexual excitement and dread, during which the patient feels that he is in a "daze" (Evans, 1970). Abel et al. (1970), however, report that most patients engage in a relatively prolonged chain of behaviors including: (1) reviewing stimulating memories of previous exposures; (2) going to the sight of the exposure; (3) locating a victim; (4) mentally rehearsing and anticipating the act; (5) exposing; and, in some cases, (6) masturbating or achieving orgasm passively. Frequently the antecedent to exhibitionist behavior is a period of intense personal conflict, often with authority figures (Bond & Hutchinson, 1960; Lowenstein, 1973; Witzig, 1968).

Mohr and his associates (Mohr, Turner, & Ball, 1962; Mohr, Turner, & Jerry, 1964) contend that the intent of the exhibitionist act is to evoke an emotional response from the victim. Ellis and Brancale (1956) claim that the offender receives the most satisfaction when the victim laughs or smiles at the exposure of his penis. Other investigators agree that an emotional response is sought, but do not agree that a pleasure or approving reaction is the exhibitionist's goal. On the contrary, the exhibitionist seems more intent on evoking fear or shock from his victim. If the female reacts strongly he may construe her reaction as a compliment to his virility, since he feels his large penis caused her reaction (Chesser, 1971). In other cases the offender may be attempting to get his victim to acknowledge his masculinity by eliciting a reaction of shock, fear, or embarrassment. It is generally agreed that the exhibitionist does not usually seek further contact with his victim and may even fear it. Like the voyeur, exhibitionists may take advantage of modern technology to enhance their sexual enjoyment. The individual who describes sexual activities to a victim over the phone while masturbating is, in our opinion, engaging in a form of exhibitionism. The voyeur-caller "looks" by listening; the exhibitionist-caller "exhibits" verbally.

Certainly, there is nothing inherently harmful in seeing another individual's genitals if one elects to do so. Like the voyeur, however, the exhibitionist denies his victim free choice in the matter; thus she is unwillingly used by the offender for his sexual stimulation and gratification. In fact, shock and humiliation of the victim may be an important factor in some cases.

Incidence

The true incidence of exhibitionism cannot be accurately determined since many such cases are never brought to legal attention. From reported cases, however, it is clear that the behavior constitutes one of the most common sexual offenses. Among individuals arrested for sexual offenses,

35 percent are charged with exhibitionism (Ellis & Brancale, 1956; Freese, 1972). Virtually all those arrested for exhibitionism are males, although a few cases of female exhibitionism are reported in the literature.

The exhibitionist act may be prosecuted as a felony or a misdemeanor, depending on the arresting officer's evaluation. Most cases are convicted only once, but 17–25 percent are repeat offenders despite severe penalties (Evans, 1970). Only about 20 percent have a record of other sexual offenses (Evans, 1970). The majority (86 percent) of instances of exhibitionism are premeditated with only a few done on impulse or in a state of drunkenness (Gebhard et al., 1965).

Victims of the Act

The exhibitionist is generally rather unspecific in his choice of victims, although most exhibitionists prefer adult females. Estimates of the percentage of exhibitionists who expose to children range from 20–25 percent. Mohr et al. (1964) claims, however, that the proportion of child victims may be higher among those charged as offenders because exposure to children is generally regarded more seriously and is more likely to be prosecuted. But whether adult or child, the victim is almost always a stranger.

A few exhibitionists have very strict criteria for the female chosen as a victim. The triggering stimulus in some cases is the sight of a victim of the preferred type, perhaps a woman with shapely legs or a large bust or a woman of a certain age:

> Middle-aged women, smartly dressed, no one else. Someone who reminds me of my mother, a doctor said once, he pointed that out to me, and I think that might be right, that I'm still trying to insult her. No, it's not a prelude to a sexual assault, there's never anything like that in my mind. Just to shock, if a woman looks disgusted and turns away, then I'm satisfied. A woman smiled at me once and came towards me instead; I ran away from her as hard as I could . . . I can't tell you why I do it; when it's happening I'm not conscious of anything except this feeling of being contemptuous toward particular women and wanting to give one a shock. (Parker, 1972, pp. 218–219).

Often the exhibitionist will choose multiple victims and expose on playgrounds, on crowded streets, and in public parks. Taylor (1947) determined that in 67 cases of exposure to adults, 34 victims were alone, two victims were together in 14 cases, and in 19 cases the victims were in groups of more than two. In 31 cases of exposure to children, 9 involved a single victm, 8 involved two victims, and 14 involved more than two victims.

Response of Victims

The reaction of the victim(s) is an important terminus in the exposure chain. For those who report feeling "in a daze" prior to and during the act of exhibiting, the spell is often broken only when the victim reacts in some way (Bond & Hutchison, 1960). The reactions of victims vary. Sometimes the victim is more amused than frightened:

> . . . I saw the erect . . . penis of a total stranger when I was ten (he was waving at me from the bottom of a hill in Central Park, where Pamela and I went sledding). Look, Pam, there's a man down there—look what he's doing. I think he's looking up our skirts. Maybe we better go down headfirst on the sled instead of sitting like this. Look at his thing—are they always red like that, or is his just cold? My brother's isn't red, but he's only twelve, said Pamela. Maybe we should move over to that hill, Pam; I'm getting scared. What're you scared for, I'm the one who started men-strew-ating. I'm the one who could get pregnant, you know. Anyway, he isn't going to do anything; he just wants to see our underpants. I think it's funny. (Gould, 1970, p. 70).

More often however, victims of exhibitionists are shocked or frightened by the experience. A young girl may be horrified if she has never seen an erect adult penis or if she has been taught that genitals are disgusting objects to be kept hidden. A woman may share some of these reactions and may also fear that she is in danger of being raped or in some way harmed by the man exposing himself to her (Davis & Davis, 1976):

> I was walking home just minding my own business, just concerned about getting home . . . and I come to this corner and I had to stop because there was this car that was going really slow and he was way over on the right hand side. I mean, apparently it looked like he was going to make a right hand turn. And I had to stop for him . . . . And, uhm, I just stood there and I wanted for him to pass [so] I could be on my way . . . . I naturally just looked in his window and he was masturbating and he looked up at me and he looked, really, he was drooling . . . and really nasty looking . . . and I really felt threatened . . . I didn't like it happening. He ended up turning left, he was way over on the right side and he ended up turning left. And I kept walking and it started bothering me. And I was thinking, you know, I didn't see that, you know, I'm just going to go home and close the door and it'll all be gone, it won't be there any more. And then . . . he came around the second time. I plainly saw him and I got really paranoid . . . . I was turning to go down a long block and he came by very slow again. He turned left and I could see his hand movements . . . [he] sort of had his face pressed up towards the window just glaring at

me. And his eyes were really wet looking. It made me paranoid because I
didn't know if he knew me and if he knew I lived by myself.

I don't know where his head was at so I don't know if he was desparate
enough to drive down an alley and grab some little kid and pull him in the car
. . . maybe he was sick, maybe this was the only way he could get his jollies
. . . maybe he never bothered anybody . . . . I think there's always going to be
a certain amount of people who are lewd, crude, and outrageous. There's nothing you can do with them, I was offended. I felt that I shouldn't have to be
exposed to it. (p. 211)

Although these fears of rape and harm are largely unfounded, since
the exhibitionist is rarely violent or aggressive and often keeps distance
from his victim, the experience can still be traumatic for the victim. Since
pursuance of further contact is not one of the goals of most exhibitionists,
they are generally regarded as a nuisance rather than a danger to their victims. The effects of this nuisance, however, can vary according to the emotional stability, intellectual adequacy, and social maturing of the victim.

There is little data regarding the effects on males who are victims of
those few female exhibitionists. Since most research documents that males
are more inclined to appreciate visual sexual stimuli than females, it is assumed that the serious psychological effects on males are minimal.

Research and Theory: Physiological Factors

Exhibitionism may be categorized as due to organic pathology, or as
psychogenic exhibitionism. Individuals who are severely retarded—both
male and female—may be unaware or partially aware of the socially disapproved nature of their behavior. In some cases organic problems such as
epilepsy, senility, and diabetes may be associated with the deviant behavior, and the act most often occurs when the individual is in a state of mental
confusion (Evans, 1970). Older male exhibitionists often suffer from senile
brain deterioration and show a lowering of behavioral controls. Alcohol
and drug abuse are also occasionally associated with decreased behavior
control and exhibitionism.

Research and Theory: Psychological Factors

Exhibitionists constitute the largest group of sex offenders apprehended by police. Traditional psychological thinking conceptualizes exhibitionism as related to various forms of psychopathology, such as sociopathic personality disorders. Such individuals are thought to have histories
of poor school adjustment and erratic work records, as well as previous dif-

ficulties with authorities as a consequence of other antisocial behaviors. Their exhibitionism appears to be just one more form of antisocial behavior, in connection with which they may or may not achieve sexual excitation and gratification (Coleman, 1972). In other cases exhibitionism is thought to be associated with manic or schizophrenic reactions. For example, Witzig (1970) claims that the only female in a group of exhibitionists studied exposed herself just prior to a complete psychotic break. In the following sections we shall discuss the psychoanalytic and behavioral formulations of exhibitionism. In addition, because of the interesting and substantial data concerning psychodynamic conceptualizations, we shall present these formulations as well.

Psychoanalytic Formulations. Psychoanalytic theory holds that exhibitionism serves as a denial of castration fears and anxieties (Radzinowicz, 1957). The young male child is said to fear castration by the father in retaliation for his competitive sexual and emotional desire for the mother. The individual who becomes fixated at the Oedipal phase of psychosexual development must seek reassurance from the reaction of females that he has a penis and that he is feared because of it (Fenichel, 1945). The shock of fear reaction is therefore extremely important to the exhibitionist, for it serves to assure him of his dominance over the female sex and to relieve castration anxieties (Radzinowicz, 1957).

Psychodynamic Formulations. According to dynamic or trait theories, exhibitionism may be divided into two major types as determined by etiology (Coleman, 1972):

1. *Exhibitionism associated with personal immaturity.* Personal immaturity is thought to be the most frequent dynamic factor in causing and maintaining exhibitionist behavior. Witzig (1968) has estimated that about 60 percent of the cases of exhibitionism referred for treatment by the courts fall into this category. The personal histories of these exhibitionists often reveal that they retain strong bonds to an overly possessive or dominating mother. Thus, the exhibitionist behavior may be seen not only as a failure to progress beyond the "showing" phase of the phallic stage, but also as an unconscious act of defiance toward the mother whose domineering has prevented the patient's progression. As an act of defiance or aggression, however, exhibiting is still childish, for as Brenner (1973) explains, the use of or the fantasy of the penis and its activity as a weapon or a means of destruction is also characteristic of the phallic stage.

The problems of the immature exhibitionist may be compounded by inadequate information about sex, feelings of shyness and inferiority in approaching the opposite sex, and/or puritanical attitudes toward masturbation. Often the exhibitionist complains that he struggles against the impulse to expose himself in much the same way that an adolescent may struggle against the impulse to masturbate, but that, as sexual or other tensions increase, he feels compelled to exhibit. Feelings of guilt and remorse frequently follow the act, particularly if the exhibitionist ejaculates. Such a compulsion for immediate gratification or discharge of cathexis is thought to be characteristic of a period of development during which the id is strong in comparison to an as yet immature ego. The defeat of the ego by the id impulses brings about the feelings of guilt, especially when the incident results in complete satisfaction of the id (ejaculation) and thus complete defeat of the ego (Brenner, 1973; Fenichel, 1945).

The marital histories of many exhibitionists seem to support the theory of personal immaturity. Many exhibitionists state that they married only because of family pressures or social expectations. Many married at a late age. Those who are married usually fail to achieve satisfactory sexual and personal relationships with their wives. According to Witzig (1968):

> These men almost never like to discuss sexual matters with their wives and frequently avoid undressing before them. The idea of living in a nudist colony is a repulsive thought to most exhibitionists, although they are periodically willing to show off their genitals in quite public places. (p. 79)

Thus many researchers believe that these individuals are essentially immature in their sex-role development, although they may be well educated and competent in other areas of their lives:

> A high school teacher had exhibited himself for several months to a 30-year-old woman who lived next door. She finally reported him, and before arresting him the police took motion pictures of his activities from the woman's apartment. In order to get a clearer picture they raised the window. At this point the teacher thought he had finally made an impression and in turn raised his own window and intensified his masturbatory activities and suggestive gestures.
>
> After his arrest he revealed a background of over-attachment to a domineering mother and an inhibited, puritanical attitude toward sex. He had rarely gone out with girls and felt extremely shy and insecure in his approach to them. His strong bond to his mother undoubtedly contributed to his difficulties in heterosexual adjustment, making even his fantasies of sexual relations with other women seem like acts of unfaithfulness toward his mother. As a result, he apparently blundered into his awkward, immature, and socially unacceptable form of sexual behavior. (Coleman, 1972, p. 464)

Coleman further claims that closely related to the exhibitionist's personal immaturity appears to be a second factor: doubts and fears about his masculinity, combined with a strong need to demonstrate masculinity and potency. Apfelberg, Sugar, and Pfeffer (1944), for example, cite the case of an exhibitionist who achieved sexual satisfaction only when he accompanied the exposure of his genitals with a question to his victim as to whether she had ever seen such a large penis. One woman, instead of evidencing shock and embarrassment, scornfully assured him that she had. On this occasion the exhibitionist claimed he received no sexual gratification.

2. *Exhibitionism associated with interpersonal stress and acting out.* A second dynamic factor is suggested by those investigators who point to the high incidence of precipitating stress. Often married exhibitionists appear to be reacting to some conflict or stress situation in their marriage, and their behavior is seen as a regression of adolescent masturbatory activity (Coleman, 1972). In these instances, an exhibitionist may state that exhibiting himself during masturbation is more exciting and tension-reducing than utilizing pictures of nude women.

Exhibitionism without genital arousal may also take place after a period of intense conflict over some problem—often involving authority figures—with which the individual feels inadequate to cope:

> For example, a Marine who wanted to make a career of the service was having an experience with a superior that made it impossible for him to reenlist. He could not admit to himself that he could be hostile to either the corps or the superior. For the first time in his life he exposed himself to a girl on the beach. Arrested, he was merely reprimanded and returned to the scene of conflict. A short time later he displayed his genitals to a girl in a parking lot. This time he was placed on probation with the stipulation that he seek treatment, and his enlistment was allowed to terminate in natural sequence. He never repeated the act. He was happily married and seemed to be acting out in this instance a vulgar expression of contempt. (Witzig, 1968, p. 77)

Behavioral Formulations. Exposing one's genitals to another person and finding pleasure and sexual arousal as a result of viewing the unclothed body of an opposite-sexed individual are similar behaviors in that both are generally considered normal components in the chain of behaviors leading to sexual intercourse. It must be remembered that these behaviors warrant a deviation classification only when they are acted out in extreme fashion, or when they represent the preferred or primary source of sexual gratification.

Many exhibitionists report their initial genital exposure occurred quite by accident, perhaps while they were urinating or masturbating in an inappropriate place. Generally they initially experienced embarrassment and concern over being discovered. Later, however, they cognitively replayed the event and became sexually aroused. McGuire et al. (1965) described two cases of exhibitionism with similar patterns. Both males had been surprised by attractive females while urinating in a semipublic place. The erotic nature of this encounter had subsequently been incorporated into their masturbatory fantasies which thereafter inclined the males to repeat the act. Predisposing factors such as a history of inadequate heterosocial relationships and heterosexual inexperience or incompetence is thought to facilitate the likelihood that an accidental exposure takes on a sexual connotation. Repeated masturbation to the cognitive rehearsal of the victim's expression of surprise or shock serves to condition the association of sexual arousal and exposure of the genitals.

A direct attempt to test this hypothesis was reported by Evans (1968). He predicted that, if the theory were correct, exhibitionists reporting normal (heterosexual) fantasies while masturbating would decondition more rapidly than exhibitionists whose masturbatory fantasies were related to their exhibitionistic behavior. He was able to form two groups of exhibitionists with an equally reported frequency of exhibitionist behavior over the previous six months, who differed according to their characteristic masturbation fantasy. The treatment involved electrical aversion after a variable delay interval while viewing slides with phrases related to their exhibitionist behavior. This procedure was carried out once a week for ten weeks, then once a fortnight for two months, then once a month during a two-year follow-up. Those subjects with normal masturbatory fantasy reported no further acting out or urges to do so after a median treatment period of four weeks, whereas the subjects with exhibitionist masturbatory fantasies achieved this status only after a median treatment period of 14 weeks.

Certainly, this study by itself is not conclusive evidence for the unequivocal acceptance of conditioning by masturbation as a major factor in the development of exhibitionism. More research into the etiology of this disorder is required. Conflict could be another source of difficulty. For example, an individual who was both fearful and attracted to heterosexual intercourse could exhibit displacement of sexual gratification down the chain of sexual behaviors leading to coitus such that primary gratification is associated with showing the genitals.

CASE HISTORY 7-3

The patient was a 29-year-old power lineman referred by the court system for psychological treatment in lieu of prior sentencing on a charge of exhibitionism. The patient had been married for five years and was the father of two young children. He had been recently suspended with pay by his employer awaiting outcome of legal processing. This charge represented the first arrest of the patient, who was described by the court social worker as a very mild-mannered individual with no significant psychopathology or history of legal problems.

The patient related that his arrest stemmed from an incident in which he exposed himself in a public library. He claimed this incident marked the third such occurrence, all of which took place in the library. He described the initial two experiences as unzipping his trousers and exposing his erect penis to a table of females approximately 30 feet away from where he stood. In both instances the females registered little emotional response, "almost like they were ignoring me." The third exposure, to three young college coeds, produced a more highly emotional response than usual with the victims screaming loudly and demanding the arrest of the patient, who bolted down the stairs and out the door. The following day the local police arrested the patient at work and escorted him to police headquarters where he was identified by the victims.

A description of the patient's sexual functioning and behavior since marriage, substantiated by his wife, revealed a frequency of intercourse of approximately once every two weeks. Although the wife desired coitus more frequently, the patient reported generally being uninterested in sex with his wife; he had, on occasion, accused the wife of being oversexed. Both partners agreed that the patient was somewhat inhibited concerning nudity and sexuality. The patient seldom undressed in the presence of his wife, frequently reprimanded his young children for walking through the house naked, and would not allow his wife to wear a bikini or a two-piece bathing suit in public. Coital functioning was characterized by frequent episodes of impotence.

The patient's sexual history revealed that at the age of 13 he was discovered masturbating in the school restroom by a group of classmates. The youths laughed uproariously at this discovery, overpowered and stripped the patient, and carried him out of the restroom through the schoolyard to the shock and dismay of the female students who gazed in disbelief at the nude patient with an erection. The patient reported being humiliated by the experience and so embarrassed that he pleaded with the school authorities to drop the investigation and charges against his perpetrators. Several weeks later, however, the patient reported frequently becoming sexually aroused while thinking of the incident and about the shocked expressions of those girls who saw his erect penis. The patient discussed his humiliation and embarrassment with an older school chum who, in an effort to comfort him, suggested that he forget the incident, and told him that "the girls probably loved it 'cause they don't get to see a big one like yours very often." After this discussion the patient began masturbating to the thought of the incident, repeatedly telling himself during masturbation how fortunate the girls were to see his large penis. The shocked expression on their faces he soon came to construe as merely a front put up to conceal what he perceived as their real enjoyment at seeing his exposed penis. The patient admitted masturbating to his fantasy daily and cognitively imagined exposing himself to nearly every young woman he encountered.

CASE HISTORY 7-4

The patient was a 21-year-old male nurse who was referred by a colleague. He reported frequent urges to expose himself to young children, particularly girls, which he acted on approximately once every three weeks. The patient's first public exposure had occurred about three years before while he was attending a nursing conference in a major midwestern city. In this incident he parked a rented automobile on a street several hundred yards from a junior high school. When school let out and students began walking home past his parked car he began masturbating. He summoned several young girls to his car on the pretext of requesting directions and exposed himself. This exposure was characterized by a spontaneous ejaculation.

The patient's sexual history revealed that he was reared in a neighborhood with few male contacts. As a child he became an accepted member of a group of neighborhood girls who, although a year or two older, included him in their daily play activities. The patient reported that he learned to enjoy playing with dolls and other tradtionally feminine toys and games. He reported that around the age of seven or eight he and his female friends would occasionally hide in a garage behind his house and ''show'' their genitals to each others. Since he was the only male he received a great deal of attention. Three or four girls closely examined his penis. When he was about ten he began experiencing penile erections when he showed his genitals to his female friends, who observed closely and occasionally touched them. When the patient was 12 years old, and his friends 13 and 14 years, the girls would talk him into taking off his clothes and masturbating while they watched. Later, when he started to ejaculate they became even more impressed. During this period the patient began masturbating to the cognition of displaying his erect penis to the young and interested female audience.

The patient dated very little during high school, claiming that his feminine mannerisms and behavior were a deterrent to obtaining dates. He masturbated to a common fantasy of exposing his genitals to young girls thoughout the high school, although he never engaged in this behavior. One of the girls with whom he had engaged in genital exposure as a child would occasionally refer to their childhood activities in a joking manner; this embarrassed him tremendously. On one evening the patient visited this girl's house with the idea of exposing himself to her. Excusing himself to go to the bathroom, he undressed and thought about opening the door and exposing his genitals. Unable to bring himself to do so, he ejaculated, dressed, and left.

Upon graduation from high school he entered nurse's training: he was the only male student in the class. During an anatomy class lecture on the male genitalia, one female student jokingly suggested that the patient undress and serve as a visual aid. This incident, characterized by good-natured student laughter and the patient's embarrassment, provided him additional masturbatory fantasies of exposing himself to the class.

The patient reported limiting his exhibitionism to young children around playgrounds, schools, and the like. He became indignant when asked if he had ever thought about engaging a child in sexual behavior and claimed he would never indulge in such "disgusting behavior." His exhibitionistic episodes were characterized by a great deal of sexual arousal and ejaculation at the moment of exposing himself, which was followed by extreme guilt and depression. The patient claimed that he was a virgin and had never so much as touched a woman's breast except on one occasion at work in the hospital when his hand accidentally slipped while helping a woman into bed.

MODIFICATION OF
VOYEURISM AND EXHIBITIONISM

Given the frequency with which voyeurism and exhibitionism are encountered both in the general population and in clinical practice, it is rather surprising to find that there are few cases of these behaviors reported in the literature (Jackson, 1969). We will focus our discussion of treatment techniques on four contrasting modification strategies: psychoanalysis, medical therapy, group therapy, and behavior therapy.

Psychoanalysis

As previously noted, psychoanalytic theory attributes voyeurism and exhibitionism to psychological fixations at specific stages of psychosexual development. A common etiologic theme is that of castration anxiety resulting from an unresolved oedipal developmental stage (Maletzky, 1974). Psychoanalytic treatment of voyeurism and exhibitionism emphasizes helping the patient gain insight into the development and maintenance of the deviant behavior. This is supposedly accomplished by the patient's free association, therapeutic interpretation and reflection, dream analysis, and the transference of the patient's castration fears onto the therapist (Fenichel, 1945). Speeling (1947) reports the psychoanalytic treatment of an exhibitionist seen five times per week for two-and-a-half years. The 600 sessions of analytically oriented psychotherapy resulted in the eventual marriage of the patient. No information indicating the success or failure of treatment was reported.

Medical Therapies

Pharmacological therapy, which is utilized primarily as an adjunct to other treatments, may provide some temporary symptomatic relief from reactive depression or anxiety associated with voyeurism and exhibitionism (Evans, 1968). If the deviant sexual behavior appears to be reinforced by masturbation and/or ejaculation, Evans suggests that a drug such as thioridazine may be useful, since it seems to depress the sex drive and may result in temporary impotence or the inability to ejaculate. However, the effectiveness and utility of this type of drug remains to be demonstrated. Other medical interventions have included electroconvulsive therapy, particularly with those individuals who do not respond to other therapeutic interventions, and with patients with suspected psychosis (Thompson, 1949). Barlow, Leitenberg, and Agras (1969) reported a case of exhibitionism associated with temporal lobe epilepsy in which a lobectomy was performed. Also, castration has been suggested by a few European clinicians, although Evans (1968) maintains that such a radical procedure could hardly be recommended. Physical and surgical methods designed to alter voyeuristic and exhibitionistic patterns of behavior have generally proven to be of little value (Yates, 1970).

Group Therapy

Group therapy in the treatment of voyeurism and exhibitionism has been reported in the literature with varying degrees of success. Witzig (1968) employed group treatment for exhibitionists, and claimed that the technique was applicable to approximately 60 percent of patients, excluding those with organic etiology, those who refuse to admit guilt, and the sociopathic exhibitionist. Typically, the group is seen once or twice weekly, and discussions center around sex education, analyses of precipitating events, discussions of alternative ways of dealing with these events, and changing the patient's passivity and self-esteem (Evans, 1968; Freese, 1972). Evans concludes that although group or family therapy may improve the patient's general living situation and/or make the patient feel better about himself, it does very little, if anything, to modify the deviant pattern of behavior.

Behavior Therapy

Learning and conditioning in connection with human sexual behavior involve the same sorts of processes as learning and conditioning in other types of behavior . . . . From its parents, from other adults, from other children, and from the community at large, the child begins to acquire its attitudes toward such things as nudity, the anatomic differences between males and females and the reproductive functions; and these attitudes may have considerable significance in determining its subsequent acceptance of avoidance of particular types of overt sexual activities . . . . Even some of the most extremely variant types of human sexual behavior may need no more explanation than is provided by our understanding of the processes of learning and conditioning. Behavior which may appear bizaar, perverse, or unthinkably unacceptable to some persons, may have significance for other individuals because of the way in which they have been conditioned. (Kinsey et al., 1953, pp. 644–646)

The behavioral treatment of voyeurism and exhibitionism is aimed at eliminating deviant sexual arousal, enhancing more acceptable sexual behaviors, and teaching alternative ways of interacting with individuals. The elimination of deviant sexual arousal is generally accomplished by use of aversion therapy (*e.g.,* electrical aversion) although it must be emphasized that care should be taken to define precisely the undesired behavior. For example, care should be exercised to avoid conditioning an exhibitionist *never* to expose his genitals since this behavior is acceptable and necessary for bathing, urinating and intercourse. Appropriate heterosexual arousal may be facilitated by positive conditioning techniques such as masturbation training. Alternative patterns of interaction may include developing heterosocial skills (*e.g.,* behavioral rehearsal) and assertive behaviors, whereas systematic desensitization may be useful if the assessment indicates a phobic element. As repeatedly noted, a broad-spectrum combination of behavioral techniques as indicated by a comprehensive and systematic assessment is the most efficacious.

Rooth and Marks (1974) compared the effects of electrical aversion, self-regulation, and relaxation training in a group of 12 chronic exhibitionists. Self-regulation, as described by Kanfer (1970), involves teaching the patient to identify the detailed chain of events leading to his undesired behavior and to adopt various strategies which disrupt this chain and instead lead to other preferred behaviors. Electrical aversion was administered to the patients as they rehearsed and described the exposure act in front of a mirror. Measures of change were based on self-report, and no physiological measures were recorded. At one year follow-up the results indicated that the aversion therapy group had engaged in significantly fewer exposures and had had fewer convictions than the self-regulation or relaxation group.

MacCulloch, Williams, and Birtles (1971) reported the use of electrical aversion in the treatment of a physically well-developed 12-year-old male exhibitionist. The patient masturbated twice daily to a fantasy of exposing his erect penis to women over the age of 25 years who, by preference, had large breasts and buttocks and well-shaped legs. Psychodynamic therapy was initially conducted, but after the patient exposed himself several more times, once to the wife of a policeman, the decision was made to refer the youth for behavior therapy.

An initial behavioral assessment indicated that the primary stimulus resulting in sexual arousal and exhibitionistic behavior was "seeing" or fantasizing well-developed mature females. As a result, the decision was made to employ electrical aversion in an effort to eliminate the exhibitionistic behavior and sexual arousal to older women. In addition, an aversion relief paradigm with slides of girls the patient's age were used to mark the offset of shock. Dependent measures included the Sexual Orientation Measure, adapted for use with an exhibitionist, and overt incidents of exposing. Results of the Sexual Orientation Measure (Figure 7-1) indicated a significant decrease in sexual orientation to older women, whereas arousal to girls of the patient's age remained high throughout treatment and follow-up. Behavioral measures at post-treatment and follow-up indicated no instances of exhibitionism.

Gaupp et al. (1971) also employed an aversion relief paradigm in the treatment of a male voyeur. The aversive stimuli consisted of 11 slides of words or phrases related directly to peeping—for example, "peeping," "wasting time while peeping," and "masturbating to peeping fantasies." The aversive stimuli were accompanied by electric shock delivered to the

SEXUAL ORIENTATION MEASURE SCORES

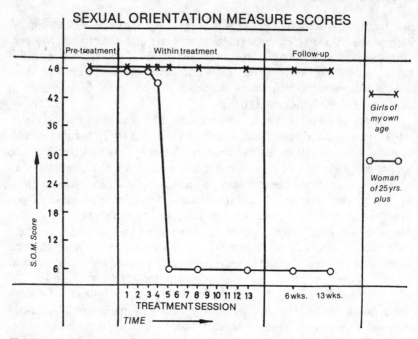

Figure 7-1. Sexual orientation measure scores. (**Source:** MacCulloch, M. J., Williams, C., & Birtles, C. J. The successful application of aversion therapy to an adolescent exhibitionist. *Journal of Behavior Therapy and Experimental Psychiatry,* 1971, *2,* 61-66. Reprinted by permission.)

patient's right ankle seven seconds after stimulus slide onset. The relief stimuli consisted of 11 slides of words or phrases related directly to the condition which led to sexual behaviors with the patient's wife and to peeping: "boredom," "frustration," and "sexual excitement from wife," and every session ended with the relief stimulus, "sexual intercourse with wife." During each session the 22 stimuli were randomly presented for 15 seconds each. GSR and EKG were measured continuously during treatment. Results of treatment and at eight-month follow-up indicated an absence of voyeuristic behavior and improved sexual relations with the patient's wife. The authors hypothesized that using written descriptions of behavior as the conditional stimuli resulted in more direct cognitive changes than pictures of imagined stimuli.

Covert sensitization has been reported as a useful substitute for electrical aversion in the treatment of voyeurism and exhibitionism. Maletzky (1974) reported excellent results with 10 exhibitionists using "assisted" covert sensitization, in which the deviant fantasy was paired not only with noxious imagery but also with the noxious smell of valeric acid. The treatment program initially consisted of progressive muscular relaxation exercises and the construction of a hierarchy of scenes collected from the patient's past and his imagination altered to include a noxious component.

Table 7-1 consists of a sample hierarchy employed with one patient. Each patient was relaxed and presented a sexual scene involving an exhibitionistic component. If the patient became sexually aroused to the imagery, he was presented the noxious component of the scene, as well as subjected to valeric acid held under his nose. As the scene progressed the patient, in imagination, escaped from the exposing situation, the odor was removed, and suggestions of calm reintroduced. An example of a covert sensitization scene follows. An asterisk indicates the point at which valeric acid was introduced and a double asterick denotes when it was removed.

You're driving down Collins Avenue, going to the laundry. You can feel yourself in the car, hands on the wheel, looking out the windows. It's dusk, and it's been raining; you can see the wet streets and puddles. Just as you make that right turn onto Andrews Drive, by the ice cream place, you see this great looking girl walking on your right. You slow down toget a better look— she's blonde—about 16, and really stacked. You can see her breasts under her tight blouse, and her skirt is so short you can see her legs all the way up! You

TABLE 7-1

**Hierarchy of Scenes Presented to Exhibitionistic Patient
Placed in Order of Sexual Pleasure to Patient**

Scene	Content	Sexual Pleasure Rating**
1.	Seeing young girls walking home from school, sitting in car across street masturbating, being discovered, getting sick to stomach.	10
2.	Standing behind tree in park, masturbating while watching young girls go by, being apprehended by police.	30
3.	Inviting young girl behind tree in park, exposing self, girl pointing and laughing at him, inviting friends to see, getting sick to stomach.	45
4.	Driving past high school, stopping and exposing self to group of girls, fearing apprehension, getting sick to stomach, having diarrhea.	60
5.	Driving through shopping center at night, approaching pretty girl in car, unzipping self, getting penis caught in zipper with much pain, bleeding.	75
6.	Driving to laundry in daytime, seeing young blond on street alone, trying to expose self, but bad smell coming in from factory producing nausea, vomiting.	85
7.	Driving to laundry at night, approaching pretty blond to expose self, getting sick to stomach, vomiting on self, girl getting license number.	100
7a.	Same as 7 but odor and sick feelings quickly removed as subject resists temptation to expose self then drives on.	

**The pleasure associated with imagining the first, or sexual, part of the scene.
Source: Maletzky, B. M. "Assisted" covert sensitization in the treatment of exhibitionism. *Journal of Consulting and Clinical Psychology*, 1974, *42*, 34-40. Copyright 1974 by the American Psychological Association. Reprinted with permission.

start to get excited just by looking and turn the car around to follow her. Now she's on your left and you slowly pull up to her as you start to play with yourself and your penis starts to get harder and stiffer. You can't help but think about touching and fondling her, and you ache just to be naked with her,* to see her be surprised and happy at how big and how hard your penis is. But as you stop the car and start to take it out, that bad smell comes back and that sick feeling in the pit of your stomach. You really get turned off as your stomach turns over and over and pieces of your supper catch in your throat. You try to gag them back down but you can't; big chunks of vomit gush out of your mouth, dribble down your chin, and go all over you. The smell is mak- you even sicker. The blonde can see you now, all soft and vomiting all over yourself, and she is starting to get your license number! People are coming out of the ice cream place to see, and you've got to get out of there! **You quickly clean yourself off and drive away, rolling down the windows to get some fresh air. As you get out of there, you start to feel much better. That bad smell is gone, and you can breathe deeply again. A fresh clean breeze comes in through the windows, goes all over you, making you feel comfortable and relaxed. Your stomach starts to settle down, and you begin to fully relax again. You drive away glad that you're out of there. (Maletzky, 1974, p. 35)

Results indicated that 9 of 10 patients ceased all exhibitionists behavior after 11–19 sessions. The remaining patient was given 10 additional sessions before elimination of the deviant behavior. Anecdotal reports collected from wives, girlfriends, and supervisors indicate that the majority of patients demonstrated improved heterosexual adjustment and job performance during treatment and at 12-month follow-up.

Maletzky (1977) continued his investigation of "assisted" covert sensitization by employing the technique in the treatment of 12 exhibitionists and 18 homosexuals. Patients were treated with covert sensitization combined with the noxious odor of valeric acid for six months. Verbal reports of behavior collected from the patients' wives, girlfriends, work supervisors, and friends were then collected over a 12-month follow-up period and indicated that seven homosexuals and four exhibitionists had relapsed and were again engaging in deviant sexual behavior (Figure 7-2). At this point booster sessions conducted once a month for three consecutive months and once every three months for the next nine months were instituted. As may be seen in Figure 7-2, the A-B-A design graphically demonstrates the efficacy of "assisted" covert sensitization as well as the effects of periodic booster sessions on the targeted behaviors.

Reitz and Keil (1971) reported the successful treatment of an exhibitionist who had been regularly exposing himself for 25 years. Treatment involved having the patient exhibit himself to four volunteer nurses under office conditions, a modification of shame aversion as described by Serber (1970). Initially, the patient reported difficulty in exhibiting. He reported being strongly embarrassed, ashamed, and guilty while engaging in the de-

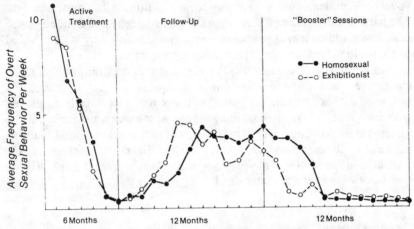

Figure 7-2. Average weekly frequency of overt homosexual or exhibitionist behavior during active treatment, follow-up, and "booster" session conditions. (**Source:** Malętzky, B. M. "Booster" sessions in aversion therapy: The permanency of treatment. *Behavior Therapy,* 1977, *8,* 460–463. Reprinted with permission.)

viant behavior. A total of 20 sessions of exposing to the nurses was conducted. A 19-month follow-up indicated no instances of exposing.

Systematic desensitization to a hierarchy of stimuli that have previously served as an antecedent to voyeurism and exhibitionism has been suggested as a useful adjunct to therapy if anxiety is found to be a preliminary link in the behavioral chain (Wolpe, 1973). Bond and Hutchinson (1960) reported the case of a 25-year-old exhibitionist who had been imprisoned nine times for this offense. A hierarchy of situations relating to anxiety experienced by the patient just before exposure took place was constructed, and systematic desensitization was employed. After a total of 30 sessions considerable improvement was demonstrated. The patient was able to attend parties and walk through supermarkets without experiencing the anxiety preceding exposure. Two relapses occurred; these involved different behavior patterns from the customary act and were quickly estinguished. No further relapses occurred during the following two months. Considering the severity of the case, as manifested by the frequency of exposure before treatment (often several times per day), and the time spent in prison, the investigators claim that the improvement can reasonably be attributed to the treatment program. A similar case was treated successfully by Wolpe (1958).

Once the deviant behavior is suppressed or is in the process of being suppressed, a treatment program to increase heterosexual arousal may be needed. If an exhibitionist or voyeur uses a deviant sexual fantasy in masturbation, it will be helpful to employ masturbation training for redirecting sexual arousal to more appropriate heterosexual stimuli (Lowenstein, 1973). Jackson (1969) utilized this procedure upon discovering that his voyeuristic patient used his viewing scenes as fantasy for masturbation. The patient was instructed that when the urge to peep appeared, he was to masturbate while viewing pornographic pictures, which were later replaced by simple female nude photos from *Playboy* magazine.

In a number of case studies on voyeurism and exhibitionism, clinicians have noted the need to institute techniques to assure better social as well as sexual adjustment. A common procedure successfully employed with such cases is assertive training. If the new assertive skills are to be directed at the wife, however, it may be useful to counsel her individually to assure that the new behaviors are not punished. In addition, training in social skills via modeling, role-playing, and role rehearsal is imperative if treatment gains are to be maintained.

Conclusions

As we have said many times throughout this text, the choice of a treatment technique(s) has to be based on a systematic and thorough behavioral assessment. In most cases of voyeurism and exhibitionism there have been excesses and deficits in several components of sexual behavior. We therefore emphasize a multicomponent treatment package as the most efficacious. In the elimination of deviant sexual arousal we have employed electrical aversion, covert sensitization, and shame aversion and have found each to be generally effective. In our opinion, covert sensitization techniques appear to be most effective with those individuals who have an active and vivid imagination and are able to graphically imagine aversive scenes. On the other hand, shame aversion appears to be most effective with those patients who experience genuine remorse, guilt, and embarrassment over their sexual orientation and behavior. We have not administered "assisted" covert sensitization with voyeurs and exhibitionists, but Maletzky (1974, 1977) reports some impressive data as to the value of this technique with a variety of sexual deviants including voyeurs and exhibitionists. Maletzky (1977) also emphasizes the importance of booster sessions, 3, 6, and 12 months in the elimination of deviant sexual arousal, a procedure we have found facilitates the permanency of therapeutic gains.

After the elimination of sexual arousal to genital exposure or clandestine peeping, arousal to more appropriate heterosexual behaviors should be enhanced. As with reorientation programs for homosexuality, we have found exposure to appropriate heterosexual behavior combined with masturbation training to be useful and effective. As previously mentioned it is often helpful to supply the patient with appropriate sexual stimuli to assist in masturbation training. If an assessment reveals that anxiety is a preliminary link in the deviant behavioral chain, systematic desensitization to the identified anxiety eliciting stimuli may be indicated.

Finally, deficits in heterosocial skills are often noted in voyeurs and exhibitionists and should be assessed carefully. These individuals frequently report discomfort and failure in heterosocial situations, including maladaptive marital interactions. In our clinical practice we have found both assertive training and behavioral rehearsal involving role playing and role reversal to be useful in instituting more adaptive heterosocial interactional skills.

CASE HISTORY 7-5

The patient was a 35-year-old businessman referred by his minister. The patient reported a 20-year history of voyeurism which had recently culminated in his apprehension while peeping into a neighborhood residence. Fearing his wife's threat of divorce, the patient contacted his minister for counsel and was referred for treatment.

A sexual history indicated that the frequency of marital coitus averaged once per month, and the frequency of masturbation to fantasies of peeping averaged twice a day. A sexual assessment in which the patient read explicit literature and viewed sexual films, slides and pictures depicting voyeuristic behaviors while penile erections were monitored via a strain gauge substantiated a sexual arousal pattern to peeping. Penile erection to fantasies of engaging in sexual intercourse with his wife or with other females did not produce sexual arousal.

Electrical aversion was employed as the treatment of choice and administered to the patient's left forearm contingent upon physiologically-measured penile arousal to films, slides, pictures, and literature depicting voyeuristic behavior. The patient brought an envelope containing polaroid pictures of his wife (ranging from fully clothed to nude) to each session, and was instructed to intently view a different photograph for two minutes following termination of each electrical stimulation. This procedure was an attempt to condition an association of the wife with aversion relief. Twelve biweekly aversive sessions were required to extinguish the deviant sexual arousal.

In an effort to redirect the patient's sexual arousal to more appropriate sexual stimuli, masturbation training was concurrently instituted. The patient was instructed that if he experienced an urge to peep, he was to masturbate immediately to a series of pornographic pictures he possessed. Over a two-month period the pornographic pictures were gradually faded out and the photographs of his nude wife faded in. Shortly after, a variant of sensate focus in which the nude wife slowly and gently massaged and masturbated the patient to orgasm replaced the photographs as sexual stimuli and activity. Gradual resumption of marital coitus followed. During this time assertiveness training sessions were also incorporated into the patient's treatment program, as were periodic individual counseling sessions with the wife to insure that assertive attempts by the patient would not be punished.

Six-months follow-up revealed that the couple was living happily together and enjoying intercourse an average of twice per week. The patient reported no voyeuristic episodes, and only two deviant urges which were immediately relieved via intercourse. Physiological follow-up data substantiated the patient's report of no voyeuristic sexual arousal.

CASE HISTORY 7-6

The patient was a 41-year-old clerk referred by his family physician. The patient had been exposing himself in the window to a neighborhood woman across the street for over three years, but had only recently been reported to the police. He had previously been arrested approximately three years before referral but was not charged, since he volunteered for psychiatric treatment. He had faithfully attended weekly intensive dynamic psychotherapy sessions with his psychiatrist for over a year, all the while continuing his exhibitionist behavior. The patient was informed by the police at his latest arrest that if he exhibited himself again he would be jailed, in treatment or not.

The patient had been married for 13 years and was the father of two boys. His exhibitionism began, as he recalled, when he was 13 or 14 years old when he exposed himself to his aunt, an attractive 25-year-old. Shortly after he had begun exposing himself quite frequently in his home to his younger sister and her girlfriends, who would laugh and make a game of his behavior. This pattern continued for almost two years, during which time he also began exposing himself to a young neighborhood married woman in her early thirties through a large picture window in the back bedroom of his home. For over a year he exhibited to this woman, who would smile and wave to him as he masturbated.

The patient estimated that he subsequently exposed himself an average of three or four times a month over the last 27-28 years. The general pattern of his behavior remained relatively constant during this time. No preference was noted regarding the places he chose for exposing himself. Typical choices were parks, street corners, swimming pools, beaches, trains, and his neighborhood. He did not show a great deal of discretion in his choice of victims, although he did admit a slight preference for young attractive women somewhere between 25 and 35 years of age. He also expressed a preference for small-breasted women, although he reported exposing himself to moderate and large-breasted women on many occasions. He typically exposed himself while in an erect state until he had the victim's attention, at which time he would begin to masturbate at a furious pace. Seldom did he reach orgasm during an exhibitionist episode, although he nearly always masturbated to orgasm soon afterward.

The patient clinically appeared to fit a general pattern frequently seen in exhibitionists—a quiet, well-mannered, submissive, nice guy, former church official, with significant feelings of worthlessness, insecurity, and depression as well as inadequate assertive and heterosocial skills. He described himself as a "candy-ass," unable to relate, meet, and stand up to people at work, home, or in social situations.

Due to the patient's hesitation and concern over the use of electrical aversion we agreed on shame aversion as the treatment of choice to eliminate his deviant behavior. A treatment plan was formulated and presented to the patient and his wife for approval. His wife refused to participate in the therapy; consequently, five young attractive women—two female clinical psychology graduate students, two nurses, and one female physician—were recruited to assist in treatment. The clinical use of the female volunteers was agreed to by both the patient and his wife. A meeting was held with the volunteers to outline the procedure and explain the rationale of the treatment program. Using a similar case presented by Reitz and Keil (1971) as a model, we decided that our office would be treated as a waiting room in which the patient would sit, while the volunteers would enter one at a time. After entering, each woman sat and read a magazine for ten minutes. The patient was instructed to exhibit himself to each woman as nearly as possible to the way he would in real life knowing that at the end of ten minutes she would get up and leave. Conversation was to be avoided by all participants, and the volunters were instructed to react to the exhibition with indifference, thus withdrawing the reinforcement of exposing and subjecting the patient to the moderate punishment of guilt, shame, and embarrassment.

The patient reported great difficulty in exposing himself to the volunteers. He reported being strongly embarrassed, ashamed, and guilty while doing so, yet he nevertheless continued with treatment. Four sessions were required before the patient reported no sexual arousal or interest in exposing himself. Ten additional sessions were conducted before a physiological assessment was conducted which substantiated his report.

In an attempt to modify the pattern of his sexual arousal, which frequently precipitated his exhibitionistic episodes, masturbation training was instituted. The patient was instructed to masturbate daily to fantasies of engaging in intercourse with his wife or to pictures from various adult magazines. The patient reported to us weekly on his frequency of masturbation, sexual urges (both for intercourse and for exhibitionism), intercourse, exhibitionistic acts, and his masturbatory fantasies. Frequency of intercourse and fantasies of intercourse increased as dramatically as the frequency of exhibitionistic urges and deviant masturbatory fantasies decreased to no exhibitionistic acts over the two-month treatment period. The patient did report, however, that the relationship with his wife continued to be inadequate both interpersonally and sexually. A private session with the wife brought out the information that she had been seeing another man for over three years and planned to leave the patient soon. Up to this point in treatment, assertiveness training had not been included in the treatment plan for fear of retribution from the somewhat domineering, hostile, and uncooperative wife. Since she was going to leave anyway, we felt that the likelihood of the patient's maintaining his therapeutic gains would be facilitated by assertiveness training. Approximately a week after the consultation with the wife, she informed the patient of her decision and left. The patient became very depressed and withdrawn, and reported renewed urges to expose himself. Masturbation training to pornographic stimuli and assertiveness training using modeling and rehearsal were immediately instituted. Female volunteers were recruited and trained to interact with the patient socially, thus allowing him to rehearse heterosocial skills. These rehearsal sessions were videotaped and reviewed by the patient at the conclusion of each session.

Despite these measures, the patient revealed that the urge to expose himself was becoming increasingly stronger. We therefore decided to offer the patient several aversive booster sessions using electrical aversion. The patient agreed to this treatment plan. A physiological sexual assessment revealed a minimal arousal to exhibitionist films and fantasy. Electrical aversion was administered contingent upon the patient's penile arousal to sexual fantasies of exposing himself. Three aversive sessions resulted in the elimination of physiological arousal to the deviant fantasy, and the patient's verbal report substantiated the termination of this urge. Social skills and assertive training were again instituted using modeling and role-playing.

Three- and six-month follow-ups revealed that the patient was functioning well both socially and sexually with no incidents of exposing himself. He was actively dating a number of different women and reported satisfaction in all aspects of his life. A third physiological sexual assessment revealed strong heterosexual arousal, and no indication of penile arousal to exhibitionistic stimuli or fantasy.

CHAPTER 8

Fetishism and Transvestism

The behaviors of fetishism and transvestism represent deviations of sexual arousal manifesting themselves in the preference for an inappropriate sexual object(s). Most individuals express a sexual preference for members of the opposite sex or members of the same sex; fetishists and transvestites are sexually aroused by some peculiarity of the human body, or, more often, to nonliving *objects* rather than people. The DSM III formally defines fetishism as sexual arousal and attraction to some special part or peculiarity of the body or by some nonliving object; it defines transvestism as recurrent and persistent cross-dressing in order to achieve sexual excitation (APA, 1978). If the fetish object happens to be clothing of the opposite sex, differentiation between fetishism and transvestism becomes difficult and perhaps unnecessary with respect to treatment. As we shall see, however, transvestism specifically describes sexual arousal as a result of dressing in clothing of the opposite sex, while fetish objects include a considerable range of items, including clothing of the opposite sex. In addition, most transvestities cross-dress in a number of articles of clothing common to the opposite sex, while fetishists usually achieve sexual arousal as a result of a single object.

The clinical data regarding fetishism and transvestism reveal a number of similarities in these behaviors. First, as previously mentioned, both fetishists and transvestites achieve sexual arousal from nonliving objects. Second, like the majority of deviant sexual behavior, fetishism and transvestism are encountered in males more frequently than in females. Third, a number of single case studies have documented deficits in heterosocial skills among these individuals. Fourth, fetishists and transvestites frequently appear socially withdrawn, isolated and lonely as a result of their sexual preoccupation. Fifth, most fetishists and transvestites demonstrate difficulties in heterosexual functioning, particularly impotence, if prohibited from engaging in their preferred fantasy or deviant behavior.

Behavioral treatment formulations for fetishism and transvestism are similar in that they advocate a multimodal treatment approach based on a thorough behavioral assessment, and frequently use an aversive component to extinguish the deviant arousal followed by education and reinforcement designed to teach and facilitate alternative skills and behavior pat-

261

terns. In the following sections, both fetishism and transvestism will be described independently. Because of the similarities in treatment considerations, however, a common treatment section will be presented.

FETISHISM

It is often difficult to differentiate objectively between a sexual preference and a fetish. Fetish behaviors, like most behaviors, lie on a continuum so that a number of individuals experience fetishism to some extent. For example, one male may prefer tall, small-breasted blondes while another is turned on by short, large-breasted brunettes. One man may find freckles particularly erotic, and another may be fascinated by a creamy, china-doll complexion. There is nothing unusual in finding certain things or individual characteristics more erotic than others. Most of us have been told, however, that only certain types of sexual behavior are normal, and any variation is labeled abnormal. It is as though we cannot respond to our own inclinations but must let society decide what is natural for each of us in our sexual activities.

In many cases the loneliness and the problems encountered by the fetishist might have been avoided if he could have found a partner who would accept and be noncritical of him. Consider the following example:

The husband was fascinated by elbow-length gloves. Unless his wife wore white kid gloves during intercourse he was practically impotent. As soon as she drew them on, however, he was powerfully stimulated. They kept a number of pairs of gloves in a special drawer. It was ceremoniously unlocked before going to bed as though beginning a sacred rite. This preliminary was a kind of symbolic love-play. (Chesser, 1971, p. 116)

On the other hand, it is often difficult to match a fetish desire with a willing partner as the following example demonstrates:

When sexually reawakened in the adolescent, KS was attracted not to women but to the fur or leather wraps they happened to wear. The attraction spread from coats and capes to gloves and shoes, women's riding boots, particularly . . . . Real female skin seemed revolting. Breasts and female genitalia were repulsive and roused intense feelings of guilt. A woman's bare foot was lifeless; that same foot in a shoe . . . . Then . . . could KS feel true sexual desire and exert full potency. Nevertheless, KS did fall in love and marry . . . . She could not understand . . . his "holy ceremony of love" which required her to put on furs or bearskin gloves before the love act, or his total impotence without resort to his fetishes. KS found that his wife could not come into his fantasy world . . . Without them, he was impotent. With them, he knew his wife's revulsion. (Ruitenbeek, 1974, p. 52)

Originally *fetish* meant an idol or an object with some magical significance (Delora & Warren, 1977). When the fetish serves as a stimulus to masturbation or intercourse, it is a partial fetish; when the fetish object serves to induce orgasm either with or without object contact but with additional stimulation, it is a "complete fetish" (Chesser, 1971). Both males and females frequently experience partial fetishism; romantic atmospheres with candlelight and soft music or the shape and movement of a sexy partner have put countless individuals in the mood for intercourse. More men than women demonstrate complete fetishism, however, although this behavior is certainly not entirely absent in women.

Fetish Objects

Fetish objects are frequently articles of female cloth: underwear, shoes, gloves, perfumes (Caprio, 1973). However, a fetish also may be part of the body, such as ankles, breasts, ears, hands, hair, or any object associated with the opposite sex that serves to sexually arouse the individual. The list of possible fetish objects is inexhaustible, although some are more common than others. Thorpe, Katz, and Lewis (1961) claim that rubber, fur, and silk are particularly popular in our culture.

Some fetishists carry on their behavior in secret, preferring to indulge in their sexual preferences with no involvement or interference from others. Problems arise when someone else is holding, wearing, or in possession of the desired object. In order to obtain the object the fetishist may occasionally commit burglary, theft, or even assault. East (1946) reported the case of a hair fetishist who was arrested for approaching a young girl on the street and cutting off a lock of her hair. At the offender's residence five plaits of hair of different colors, as well as 72 hair ribbons, were discovered.

Foot Fondler Tripped Up?

San Antonio, Tex.—Police said yesterday they believe they have nabbed the phantom female foot fondler. Several women residents on the affluent north side of the city have reported being attacked by a young man who grabbed their feet, slipped off their shoes then kissed and carressed their toes. Thursday, officers said a man pushed a 30-year-old woman shopper against her car, grabbed her ankle and removed her shoe. But he ran away, with her shoe still in his hand, when the woman struggled and screamed. An off-duty officer and passerby subdued the man, who was charged with stealing a shoe and jailed in lieu of $10,000 bond. (*Providence Journal Bulletin*)

Probably the articles most commonly taken by fetishists are women's undergarments. Coleman (1972) described the case of a young man who

was found to have accumulated over a hundred pairs of panties from a lingerie shop when he was apprehended. It is also quite common for a fetishist
to be arrested for stealing panties and bras from clotheslines. In such cases
the excitement and suspense of the criminal act itself may reinforce the sexual stimulation and in some cases actually constitute the fetish, the article
stolen being of little importance. For example, Coleman (1972) described
one youth who admitted entering a large number of homes in which the entering itself usually sufficed to induce an orgasm. When it did not, he was
able to achieve sexual satisfaction by taking some "token" such as money
or jewelry.

Sometimes the fetishist becomes so obsessed with his favorite objects
that he becomes a collector, keeping careful records of the date and origin
of the acquisition. We treated one fetishist who kept a detailed diary describing the date, time, location, and owner of every pair of panties he
stole. Although this fetishist's usual approach involved stealing garments
off clotheslines and from laundry rooms, he reported that on one occasion
he patiently followed a woman as she strolled through a park. When she
finally entered the restroom he burst into the toilet, literally catching her
with her pants down, and snatched the panties from around her ankles before hurrying out of the door.

Fetish Behavior

Although most fetishists are capable of participating in heterosexual
relations, their sexual arousal is often contingent upon fantasies of the
fetish object or the actual wearing of the object. In many cases the heterosexual partner is aware of the fetish and participates by wearing the valued
object. One married patient, for instance, exhibited a fetish for garter belts
and women's seamed hoisery. He and his wife had a collection of garter
belts, one of which the wife would wear with seamed hose during sexual activity. During nonsexual activities she wore pantyhose which was nonarousing to the patient. The fetish garter belt and seamed hose, however,
had the effect of transforming an otherwise impotent husband into an "insatiable romantic."

Another fetish behavior is masturbation in association with the fetish
object. Here, of course, it is difficult to differentiate fetish behavior and
the effort to increase the sexual arousal, excitation, and satisfaction of
masturbation through the use of pictures and other articles associated with
the desired object. Utilization of such articles and fantasy in masturbation
is generally thought to be a rather common practice and is usually not considered pathological. However, when antisocial behavior, such as theft or
breaking and entering, is involved, or when masturbation to the object be-

comes the individual's preferred or exclusive sexual behavior, the practice is likely to be labeled as fetishistic.

A somewhat different, but not atypical, pattern of fetishistic behavior is illustrated in the case of a man whose fetish was women's shoes and legs:

> The fetishist in this case was arrested several times for loitering in public places, such as railroad stations and libraries, watching women's legs. Finally he chanced on a novel solution to his problem. Posing as an agent for a hosiery firm, he hired a large room, advertised for models, and took motion pictures of a number of girls walking and seated with their legs displayed to best advantage. He then used these pictures to achieve sexual satisfaction and found that they continued adequate for the purpose. (Grant, 1953, p. 221)

For those individuals who seek partners for fetishistic or other unusual sexual acts, personal ads in various gay and straight underground newspapers serve to match sexual partners. For a small fee, and often at no cost to females, these newspapers print advertisements for partners to engage in practically any sexual behavior. Delora and Warren (1977) provide examples:

> TOY BALLOONS—BiWM [bisexual white male] professional with unique fetish—kids' balloons turn me on! If you have same or complementary turn on, would like to hear.

> BOXING FANS—WM uni grad, turned-on by prizefights, leather boxing great, etc., wishes to hear from ringsiders, any age. Object: Friendship. Also research amateur boxing hist. See info and pics of stag smoker battle royals, clandestine newsboy B.A. fight shows, etc.

Fetishists are also considered good customers by many prostitutes who specialize in fulfilling unusual sexual preferences as this exerpt from our files shows:

> Most of my customers are repeats, you know, regulars who know that I'll do the kinky stuff. I like it that way cause there's a hell of a lot more green [money] in it and lots of times I don't even have to put out . . . . It's really weird you know, these guys put out a lot of green to do some of the damnedest things . . . like dressing up like a cheerleader and letting them feel me up under my sweater while they jerk off. Another guy pays me $50.00 every other Friday to sit on the john and take a leak while he stands in front of me and jerks off. Another kinky wants me to dress in this leather outfit I wear to ride my cycle and let him rub his joint all over me . . . . I don't know, you guys are shrinks, you explain it. I guess it's just that they're looking for something they don't get at home. Probably afraid to tell their wives what turns them on. Maybe just easier to fluff my nest [pay her for sexual services]. All I know

is that I tried hooking the straights [those men desiring only intercourse] once and damn near went broke . . . too many good lookers out there [attractive nonprostitutes available]. Working with the kinkies keeps me in fat city [financially comfortable].

Research and Theory: Physiological Factors

Biological theories vary but generally state that fetish behavior is frequently the result of organic pathology. An occasional association with temporal lobe epilepsy has been noted (Davies & Morganstein, 1960), although the association is infrequent and not well understood. Some researchers attribute the behavior to a unique result of electrical discharge from cortical cells. Other organic theories attribute fetish behavior to encephalopathy such as brain tumors, especially meningiomas, astrocytomas, and oligodendrogliomas; little substantiative data exist, however.

In 1961, Epstein described four fetishist patients, three of whom showed electroencephalographic (EEG) abnormality of temporal lobe origin and one who showed a temporal lobe focus and a generalized abnormal EEG. One of the four patients had clinically verified epileptic convulsions. Certain other clinical features were also cited to substantiate brain dysfunction in these subjects: (1) hyperactivity; (2) disturbed sleep patterns in infancy; (3) early enuresis; (4) learning difficulty; and (5) somnambulism. In addition, Epstein described a case of episodic transvestism combined with epilepsy in which the EEG showed diffuse dysrhythmia, though not distinctly localized over the temporal lobes. In one of the cases Epstein followed for years, the EEG was initially considered only slightly abnormal but became increasingly abnormal through the years and eventually showed spikes coming from one of the temporal lobes.

Epstein summarized his findings by suggesting that although clinical manifestations of dysfunction in the temporal (more properly limbic) system are not well understood and cannot be fully explained, they appear to be associated with fetishist behavior. Recent advances in electroencephalographic and other neurological diagnostic techniques do not usually support Epstein's work (Lansdell, 1971).

Research and Theory: Psychological Factors

An endless number of stimuli can come to be associated with sexual arousal in everyday life. Probably most people are stimulated to some degree by intimate articles of clothing and by perfumes and odors associated with the opposite sex. In many instances, however, such associations are not easy to explain. In this section we shall discuss two popular yet contrasting theories as to the ediology and maintenance of fetishism.

Psychoanalytic Formulations. Psychoanalytic theories of fetishism are legion. In fact, fetishism is one of the few specific sexual disorders to which Freud (1928), in his latter years, devoted a complete paper. Freud regarded the fetish object as a substitute for the penis which, as a young child, the fetishist believed his mother possessed. The child's perception of the mother's penis is modified as the child grows older so that a penis in a true anatomical sense is correctly denied. Yet the afflicted child persists in his belief that the mother does possess some type of mysterious penis, and the fetish object is thought to substitute for it. Psychoanalysts also associate certain personality characteristics and patterns with fetishists. According to Epstein (1960), the fetishist tends to be obsessional and reserved, to have sexual fears relating to body mutilation, to show strong maternal attachment, to manifest an early interest in sexual matters, and be anal-sadistic.

Behavioral Formulations. In considering the behavioral formulation for the etiology and maintenance of fetishism, we emphasize that the sexualization of certain objects is normal. For example, there are stores that specialize in the sale of women's erotic, sexy undergarments and lingerie, with names like Frederick's of Hollywood, Sarah Ann's Undercover World, and Lynn's Lingerie. These businesses demonstrate the fact that women's erotic underwear has popular sexual appeal. In many instances, however, the sexualization of certain objects is difficult to explain. For example, Bergler (1946) cited an unusual case in which a man's sexual behavior was almost completely dominated by a fetishistic fascination for exhaust pipes of automobiles. Nor would just any exhaust pipe do; it had to be in perfect shape, that is to say, undented and undamaged, and it had to emit softly blowing gases. This fetish behavior was deemed far more sexual than erotic activities associated with women.

The genesis and maintenance of fetishism is undoubtedly difficult for the average person to comprehend. In fact, fetishism is a source of much humor for many individuals with normal sexual orientation. It is a source of extreme consternation for most fetishists. To understand the etiology of this behavior we must trace the behavior through a series of logical progressions.

The first prerequisite in fetishism appears to be a conditioning experience. In many instances this original conditioning experience may be quite accidental, as when sexual arousal and orgasm—which are both reflexive responses—are elicited by a strong emotional experience involving some particular object or part of the body (Coleman, 1972). For example, one patient was able to achieve an erection only when his leg was encased in a plaster case, the kind that is usually used to restrict the movement of a broken leg. The patient had gone to considerable length to collect a number of casts which he used in masturbatory and coital activities. A sexual assessment revealed that as an 11-year-old boy the patient had suffered a broken leg. During the casting of his leg, the physician was assisted by a young, attractive nurse who was required to hold the patient's bare leg as a plaster cast was placed from his foot to his hip. Tactile stimulation of his thigh by the nurse resulted in the patient's experiencing an erection. The patient reported repeatedly masturbating to this memory throughout his teenage years.

The endowment of a formerly neutral stimulus with sexual properties has also been demonstrated in an interesting classical conditioning experiment by Rachman (1966). Rachman conditioned a mild fetish, under laboratory conditions, in several male clinical psychology graduate students. A photograph of women's boots was repeatedly presented to the subjects followed by photographs of nude females which the subjects had chosen as sexually stimulating. As a result of this conditioning paradigm, subjects came to exhibit sexual arousal, as measured by changes in penile volume, to photographs of the boots alone. Further investigation revealed that this response soon generalized to other types of women's shoes as well.

The second prerequisite of fetishism seems to be the strengthening and maintenance of the initial conditioning experience through the reinforcement of masturbation and orgasm. In addition, variables such as heterosocial and heterosexual skills deficits, as well as the availability of receptive members of the opposite sex, frequently pay an important role in the etiology and maintenance of the deviant behavior. For example, we treated a 21-year-old veteran of the Vietnam war who exhibited a fetish for women with amputated limbs. The patient had collected a variety of pictures of multilated bodies and also *Playboy* photographs of women from which he had cut off one of the arms or legs. These pictures were regularly used in masturbation or for penile erection just prior to coitus with his wife. A sexual history revealed that, while in Vietnam, the patient frequently encountered mutilated bodies of partially nude Vietnamese females killed during enemy bombings and attacks. In addition, the patient had lost his virginity during the war to a Vietnamese prostitute who had lost one leg as a result of an automobile accident. The patient began to incorporate memories of the partially nude mutilated bodies as well as photographs of the ghastly scenes into his masturbatory practices. Conditioning was further strengthened by repeated sexual activity with the prostitute. At the time of referral the patient was totally impotent without his deviant visual stimuli.

CASE HISTORY 8-1

The patient was a 24-year-old salesman referred for treatment of a fetish for women's underwear. The patient reported his usual sexual behavior consisted of dressing in women's panties and masturbating to orgasm. He estimated his frequency of heterosexual dating to be six or seven times per month, primarily with the same woman. Intercourse with this woman was estimated to occur approximately one or two times per week. The patient reported being impotent during sexual activities unless he wore women's undergarments. He complained that while he did not really enjoy regularly dating the same woman, she appeared to understand and accept his unusual sexual behavior. The patient reported no desire to dress in women's underwear at any time other than during masturbation or intercourse.

A sexual history revealed that the patient first remembered masturbating as a youth by rubbing his penis to orgasm with a pair of his mother's silk underwear. This activity was repeatedly engaged in whenever he was alone in the house. After a while the patient stole a pair of underwear from a neighbor's clothesline, hiding it in his room where he would employ the garment in masturbation almost nightly.

When the patient was approximately 14 years old he began regularly dating a girl from his school. During the first several months of this relationship the patient continued masturbating with the aid of women's underwear while fantasizing the young girl. Sexual activities between the two gradually progressed to the point where the girl would allow the patient to unbutton her blouse, pull up her skirt, lie between her legs, and masturbate himself to orgasm by rubbing his penis against her panties and mons pubis. During this time he confiscated a piece of his partner's underwear which he would enjoy in masturbation.

During the patient's teenage years he continued masturbating to fantasies and photographs of women in underwear, collecting a scrapbook of pictures of women's underwear advertisements from catalogs and magazines. During this time the patient also began regularly stealing undergarments from laundry rooms and clotheslines. This unusual behavior later generalized to stealing from a number of women, most of whom he knew, until he was stealing approximately once a week. Each pair of panties stolen was carefully labeled to note the name of the owner and the date taken. Masturbation activities during this period involved carefully choosing a pair of panties from his collection, fantasizing the owner dressed in the underwear, and rubbing his penis to orgasm.

The patient reported one episode of sneaking into the girls' locker room and stealing several pair of panties while the girls' swimming team was practicing in the gymnasium pool, and using these garments as both olfactory and tactile masturbatory aids. He later found an advertisement in an underground newspaper offering to sell soiled panties by mail. He purchased several pair of panties by mail which aroused him because of their odor and texture.

The patient had never been discovered stealing, although in one adventure he was chased by a dog, collided with a lawn mower in the dark, and suffered a leg wound that required 15 stitches. He told us he had revealed his sexual orientation to three different women with no immediate adverse reaction from any of them. Two of the three women allowed him to wear feminine undergarments during intercourse but later refused further dates with him. The third woman was his regular sexual partner. At the time of referral the patient reported that he frequently wore women's underwear under his usual clothing, especially on weekends. He claimed he found the thought and texture of the garments so extremely arousing that he would feel the desire to masturbate repeatedly.

TRANSVESTISM

Transvestism, or cross-dressing, involves wearing the dress of the opposite sex in order to produce sexual arousal. The terms transvestism and transsexualism are frequently confused and are sometimes used interchangeably. They are, however, two distinct patterns of behavioral disorders. Clinical evidence suggests that transvestites feel and think in ways that are consistent with their biological gender identity and exhibit, primarily, a heterosexual orientation. Transsexuals, however, are often deeply unhappy as members of their anatomically structured gender. Male transsexuals are popularly described as feeling like "a woman trapped in a man's body." Transsexualism will be discussed in Chapter 11.

Differentiation between fetishism and transvestism is also frequently difficult (Yates, 1970). Some authorities (Stroller, 1971) claim that transvestism is little more than fetish cross-dressing and should therefore be considered as simply one behavior along the fetish continuum. Disagreements concerning the taxonomy of transvestism need not be discussed here; for our purposes it is enough to consider transvestism, as well as fetishism, deviations of sexual object.

Transvestism is primarily thought to be a sexual behavior exhibited by males. Yates (1970), however, disagrees; he claims that cross-dressing among women is relatively common but is not considered pathological unless accompanied by other deviant behaviors. Apparently women do not engage in transvestism in its strictest definition, or if they do, most of the cases have not been reported in the literature. Many women dress in men's clothing on occasion, if slacks are considered male clothing; but the vast majority do not appear to become sexually aroused by this act.

There are two different types of transvestities. Many are sexually excited by a single feminine garment or a few garments, and this preference remains relatively constant throughout life. For example, a male may find it highly arousing to don a pair of women's lace panties, and may wear them often under his usual masculine outer garments (Delora & Warren, 1977). Although the other type of transvestities' may initially start with only a few feminine garments, they gradually include more and more garments until they dress completely in feminine clothing. They may succeed in passing as a woman, and they enjoy the thought that they are fooling the world and may at any moment reveal their secret (Stoller, 1971).

Life as a Transvestite

The typical male transvestite will cross-dress in female clothing, including underwear and makeup, and may masturbate while observing himself in the mirror. Other transvestities will stroll through public places dressed in feminine attire to obtain sexual excitement and admiring glances. Later, these individuals may masturbate to the memories and fantasies of these public excursions. Still other individuals may cross-dress for the purpose of inviting a homosexual experience. A vivid example is Miss Destiny in John Rechy's book, *City of Nights* (1963):

> . . . I went to Philadelphia. And the first thing I did why, I bought myself a flaming red dress and high heeled sequined shoes and everyone thought I was Real, and Miss Thing said, "Hurry honey; You've done it—stick to it"; and I met a rich daddy, who thought I was Real, and he flipped over me and took me to a straight cocktail party. (p. 106)

Incidence

It is important to note that transvestism is not necessarily associated with homosexual behavior, although it may be so oriented. Prince and Bentler (1972) reported a survey of 504 subscribers to the magazine *Transvestia*. The following is a summary of the major findings:

1. Only 22 percent were single men, the remainder being married or divorced. Eighty percent of the wives were aware of the problem and expressed the full gamut of reactions ranging from acceptance to rejection. Seventy-four percent of the married sample had one or more children.

2. Eighty-nine percent of the married sample considered themselves heterosexual, and 86 percent said that interest in females was normal or above average.

3. Sixty-six percent had never seen a psychiatrist or clinical psychologist and were not motivated to do so. In fact, 41 percent regarded cross-dressing favorably, despite an awareness of societal disapproval.

4. Sixty-nine percent described themselves as a man who "has a feminine side seeking expression," but by far the majority did not wish sex conversion surgery and were thus clearly distinguishable from transsexuals.

5. There was no evidence to support suggestions in the psychodynamic literature that disturbed families or childhood upbringing contributed to the problem; 83 percent replied that they had always been brought up and treated as a boy.

6. There was a general tendency to prefer wearing feminine clothing during heterosexual intercourse, the most commonly cited clothing preferences being for lingerie items.

7. Eighteen percent had appeared in public and 16 percent more were thought to have done so. Those who went out most frequently tended to have the strongest transvestic desires.

8. Approximately 50 percent remained secretive about their transvestism; 69 percent had at one time tried to discontinue the activity and had given away or destroyed their female clothing.

This discussion suggests that most transvestities are heterosexually oriented and many are married and have children. Bruckner (1970) formulated a description of the "ordinary" transvestite from an earlier survey of 262 subscribers to the magazine *Transvestia*.

> He is probably married (about two-thirds are); if he is married he probably has children (about two-thirds do). Almost all of these transvestites said they were exclusively heterosexual—in fact, the rate of homosexuality was less than the average for the general population. The transvestic behavior generally consists of privately dressing in the clothes of a woman, at home, in secret. . . .The transvestite generally does not run into trouble with the law. His cross-dressing causes difficulties for very few people besides himself and his wife. (p. 381)

As these surveys indicate, the wife of a married transvestite is often fully aware of her husband's cross-dressing. Occasionally, in fact, the wife participates in heterosexual intercourse with her husband when he is cross-dressing.

> When she got home, the lights were out in the foyer. The servants had all gone to bed, thinking she was in the bedroom with Tzigie. That probably meant that Tzigie was sleeping. She slipped out of her Valentino shoes, made her way quietly across the apartment floors, and gently opened the door to the master suite. He was standing in front of the full-length mirror by the marbletopped console. He had on one of her black chiffon scarves and a necklace of imitation rose quartz from Kenneth Lane, with matching earrings. His dress was the black and white vinyl she had discarded before the party. "Oh," he said, and brought up his hands, as if to shield himself from his own reflection.
>
> She closed the door and locked it, behind her back, watching him the entire time. He did not move.
>
> "I'm sorry," he said. "I'm really sorry."
>
> "That's all right," she swallowed. "If it makes you happy."
>
> "I didn't think you'd be home so early."
>
> "It isn't as if you're hurting anyone, is it?"
>
> "I didn't want you to know."
>
> "Why not?" Diane asked. "People do all kinds of things. As long as you don't hurt anybody. You make a very good-looking woman."
>
> "You're laughing at me?"
>
> "Not at all."
>
> She looked at him in the reflection, and then she looked at him directly. "As a matter of fact, I never realized until this very moment how much like me you really looked."
>
> "I take that as a great compliment," he said.
>
> "So you should," she said, and went to him.
>
> That evening they made love with a ferocity they had never had before,

she wanting him more than she had ever done, and he hungering to please her. Shortly after that he shaved off his moustache. From then on, she never went shopping, even for a brassiere, without him coming along. And whenever she wanted him, she had only to set out something of hers on the bed, or the chaise, so he would know, and make himself ready for her. (Davis, 1969, pp. 308–309)

Frequently, however, the transvestite's marriage is endangered. Many wives cannot tolerate seeing their husbands in feminine attire, as Stroller indicates:

"We fell in love and as soon as I felt we could we were married. We have been as happy as two people can be and the best part of it is that she knows all about me and not only accepts me as I am but assists in my transformation and then admire me . . . ."
    This is the way the relationship looks at first, when the wife is pleased to see her husband's femininity. She does not know yet that as he becomes a more successful transvestite her enthusiasm will wane. Then he will be hurt that she is no longer interested in his dressing up, his sexual needs, his work. The fighting will start, neither will understand what has happened, and they will divorce. (1967, p. 336)

Homosexuals may also cross-dress or "go in drag" on occasions, although it is generally believed that this behavior is not sexually arousing to them and may have little or no sexual motivation (Delora & Warren, 1977). Among gay males there are three general reasons for wearing feminine attire: (1) transvestism; (2) professional female impersonation—female impersonators are often star entertainers in many gay and straight nightclubs; (3) casual "camping," that is, having occasional fun as a "drag queen." Among gay males the drag queen represents a humorous caricature of femininity and effeminacy (Warren, 1974).

Individual gay males may be openly hostile to those who wear female clothing for a reason different from one that is acceptable to them; for example, some gays dislike all drag while others like it only in the casual sense (Warren, 1974). The annual San Francisco Beaux Arts Ball is a social occasion in which many homosexuals dress in feminine attire.

Female impersonators may also disdain transvestities:

Female impersonators do not refer to themselves as transvestites. Sometimes in interviews one would reluctantly say, "Well, I guess I'm sort of transvestite," but then he would quickly add, "but I only do it for a living," or "this is my job." To female impersonators, the real transvestites are the lone wolf isolates whose individual and private experiments with female attire are described as "freakish." To them the transvestite is one who dresses as a woman for some "perverted" sexual purpose. (Newton, 1972, p. 51)

Transvestites may make a genuine attempt to look like women and wear ordinary feminine clothing; drag queens and female impersonators usually wear outrageous, flamboyant, and out-of-the-ordinary evening costumes, with elaborate hair styles and glittering makeup (Newton, 1972).

Like male homosexuals, some female homosexuals also enjoy dressing in drag to attend a gay costume party or drag ball. A minority of female homosexuals consistently dress as males or do so in their leisure hours. However, unlike male drag queens, their masculine clothing usually resembles that of the blue-collar, jean-clad man rather than one who is elegantly attired. Lesbians who consistently dress as men often have very feminine sexual partners with whom they act out traditional male-female social, and often sexual, roles (see Chapter 6). There are very few professional male impersonators (Newton, 1972).

The exact incidence of transvestism is unknown, since individuals without homosexual involvement rarely seek treatment. The level of public condemnation is generally considered rather low. It is quite possible for an individual to participate in private cross-dressing all his life without the knowledge of interference of society.

Research and Theory: Physiological Factors

In the late 1950s and early 1960s a moderate degree of research on the association of cerebral dysfunction and transvestism was done. Thompson (1955) first suggested that there might be a cerebral center "discharging without normal cortical control" in cases of transvestism, and that the deviant behavior might be a form of cortical release phenomenon. He also drew attention to a proposed association of sexual psychopathology and psychomotor epilepsy. Hill, Pond, Mitchell, and Falconer (1957) later reported studying 27 patients who had undergone lobectomies for epilepsy, including three transvestites. These authors reported that following surgery the transvestite patients "acquired normal libidinal interest and sexual activity." Hunter, Logue, and McMenemy (1963) further popularized the hypothesis of cerebral dysfunction in transvestites by reporting a case of transvestism combined with temporal lobe epilepsy in a 39-year-old man who had begun engaging in cross-dressing when he was nine years old. The authors reported that at first both the sexual and convulsive disorders responded well to anticonvulsant treatment but after a time grew worse until a temporal lobectomy was performed. "After surgery both the convulsions and transvestism disappeared." Walinder (1965) found a similar occurrence of cerebral dysfunction in 8 of 18 electroencephalograms of transvestite subjects. While cerebral dysfunction is occasionally diagnosed in transvestites, recent research indicates that its incidence is no higher than in the general population, and the cerebral dysfunction hypothesis as a causal factor in transvestism has largely been discounted (Lansdell, 1971).

Research and Theory: Psychological Factors

Psychological theories proposed to explain the genesis and maintenance of transvestism cover an exceedingly broad range. Among these theories the oldest, that of "divine origin," has its roots in myth and magic. Herodotus explained the "Skythian illness" as a divine punishment, a curse upon the Skyths and their male posterity by the goddess Aphrodite, enraged with their plundering of her temple in Askalos.

The idea that dressing children in the clothing of the opposite sex leads to transvestic development is a contemporary etiological theory. Many transvestites report being dressed in girl's clothing as children. Such dressing supposedly puzzles and perplexes the child and prevents him from identifying with members of his own sex.

A variation of dressing children in opposite-sex clothing is cross-dressing children for punishment. Theoretically this behavior is supposed to precipitate transvestite tendencies by way of traumatic fixation. This variant applies only to male subjects since only the female dress for men has a humiliating connotation in our culture. London (1957) reported a patient punished by his mother by being forced to wear girl's clothing at the age of six. At first he felt "so shy and humiliated that when visitors came he would hide under the table." However soon he developed an interest in the feminine garments and would put them on at every opportunity.

The favored status of being a little girl in the family group is also thought to play a causative role in many transvestite cases. The psychological symbolism of transvestism here is self-explanatory. Through assuming the dress of the preferred sex (and thus pretending to belong to it), the child hopes to participate in the preferential treatment of the feminine sex; then as the boy matures, his sexual arousal is generalized and oriented to feminine clothing.

Psychoanalytic Formulations. Most psychoanalysts base their interpretations of transvestism on the writings of Freud (1928). Their etiological theory views transvestism as an attempt to overcome the fear of castration by creating an imaginary phallic woman and identifying with her. Fenichel (1949), for example, gave this symbolic formula of transvestism: "Phallic women exist; I myself am one." He elaborated further:

> The fantasy of a phallic girl is a substitute for a phallic exhibition which is inhibited by castration anxiety, and is composed of the two kinds of castration denial. I keep my penis by acting as if I were a girl. Girls are really no different from myself. (p. 81)

All this is condensed into the symbolic equation: "I = my whole body = a girl = the little one = the penis." Sadger (1921) reconstructs the train of thought of a male transvestite as follows: "When I put on my mother's dress I feel as if I were she herself, and so could arouse sexual feelings in myself and in my father, and possibly supplant her with him."

In the act of transvestism both object love and identification are supposedly present, the forms in which each manifests itself being modified by the castration complex and the patient's obstinate retention of his belief that the woman possesses a phallus. The act has a twofold significance: (1) object-erotic, and (2) narcissistic (homosexual). Instead of having coitus with the mother or ner substitute the patient enters into sexual relations with her clothes, which he brings into as close contact as he can with his own person and particularly with his genital organ. This theory explains why transvestites frequently prefer that the feminine garments should have been used, and, if possible, should still retain something of the warmth and odor of the woman's body. This intercourse is conceived of in typically sadistic terms. The patient himself represents a woman with a penis, and the penis is represented in twofold manner: (1) in the patient's genitals, and (2) in the articles of clothing which are a symbolic substitute for the penis and which the transvestite (even if he cross-dresses secretly) always wants to display. This desire is considered a form of displaced exhibitionism which, according to analytic thinking, is also designed to refute the idea of castration.

Behavioral Formulations. Sexual deviations may be viewed as a problem of stimulus control since sexual arousal occurs in the presence of an inappropriate stimulus (Barlow & Agras, 1973). Transvestism, therefore, may be viewed as a problem of stimulus control since sexual arousal occurs in the wearing of women's clothing.

Nonsexual objects may be eroticized by frequent and repeated associations with actual sexual parts and functions or because of chance associations under emotionally charged conditions (Rachman, 1966). If a powerful reinforcer such as sexual arousal and masturbatory orgasm to an object is introduced, the conditioning process becomes even more potent. Given certain predisposing factors such as deficits in heterosocial and heterosexual skills combined with selected environmental variables, and theoretically the stage is set for the development of transvestism, as illustrated in the following case history.

CASE HISTORY 8-2

The patient was a 28-year-old attorney who referred himself for treatment following his third failure to pass the bar exam. He reported cross-dressing since the age of 14, and claimed that his sexual behavior was responsible for his examination failure because he spent an excessive amount of time in sexual activities. He also claimed that he had virtually no social life during or since high school because of cross-dressing and reported no experiences with heterosexual intercourse. At the time of the initial interview the patient reported cross-dressing approximately five to seven times per week. He had never entertained thoughts about or desire for a sex-change operation, and had no homosexual experience or fantasies. A detailed physiological assessment substantiated the patient's heterosexual orientation and transvestic preferences. The patient reported his heterosexual experience had been limited to heavy petting with occasional girlfriends and mutual masturbation with one woman. None of his heterosexual relationships had lasted more than a few weeks. The patient reported his current sexual behavior consisted of dressing in women's clothing (including makeup and underwear) and masturbating as he viewed himself in a full-length mirror. He claimed never to have appeared in public while cross-dressing.

A sexual history revealed the patient's first transvestic experience occurred during the summer of his fourteenth year when an older female cousin spent several months visiting his family. The patient remembered being sexually attracted to the cousin at the onset of her visit. During one particular family outing at a lake he accidentally viewed the cousin nude as she was changing into her swimsuit. The patient reported being highly aroused by this sight, but hurried back into the water to avoid being discovered. The patient reported fantasizing the sight of his nude cousin the remainder of the day and became increasingly aroused. Later the same day he took the girl's swimsuit from the clothesline and masturbated by rubbing his penis against the crotch of the suit while fantasizing the woman.

For the next week or so the patient frequently fantasized the female cousin and attempted to repeat his voyeuristic experience by looking up her dress and peeping through the keyhole to her room. These efforts met with failure and frustration. Finally he slipped into her room to remove a pair of her panties which he again employed in masturbation. Several days later he removed a pair of her soiled panties from the laundry room, and during the course of masturbastion slipped the garment on. He then ejaculated by lying on his stomach and rubbing his penis against the garment and the bed.

The patient reported that he gradually stole more and more articles of clothing from his cousin's room to use in masturbation until he eventually could dress completely in them, including shoes, stockings, underwear, and dress. After several experiences of complete cross-dressing and masturbation, he was accidentally discovered by his mother and cousin during one such episode. The patient reported that since he was not masturbating at the time of discovery he informed his startled mother and cousin that he was "just doing it as a gag." His mother announced that if he wanted to dress like a girl he should "do it right," and forced him to let her and the cousin put facial makeup on him. The mother soon tired of this punishment and left the cousin to complete the task, after which the cousin asked the patient if he were wearing a bra. When he answered no, she made him take off the dress so that she could put a bra on him. While she was doing this, he became sexually aroused and tried to hide his erect penis from his cousin, but she noticed his arousal, laughingly called attention to his "big boy hard-on," and playfully thumped his penis with her finger. The patient reported masturbating to the fantasy of this experience while cross-dressed for several years afterward.

Throughout college and law school the patient spent most of his time either studying or cross-dressing. He reported frequently cross-dressing and spending an entire afernoon or evening wandering around his apartment in a state of sexual arousal, delaying masturbation as long as possible. Although he felt socially uncomfortable around women, he dated on occasion and had engaged in heavy kissing and fondling of genitalia with several women. His only heterosexual experience of significance was with a woman to whom he had admitted his sexual preference. Over a period of some eight or nine weeks this relationship gradually evolved to where the couple would lie nude together kissing and fondling each other. The patient would then perform cunnilingus on the woman for long periods of time until she reached orgasm. The couple would then engage in a very ritualistic sequence of behaviors in which the patient watched as the woman carefully dressed completely (always in a dress) as the patient became slowly aroused. When fully dressed she would begin dressing the patient in women's clothing, beginning with makeup, underwear, hose, wig, and finally a dress. By the time the patient was fully dressed, he was highly aroused. The patient would next stand in front of a full-length mirror as the woman reached under his dress and masturbated him to orgasm. He reported these sexual encounters would frequently take as long as four hours to complete.

As this case history illustrates, the etiology and maintenance of transvestism cannot be attributed to one factor, but rather the interplay of several variables in combination. This patient originally reported a measure of sexual arousal to his female cousin. This arousal in a 14-year-old boy to an older attractive woman may be considered appropriate or normal. The chance discovery of his cousin nude provided additional sexual valence to her and resulted in increased sexual arousal. Again, increased sexual arousal is appropriately targeted toward a member of the opposite sex and no deviation of object is suggested. Next, in an effort to relieve his sexual arousal the patient masturbated using his cousin's swimsuit as a masturbatory aid, yet fantasizing the nude woman. Here the sexual stimulus during masturbation remains the woman, although an article of clothing as a masturbatory aid is introduced into the masturbatory act. The ensuing week provided no additional novel sexual stimulation; therefore the patient resorted to repeated masturbation, this time with underwear belonging to the cousin. During this time the patient first put on an article of women's clothing and experienced a powerful orgasm. This reinforcement led to additional masturbatory episodes in which the patient's sexual arousal was satisfied with a variety of his cousin's garments. Here we see the patient's sexual arousal generalizing to various articles of clothing which he would wear during masturbation.

In the next sequence of events the association of the patient's sexual arousal to his female cousin and also to articles of women's clothing was reinforced by the cousin who carefully put makeup on the patient, had him stand partially nude in front of her, and acknowledged his erection both verbally ("big boy hard on") and physically (briefly touching his penis).

The patient admitted that the fantasy of his experience served as a powerful sexual stimulus for several years of masturbatory conditioning. Finally the patient's sexual history reveals a period of solitary cross-dressing and masturbatory reinforcement as well as episodes of cooperation in acting out his sexual preference. The pattern of sexual behavior was thus maintained through repeated reinforcement, so that what he later perceived as periodic aversive consequences such as guilt over his lack of a better social life and failure to pass his licensing examination, were of insufficient strength, frequency, and duration to offset his cross-dressing.

MODIFICATION OF FETISHISM AND TRANSVESTISM

Treatment techniques for fetishism and transvestism encompass a variety of strategies from psychological to pharmacological, few of which have proven successful. Benjamin (1953) admits that, "Medical science is rather helpless in the more pronounced instances of deviated behavior . . . . this applies to transvestism." Other researchers echo Benjamin's pessimistic opinion while maintaining a genetic etiological adherence, "The tragedy in the life of these human beings is innate and inborn and can't be completely remedied in any way, neither by medical nor administrative means" (Glaus, 1952).

Medical Therapies

As with most deviant or abnormal behaviors, treatment of fetishism and transvestism originally fell within the domain of medicine. The literature documents three general categories of medically oriented treatment of these disorders: physical methods, glandular methods, and pharmacological methods.

> Physical treatment techniques cannot cure transvestism and fetishism as such, but can relieve the patient from some accompanying psychoneurotic symptoms, such as depression, feelings of guilt, and anxiety and thus enable him to cope more efficiently with his difficulties, and eventually make a more satisfactory adjustment. (Lukianowicz, 1959, p. 303)

Techniques such as electroconvulsive therapy and modified insulin therapy have been advocated as therapeutic in the sense that the patient "feels better" about his deviant behavior. In addition lobectomies used to be performed occasionally on fetishists and transvestites whose behavior was thought to be associated with cerebral dysfunctions (McMenemy, 1963). A review of the literature produces little reliable data documenting the efficacy of these techniques.

Glandular methods of treatment, which amount to chemical castration, have been applied to some male transvestites with the therapeutic aim of inhibiting the testicular function and causing a secondary feminization. Fortunately there are few advocates of this type of therapy in which large doses of estrogen are administered to the patient. Benjamin (1953) recommends that endocrine treatment at the earliest possible stage be administered to milder cases of fetishism and transvestism. Hamburger (1953) also advocates glandular treatment, though he recommends it as a preparatory measure for the subsequent operative castration that should follow, and not for the treatment effects *per se*.

A variety of pharmacologic agents have been suggested in the treatment of fetishism and transvestism. Included in the list are depressants (barbiturates and alcohol); anti-depressants (MAO-inhibitors); anti-psychotics (phenothiazines); and tranquilizers (benzodiazepines). While the effects of pharmacologic agents may be worthwhile in the treatment of behaviors, such as depression, associated with the deviant behavior, little evidence exists that chemotherapy is an effective treatment for fetishism and transvestism.

Psychoanalysis

As previously noted psychoanalysts regard fetishism and transvestism as the result of intense castration fears. As a result, treatment techniques such as developing insight into the dynamics of the deviant behavior through free association, dream analysis, and transference are commonly employed.

Peabody, Row, and Wall (1953) reported the psychoanalytic treatment of two cases of transvestism and one case of glove fetishism. In one case, transvestism was associated with psychopathic behavior, and the author claimed that treatment was unsuccessful. The second transvestite was still undergoing analysis at the time of the report, and the glove fetishist, who reportedly also suffered from schizophrenia, was still engaging in the fetish behavior after two years of analysis. Nonetheless, the authors claim that "the analytic approach with emphasis on dynamic understanding and guidance offers the best results."

Behavior Therapy

A number of reports exist about behavioral treatment programs aimed at modifying fetish and transvestic behavior (Barker & Miller, 1968; Bond & Evans, 1967; Clark, 1963; Kushner, 1965; Marks & Gelder, 1967; McGuire & Valance, 1964; Raymond, 1956; Raymond & O'Keefe, 1965; Thorpe et al., 1964). Most of these behavioral treatments have consisted of little more than aversion therapy. In retrospect, however, many of the early behavioral conceptualizations of fetishism and transvestism seem naive since they tend to consider behaviors in terms of oversimplified general categories; fetishism, for example, does not include a detailed description of the complex of behaviors involved. This tendency results from inadequate analyses of behavioral excesses and deficits in various components of sexual behaviors all of which imply the need for a combination of treatment techniques. An argument for the efficacy of a multicomponent treatment program has been made elsewhere (Adams & Sturgis, 1977; Marshall, 1971) as well as throughout this text. In this section we will present several cases selected to illustrate the multicomponent behavioral treatment of fetishism and transvestism.

Rosen and Rehm (1977) described the treatment of two cases of transvestism that illustrate the importance of a multicomponent treatment program and especially the importance of enhancing appropriate alternative sexual behaviors. In an effort to eliminate sexual arousal as a result of cross-dressing, both patients were initially administered electrical aversion therapy contingent upon imagining dressing in women's clothing. Following six trials the treatment format was altered to involve the administration of electrical aversion as the patients actually dressed in feminine clothing. A total of 31 aversion therapy sessions were massed within a three-week period. Verbal report measures from both patients indicated complete cessation of cross-dressing and no desire to engage in this deviant behavior. At followups of 15 and 24 months, respectively, however, both patients reported again engaging in cross-dressing at pretreatment baseline frequencies. The results of this study document the need to tailor the treatment of transvestism to insure long-term therapeutic maintenance. Toward this effort the authors suggest use of electrical aversion booster sessions and attention to strengthening alternative responses based on a systematic analysis of the individual case. On the other hand, the relapses noted in their investigation may also illustrate the unreliability of verbal report. The importance of substantiating verbal report of sexual arousal with physiological measures of penile erection cannot be overemphasized.

Marshall and Lippins (1977) employed a unique approach in treating a 27-year-old married male with a fetish for pantyhose or nylon stockings. The patient had a history of sexually assaultive behavior and was serving a prison sentence for rape at the time of treatment. His typical behavior pattern was to become sexually aroused when seeing a woman wearing pantyhose or nylon stockings; and he would either follow her to a deserted place where he would rape her, or hurry home to masturbate to the fantasy of pantyhose. When engaging in intercourse with his wife the patient could only achieve an erection when she was wearing pantyhose with the crotch cut out to permit insertion of his penis. The authors reported that a comprehensive sexual assessment indicated that the patient did not incorporate rape fantasies into his masturbatory fantasies and did not demonstrate penile erection to rape stimuli. He did, however physiologically respond to stimuli depicting the fetish object. Upon completion of the sexual assessment and a three-week baseline self-monitoring of fetish urges, a treatment program involving electrical aversion therapy and concomitant orgasmic reconditioning was initiated. Aversion therapy consisted of three sessions per week during which electric shock was delivered to the patient's leg contingent upon penile erection as a result of fantasizing or holding pantyhose or nylons. Orgasmic reconditioning involved instructing the patient to masturbate to a fantasy of pantyhose and switch to an appropriate fantasy of intercourse with his wife at the moment of orgasm. An assessment following 12 weeks of treatment indicated no decrease in sexual arousal to the fetishistic object as compared to baseline measures. As a result, the authors initiated a novel treatment approach which involved having the patient continuously masturbate beyond ejaculation for a prolonged period of time (1.5 hours) while fantasizing the fetish object. Continual fantasizing was controlled by having the patient verbalize his fantasies throughout each masturbatory session. After six sessions the patient reported extreme difficulty in fantasizing the fetish object and expressed displeasure at having to go through "that boring procedure again." A sexual assessment following nine treatment sessions indicated no physiological arousal to pantyhose or nylons, and an increase in sexual arousal to more appropriate heterosexual stimuli. A one-year followup verified the maintenance of treatment effects.

Marshall (1973) reported the case of a male fetishist which illustrates the importance of an adequate behavioral assessment and the value of combining various therapeutic techniques in the treatment of deviant sexual behavior. The patient had a long-standing fetish for young men's trousers, and at first described his behavior as limited to masturbating which he carried out by rubbing a chosen pair of trousers against his penis. Further questioning, however, revealed that masturbatory fantasies were exclusively related to trousers which he would view and touch during masturbation as well as at times when masturbation did not follow, as at school. Furthermore, the patient occasionally entered locker rooms during athletic contests and stole trousers. A sexual assessment involving measurements of penile erection to slides depicting the deviant stimulus along with slides of nude males and females substantiated the patient's verbally reported arousal pattern.

Treatment initially consisted of electrical aversion therapy contingent on sexual arousal as a result of feeling and rubbing trousers against his body. In addition, shock was delivered as the patient fantasized masturbating with chosen pairs of trousers. Treatment was continued over a three-week period in which electrical aversion was administered more than 1,000 times. Physiological assessment at the conclusion of this treatment indicated only a slight decrease in sexual arousal to male trousers and no change in sexual arousal to heterosexual stimuli. In addition the patient verbally reported no change in his masturbatory fantasies. As a result of no change in masturbatory fantasies and no decrease in sexual arousal to trousers, orgasmic conditioning was instituted. The procedure was explained to the patient who was provided materials describing heterosexual activities and a series of photographs of nude women. A sexual assessment following four weeks of orgasmic conditioning indicated a decrease in sexual arousal to trousers and an increase in arousal to women such that the level of penile erection to both stimuli was approximately equal.

At this time a third phase of treatment was initiated which involved giving the patient a bottle of smelling salts which he was advised to carry with him at all times. Whenever a deviant sexual fantasy began to occupy his thoughts, he was instructed to take a quick nasal inhalation. The patient reported using this simple self-punishment procedure on nearly 90 per cent of appropriate occasions during the two-week treatment phase. Orgasmic conditioning was continued concomitant with the self-punishment procedure. A final physiological sexual assessment indicated the elimination of sexual arousal to trousers and an increase in sexual arousal to heterosexual stimuli. Since a pretreatment heterosocial skills assessment had indicated no deficits in social skills, the patient's treatment was terminated. Three- and six-months followups showed that treatment gains had been maintained.

CASE HISTORY 8-3

The patient was a 29-year-old married male referred for treatment of cross-dressing. The patient and his wife had originally contacted a colleague for marital counseling and were subsequently referred to us when it became apparent that the patient's cross-dressing was a constant source of friction between the couple.

A sexual history revealed that the patient had been cross-dressing since the age of 12. Although he had refrained from this behavior for short periods of time, he confessed that dressing in women's clothing was his preferred mode of sexual activity. He maintained that he had never experienced difficulty in achieving or maintaining an erection during sexual intercourse. However, the frequency of intercourse (approximately once every three weeks) was considered a significant problem by the wife who claimed that it was one of the main causes of their marital discord. The patient engaged in cross-dressing approximately every other day. His transvestic behavior consisted of dressing in women's clothing and masturbating to orgasm as he walked around the house. Since the wife worked until early evening and the patient arrived home in the afternoon, he would engage in this behavior during his wife's absence. The patient had concealed his sexual preference from his wife for the first four years of the five-year marriage. During this time the couple would frequently argue and disagree over the frequency of sexual intercourse, the wife claiming that she could not understand why the patient did not desire sexual relations more often. It was only after being accidentally discovered by the wife that the patient admitted his cross-dressing. Both partners agreed that the wife initially accepted the patient's behavior and, in fact, claimed that the marriage improved for a short while afterward. During this period of marital improvement the couple would engage in intercourse approximately three to four times weekly with the patient dressed in his wife's clothing and the wife nude. The wife claimed that she had originally accepted the idea because of the novelty and the pleasure of increased coital frequency. However, she soon tired of the patient's transvestism and claimed to be disgusted at the sight of her husband dressed in her clothing. During the year prior to seeking therapy, the frequency of intercourse had again decreased to approximately once every three weeks, and arguments and discord had increased.

A physiological sexual assessment was conducted which included monitoring penile responses to a variety of sexual stimuli including films, slides, magazines, literature, and fantasies of cross-dressing. The stimuli were both homosexually- and heterosexually-oriented, and included a series of transvestic-oriented stimuli. While the patient demonstrated moderate sexual arousal to stimuli depicting sexual intercourse, his primary penile arousal was to stimuli depicting transvestic behaviors. No homosexual arousal was noted during the assessment.

A treatment plan was formulated and presented to the couple as follows: (1) electrical aversion to both the cross-dressing fantasy and the transvestic behavior *per se*, in an effort to extinguish both the deviant behavior and the arousing fantasy; (2) masturbation training and modified sensate focus in an effort to increase the patient's heterosexual arousal and direct the arousal to coital activities; and (3) assertive training in an effort to improve the patient's interactions with his wife as well as with his colleagues and superiors at work. The total treatment package was carefully explained to the couple and included warnings of potential transient impotence and the effects that assertive training could have on their marital interactions. After several questions from the couple, both agreed to the treatment program. However, to insure agreement and understanding we encouraged the couple to discuss it between themselves before calling us with a final decision. Several days later the couple phoned to register their agreement with the treatment plan, and the patient was scheduled for an appointment the following week.

At his next appointment he selected stimuli considered sexually arousing and was introduced to the treatment laboratory. He chose 15 slides depicting men in various stages of cross-dressing from a file of over 300 slides of various sexual stimuli. Various intensity levels of electrical shock were administered to the patient to allow him to choose an intensity that he considered painful, yet not unbearable.

The patient was administered 18 sessions of electrical aversion over the next four weeks. The patient's penile responses were monitored via a strain gauge, and shock was delivered contingent upon sexual arousal to both the sexual slides and fantasy. After several sessions the patient reported that he found it difficult to conjure the transvestic fantasy; therefore visual stimuli were emphasized to increase his sexual arousal. After 12 aversion sessions the patient showed no penile arousal to the transvestic stimuli and reported no cognitive arousal to the thought of cross-dressing. He had to miss the next week of treatment because of an out-of-town business trip, and thus could not return for treatment for ten days.

At this next appointment the patient was terribly distressed. While he had been out of town, he had experienced recurrent desires to cross-dress and had masturbated to this fantasy several times. He claimed that the transvestite magazines that he had previously used as masturbatory aids no longer aroused him, but the desire to actually engage in cross-dressing had recurred. We felt that this desire had been partially influenced by the patient's absence from his wife and from therapy during a critical point in treatment, but nevertheless decided to reinstitute aversion therapy as the patient actually engaged in cross-dressing behavior. The patient agreed to this procedure and was administered eight additional aversion sessions over the next two weeks. Shock was delivered contingent upon the patient's penile arousal while cross-dressing. After three sessions the patient verbally reported and physiologically demonstrated no sexual arousal to this behavior.

Masturbation training to heterosexual magazines and fantasy as well as prolonged sessions of sexual foreplay were instituted concurrent with aversion therapy. After several weeks of training the couple was given permission to engage in intercourse at their discretion.

Because of the patient's maladaptive style of social interaction with his wife and others, assertiveness training was also instituted, employing role playing. Both male and female assistants were employed to play the roles of the patient's wife, employer, co-workers, and significant others. These interactions were videotaped and replayed to allow the patient to review his behavior. He was encouraged to offer alternative responses at times, and instructed to institute his new interactional skills at home and place of employment.

The patient was scheduled for followup visits at three, six, and twelve months. All followups indicated, both through the couple's self-report and the patient's physiological assessment, that treatment progress was maintained. The couple reported the marriage as stable and the patient reported no instances of desires to cross-dress. Self-monitoring revealed the frequency of sexual intercourse to be approximately twice weekly.

CHAPTER 9

Sadism, Masochism, and Rape

Sex with violence goes through a continuum of behaviors, from sex with extreme violence, through sex with wanted force, to boisterous sexual interactions with consent. Three major types of sexual behavior that involve violence are sadism, masochism, and forcible rape. Rape is frequently considered a sadistic behavior, since the behavior is aimed at inflicting physical harm and/or mental humiliation and pain upon the victim.

The terms *sadism* and *masochism* are often combined in a third, *sado-masochism,* reflecting the common belief that individuals who are sexually stimulated by one activity will also be stimulated by the other (Moore, 1969). Other researchers call sadistic and masochistic behaviors by the term *algo-langia,* which indicates that the sexual urge has become linked to the experience of pain or to a rite, a punishment, or an act of violence that causes pain (Ullerstam, 1970). Algolangia may be more accurate in our context, since *sadism* and *masochism* are often loosely used to refer to many behaviors that have little or no sexual connotation.

SADISM

The term *sadism* is derived from the name of the Marquis de Sade (1774–1814), who for sexual purposes inflicted such cruelty on his victims that he was eventually committed as insane. The French author wrote extensively of his cruel erotic fantasies and exploits, one of which was to hang women from the ceiling and whip them as his servant manually stimulated his genitals. Although its meaning has broadened to denote cruelty in general, we shall use *sadism* only to mean achievement of sexual gratification through the infliction of pain on a partner. The pain may be inflicted by such means as whipping, biting, and pinching and the act may vary in intensity from fantasy through mild sadism to severe mutilation, and in extreme cases even to murder. Mild or relatively harmless sadistic behaviors appear to be prevalent in the general population. Some sex manuals, in fact, advise mild forms of sadistic behaviors for enhancing sexual pleasure. For example, *The Joy of Sex* by Alex Comfort (1972) suggests the use of "bondage" (tieing the partner's hands and feet) to increase sexual arousal and satisfaction. Comfort carefully warns against dangerous and coercive bondage and distinguishes between real and feigned pain. Thus, although such bondage resembles a sadistic act, it lacks the ingredient of forcibly rendering a victim powerless. Many sex shops also cater to sadistic behavior by selling shackles, chains, tethers, and whips. In addition, there are movies, books, and magazines that cater exclusively to sadistic interests by depicting sadistic scenes that defy the imagination.

Types of Sadism

All sadistic sexual behavior involves violence, either physical, mental, or both. In some cases sadistic activities lead up to or terminate in actual sexual relations; in others, full sexual gratification is obtained from the sadistic act alone. Generally sadistic sexual behavior may take three identifiable forms.

1. *Violent and forcible sadistic behavior involving a lack of consent.* The following is an example, adapted from Berg (1954):

> The offender, Peter Kursten, was 47 years old at the time of his apprehension in Dusseldorf, Germany, for a series of lust murders. He was a skilled laborer, well groomed, modest, and had done nothing that annoyed his fellow workers.
>
> Peter came from a disturbed family background, his father having been an alcoholic who had been sent to prison for having intercourse with Peter's older sister. Peter's own earliest sexual experiences were with animals. When he was about 13 years old, he attempted to have intercourse with a sheep, but the animal would not hold still and he took out a knife and stabbed her. At that moment he had an ejaculation.
>
> As a consequence of this experience, Peter found the sight of gushing blood sexually exciting; and he turned from animals to human females. Often he first choked his victim, but if he did not achieve an orgasm he then stabbed her. Initially he used scissors and a dagger, but later he took to using a hammer or an axe. After he achieved ejaculation, he lost interest in his victim, except in taking measures to cover up his crime. The offender's sexual crimes extended over a period of some 30 years and involved over 40 victims. Finally apprehended in 1930, he expressed a sense of injustice at not being like other people who were raised in normal families.

Other cases in which women have been strangled and mutilated in association with sadistic behaviors could be cited. In these cases, the offender appears unable to control his sadistic impulses, and unless apprehended his violent acts tend to be repetitious. And, as Hirschfeld (1956) has stated:

In genuine cases of sexual murder the killing replaces the sexual act. There is often no sexual intercourse at all, and sexual pleasure is induced by cutting, stabbing, and slashing the victim's body, ripping open the abdomen, plunging the hands into her intestines, cutting out and taking away her genitals, throttling her, sucking her blood. These horrors . . . constitute the—so to speak—pathological equivalent of coitus. (p. 388)

Violent and forcible sadistic behaviors involving a lack of consent do not necessarily involve murder. Coleman (1972) cites the case of a young man who entered a strange girl's apartment, held a chloroformed rag to her face until she lost consciousness, and then branded her on the thigh with a hot iron. She was not molested in any other way. Violent acts may also be associated with animals or with fetishistic objects instead of other human beings. East (1946) cited the case of a man who stole women's shoes, which he than slashed savagely with a knife. When he was in prison, he was found mutilating photographs that other prisoners kept in their cells by cutting the throats of the women in them. He admitted that he derived full sexual gratification from this procedure.

Violent and forcible sadistic behaviors involving lack of consent also need not necessarily involve physical violence. Humiliating sarcasm can often hurt more than a physical blow and can be kept up much longer. It is not unusual for some couples to report they have their best lovemaking after a big fight. A similar pattern is found in the animal kingdom. For example, some monkeys engage in battle before beginning copulation. At the conclusion of mating, the female monkeys may be severely wounded (Chesser, 1971).

2. *Violent and perhaps forcible sadistic behavior involving at least initial consent.* This type of sadistic behavior involves those sexual acts that begin as novelty with consent and terminate in sadistic behaviors, as the following example from our files indicates:

I don't know what got into him. It started out as just a game. I trusted him and thought he was just playing. He wanted to tie me down to the bed during sex. I thought it might be kinda fun so I agreed. I had no idea what would happen. He seemed content at first but after a while he started talking mean to me and slapping me on the face and breasts. I was getting scared and begged him to untie me. He went to the dresser and got a hairbrush and shoved it up my vagina over and over again. I screamed and thought he was going to kill me. I told him I was going to call the police. He seemed to lose control, slapping me and pushing the hairbrush up my vagina. I nearly passed out from the pain.

3. *Sadism that involves mock rather than real or painful volence of force.* This type of sadism is usually done by mutual consent of both partners and is not carried to the point of injury. An example is the following

agreement that Leopold Baron von Sacher-Masoch drew up and had Madam Wanda von Dunajew sign. It specifies the conditions of her "slavery" to him.

> My slave, the conditions upon which I accept you as my slave and agree to tolerate you near me are as follows:
>> Unconditional surrender of self.
>> You have no will besides my own.
>> You are a blind fool in my hands, executing all my commands without the least demur. Should you forget that you are a slave and fail to give me absolute obedience in all things I shall be entitled to punish and chastise you entirely at my discretion without any right of complaint on your part.
>> Any pleasure and happiness I may grant you must be acknowledged by you as such; I am under no debt or obligation to you. You must be neither son, nor brother, nor friend, nothing but a slave lying in the dust. Your body as well as your soul belongs to me, and no matter how much suffering this will cause you, you must subordinate your feelings and emotions to my will.
>> I am entitled to practice the worst cruelties upon you and you must bear them without complaint. You must work for me like a slave and if I revel in plenty and nevertheless starve you and trample you underfoot, you must, without a murmur kiss the foot that is trampling you.
>> I may dismiss you at any time, but you must never leave me without my consent, and should you attempt to escape you authorize me to torture you to death by every imaginable means.
>> Apart from me you have nothing, I am your all, your life, your future, your happiness, your misfortune, your joy and your sorrow. (Sacher-Masoch, 1907)

Many sadistic behaviors may also involve such things as enacting a rape scene in which one of the partners pretends to force the other to submit while she or he vehemently protests this indignity. The use of sadistic games in this manner assumes a tacit understanding that the partner playing the sadistic role will not inflict punishment beyond the point where the other partner's protests and fears become real rather than feigned (Comfort, 1972).

Incidence of Sadism

While it may be inconceivable to many people that inflicting pain on someone could be sexually gratifying, it is not an uncommon phenomenon. Kinsey et al. (1953) reported that 3 percent of females and 1 percent of males admitted a definite or frequent erotic response to sadistic stories. Hunt (1974) found that males are more inclined to inflict pain, while females are more likely to be the recipients of pain during erotic activities.

Unmarried males below the age of 35 appear to represent the most frequent participants in such activities. Most deliberate infliction of pain was found to be biting, although hitting, scratching, and pinching were preferred by some. Some individuals reported engaging in activities that resulted in pain but were not deliberately done for that purpose, such as unduly hard kissing or anal intercourse (Hunt, 1974).

Sadism and Prostitution

Frequently individuals who enjoy sadistic activities do not have a sexual partner who is inclined to cooperate. This being the case, some may seek prostitutes who are willing to cater to their desires. Houses of prostitution that specialize in a clientele with sadistic preferences may be furnished with torture chambers where the prostitutes will not only receive pain (within limits, of course, and normally with an armed guard secretly observing or standing close by to protect the girl from an overly zealous client) as the client prefers, but also feign sexual pleasure while doing so (Delora & Warren, 1977). Similarly, homosexual gathering places may have special rooms where sadistic and masochistic customers may meet and act out their sexual preferences. People without a sexual partner may use pornographic films, books, and magazines that concentrate on sadistic themes. Such material frequently uses red paint or food dye as a substitute for blood in the color photographs.

Sadistic behavior with a consenting adult partner, with a prostitute, or in masturbatory fantasy is likely to pose no special social problem. The most extreme form of sadistic behavior, however, may involve the use of violence and force to the point of serious injury or even murder. While many people may be somewhat sexually aroused by fantasies or behavior involving sadistic activities, in clinical practice it is relatively rare to encounter a person totally dependent on these activities for sexual arousal and gratification.

Research and Theory: Physiological Factors

Organic theories that try to explain the genesis and maintenance of sadism emphasize the behavioral effects of various physical and neurological dysfunctions. Dyscontrol syndrome, psychomotor epilepsy, and temporal lobe epilepsy frequently underlie sadistic behaviors, according to these theorists. Clinical data do substantiate the various behavioral effects of these neurological dysfunctions, including episodic sadistic-type behavior: but any cause-and-effect relationship is rare. Research has indicated that only a small percentage of those exhibiting sadistic behaviors suffer from neurological impairment, and only a small percentage of those neurologically impaired exhibit sadistic behaviors. Research done so far supports the idea that sadism is due to psychological factors in the vast majority of cases.

Research and Theory: Psychological Factors

A considerable number of psychological hypotheses have been advanced to explain the development and maintenance of sadism. Freud (1953), for example, wrote a paper explaining the psychoanalytic theory of sadism and masochism. More recent literature reports that conditioning plays a critical role in the etiology of sadism.

Psychoanalytic Formulations. Psychoanalytic theory considers sadism and exhibitionism as similar behaviors in that the threatening nature of each serves to make victims powerless and, as a result, relieves the anxiety that has become associated with sexual pleasure. In other words, analysts believe that sadists have the slogan, "Do unto others *before* they do unto you!"

> If a person is able to do to others what he fears may be done to him, he no longer has to be afraid. Thus anything that tends to increase the subject's power or prestige can be used as a reassurance against anxieties. What might happen to the subject passively is done actively by him, in anticipation of attack, to others. (Fenichel, 1945, p. 354)

A variant of psychoanalytic theory is espoused by Stekel (1953), who wrote two volumes on the psychology of sadism and masochism. Stekel's main thesis is that sadism is a disturbance or fixation in the psychosexual development of an individual. According to this view, patients suffering from sadistic behaviors have a predominantly "retrospective" orientation which forces them to relive again and again certain conflict situations of their early lives by the use of symbolizations, projections, condensations, role exchanges, and the like. Stekel's theory of bipolarity of all psychic phenomenon stipulates that hate and aggression, as primal reactions to forces impeding the individual's narcissistic pleasure demands, are "older" than reactions of love. Man, thus, has an inherent "need" to hate, and the fact that religion and other ethical movements try to stem the hate demonstrates that the sadistic neurosis is a compromise between the polarities of life's creative and destructive forces.

Behavioral Formulations. Behavioral theorists believe that sadistic behaviors develop when sexual arousal and orgasm become associated with viewing pain or administering pain to another individual. Unfortunately, the data to substantiate this hypothesis are presently lacking. However, considerable secondary evidence indicates that both animals and humans become more aggressive if aggressive behavior is rewarded. For example, Geen and Pigg (1970) deceived subjects into believing that they were helping teach other subjects a task by delivering electrical shocks to the subjects contingent upon mistakes in learning. The "teachers" were divided into two groups; the first group was verbally praised for delivering shocks; while the second group was not praised. Results indicated that the reinforced subjects delivered more frequent shocks at higher intensities and later emitted more aggressive words on a word association test than did the nonreinforced subjects. Dreyer and Church (1970) found that rats will inflict pain on other rats for a variety of reinforcers, including food, drink, exercise, and the opportunity to copulate with a female rat.

Another aspects of pain-inflicting behavior in humans may involve self-esteem (Johnson, 1972). Often manliness is equated with pride and self-esteem, as in the traditional warrior or caveman definition of masculinity. By inflicting pain and dominating others we demonstrate status and power; being dominated or controlled is a significant blow to self-esteem (Johnson, 1972). Fesbach (1971) has argued that threats to self-esteem and humiliation may be among the most powerful elicitors of aggressive behaviors in humans. Skinner (1953) claimed that the primary motivation of the neighborhood bully is likely to be the acquiescence of the bullied individual. Scott (1958), in fact, found that rats can be trained to fight by matching them with a restrained rat which has difficulty fighting back. The "free" rat soon becomes encouraged and rewarded by his "success," and develops the habit of inflicting pain on all rats, including females during sexual activity.

CASE HISTORY 9-1

The patient was a 45-year-old laborer referred by a social services organization for treatment of episodic, violent attacks on women during sexual activities. His most recent attack had resulted in a prison confinement for 23 months. Reports from prison officials were that he was a model prisoner; he served as a trusted aid and was released early for good behavior. The patient appeared eager for treatment, and offered the following sexual history.

His parents had divorced when he was five, and he had been raised by his elderly grandparents. He claimed he learned about sex at a relatively early age of 10. As a child he belonged to what he described as an "older rough neighborhood gang always looking for sex and trouble." He began drinking at the age of 12, and quit school in the 8th grade.

The patient's first sexual experience occurred at the age of 11 when he was initiated into a neighborhood "gang." Part of the initiation rite included his having intercourse with a large dog while the other members (several years older than he) watched. After completion of intercourse, he was forced to carve the insignia of the gang into the stomach of the dog with a knife.

The patient recalled that his gang would frequently play a game they called "rip and run." It involved the group's searching for a woman walking alone in a semi-secluded area; when they found one; different members of the gang would attack her from behind knocking her violently to the ground. They would then rip her panties from her and run.

The patient claimed he and other gang members frequently solicited dates and prostitutes for the sexual gratification of all the gang members. Most often this involved physical violence or threats of violence if the woman did not cooperate. On several occasions the group would bet money on who could ejaculate the fastest, and different members would beat a willing, although most often a non-willing, female brought to fellate the gang, with their belts to increase her speed and intensity of fellatio so that they would ejaculate more quickly.

When the patient was 17 years old he began dating a woman who resisted all his sexual advances. On one occasion of heavy petting the couple began playfully struggling, and she became receptive for intercourse. The patient gradually began getting increasingly rough with her, which seemed to heighten her sexual desire and satisfaction. This relationship soon evolved into a classic sadomasochistic pairing in which the patient forced every imaginal sexual degradation and physical abuse on the partner who offered him "total and complete" sexual satisfaction in return. Several of these sexual encounters resulted in the patient's carrying his partner to the hospital for suturing of various cuts and abrasions.

When the patient was 18 years old, he joined the military and was stationed overseas. He discovered a house of prostitution in a nearby city that catered to unusual sexual preferences, including sadism, for what he considered a small price in American money. He frequented this establishment for over a year. Sexual activities included bondage, whipping, hair pulling, forced anal intercourse, and the like. The patient said, "You wouldn't believe what they would let you do to them for money." His first brush with the law came as a result of an over zealous encounter with a prostitute who required hospitalization for her multiple injuries.

The incident that resulted in his imprisonment involved a woman he met in a bar and escorted to a motel. During the course of sexual activity she refused to engage in several sexual behaviors he requested. He therefore began hitting the woman repeatedly until she was unconscious. He then gagged and tied her to the bed with strips of bed sheets, engaged in anal intercourse, defecated on her, and left her alone. She was later found to have vaginal and rectal lacerations and bleeding, as well as a concussion.

The patient proceeded to describe dozens of relationships and instances of sexual activity associated with inflicting pain on his partners. An interesting incident occurred which involved his sister only weeks before he first came for treatment. He was visiting his sister and brother-in-law over a weekend, and slapped his sister several times in the face for walking from the bedroom to the bathroom in her bra. He claimed he did not intend to strike her, but "she shouldn't walk around like a whore."

MASOCHISM

The term *masochism* is derived from the name of the Austrian novelist Leopold Baron Von Sacher-Masoch (1836-1905), whose fictional characters dwelt lovingly on the sexual gratification and pleasure of pain. The meaning of masochism has been broadened beyond sexual connotations so that it includes the deriving of pleasure from self-denial, expiatory physical suffering such as that of the religious falgellants, and various hardships and suffering in general. Our discussion will be restricted to the sexual aspects of masochistic behavior. In contrast to sadism, masochism denotes achievement of sexual gratification and pleasure through the infliction of pain on the self instead of on others.

Incidence of Masochism

It may be inconceivable to many people that the element of pain can be sexually exciting; however, according to published data, masochistic behavior is not an uncommon phenomenon. Kinsey and his associates (1953) found that over 25 percent of both males and females reported definite or frequent erotic response to being bitten in foreplay. More recent data (Hunt, 1974) show some interesting trends and results. Males are more likely to inflict pain; females are more likely to be the recipients of pain in erotic encounters. Hunt (1974) found that 10 percent of the unmarried females sampled admitted obtaining sexual pleasure from receiving pain, while 6.3 percent of the unmarried males sampled admitted this pleasure. If these data are assumed to represent the population at large, masochistic behavior is one of the very few sexual deviations more prevalent among women than men. The receiving of sexual pleasure from pain was also found to be more common in both males and females under the age of 35. Bondage and disciplin (being tied and being whipped), described in the literature as classic masochistic behaviors, were relatively rare in this sample. The most deliberate infliction of pain was found to be biting, although some samples reported activites such as hitting, beating, scratching, rough coital thrusting, and pinching. The masochist poses no serious threat to society and is rarely arrested. The number of masochists seeking psychological treatment for their sexual preference is also thought to be quite small.

One fictional account of this behavior occurs in Gore Vidal's novel, *Myra Breckenridge.*

> It began upstairs when he tore my clothes off in the closet. Then he raped me standing up with a metal clothes hanger twisted around my neck, choking me. I could hardly breathe. It was exquisite! Then one thing led to another. Those small attentions a girl like me cherishes . . . a lighted cigarette stubbed

out on my derriere, a complete beating with his great thick heavy leather belt, a series of ravenous bites up and down the inner thighs, drawing blood. All the fun things, except that this time he went beyond anything he had tried before. This time he dragged me to the head of the stairs and raped me from behind, all the while beating me with his boot. Then, just as I was about to reach the big O, shrieking with pleasure, he hurled me down the stairs, so that my orgasm and the final crash with the banister occurred simultaneously. I fainted with joy! Without a doubt, it was the completion of my life. (1968, p. 270)

Masochistic Games

Masochistic behavior may be confined to sexually stimulating fantasies of ill treatment, or it may involve a wide range of pain-inflicting activities such as binding, trampling, semistrangulation, switching, spanking, stricking with pins, and verbal abuse. Such behavior is more common among women than men (Coleman, 1972), but it is certainly not restricted to- females. These games may involve such activities as enacting a rape scene in which the man pretends to force the woman to submit while she violently strugges in protest, or may involve fantasies of being taken by force.

Ever since I was a little girl, I have been turned on by the idea of getting spanked. My parents never did so I don't know how it happened to appeal to me—but it did. As I got older and knew more about sex, my horizons broadened a bit, and I enjoyed the idea of being beaten with a belt. My whole personality is geared toward male domination—I hate guys who let women walk all over them. Taking this into consideration, my husband is the perfect partner for me, the kind who treats a girl fantastic in return for a little deference and obedience. But to get back to the subject, sometimes when were were [having intercourse], I'd ask him to slap me, and he always would, although he seemed a little resistant . . . . I got him started slapping me, and after it was over I thought, "What the hell," he knows other women like weird things, so I'll ask him. I said, "Do you like hitting me?" and he said, "Yes." I asked if he had ever thought of trying it with something else. "Like what?" he asked me, and I said, "Like a belt." I suggested we start with a spanking to sort of warm up. He took me across his knee and spanked my buttocks about ten times . . . . At first, I was nervous that the whole thing would be a disappointment, but after he hit me just once, I knew there was no danger of that. It was fantastic! It hurt but I wanted it to go on forever. I can't really describe the feeling, except that I loved feeling helpless, and that he was so much stronger, more dominant than I was. (Friday, 1975, p. 63)

Other masochistic games may involve verbal abuse. One young woman we treated could achieve orgasm only when verbally abused in the worst possible manner by her sexual partners.

Deaths resulting from masochistic activities are rare, but occasionally are reported. Most often, serious injuries are self-inflicted during masturbatory activities. Some individuals inflicting pain on themselves have died as a result of knifing themselves in arteries, burning themselves, or accidentally hanging themselves.

Masochism and Prostitution

Individuals with masochistic orientations and no willing sexual partner must either satisfy their sexual desires through fantasy, inflict pain on themselves during masturbation, or solicit the cooperation of a willing prostitute. While many women engage in masochistic activities, more men than women frequent prostitutes for painful sexual pleasures.

Both in this country and abroad a person can pay to have himself whipped. This type of service is normally provided by specialized prostitutes and is more likely to be found in large cities. Houses of prostitution that specialize in a clientele with masochistic preferences may be furnished with "torture chambers" complete with whips, chains, ropes, gags, belts, cuffs, plugs, enema bottles, and racks. In this country, elaborate torture chambers and prostitutes willing to inflict pain on individuals may be very expensive. Because of the high risk of physical injury, many of these prostitues accept only regular clients.

A few women who specialize in inflicting pain and humiliation on clients may actually advertise their unique services in various men's, swingers', and underground magazines. One well-known dominatrix is "Miss Vickie," who is called the "Queen of American Dominants," and who writes a column on domination and masochism for a popular men's magazine, *Cheri* (1978).

Not your average sweetheart Southern belle, folks, Miss Vickie, our nation's most devilish dominant, hails from Atlanta where she's discovered there's mental health in them there welts. . . .She is a legend in her own time. Still in her twenties, gorgeous, willowy Vickie Lou of Atlanta has, over the years, established an unchallengeable reputation as the premiere dominatrix of her time. Slaves say it. Rival S's say it. And, if you're at all hip to punishment, you yourself have been aware of it for at least two years. Vickie's fame is not limited to Dixie. From San Francisco to The Bronx, from Brownsville to Bangor, in dungeon and in closet, submissochists and fantasy freaks tremble at the mere mention of her name. Her reputation for creative cruelties and titillating tortures is nonpareil. Her beauty is legend.

A small percentage of masochistically oriented people may engage in such behaviors with prostitutes; but the vast majority restrict their activi-

ties to viewing pornographic films or reading magazines that feature car-
toons or photographs of women dressed in leather and spike-heeled shoes
looking menacing as they gag, bind, chain, whip, and variously "torture"
their victims. Artificial coloring is used for blood in these photographs and
films, and the men and women who buy these masochistic movies and magazines are generally considered harmless (Katchadourian & Lunde, 1972).

Research and Theory: Physiological Factors

Masochistic behaviors have been reported in association with severe
mental retardation and various types of neuroencephalopathy. Severe schizophrenic and autistic individuals occasionally engage in head-banging
and other self-inflicted behaviors such as biting. The sexual gratification
resulting from these types of behaviors is, however, certainly questionable.

Research and Theory: Psychological Factors

Some developmental theories regarding masochistic behavior focus
on deeply ingrained fears of abandonment, neglect, or rejection. These
fears in the masochistic adult are thought to be traceable to traumatic childhood events and/or relationships, especially with the mother. For example, if punishment has been the only evidence of love and affection that a
child received, he may later, in sexual relations, offer to submit to being
hurt by a sex partner as a means of feeling wanted and loved (Coleman,
1972). In fact, if his basic need for love, affection, and acceptance is great
enough, he may actually solicit pain as a demonstration of being cared for,
rejecting tender and loving sexual relations as unacceptable proof of acceptance.

Psychoanalytic Formulations. Psychoanalytic theory is that masochism is merely the expression of sadism turned inward. Thus, masochistic
behavior is explained on the basis of the patient's fixation in psychosexual
development. As a result, the patient later develops a retrospective personality which forces him to relive the unresolved conflicts of psychosexual development and the painful consequences of childhood (Fenichel, 1945).

Behavioral Formulations. The intentional and repeated infliction of
pain upon oneself is a puzzling behavior. The first question that comes to
mind is, "What is the reinforcement for engaging in such painful behavior?" While the reinforcement for engaging in sexual masochism, autistic
headbanging and other pain inflicting behaviors is not overtly clear, it must
be emphasized that although aversive stimuli have their own specific properties that account for their most typical behavioral effect, response elim-

ination, they are also stimuli. As such they have the capacity to serve as discriminative cues or information-producing signals. In the latter capacity stimuli employed as painfully aversive can, under certain conditions, produce a paradoxical effect upon behavior in that their application results in response facilitation rather than response elimination.

Behavioral theories of masochistic development and maintenance are based on animal experimentation emphasizing the importance of conditioned learning. For example, Masserman and Jacques (1948) trained cats to punish themselves by using a blast of air as a discriminative stimulus for food reward. Similarly, Schaefer (1970) conditioned monkeys to inflict serious injury on themselves by feeding them when they repeatedly struck their heads with their fists. Although food was used as reward in the animal experiments, Rachman (1966) and Rachman and Hodgson (1968) have demonstrated that sexual arousal may also serve as a powerful reinforcer. The development of masochistic behavior may, therefore, be the result of early experiences in which the individual learns to associate pain with sexual arousal and orgasm. For example, the early history of a masochist may include the experience of being spanked on the naked bottom while being caressed on the genitals by a perverse mother or father (Rimm & Somerville, 1977).

CASE HISTORY 9-2

The patient was a 27-year-old unmarried female who came for treatment of what she described as "masochism." The patient claimed she was unable to enjoy sexual activities unless she were whipped, beaten, verbally abused, or defiled in some manner. She had avoided all contact with males, both socially and sexually, for the five-month period prior to seeking treatment, claiming that all such contacts reminded her of her sexual preference which she abhorred. Before the five-month abstinence, she estimated her frequency of sexual activity at once per week, although she had two long-term relationships in which the frequency of intercourse had been much higher. Her masturbatory frequency was estimated at twice per week and consistently involved fantasies of being beaten, raped, forced to engage in sexual activities with multiple partners, and other behaviors involving violence and pain. A detailed sexual history revealed the following data.

The patient was reared by her mother and alcoholic father. She described her parent's relationship as "one violent fight after another," claiming that her mother "constantly ran around on my father" and her father "was drunk all the time." She was physically abused as a child on numerous occasions, and at one point was taken from the home by her aunt and uncle with whom she lived for three months. Her parents would frequently invite couples to their home for drunken parties during which she and her older brother would be locked in a bedroom. She claimed she did not know precisely what went on at these parties but was certain they involved open sex, mate swapping, and pornographic films.

The patient recalled three traumatic sexual experiences as a child. When she was approximately nine years old her father, while intoxicated, forced her to masturbate him while he examined a pornographic magazine. When she refused, she was beaten into submission. The second traumatic event occurred about the age of 12 during one of her parent's parties. She was escorted by her mother from her locked room to the living room where she was instructed to remove her blouse and expose her developing breasts to four or five couples. She reported being slapped by her mother for refusing and told she would be beaten if she did not cooperate. She admitted being tremendously embarrassed and humiliated as her mother also removed her blouse and compared the patient's small breasts to the mother's mature breasts as the crowd laughed uproariously. The third traumatic experience occurred when the patient was approximately 14 years old, at which time she was physically beaten and forcefully raped by her brother and three friends.

The patient left home at the age of 16 and moved to a nearby city where she soon married. Her five-year marriage was described as "very unhappy," and involved physical and mental abuse by her husband who often deserted her for weeks at a time. Sexual activity between the patient and husband was characterized by his rough and crude manner which frequently involved his slapping her. He would occasionally tie her to the bed and have intercourse while he took photographs that he would show to his friends. While she was frequently orgasmic with her husband, it was only when he was physically abusive that she was able to achieve sexual gratification. She reported that while she hated her husband because of the violence, she was unable to experience coital orgasm in any other manner. She also found that she had little difficulty achieving orgasm during masturbation with masochistic fantasies, and began employing such fantasies regularly.

Upon divorcing her husband the patient again moved to another city and began dating a variety of men. She discovered, however, that she was totally nonorgasmic with these partners, and reported becoming frustrated and masturbating frequently. She later had two long term relationships, each lasting close to a year. She admitted her sexual preference for her first partner who engaged in sexual behaviors for her sexual pleasure and satisfaction. She did not inform her second partner of her masochistic orientation because she wanted to have what she considered "a normal sexual relationship." The failure of the second relationship resulted in her decision to avoid all heterosexual contacts.

MODIFICATION OF SADISM AND MASOCHISM

Five major treatment strategies have attempted to modify sadistic and masochistic behaviors. These include psychotherapy, psychoanalysis, group therapy, chemotherapy, and behavior therapy. Few individuals with sadistic or masochistic orientations seek treatment for their sexual preferences; consequently, the literature concerning such treatment strategies is somewhat scarce.

Dynamic Psychotherapy

Dynamically oriented psychotherapy aims to alter sadistic and masochistic behaviors by enabling the patient to gain insight into his or her behavior. Counseling, guidance, and interpretation are tools used by the psychotherapist in an effort to explain the patient's behavior in the belief that behavior change occurs through understanding of the dynamics of the undesired behavior (Eysenck & Rachman, 1966).

Psychoanalysis

Psychoanalysis attempts to free the sadistic or masochistic patient from his stunted developmental psychosexual fixation. Through the use of dream interpretation, free association, and transference, the analyst attempts to uncover the unconscious intrapsychic roots mandating the patient's deviant behavior. Normally, psychoanalysis requires from 12 to 36 months, and its success is documented by very few reliable investigative studies (Friedman, 1973).

Group Therapy

Group therapy appears to be a common treatment strategy for sexual deviations. Group efforts are often targeted toward facilitating communication and interpersonal skills as well as educating the patients in the basis of their behavior through affiliation with other patients. Group therapy geared to teach effective heterosocial skills may be an effective adjunct to more directive therapy, but its utility as a primary treatment modality has yet to be demonstrated (Coleman, 1972).

Medical Therapies

Operating on the assumption that sadistic and masochistic behaviors are related to anxiety and tension levels, many psychiatrists and physicians attempt to reduce anxiety through the use of minor tranquilizers. Anti-anxiety agents such as Valium, Librium, Serax, and Tranxene have been prescribed for control of deviant behaviors (Chesser, 1971). However, there are few reliable data to suggest that such pharmacological agents modify sadistic and masochistic sexual orientations and behaviors (Solomon & Patch, 1974).

Behavior Therapy

The behavioral treatment of sadism and masochism also suffers from a dearth of definitive data, possibly because so few sadists and masochists seek professional assistance, but also because of some common misconceptions about masochists. Perhaps some therapists believe aversion therapy, an important component in the multicomponent behavioral treatment program for sexual deviations, would be useless in eliminating deviant sexual arousal in masochists. According to Marks, Rachman, and Gelder (1965), this is not true.

Marks et al. (1965) treated a 34-year-old masochist who was aroused both in fantasy and *in-vivo* by being kicked in the genitals and back with high-heeled shoes and boots. The patient's masturbatory activity involved slapping his genitals with a boot while fantasizing being kicked to death.

In order to determine whether electrical aversion therapy would be aversive to the patient a simple operant conditioning task was employed. The patient sat in front of a lever and was instructed to rotate the lever in a clockwise direction at whatever speed he found most comfortable. His response rates were measured under three conditions:

1. *Control:* The patient stabilized his responses at 70 rotations per minute over several control periods.

2. *Sexual stimuli:* the patient was asked to continue as before but to hold a pair of prized rubber boots in one hand while rotating the lever with the other. Immediately the number of rotations increased to an average of 85 rotations per minute over a five-minute period.

3. *Sexual stimuli and shock:* After a five-minute rest the patient was asked to continue rotating the lever while holding the boots but was told that he might be shocked periodically.

Without the patient's knowledge, the shocks were predetermined to occur when the response rate reached 70 rotations per minute or more. Soon after the shocks were initiated, the patient's rotations decreased below the original control rate of 70 per minute. The authors claim that the patient was clearly avoiding the shock even in the presence of the sexual stimuli. This finding was confirmed with a second test several days later. Electrical aversion therapy contingent on the patient's fantasizing masochistic behaviors resulted in the elimination of the deviant fantasy and behavior.

Davison (1968) utilized masturbation training and covert sensitization in the treatment of a 21-year-old male with sadistic sexual fantasies. The patient regularly masturbated to fantasies of beating and whipping women to force them to engage in deviant sexual activities. Treatment was initiated by instructing the patient to masturbate while looking at pictures of nude women and imagining normal heterosexual intercourse. If the patient was unable to become sexually aroused using this fantasy, he was instructed to employ his deviant fantasy to achieve arousal at which time he was to switch to the appropriate sexual fantasy. After fantasies of normal heterosexual intercourse had acquired sexual arousing value, a second procedure was introduced in which sadistic fantasy was impaired with nauseous imagery, such as "steaming urine with reeking fecal boli bobbing on top while he drank." At the end of six treatment sessions the patient demonstrated no arousal to sadistic sexual fantasies.

Hayes et al. (1978) used a variation of covert sensitization in the treatment of a 25-year-old male with multiple sexual deviations including sadism and exhibitionism. The patient reported his sadistic fantasies included bondage of a female; forced intercourse and fellatio; forced sexual behavior with animals or women; forced masturbation with bottles and other objects; and physical infliction of pain on a victim with pins, whips, or static-electricity generators. The patient claimed that such sadistic thoughts occupied four to six hours of each day. In addition, the patient had been arrested for attempted rape and for exhibiting himself.

Assessment of the patient's sexual arousal included both physiological and self-report data. Physiological data involved measuring the level of penile erection with a strain gauge as the patient viewed several slides from each of three categories: exhibitionistic, sadistic, and heterosexual. The self-report measure was the card-sort technique (Barlow et al., 1969) in which five scenes each were generated relating to exhibitionism, sadism, and appropriate heterosexual activities. Each scene was placed on an index card and presented to the patient, who rated the scenes according to the degree of sexual arousal each elicited.

Treatment was initially targeted toward the elimination of sexual arousal associated with exhibiting himself. Covert sensitization scenes were generated by the therapists and the patient which involved themes of being arrested by the police, or discovered by his family, and public ridicule at losing his job and going to prison. The patient was instructed to self-administer the aversive scenes several times daily. After six days of self-administered covert sensitization treatment for exhibitionism, the procedure was targeted toward the sadistic arousal pattern. Following six days of sadistic arousal treatment the patient was discharged from the hospital and instructed to practice self-administered covert sensitization whenever he felt a deviant urge. At the end of treatment the patient displayed low levels of arousal to exhibitionistic and sadistic stimuli while maintaining appropriate heterosexual arousal (Figure 9-1). These treatment effects were sustained during a two-month follow up period.

CASE HISTORY 9-3

The patient was a 30-year-old male referred by a psychiatrist colleague for treatment of sadistic sexual fantasies and behaviors. A sexual history revealed that the patient masturbated almost daily to pictures of mutilated bodies and women tied and gagged, as well as various sadistic films and fantasies of beating nude women. In addition, he had engaged in a variety of sadistic sexual behaviors with a woman with whom he had once lived for over a year. He estimated his frequency of dating at least once every three months, and reported engaging in few activities other than working and masturbating to sadistic stimuli. He reported being impotent without the aid of sadistic fantasies which he relied on during both masturbatory and coital activities. A detailed and comprehensive physiological sexual assessment

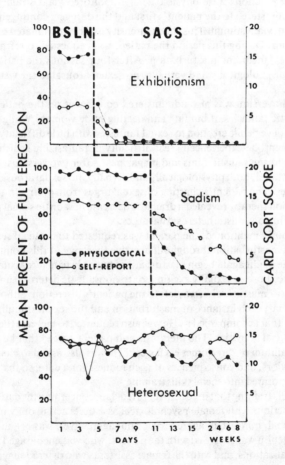

Figure 9-1. Percentage of full erection and self-reported arousal to exhibitionistic, sadistic, and heterosexual stimuli during baseline treatment and follow-up phases. Card sort data are daily averages in the baseline and treatment phases and weekly averages in the follow-up phase. (**Source:** Hayes, S. C., Brownell, K. D., & Barlow, D. H. The use of self-administered covert sensitization in the treatment of exhibitionism and sadism. *Behavior Therapy*, 1978, *9*, 283–289. Reproduced by permission of Academic Press.)

that covered a wide range of sexual stimuli substantiated the patient's reported sadistic heterosexual orientation.

In collaboration with the patient, a treatment program was formulated which consisted of electrical aversion contingent upon sexual arousal to the deviant stimuli, masturbation training in an effort to modify heterosexual arousal, attempts to increase the frequency of dating, and social skills training. The complete treatment program was carefully explained in detail to the patient who was encouraged to ask questions.

Treatment was initiated with electrical aversion. The patient was requested to bring several favorite films and magazines that he frequently used as masturbatory stimuli. Penile erections were physiologically monitored via a strain gauge, and shock was administered to the patient's first and third fingers contingent on sexual arousal to the deviant stimuli. This shock intensity had been evaluated before treatment was begun. During this period the patient was requested to refrain from all sexual activities, including masturbation. After four sessions the patient demonstrated, both physiologically and verbally, no sexual arousal to the visual sadistic sexual stimuli.

Electrical aversion was also administered contingent on the patient's sexual arousal to erotic fantasies of binding and beating nude women. While the patient was able to achieve penile erection to sexual fantasies with little difficulty during the sexual assessment, he experienced great difficulty in fantasizing sadistic activities after aversion to the sadistic films and magazines. After two sessions, the patient again demonstrated, both physiologically and verbally, no sexual arousal to sadistic sexual fantasies. The patient's charting of sexual urges from pretreatment baseline through aversion therapy revealed a dramatic decrease in sadistic sexual urges and a slight increase in nonsadistic heterosexual urges.

As previously mentioned, the patient was requested to cease all sexual activities, including masturbation throughout aversive therapy. At this point he was instructed that he might again begin masturbating, but only to heterosexual films and pictures that he chose as sexually exciting, or to nonsadistic heterosexual fantasies. The frequency of masturbation was left to the patient's discretion, although he was requested to chart each instance of masturbation and the sexual stimuli, either visual or fantasy, that accompanied it. He was also requested to increase the frequency of his heterosocial activities. The therapists and patient agreed that he should ask for dates a minimum of three times each week. He was also asked to chart the antecedents, behaviors, and consequences of each request for a date, so that these data could be incorporated into social skills training.

Social skills training that used self-reported data concerning his dates, plus videotaped interactions with female psychological assistants acting out various social behaviors (verbal, nonverbal, aggressive, or nonaggressive), was begun. Each videotaped interaction was reviewed with the patient, who was encouraged to offer alternative verbalizations, and with the female assistants who offered suggestions and praise. The patient was encouraged to apply the skills developed in training to real life heterosocial situations. Charting of antecedents, behaviors, and consequences of each heterosocial interaction indicated that the patient was successfully requesting dates from a variety of women and subjectively feeling more comfortable and confident in dating behaviors. He engaged in intercourse on several occasions with no instances of impotence and no utilization of sadistic sexual fantasies.

At six weeks follow up an equipment malfunction prohibited a physiological assessment, although the patient's verbal report indicated that the treatment results were being maintained. Another follow up assessment was scheduled for three months. A month later, however, the patient called to report his arrest on charges of sexual assault. Further questioning revealed that the patient had suggested bondage to a date as part of their sexual activity. The woman agreed, thinking it was "all in fun." The patient tied her nude to his bed and initially only playfully struck her with his belt. As he became sexually aroused, however, he began striking her increasingly harder until he lost control and really began beating her. This assault lasted until the patient masturbated to ejaculation and the woman fainted as a result of her injuries. Although the woman later dropped charges against the patient, the decision was made to again initiate aversion therapy on a more frequent and intensive schedule. Eight three-hour sessions of electrical aversion were administered to the patient over the next three months. A three-month, six-month, and one-year physiological follow up assessment indicated no arousal to sadistic fantasies or pictures and moderate sexual arousal to appropriate heterosexual stimuli.

CASE HISTORY 9-4

The patient was a 22-year-old female student whose presenting complaint was an inability to enjoy sexual activities or achieve orgasm without receiving pain or humiliation in some fashion. She complained that normal heterosexual activities were completely nonarousing. Pleasurable sexual activities included being spanked, slapped, or verbally abused during sexual encounters. The patient's sexual history revealed a considerable number of sexual partners, of which only a few had fulfilled her sexual desires and expectations. She reported her most satisfying relationship had been a four-month encounter with a partner whose imaginative innovatious for inflicting pain and satisfaction were matchless. The patient's masturbatory behavior including forcing large objects into her vagina and rectum while fantasizing being raped by groups of men. On one occasion she lay in a bath of scalding water and masturbated to orgasm, a feat that later required medical treatment for burns. For several years she would periodically frequent bars in search of multiple sexual partners. Locating several men together, she would "allow" herself to be taken by the group to a motel where she would engage in sexual activities with several males simultaneously. At the time of treatment she had been living with a man for several months who was agreeable to assisting in treatment.

The initial stage of treatment centered on eliminating the deviant masochistic arousal by using covert sensitization. The patient assisted in formulating several aversive scenes which centered on her dreaded fear of snakes. For example:

You become highly aroused as Jim pulls you down on the bed by your hair, ripping the buttons off your blouse as he kisses you roughly. Your body trembles with excitement as he stands to remove his pants and takes the giant leather belt from his jeans. "Suck me off, bitch," he commands as he violently strikes his belt across your naked breasts. Your body trembles with excitement and you feel as if you're going to have an orgasm as he continues thrashing you with his belt as you frantically go down on him. Just as you are about to climax he pulls from your mouth and reaches under the bed. "I've got a surprise for you bitch,'' he laughs, reaching into a large box. Suddenly you freeze in terror as he throws a giant, slimy snake on your naked stomach. You scream in terror as Jim laughs and throws another snake on you. The snakes are crawling over your body as he laughs while you scream and try to get away. Suddenly you manage to free yourself from the snakes and race from the room. As you slam the door you can still hear Jim laughing at you. You begin to feel better as you get in your car and ride away.

Masturbation training was initiated concurrent with covert sensitization. Since the patient was particularly responsive to verbalizations of sexual activities, it was decided to utilize this medium in an effort to redirect her sexual activities. An audiotape describing various heterosexual behaviors was produced with the assistance of a male graduate student. The patient was given the tape and instructed to attempt manual masturbation while playing and attending to the audio stimulus. Progressive muscular relaxation was also taught to the patient in an effort to facilitate relaxation. The couple was requested to avoid all heterosexual activities during this stage of treatment.

The patient originally reported only minimal sexual arousal as a result of the audio stimulus. However, within two weeks she had experienced her first orgasm to the nonmasochistic stimulus. Within a month after the initiation of masturbation training she was frequently able to achieve orgasm utilizing the audio stimulus, and permission was given to begin heterosexual intercourse. An appointment for a follow-up assessment was scheduled in one month.

At follow-up a physiological assessment utilizing a vaginal probe indicated no sexual arousal to masochistic stimuli and moderate to strong arousal to heterosexual stimuli. The patient reported strong arousal to heterosexual intercourse, but she complained of being orgasmic only during masturbation. At this point it was decided to initiate sensate focus exercises with her male partner. Again the patient initially reported only minimal sexual arousal to this activity. Within three weeks, however, she was frequently experiencing sexual pleasure and orgasm as a result of manual and oral stimulation by her partner, as well as during intercourse.

Two- and five-month follow-ups indicated that the patient was continuing to experience satisfaction through nonmasochistic sexual behaviors. She reported only occasional masochistic urges and no masochistic masturbatory fantasies or behaviors. At the five-month follow-up she had discontinued her relationship with her boyfriend, but was continuing to enjoy sexual activities with a variety of partners. Approximately a year later we received a letter from the patient reporting that she had married and was expecting a child. She reported being very happy with no sexually related problems.

RAPE

Definitions of rape vary considerably, but usually include the idea that rape involves sexual activity with an individual other than one's spouse under conditions of force, threat of violence, or trickery, or with a person not competent to give consent. This definition is interpreted as including sexual activity with an individual who is drugged, drunk, mentally unsound, unconscious, or under the age of 18. As such, rape is usually committed by men against women, although homosexual rapes do occur and will be discussed. Legally, rape is divided into *statutory rape,* involving sexual activity with an individual under legal age (usually 18) either with or without consent, and *forcible rape* or intercourse without consent. It is with the latter that we are here primarily concerned.

The Act of Rape

By definition, rape is a crime that combines sexual and aggressive behavior. Nevertheless, rape tends at times to be viewed as primarily or exclusively sexual or aggressive in nature. But rape is not simply unbridled sexuality. Even rape committed following the prolonged absence of an available sexual partner usually involves much aggression and humiliation. Furthermore, many rapists do not lack available sexual partners. Neither is rape pure aggression, a singular desire to injure the victim, nor, as has been frequently suggested recently (Brownmiller, 1975), simply another aggressive tactic of men directed toward women. Rape is a combination of sexual and aggressive behaviors. In contrast with those of the rapist, however, the sexual and aggressive behaviors of normal adults are fused in such a manner as to allow for mutually enjoyable sexual relationships. In the rapist, this fusion has gone awry.

Degree of Force. Forcible and violent rape is what usually comes to mind when one thinks of rape. Forcible rape is highly feared by most women and regarded as reprehensible by society at large. However, not all instances of rape labeled as forcible involve the use of physical force sufficient to produce injury. Some rapists use force only to achieve their sexual aims (usually coitus, fellatio, or anal intercourse). They are not interested in hurting the victim, occasionally, in fact, pleading with the victim to cooperate to avoid violence. Other rapists use more force than necessary, and it is sometimes difficult to tell whether the primary purpose of the attack is sexual or aggressive. A currently unresolved and controversial issue is how much force must be employed to label clearly an act of sexual intercourse as forced on the victim (Selkin, 1975). Many people in our society feel that a virtuous woman should appear to resist sexual activities with a man to whom she is not married, even though she may actually desire a sexual relationship with him. Similarly, society teaches men that they are expected to use persuasion, coercion, and trickery in efforts to seduce women as proof of their virility and masculinity and as a means of allowing women to experience the pleasure of sex while maintaining an appearance of purity and virtue. The question remains: how much force, both physical and psychological, is required to label an act of rape?

> There is a footnote to this excavation. The strain of climatic discovery had evidently been too much for my men. As I was getting into bed one night they surrounded my tent to serenade me first, and then had the effrontery, with lots of jokes and lots of shouts, to come in and pull me out of my cot in my nightgown. Tugging at my hands, they insisted on leading me, over my protests, over my laughter, with lots of flashlights and song, to the nearby Cave of the Throat. I was irritated at being dragged into an unlighted cave at night by so many aroused old men. But for group morale I decided to be a good sport about the whole thing and confined my objections to nervous reprimands. When we reached the cave, they hauled me in all the way under the arch to that inflamed pink-and-purple-and red stalagmite poking up out of the floor, engorged and glistening. They pulled my legs apart and rudely lifted my nightgown out of the way. Even Totonedu. I was paralyzed with shock; worse, I was plain speechless. With all the cackling together, intoning some unctuous local chant, and holding me up by my spread thighs over the ancient protruding deposit, rather gently they wedded me to the rock.
>
> As their boss I was outraged. As a poet, however, I was impressed to the core and upon reflection realized that I had experienced a rape that deserved reverence. How else was I to interpret it? Some obscenities are sacred, certain violations sacramental. (Taken from *Hermaphrodeity,* Friedman, A., 1973)

Because of fixed societal notions of appropriate behavior for men and women in their initial sexual encounters, it is not surprising that misunderstanding may arise as to precisely how much force and resistance is necessary in a given case to accurately describe it as rape. Consider, for example, the woman who becomes so terrified as to be speechless and motionless at the physical persistence of an aggressive male. Or consider also that the resistance offered by a small woman may be felt by her to be a real struggle, while her stronger assailant interprets the struggle as no more than a coy ritual prostestation of virtue.

Stages of Rape. In more than half the cases of reported forcible rape, the rapist is a stranger to the victim. In these cases the rape usually has a discernible number of stages (Selkin, 1975). The first stage involves locating a victim. Some rapists choose victims vulnerable to attack, such as elderly women, mentally retarded or handicapped women, or women who are intoxicated. Other rapists attempt to locate defenseless women by searching out easily entered locations where women live alone. Some rapists search telephone books for listings of women's names or canvas apartments looking for listings in women's names.

After locating a likely victim, the next stage is to determine if she will react with submission or fear. Once the rapist has assessed his ability to intimidate the victim, he assumes she is likely to submit to his demands.

The third stage is characterized by threat; the offender tells the victim what he wants from her and what he will do to her if she resists (Selkin, 1975). It is very important that the rapist frighten the victim into submission so that he secures controlled behavior on her part which permits him to carry out the sexual act. Intimidation may come as a result of verbal threat or the presence of a weapon.

The fourth and final stage in rape is the sexual transaction itself. Vaginal intercourse occurs in about half the rape cases; oral and anal intercourse in most of the others (Selkin, 1975). One rape is described in Parker (1972) as follows:

> There was a sort of shed, a big shed where you keep garden tools and things. I caught hold of her arm, I said, "Come on, come in here." She started yelling. I said, "Keep quiet, I won't hurt you, I'm not going to hurt you if you keep quiet." She said, "What do you want, do you want money, I've got some money in the house . . . . I'll give it to you if you want it." I said . . . "I don't want money, you can keep your money. Just keep quiet and then I won't hurt you." There was a lot of room in that shed, a big place it was; all garden tools and a big lawn-mower and a lot of old sacks. I said, "Get down on those, you'll be all right, I just want a bit quick and then I'll leave you alone." . . . She didn't make any noise, then I had intercourse with her. (p. 264)

The Rapist

Many researchers believe that both sexual and aggressive impulses motivate the act of rape. Cohen, Garofalo, Boucher, and Seghorn (1971) conducted an investigation of 27 convicted rapists and formulated a typology or scheme for categorizing rapists based on the motivation of the rapist for committing the crime, in particular whether he was motivated by sex or by aggression. According to this typology, there are four categories of rapists: the *aggressive-aim* rapist, the *sexual-aim* rapist, the *sex-aggression-fusion* rapist, and the *impulse* rapist.

Categories of Rapists.

1. *Aggressive-aim rapists.* In the aggressive-aim pattern the rapist is motivated by a desire to humiliate, defile, and injure the victim. Sex has little to do with the act except insofar as the rapist uses it to hurt the victim. Those parts of a woman's body which usually are sexually exciting fre-

quently become the foci of the aggressive-aim rapist; he may attempt to damage the victim's breasts or genitals or insert objects into the victim's vagina (Selkin, 1975). The emotional state of the rapist during the act is one of anger, and the victim is usually a complete stranger. Aggressive-aim rapists frequently have an adequate occupational history and are often married, although they have a history of irritating or even violent relationships with women.

2. *Sexual-aim rapist.* In the sexual-aim pattern the rapist is motivated by sexual desires. There is a relative absence of violence and brutality—only what is needed to accomplish the sexual act. During the act the rapist is very much sexually aroused, and rather than being impulsive, the rapist usually rehearses the act in masturbatory fantasy in which the victim initially resists but later falls in love with him. The sexual-aim rapist frequently has a childhood and adolescent history of voyeurism, exhibitionism, and inadequate heterosocial skills. During the rape he may use some force to subdue the victim, but is likely to release the victim and flee if she puts up a significant struggled (Rada, 1978)

3. *Sex-aggression-fusion rapist.* In the sex-aggression-fusion pattern a strong sadistic component is present and some degree of violence is necessary to achieve sexual arousal. Indeed, the rapist may be impotent unless the woman resists. Rapist-murderers are an extreme version of this type; most sex-aggression-fusion rapists use violence only to become aroused, and employ no further violence once the act is over. Such a rapist often projects his own confusion of sex and aggression onto the victim—"Women like to get roughed up during sex; it turns them on." The behavior of the sex-aggression-fusion rapist may resemble that of the psychopath; he has a history of antisocial behavior, an inability to form stable relationships, a noncaring attitude toward others, little control over his impulses, and no feeling of guilt over his behavior. Paranoid features are more common in this group and may reach psychotic proportions (Rada, 1978).

4. *Impulse rapist.* In the impulse pattern the rapist has neither a sexual nor an aggressive motive. Rather, he commits the rape on impulse. For example, he may be involved in robbing an apartment when he notices that it is unoccupied except for one woman who is asleep in bed. He notes the opportunity for committing rape and seizes it for no other reason than sexual satisfaction. This type of rapist has also been referred to as the *predatory* rapist (Selkin, 1975).

Many other classifications and typologies of the rapist have been suggested (Amir, 1971; Ellis & Brancale, 1956; Wile, 1941) based on motivation, degree of violence used, modus operandi of the rapist, presence of organic or psychological abnormalities, repetitiveness of offenses, personality type, and so on. All of these classification systems are to some extent arbitrary and artificial. Care should be taken when classifying any behavior that the classification system is not used in a manner that obscures the individuality of each offender.

The Date Rapist. Although seldom classified as rape, some acts of sexual intercourse on dates involve a good deal of force and could at least be termed sexual aggression. Kanin (1969) investigated incidents of this type by contacting a random sample of unmarried male university students of whom 95 percent cooperated. Of those who responded, 25 percent reported having performed at least one act of sexual aggression, defined as making a foreceful attempt at coitus to the point of being disagreeable and offensive to the woman and having the woman respond by fighting or crying. The 87 males who had engaged in such behavior reported 181 episodes with 142 females.

In some cases sexual aggression on dates may result from miscommunication between the partners (Kanin, 1969):

> I picked up M and she suggests we go park and "talk." Talk shifts to "old times." I move over and kiss her. One thing leads to another and I am petting her breasts. M begins to complain about her girdle and removes it. The pace increases to the point where I try to lay her down on the front seat of the car. She resists and I keep going until she suddenly starts fighting and screaming at me. I finally told her to shut up and took her home. She was really sore. (p. 129)

In this case the sexual aggressor was not a deviant rapist but rather guilty of nothing more than misinterpreting the woman's taking off her girdle as an invitation to intercourse. In some cases miscommunications and misunderstanding are so great as to be nearly unbelievable. For example, Hyde (1979) reports that some rapists have been known to ask, after the rape, whether the victim had an orgasm.

The Homosexual Rapist. An unusual but not uncommon subcategory of rape involves assault by a male on another male or assault by a woman on another woman. Such rapes are not uncommon in prisons where a new prisoner may be repeatedly raped by other prisoners unless he/she is particularly strong or quickly locates another prisoner who will help or protect. Unfortunately, however, those prisoners who offer protection to a new prisoner frequently do so under the conditions that he/she will reciprocate with sexual favors exclusively to the protector. The new prisoner is thus forced to make a rather difficult decision.

In men's prisons rape may involve forcing the victim to perform fellatio on the offender(s) or mutual fellation, but most often involves the victim to submit to anal intercourse. In women's prisons rape may involve forcing the victim to perform masturbation or cunnilingus on the offender(s), mutual masturbation or cunnilingus, or more violent acts involving vaginal or anal rape with foreign objects. Prison rape, however, if frequently considered to be as much a part of the power struggle in the institution as it is a sexual release. For example, in 1973 a 28-year-old Quaker pacifist named Robert A. Martin held a press conference in which he told the story of his experience of homosexual rape (Aiken, 1973). Arrested during a peace demonstration, Martin had chosen to go to jail rather than post a $10.00 bond. His first week in the District of Columbia jail was uneventful. The next week, however, he was transferred to another cellblock and during the recreation period on the first evening he was invited into a cell by some other inmates. Then, "my exit was blocked and my pants were forcibly taken off me and I was raped. Then I was dragged from cell to cell all evening." He was promised protection from further assaults by two of the men. The next night his "protectors" initiated a second round of oral and anal rape, collecting cigarettes from prisoners wanting a turn. When he was given a brief rest to overcome gagging and nausea he escaped, alerted a guard, and was taken to a hospital.

Female Rapists. Perhaps one of the many sexual fantasies of the average American male is to be raped or erotically used by a group of beautiful women, all of whom are delirious with desire. It is a safe bet, however, that few of the fantasies include the pain, brutal force, and humiliation which often characterizes the act of forcible rape. There are, in fact, some rare instances in which a woman is charged with rape. However, in the majority of these cases the woman served only as an accomplice, assisting a man in raping another woman. For example, in one case a man and his wife were both charged in the rape of their 13-year-old niece. The girl reported that her aunt took her by force to her uncle's bedroom, took off her pajamas, and held her down while her uncle raped her (MacDonald, 1971). And in some states an adult female who entices a boy under the age of 18 to have sexual relations can be prosecuted for statutory rape. However, forcible rape of a man by a woman is quite rare and often considered physically impossible because some degree of erection in the male is necessary for penile-vaginal intercourse. However, it is possible for a woman to forcibly rape a man. MacDonald (1971) provides an example of female rape in a description of sexual assaults by women of Vakuta (in northwestern Melanesia) on men from other villages:

> First they pull off and tear up his pubic leaf, the protection of his modesty and, to a native, the symbol of his manly dignity. Then, by masturbatory practices and exhibitionism, they try to produce an erection in their victim and, when their maneuvers have brought about the desired result, one of them squats over him and inserts his penis into her vagina. After the first ejaculation he may be treated in the same manner by another woman. . . . Sometimes these furies rub their genitals against his nose and mouth, and use his fingers and toes, in fact, any projecting part of his body, for lascivious purposes. (p. 75)

The Victims of Rape

The victims of rape may be of any age from small infants to very elderly women. Often the rapist shows very little esthetic preference in his choice of victims. Sometimes he simply decides that he will rape the next woman he sees, conditions permitting. East (1946) cited a case in which an unprepossessing woman over 70 years of age was raped and then murdered by a man who was not drunk, mentally retarded, or psychotic. More recently, a man in his late 20s broke into a 72-year-old woman's home in Los Angeles; he raped and beat the woman, and afterward, sat down to smoke a cigarette and watch television. In another instance, a young woman volunteer worker in a rape crisis center located in a major southern city was raped in the crisis center itself, located in a deserted part of a large hospital. The majority of rape victims, however, are between the ages of 15 and 25 years of age, unmarried, and come from the lower social classes (Delora & Warren, 1977).

It is not uncommon for women who struggle against their attacker to receive broken ribs, fractures, and bruises. Occasionally several offenders join together and rape a victim consecutively or simultaneously. In addition to the physical trauma inflicted on the victim, the psychological trauma varies greatly with the victim but may be severe. Effects of rape on marital relationships are particularly severe, especially if the husband has been forced to watch the rape. In a study of 13 female rape victims, ages 18 to 24, Sutherland and Scherl (1970) reported a rather typical response pattern, which involved three phases:

Reactions to Rape.

1. *Acute Reaction.* In the moments, hours, and days immediately following the rape, the victim's acute reactions may take a variety of forms including shock, disbelief, and dismay. She often appears at the police station or the hospital in an agitated, incoherent, and highly volatile state. Frequently she is unable to talk about what has happened to her or to describe the man who has assaulted her. Sometimes the victim will initially appear stable only to break down at the first unexpected reminder of the incident. In addition, many women report an overwhelming fear of physical violence and say that they had believed they would be murdered during the attack. Self-blame also occurs, with the woman spending hours agonizing over what she may have done to provoke the rape: "If I hadn't worn that tight sweater. . . ." The acute reaction usually resolves within a period of a few days to a few weeks.

2. *Outward Adjustment.* After the immediate anxiety-arousing issues have been temporarily settled, the patient generally returns to her usual work, school, or home pursuits. She announces all is well and says she needs no further help. During this phase the woman deals with her feelings

about the assailant. Anger or resentment are often subdued in the interest of a return to ordinary daily life. The victim may rationalize these feelings by attributing the act to blind chance (it could have happened to anyone), to sickness on the part of the assailant, or to an extension of the social struggle of black against white or of poor against rich. In similar fashion and for the same reasons the victim's doubts about her role in the assault are also set aside.

3. *Integration and Resolution.* This phase begins when the victim develops an inner sense of depression and of the need to talk. It is during this period that the resolution of the feelings aroused by the rape usually occur. Concerns which have been dealt with superficially or denied successfully reappear for more comprehensive review. The depression of phase three is psychologically normal and occurs in most young women who have been raped (Brodsky, 1976).

Burgess and Holmstrom (1974) interviewed 92 victims of forcible rape and reported a *rape trauma syndrome* consisting of acute and long term reorganization phases similar to those described above.

Incidence. The scientific study of rape and rapists, like the study of other illegal sexual variations, is limited because the vast majority of data are derived from cases that come to the attention of the law. Statistics concerning reported cases of rape are especially biased because rape is an underreported crime, possibly by as much as 80 percent (Amir, 1971). A detailed interview study by the National Opinion Research Center of the University of Chicago suggests that actual incidence figures are probably more than 3.5 times the reported rate (President's Commission, 1967). In 1973 there were 51,000 reported rapes in the United States. In 1974 there were 26.1 forcible rapes per 100,000 women, an increase of 175 percent over 1960. It is estimated that the actual incidence of rape is presently between 28 and 70 victims per 100,000 women per year (Rimm & Somerville, 1977). Let us make these statistics more meaningful: on the basis of crime and census statistics for the city of Los Angeles, the chances of a Los Angeles woman's meeting a rapist at some time during a 30-year period is conservatively estimated as approximately one in ten (Offir, 1975).

The reasons for the dramatic increases in rapes are not well understood. Certainly crime in all major cities has increased since 1960, and rape may be influenced by many of the same contributory factors of overcrowding, increasing use of drugs and alcohol, umemployment, availability of firearms, and unfavorable living conditions. In addition, the *reported* incidence of rape may be increasing because the victims are more willing to come forward and press charges. Most major cities now have rape crisis centers, and many women's groups support and actively encourage rape victims to come forward. In addition, supportive procedures have been developed to assist the rape victim adjust to her traumatic experience and even to help her legally (Medea & Thompson, 1974; Oliver, 1974). The purpose of the rape crisis centers is mainly to provide psychological support, although a large number of victims require medical treatment for lacerations and various other injuries, and about one percent of all rape victims become pregnant as a result of the assault. Many people feel that rape crisis centers provide beneficial aid to the victims of rape, yet comprehensive and reliable research on the effects such centers have has yet to be done. Opponents of rape crisis centers, which are usually staffed by nonprofessional volunteers or minimally trained paraprofessionals, claim that a victim of rape should be evaluated and treated by a competent psychiatrist or clinical psychologist as soon as possible after the assault.

Defending Against Rape

Selkin (1975) claims that a familiarity with the patterns of rape may make it possible to avoid it. Selkin suggests that women should avoid being alone in isolated areas and should also avoid being friendly or helpful to strangers when they live alone or are unaccompanied. If they are approached by a stranger, their best defense is to refuse to be intimidated and resist from the very beginning. Screaming, running away, and fighting back may induce a would-be rapist to look for a more cooperative and easily intimidated victim.

In every rape attempt, particularly when the assailant has a weapon, the woman who resists runs a risk of injury or death. Fortunately, this risk is not as large as one might suppose. For example, fewer than 9 percent of the rape victims in Denver from 1970 to 1972 suffered anything more serious than a cut or bruise (Delora & Warren, 1977). Selkin (1975) estimates that probably less than one percent of all murders involve sexual assault.

In *Hail to the Chief* (McBain, 1973) Detective Meyer of the 87th Precinct gives a lecture to a group of college coeds that contains some interesting and thought provoking ideas:

I don't want you to become neurotic about rape, I don't want you to start screaming if a panhandler taps you on the shoulder. He may only want a quarter for a drink, and you'll start screaming, and he'll try to shut you up, and the next thing you know he's broken your neck. That's as bad as being assaulted by a real rapist . . . . [Rape] has nothing to do with the way you look. You can be standing on a corner wearing a potato sack, with your hair in curlers, and a fever sore on your lip, and that won't discourage the rapist. He is a sick man; you are presumably a healthy individual. Don't, for God's sake, foolishly place yourself in hazardous or vulnerable situations.

If you're out on a date with a man you know, and you're necking in his automobile, and he decides to take you by force, against your will, that's rape

—even if you've known him since he was six years old. In a situation like that, I would advise you to stop necking for a moment, stick your finger down your throat, and vomit into his lap.

Remember that the unexpected is the best approach. You are flat on your back, and this man is about to rape you. Instead of trying to twist away, begin to fondle him. That's right. Fondle his genitals. Then drop your hand to his testicles and squeeze. Squeeze as hard as you can. You are going to hurt this man, but you are also going to end the rape that very minute. You may wonder whether he will be able to chase you afterwards, perhaps hit you harder than he did before, perhaps even kill you. I can guarantee that you can run clear to California and back, and that man will still be lying on the ground incapable of movement. There is another way and I suspect your reaction to it will be 'I'd rather get raped.' That, of course, is up to you. I can only offer you options. Again, do the unexpected. Put your hands gently on the rapist's face, palms against his temples, cradle his face, murmer words of endearment, allow him to think you're going along with his plans. Your thumbs will be close to his eyes. If you have it in yourself the courage to push your thumbs into a hard-boiled egg, then you can also push your thumbs into this man's eyes. You will put out his eyes, you will blind him. But you will not be raped.
. . . The choice is yours. (pp. 113–117)

Research and Theory: Physiological Factors

The act of rape involves both sexual and aggressive behavior and has produced a considerable volume of literature on the biological aspects of each. In this section we will briefly discuss three major biological areas of etiological research: genetic factors, neuroanatomical and neurophysiological factors, and endocrinologic factors. The interested reader may find more detailed discussions of these topics elsewhere (Lloyd & Weisz, 1975; Sandler & Gessa, 1975).

Genetic Factors. The development of laboratory techniques for assessing human chromosomes (karyotypes) and sex chromatin has produced the description of several syndromes resulting from abnormal sex chromosome patterns, namely Turner's syndrome—45, X—in the female and Klinefelter's syndrome—47, XXY and 47, XYY in the male. Various personality and behavioral characteristics, including antisocial and aggressive behavior, have been reported in Klinefelter's syndrome and 47, XYY males. For example, Baker, Telfer, and Richardson (1970) compared men in prisons and facilities for the mentally ill and mentally retarded who showed Klinefelter's syndrome or the XYY chromosome pattern. These authors reported that sexual assault was prominent in both groups and cited several case histories of men with XYY chromosome patterns who were rapists. Money (1975), however, reviewed the literature involving each of these syndromes and noted a number of errors in the research, most notably the possible sampling errors and lack of conclusive data regarding the frequency incidence of 47, XYY males in the general population and among antisocial males who are not confined. Money concluded that the stereotype of the 47, XYY male as an aggressive, violent rapist is not confirmed.

Neuroanatomical and Neurophysiological Factors. While it is clear that brain pathology can lead to personality changes (Blumer & Benson, 1975), it is not clear to what extent, if any, central nervous system dysfunction can produce sexual deviation or abnormal aggression (Rada, 1978). Investigators have explored several avenues of inquiry.

As far back as 1939, Kluver and Bucy described a specific syndrome associated with bilateral temporal lobectomies in rhesus monkeys. This syndrome, known as the Kluver-Bucy syndrome, includes hypersexuality and was for a short while thought by many to explain rape. In the 1940s Cook (1949) supported the idea that antisocial behavior and sexual psychopathology were associated with abnormal electroencephalograms (EEGs). Rada (1978) claims that despite the evidence that criminal sexual behavior such as rape is the result of brain pathology, there are data suggesting a close association between epilepsy and abnormal sexual behavior in some patients. Of all the epilepsies, temporal lobe epilepsy is most clearly associated with abnormalities in sexual and aggressive behavior. Brain and Walton (1969), however, claim that this association is, in fact, weak and based largely on faulty investigative methodology. Goldstein (1975) did a detailed review of the animal and human literature on brain research and violent behavior, including rape, and concluded that more research is needed in this area before definitive statements can be made.

Endocrinologic Factors. Studies of testosterone and aggressive behavior have been reported in a number of species, including deer, dogs, hamsters, mice, monkeys, and rats (Rada, 1978). In general these studies indicate the importance of androgens in establishing a biological readiness to aggressive behavior and in facilitating the expression of aggressive behavior in adult animals. However, they also indicate the importance of social factors and learning on the actual expression of aggression in adulthood. The reported relationship between testosterone level and both sexual and aggressive behavior in animals led to an investigation of testosterone level in rapists. Rada, Laws, and Kellner (1976) measured plasma testosterone levels in 52 rapists and 12 pedophiles. The rapists were classified according to the degree of violence used in the deviant behavior and were administered a paper and pencil measure of aggression. Results indicated that the group of rapists who were judged to be most violent had a significantly higher mean plasma testosterone level than normals, child molesters, and other rapists in the study. Mean aggressive-hostility ratings for the rapists were significantly higher than the mean for normals, although there was no correlation between individual aggressive-hostility scores and plasma testosterone levels. It should be noted, however, that this study did not control for the effects of medication that the rapists were taking. In fact, it was reported that several of the rapists were on a drug regimen of thioridazine (Mellaril) which has been found to decrease plasma testosterone levels (Beaumont, Corker, & Friesen, 1974).

Research and Theory: Psychological Factors

It may seem logical to assume that the major cause of rape is an abnormally heightened sexual drive. It is interesting that no major clinician or researcher currently believes that rapists act out of unbridled, uncontrollable hypersexuality. The rapist's lack of proper control over his sexual and aggressive impulses is not disputed; but most clinicians agree that rape represents overcompensatory behavior in an individual suffering from hyposexuality or at least inadequate heterosocial/sexual skills. There are three major psychological theories as to the development of rapist behavior.

Psychoanalytic Formulations. Psychoanalytic thinking regarding rape often includes emphasis on the rapist's relationship with his mother. Faulty mother-son relationships may result in the adult male's hatred of women. He may project his disgust felt toward the mother onto women in general, feeling that women should be punished and defiled. Psychoanalytic thinking views the rape of a stranger as retribution against the mother who fosters such negative and hostile perceptions in the child, but who remains unpunishable because of the sanctity of motherhood. A love-hate conflict thus exists in relationship to the mother which must be resolved by the man's punishment and hatred of women (indirectly targeted toward the mother), while maintaining love and affection in direct dealings with the mother.

Psychodynamic Formulations. Dynamically oriented psychological thinking views the etiology and maintenance of rape as a function of severe psychopathology. In a study of 100 rapists, Kopp (1962) found a high incidence of antisocial or psychopathic personalities, which he described thus:

> This antisocial psychopath is a cold, seemingly unfeeling man who has always taken what he wanted from others without apparent concern for the feelings of his victims or for the consequences of his act. For him, rape is just another instance of aggressive taking, except that in this case he steals sexual satisfaction rather than money or property. When questioned about his offense, he often responds with callous sarcasm, completely devoid of guilt or

concern. He may well simply respond with the statement, "I wanted it so I took it." The rape fits so well with his character structure and is so typical of his general behavior pattern that he can see nothing wrong with the act, and often goes on to rationalize that his victim probably enjoyed it. He wants no part of therapy unless he sees it as a means of manipulating his way out of incarceration. (p. 66)

Although most dynamic theories hypothesize psychopathic personality structures, other categories of psychopathology have been emphasized. In men suffering from manic reactions, schizophrenia, and various organic psychoses, for example, lowering of inner controls may possibly lead to physical assault and occasionally to forcible rape. However, during acute psychotic episodes the individual is likely to be so disorganized as to be capable only of indiscriminate physical assault rather than the coordinated behavior required for forcible rape (Coleman, 1972).

Behavioral Formulations. As previously mentioned, many researchers believe that the act of rape may be motivated by either sexual or aggressive impulses (Cohen et al., 1971). Sexually motivated acts of rape may be viewed as resulting from faulty patterns of learning regarding impulse control and delayed gratification, as well as a severe lack of appropriate heterosocial/heterosexual skills. If an individual is so deficient in heterosocial and/or heterosexual skills that he lacks knowledge of the basics of heterosexual seduction, his avenues of appropriate sexual behavior become greatly limited. Often the issue is compounded by an environment in which control of sexual and aggressive impulses and delayed gratification are only minimally or even negatively valued. In these circumstances, the individual may simply learn that if he cannot obtain his goals through proper channels, he must rely on force, trickery, or deceit.

Rape that is due to aggressive motivation may result from a set of learning circumstances that resemble those that cause sadistic behavior. Abel, Barlow, Blanchard, and Guild (1977) found that, like the voyeur and the exhibitionist who become aroused, at least in part, by the victim's lack of consent, some rapists were sexually aroused to aggressive scenes as much as they were aroused to verbalized descriptions of actual rape. These rapists verbalized a distinct preference for physically forcing themselves on their victims even when the victim freely offered herself without force being necessary.

CASE HISTORY 9-5

The patient was a 19-year-old male serving a prison sentence for forcible rape and assault. One of us, was asked to see the patient and consult on a rehabilitation program proposed by a colleague.

The patient's social history revealed a number of confrontations with the law, beginning at the age of 11 when he was arrested and later released for stealing. Since then he estimated he had been arrested seven or eight times for stealing, breaking and entering, public drunkenness, and assault. The patient had escaped a prison sentence for all these crimes, and his incarceration as a result of conviction on charges of forcible rape and assault represented his first prison sentence.

The patient's sexual history revealed his first heterosexual experience at the age of 12. This incident involved waiting his turn to have intercourse with a prostitute while several older friends preceded him. As a teenager he asked many girls for dates but was seldom successful. As he put it, "I came from a rough neighborhood, I wasn't much to look at, I had no money, and I was always in trouble with the law. Now who wanted to date me?" The patient's sexual experiences were almost exclusively limited to engaging in sexual activities with neighborhood prostitutes, one of whom was his cousin. His only other sexual experience was with a mentally retarded neighborhood girl to whom he once gave a soft drink to fellate him.

The patient assessed his problems as follows: I always wanted the good-looking women; wouldn't settle for nothing else. When they wouldn't go out with me cause I wasn't good enough for them, it began to piss me off. I could feel it building up in me. I finally decided if I couldn't date it or buy it, I'd just take it.

And so he did. He was charged and convicted of abducting, raping, and beating a 24-year-old college beauty queen. The assault resulted in a five-day hospitilization for the young woman who resisted the attack and suffered multiple lacerations, bruises, and a broken jaw. The patient expressed no remorse over his behavior.

Modification of Rapists' Behavior

Rapists have traditionally been handled through the legal system and because they cause their victims so much physical and psychological suffering, they are usually given long jail sentences. Imprisonment seems to have little value for them, although it does protect society from further assaults by the offender during his incarceration.

Psychological treatment for the rapist is frequently not available; when it is, it is lengthy and difficult (Wincze, 1977). When professional help is available, it must be offered within the confines of a prison, which makes it subject to the limitations and inadequacies inherent in the penal system. Personnel inadequately trained in the management of sexually related behaviors, lack of financial resources, over crowded conditions, and the fact that sex offenders are not separated from other inmates all severely limit an efficient management of sexually related offenders. California's Atascadero State Hospital is one of the few state institutions that specialize in treating sexually related offenses and offenders.

Medical Therapies. Throughout history castration has been used to prevent the procreation of those deemed undesirable, as retribution for crimes, and more recently, as a preventive and treatment technique for violent sexual offenses (Rada, 1978). According to Karpman (1959), castration was first recommended as a treatment for sexual overexcitement in the late eighteenth century and was first utilized as therapy in 1889. The rationale is quite obvious; to remove the organ producing the hormone of sexual desire, and sexual interest and performance will be arrested. However, those researchers who view rape as motivated by aggression do not agree that castration will modify the rapist's behavior. At the present time castration of rapists is confined to Europe; there are no reports of the techniques' being used in the United States.

Psychosurgery has been recommended in the treatment of a variety of mental disorders, some violent disorders, and certain sexual disorders, including rape (Valenstein, 1973). As with castration, psychosurgery has strong proponents but an equally vociferous group of critics.

Although the use of psychosurgery has declined significantly in the past ten years, there are occasional scattered reports of its use in treating certain sexual disorders including rape (Valenstein, 1973). As with castration, psychosurgery has strong proponents but an equally vocal group of critics. The legality of experimental psychosurgery has received considerable attention because of the Kaimowitz case tried in Michigan. John Doe, the patient in question, had been committed many years earlier for murdering and then raping a young woman. A group of investigators proposed an experiment to compare the effects of psychosurgery on the amygdaloid portion of the limbic system with the effects of the drug cyproterone acetate, an antiandrogen agent. Although the surgery was officially approved and the patient had agreed, a lawyer filed a writ of habeas corpus alleging that the patient as a convicted rapist could not give an objective consent. The court ruling upheld the writ, claiming that the patient could not give a truly informed consent. Many think this ruling marks the end of psychosurgery, at least in the U.S. (Rada, 1978).

A number of investigators have reported on the use of various drugs in the treatment of rapists and other sexual deviates. Although the exact mechanism of action of all these drugs is not completely understood at this time, most appear to affect the circulating levels of plasma testosterone, thereby producing an alteration in sexual desire or function.

In 1970, Money reported on the use of medroxyprogesterone acetate in depot injectable form (Depo-Provera) in the treatment of male sexual offenders; he found that the agent produced a significant decrease in circulating testosterone. Money studied the use of Depo-Provera in eight male sexual offenders and reported the elimination of deviant behavior in all subjects.

Various phenothiazines have also been recommended in the treatment of sexual offenders. The side effect of impotence frequently associated with thioridazine (Mellaril) has resulted in this becoming a popular drug in the treatment of outpatient rapists. The phenothiazines can also produce a decrease in circulating plasma testosterone levels (Beumont et al., 1974). Other phenothiazines reportedly used in the treatment of sexual offenders such as rapists include fluphenazine enanthate (Prolixin) (Bartholomew, 1968), and chlorpromazine (Thorazine) (Tennent, Bancroft, & Cass, 1974), as well as the butyrophenone agent haloperidol (Haldol) (Field, 1973).

Behavior Therapy. Behavioral treatments of rapists have been only sparcely reported. One reason is that because of misunderstanding about behavior modification, behavioral treatment techniques are prohibited in many prison systems housing sexual offenders.

Assessment of rapists' sexual arousal to appropriate and deviant sexual stimuli has been the object of three important investigations using appropriate control groups. Neither of the first two studies showed differences between rapists and nonrapists. Karacan, Williams, and Guerrero (1974) measured nocturnal penile tumescence, sleep EEG, and eye movement patterns in rapist prisoners, nonrapists, and nonrapist prisoners. Although a variety of EEG changes were noted, no difference was noted between the erection measures of the rapists and nonrapist prisoners.

Kercher and Walker (1973) presented rapist and nonrapist prisoners with a variety of sexual stimuli while recording their penile erections and GSRs. Again, no difference in erections was noted between the groups, although rapists did show greater GSR changes while viewing slides of sexual activities and did rate the sexual stimuli less appealing than did the nonrapists. However, a variety of factors may have influenced the lack of difference in erection measures. First, subjects were not presented rape stimuli, only nonrape sexual cues. Second, slides have been reported as less sexually arousing than movies (Tollison et al., 1977) and the brief slide presentation (20 seconds) may not have allowed sufficient time for erections to occur. Finally, GSR changes are not specific to sexual arousal; thus the GSR differences between the rapists and nonrapists may have reflected some other emotional state differing between the groups (Zuckerman, 1971).

Abel et al. (1977) have provided some physiological evidence to help discriminate rapists from nonrapists and to help identify subcategories of rapists. These investigators used audio descriptions of various rape and nonrape sexual scenes, and measured penile circumference changes in groups of rapists and nonrapists. Results indicated that rapists as a group responded to both rape and mutually enjoyable intercourse scenes, whereas nonrapists only responded to the mutually enjoyable intercourse scenes (Figure 9-2). A "rape index" was compiled by dividing erection-to-rape cues by erection-to-mutually-enjoyable-intercourse cues. This index was useful not only in distinguishing rapists from nonrapists, but also in identifying rapists with a high frequency of rape, rapists who commonly injured their victims, and rapists who chose children as victims. Such a specific identification of a rapist's arousal pattern may be helpful in understanding

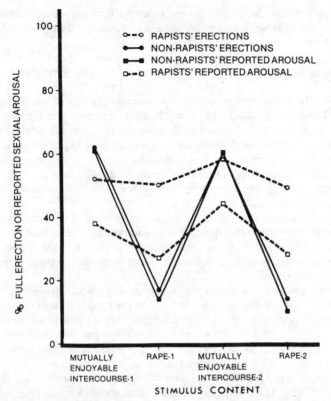

Figure 9-2. Comparison of erection and subjective arousal of seven consecutive rapists and nonrapists. (**Source:** Abel, G. G., Barlow, D. H., Blanchard, E. B., & Guild, D. The components of rapists' sexual arousal. *Archives of General Psychiatry*, 1977, *34*, 895–903. Reproduced by permission of the American Medical Association).

the rapist and in designing treatment programs. Abel et al.'s technique may also be useful as a preventive measure for identifying and treating potential rapists (Wincze, 1977).

A review of the behavioral literature indicates several treatment studies involving rapists with other sexual deviates (Marshall, 1973), patients who were treated for multiple sexual deviations including rape (Hayes et al., 1978), or more often multiple sexual deviations including rape fantasies. Unfortunately, no behavioral intervention studies specifically targeting on the treatment of rapists have been reported in the literature to date.

CASE HISTORY 9-6

The patient was a 27-year-old male serving a prison sentence for assault and forcible rape who volunteered to participate in an investigation of different treatment techniques. At the time of treatment he had been incarcerated for 18 months of a six-year prison sentence. The patient was described by prison officials as well-mannered, friendly, likable, and orderly, and a good candidate for early parole in approximately six months.

The patient was offered a treatment program consisting of electrical aversion therapy contingent on sexual arousal to deviant sexual stimuli depicting rape and other violent sex acts, and heterosocial skills training in an effort to facilitate his interactional skills with women. A special effort was made to explain the details of the treatment program to the patient since, being incarcerated, his freedom of choice was suspect. When he had agreed to all components of the treatment program, he was asked to cooperate in a physiological sexual assessment which measured the percentage of penile circumference change to various sexual stimuli. In addition, the patient was instructed to verbally rate the degree of sexual arousal produced by each visual stimulus. The stimuli consisted of a variety of heterosexual and homosexual photographs and slides. Those stimuli depicting force or violent sexual acts and rated as highly arousing by the patient, and whose physiological measurement corresponded with the high verbal rating were selected as stimuli to be used in aversion therapy. The results of physiological assessment indicated that the patient experienced sexual arousal to both normal heterosexual stimuli and to visuals depicting force and violent sex acts.

A modified version of aversion therapy was employed in which the patient controlled the duration of electrical stimulation. While the patient's penile responses were monitored via a strain gauge, deviant stimuli rated by the patient as arousing, and physiologically assessed to be so were presented in varying order. When penile erection was assessed at 25 percent of full erection (previously assessed by having the patient masturbate to a point just prior to orgasm and taking this measure as 100 percent erect), electrical stimulation was administered to the patient's first and third fingers of the left hand. The intensity of the electrical shock was assessed prior to the onset of treatment. Electrical stimulation was continuously administered until the patient tripped a switch attached to his chair which terminated both the aversion and the deviant stimulus. Eleven sessions of aversion therapy were administered before the patient both reported verbally and demonstrated physiologically no sexual arousal to the deviant stimuli. Twenty sessions of electrical stimulation were administered totally.

Because of the serious illness of the patient's father, he was transferred to another prison closer to his home before social skills therapy could be offered. Post-treatment physiological followup assessments at two and four months, however, indicated no sexual arousal to sexual stimuli depicting force or violent sexual acts, while arousal to those stimuli considered sexually appropriate was virtually unchanged and remained highly arousing. Another follow-up after the patient's parole and approximately 13 months from the onset of treatment demonstrated the maintenance of treatment gains.

CHAPTER 10

Pedophilia

When the sexual object for an adult is a child, the sexual act is classified as *pedophilia* (Greek for "love of children") or child molesting. Problems arise, however, in any operational definition of pedophilia. In legal terminology, pedophilia charges may be brought against an adult who engages in sexual contact with a minor (usually considered an individual under the age of 18. Using this definition, however, legal charges could be brought against an 18-year-old for engaging in sexual activity with a 17-year-old. For this reason, some researchers have attempted to define pedophilia in more useful and meaningful terms. Quinsey (1977), for example, defines pedophilia as sexual activity between an adult and a child 13 years of age or under when the adult is 16 years of age or older and at least five years older than the child. Unfortunately, this definition also is almost meaningless. Does an 18-year-old boy who engages in sexual activity with a physically mature and willing 13-year-old girl really warrant a diagnosis of pedophile? Classification of pedophilia according to the sexual act is also inappropriate, since heterosexual pedophiles may engage in the same sexual activities with their partners as do heterosexual adult partners. Thus, the definitions of pedophilia present many difficult problems for which there are no obvious solutions. A meaningful, useful, and appropriate definition of pedophilia has yet to be offered.

An adult, almost always a male, who engages in sexual relations with a child in our society has committed one of the most serious sex offenses and is traditionally regarded by the public as extremely degenerate. Hardly any other behavior, sexual or otherwise, can generate more social disgust and anger than pedophilia. In fact, even among imprisoned sexual offenders, pedophiles are regarded as guilty of the most degenerate sexual crime and are frequently the object of physical and psychological abuse by other inmates (Katchadourian & Lunde, 1972). Our legal system mirrors society's perception of the pedophile. In many states the penalty for the offending adult is life imprisonment, and in a few it has been death (Thorpe et al., 1961).

Pedophilic behavior may involve caressing a child's body, manipulating a child's genitals, or inducing a child to manipulate an adult's genitals. Occasionally, the behaviors also include penile penetration (partial or complete—vaginal or anal), oral sex, and any practice utilizing the sexual parts or organs of a child so as to bring the person in contact with the child's body in any sexual manner. Pedophilic acts may be homosexual or heterosexual in nature and may include touching, caressing, masturbation, oral-genital contact, and intercourse, as well as pedophilic exhibitionism, voyeurism, rape, sadism, and masochism.

The pedophile is frequently thought of as a stranger who lurks about the schoolyard and abducts an unsuspecting child who is taken by force to some secluded place and ravished. Investigative data rarely support this stereotype. While violent and brutal pedophilic sexual instances do occur, studies have shown that in about 85 percent of pedophilic cases the pedophile is either a relative, a family friend, a neighbor, or an acquaintance. The adult usually makes sexual advances to the child either in the child's home where the adult is visiting or living, or in the adult's home where the child is visiting or is enticed. Vetter (1972), in fact, reported that 79 percent of pedophilic instances occur in homes, 13 percent in public places, and 8 percent in cars. Physical violence to the child occurs in only 2 percent of instances, although threats of violence or some degree of physical restraint is present in about 33 percent of instances in which arrests and convictions follow (Vetter, 1972).

The adult who engages in sexual behavior with a child is condemned by society even when force is not involved and the child is either the aggressor or a willing partner. This horror is apparently based on the assumption that all children are sexually pure and innocent and that the pedophile is corrupting this innocence (Delora & Warren, 1977). This assumption of childhood innocence persists in spite of repeated research (for example, that of Kinsey et al., 1953) that children are often willing participants.

Societal attitudes and legal statutes against adult-child sexual relations are not imposed in all cultures with the same intensity as in the United States (Ullerstam, 1970). Among the Balinese, for example, fretful infants are frequently comforted by manipulation of their genitals, an act considered perfectly normal in Balinese culture (Martinson, 1973). The ancient Greeks also commonly enjoyed adult-child sex. In fact, it was considered a duty and privilege of the Greek adult to engage in such relations in order to prepare the child for citizenship.

All sexual relations between adults and children are presently considered criminal in our culture, even though there are varying degrees of coercion by the adult, and the child's reaction may range from strong resistance to cooperation and even seduction. When psychological or physical force is directed toward the child, the act is termed *rape*. Delora and Warren (1977) point out that the term "child molesting" is judgmental and reflects the common assumption in our culture that the child is an unwilling victim, even though he or she may have been cooperative or even aggressive. If the sex act involves anal intercourse between an adult and a boy, the activity is commonly called pederasty. When an adult has sexual relations with a willing and cooperative adolescent who is not of legal age, the act is *statutory rape*. In most states the legal age of consent is eighteen.

CHARACTERISTICS OF PEDOPHILES

Data concerning the pedophile indicate that most pedophilic behavior is distributed among three distinct age groups, with peaks in puberty (adolescent group), the mid-to-late thirties (middle-age group), and the mid-to-late fifties (senescent group). According to Mohr et al. (1962), studies of offenders, especially those who have been convicted and institutionalized, having consistently demonstrated that the middle-age group represents the largest total number of offenders. The majority of heterosexual pedophiles in the middle-age and senescent groups either are, or have been, married, and many have children of their own. Only one-third to one-half of homosexual pedophiles have ever been married. In a study of 36 convicted pedophiles, Revitch and Weiss (1962) found that older offenders tended to seek out immature children, while younger offenders preferred adolescent girls between 12 and 15. Girls outnumbered boys as victims, at a ratio of 2 to 1. For the majority of pedophilic offenders, acts of pedophilia are more or less incidental occurrences. It is only for a very small group of individuals that the behavior becomes chronic (Vetter, 1972).

TABLE 10-1

Heterosexual Pedophiles

At the receiving center of the California Department of Corrections, a study was made of 100 consecutive cases in which males were convicted of sexual offenses against female children. The number of victims molested by a single offender varied from 1 to 6; however, the prosecution usually sought convictions on only one count and dropped the other charges. There were 147 victims in all, ranging in age from 3 to 17 years, with a mean age of 10.5 years. Sixty-seven percent of the molested children were known to the offenders. Other information about the offenders is as follows:

Age range	23 to 70 years; mean age, 37
Marital status	Single, 22; married, 43; divorced, 24; separated, 8; widowed, 3
Race	White, 73; black, 11; Mexican-American, 15; Oriental, 2
Victim's relationship to offender	Own child, 18; child of a relative, 21; child of a friend, 21; stranger, 32; own child plus child of á relative, 4; own child plus child of a friend, 2; own child plus stranger, 1; child of a friend plus stranger, 1

Source: Fisher, G. Psychological needs of heterosexual pedophiliacs. *Diseases of the Nervous System*, 1969, *30*, 419-421.

Types of Pedophiles

A number of investigations have been made into the characteristics of pedophiles, and attempts have been made to categorize them into types on the basis of age (Mohr, 1962; Monr & Turner, 1967), adequacy of social skills (Cohen, Seghorn, & Calmas, 1969), or a combination of victim type and presumed etiology (Gebhard et al., 1965; McCaghy, 1968). In a study of 38 pedophilic offenders living in a segregated treatment center, Cohen et al. (1969) noted three distinguishable types of offenders:

1. *The personally immature offender,* who has never been able to establish or maintain satisfactory interpersonal relationships with male or female peers during his adolescent, young adult, or adult life. This represents the most common type of offender. He is sexually comfortable only with children and in most cases knows the victim. Usually the act is not impulsive but begins with a type of disarming courtship which eventually leads to sexual play. Either male or female children may be the victims.

2. *The regressed offender,* who during adolescence shows apparently normal development with good peer relationships and adequate social and heterosocial skills as well as heterosexual experience.

> However, throughout this period there exist increasing feelings of masculine inadequacy in sexual and nonsexual activities. And as he enters adulthood, his social, occupational, and marital adjustment is quite tenuous and marginal. There is frequently a history of an inability to deal with the normal stresses of adult life and alcoholic episodes become increasingly more frequent and result in the breakdown of a relatively stable marital, social, and work adjustment. In almost all instances the pedophilic acts are precipitated by some direct confrontation of his sexual adequacy by an adult female or some threat to his masculine image by a male peer. (p. 251)

One of the more frequent precipitating events is the discovery that the offender's wife or girlfriend is involved in an affair with another man. In most of these cases the victim is a female child.

In contrast to the personally immature offender, the regressed offender is generally not acquainted with his victim, and the act is characteristically impulsive. For example, the offender may be driving in his car, see a child, and become overwhelmed with sexual excitation (Coleman, 1972).

3. *The aggressive offender* describes the offender whose motivation for pedophilic behavior is both aggressive and sexual. Cohen states:

> The primary aim is aggression, and is expressed in cruel and vicious assaults on the genitalia or by introducing the penis or elongated objects into the victim orally or anally. The sexual excitement increases as an apparent function

of the aggression, but the orgasm itself either does not occur or must be reached through masturbation (p. 251)

Such offenders usually have a history of antisocial behavior and frequently are characterized as hostile, aggressive psychopaths. Ordinarily they select a boy as the object of their aggressive act.

Unfortunately, offenders of this type have not been studied in regard to treatment variables or subsequent recidivism. Furthermore whether these offenders are representative of pedophiles in general is highly questionable.

Intelligence

Much is said about the deteriorated mental state of all sexual offenders (Rooth, 1969). In fact, in the early studies of pedophilia the majority of pedophiles were believed to be suffering from mental retardation or senile dementia. According to Mohr et al. (1964), however, recent studies have demonstrated that their intelligence levels are comparable to those of the general population with a tendency toward the lower end of the scale. In educational level pedophiles generally conform to that of the population at large.

Personal, Social, and Family Characteristics

Studies exist that demonstrate pedophiles are present in all occupational groupings; nonetheless, there is a stereotyped popular myth that most pedophiles are youth counselors or elementary school teachers. No evidence exists to show that particular occupational choices are favorites among pedophiles, but there are data suggesting their general occupational orientations. Heterosexual pedophiles tend to be found in the trades and the semiskilled occupations; homosexual pedophiliacs are generally found among the business and service occupations (Vetter, 1972).

One factor which seems to emerge as common to both heterosexual and homosexual pedophiles is their relative isolation from adult social contacts. In the vast majority of cases, convicted pedophiles are characterized as loners or socially unskilled individuals who avoid social contacts (Vetter, 1972). The majority of social contacts of the hard core pedophiliac are with children in youth work or youth religious activities.

Little data exist on the family background of pedophiles. The existing data document no unusual pattern of birth order or sibling relationships with the exception of the relationship of the pedophile to his parents, an etiological consideration to be discussed below. The only consistent fact concerns the predominance of male offenders.

Child Sexuality Organizations

The actual incidence of child-adult sexual contacts is unknown, but the incidence may be higher than many authorities believe. The majority of society, including most pedophiles, feel that adult-child sexual contacts are shameful and should be forbidden: but a few small organizations exist dedicated to the promotion of childhood sexuality, specifically child-adult sexuality. These groups, much like the gay liberation groups for homosexuals, view their sexual practices as "healthy and normal." For example, the Rene Gunyon Society of Los Angeles works to bring about decriminalization of child-adult sexuality. The slogan of this group is "Sex by age eight, or else it's too late!" Similarly, the Better Life organization wishes to legislate and promote child-adult sexual contacts:

> Better Life is an educational service organization serving the interests of pedophiles and children's sexual rights worldwide. For the record, a pedophile is an adult who enters into emotional/physical relationships with children under the age of 15 or 16. (Wright, 1975, p. 71)

These organizations solicit memberships and donations to carry on their work nationwide. Most authorities believe, however, that the number of active members is relatively small.

THE PEDOPHILIC VICTIM

Kinsey et al. (1953) sampled a population of twelve-hundred women about prepubescent sexual activities. Twenty-eight percent reported a sexual experience with an adult before the age of 13, but in only 6 percent of the cases could the subject recall the event's being reported to the police. In less than 2 percent of the cases did the women report they were coerced in this childhood encounter, and less than 8 percent collaborated in the sexual activity. The remaining 90 percent were accidentally involved by someone exposing himself to them or unexpectedly fondling or patting their genitals (Gagnon, 1965).

A vast majority of the women sampled reported reacting negatively to the adult-child sexual experience. Most were simply frightened as they would be if they had seen a spider; a few had extreme negative reactions such as hysteria or vomiting; some reacted positively with sexual arousal up to and including orgasm. It is interesting to note that of the 333 women admitting sexual contacts with adults in their childhood, only 3 of them had severely damaged adult lives that they attributed to their early adult-child sexual experience (Gagnon, 1965).

According to the data gathered by Kinsey and his associates, it is estimated that between 20–25 percent of girls reared in a middle-class environment experience sexual interaction with an adult while they are still children. The vast majority of these sexual interactions, however, were limited to simple exhibitionism or genital touching.

Girls reared in a lower-class environment are exposed to a much higher risk of adult-child sexual acts, including offenses against them of a more intimate nature, such as intercourse and oral-genital contact. As might be expected, most of these contacts are never reported to the police, and even if they were, considering the structure of our legal system, it is not clear that any such report would be the best decision for the child. As is true also of rape victims, the interrogation by authorities and the adversary proceedings of the courtroom might be even more traumatic than the sexual offense itself. Gagnon (1965) claims that becoming involved in the legal system might indelibly imprint a traumatic event on the child's mind that she might otherwise quickly forget.

Age of Victim

According to Mohr et al. (1964), the majority of heterosexual pedophilia victims fall between the ages of 6 and 12, peaking between the ages of 8 and 11. Homosexual pedophilia victims increase in numbers into puberty, the result being a statistical overlap with adult homosexuality victims; but peak ages are between 12 and 15.

Relationship of the Victim to the Pedophile

Mohr et al. (1964) claim that, "Contrary to public opinion, . . . the victim of pedophilia is seldom a total stranger to the offender" (p. 28). More often, the victim is the pedophiliac's own child, stepchild, nephew, niece, friend, or neighbor's child. Sometimes the pattern follows that described by MacNamara (1968):

> The prepubescent, non-sexually agressive or adventuresome girl may awake biological urges by her uninhibited affection for a male relative, acquaintance, or neighbor who, if his social inhibitions are weak because of loneliness, depression, alcohol, or other emotional state, may respond sexually. (p. 153)

Because of the social or family relationships that often exist, pedophilic victims are frequently caught quite unaware and unprepared.

Uncle Frank is not someone considered by mother or father as the "beware of the stranger" type, and the child is usually unprepared for his advances. Homosexual pedophiles are more likely to engage in acts with strangers as their victims (Quinsey, 1977).

THE PEDOPHILIC ACT

In assessing the nature of the pedophilic act, we shall consider two things: the act itself, and the direction or intentionality of the act. Various kinds of deviant acts are open to the pedophile: heterosexual, homosexual, and what we shall call "miscellaneous" pedophilic behaviors.

Heterosexual Pedophilia

Sexual acts which engage a child of the opposite sex seem to be more frequent than those that involve a child of the same sex. The stereotype of the child molester is an old man who is approaching or has reached senility. Statistics, however, do not support the idea of this stereotype. One study of child molesters convicted for heterosexual offenses against girls under the age of 12 found the offenders averaged 35 years of age, with only one-sixth of them over age 50. Roughly one-third of them were married at the time of the sexual contact. Although about one-fourth of the men were drunk at the time of the offense, most of the acts were obviously planned in advance (Gebhard et al., 1965).

Among heterosexual pedophiles only a small minority engage in penetration and intravaginal coitus with their victims, and then mainly with the age group over 14 and with their permission (Vetter, 1972). Usually vaginal penetration is not the intention of the pedophile and is in many cases anatomically unfeasible.

The majority of sexual acts in heterosexual pedophilia consist of sex-play and include such behaviors as exposing, fondling, or being fondled.

> Always the same age group, six to eleven; no younger and no older, outside those limits it didn't appeal to me at all. Playing about with them with my hands under their skirts, tickling their bottoms, getting them to let me take their knickers (panties) down. . . . I'd sit them on my knee and play with them, and at the same time I was able to masturbate myself without using my hands. Five, ten minutes at the outside, then I got my ejaculation and that was it. (Parker, 1972, pp. 27–28)

According to Mohr et al. (1964), many heterosexual pedophiles are characterized by their inability or unwillingness to defer sexual gratification until a more suitable sexual partner can be found:

> The predominant intentionality of the pedophilic act is therefore one of immature gratification. The pedophilic act represents an arrested development in which the offender has never grown psychosexually beyond the immature pre-pubertal stage, or a regression or a return to this stage due to certain stresses in adult life, or a modification of the sexual drive in old age. (p. 19)

While some heterosexual pedophiles are admittedly amoral, the majority are moralistic, conservative, and extremely guilt-ridden as a result of their sexual activities with children (Marshall & McKnight, 1975). However, even the guilt-ridden tend to repeat their acts.

Homosexual Pedophilia

Homosexual pedophilic offenses are believed to occur less frequently than heterosexual offenses. One study of men convicted of sexual activities with boys under the age of 12 found that most of these men were fairly young (average age, 31 years) and that only 16 percent were married at the time (Mohr et al., 1964). Most of these men also indicated interest in sexual contacts with adolescent boys (age 13 to 15) and very young girls (age 6 to 10); however, some were interested in reaching orgasm with any warm-blooded animal and would use whatever was convenient (Gebhard et al., 1965). According to Mohr et al. (1964), homosexual pedophilic offenses account for approximately 30 to 45 percent of all sexual offenses against children. Homosexual pedophiles are less likely to have close relationships with their victims as compared to heterosexual pedophiles, and, if convicted, are far more likely to recidivate (Quinsey, 1977).

The most common form of homosexual pedophilic contact (in approximately 45 percent of cases) is masturbation—usually done to, rather than by, the boy. Fellatio occurs in 38 percent of cases, anal intercourse in only 4 percent (Gebhard et al., 1965). Parker (1972) describes one case:

> One Saturday afternoon there was two of them, two little boys, I said all right they could come out with me because they'd helped me push by boat down into the water from the shed. A very hot day it was. They went over the side for a swim. They'd no costumes on. . . .And I did, you know, I must admit I did go so far as to forget myself, I laid hands on them. Nothing seriour, please don't think that, I didn't attack them or anything of that kind. Only playing about, touching them, that as far as it went. They didn't object, they didn't complain . . . .
>
> That was why it was such a surprise to me that next week-end those two plain clothes policemen . . . asked me exactly what it was had happened . . .

and I told them . . . . The police took me to court straight away for it, and I was given six months. (p. 70)

According to a study by Rossman (1973) of self-identified homosexual pedophiles willing to be interviewed, many such individuals never come to the attention of the law because they tend to have impersonal sex with young male prostitutes when away from home and affectionate nonsexual relationships with boys at home. Most of those who have sexual contacts with boys who are not prostitutes are careful to secure the boy's affection first and become sexually active only as the affection grows and the boy agrees. Young male prostitutes often work for organizations that cater to the desires of homosexual pedophiles. An interesting case was reported in the *Chicago Tribune,* for May 16, 1977.

A nationwide homosexual ring with headquarters in Chicago has been trafficking in young boys, sending them across state lines and the nation to serve clients willing to pay hundreds of dollars for their services. Existence of the ring was uncovered by the *Chicago Tribune* investigation of child prostitution throughout the country.

The ring goes under the name Delta Project and according to police in Chicago, Los Angeles and Dallas, is masterminded by a 49-year-old convicted sodomite serving a four-year sentence in the Illinois state prison at Pontiac. His close associate is a 25-year-old convicted murderer and thief now on probation.

Unknown to jail officials the suspected mastermind used the jail's printing facilities to send out three "newsletters" about the project to homosexual clients throughout the country and to people who answered his advertisements in gay publications. The newsletters said the aim of the Delta Project was "to provide educational, travel and self development opportunities for qualified young men of character and integrity." To this end "Delta Dorms" were being established around the country. "Each is a private residence where one of our sustaining members acts as a *don* for two or four *cadets* . . . . The nature of the relationship is left entirely up to the two of them."

In a prison interview with the *Tribune [the suspected mastermind]* said the Delta Project was a program to provide self-development and training for young men: "This has nothing to do with sex. I didn't want to get your kids involved in sex." But police say the *dons* are pedophiles—adults with a sexual preference for children—and the *cadets* are boy prostitutes recruited in the Chicago area . . . . "It was quite a project and I would work all day, 16 hours, and I paid another inmate to do the typing and other work during the other eight hours of the day." [The leader] said he also plans to go into the business of selling pornographic TV cassettes when his prison term is up but denied that children would be involved.

The Delta Project was only the latest of a series of organizations he set up to supply boy prostitutes to male customers around the country, police said. Earlier, his operation had gone by such names as the Norman Foundation, Epic International and the Odyssey Foundation.

The *Tribune* investigation has also disclosed that a clandestine "boy love" newsletter, *Hermes,* is being published in Chicago. A bimonthly publication, it contains line drawings and photographs of naked boys, articles on "boy love" and advertisements listing coded names that enable subscribers to contact one another and to engage children for pornographic modeling and prostitution.

It is one of the three principal "boy love" newsletters in the United States. The others are *Better Life Monthly,* published in California, and the *Broad Street Journal,* published in Milliken, Colorado. According to police, *Hermes* sells more than 5,000 copies nationally every two months and, at $10 a copy, grosses more than $300,000 a year.

Miscellaneous Pedophilic Behaviors

Pedophilia refers only to children as sexual objects and does not indicate or delineate actual sexual behaviors. A variety of pedophilic oriented behaviors are possible with same-sex or opposite-sex children. Therefore, both homosexual and heterosexual pedophilia may include other deviant sexual behaviors such as exhibitionism, voyeurism, fetishism, incest, rape, sadism, and masochism.

In milder forms voyeurism and such fetish acts as spanking may be engaged in expressly for the purpose of an adult's sexual gratification and thereby be considered deviant; this behavior is seldom brought to the attention of clinical psychologists or psychiatrists, and seldom legally prosecuted. In more serious forms, sadism, masochism, and rape may be directed toward children. On occasion, newspapers report the occurrence of a brutal physical and sexual assault of a child. Finally, some cases of pedophilia are incestuous and include actual sexual union between members of the same family, most often between father and daughter. The actual incidence of incest is unknown, although Kinsey et al. (1948) reported an incidence of about .05 percent. Incest is prohibited in most all cultures, presumably because of the dangers of genetic inbreeding. A sexual relationship between family members usually represents profound psychopathology; it often results in disturbed sexual functioning in adults who were the victims as children.

RESEARCH AND THEORY: PHYSIOLOGICAL FACTORS

Some researchers suggest that pedophilic behavior may result from weakened inhibitory controls as a function of brain damage and other neuroencephalopathy (Dix, 1975). There are data indicating that pedophilia and exhibitionism are the most common sexual offenses committed by senile and arteriosclerotic individuals (Quinsey & Bergersen, 1976). There are also data indicating that close to 30 percent of pedophilic offenses occur when the adult is under the influence of alcohol; among repeated pedophilic offenders, alcohol abuse is common (Vetter, 1972).

RESEARCH AND THEORY: PSYCHOLOGICAL FACTORS

A number of investigators have pointed to the high incidence of severe psychopathology, in addition to psychopathic personality, among pedophiles. In a study of 25 offenders, Swanson (1968) found a high incidence of sociopathic personalities, mental retardates, neurotics, schizoid personalities, and borderline schizophrenics. In over 50 percent of these cases, the pedophile was experiencing conflict over the loss of his usual source of sexual gratification.

Psychoanalytic Formulations

Psychoanalytic theory relates the causes for pedophilia to the weaning process; phallic and castration anxieties, psychic impotence, and incestuous wishes, all basic to an unresolved oedipus complex which makes the choice of an immature sexual object understandable (Fenichel, 1945). It is, according to Freud (1905):

> only exceptionally that children are . . . exclusive sex objects. . . . They usually come to play that part when someone who is cowardly or has become impotent adopts them as a substitute, or when an urgent instinct (one which will not allow of postponement) cannot at the moment get possession of any more appropriate object. (p. 148)

In the House-Tree-Person test administered by Hammer (1954) to 33 pedophiles in Sing Sing Prison, the woman drawing was significantly older than the man. She appeared as a sexualized maternal figure.

> We may, then, postulate that as a child the pedophile originally desired, psychosexually speaking, the mother-figure because she was the nearest and most significant female. Having failed to resolve his original entanglement in oedipal feelings, he now tends to view the mature female as an object arousing his forbidden oedipal attitudes . . . reflecting the strikingly immature confusion of sexual and maternal figures. The pedophile is plagued by forbidden sexual desires toward the mother-figure. His frightening desires cause [him] to renounce adult females as available sex objects and to throw himself into a regressive flight into immaturity. He falls back, or has remained fixated, upon intermediate goals in regard to both sexual object and sexual activities, the latter usually involving seeing, touching, and manipulating of a child's genitals. (pp. 352–353)

The formula Cassity (1927) arrived at, the weaning trauma, with its various hazards, is hypothesized to play a dominant role in later pedophilic formation. Among the hazards are resulting psychic emasculation, the subsequent narcissistic effort to compensate for the imagined impotency, and the eventual occurrence of the precipitating factor of the neurosis itself. All these hazards are felt to contribute extensively to the final use of the unique expedient of pedophilia in order that the neurotic may cope more satisfactorily with the rapidly accumulating psychic entanglements. Thus the early loss of the breasts provokes strong retaliative tendencies that are alleviated by forcing the love object to gratify oral cravings, and at the same time dominating and controlling it, as well as avoiding castration anxiety by choosing a love object like oneself. Selecting a little girl as an object "represents a narcissistic object choice, that is treating these girls as they would have like to be treated by their mothers" (Fenichel, 1945, p. 333). Thus, while the mature woman represents a maternal and therefore tabooed incestuous figure, the child represents the patient as he would prefer to be himself, that is, a small child (Hirning, 1947). This is a recurrent theme in the psychoanalytic literature on pedophilia. Traditional psychological tests supposedly indicate oral deprivation and need for maternal warmth among pedophiliacs, according to Kurland (1960), who adds,

> Another common finding in keeping with the emphasis on oral needs was the preoccupation of each man with oral-genital perversion and its prominence in their fantasy life. This further substantiates . . . the polymorphous perverse nature of these patients' pathology and their deeply rooted and fixated immaturity. (p. 402)

In their study of the psychosexual development of Norman, a child molester, Bell, and Hall (1971), working independently, made a content analysis of his 1,368 dreams recorded over a three-year period. The study includes Norman's account of himself during an extended intake, plus 20 interviews held over a seven-month period, and a battery of projective and intelligence tests. Data from institutions where the patient had been confined periodically over 15 years were also obtained, along with subsequent letters mailed to the therapist. Thus five different kinds of information were utilized: dreams, interviews, tests, institutional reports, and personal correspondence. The dream material was given the role of principal datum.

> The most outstanding feature of [the patient's] personality is his extraordinary emotional immaturity. On every level of his existence, he remains a child. His infantile status if reflected in a polymorphously perverse disposition which fails to distinguish between one sexual object and another or one sexual act and another. . . . Most of his sexual feelings are not acted out. In fact he is less sexually active than most males his age. . . . Another reflection of Norman's childlike personality is his unusual dependence upon his mother

and sister for emotional security. This dependency is of long standing. During his childhood . . . Norman had few friendships. Then, as now, Norman invested little of himself in others with whom he remained only superficially friendly. Another reason that Norman remains a "loner" is that his associations with other children were very painful. In fact, it is reasonable to suppose that Norman's sexual activities with children represent, in part, the efforts to make up for his original experience of loneliness in childhood. (pp. 83–84)

The analytic portrait that evolves of the pedophile is, in summary, an essentially immature, shy person who is orally deprived and in need of maternal warmth not provided by the phallic mother. The pedophiliac suffers from castration anxiety and an unresolved Oedipus complex, and uses pedophilia as a defensive measure against introjected and projected anxieties of early childhood in an attempt to avoid anxiety, guilt, and pain (Socarides, 1959). A hallmark of the pedophile is his immature character, with strong feelings of sexual inadequacy and impotence (Karpman, 1959), who lacks the courage to attempt sexual contact with adult women (Guttmacher, 1951). Such a man usually avoids close relationships with people his own age, does not feel group up, and is unable to carve out any satisfying or self-sustaining role in the adult community.

Behavioral Formulations

The major question in the behavioral formulation of pedophilia is why some individuals become sexually aroused to children. Behavior therapists have not attempted to advance an etiological theory of pedophilia. As noted by many (Goldfried & Linehan, 1977), behavioral etiological theories and behavioral assessment techniques have yet to achieve the same level of sophistication that is associated with many behavior therapy treatment procedures. Nevertheless, several variables are thought to be important contributing factors in the development and maintenance of pedophilia.

The conditioning of children as sexual stimuli probably follows the same laws of learning as for other sexual deviations. However, important precipitating factors may facilitate the likelihood of sexual arousal to children. For example, inadequate heterosocial skills are frequently detected in the pedophile (Marshall & McKnight, 1975). Pedophiles we have seen in our clinical practice are often sexually neutral; they may even be phobic to adult peers or averse to secondary sex characteristics, such as breasts and/or pubic hair. Many of these individuals report being rejected by their peers as children and have a history of social isolation and infrequent peer contact. As a result, they sought affiliation with younger companions where the chances of rejection were decreased. These contacts frequently resulted in sexual experimentation and subsequent sexual arousal and masturbation. In fact, many pedophiles report that their preference for youthful companions began when they were children themselves and only later resulted in a sexual preference for youthful sexual objects. As adults, it may be that these individuals never developed adequate heterosocial skills and appropriate sexual arousal as a result of their long history of pedophilic preference and consequent avoidance of adult companions.

CASE HISTORY 10-1

The patient was a 30-year-old married male who reported that his presenting problem was, "I am bisexual and I don't want to be." According to the patient, for two years he had been intimidating young boys into engaging into homosexual acts with him. He described the typical intimidation sequence, which he referred to as *bluffing,* as follows: He drove his car through residential areas and around playgrounds. If he found a young boy alone, he invited him to take a ride. He would then drive to a secluded wooded area and begin to manipulate the boy's genitals. He would "bluff" the youth, threatening physical violence if the boy did not capitulate and agree to engage in mutual fellatio. Grasping the boy by the arm, he would lead the youngster into the woods where he would remove the boy's pants and fellate him. The boy was usually too intimidated to resist. The patient would next remove his own pants and force the boy to fellate him.

The patient reported forcing young boys into submitting to anal intercourse 15-16 times during the year prior to contacting us. He found this more sexually arousing than mutual fellatio, and acknowledged that it required a more intense threat of violence than mutual fellatio. He further acknowledged that the added fear and pain experienced by the boys during anal intercourse, as well as their increased resistance, were arousing for him.

The patient reported maximum attraction to boys 7–10 years of age who have youthful, innocent, childlike appearances. Additional stimulus characteristics included a trim body with minimal masculature and tight pants with a protruding penis. The patient stated that a homosexual encounter with a peer or older adult male would be repulsive.

The patient reported engaging in homosexual behavior since the age of nine, when he and his younger brother began engaging in mutual masturbation. Soon afterward he began engaging in group masturbation with neighborhood boys of his own age. The patient experienced his first orgasm shortly after puberty when he was fellated by a boy six years his junior; he recalled this as a sexually arousing and enjoyable experience. Since that time the patient had engaged in a series of pedophilic homosexual experiences including anal intercourse and mutual fellatio. He reported he had recently threatened children to make them submit to sexual activities and he feared that he might physically harm a child if he refused anal intercourse.

The patient's heterosexual experience was minimal: a total of two dates in high school with the same girl. He reported no sexual advances were made with the girl because he feared her and felt extremely uncomfortable. In college he dated several women but again made no sexual advances, and described himself as being very nervous around women.

The patient's first attempt at heterosexual intercourse was with his fiancee approximately two months prior to marriage. This occurrence was distressing to the patient as he failed to maintain an erection. His second attempt was successful; he attributes his success partly to his wife's reassurance and support, and, partly to a fantasy of homosexual activities with children he concentrated on during heterosexual intercourse.

According to the patient, he masturbated almost daily until marriage. He typically masturbated to fantasies of his most recent pedophilic homosexual encounter, although occasionally he masturbated to a particularly arousing past pedophilic encounter. He reported not having masturbated since his marriage.

As previously noted, pedophilic behavior, like the majority of deviant sexual behaviors, is almost exclusively associated with males. However, this is not always the case, as the following case history illustrates.

CASE HISTORY 10-2

The patient was a 45-year-old divorced female referred by the court system for psychological evaluation. She had a history of arrests for alcohol and drug abuse violations and had recently been convicted on two counts of contributing to the delinquency of a minor. The most recent charges stemmed from her sexual involvement with two young males. The patient readily admitted this involvement.

The patient claimed her first coital experience occurred at the age of 10 with an older neighborhood youth, and reported being sexually active with a variety of men since that time. She married at the age of 15 to a man 30 years her senior. She described the 12-year marriage as brutal, claiming she was frequently beaten by her alcoholic husband. She reported the sexual relationship with her husband was also unsatisfactory and admitted engaging in a two-year affair during the latter part of her marriage with a teenaged youth who lived in the apartment complex.

Upon the patient's divorce she took a job as a waitress in a small diner known to be a hang out for teenagers dealing in illegal drugs. Although her abusive drinking pattern was already established, she was introduced to drugs by several youths who frequented the diner. She soon began spending considerable time with the youths, many of whom were 12 to 15 years her junior, and her apartment became a hang out for the group. She reported her involvement with the youths began because "they treated me so nice, with respect, like they really liked me." She admitted becoming addicted to heroin during this time.

The patient also reported becoming sexually involved with the group. As the only female member she would frequently engage in sexual activities with five or six males in a single night. The ages of the youths ranged from 12 to 18 years although a group member would occasionally bring boys to her for sexual favors who would be as young as 8 or 9. She admitted enjoying sexual activities with the youthful group because "unlike older guys, including my husband, they seemed to appreciate me so much and were always concerned that I climaxed too." Her involvement with the group lasted over three years, during which time she became increasingly addicted to a variety of drugs, including alcohol.

She had lived in many cities, each move being the result of a decision to change locations and start over; however, her pattern of sexual involvement with children remained unchanged. To meet the expense of her drug habit, she resorted to prostitution and was once paid to fellate a 5-year-old boy while being observed by an older client. She actively encouraged high-school boys to view her as a "mistress without pay"; a group of them would visit her several nights each week for sex.

Approximately five years before referral the patient was arrested and hospitalized for drug addiction. She became completely free of drugs and later got a job in a local factory. However, she admitted that her preference for youthful sexual partners remained unchanged. Her recent arrest, which prompted her referral, came after two brothers informed their parents of the patient's seducing them to her apartment with promises of soft drinks and then engaging them in sexual activities. The boys' ages were 8 and 13.

MODIFICATION OF PEDOPHILIC BEHAVIOR

In most states pedophilia is punishable by confinement in prison or a mental hospital. For some offenders imprisonment appears to be the only course to take; although it may do little to modify the offender's behavior, it does protect society. However, since many pedophiles experience genuine remorse and want to change their maladaptive behavior, an increasing number are being screened for treatment and given indeterminate sentences in state mental hospitals or other facilities for sexual offenders. Unfortunately, such facilities usually offer only traditional therapies.

Electroconvulsive Therapy

The pedophile is considered by some to be schizophrenic if for no other reason than that he/she engages in adult-child sexual behavior. Since pedophilia is considered severe psychopathology, it is not surprising that electroconvulsive therapy (ECT) is frequently offered as a treatment modality, particularly in institutional settings where the patient's personal freedoms are somewhat limited. (Radzinowicz, 1957).

The administration of ECT usually follows a regimented procedure (Batchelor, 1969). Half to one hour before treatment the patient is given a subcutaneous injection of atropine sulfate to prevent salivation and vomiting. At this time the very anxious patient may also be given a small dose of amylobarbitone sodium. Immediately before treatment the patient is instructed to empty his bladder and bowels. His clothes are then loosened at the neck and waist, and dentures, hairclips, and jewelry are removed.

Shortly before treatment the patient is usually given a muscle relaxant which modifies the force of the electrically-induced convulsion and helps decrease the risk of fractures and dislocations. Since the onset of paralysis is often frightening to the conscious patient, a light anesthesia (Intraval Sodium) is given. Before switching on the electrical current a few breaths of oxygen are administered to the patient through a mask.

To conduct the electrical current electrodes, covered by pads with saline or sodium bicarbonate, are placed firmly on the temples. A mouth gag is inserted and the current is administered. A typical setting of a McPhail-Strauss machine might be 120 volts for 0.3 seconds. The object is to produce a major convulsion.

Oxygenation is continued by mask after the seizure until the patient's breathing has restarted, which usually takes three to five minutes. Occasionally, apnea (cessation of breathing) may occur to such an extent as to require oxygenation with a pressure bag for as long as 20 to 30 minutes. On rare occasions an intratracheal tube must be implanted.

After treatment the patient is returned to bed. He may regain consciousness quickly, be restless, and emotional, and complain of a severe headache, or he may sleep for several hours or longer. Presently little supportive data exist for the efficacy of ECT in the treatment of pedophilia.

Chemotherapy

While most clinicians recognize that no pharmacological agent can by itself alter preferences in sexual arousal, many utilize estrogens to reduce the strength of the sexual drive. Estradiol (0.02–0.05 mg, daily) is frequently prescribed (Renshaw, 1978). Common side effects of estrogen therapy include nausea and gynecomastia (enlargement of the breasts in males). More recently, antiandrogen compounds have been systhesized which are nonfeminizing. Agents such as cyproterone and provera are claimed to reduce sexual desire (Walen et al., 1977).

Group Therapy

Group therapy is a form of treatment in which selected patients form a group, guided by a therapist, to help each other effect personality change. By using technical maneuvers and theoretical constructs, the leader manipulates the group members' interactions to bring about this change.

The dynamics of group therapy are relatively simple. Although techniques and orientations vary, the object of many group therapies is the undoing of a faulty sociodynamic pattern of human maturation (Walen et al.,

1977). That is, the development of the infant from helplessness and dependency to tempered autonomy and acculturation is believed to take place through a continuing series of transactions within the family and a series of extrafamilial social relations. If maladjustments, such as pedophilia, develop as a result of inadequate group situations during the formative periods of life, it should be possible to undo and modify them by exposing the maladaptations to continuous, structured group action in a more adequate environment (Kolb, 1968).

A group therapy program for pedophiles confined to a security hospital has been described by Costell and Yalom (1972). The goal of this group therapy was impulse modification or impulse control, since sufficient evidence exists to indicate that the goal of sexual reorientation to adult women was unrealistic for confined pedophiles. Heterosexual and homosexual child molesters were treated similarly and in the same group. During therapy sessions the pedophiles shared their strategies for dealing with deviant impulses of both a sexual and nonsexual nature. In addition they discussed their fears of masculine competition and were encouraged to try out new behaviors. The investigators reported encouraging the offenders to modify their masturbatory fantasies and to reduce their homosexual behavior. No results of the treatment program were given.

Group therapy remains the most widely employed treatment for pedophilia, although its efficacy is still unproven, perhaps the majority of pedophiles in therapy are those in prisons where lack of professional personnel usually means that if treatment is offered at all, it is offered on a group basis. Nevertheless, despite Hartman's (1965) claim that "group psychotherapy may be regarded as the treatment of choice for certain types of personality disorders, pedophilia being one of them," the group therapy approaches described in the literature appear to be based on contradictory premises (Quinsey, 1977). Furthermore, few data have been reported to indicate that changes in behavior occur as a result of group therapy, and no studies have been conducted that compare group therapy to other types of treatment.

Behavior Therapy

Behavioral literature consistently utilizes three principal approaches to pedophilic behavior. The first approach is based on the hypothesis that many pedophiles are phobic to adults and find appropriate sexual stimuli aversive. This means neutralizing the anxiety-provoking valence of adults through desensitization so that the pedophile's approach behavior to appropriate sexual stimuli can be increased. The second approach is based on the hypothesis that most pedophiles demonstrate deficits in heterosocial skills. This approach thus involves individually tailored programs in social skills training. The final approach involves eliminating the pattern of sexual arousal to children, through the use of aversion therapy.

Quinsey, Bergersen, and Steinman (1976) reported classical conditioning type aversion therapy with 10 institutionalized homosexual and heterosexual pedophiles. Each subject was seen a total of 24 sessions in which physiological measures were recorded: one preliminary assessment session, 20 aversion therapy sessions, and 3 assessment sessions. The preliminary assessment session in which changes in penile circumference and skin conductance were monitored while subjects viewed a series of slides of nudes ranging from young prepubescents through teenage children was conducted in order to measure each subject's pattern of physiological responding. Data from this session dictated the age group and gender classification of sexual stimuli to be used in the aversion sessions. In addition to the photographic slides of children, slides of adults were chosen on the basis of the sex to which each subject reported he would like to respond.

The three assessment sessions were identical; the first was performed before aversion therapy began, the second after 10 treatment sessions, and the third, posttreatment. Each assessment session consisted of the presentation of 20 slides: 10 slides of nude children, 5 of either adult males or females, depending on the subject's preference, and 5 neutral slides. These slides were presented in a fixed random sequence with each slide presented for 30 seconds with an interslide interval of 60 seconds unless the subject experienced an erection in which case the presentation of slides was halted until the erection declined to baseline levels.

Each aversion session incorporated the presentation of 10 adult (male or female) slides and 10 slides of children. Electrical shock was administered to the inside of each subject's upper left arm during the presentation of 80 percent of the slides of children. Shock was not paired with the slides of adults. The results of this investigation indicated decreased sexual arousal to children as well as a slight increase in arousal to adults. Since the subjects employed in this investigation were institutionalized, measures of behavior change could not be obtained. No followup data were reported.

Forgione (1976) has provided an interesting variation of aversive therapy for pedophilic behavior. Two males with court histories of nonviolent heterosexual child molesting were initially assessed by photographing each patient's enactment of his molesting behavior with life-sized mannequins. The assessment procedure revealed large discrepancies between each subject's verbal report of pedophilic behavior and the photographed enactment of the actual behavior with the mannequin (Table 10-2). The use of photographed behavior with mannequins, rather than reliance on verbal report, provided an objective measure of deviant sexual behaviors and fantasies. The photographic slides were then employed in electrical aversion therapy. Assertiveness training and family counseling were also instituted.

TABLE 10-2

Child-Molesting Behavior

Reported at Interview	Acted with Mannequins
Case I	
Coaxes child into confined space	Coaxes child into confined space
Kneels before standing child	Kneels before standing child
Strokes child's hair	Approaches with hands on child's shoulders, back, buttocks (ritualized)
Strokes child's genital area through panties	Pulls down panties of clothed child
Bribes child to remove all clothing except panties	Removes all child's clothing
	Places child in supine position
	Licks labial and vaginal areas
	Probes vagina with tongue
	Kneels astride supine child, exposes penis
	Attempts intromission, fails
	Masturbates, ejaculates on genital area
	Probes vagina manually
	Probes anus manually
	Fondles nipples
Case II	
Coaxes children to "play doctor"	Places children astride broom handles or sticks
Coaxes children to assume sexual sexual positions	Strokes children's genital areas with instruments
Coaxes children to rub his penis through trousers	Grabs girl from behind
Places children astride his lap to "play horses"	Rubs penis between girl's buttocks
	Exposes penis
Coaxes children to look at his penis	Coaxes children to look at his penis
	Coaxes boys and girls to hold his penis, masturbate him
	Places children in sexual positions
	Coaxes children to rotate genital areas
	Places girl in supine position
	Coaxes boy to watch him kneel astride clothed and unclothed girls
	Rubs penis on vulva
	Masturbates, ejaculates on girl's abdomen
	Masturbates boys and girls, single and simultaneously

Source: Forgione, A. G. The use of mannequins in the behavioral assessment of child molesters: Two case reports. *Behavior Therapy*, 1976, *7*, 678-685. Reprinted with permission of Academic Press.

Follow-up studies of one, two, and three years revealed no recurrence of pedophilic behavior.

Covert sensitization has also been successfully employed in the treatment of pedophilic behavior. Levin, Barry, Gambaro, Wolfinsohn & Smith (1977) reported the use of covert sensitization and two variations of the standard covert sensitization procedure in the treatment of a patient with a 19-year history of pedophilic behavior. The covert sensitization period was divided into four successive phases with each phase lasting four weeks. The initial treatment phase, standard covert sensitization, involved physically aversive imagery, mainly of nausea and vomiting, with sexual arousal to young girls. During the second phase the physically aversive imagery was accompanied by exposure to valeric acid. The vial was uncorked just prior to the patient's imagining, and the aversive odor was covered immediately preceding cessation of the noxious imagery. The third phase of treatment involved psychologically aversive imagery. During this phase the patient imagined past aversive events that had been consequences of his pedophilic behavior. For example, he reported experiencing significant shame and guilt as a result of his wife's once discovering him in a closet with a young girl who was related to him. The final phase of treatment involved covert sensitization with mixed imagery.

During the first three phases of treatment the specific girls imagined were limited to two young children known to the patient. During the fourth treatment phase, however, aversive imagery was shifted to two other young girls not previously used in the treatment process. Sexual arousal to one of the new girls was followed by physically aversive imagery with valeric acid, while arousal to the second new child was associated with psychologically aversive imagery. Pictures and slides of adult nude women were presented immediately following cessation of each covert sensitization trial. Subjective reports and penile erection measures served as the dependent measures and were recorded during each session.

The results of this study indicated a significant decrease in sexual arousal to young girls with most of the decrease occurring during covert sensitization using psychological imagery and chemically supplemented physical imagery (Figure 10-1). Sexual arousal to women increased. A 10-month followup assessment indicated that the improvements were stable over time.

Beech, Watts, and Poole (1971) reported the classical conditioning (without aversion therapy) treatment of a 21-year-old male heterosexual pedophile. A series of photographs of nude females, ranging from the immature (totally without secondary sexual characteristics) to the fully mature (well-developed adults) was presented to the patient in random order for 10 seconds each. He was instructed to fantasize sexually to each photograph while the latency and amplitude of his penile response to each stimulus was recorded. The patient also was asked to rate each photograph on a 5-point scale extending from "very attractive" to "repugnant." The investigators claimed that the two measures were well correlated, and confirmed that the most immature females proved to be most sexually arousing and that no

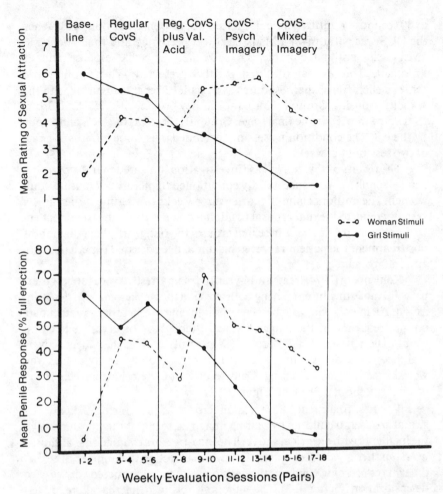

Figure 10-1. Ratings and penile responses to girl and woman stimuli. (CovS = covert sensitization; Val. acid = valeric acid; Psych = psychological.) **(Source:** Levin, S. M., Barry, S. M., Gambaro, S., Wolfinsohn, L., & Smith, A. Variations of covert sensitization in the treatment of pedophilic behavior: A case study. *Journal of Consulting and Clinical Psychology*, 1977, *45,* 896–907. Copyright 1977 by the American Psychological Association. Reprinted by permission.)

penile response was elicited to the pictures of the more mature females. Four groups of pictures were then assembled, ranging from very young prepubertal girls (Group I) which served as the initial unconditioned stimuli (UCS) to the fully mature adult women photographed in provocative positions (Group IV).

At the beginning of treatment, Group I stimuli were used as the UCS and Group II the conditioned stimuli (CS). A CS was presented for 5 seconds, then removed and replaced by a UCS which was presented for a maximum of 30 seconds or until a penile circumference response was obtained. When the UCS was withdrawn a blank card was presented and the patient was given mental arithmatic problems to solve until the penile response returned to baseline. The next pair of stimuli was then presented. When Group II had come to elicit full sexual responses as a result of repeated pairing with the sexually arousing Group I photographs, they became the UCS and Group III became the CS. In the final stage, Group III served as the UCS and Group IV the CS. The conditioning sessions extended over three months at a rate of two sessions per week.

The results of this single-case investigation indicated that the patient's penile responses were successfully conditioned to pictures of mature adult women. The authors claim that after three weeks of treatment the subject verbally reported sexual arousal to adult women outside the treatment environment, and a decrease in sexual arousal to young girls. Several months posttreatment the patient reported his initial heterosexual experience with an adult woman.

Kohlenberg (1974) treated a 34-year-old male arrested twice for homosexual child molesting by employing both aversion therapy and *in-vivo* desensitization. An initial four-week baseline was implemented in order to gather data on the frequency of the patient's sexual "thoughts" or urges centered on young males; the number of "prowling" incidents in which the patient actively searched for sexual victims; and the number of contacts with adults who were deemed sexually arousing. Daily records of these behaviors were monitored throughout treatment (Figure 10-2).

The first treatment phase was directed toward reducing the patient's sexual arousal to children by pairing imagined sexual thoughts and prowling incidents with electrical shock. The investigators claimed that although aversion therapy did not appear to have an effect on the number of sexual thoughts concerning children, the decision was made to proceed with *in-vivo* desensitization (Figure 10-2). The authors also claimed that the failure of aversion therapy may have been the result of an insufficient number of pairings between the shock and imagined sexual stimuli, as well as inadequate shock intensity. It is also possible that the failure may have also been the result of using only imagined stimuli rather than combining imagined stimuli with films, pictures, or slides of sexually arousing scenes.

In-vivo desensitization followed the sensate focus format outlined above in Chapter 3. Since the patient desired to maintain his homosexual orientation, a willing adult male served as the sexual partner in these exercises.

The results of this investigation indicated that the patient became sexually aroused to adult males and that pedophilic thoughts and incidents of prowling decrease during treatment. Followup data demonstrated a maintenance of treatment effects (Figure 10-2).

The obvious deficits in the social behavior of many child molesters have prompted a number of therapists to try and teach pedophiles appropriate ways of interacting with potential adult sexual partners. Some programs reported in

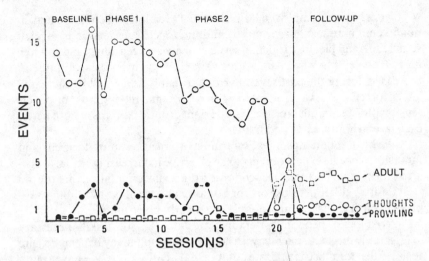

Figure 10-2. The number of "thoughts" and "prowling" incidents concerning children and "adult contacts" for the three treatment phases and follow-up. The follow-up data are means for each of the six months following treatment. (**Source:** Kohlenberg, R. J. Treatment of a homosexual pedophiliac using in vivo desensitization: A case study. *Journal of Abnormal Psychology,* 1974, *2,* 192–195. Copyright 1974 by the American Psychological Association. Reprinted with permission.)

the literature (Marshall & McKnight, 1957) include a social-skill-training component, but do not present information concerning its effectiveness in isolation from other treatment components.

Laws and Serber (1975) discussed the targeting of various aspects of heterosexual social behavior using observations on a pedophilic individual. From these observations they concluded that independent observers could reliably code such variables as the patient's dysfluencies and "closed" body posture from videotaped recordings of his interactions with a female therapist, but that measures of inappropriate speech content would also need to be devised for use in evaluating a social skills program. Serber and Keith (1974) described an innovative social skills training program for homosexual pedophiles in which members of the gay community were used as models of appropriate homosexual social behavior. Videotape feedback was employed in conjunction with behavioral rehearsal of common social situations. Although this approach appears promising, no evaluative data have as yet been published.

Conclusions

The effective modification of pedophilic behavior involves eliminating the pattern of sexual arousal to children, increasing sexual arousal to adults, instructing appropriate heterosocial skills, and, on occasion, desensitizing the patient to adult heterosocial—heterosexual contacts. In our practice we have effectively employed both electrical aversion and covert sensitization to eliminate sexual arousal to children. Electrical aversion to explicit sexual films and pictures depicting sexual activity between adults and children may be difficult however, since the availability of such sexual stimuli has decreased during the past several years, probably as a result of increased law enforcement. As a result we have recently begun relying more on covert sensitization techniques to eliminate deviant arousal patterns in both heterosexual and homosexual pedophiles.

We have found masturbation training to pictures of nude adults and fantasies of adult sexual contacts to be effective in increasing sexual arousal to older sexual partners. Depending on the sexual orientation that the patient desires, either heterosexual or homosexual, we make available a supply of explicit sexual stimuli to assist in masturbation training.

A number of pedophiles demonstrate deficits in social skills necessary to effectively meet and interact with adults. As a result many patients require social skills training to facilitate adult sexual involvement. We have found modeling and response practice with a variety of adult partners to be effective teaching techniques. Laws and Serber (1975) recommend that members of the gay community be recruited for modeling with patients desiring an adult homosexual orientation.

Finally, the development of sexual skills and an adult-oriented pattern of sexual arousal are greatly facilitated by the assistance and cooperation of an adult sexual partner.

CASE HISTORY 10-3

The patient was a 30-year-old married male with a history of homosexual pedophilic behavior. A sexual history and assessment indicated that physical abuse and violence were playing an increasingly important role in the patient's sexual fantasies and behavior. Because of this potential danger, rapid and effective intervention was required. As a result, aversion therapy to inhibit sexual arousal to pedophilic homosexual stimuli was proposed. In addition, programmed masturbation training to enhance arousal to appropriate heterosexual stimuli and heterosocial skills training were consecutively prescribed.

Several difficulties arose during the course of treatment. First, it was difficult to find a regimen of electrical shock that was effectively aversive for the patient. His ability to anticipate and prepare himself for the administration of electrical shock contingent on sexual arousal to literature picturing and describing homosexual pedophilic behavior mitigated the pain from the shock. Therefore, it was necessary to modify the aversion regimen so that electrical shock was administered independent of penile erection.

A second problem involved the patient's failure to regularly complete the masturbation training exercises. Several weeks into treatment the patient admitted incorporating a fantasy of sexual activity with a young girl into his masturbatory practices. Although the potential for conditioning sexual arousal to young girls (ags 8–12 years) was carefully explained to the patient, we later discovered that he had continued incorporating these fantasies on subsequent occasions of masturbation and intercourse with his wife.

A third difficulty involved the patient's motivation for behavior changes which was somewhat questionable by his own admission. He frequently did not report for scheduled appointments and was chronically late for treatment sessions. After 12 sessions of electrical aversion therapy combined with masturbation training, the patient informed us of his decision to terminate therapy. He reported control over his pedophilic arousal and maintained that there had been no occurrences of pedophilic behavior since he began treatment. A physiological assessment, however, indicated that while the patient's arousal to heterosexual stimuli had increased somewhat during treatment, sexual arousal to pedophilic stimuli had remained unchanged. Although these data were presented and carefully explained to the patient, he maintained he had no further need or desire to continue treatment. At this point we had no choice other than to re-emphasize the legal and social consequences of pedophilic behavior, and to tell him we would be available should he desire to resume treatment later on. He is now serving a 15-year prison sentence for child molesting.

Patient motivation is a critical factor for effective behavior change. Unfortunately, in the treatment of sexual deviations many times the patient's sexual behavior, while distressing, is also powerfully reinforcing via sexual arousal and orgasm. As a result sexual deviates are occasionally not as therapeutically motivated as patients suffering from other types of problems such as anxiety or depression in which such reinforcement is absent. In addition to explaining to the patient during the initial interview that his/her cooperation and motivation is imperative throughout treatment, the clinician should also watch for subtle signs of patient noncooperation and attempt to modify this behavior at the outset. The following case history illustrates the treatment of a more highly motivated pedophile.

CASE HISTORY 10-4

The patient was a 37-year-old single male elementary school teacher referred for treatment of homosexual pedophilia. Approximately 10 years prior to treatment he had been arrested twice for exposing himself to groups of male children. At the time of the initial interview the patient denied any urge to exhibit himself and reported no incidents of exhibitionism in the last six years. However, he readily admitted strong sexual arousal to children and reported a desire to engage in mutual masturbation and oral-genital contact with young males, particularly those between the ages of 8 and 12. The patient reported no sexual experiences with females or adult males, and described female breasts as particularly revolting. Socially he described himself as a "loner" and an "isolate." He reported few social contacts and maintained he would "rather not have to interact with men and women, but rather spend his time with children and his hobby of bicycling." During the initial interview he exhibited exaggerated effeminate motor behaviors and spoke in a high-pitched voice.

The patient reported that as a child he led a sheltered life before beginning school, and because of his mother's restrictions he did not play with other children in the neighborhood. His only playmate was his older sister. He started school at age six and reported that he wasn't happy because the other kids "picked" on him. He guessed the reason for this was that "the other kids always wanted to play the same old games" and his ideas were more "creative" than theirs. He reported first noticing his attraction to other boys when he was approximately 12 years old.

During high school the patient played in the band but remained socially isolated from other students and never dated. After high school he attended college and graduate school and again never dated.

In order to obtain objective measures of the patient's pattern of sexual arousal, a sexual assessment was conducted which involved the patient's ranking a series of photographic slides in a hierarchy of attractiveness. The slides depicted nude and clothed adult males and females as well as nude and clothed male and female children. In addition, literature describing explicit homosexual and heterosexual pedophilic behavior and homosexual and heterosexual pedophilic exhibitionism were ranked in a hierarchy of elicited sexual arousal. The erotic slides and literature were randomly presented to the patient who verbally estimated his level of sexual arousal to each sexual stimulus while penile erections were continuously monitored via a strain gauge. Results of the sexual assessment verified the patient's reported exclusive sexual arousal to young male children and lack of arousal to female children, adult males, and adult females. In addition, only minimal arousal was measured in response to explicit descriptions of pedophilic exhibitionism.

Assessment was also made of heterosocial skills and appropriate gender behaviors. Heterosocial skills were assessed by having the patient role-play situations involving approaching a female and asking for a date both in person and on the telephone, telephoning a female to confirm a date, picking up a date at her residence and engaging in casual conversation, and taking a female home after a date. Each situation was videotaped and rated by independent observers. In addition, the Barlow et al. (1977) behavioral checklist was used to assess voice, form of conversation, and affect. Gender role behaviors were assessed using the Barlow et al. (1973) masculine-feminine rating scale which measured the gender appropriateness of sitting, standing, and walking (see Chapter 2). Assessment of heterosocial skills and appropriate gender behaviors indicated severely deficient social skills and exaggerated effeminate motor behaviors.

A treatment plan involving electrical aversion therapy, systematic desensitization to female genitalia and breasts, masturbation training, heterosocial skills training, vocal retraining, and grooming skills was formulated and presented to the patient. Given the potential consequences of continued homosexual pedophilic behavior, we suggested he begin aversion therapy immediately, and the patient agreed. We carefully explained that his pattern of sexual arousal could be reoriented to adult males *or* adult females, depending on his preference. He adamantly maintained that we should target our efforts toward establishing a heterosexual arousal pattern since he considered the thought of sex with an adult male as "filthy, disgusting and unacceptable."

Electrical aversion therapy was administered for 15 sessions over a six-week period. Each session involved 3–5 trials of shock (approximately 5 milliamps) to the patient's left hand, delivered contingent on sexual arousal to deviant sexual stimuli similar to those employed in the sexual assessment. At the same time six sessions of systematic desensitization to female sex characteristics were instituted, followed by masturbation training during which the patient became sexually aroused using deviant fantasy and switched to appropriate heterosexual fantasy earlier in successive masturbatory sessions. These sessions were continued until the patient was able to employ heterosexual fantasy throughout each masturbatory session.

Inappropriate gender-role behaviors were modified by having the patient observe a male clinical-training student who modeled typical masculine methods of sitting, standing and walking. After each demonstration the patient practiced imitating the behaviors in sessions that were videotaped and replayed. In addition, more masculine speech patterns and voice pitches as well as grooming skills were taught. The patient was taught to lower the pitch of his voice and instructed to practice more masculine speech patterns and voice pitches by using a metronome to pace the rate of speech and by recording a 10-minute audiotape daily which he brought to each therapy session. Grooming skills focused on changing the patient's hair style and increasing his awareness of clothing styles. Severeal male and female clinical training students accompanied the patient on a shopping trip to buy a more stylish wardrobe.

Heterosocial skills training involved role-playing of social situations with female clinical-training students. These interactions were videotaped and discussed at the end of each treatment session. Particular emphasis was placed on situations involving asking females for dates and casual conversations with females.

A second sexual assessment was then made of gender role behavior and heterosocial skills. Results of this assessment indicated no sexual arousal to male or female children and moderate arousal to adult females. Gender role behaviors were rated as approximately masculine, and heterosocial skills judged moderately good by a group of independent raters. The patient responded to our encouragement to begin searching for a date by taking a female teacher from his school to dinner and a movie. In addition, a female clinical psychology student accompanied him to a meeting of an organized social club for singles. At six-months and two-years follow-up the patient demonstrated moderate to strong sexual arousal to adult females and no arousal to children. He was dating regularly and reported satisfaction with his new sexual and social skills.

CHAPTER 11

Other Variations in Sexual Behavior

In this chapter we shall discuss a number of behaviors that vary in how greatly they are condemned both socially and legally. Most of these behaviors are thought to be sexual, although they do include prostitution, nudism, and transsexualism, which are not directly motivated by sexual arousal. Some, such as incest and beastiality, have been recorded since earliest times, and have always fascinated writers and researchers. Others, such as polaroid parties and film clubs, use modern technology, and are recent phenomena whose longterm psychological and sociological effects remain to be seen. Still others, such as mate swapping, group sex, and nudism are not innovations of contemporary society, but have recently become more evident.

Not much psychological research has been done on these behaviors, for three major reasons. The first may be that on the relatively recent phenomena of polaroid parties, film clubs, and organized swingers clubs, we have not had time to develop a literature. Secondly, the sexual behaviors we are now talking about are largely victimless behaviors with the exception of some cases of incest. Nudism and mate swapping involve individual preferences or mutual consent among couples, and consequently are not as easily researched as are sexual behaviors inflicted upon unwilling and complaining victims. And finally, these behaviors are only infrequently presented to clinical psychologists and psychiatrists. Mate swapping, group sex, nudism, polaroid parties and semipublic sex are recreational; and even if incest is reported to authorities these cases do not usually result in a verdict of guilty, and so we do not have many available subjects to do research on.

In the first part of this chapter we will discuss a number of behaviors motivated by sexual arousal; we will then discuss behaviors in which a sexual motivation is considered secondary, such as prostitution, transsexualism, and nudism.

INCEST

The term *incest* (from the Latin for "impure" or "soiled") is commonly used to denote sexual relations between parents and offspring; it actually also includes sexual activity between an individual and any close relative (such as a grandparent, uncle or aunt, stepfather, stepmother, or brother or sister. The studies of incest conducted in the United States are largely based on persons institutionalized after arrest and conviction. This methodology may limit our understanding of the phenomenon, because this population probably is not representative.

Types of Incest

Father-daughter incest is the most common type reported, mother-son the least reported (Cavallin, 1973). The father most often initiates the sexual relationship with the daughter, although in many cases the daughter is a willing participant. Father-daughter incest is usually detected not when the wife learns of the relationship, but rather when the daughter tires of the activity or becomes angry with the father and reports it (Weinberg, 1955). The wife, in fact, may have full knowledge of the relationship, yet do little about reporting or discouraging the activity (Katchadourian & Lunde, 1972).

Incestuous behavior between brother and sister who are in their early teens or younger is the most frequent type, but is only rarely reported (Weinberg, 1955). This type of relationship is seldom discovered, and when discovered is usually not treated as a serious matter (Delora & Warren, 1977). However, incest among teenage or older participants is sometimes reported, usually by the sister (Cavallin, 1973). Brother-sister incest occurs most often in families in which children are given considerable sexual freedom; in which one of the participants cannot secure appropriate sexual partners outside the family for various reasons; or when brothers and sisters share the same bedroom (Delora & Warren, 1977). Females engaging in sexual relations with their brothers are more likely to be willing participants or even sexual aggressors than are females engaging in such behavior with their fathers (Weinberg, 1955). Greenwald & Greenwald (1973) report that a woman in her forties recalls:

> Looking in my brother's room I found him asleep also, but the covers of his bed had fallen to one side, and I could see my brother lying down, wearing nothing but an undershirt which was worked up above the waist leaving the rest of his body exposed. I stood for about 20 minutes just looking at his fairly well-developed penis and testicles. . . . My brother actually possessed more

than my husband. . . .I removed my night clothes, went into bed with him and snuggled up close, molding my body with his. I must have dozed off for when I awoke it was four o'clock. My brother had changed his position and was now facing me. He was awake and also sexually excited. Without any warning, I forced one leg under him and the other over him, sliding his penis into me. Although I had to help him all the way to his release he completed the act beautifully, and we had sexual intercourse two more times that day. (p. 236)

Prevalence of Incest

Morton Hunt's national survey (1974) gives some ideas of the prevalence of incestuous behavior in the United States. Approximately 15 percent of respondents indicated some sexual contact with relatives, including petting as well as coitus (Table 11-1). Most of this contact was with siblings or cousins; rarely was it between parent and child (see Table 11-2). Much of the contact took the form of childhood sex play, as evidenced by the fact that one-third of the males and half of the females had these experiences before age twelve. In addition, more than a quarter of the males and over half of the females went no further than light petting in these activities.

Hunt found that by discounting those incestuous contacts that involved petting and considering only those contacts that involved coitus, only 7 percent of his sample reported engaging in such behavior. Again this activity occurred most often between siblings or cousins (Table 11-3). In contrast to the findings of studies based on institutionalized offenders, Hunt found incestuous acts are more common among better educated and white-collar people than among the blue-collar population or those who had not attended college.

The Incest Taboo

Taboos against incest have been found in virtually all human societies, although some exceptions have been documented. Scientists and laymen advance a number of arguments for the necessity of the incest taboo: incest

TABLE 11-1

Ever Had Any Sexual Contact with Relatives
(Corrected to allow for experience by half of nonrespondents, percents)

	Under 35	35 and over
Males	18.9	13.4
Females	12.6	11.3

Source: Hunt, M. *Sexual behavior in the 1970's.* Chicago: Playboy Press, 1974. Reprinted with permission of Playboy Press. Copyright © 1974 by Morton Hunt.

TABLE 11-2

Ever Had Any Sexual Contact with Relatives
(Total national sample, by sex and by relationship of partner, percents)

Had Incestuous Contact with:		Males	Females
Nuclear family	Father	0	0.5
	Mother	0	0
	Son	0	*
	Daughter	*	0
	Brother	*	3.6
	Sister	3.8	0.7
Other close relatives	Uncle	*	0.6
	Aunt	*	0
	Nephew	0	0
	Niece	*	0
	Grandfather	0	*
	Grandmother	0	0
Marginally consanguineous and nonconsanguineous relatives	Male cousin	*	3.2
	Female cousin	9.2	*
	Brother-in-law	0	*
	Sister-in-law	*	0
	Stepfather	0	*
	Stepmother	0	0

*Less than 0.5 percent

Source: Hunt, M. *Sexual behavior in the 1970's*. Chicago: Playboy Press, 1974. Reprinted with permission of Playboy Press. Copyright © 1974 by Morton Hunt.

prohibitions are instinctive, incest taboos are necessary to maintain family structures, and incestuous breeding causes biological degeneration (Delora & Warren, 1977).

The most popular of these arguments is that incest will cause a deterioration of genetic quality by increasing sickliness, degeneracy, idiocy, and sterility (Cavallin, 1973). Experiments of inbreeding among animals and studies of children born of incestuous relationships, however, largely contradict this claim (Bagley, 1958). Obviously, inbreeding intensifies the inheritance of traits, both good and bad, but the risk of defective offspring from recessive hereditary disease is negligible if the disease has not previously manifested itself in the family (Ullerstam, 1966).

Modification of Incestuous Behavior

Very little work with behavioral treatment methods of incest have been reported. Barlow and his colleagues (Brownell & Barlow, 1976; Brown-

TABLE 11-3

Ever Had Heterosexual Coitus with Relatives
(By sex and by relationship of partner, total national sample, percents)

	Males	*Females*
Had coitus with:		
Sister	1.5	
Aunt	*	
Niece	*	
Sister-in-law	*	
Female cousin	3.9	
Brother		0.8
Uncle		*
Stepfather		*
Male cousin		0.5

*Less than 0.5 percent.

Source: Hunt, M. *Sexual behavior in the 1970's.* Chicago: Playboy Press, 1974. Reprinted with permission of Playboy Press. Copyright © 1974 by Morton Hunt.

nell, Hayes, & Barlow, 1977; Harbert et al., 1974) reported the successful use of covert sensitization with several males convicted of incestuous behavior. Their works essentially represent the behavioral research reported to date. These cases have been previously described in this text.

CASE HISTORY

Ralphing, Carpenter, and Davis (1967) reported the case of a 39-year-old white male who learned incestuous behavior from his father and in turn transmitted the knowledge to his son. The male sought professional help at the insistence of his wife. Their psychiatric examination showed the following results:

The father is described by the patient as being similar to himself, both in physical appearance and personality type. . . . As a unit the family was loosely bound and little affection was expressed. The mother and father remained emotionally isolated from each other and were openly hostile to one another . . . . The patient received his sexual education from his peers and from what he observed in his own home.

He recalls having observed sexual relations between his father and older sister when he was 11. Shortly thereafter the patient himself began to experiment in sexual relations with his sister. He denies ever having had orgasm with her as a sexual partner. He also states that she appeared to accept the incestuous relationship.

The patient states that his mother was aware of her husband's special relationship with his 13-year-old daughter, and passively accepted this behavior. Indeed, the father would manipulate the daughter's genitals while he was in bed with both her and his wife. The patient and his father, quite independently, continued to have relations with the oldest girl until she ran away from home at 14 to marry.

The patient left home at 16. During his absence the father commenced incestuous relations with his two younger daughters, who were just reaching puberty. When the patient returned home at 18, he soon followed in his father's footsteps and began to have sexual relations with his two younger sisters; he continued this practice sporadically until they left home.

The patient married an 18-year-old farm girl when he was 21. . . . .The couple have five children: four daughters whose ages are 17, 16, 10, and 5 years, and one son, age 14. When the first daughter reached puberty at age 12, the patient states he initiated her into sexual relations while his wife was in the hospital delivering their youngest child. Subsequently he has had intercourse with her on an average of two to three times per week for the last five years.

The daughter passively accepted her father's proposals, but states that she derives no sexual pleasure from these acts. On the contrary, the patient has been able to achieve orgasm whenever intercourse was carried to completion. The daughter states that she allowed this relationship to continue because her father expected her to participate, because she felt sorry for him after she refused him, and because she feared she would lose any affection which he might have for her if she did not submit.

When the patient next approached his second eldest daughter he was vehemently refused by her; consequently, he has rarely been able to complete the sexual act with her. He nevertheless persisted in his sexual pursuit . . . . having already had sexual relations with two daughters, he next attempted manual manipulation of the next-to-youngest daughter, then age 8. She protested so strenuously that he has made no further sexual advances to her.

When his only son reached puberty the patient took great care to instruct him in the details of sexual behavior and urged him to have sexual relations with his own mother. The son did eventually make vague sexual advances to his mother which greatly angered her. In addition, the patient implicitly gave his son permission to have sexual relations with his sisters. The eldest daughter denies having submitted to her brother; he, however, contradicts this, and further states that he derives great pleasure from sexual relations with his sisters, but denies any other sexual contacts to date.

On examination the patient appeared anxious but was able to express himself without hestitation. . . .

Although he feels unhappy and guilty about this incestuous behavior, he readily admits that this has not prevented him from continuing to have sexual relations with his daughters. He . . . has . . . reassured himself that he is doing his daughters a favor by initiating them into sexual relations. Paradosically enough, he is a prudish man who dictates high moral standards to his family at the same time he commits incest. . . .

He has few social contacts other than with those who work with him. His work record has been good and he has carried out duties which involve great responsibility. . . . (pp. 507–509; reproduced with permission of the American Medical Association)

MATE-SWAPPING

In mate-swapping, wife-swapping, or swinging couples who are usually married exchange spouses with other married couples with the full consent of all involved (Delora & Warren, 1977). Mate-swapping can be differentiated from extramarital "affairs" or open-ended marriages because it is a sexual exchange in which the husband and wife participate simultaneously and in the same place, although sometimes in different rooms.

The age range of couples who engage in mate-swapping is quite wide with the youngest reported as 18 and the oldest as 78 (Bartel, 1970). The social class range of the swinging groups studied so far is fairly narrow: predominately middle-class and upper-middle class (Bartel, 1970). Spanier and Cole (1975) estimate that 2 percent of couples have tried mate swapping on at least one occasion.

Initiation into Mate-Swapping

In most instances when the decision is made to experiment with mate-swapping, the idea is initiated by the husband and the wife agrees only after considerable discussion (Rosen, 1971). For example:

> Swinging was something Don and I had read about and occasionally joked about, and I must admit the idea was somewhat intriguing at that point. But when Don suggested that we ask Jim and Myrna if they would be interested, I was horrified. It was a fun thing to joke about, but when I had to think of it in terms of actually switching off and having sex with friends, it suddenly seemed unthinkable. I insisted it would be impossible for me to repond in bed with someone I did not really love. But Don kept bringing up the subject. . . . Finally I agreed that we might just go over to Jim and Myrna's house to see some porno movies he had just gotten, but if I did not feel like switching partners, we did not have to. That made me feel a little better, but I was still nervous. (Delora & Warren, 1972, p. 225)

Mate-Swapping Contacts

Couples interested in mate-swapping contact other willing couples in a variety of ways. Occasionally, couples who are close friend simply drift into a sexual exchange. More often, however, swingers contact couples whom they do not know. These contacts may be made through a mutual friend or through advertisements in swinging magazines or at swinging parties or bars (Bartel, 1970).

Mate-swapping parties may assume several forms. A party may be of the "closed" or "soft-swing" type, which at first glance resembles any other cocktail party. The difference is that couples occasionally drift off to bedrooms, returning later, fully dressed, to resume their socializing.

At the other extreme is the "open" or "hard swing" party—more commonly called an *orgy*. At these parties the motto is that anything goes. In many instances, nude participants pile in the middle of a room, touching and being touched by whomever is within reach (Palson & Palson, 1972). Any given party may fall somewhere between the soft and hard or may include both open and closed mate-swapping in different rooms (Bartel, 1970).

Some degree of homosexual behavior is usually present at most large parties; female homosexuality may be encouraged and male homosexual behavior is usually discouraged (Varni, 1972). Ordinarily the men sit and passively watch as two or more women engage in sexual behavior; they rate these scenes as extremely arousing. After a time the men may join the women, and the orientation of the sexual activity changes from homosexual to heterosexual (Palson & Palson, 1972).

The Experience of Mate-Swapping

Mate-swapping is apparently an enjoyable social and sexual activity for some participants; they emphasize the variety of impersonal sexual partners and the satisfaction of realizing that a number of individuals find them sexually desirable.

> You can meet and be with physically the most attractive, good, intelligent people with your wife's consent and be as sexually stimulated as you want to be and still have a great home life—dinner cooked when I get home from work, a beautiful mother for our children, and have my wife as a great bed partner and still have all the variety any man could want when it comes to sex. (Margolis & Rubenstein, 1971, p. 54)

For others, however, mate-swapping may prove to be a negative experience for a variety of reasons. First, participants often find that their fantasies of sexual prowess and attractiveness exceed the realities of the situation. The male participant is particularly vulnerable to this negative experience. According to our study of swingers, less than 25 percent of the men become sexually aroused regularly at large parties although most report they get aroused more frequently at small parties (Bartel, 1970). Second, the wife of a mate-swapping couple often becomes more enthusiastic about swinging than the husband after she overcomes her initial shyness and anxiety (Palson & Palson, 1972), particularly if the wife is attractive and popular with other men. The husband must often watch his wife engage in sexual activity with a number of men either one at a time or in group sex while he attracts less attention. The husband's inability to respond sexually to every woman can become quite apparent while the wife is capable of many orgasms in one evening, and any failure she has at becoming sexually aroused is not as visible (Varni, 1972). Finally, mate-swapping may lead to jealousies and problems in a marriage if one of the partners suspects his/her spouse of becoming emotionally attached to another person (Spanier & Cole, 1975).

Polaroid Parties and Film Clubs

Polaroid parties and film clubs are variants of mate-swapping. Most often they are mate-swapping parties during which participants are allowed to photograph or film the action; or they are organized clubs whose members mail sexually explicit photographs or films of themselves to other members who likewise reciprocate (Penthouse, 1977). The object of mailing such photographs and films may be to interest other mate-swapping couples in future get togethers, or they are simply meant to serve as a visual stimulus for arousal. There are a number of national publications that organize the exchange of sexual photographs and films, for instance, *Swinger's World* and *Adam*.

SEMIPUBLIC SEX

In our society, norms prescribe that sexual activity take place in private, away from the view of individuals who do not give their consent to the observation of sexual behavior. It would seem, however, that the popularity of semipublic sex is increasing. Participants in semipublic activity usually consider the behavior an occasional turnon rather than a preferred and regular pattern of behavior. It is unclear whether the sexually arousing value of this behavior is similar to that of exhibitionism or is merely the result of fear of being discovered. The following example is from *Gallery,* August, 1976:

> . . .we have spent other fun weekends at motels. After all have retired in their rooms, my wife and I will roam around with her wearing only her coat, completely nude under it. We will stop at a pop machine, or whatever, and she will remove her coat. I take nude photos of her then and there. Sometimes we even get it on by the ice machines. She likes to get rooms next to stairways so she can walk out stark naked into the hallway or steps. Later we screw in our motel room with the door completely open. When we do that we are usually lying on the floor just inside the doorway. We have often wondered how

many people see in on us as they walk down the hallway. (*Gallary*, August, 1976)

NECROPHILIA

Necrophilia is defined as sexual gratification obtained from corpses. It is a rare form of behavior, and may involve viewing a corpse or actually having intercourse with it; the corpse may be mutiliated afterward (Solomon & Patch, 1974). If the victim is first killed and then sexually assaulted, the behavior is an extreme form of sadism. Most necrophiles are considered psychotic and extremely deviant (Hyde, 1979).

Necrophiles may take considerable risk such as removing corpses from graves. Others may obtain jobs in morgues and funeral homes. Although most necrophiles are not sexually aroused to living persons, some are able to perform coitus if the woman lies absolutely motionless. Some larger cities have prostitutes who cater to this preference; they use wax or powder to give their skin a lifeless appearance, dress in a shroud, and lie in a coffin for the benefit of the client (Solomon & Patch, 1974).

A client took me back to his place, and as soon as I got in the door there was a dirty great coffin standing open. He put me in a white nightie with a rosary in one hand and a Bible in the other and a wreath of roses on my head. Then I had to lie down in the coffin. . .he started nailing the lid down and all the time he was shouting: "You're dead now, God damn you to hell." He told me his wife had died. (Young, Goy, & Phoenix, 1964, p. 65).

FROTTAGE

Frottage is defined as sexual arousal as a result of rubbing or pressing the penis against an object, usually the buttocks of a fully clothed woman (Solomon & Patch, 1974). It is thought to be a rare disorder, and usually occurs in subways, buses, or other crowded situations. It may pass unnoticed by the victim. Frotteurs are usually impotent in normal sexual situations and this deviant behavior is their sole avenue of sexual gratification (Allen, 1969).

COPROPHILIA AND COPROPHAGIA

Coprophilia involves an abnormal sexual interest in excretion, while *coprophagia* is defined as sexual gratification as a result of eating excretions and/or secretions (Delora & Warren, 1977). These disorders are quite rare and are often associated with other deviant behaviors. For example, a prerequisite for sexual arousal may be sadism through urinating on the partner; or masochism by being urinated on; or voyeurism by observing excretory functions. Other researchers consider these behaviors associated with sexual analism (Delora & Warren, 1977). Orgasm is most often achieved by masturbation (Solomon & Patch, 1974).

SEXUAL URETHRALISM

Sexual urethralism is sexual arousal as a result of urethral stimulation by some object (Delora & Warren, 1977). Although social problems resulting from this behavior are few, medical problems are many, since the object used to stimulate the urethra may slip into the bladder. The relatively longer length of the male as compared to the female urethra makes this accident less common in males. However, almost every type of small object has been surgically removed from both male and female bladders at one time or another—including even a small snake (Allen, 1969).

Closely related to sexual urethralism, coprophilia, and coprophagia is *urophilia*, which is sexual arousal to and interest in urine. Sexual arousal may be achieved by watching persons or animals urinate, by urinating on others, being urinated upon, or by drinking urine (Allen, 1969). Occasionally persons who become sexually aroused by such acts term them "water sports" or "golden showers," and advertise in underground newspapers for sexual partners.

WET PANTS, WET BEDS, DIAPERS—Are you turned on by wetting your pants or bed, wearing pants or diapers? Let's make contact; Esp. Florida wetters: W/m 40, 6', 32" waist.

ZOOPHILIA

The use of animals as sex objects is commonly called *zoophilia, beastiality,* or *beastiosexuality.* The DSM III (APA, 1978) states that the essential features of zoophilia are the use of animals as the preferred to exclusive method of producing sexual excitement; and the repeated production of sexual arousal as a result of fantasy or the act of engaging in sexual activity with animals. Many different types of animals and types of sexual contact may be used. The animal may be the object of intercourse or may be trained to sexually excite the human partner by licking or rubbing the individual's genitals. Other behaviors include masturbating the animal or performing oral sex on the animal (Kinsey et al., 1953, p. 509).

It is not unusual for the person engaging in sexual activities with an animal to have affectionate feelings for the animal, which may be a pet (Delora & Warren, 1977). Quite often, though, the contact is made simply through curiosity, desire for novelty, or a desire for sexual release when other sex objects are unavailable. Occasionally, zoophilia involves sadistic elements that may result in injury or even death to the animal.

Research has indicated that as many as 17 percent of male adolescents who live in rural areas have sexual contact to orgasm with animals, and probably as many more have sexual relations that are not carried through to orgasm (Kinsey et al., 1948, p. 459). Usually these contacts become less frequent with age and as the adolescent encounters available human sexual partners. It is not surprising that sexual contact with animals is less common for males raised in urban areas, since they often have less access to animals. The incidence for urban males is only one-half to one-fifth that found among rural males (Kinsey et al., 1948, p. 459–463). The total number of adult males who reported sexual contact, including orgasm, with animals at some point in their lives was close to 8 percent (Kinsey et al., 1948).

Females in the United States are believed less likely than males to engage in sexual activities with animals; the reported incidence for women is about 4 percent, with very few of these incidents involving contact to orgasm (Kinsey et al., 1953, p. 509). Females are most likely to have sexual contacts with cats and dogs. They usually involve general body contact, but may include the animal's licking the female's genitals, masturbation of the animal, oral sex performed on the animal, or intercourse. We have read and heard of dogs that are specially trained and sold for purposes of zoophilia, but these reports are difficult to confirm. There are, however, establishments that feature exhibitions of coitus between women and dogs or donkeys; these places cater primarily to the interests of males (Katchadourian & Lunde, 1972). In addition, sexual activity between women and animals seems to be a popular theme in many stag films.

SATYRIASIS AND NYMPHOMANIA

Satyriasis and *nymphomania* refer to males and females respectively who experience almost continual sexual desire and arousal, and who focus their lives largely around their activities. Historically, these behavioral patterns have been assumed to be abnormal; but in the light of available evidence and current thinking concerning sexual behavior, it is difficult to ascribe much meaning to these labels, or to attach much validity to their application. Research has demonstrated that there are wide variations in frequency and strength of sexual arousal and activity; and a high incidence of sexual behavior should not be considered abnormal unless such sexual patterns impair ability to establish satisfying interpersonal relationships or make other life adjustments.

Etiology of Satyriasis and Nymphomania

It is presently unclear whether the development of satyriasis or nymphomania is due to psychological or physiological factors. Psychological theories forwarded to explain these behaviors include parental conditioning and compulsivity. For example, Ellis and Sagarin (1964) cite the case of a middle-aged nymphomanic:

> She performed obsessive-compulsive rituals while eating, washing, cleaning house, and working . . . she did the same thing in her sex relations. She would start, for example, with an Italian boy . . . and then could not consider another Italian bedmate for a while. . . . She'd go through a good many different males, and then allow herself another Italian. (p. 55)

Other psychological theories consider some cases of satyriasis and nymphomania to be the result of a variable ratio reinforcement schedule (Vetter, 1972). If the assumption is correct that persons suffering from satyriasis and nymphomania are usually unable to achieve orgasm, then the person may "wander from partner to partner to partner in the hope that the next sexual encounter will be more adequate and will succeed in giving release where others have failed" (Mindlin, 1967, p. 196).

Physiological theories emphasize the importance of certain structures in the brain in regulating and controlling sexual arousal. For example, if the amygdala (a portion of the brain lying below the frontal lobes) is destroyed by disease or injury or blocked as a result of surgery, the result is an almost insatiable desire for sexual activity (Wilson, 1963). An interesting case was reported in the *Los Angeles Times* (1970) in which a woman filed suit against the owner of a cable car company for injuries received in an accident in which she received a blow to the head. The woman, a Sunday School teacher, complained of developing an uncontrollable sexual drive after the accident and had engaged in intercourse with over 100 men as a result. In addition, she complained of losing several jobs because of her intense sexual desire. The woman was awarded a monetary settlement.

PROSTITUTION

The word *prostitute* comes from the Latin *prostituere,* meaning "to expose." It implies the offering of one's body for sale *passim et sine dilectu* ("indiscriminately and without pleasure"), in the legal phrasing of ancient Roman law. Today prostitution is defined as the provision of sexual relations in return for money, and represents the only sexual offense for which women are prosecuted to any significant extent. To this rather narrow definition we may add that such relations are promiscuous, fairly indiscriminate, largely without affection, often anonymous, and are not rendered legitimate by marriage (Delora & Warren, 1977). Even with all these qualifications, it is difficult to distinguish those cases in which mistresses, girlfriends, and wives accept money or gifts in exchange for sexual favors (Gebhard, 1966).

Prostitution has always existed despite repeated attempts to eliminate it through religious and legal sanctions. In various ancient cultures prostitution was associated with the religious rites, the so-called "sacred" or "temple" prostitution. In Mesopotamia around the middle of the fifth century B.C., for example, every woman had to give herself once to a stranger in the temple before she married. This obligatory prostitution was regarded as a purely religious act, a sacrifice to the goddess, Ishtar, to whom every woman must belong for a night (Lewinsohn, 1958). Commercialized prostitution, as we know it today, dates back at least to ancient Greece (Katchadorian & Lunde, 1972). Solon is credited with having been the first public official to establish, in 550 B.C., licensed public houses of commercialized prostitution. The revenue from the brothels were used to lower the taxes of the citizenry and to build a temple to Aphrodite.

Technically, there are four categories of prostitution, the most common of which is a heterosexual relation for which the female is paid. There is also heterosexual prostitution for which the male, called a "gigolo," is paid by the female. In addition, there is male homosexual prostitution in which a male provides sexual relations for another male; and female homosexual prostitution, in which a female provides sexual relations for another female. Since female prostitutes who are paid by male clients are most numerous, more data are available on them than on any other type of prostitute, and we shall focus our discussion on heterosexual relations for which the female is paid. However, even these data are limited because of the problems in obtaining a representative sample of prostitutes. Most of the available literature is based on prostitutes who are in prison or in psychotherapy; however, these women are certainly not representative of all prostitutes (Delora & Warren, 1977).

The World of Prostitution

In the world of prostitution, men, and more rarely, women, who live in whole or in part off the earnings of prostitutes are called pimps (Benjamin & Masters, 1964). Criminal subculture prostitutes and streetwalkers are most likely to share a pimp with other prostitutes (Benjamin & Masters, 1964); on the other hand, massage parlor and other middle class prostitutes are more likely to have husbands who may or may not act as pimps (Jackman, O'Toole, & Geis, 1963). Call girls are least likely to have pimps, but may have them for protection from clients and the police.

The pimp serves as the prostitute's protector, employment agent, and emotional anchor. She often becomes emotionally attached to him and may even turn over more of her earnings to him than is required. A pimp may also provide an underworld connection for getting drugs and for protecting the prostitute from arrest or conviction (Benjamin & Masters, 1964). In the criminal subculture, the pimps' fancy clothes and car functions as symbols of the prostitutes' prestige and earning power (Young, 1970).

> And before I could even open my mouth, they'd made a deal for monthly payoffs of $1,100 to the police for protection. When I complained about the high monthly figure, Abe told me I'd better cooperate, since I needed the protection, or else I would get deported. . . . Meanwhile, another deal was made. This had to do with my previous arrest. After discussions back and forth with Abe and the arresting police officer, Nick fixed a price of $3,500 to get me off the hook completely. Originally the arresting officer had suggested wryly that the "golden goose" ought to pay $10,000 to get her case dismissed, but as that figure was rather outrageous they settled for $3,500. Again there was really nothing I could do about it other than get up the money. (Hollander, 1972, pp. 303–304)

A less important role in the prostitutes' affairs is played by the madam, who is, according to some thought, merely the prostitute's employer.

> The madam . . . hires and fires, makes rules, punishes those who break them, and generally supervises the activities of girls on the job. She often keeps lists of customers and girls who may be available if extra help is needed. She may find it necessary to employ accessory personnel such as maids, cooks, bouncers, and spotters. Her contacts with madams in other cities enable her to assist girls at finding new positions. Her problems include those involved in meeting the sometimes rapidly changing tastes of her customers and of working some sort of stable arrangement with city officials and the police. Although the prostitute usually sees or works for a madam during the course of her career. . . there is little doubt that she is less important as an associate than either the pimp or the fellow prostitute. (Hirschi, 1962, p. 203)

The amount of money a given prostitute can earn depends upon a variety of factors: her sexual skills, the variety of sexual services she will perform, her attractiveness, her initiative, the amount of time she puts in, where she works, and the socioeconomic level of her customers (Delora & Warren, 1977). Probably the lowest priced prostitutes in the United States are the older and less attractive women working in slum areas who may receive only a few dollars for a rushed session of sexual intercourse in a darkened alley, or for masturbating a customer under the table in a slum bar or darkened X-rated theatre. Most desirable massage parlor prostitutes and streetwalkers often get as much as 20 to 50 dollars per customer. At the top of the economic scale are the call girls who frequently receive from 50 to several hundred dollars for each session, and on occasion, even more (Greenwald, 1970).

Prostitutes usually pay little or no taxes on their income, but they often have relatively high business-related expenses, such as attractive clothes, liquor, and sexually related devices like erotic films. If a call girl works out of her apartment she may also have to give generous tips to the apartment manager, doorman, and elevator operator.

Because prostitution is against the law in all states except Nevada, the prostitute constantly runs the risk of arrest. Most arrests are made when prostitutes solicit customers or plainclothes police officers on streets or in public places like hotels, bars, or movie houses. The experienced prostitute exercises extreme caution in the wording of her offer in order to avoid arrest. She will mention no sexual activity at all but will speak vaguely of "wanting to have a good time" or "some fun." She will also be wary of speaking directly of money for sexual services to be rendered. Rather, she may mention that she needs a certain amount of money to pay her rent or for some new clothes. In addition, she will usually avoid taking money from the customer until after the sexual activities have been completed, thus forcing a plainclothes policeman to engage in sexual activity with her before he can arrest her for prostitution. These ploys are not always successful, however, and courts have sustained convictions when there was sufficent reason to believe, on the basis of circumstances and general behavior, that the women had been soliciting, regardless of whether or not they specifically "offered their bodies for hire." Usually a convicted prostitute is merely fined and released to resume her occupation, which amounts to imposing a type of excise tax, the cost of which is passed on the customer.

Types of Prostitutes

Female prostitutes who cater to male clients may be roughly divided into four types based on the means by which they conduct their business. During a long-term career, prostitutes may often work in all these ways. Some prostitutes originally may begin by working in massage parlors and then, due to their physical attractiveness and sexual skills, become more prestigious call girls. On the other hand, some former call girls may find that as they grow older and less attractive, massage parlors, brothels, or streetwalking are all they can do.

Streetwalkers. The first type of prostitute is called a "streetwalker" or "bar girl." Among prostitutes these are probably lowest on the social scale in terms of income and prestige (Delora & Warren, 1977). The streetwalker solicits business by approaching men on the street in particular areas of the city; the bar girl solicits men who frequent a particular bar in which she plys her trade. In addition, some streetwalkers solicit business in X-rated movie houses. In all cases the prostitute must approach the man in a manner that indicates to him that she is willing to exchange sexual services for money. However, the prostitute must exercise a degree of caution, for the potential customer may be a police officer in plain clothes who could arrest her for soliciting. Once she and her customer have agreed on the particulars of the arrangement they go to her apartment, a nearby hotel, his hotel room, or occasionally engage in sexual behavior in a darkened movie house, bar, or alley (Woolston, 1969). The following case study is from our files:

CASE HISTORY 11-1

Name: Judy
Age: 17
Education: Ninth Grade

    I been at this now for about six months. It's tough getting started you know but after a while you can smell a cop a mile away. I got busted twice before I learned the ropes. . . . The money's good, it keeps us in grass and groceries. . . . Fifteen dollars buys you fifteen minutes. What they do with their time is their business. If they want to talk, I'll talk. If they wanna screw, I'll screw. If they want me to stand on my head and whistle *Dixie* while I'm going down on them then I'll do that. It's their money, I don't really care one way or the other. The only thing I won't do is the backdoor [anal intercourse]. Two guys held me down one time and did the backdoor on me and almost killed me. . . . My old man, the guy I live with, he's a musician and ain't got a gig now. He's really good though and someday he'll make it big, like Elton John or somebody. When that day comes it's goodbye hooking and hello money. . . .

    Prostitutes in Brothels, or "Red Light Workers." Some prostitutes may work in brothels, or whorehouses that are usually found in what are called "red light districts" of a city. These women turn over a percentage of their fees to the owner of the house, and in exchange get a place to conduct their business as well as some measure of protection from arrest or brutal clients (Delora & Warren, 1977). Brothels vary in their arrangements, but often have a large sitting room where the client makes his choice among women who are available at the time. The chosen woman then takes the client to her room. The activities she performs, the prices she charges, and the time she devotes to the sexual session are agreed upon either in the sitting room or as soon as they get to the prostitute's room (Woolston, 1969). The following is from our files:

CASE HISTORY 11-2

Name: Elaine
Age: 44
Education: Sixth Grade

I've had a really weird life. I guess. I've been married three times and none of my husbands was worth a damn. Sometimes I wonder how I could have gotten four losers. . . . My second husband got me into tricking. One of my kids got sick and it took lots of money to pay the bills. My husband was too busy drinking to help make any money. He finally talked me into hooking and I've been at it off and on since then, 20 years or so. What the hell else can I do for a living? I got a drinking problem now and I can't do much else. . . . Money, that's a joke. Look at me, I'm 44 years old. The money used to be good when I was younger but now, after I give the owner his cut I hardly make a living. . . . I don't do nothing but blow jobs these days. Most of my customers are old drunks and young kids looking for some fun. Who else is gonna come in this dump?

Prostitutes in Massage Parlors. The next type of prostitute is one who plys her trade in massage parlors. While customers may go to a massage parlor for a legitimate massage, in many instances these massages are conducted in small private cubicles where it is quite likely that sexual services can be and are sold to the customer (Delora & Warren, 1977). To protect herself legally, the masseuse does not directly offer sexual services, but is generally understood that they are available in most massage parlors when the customer requests them (Rasmussen & Kuhn, 1976). Intercourse is not a common activitiy in massage parlors because by law they may not have beds, but fellatio and masturbation often are quite common (Delora & Warren, 1977). The fee charged a customer depends on the type of sexual services offered in addition to the massage. The advantages of the massage parlor for both the woman and her customer is that it is not illegal in most states, whereas houses of prostitution are illegal in all states except Nevada (Winick & Kinsie, 1971). The following is from our files.

CASE HISTORY 11-3

Name: Marla
Age: 22
Education: Completed high school

I've been working here for close to a year now and a joint up the street for a couple of months before coming here. I worked for an insurance company as a secretary before getting into this business. . . . Mostly I do it for the money. My husband works the second shift and doesn't get home till midnight and so my hours work out well with his, but mostly it's the money. Fifteen dollars for a 15 minute massage and I get half the money. On top of that we can negotiate a price for anything extra the customer wants and we get to keep all of that. A good week and I make 350 to 400 dollars. How many secretaries do you know that make that kind of money? If they do, they're probably doing the same thing I'm doing. . . .Mostly handjobs but occasionally I'll go down on a guy if he looks clean and the money is right. Some of the girls will have intercourse but not me. My husband and I agreed that I wouldn't do anything but handjobs and go down. Anyway, it's too risky having intercourse. The last thing I want is to get arrested.

Call Girls. The call girl represents the most prestigious type of female prostitute and is likely to be at the top of the economic hierarchy. Generally she does not hustle clients on the street, in bars, or in X-rated movie houses, nor does she work in a massage parlor or brothel. Instead, the call girl most often has regular clients, and accepts new clients only through personal referral. Some call girls have only a few wealthy sugar daddies who provide their total income. Others may work with an organized "escort service" which serves as an intermediary between the client and the prostitute. It is not uncommon for a call girl to ask a prospective client for his name, driver's license number, and place of business (Delora & Warren, 1977). This information enables her to check and see if he is a member of the vice squad or a legitimate client. In addition, it gives her some added protection against the client's being brutal or psychopathic (Delora & Warren, 1977). The behavior of clients is a constant source of concern to any prostitute, since she has no legal recourse if she is cheated out of her money, or worse, brutally beaten.

The call girl may perform her services either by visiting the client or in her own home or apartment. On occasion, she, and perhaps several other prostitutes, are hired to provide entertainment or serve as dates for groups of men at private parties. Large corporations sometimes use call girls in this way to entertain prospective clients or other business associates (Delora & Warren, 1977). The call girl, more so than the other types of prostitutes, is likely to provide services other than direct sexual ones, such as serving as an attractive date for dinner or a party or possibly a weekend vacation (Winick & Kinsie, 1971).

Call girls may work full-time or part-time. Full-time call girls are likely to be single, well educated, and have clients who visit her on a regular basis. One such woman's story is from our files.

CASE HISTORY 11-4

Name: Hope
Age: 27
Education: Masters Degree in Education

I went into this business about five years ago on a part-time basis and about three years ago full-time. I wasn't very happy teaching and surely wasn't making near the money teaching that I make now. I originally started when a friend who was also working talked me into it. She lined me up with some tricks and I gradually got busier. I'm trying to hold my business down now, no sense in working yourself to death, is there? . . . I only take regular clients that I know or who are introduced to me by some I know well. It's much more than just sex, believe me. Many of my clients want to go to dinner or a play and some want an occasional quiet evening to be alone and talk. I probably don't have sex with many more different men than some women who don't hook but date a variety of men. . . . The money is good. I live in a nice apartment, buy a new car every year and spent three weeks in Europe this summer on vacation. In addition, I'm saving four times as much money each year than I made teaching. Someday when I go back to teaching I'll have money saved . . . . I've read all the stories of prostitutes who really hate men, who come from terrible families, who give their money to pimps, and who are really miserable. Do I look like I'm miserable? I'm very happy and content. It's not a bad way to make a living at all. In fact, I can't think of an easier way.

Part-time call girls may be secretaries, teachers, housewives, or college students, and are apt to see their work as temporary. The following case is from our files:

CASE HISTORY 11-5

Name: Jennifer
Age: 20
Education: College Junior

I suppose I've been working about two years now. During my freshman year in college I needed some extra money so I took a job as a hostess for a weekend automobile dealers' convention. It was innocent enough, one of these deals that lots of college girls take to make some extra money for an afternoon. All I had to do was stand around in a low-cut blouse and short skirt and let all the dirty old men try to put the move on me. Anyway, after that one of the guys at the promotion company that booked conventions told me I could make money dating guys who come to town for different business meetings. I gave it a try and liked it okay so I stayed at it. I go to college so finding time to work at a regular job is difficult. With this job the promotion company man calls me when someone is coming to town and wants a date and if I'm not busy I go. Easy way to pick up a hundred dollars for a few hours work. . . . I'm hoping to go to graduate school in social work when I graduate from college and so I guess I'll keep doing this until I finish school. The guys are all businessmen, educated, and wealthy who want to have a little fun and a little sex and then hurry home to their families. I think it's a pretty good deal.

How and Why Women Become Prostitutes

There are apparently many people who cite psychological aberrations as the reason why women decide to enter prostitution. Prostitutes themselves, however, are likely to say it was nothing more than simple economics. Laner (1974) claims that these explanations are not mutually exclusive; prostitutes may seek as the rewards of prostitution both "feelings of personal worth as desirable women and financial proof of that worth.'' (p. 414). Other possible motivations for prostitution include the chance to earn a substantial income in nonroutine work, the chance to live a glamorous life and mingle with clients of a higher socioeconomic level, and the excitement of an illegal profession (Delora & Warren, 1977). For some women, prostitution represents the only way to earn enough money to finance a drug or alcohol habit. Other women may be encouraged to enter prostitution by husbands or boyfriends who recognize the economic potential of providing sexual services for a fee. On occasion, a woman with a very high sex drive will seek prostitution as a logical way to earn money at the same time she satisfies her sexual needs (Gebhard, 1966; Woolston, 1969).

Research studies have ascribed widely different motives and characteristics to girls who become prostitutes. Contrary to popular myth, there does not appear to be any systematic process of recruiting females into the profession. Women may enter prostitution almost by accident, by deliberately seeking contacts, or by any combination of both. As Gagnon and Simon (1968) have stated, "We are dealing with the phenomena of enlistment rather than recruitment." (p. 117) Many studies report that the majority of girls who enlist in prostitution appear to come from lower class or lower middle class homes. Frequently they come from unstable families and have histories of sexual promiscuity during adolescence (Coleman, 1972). It is probable that at some point they may receive gifts or money for providing sexual favors and thus become interested in the possibility of engaging in prostitution on a regular basis. Young (1970) indicates that in western societies very few women are forced into prostitution.

The decision to enter prostitution must be implemented by some actual means of entering the profession. Jackman et al. (1963) found that among 15 call girls interviewed, all but one had entered prostitution by making contact with another call girl. Bryan (1965) found that all but one of the 33 call girls he interviewed in the Los Angeles area had personal contact with someone engaged in call girl activities. He claims that in some instances the girls had been friends; sometimes the contact had started with a homosexual relationship between the two. The initial contact appears to greatly determine the type or social level of prostitution at which the girl began. Young (1970) reports that other prostitutes merely drift into the game through occupations such as restaurant or hotel work.

After the decision has been made to enter prostitution and a contact in the business is made, the novice typically enters a period of apprenticeship, which may last from two to eight months or even longer (Coleman, 1972). Generally, clients are perceived as basically exploitive and hence open to exploitation. Most girls view prostitution as simply an occupation, certainly no more dishonest than marrying for money. Tollison, Nesbitt, and Frey (1977), in fact, compared attitudes toward sexual intimacy in prostitutes and college girls, and found that prostitutes had more conservative ideas and attitudes toward premarital sex and sexual intimacy than did the university population.

Prostitute-Client Relationship

There exists a common assumption that the prostitute views her behavior strictly as a matter of business and does not experience orgasm or emotional arousal during a professional contact. However, relationships between prostitutes and clients vary greatly. Young (1970) studied groups of prostitutes and found that most disliked their clients, especially the kinky ones. According to Jackman et al. (1963) many prostitutes from the criminal subculture disliked middle-class values. Alienated prostitutes were apathetic, while middle-class prostitutes had a rather ambivalent attitude both to the middle class and to clients. For streetwalkers in large cities who may never expect to see their clients again, it is assumed that the sexual encounter is brief and business like, with no emotional attachment involved.

In contrast, Bryan (1966) found that a wide variety of relationships existed between prostitutes and their clients, ranging from coldness and hostility on the girls' part to friendship and sexual gratification. He found that call girls often mistrusted other call girls more than their clients, and had higher esteem for their clients than other prostitutes. In general, prostitutes' attitudes toward their clients correspond to the social level of the client: that is, prostitutes who service lower-class men are less likely to like them than those who service upper-class men.

Why Men Frequent Prostitutes

Among the reasons that Kinsey et al. (1948) reported for men's frequenting of prostitutes were: (1) insufficient opportunity for other types of heterosexual experience, as is often the case with military personnel; (2) desire to discover what such an experience may have to offer, and, in the case of some older men, to have sexual relations with a younger woman; (3) the desire to avoid responsibilities generally associated with sexual relations; (4) difficulty in securing sexual relations with other women, possibly of timidity or a physical defect; and (5) desire to find a partner willing to engage in deviant sexual practices.

NUDISM

The rationale for prohibiting public nudity in our society is similar to that for prohibiting exhibitionism: the display of one's genitals to others without their consent. However, places have been set aside for social nudism, where adults and sometimes children consent to congregate without clothes.

Nudist Camps

Nudist camps are generally governed by a very rigid set of rules of conduct. Individuals without partners are prohibited or discouraged from joining, and visitors and new members are carefully screened. Sexual arousal and activity at nudist camps is reportedly rare, due in part, to the self-consciously asexual atmosphere in most camps. Delora & Warren (1977), in fact, claim that the attitude toward public sexuality in most nudist camps is "prudish" by most non-nudist standards. Sexual suggestiveness is quite restricted, and accentuation of the body is frowned upon, as in making inviting remarks or sitting with the legs spread. In addition, body contact is usually considered taboo and alcoholic beverages are forbidden (Weinberg, 1971).

Most participants report being surprised upon first visiting a nudist camp to find that they readily adjust to nudity and experience little or no self-consciousness in socializing with others while nude (Weinberg, 1971). A problem that often faces nudists however is that the practice is not accepted in most social circles. As a result, they majority of nudists keep their nudity secret because they fear the social consequences if it were known. Because of the stigmatization of nudists by many others in our society, it is not surprising that most nudists, like others whose behavior violate sexual taboos, lead something of a double life and feel isolated from much of the rest of the society (Hartman & Fithian, 1971).

Nude Beaches

In contrast to the somewhat conservative, largely middle-aged individuals who belong to organized nudist camps, nude beaches are public rather than private, attract a younger group of participants, and do not enforce the rules for conduct found in most nudist camps. As a result, body contact and displays of affection are frequently encountered. In addition, alcohol and marijuana, although usually illegal, are often a part of the social environment at these beaches (Delora & Warren, 1977).

TRANSSEXUALISM

Transsexuals are individuals who consider themselves to be of the sex opposite their biological sex. A biological male who is a transsexual may feel that he is really a woman who happens to be trapped in a man's body. Similarly, a female transsexual feels she is really a man encased in the body of a woman. The experience is not new in our time; in Greek mythology Venus Castina was the goddess who responded with sympathy and understanding to those feminine souls who were locked up in male bodies.

Socarides (1977) claims that transsexualism may be characterized by: (1) an intense insistence and overriding wish for sexual transformation into a person of the opposite sex. Such a transformation may be effected directly through surgical alteration of the external and internal sexual apparatus and secondary sex characteristics of the body, and indirectly through the administration of endocrinological preparations. (2) The conviction that one is basically of the opposite sex; (3) Concomitant behavior imitative of the behavior of the opposite sex such as alteration in dress, interests, attitudes, and choice of sexual objects. In part, this is a desperate attempt to strengthen the wish for a transformation; (4) The insistent search for surgical transformation, even to the point of self-inflicted mutilation.

Transsexuals should not be confused with transvestities or homosexuals. Transsexuals, unlike transvestites, usually feel relaxed rather than sexually aroused when dressed in the clothing of the opposite sex (Green, 1971). The vast majority of transsexuals do not identify with the homosexual community and may even be hostile to it. A homosexual is attracted to people of the same sex, but transsexuals consider themselves to be heterosexual because they feel they do not belong to their biologically assigned sex and are therefore actually attracted to people of the opposite sex (Delora & Warren, 1977). Transsexuals are relatively rare in our society; most are male. Estimates of the ratio of the two sexes in the transsexual population range from 95 percent male and 5 percent female to 50 percent male and 50 percent female (Block & Tessler, 1973).

Variations in Gender Identity

Case histories of transsexuals indicate that their cross-gender identification begins in childhood and continues into adulthood. Money and Primrose (1968) studied 14 male transsexuals, 12 of whom had undergone sex-reassignment surgery, and found that in every case the men had been regarded as "sissies" during childhood. All 14 transsexuals expressed a strong wish to adopt children, though their preference was for small children rather than new born babies.

> In general, the group appeared to possess a feminine gender identity, except for a masculine threshold of erotic arousal in response to visual imagery and an unmotherly disengagement from the helplessness of the new born. (p. 472)

Money and Brennan (1968) studied the performance of six female transsexuals on a personality inventory and found a relatively high score on masculinity and a low score on femininity. The subjects had also not shown girlist interests in childhood such as playing with dolls; they were described as having been "tomboys," prone to fighting with boys and playing "rough." Five of the females were living as males, and all showed hatred of their breasts and rejection of pregnancy and motherhood.

Etiology of Transsexualism

Research indicates that most cases of transsexualism appear to be established early, probably during the first three years of life, and are highly resistant to change. One hypothesis is that there is a sex center in the brain that directs the organism's development as male or female, and that this development always starts as female, becoming male only when adequate male hormones are secreted during an early critical period in development (Coleman, 1972). However, this hypothesis is based on evidence from studies of lower mammals. Whether such a "sex center" actually does exist in the human brain and whether a comparable pattern of virilization takes place in human development are not presently known (Coleman, 1972).

Behavioral theories frequently cite the role of early learning as important in the etiology of transsexualism. Lukianowicz (1959) suggests four instances in early development that may account for the etiology of many transsexuals.

1. *Dressing of children in the garb appropriate to the opposite sex.* Many male transsexuals report being dressed in girl's clothes until the age of three or four years.

2. *Cross-dressing for punishment.* On occasion some transsexuals will report being dressed in clothing of the opposite sex as punishment for some wrong doing. This is especially true with males, since only feminine dress for men has a humiliating connotation in our culture.

3. *The favored status of "a little girl."* Lukianowicz (1959) claims that some male transsexuals attempt to participate in the preferential sex and thus pretend to belong to it.

4. *Close contact with a female.* Some transsexuals report being reared by mothers, aunts, or grandmothers, with no opportunity to model male behavior. It is thus expected in these cases that transsexual behavior is the result of an identification with a parent of the opposite sex.

Modifications of Transsexualism

No form of psychological intervention has been shown to be consistently effective in modifying transsexualism. Pauley (1965), for example, reports 26 cases in which a change in sexual identify was unsuccessfully attempted through dynamic psychotherapy. Nor has behavior therapy fared much better. Gelder and Marks (1969) treated both transsexuals and transvestitites by electrical shock for cross-dressing in an aversion therapy program. Although 18 of 20 transvestites were not cross-dressing at followup, all five transexuals continued to cross-dress and request sex change through surgery.

Surgical Treatment. The vast majority of transsexuals who come to clinicians for treatment are referred for surgical transformation. F. Z. Abraham is said to have performed the first transsexual operation in the 1930s. While occasional reports of similar operations were forthcoming for the next two decades, it was not until 1953, when Hamburger reported the case of Christine Jorgensen, that surgical sex reassignment became well known. Johns Hopkins University Hospital and the University of Minnesota Hospital were among the first in this country to give official support to sex change surgery; each has since had thousands of requests from individuals for evaluations and management of their cases.

The surgical transformation of a woman to a man requires a complex, three-stage course of surgery that takes at least six months to a year. The breasts and internal sex organs are first removed. A scrotum is made from labial tissue and filled with plastic testicles. A penis is next created in stages; First a skin graft from the abdominal wall is built into a tube that hangs down to enclose an artificial urethra, and then the clitoris is embedded in the artificial penis so that the capacity for orgasm is retained. At best the penis is not very large or realistic, and it cannot become erect; to penetrate a vagina it must be given artificial support.

The surgical mechanics of the male-into-female operation involve amputation of the penis with resultant transsection of the urethra; perieneal dissection like that used in a perineal prostatectomy, in order to secure a suitable vaginal cavity; and lining of this cavity posteriorly with a still-attached flap of scrotal skin and anteriorly with a flap developed from the ventral skin of the penis, after which the newly created space is packed to prevent contraction. A vaginal form must be worn continuously by the patient for at least three months postoperatively and on a less constant basis for another three months. At the end of this time the vaginal size should be maintainable with physiological dilation two or three times a week. The greatest postoperative problem is the narrowing of the vagina; in a majority of cases this can be treated successfully with dilation by the physician. Weekly injections of sex hormones stimulate breast development, give more feminine texture to the skin and also lessen beard growth, though electrolysis is usually needed to remove excess hair.

Various evaluative studies of the outcome of such operations have been reported, perhaps the best known being that of Benjamin (1966). This investigator interviewed 50 transsexuals who had their gender surgically changed from male to female. Their ages at the time of surgery ranged from 19 to 58 years, with an average of 32 years. Of the subjects, 44 reported contentment sexually and socially with their new roles as women; five complained either about their ability to perform sexually or about their appearance; and one was totally dissatisfied with the results. In a similar study Pauley (1968) reviewed the postoperative course of 121 male transsexuals who had received sex reassignment surgery and found that satisfactory outcomes outnumbered unsatisfactory ones at a ratio of 10 to 1.

Behavior Therapy. Behavior therapy, like other psychological interventions, has not been resoundingly successful in the modification of transsexualism. The one exception is a comprehensive and detailed behavioral treatment program reported by Barlow et al. (1973).

The patient was a 17-year-old male who was a disappointment to his mother since she desired a girl. Nevertheless, he became her favorite child. His father worked long hours and had little contact with the boy. For as long as the patient could remember he had thought of himself as a girl. Spontaneous cross-dressing, as reported by the patient and confirmed by his parents, began before the age of five years and continued into junior high school. The patient's mother reported that during this time he developed an interest in knitting, cooking, crocheting, and embroidering; and that he was scolded by his older brother for his distaste of masculine activities like hunting. In his sexual fantasies, which developed about 12 years of age, he pictured himself as a female having intercourse with a male.

Upon referral the patient was moderately depressed, withdrawn, and attending secretarial school where he was the only boy in his class. He was reported to have a strong desire to change his sex. When he was informed that surgery was not possible at his age, he agreed to enter a treatment program designed to change his gender identity on the premise that it might at least make him more comfortable and that surgery was always possible at a later date.

Barlow et al. (1973) report that early attempts to depress deviant arousal and transsexual interest through aversion therapy failed, as did attempts to increase heterosexual arousal. At this point an attempt was made to modify the patient's extremely effeminate motor behavior, for which he was often ridiculed. To this end, a behavioral checklist of gender-specific motor behaviors was developed by observing males and females in the natural environment and noting characteristic ways of sitting, walking, and standing chosen on the basis of uniqueness to sex. Direct modification of sitting, standing, and walking was then attempted by modeling and videotape feedback. Independent raters judged that the patient learned to behave in a more masculine manner while sitting, standing, and walking.

Vocal characteristics that were initially feminine were next modified to masculine through a series of feedback and reinforcement techniques. Upon successful completion, assessment revealed that all desire for change of sex was absent and male sex role behavior relatively strong. Patterns of sexual arousal, however, were still homosexual, and procedures to increase heterosexual arousal and suppress homosexual arousal which had failed nearly a year before were once again introduced. Unlike the first attempt, this procedure was effective and the client assumed a heterosexual orientation which was maintained at a one-year followup.

CHAPTER 12

Legal, Ethical, and Professional Issues

The treatment of sexual dysfunctions and deviations represents involvement in one of the most exploitable, sensitive, intimate, and explosive aspects of a patient's life. Therefore, the legal, ethical, and professional issues which should be of the uppermost concern to all health-care professionals should become even more important to the clinician tho treats sexual cases. In this chapter we will briefly discuss some of these issues, recognizing that many of the questions to be raised have no definitive agreed-upon solutions.

LEGAL ISSUES

Legislation of sexual behavior dates back to ancient times, certainly to the time of the Old Testament (Hyde, 1979). Throughout history attempts to regulate public morals have been the rule in countries in which the Judeo-Christian tradition is influential. Contemporary thought generally regards most sexual behavior as a private matter of concern only to those involved, but historically sex has been seen as a matter which very much affects society and therefore as a fit subject for law. Not all restrictions are historical. For example, on June 13, 1969, a jury in Patterson, New Jersey found a man and a woman guilty on three counts of fornication; that is, the defendants were convicted of a crime of sexual intercourse between consenting unmarried adults. According to Municipal Judge Ervan F. Jushner, "I saw a crime being committed when an unmarried woman walked into my courtroom pregnant."

Legislation governing sexual behavior between consenting adults may seem somewhat unnecessary, but other types of sex laws are probably legitimate and necessary. Herbert Packer (1968) argues that the following might be rationally included in law: protection "against force and equivalent means of coercion to secure sexual gratification, protection of the immature against sexual exploitation, and the prevention of conduct that gives offense or is likely to give offense to innocent bystanders," (p. 16).

While it is generally agreed that sexual behavior that involves force or children or that constitutes some sort of public nuisance should continue to be prohibited by law, there is obvious disagreement among legislators, psychologists, and the courts on how offenders should be dealt with under the law. Individuals who commit offenses of the sort to be described in this section are generally designated legally as *sexual psychopaths*. It should be noted however that this phrase does not correspond to any well-defined and accepted constellation of behaviors recognized by clinical psychologists or psychiatrists. Rather, it is a legal term that poses some of the same problems as does the legal term "insanity," which also does not correspond to any particular form of mental illness (Katchadourian & Lunde, 1972). The elements that appear to constitute sexual psychopathy under the law include compulsiveness, repetition, and a certain bizarre, or disconcerting quality in sexual behavior.

Thirty of the 50 states and the District of Columbia now have laws applicable to sexual psychopaths (Katchadourian & Lunde, 1972). The first state to pass such a law was Michigan, in 1935. Most of these laws as written incorporate two important factors. First is the *indeterminate sentence,* under which the sexual psychopath can be imprisoned or hospitalized for the rest of his life or any lesser period depending on the attitude of the court. The indeterminate sentence is supposedly acceptable on the grounds that society must be protected from habitual sex criminals and that the court, with the assistance of prison wardens, hospital administrators, state psychologists and psychiatrists, should prohibit the criminal from being released early and re-enacting the crime. However, some research indicates that the only group of individuals convicted of major crimes and having recidivism rates lower than those of sex offenders are those convicted of homicides. The Report of the New Jersey Commission on the Habitual Sex Offender (1965) indicated that among the 7 percent of sex offenders who do repeat their offenses the majority are nonviolent offenders such as voyeurs, exhibitionists, and homosexuals.

The second significant factor in the laws on sexual psychopaths is the recognition of sex offenders as *mentally ill* and in need of treatment or rehabilitation rather than punishment. Many times the provisions for treatment are part of an indeterminate sentence so that the offender is sentenced to confinement and treatment until he is no longer considered a menace to society. However, many individuals are sentenced to prison for sexual offenses and offered none or only inadequate treatment by poorly trained and overworked paraprofessionals. To our knowledge California is the only state to provide a special institution to deal with the legally convicted sexual psychopath at Atascadero State Hospital.

We will describe here some of the legal aspects of specific sexual offenses that are considered as sexual psychopathy. Details on the kinds of individuals and behavior patterns involved in these offenses have been described in previous chapters.

Public Nuisance Offenses

Behaviors subsumed under the general category of public nuisances include exhibitionism, voyeurism, and transvestism. These behaviors do not involve physical contact with victims, and as far as voyeurism is concerned, the victim may be totally unaware that a crime has even taken place. These acts are considered criminal on the grounds that they offend public decency, disturb the peace, violate community standards of taste and delicacy, and tend to subvert and corrupt the morals of the people. Statutes governing these behaviors are by and large vague; they punish acts that are offensive, or likely to be offensive, to someone. Probably the greatest controversy over this general category of offenses involves exhibitionism. Here is a typical statute from the New Jersey State Penal Code:

314. *Indecent Exposure*—Every person who willfully and lewdly, either
1. Exposes his person, or the private parts thereof, in any public place, or in any place where there are present persons to be offended or annoyed thereby; or
2. Procures, counsels, or assists any person so to expose himself or take part in any model artist exhibition, or to make any other exhibition of himself to public view, or the view of any number of persons, such as if offensive to decency, or is adapted to excite to vicious or lewd thoughts or acts, is guilty of a misdemeanor.
Upon the second and each subsequent conviction under subdivision 1 of this section, or upon a first conviction under subdivision 1 of this section after a previous conviction under Section 288 of this code, every person so convicted is guilty of a felony, and is punishable by imprisonment in the state prison for not less than one year.

Various ambiguities in the wording of such laws are apparent. One is that a person can be convicted of indecent exposure for an offense that occurs in comparative privacy, as long as someone present claims to have been offended. There have also been instances in which no one present was offended, yet the person or persons involved were convicted of indecent exposure. Most of these cases involved people bathing in the nude, sunbathing in their backyards, or frequenting nudist camps (Boggan, Haft, Lister, & Rupp, 1975). Conviction of a public nuisance offense may carry penalties of from 30 days to 5 years in jail with fines of $5.00 to $5,000.00.

Homosexuality

Being sexually aroused and attracted to members of the same sex is not illegal in any state. In fact, laws defining various common homosexual behaviors (oral-genital contacts, anal intercourse, mutual masturbation) as crimes do not specify the sexes of the participants. However, the sexual acts involved in most homosexual contacts are illegal whether performed by a man and woman (adultery, fornication), two men, or two women. Homosexuals, and particularly male homosexuals, are prosecuted far more often than heterosexuals for engaging in these criminal behaviors (Rosenblatt & Pariente, 1973).

The legal penalties for these offenses can be quite severe but relatively few homosexuals are arrested for such violations, probably because most homosexual contacts take place in private and the participants are thus protected by the search-and-seizure provisions of the Constitution. When homosexuals are arrested, the arrest is usually the result of the criminal acts transpiring in public places such as rest rooms, theaters, or parked automobiles. In approximately 90 percent of these arrests the criminal act is oral-genital contact (Katchadourian & Lunde, 1972). While this act is usually considered a felony, judges in many states are authorized to reduce the charges to a misdemeanor. Anal intercourse is considered a felony in most all states, and few states allow judges to reduce the charge.

In many cases homosexuals are arrested not for engaging in a specific criminal act but for solicitation or loitering in public places. For example, the California Criminal Code reads:

> 647. *Disorderly Conduct Defined—Misdemeanor.*—Every person who commits any of the following acts shall be guilty of disorderly conduct, a misdemeanor:
>
> (a) Who solicits anyone to engage in or who engages in lewd or dissolute conduct in any public place or in any place open to the public or exposed to public view.
>
> (b) Who loiters in or about any toilet open to the public for the purpose of engaging in or soliciting any lewd or lascivious or any unlawful act.
>
> 650 ½. *Injuries to persons, Property, Public Peace, Health or Decency; False Personation for Lewd Purpose.*—A person who willfully and wrongfully commits any act which seriously injures the person or property of another, or which seriously disturbs or endangers the public peace or health, or which openly outrages the public decency, . . . for which no other punishment is expressly prescribed by this code, is guilty of a misdemeanor.

A highly controversial mode of homosexual arrest involves Section 647a of this California Criminal Code. In many instances police use young and attractive decoys who loiter in public rest rooms or similar locations for the express purpose of enticing homosexuals to solicit "a lewd and lascivious act.'' The arrest is usually made by a second officer who stations himself close by, and the first officer serves as a witness against the defendant. Many consider this mode of police work entrapment, that is bringing a person to commit a criminal act which he would not otherwise commit. Entrapment is also a technique frequently used when arresting prostitutes.

Arrest and conviction are far more likely to affect the male homosexual than the lesbian, probably because of the rather prevalent belief that male homosexuals are likely to commit crimes of voilence and crimes against children. Although research does not substantiate this belief (Gebhard et al., 1965), the idea persists. In an effort to control the behavior of homosexuals and other persons convicted of sexual offenses some states require the registration of convicted individuals. For example, the California State Penal Code:

> 290. *Person Convicted of Certain Lewd Crimes Must Register with Sheriff—Facts to State.*—Any person who, since the first day of July, 1944, has been or is hereafter convicted in the State of California of the offense of assault with intent to commit rape or the infamous crime against nature, under Section 220, or of any offense defined in Sections 266, 267, 268, 285, 286, 288, 288a, subdivision 1 of Section 647a, subdivision 3 or 4 of Section 261, subdivision (12) (a) or (d) of Section 647, or subdivision 1 or 2 of Section (14) 314 of this code or of any offense involving lewd and lascivious conduct . . . shall within 30 days after the effective date of this section or within 30 days of his coming into any county or city, or city and county in which he resides or is temporarily domiciled for such length of time register with the chief of police in the city in which he resides or the sheriff of the county if he resides in an unincorporated area.

This requirement for registration and disclosure renders the convicted homosexual susceptible to being picked up for questioning and generally harassed whenever a sex crime has been committed in the area in which he is living. In addition, homosexuals are generally prohibited from holding jobs that require security clearance or involve the handling of sensitive information. This requirement is thought to be based on the idea that such individuals are both unreliable and vulnerable to extortion and blackmail (Katchadourian & Lunde, 1972).

Crimes Against Children

Laws that seek to prevent the sexual exploitation of children are often difficult to prosecute since, in many cases, the only witnesses are children who are not always able to provide reliable, consistent evidence necessary for conviction (Slovenko, 1965). Most states have laws against what is termed *carnal knowledge of a juvenile* or *statutory rape*. These laws prohibit a male over the age of 17 or 18 from having intercourse with a female under the age of consent. The age of consent may be as young as 12 or as old as 17. The law applies regardless of consent or of the victim's previous sexual history (Slovenko, 1965). As noted in the chapter on Pedophilia, such laws make it possible for an 18-year-old male to be arrested for engaging in intercourse with his 16-year-old girlfriend.

Child molestation laws prohibit certain acts (other than intercourse) with the "immature." Such laws are usually extremely vague, and cover physical or genital contact, use of sexual language, exhibitionism, or showing a child pornography (Slovenko, 1965). The California State Penal Code for example, states:

> 288. *Exciting Lust of Child Under Age of Fourteen.*—Any person who shall willfully and lewdly commit any lewd or lascivious act including any of the acts constituting other crimes provided for in part one of this code upon or with the body, or with any part or member thereof, of a child under the age of fourteen years, with the intent of arousing, appealing to, or gratifying the lust or passions or sexual desires of such person or of such child, shall be guilty of a felony and shall be imprisoned in the State prison for a term of from one year to life.

Finally, all 50 states have laws against incest. The law usually treats incest in special statutes prohibiting marriage or sexual activity between immediate family members and relatives of varying degrees of consanguinity. This offense is most always considered a felony and is punishable by as much as 50 years in prison in some states (Slovenko, 1965).

Rape and Related Offenses

Sexual intercourse with a woman other than a spouse under conditions of force or threat of force is considered one of the more serious of all sexual offenses under criminal law. Penalties for rape vary from prison sentences of several years to life in confinement, and in some states include a death sentence. Although capital punishment has not been carried out in cases of rape in recent years, from 1930 to 1948 over 300 men were executed for rape in the United States (Katchadourian & Lunde, 1972).

There are a number of difficulties in defining rape, as illustrated by the following California statute:

> 261. *Rape—Acts Constituting.*—Rape is an act of sexual intercourse, accomplished with a female not the wife of the perpetrator, under either of the following circumstances:
> 1. Where the female is under the age of eighteen years;

2. Where she is incapable, through lunacy or other unsoundness of mind, whether temporary or permanent, of giving legal consent;

3. Where she resists, but her resistance is overcome by force or violence;

4. Where she is prevented from resisting by threats of great and immediate bodily harm, accompanied by apparent power of execution, or by any intoxicating narcotic, or anesthetic substance, administered by or with the privity of the accused;

5. Where she is at the time unconscious of the nature of the act, and this is known to the accused;

6. Where she submits under the belief that the person committing the act is her husband, and this belief is induced by any artifice, pretense, or concealment practiced by the accused, with intent to induce such belief.

262. *Minor Under 14 Presumed Incapable of.*—No conviction for rape can be had against one who was under the age of fourteen years at the time of the act alleged, unless his physical ability to accomplish penetration is proved as an independent fact, and beyond a reasonable doubt.

263. *Essential Elements—Penetration.* The essential guilt of rape consists in the outrage to the person and feelings of the female. Any sexual penetration, however slight, is sufficient to complete the crime.

264. *Punishment.*—Rape is punishable by imprisonment in the State prison not less than three years, except where the offense is under subdivision 1 of section 261 of the Penal Code, in which case the punishment shall be either by imprisonment in the county jail for not more than one year or in the State prison for not more than 50 years, and in such case the jury shall recomment by their verdict whether the punishment shall be by imprisonment in the county jail or in the State prison; provided, that when the defendant pleads guilty of an offense under subdivison 1 of section 261 of the Penal Code the punishment shall be in the discretion of the trial court, either by imprisonment in the county jail for not more than one year or in the State prison for not more than 50 years.

One difficulty in defining rape involves the question of consent by the the female. If a woman is seriously ill, mentally retarded, or rendered unconscious by a blow to the head or by a drug, it is evident that she is incapable of granting responsible consent. However, in the vast majority of cases the issue is far from being that clear. Suppose, for example, that a man has intercourse with a woman he met at a bar after both had been drinking heavily. That the man was drunk at the time is no defense, yet the woman can claim that because she was drunk (even though voluntarily), she was incapable of giving responsible consent though she offered no resistance. According to the manner in which many state sex laws are written, the man can be legally charged with rape (Katchadourian & Lunde, 1972).

Another controversial aspect of many of the laws that prohibit rape is the amount of resistance a woman must put up in order to prove that she did resist the attack. Some courts require evidence that the woman adamantly resisted while others do not emphasize the point so greatly. Some courts appear to believe that a woman should resist rape to the utmost, while others believe that considerable resistance may result in additional bodily harm to the woman. Many states allow the victim's prior sexual activities to be considered as evidence of her consent, an allowance that many people feel results in putting the victim on trial. The women's movement has argued that reform of rape laws is desperately needed to protect women from what they consider to be a crime of aggression rather than a sexual crime (Brownmiller, 1975).

Criminal Commercial Sex

The law has also deemed it illegal to make money from sex, at least in certain circumstances. While it is not illegal to sell products with subtle promises of sexual fulfillment, it is illegal to actually provide such fulfillment either in direct form, as in prostitution, or indirect form, as in pornography. Prostitution is the only sexual offense for which women are prosecuted to any significant extent. In itself this phenomenon is interesting, for the most common form of prostitution involves women performing sexual services for men in return for money, and it is men who write and administer the law in our society. Prostitution can exist only because men demand such services. Many people never question whether instead of being a criminal offense prostitution should not be decriminalized and governed, controlled, and taxed by local and state governments.

The laws dealing with prostitution are numerous and encompass various types of behavior. The most common form of prosecution is for the offense of soliciting. Soliciting is usually vaguely defined to include a wide range of behaviors as the following statute from the Colorado Penal Code attests:

> Any prostitute or lewd woman who shall, by word, gesture or action, endeavor to ply her vocation upon the streets, or from the door or window of any house, or in any public place, or make a bold display of herself, shall be guilty of a misdemeanor, and shall be fined not more than $100 or imprisoned in the county jail for not less than ten days nor ore than three months, or both.

Individuals involved in the enterprise of prostitution are also subject to legal arrest since they are often viewed as profiting most from the practice and considered the major exploiters of prostitutes. They include procurers, pimps, operators, facilitators of houses of prostitution, and those who traffic in women. These activites are usually covered under state law but may violate federal law (the Mann Act) if women are transported across state lines for "immoral and illegal purpose."

Prostitution is illegal in every jurisdiction in the United States with the exception of Nevada where counties may vote to legalize the practice. Laws prohibiting prostitution have proved so difficult to enforce that the world's oldest profession goes on unabated.

Therapist-Patient Relationship in Criminal Sexual Behavior

The therapist who plans to treat individuals with sexual deviations should recognize and carefully consider the potential problems of confidentiality and privileged information that may surface in the therapist-patient relationship. Consider, for example, a rapist or pedophile who reports engaging in criminal sexual behavior during the course of treatment. Does the therapist respect the patient's rights of confidentiality and privileged communication and risk a criminal charge of being an accessory to a crime? Or does he/she violate the patient's rights by reporting the incident(s) to authorities and risk a lawsuit by the patient for violating the rights of a professional relationship?

We attempt to avoid this uncertain situation by carefully explaining to the patient during the initial interview that whether or not he/she is accepted as a patient is contingent, in part, on agreement to halt all illegal sexual behavior during the course of treatment. This agreement is subsequently incorporated into a written contract between the therapist and the patient, which clearly stipulates that the patient agrees that violation of the contract may necessitate the therapist's reporting the patient's behavior to the authorities. We recognize that this procedure is not ideal, since the patient may simply avoid reporting his or her behavior; however, we feel that it does impress upon the patient the necessity of halting criminal behavior and, according to legal opinion, does protect the therapist from legal recourse. While less serious behaviors such as voyeurism and exhibitionism may not require such measures, we feel that protection of the patient, the therapist, and the public from more serious criminal sexual offenses is warranted. Professional judgment, of course, must be exercised.

ETHICAL AND PROFESSIONAL ISSUES

The treatment of sexual disorders is fast becoming a highly exploitive and financially lucrative practice. In this situation, serious and ethical practitioners and researchers must be aware of a number of important ethical and professional issues which are directly related to the specialty of practice and research.

The Practice of Sex Therapy

In the 1940s and 1950s clinical psychologists and psychiatrists had little to offer those individuals suffering from sexual dysfunctions or deviations.

American psychology and psychiatry were primarily Freudian and psycho-analytic. However, the late 1950s saw the advent of short-term approaches based on learning theory, stressing direct behavioral retraining procedures in the here and now. These novel approaches were remarkably successful, with reported success rates of 60–80 percent, but were for the most part ignored by both professionals and the media. It was only with the publication of the book *Human Sexual Inadequacy* (Masters & Johnson, 1970) that the general public as well as many professionals became aware of this new form of effective sex therapy (LoPiccolo, 1977).

In the years since 1970 interest in sexual disorders and sex therapy has increased. This increase is due, in part, to the effectiveness of behavioral techniques of treatment as well as the publicity of sex therapy in the media. As a result, increasing numbers of individuals are seeking sex therapy. This sharp increase has created a number of problems, however, among them a drastic shortage of competently trained professionals to deal with the number of individuals requesting sex therapy. This supply and demand imbalance has caused a number of ethical and professional problems.

Who Should Practice Sex Therapy? The publicity about behavior therapy for sexual dysfunctions and deviations has undoubtedly meant that a number of individuals have been able to get direct and effective modification of their disordered sexual behaviors. On the other hand, this publicity has also attracted many unqualified "therapists" into the field. As incredible as it may seem, anyone may call himself/herself a sex therapist and practice in any state in the United States. He/she need not hold a doctorate in clinical psychology or medicine, or have any formal training whatsoever. He/she need not have a masters degree, college diploma, or high school diploma, or even have completed elementary school. He/she must pass no boards or examinations and must convince no one of his/her competency. He/she may practice ethically or unethically and need answer to no one. In order to practice sex therapy one need only title himself/herself a "sex therapist," purchase a business license, and lease an office. Having done so, he/she may legally treat problems whose etiology may be associated with a complex interplay of psychological variables, systemic, local, and genital diseases, endocrine and neurological disorders, pelvic pathology, and surgical conditions. With little or no training, sex therapists may legally dabble, counsel, suggest, recommend, attempt to alter, and assume responsibility for one of the most exploitable, sensitive, intimate, and explosive aspects of a patient's life. Unfortunately, many apparently do. Masters and Johnson (1977) claim that the practice of sex therapy:

> . . . is dominated by an astounding assortment of incompetents, cultists, mystics, well-meaning dabblers, and outright charlatans. . . . Approximately 3,500 to 5,000 new "clinics," "treatment centers," and "practices" devoted to sex problems have been established in the United States in the last six years.

Of these, the most charitable estimates cite perhaps 100 that are legitimate. Our instinct says that 50 would be a better guess . . . . Only 50 out of a possible 500 offer treatment methods that have been developed with proper scientific care; have been subjected to long, conscientious testing and evaluation; and are administered by trained, fully competent personnel. The rest of the clinics offer little more than a superficial sex education at best and dangerous quackery at worst. They offer unevaluated theories, mystical cant, pop-psychological remedies, and simplistic pseudoscience. Although some of the untested approaches sound imaginative, appealing, and interesting, and some of the practitioners can present seductive sounding justification for their theories, few or none can offer a truly believable promise that they will lighten your sexual difficulties. They can promise only to lighten your wallet. (p. 6)

There are presently at least two schools of thought concerning who is qualified to practice sex therapy. On the one hand, the established mental health professionals tend to argue that sex therapy is a set of specialized procedures for use only by trained therapists competent and licensed to engage in psychotherapy at the independent practitioner level. On the other hand, a number of the new sex therapists argue that sex therapy is a separate new profession. The point of view held by many if not most clinical psychologists and psychiatrists is that sex therapy is a subspecialty of psychotherapy. It logically follows, then, that only those persons who are qualified by experience and training and who have passed licensing examinations should be doing sex therapy. Sexual dysfunctions and deviations do not exist in a vacuum; they are often related to a number of psychological and medical conditions. The complex interplay of variables that may exist in sexual disorders frequently taxes the competency and ability of clinical psychologists and psychiatrists who have had years of supervised training. Given the complexity involved in many cases, we find it difficult to see how treatment by lesser trained paraprofessionals or individuals with no formal training is in the best interest of the patient.

It should not be assumed, however, that the practice of sex therapy is a bipolar phenomenon with competent and well-trained clinical psychologists and psychiatrists on one end and quacks and con men representing the other. The legitimacy of sex therapists may best be described as a continuum, with trained and competent clinical psychologists and psychiatrists at one end; clinical psychologists and psychiatrists who have not had adequate and supervised training in the treatment of sexual disorders along with health educators, social workers, sociologists, clergy, and experimental, educational, and counseling psychologists, and nurses in the middle; and the incompetent exploiters at the other end.

In an effort to protect the public by insuring competency and by regulating who may practice sex therapy as an adjunct to other medical and psychological treatments or as a full-time specialty, some national associations have tried to institute certification of sex counselors and therapists. The reasons why this has failed may be due to the multiplicity of disciplines practicing sex therapy; the fact that certification by professional associations carries no legal implications; and the unfortunate fact that practically anyone can meet the ill-defined, ambiguous requirements that characterize most of the certification agencies. For example, Patricia Schiller, an attorney, is director and founder of the American Association of Sex Educators, Counselors, and Therapists (AASECT). One of the largest professional associations in the field of sex therapy, this group's membership has grown from 1,700 members in 1974 to over 4,500 members in 1977 (Wykert, 1977). Certification as a "Sex Therapist" by this group requires nothing more than a doctorate (M.D., Ph.D., Ed.D., D.D., D.D.S., Th.D., J.D.); a Masters degree in a clinical field (counseling, social work, nursing,); or attendance at a AASECT sponsored workshop if the degree is not in a clinical field; 1000 hours as a paid sex therapist or the equivalent; a written examination; and attendance at a two-day workshop where "the applicant will have an opportunity to sift through and sort out his/her attitudes and values concerning human sexuality." The certificate costs $50.00 and "may be framed and displayed," and annual dues are $25.00. There may be those who think highly of this group's certification, but most discount its standards and value. Other certifying associations include the Eastern Association of Sex Therapists, Family Services Association of America, and the National Council on Family Relations.

Fees and Third Party Payment. Fifteen hours of outpatient psychotherapy in the United States generally costs somewhere between $600 and $900. Fifteen hours of sex therapy from one of the many new sex therapy centers or clinics runs between $2,500 and $5,000 (LoPiccolo, 1977). The explanations offered by these expensive clinics do not appear to justify their outrageous fees, especially since many sex therapists often have less formal training and experience than do clinical psychologists and psychiatrists. In addition, those clinical psychologists and psychiatrists who treat sexual disorders as a subspecialty of their practice invest no more additional time in training to treat sexual disorders than is required in their formal training programs. The clinician treating sexual disorders also is not required to purchase significantly more expensive equipment than most behavior therapists—for instance, a polygraph, or electrical aversion stimulators. Many clinics utilize a male and female cotherapy team, expecially in the treatment of sexual dysfunctions, but research has indicated that a single therapist can be as effective as cotherapy teams (Kaplan, 1974). Therefore, the reasons usually offered to explain the higher fees of specialty practitioners—longer training, expensive equipment, and the use of a cotherapy team—do not appear to be rationally related to the four to five times higher fee frequently charged for treatment of sexual disorders. To expect patients to pay this much is both unreasonable and unethical.

It would appear that the United States is moving slowly toward a system of national health care. As a result the issues of licensing mental health practitioners and determining who will qualify for reimbursement under such a program are currently the focus of much lobbying in Washington. If coverage of mental health problems—including sexual dysfunctions and deviations—under national health care insurance is to become a reality, someone must first make some hard decisions concerning *who* may provide psychotherapy.

If the problems of which practitioners should be eligible is resolved, it is still doubtful that treatment of sexual dysfunctions and some forms of sexual deviation would be covered. Most private insurance companies pay for professional services rendered by clinical psychologists and psychiatrists, but remuneration for the treatment of marital and/or sexual problems is usually specifically excluded. Some clinical psychologists and psychiatrists probably give their sexually dysfunctional and sexually deviant patients fradulent diagnoses on insurance forms so that the insurance company will pay for the cost of therapy, and the patient will be spared the embarrassment of a diagnosis of sexually deviance. This practice may represent questionable ethics, but LoPiccolo (1977) makes the point that it is unreasonable for anxiety and depression caused by job problems to be covered by insurance while treatment of anxiety and depression caused by marital or sexual problems is not. LoPiccolo adds that given the social and monetary costs of broken marriages (welfare aid to dependent children, tying up the court system with divorce cases, and so on) as a result of sexual dysfunctions as well as sexual deviations, including court trials and incarceration, the inclusion of sexual disorders as a legitimate form of mental health care performed by competent and well-trained professionals might be a bargain at almost any price.

Sexual Activity Between Clinician and Patient. The treatment techniques used with sexual disorders as described in this text have a firm theoretical basis in learning and behavior therapy and are empirically based in that they have a body of research substantiating their efficacy. In direct contrast to this scientific approach is a growing trend for the treatment of sexual disorders that include some form of quasi-sexual or direct sexual contact between the clinican and the patient (LoPiccolo, 1977). A description of and the ethics involved in these types of therapies have been described in Chapters 3, 4, and 5; here let us simply add that in all procedures involving nudity, touching, and sexual activity between the patient and the therapist even the most charitable observer must question the therapist's motives for using such procedures. We know of no data substantiating the effectiveness and utility which leads us to believe that a major factor in the decision to use such procedures is the therapist's enjoyment and pleasure rather than the welfare of the patient.

Sexual Surrogates. The International Professional Surrogates Association is an organization primarily of women who make their services available to those who wish to use them. The clinical efficacy of using sexual surrogates in the treatment of sexual disorders and the ethical issues involved in their use remains a sharply divided and controversial topics. For example, the use of surrogates with those patients who do not have a sexual partner is a logical and beneficial procedure, according to the advocates of surrogate therapy. However, as previously discussed in Chapter 3, Holden (1974) has described the use of sexual surrogates as nothing more than "thinly veiled prostitution." Advocates of surrogate therapy claim high success in the treatment of sexual disorders, but scientific data that substantiates the generalization of treatment gains from the surrogate to a real life sexual partner are almost nonexistent. Until a legal interpretation governing the use of sexual surrogates is rendered, clinicians should take notice that many law enforcement personnel may consider the practice illegal.

Confidentiality. Safeguarding information about an individual that has been obtained by the psychologist in the course of teaching, practice, or investigation is a primary obligation of psychologists, according to Principle 6 of the *Ethical Standards of Psychologists* (APA, 1972). The intimate, personal qualities most people attach to information about their sexuality requires that therapists working with sexual disorders exercise extraordinary precautions to protect the confidentiality of knowledge gained in the course of evaluation, treatment, and followup of patients.

Under the sponsorship of Masters and Johnson's Reproductive Biology Research Foundation, a conference on the ethical issues of sex therapy and research led to a set of guidelines. These guidelines were formulated primarily for therapists working with sexual dysfunctions, but the issues of confidentiality are appropriate and pertinent for therapists treating sexual deviations as well:

1. There is a general responsibility on the part of sex therapists to treat all information received in a therapist-client relationship as confidential, even if some portions of the information appear trivial, irrelevant, or not to require confidentiality.

2. The very existence of a therapist-client relationship is a confidential matter, since there are circumstances under which the identification of such a relationship would imply the presence of sexual problems or difficulties on the part of the client.

3. Information received by the sex therapist from a client or prospective client or from diagnostic evaluation, treatment, or follow-up of a client may be divulged to the extent required only in the following circumstances:

a. When the client provides written consent (except when the information has been obtained from another person whose privacy would be violated by unauthorized disclosure). Special precautions should be taken when the release of confidential information has a high risk of being harmful to the client.

b. When there is clear and imminent serious danger to the life or safety of an individual and when no other reasonable alternative can be found. In such an instance, disclosure should be made only to appropriate family members, public authorities, or professional workers (in assessing the necessity for such an action, it is permissible for the therapist to consult with other professionals, including a lawyer, as long as the consultation protects the identity of the client involved).

c. When such information is required to defend the sex therapist, employees or associates of the sex therapist, or the institute or employer of the sex therapist against formal accusation (for example, court proceedings or hearings of an organizational ethics committee) by the client of wrongful conduct.

4. In cases in which a subpoena is served to obtain confidential information about a client, sex therapists should protect their material by claiming a privileged relationship in jurisdictions where this privilege is recognized. When such privilege is not clearly recognized, the sex therapist may obtain legal counsel and attempt to resist the subpoena. A sex therapist who believes that an unjustified violation of the confidentiality and trust of the therapist-client relationship would occur if such material were divulged under legal ediction in response to a subpoena may properly refuse to comply and will not be viewed as acting in other than an ethical manner within the context of these guidelines.

5. If a sex therapist wishes to use identifiable information about a client or materials related to the evaluation, treatment, or follow-up of a client for purposes of education, training, research, or publication, the express free and informed consent of the client must be obtained.

6. A sex therapist may discuss in a professional manner information about a client or matters related to the evaluation, treatment, or follow-up of a client for purposes of consultation with professional colleagues, when there is reasonable assurance that the identity of the client will not be disclosed.

7. Since the normal functions of an office, clinic, agency, or institution where sex therapy may be conducted include exposure of confidential information to persons who are neither sex therapists nor health-care professionals, particularly secretaries, students, trainees, and assistants, it is important that the degree of this exposure be minimized insofar as possible and that careful methods be used to select employees, students, and trainees. Sex therapists should specifically instruct such persons in areas related to confidentiality.

8. Sex therapists are responsible for planning and maintaining the confidentiality of all client-related records, including (but not limited to) correspondence, evaluation notes, results of diagnostic testing, notes about therapy sessions, tape recordings (audio or audiovisual), and case summaries. This responsibility extends to the ultimate disposition of such confidential records.

9. It is permissible for sex therapists to provide such information about a client to an outside agency as is necessary for matters of accounting, bookkeeping, data processing, banking, collecting, duplicating, microfilming, printing, or other legitimate purposes. Care should be exercised in the selec-

tion of such an agency, and the agency should be notified of the strict need for confidentiality.

10. When sex therapy involves one or more therapists working with a client couple, whether married or not, unusual circumstances pertaining to confidentiality may arise. In such instances. considerations apply:

a. Disclosure of information that one client has requested be kept confidential from his or her partner should not be made without the express consent of the person providing the confidential information.

b. When only one client of a client couple provides consent to the release of confidential records or information, the sex therapist is responsible for releasing only information about the consenting client and must protect the confidentiality of all information deriving from the nonconsenting client.

11. When sex therapy is done in a group therapy format, special and complex circumstances pertaining to confidentiality may apply. It is important for sex therapists to recognize this risk and inform prospective clients of it. Group therapy leaders should remain alert to the potential loss of confidentiality when other clients, not bound by professional ethics, may learn information of a private, intimate, or secret nature.

12. All considerations related to confidentiality in the sex therapist-client relationship continue after the termination of this relationship.

Research in Sex Therapy

Research in human sexuality requires that researchers conduct their investigations with respect for the dignity, rights, and welfare of their subjects. Principle 16 of the *Ethical Standards of Psychologists* (APA, 1972) states that

the decision to undertake research should rest upon a considered judgment by the individual psychologist about how best to contribute to psychological science and to human welfare. The responsible psychologist weighs alternative directions in which personal energies and resources might be invested. (p.6)

Every research proposal involving human sexuality should be carefully screened for ethical issues and is never justified solely on the basis of outcome data. These considerations should apply whether the research is in conjunction with clinical treatment or not.

The Ethics Congress sponsored by the Reproductive Biology Research Foundation (1978) issued the following outline for the ethical welfare of subjects involved in sexual research:

1. Sex research should be carried out only by persons qualified to do such investigations or under the direct supervision of persons so qualified.

2. For each research project, a person or persons who assume the ethical and scientific responsibility for the conduct of the investigation should be designated and identified to potential subjects (in writing whenever practicable).

3. All research that places human subjects at risk should be designed to require the free and informed consent of these subjects. Such requirement consists of the following:

a. The general purposes, procedures, and details of study participation are explained accurately to the potential subject.

b. The physical, social, psychological, legal, and economic risk of study participation are fully and accurately described to the potential subject, along with a description of any potential benefits.

c. The potential subject must be free to choose whether or not to participate, without any element of coercion, force, or deceit.

d. The potential study subject must be aware of his or her right to withdraw from the study at any time without prejudice.

e. If the study is in a context of clinical treatment, the subject must be assured that his or her decision not to participate or to withdraw will not affect his or her continuing treatment.

f. The researcher should attempt to ensure that the subject understands the points outlined above.

4. When subjects have diminished capacity (e.g., children, the mentally retarded, and the mentally ill), diminished autonomy (e.g., prisoners and students), or increased vulnerability to social consequences (e.g., transsexuals and minority groups), the investigator should attempt to obtain from those subjects consent that is as informed and voluntary as the circumstances permit. In these instances the researcher has a compelling responsibility to observe safeguards that perserve the rights, dignity, and welfare of subjects.

a. In the case of those legally incompetent and/or incapable by reason of diminished capacity, participation in research requires the informed permission of legal guardians and the assent of subjects to the degree possible. That permission can be validly granted if no more than minimal risk to subject is involved or if more than minimal risk is justified by potential direct benefit to the subject.

b. In sex research involving adolescents, similar principles apply, except that permission of parents or guardians need not be obtained if risk is minimal.

c. In the case of persons whose freedom of choice is limited by institutionalization or other constraints, subjects may participate after giving informed consent only when there are adequate guarantees that no undue inducement or coercion exists. In such circumstances it is desirable that an outside advocate be available to subjects.

d. In the case of persons particularly vulnerable to social consequences as a result of participation in research, the investigator must inform them of that risk.

5. Sex researchers must protect the confidentiality of research data, including the identity of participants.

a. All information obtained by the researcher is confidential except information in the public realm or information that cannot be linked to the specific subject.

b. The investigator must take adequate measures to ensure that subjects' participation or identities are not revealed through exposure of records, publication, presentation, or other means.

c. All research-related records must be maintained with diligent and continuing attention to safeguarding confidentiality. It is the responsibility of the sex researcher to ensure his protection in regard to data collection, data processing, data analysis, and, finally, the disposition of research records.

d. Potential research subjects should be informed of the limits that may apply to confidentiality, such as the possibility of access to research records by subpoena.

e. All considerations related to confidentiality in sex research remain in effect on conclusion of a subject's participation in a study and after the study has been completed.

f. Information received from a research subject may be divulged to the extent required only in the following circumstances:

(1) When the subject provides written consent

(2) When there is clear and imminent serious danger to the life or safety of an individual and when no other reasonable alternative can be found

(3) When the information is required to defend the sex researcher, employees or associates of the sex researcher, or the institute or employer of the sex researcher against formal accusation by the research subject of wrongful conduct

6. Sex researchers should strive for honesty and accuracy in their dealings with research subjects. Concealment or deception may be used as a part of the research design only when alternate methodologies have been considered and found inadequate. In such cases, unless the risk is minimal *and* there is potential direct therapeutic benefit, subjects must be informed during the consent process that concealment or deception may be used. Explanation of the specific nature of the concealment or deception must be made as soon as possible after the subject's participation has ended.

7. The researcher has a dual responsibility to protect the welfare of subjects and to provide or arrange treatment for adverse physical or psychological effects that may occur during or after the study as a result of research participation, if the subject desires such treatment. Although this responsibility encompasses all phases of research, it applies specifically to situations of research in a context of therapy in which a subject is assigned to a no-treatment group, placebo control group, or minimal-treatment group and a determination is made that failure to receive full treatment is producing adverse consequences.

8. Research subjects are entitled to an explanation of the results and pur-

poses of their participation in the study, including an opportunity to react to the research, ask questions, and receive responses.

9. Research involving the risk of medical complications should be conducted only when adequate medical resources are readily available.

10. It is recommended that sex research protocols be submitted to an institutional review board for evaluation of ethical propriety. Investigators not affiliated with an institution that has an accredited review board are encouraged to arrange voluntarily to have their protocols reviewed and to accept the judgment of the reviewing body.

A Guide to Choosing a Sex Therapist

Given the problems that exist in treating sexual deviations and dysfunctions, how can an individual or couple with a sexually related problem locate a competent and qualified therapist? Unfortunately, there is no way to guarantee insure competency, but several precautions may be listed.

1. Insure that the prospective therapist is licensed and trained as a clinical psychologist or psychiatrist. Note that the title *psychologist* is a generic term similar to the title *physician*. Just as there are a number of specialties of physicians—neurologist, dermatologist, psychiatrist—so too are there a number of specialties of psychologists—clinical, social, experimental, counseling. Because of the chaotic state of licensing laws in most states, practically all psychologists can meet the minimum requirements for licensure, including those psychologists whose training has been mainly laboratory or academic. Only the *clinical* psychologist receives intensive applied, research, and academic training in the diagnosis and treatment of emotional and certain physical disorders. Of course, not all clinical psychologists and psychiatrists are competently trained in the treatment of sexual disorders, but a patient who goes to one of these specialists does insure that he has a certain amount of legal protection that may prove to be important. Employees of state agencies are often exempt from licensure, so this suggestion is less relevant if therapy is being sought at a university-based therapy program.

2. Do not seek treatment from therapists or clinics who advertise in any medium. In most states, clinical psychologists and psychiatrists are prohibited by law from advertising for patients. On the other hand, stories about university or medical school programs for treating sexual disorders are not considered advertising, and they are often a very good way to locate a competent therapist.

3. Investigate the qualifications and training of the therapist. In addition to holding state licensure, the clinical psychologist may be board-certified by the American Board of Professional Psychology (ABPP); the psychiatrist may be board-certified by the American Board of Psychiatry and

Neurology. Find out if the therapist has received extensive supervised training in the treatment of sexual deviations and dysfunctions. A competent and qualified therapist will welcome the investigation of his/her credentials.

4. A referral by a family doctor, minister, or other professional or a call to the county or state psychological or medical association may help, but will not guarantee the competency of the therapist. Often individuals will refer patients to their friends or acquaintances without thought as to whether the therapist has specialized training in the treatment of sexual deviations and/or dysfunctions. Psychological and medical associations may be required to offer the names of two or three therapists who are members of the association and who may, or may not, be trained in the modification of sexual disorders. A telephone call to a university-based department of clinical psychology or psychiatry is most often the best way to locate a competently trained and qualified therapist.

References

Abarbanel, A. R. Diagnosis and treatment of coital discomfort. In J. LoPiccolo & L. LoPiccolo (Eds.) *Handbook of sex therapy.* New York: Plenum Press, 1978.

Abbott, M. S., & Love, J. V. Children of incest. *Pediatrics,* 1972, *40,* 55–62.

Abel, G., Barlow, D., Blanchard, E., & Guild, D. *The components of rapist's sexual arousal.* Paper presented at the 128th Annual Meeting of the American Psychiatric Association, Anaheim, California, May 5, 1977.

Abel, G. G., Barlow, D. H., Blanchard, E.B., & Mavissakalian, M. Measurement of sexual arousal in male homosexuals: Effects of instructions and stimulus modality. *Archives of Sexual Behavior,* 1975, Vol. 4, No. 6.

Abel, G., Blanchard, E., Barlow, D., & Movissakalian, M. Identifying specific erotic cues in sexual deviations by audiotaped descriptions. *Journal of Applied Behavior Analysis,* 1975, *8,* 247-260.

Abel, G., Levis, D., & Clancy, J. Aversion therapy applied to taped sequences of deviant behavior in exhibitionists and other sexual deviations: A preliminary report. *Journal of Behavior Therapy and Experimental Psychiatry,* 1970, *1,* 59–60.

Abelson, J. H. Apprenticeship in prostitution. *Social Problems,* 1974, *12,* 287-297.

Adams, H. E., Doster, J. A., & Calhoun, K. S. A psychological based system of response classification. In A. R. Cimminero, K. S. Calhoun, & H.E. Adams (Eds.). *Handbook of behavior assessment.* New York: Wiley, 1977.

Adams, H. E., & Sturgis, E. T. Status of behavioral reorientation techniques in the modification of homosexuality: A review. *Psychological Bulletin,* 1977, *84,* 1171–1188.

Adams, H. E., & Sturgis, E. T. Status of behavioral reorientation techniques in modification of homosexuality: A review. *Psychological Bulletin,* 1978, *84* (6), 1171–1188.

Aiken, D. L. Ex-sailor charges jail rape, stirs up storm. *The Advocate,* Sept. 26, 1973, 203–209.

Allen C. *A textbook of psychosexual disorders.* London: Oxford University Press, 1962.

Allen, C. *A textbook of psychosexual disorders.* London: Oxford University Press, 1969.

Amelar, R.D. Therapeutic approaches to impotence in the male: Urologic aspects of the therapeutic approach to impotence. *Journal of Sex Research,* 1971, *7,* 163–167.

American Psychiatric Association. *Diagnostic and statistical manual of mental disorders* (3rd. ed.). Washington, D.C.: American Psychiatric Association, 1978.

401

American Psychological Association. *Ethical standards of psychologists.* Washington, D.C.: American Psychological Association, 1972 (revised).

Amir, M. *Patterns in forcible rape.* Chicago: University of Chicago Press, 1971.

Annon, J. S. The extension of learning principles to the analysis and treatment of sexual problems. *Dissertation Abstracts International,* 1971, *32* (6B), 3627.

Annon, J. *The behavioral treatment of sexual problems: Brief therapy.* New York: Harper & Row, 1976.

Annon, J. S., & Robinson, C. H. The use of vicarious learning in the treatment of sexual concerns. In J. LoPiccolo & L. LoPiccolo (Eds.), *Handbook of sexual therapy.* New York: Plenum Press, 1978.

Apfelbaum, B. *Theoretical and clinical issues in individual body-work sex therapy.* Paper presented at the University of California Conference on Progressive Issues in the Use of Surrogate Partners in Sex Therapy, May 1976.

Apfelberg, B., Sugar, C., & Pfeffer, A. A psychiatric study of 250 sex offenders. *American Journal of Psychiatry,* 1944, *100,* 762–770.

Argyle, M. *Social interaction.* London: Methuen, 1967.

Arkowitz, H., Lichtenstein, E., McGovern, K., & Hines, P. The behavioral assessment of social competency in males. *Behavior Therapy,* 1975, *6,* 3–13.

Athanasiou, R., Shaver, P., & Travis, C. Sex. *Psychology Today,* July, 1970, 39–52.

Azrin, N. H., & Holtz, W. C. Punishment. In W. K. Honig (Ed.), *Operant behavior: Areas of research and application.* New York: Appleton-Century-Crofts, 1966.

Baer, D. M. Some current dimensions of applied behavioral analysis. *Journal of Applied Behavioral Analysis,* 1971, *1,* 91–97.

Bagley, C. Incest behavior and incest taboo. *Social Problems,* 1968, *16,* 505–508.

Baker, D., Telfer, M.A., & Richardson, C.E. Chromosome errors in men with antisocial behavior. *Journal of American Medical Association,* 1970, *214,* 869–878.

Bancroft, J. Aversion therapy of homosexuality. *British Journal of Psychology,* 1969, *115,* 1417–1431.

Bancroft, J. A comparative study of aversion and desensitization in the treatment of homosexuality. In L. E. Burns & J. L. Worsley (Eds.), *Behavior therapy in the 1970s.* Bristol, England: Wright, 1970.

Bancroft, J. The application of psychophysiological measures to the assessment and modification of sexual behavior. *Behavior Research and Therapy,* 1971, *9,* 119–130.

Bancroft, J., Jones, H. G., & Pullan, B. P. A simple transducer for measuring penile erection with comments on its use in the treatment of sexual disorders. *Behavior Research and Therapy,* 1966, *4,* 239–241.

Bancroft, J., & Matthews, A. Autonomic correlates of penile erection. *Journal of Psychosomatic Research,* 1971, *15,* 159–167.

Bandura, A. *Principles of behavior modification.* New York: Holt, Rinehart & Winston, 1969.

Bandura, A. Analysis of modeling processes. In A. Bandura (Ed.), *Psychological modeling: Conflicting theories.* New York: Aldine-Atherton, 1971.

Bandura, A., Blanchard, E. B., & Ritter, R. The relative efficacy of desensitization and modeling apparatus for inducing behavioral, affective, and attitudinal changes. *Journal of Personality and Social Psychology,* 1969, *13,* 173–199.

Bandura, A., & Menlove, F. L. Factors determining vicarious extinction of avoidance behavior through symbolic modeling. *Journal of Personality and Social Psychology,* 1969, *8,* 99–108.

Banks, W. C. The effects of perceived similarity upon the use of reward and punishment. *Journal of Experimental Social Psychology,* 1976, *12,* 131–138.

Barker, J. C., & Miller, M. E. Some clinical applications of aversion therapy. In H. Freeman (Ed.), *Progress in behavior therapy.* Bristol, England: Wright, 1968.

Barlow, D. H. The treatment of sexual deviation: Towards a comprehensive approach. In K. S. Calhoun, H. E. Adams, & K. M. Mitchell (Eds.), *Innovative treatment methods in psychopathology.* New York: Wiley, 1974.

Barlow, D. Assessment of sexual behavior. In A. R. Ciminero, K. S. Calhoun, & H. E. Adams (Eds.), *Handbook of behavioral assessment.* New York: Wiley, 1977.

Barlow, D. H., Abel, G. G., Blanchard, E. B., Bristow, A. R., & Young, L. D. A heterosocial skills checklist for males. *Behavior Therapy,* 1977, *8,* 229–239.

Barlow, D. H., & Agras, W. S. Fading to increase heterosexual responsiveness in homosexuals. *Journal of Applied Behavior Analysis,* 1973, *6,* 355–367.

Barlow, D., Becker, R., Leitenberg, H., & Agras, S. A mechanical strain gauge for recording penile circumference change. *Journal of Applied Behavior Analysis,* 1970, *3,* 73–76.

Barlow, D., Leitenberg, H., & Agras, H. S. The experimental control of sexual deviation through manipulation of the noxious scene in covert sensitization. *Journal of Abnormal Psychology,* 1969, *74,* 596–601.

Barlow, D. H., Reynolds, E. H., & Agras, W. S. Gender identitiy change in a transsexual. *Archives of General Psychiatry,* 1973, *28,* 569–579.

Barr, R. G., & McConaghy, N. Penile volume responses to appetitive and aversive stimuli in reaction to sexual orientation and conditioning performance. *British Journal of Psychiatry,* 1971, *119,* 377–383.

Barr, R. F., Raphael, B., & Hennessey, N. Apparent heterosexuality in two male patients requesting change of sex operations. *Archives of Sexual Behavior,* 1974, *3,* 325–330.

Barron, R. A., & Byrne, D. *Social psychology: Understanding human interaction.* Boston: Allyn & Bacon, 1977.

Bartel, G. D. Group sex among mid-Americans. *Journal of Sex Research,* 1970, *6,* 113–130.

Bartholomew, A. A. A long acting phenothiazine as a possible agent to control deviant sexual behavior. *American Journal of Psychiatry,* 1968, *124,* 917–923.

Bartlett, R.G. Physiologic responses during coitus. *Journal of Applied Physiology,* 1956, *9,* 469–471.

Bass, B. A. Sexual arousal as an anxiety inhibitor. *Journal of Behavior Therapy and Experimental Psychiatry,* 1974, *5,* 151–152.

Batchelor, I. R. C. *Textbook of psychiatry.* London: Oxford University Press, 1969.

Bates, J. E., & Bentler, T. M. Play activities of normal and effeminite boys. *Developmental Psychology,* 1973, *9,* 20–27.

Bates, J. E., Bentler, T. M., & Thompson, S. Measurement of deviant gender development in boys. *Child Development,* 1973, *44,* 591–598.

Beech, H. R., Watts, F., & Poole, A. D. Classical conditioning of a sexual deviation: A preliminary note. *Behavior Therapy,* 1971, *2,* 400–402.

Begelman, D. A. The ethics of behavioral control and a new mythology. *Psychotherapy: Theory, research and practice,* 1971, *8,* 165-169.

Begelman, D. A. Ethical and legal issues of behavior modification. In M. Hersen, R. Eisler, & P. M. Miller (Eds.), *Progress in behavior modification.* New York: Academic Press, 1975.

Bem, S. L. The measurement of psychological androgyny. *Journal of Consulting and Clinical Psychology,* 1974, *42,* 155-162.

Benjamin, H. Transvestism and transsexualism. *International Journal of Sexology, 7,* 12, 1953.

Benjamin, H., & Masters, R. E. L. *Prostitution and morality.* New York: Julian Press, 1964.

Benjamin, H. *Prostitution and morality.* New York: Grove Press, 1966.

Bentler, P. M. Heterosexual behavior assessment—II females. *Behavior Research and Therapy,* 1968, *6,* 27-30.

Berg, A. *The sadist.* New York: Medical Press of New York, 1954.

Bergler, E. Analysis of an unusual case of fetishism. *Bulletin of the Menninger Clinic,* 1946, *2,* 67-75.

Bernick, N., Kling, A., & Borowitz, G. Physiological differentiation, sexual arousal, and anxiety. *Psychosomatic Medicine,* 1968, *65,* 427-433.

Bernstein, L., Bernstein, R. S., & Dana, R. H. *Interviewing: A guide for health professionals.* New York: Appleton-Century-Crofts, 1974.

Berscheid, E., & Walter, E. A little bit about love. In T. L. Huston (Ed.), *Foundations of interpersonal attraction.* New York: Academic Press, 1974.

Beaumont, P. J. V., Corker, C. S., & Friesen, H. G. The effects of phenothiazines on endocrine functions: Effects in men and post-menopausal women. *British Journal of Psychiatry,* 1974, *124,* 420-430.

Bieber, I. *Homosexuality: A psychoanalytic study of male homosexuals.* New York: Basic Books, 1962.

Bieber, I. On behavior therapy: A critique. *Journal of the American Academy of Psychoanalysis,* 1973, *1,* 39-52.

Bieber, I. Homosexuality: The ethical challenge. *Journal of Consulting and Clinical Psychology,* 1976, *44,* 163-166.

Bieber, B., Bieber, I., Dain, H. J., Dince, P. R., Drellich, M. G., Grand, H. G., Frundlach, R. H., Kremer, M. W., Wilber, C. B., & Bieber, T. D. *Homosexuality.* New York: Basic Books, 1963.

Binet, A. *Etudes de psychologie experimentale.* Paris, 1888.

Block, N. L., & Tessler, A. N. Transsexualism and surgical procedures. *Medical Aspects of Human Sexuality,* 1973, *7,* 158-161.

Blumer, D., & Benson, D. F. Personality changes with frontal and temporal lobe lesions. In D. Blumer & D. F. Benson (Eds.), *Psychiatric aspects to neurological disease.* New York: Grune & Stratton, 1975.

Boggan, E. C., Haft, M. G., Lister, C., & Rupp, J. P. *The civil rights of gay people.* New York: Discus Books, 1975.

Bond, I. K., & Evans, D. R. Avoidance therapy: Its uses in two cases of underwear fetishism. *Canadian Medical Association Journal,* 1967, *20,* 1160-1162.

Bond, I. K., & Hutchison, H. C. Application of reciprocal inhibition therapy to exhibitionism. *Canadian Medical Association Journal,* 1960, *83,* 23-25.

Borkovec, T. D., Stone, N. M., O'Brien, G. T., & Kaloupek, D. Evaluation of a clinically relevant target behavior for analog outcome research. *Behavior Therapy,* 1974, *5,* 503–513.

Brady, J., & Levitt, E. The scalability of sexual experiences. *Psychological Record,* 1965, *15,* 275–279.

Brain, W. R., & Walton, J. N. *Brain's diseases of the nervous system* (7th ed.). London: Oxford University Press, 1969.

Brenner, J. *Asexualization: A follow-up study of 244 cases.* Oslo, Norway: Oslo University Press, 1973.

Brodsky, C. M. Rape at work. In M. J. Walker & S. L. Brodsky (Eds.), *Sexual assault: The victim and the rapist.* Lexington, Mass.: Lexington Books, 1976.

Brown, C. C. The techniques of plethysmography. In C. C. Brown (Ed.), *Methods in psychophysiology.* Baltimore: Williams & Wilkins, 1967.

Brown, D. G. Sex-role development in a changing culture. *Psychological Bulletin,* 1958, *35,* 232–242.

Brown, D. G. Female orgasm and sexual inadequacy. In R. Brecker & F. Brecker (Eds.), *An analysis of human sexual response.* New York: Signet Books, 1966.

Brownell, K. D., & Barlow, D. H. Measurement and treatment of two sexual deviations in one person. *Journal of Behavior Therapy and Experimental Psychiatry,* 1976, *7,* 349–354.

Brownell, K. D., Hayes, S. C., & Barlow, D. H. Patterns of appropriate and deviant sexual arousal: The behavioral treatment of multiple sexual deviations. *Journal of Consulting and Clinical Psychology,* 1977, *45,* 1144–1155.

Brownmiller, S. *Against our will: Men, women, and rape.* New York: Simon & Schuster, 1975.

Bryan, J. H. Apprenticeships and prostitution. *Social Problems,* 1965, *12,* 278–297.

Bryan, J. H. Occupational ideologies and individual attitudes of call girls. *Social Problems,* 1966, *13,* 441–450.

Buckner, H. T. The transvestic career path. *Psychiatry,* 1970, *33,* 381–389.

Burgess, A. W., & Holmstrom, L. L. Rape trauma syndrome. *American Journal of Psychiatry,* 1974, *131,* 981–986.

Burgess, T. D., & Sales, S. M. Attitudinal effects of more exposure: A re-evaluation. *Journal of Experimental Social Psychology,* 1971, *7,* 461–472.

Byrne, D., Rasche, L., & Kelley, K. When "I like you," indicates disagreement: An experimental differentiation of information and affect. *Journal of Research in Personality,* 1974, *8,* 207–217.

Caird, W. K., & Wincze, J. P. Videotaped desensitization of frigidity. *Behavior Research and Therapy,* 1974, *5,* 175–178.

Caird, W. K., & Wincze, J. P. *Sex therapy: A behavioral approach.* Hagerstown, Md.: Harper & Row, 1977.

Caprio, F. S. "Fetishism." In A. Ellis & A. Abarbanel (Eds.), *Encyclopedia of sexual behavior.* New York: Jason Aronson, 1973.

Cassity, J. H. Psychological considerations of pedophilia. *Psychoanalytic Review,* 1927, *14,* 189–199.

Cautela, J. R. Covert sensitization. *Psychological Record,* 1967, *20,* 459–468.

Cautela, J. R., & Wiscocki, P. A. The use of male and female therapists in the treatment of sexual behavior. In R. Rubin & C. Franks (Eds.), *Advances in behavior therapy.* New York: Academic Press, 1969.

Cavallin, H. Incest. *Sexual Behavior,* 1973, *3,* 19–21.

Chapman, J. D. Frigidity: Rapid treatment by reciprocal inhibition. *Journal of the American Osteopathic Association,* 1968, *67,* 871–878.

Chapman, L. J., Chapman, J. P., & Brelje, T. Influence of the experimental or pupillary dilation to sexually provocative pictures. *Journal of Abnormal Psychology,* 1969, *74,* 396–400.

Cheri, May 1978, 42.

Chesser, E. *Human aspects of sexual deviation.* London: Jerrolds Publishing, 1971.

Christensen, A., & Arkowitz, H. Preliminary report on practice dating and feedback as treatment for college dating problems. *Journal of Counseling Psychology,* 1974, *21,* 92–95.

Christensen, A., Arkowitz, H., & Anderson, J. Beaus for cupid's errors: Practice dating and feedback for college dating inhibitions. *Behavior Research and Therapy,* 1975, *13,* 321–331.

Ciminero, A. R. Behavioral assessment: An overview. In A. R. Ciminero, K. S. Calhoun, & H. E. Adams (Eds.), *Handbook of behavioral assessment.* New York: Wiley, 1977.

Ciminero, A. R., Nelson, R. O., & Lipinski, D. P. Self-monitoring procedures. In A. Ciminero, K. S. Calhoun, & H. E. Adams (Eds.), *Handbook of behavioral assessment.* New York: Wiley, 1977.

Clark, D. F. Treatment of fetishism by negative conditioning—A further note. *British Journal of Psychiatry,* 1963, *109,* 695–696.

Cohen, M. L., Garofalo, R., Boucher, R., & Seghorn, T. The psychology of rapists. *Seminars in Psychiatry,* 1971, *3,* 307–327.

Cohen, M.L., Seghorn, T., & Calmas, W. Sociometric study of the sex offender. *Journal of Abnormal Psychology,* 1969, *74,* 249–255.

Cohen, H. D., & Shapiro, A. A method for measuring sexual arousal in the female. *Psychophysiology,* 1970, *8,* 251–252.

Coleman, J. C. *Abnormal psychology and modern life.* New York: Scott, Foresman, 1972.

Comfort, A. *The joy of sex.* New York: Crown, 1972.

Cook, G. H. Problem of the criminal sexual psychopath. *Diseases of the Nervous System,* 1949, *10,* 137–142.

Cooper, A. J. A case of fetishism and impotence treated by behavior therapy. *British Journal of Psychiatry,* 1963, *109,* 649–652.

Cooper, A. J. A factual study of male potency disorders. *British Journal of Psychiatry,* 1968, *104,* 719–731.

Cooper, A. J. A clinical study of "coital anxiety" in male potency problems. *Journal of Psychosomatic Research,* 1969, *13,* 143–147.

Cooper, A. J. Treatments of male potency disorders: The present status. *Psychosomatics,* 1971, *12,* 235–244.

Corman, C. *Physiological response to a sexual stimulus.* Unpublished thesis, University of Manitoba, Canada, 1968.

Costell, R., & Yalom, I. Institutional group therapy. In H. L. Resnick & M. C.

Wolfgang (Eds.), *Sexual behavior: Social, clinical, and legal aspects.* Boston: Little, Brown, 1972.

Craighead, W. E., Kazdin, A. E., & Mahoney, M. J. *Behavior modification.* Boston: Houghton Mifflin, 1976.

Curran, J. P. An evaluation of a skills training program and a systematic desensitization program in reducing data anxiety. *Behavior Research and Therapy,* 1975, *13,* 65-68.

Curran, J. P. Skills training as an approach to the treatment of heterosexual-social anxiety: A review. *Psychological Bulletin,* 1977, *84,* 140-157.

Curran, J. P., & Gilbert, F. S. A test of the relative effectiveness of a systematic desensitization program and an interpersonal skills training program with date anxious subjects. *Behavior Therapy,* 1975, *6,* 510-521.

Curran, J. P., Gilbert, F. S., & Little, L. M. A comparison between behavioral training and sensitivity training approaches to heterosexual dating anxiety. *Journal of Counseling Psychology,* 1976, *23,* 190-196.

Curran, J. P., & Lippold, S. The effect of physical attraction and attitude similarity on attraction in dating dyads. *Journal of Personality,* 1975, *43,* 528-539.

Davies, B. M., & Morganstern, F. S. A case of cysticercosis, temporal lobe epilepsy, and transvestism. *Journal of Neurology and Neurosurgical Psychiatry,* 1960, *23,* 247-249.

Davis, A. J. Sexual assault in the Philadelphia prisons and sheriff's vans. *Transaction,* 1968, *6,* 28-35.

Davis, G. *The pretenders.* New York: World, 1969.

Davis, S. K., & Davis, P. W. Meaning and process in erotic offensiveness: An exposé on exposées. *Urban Life:* Special issue on *sexuality, encounter, identities, and relationships,* October 1976, 671-677.

Davison, G. Elimination of a sadistic fantasy by a client-controlled counterconditioning technique: A case study. *Journal of Abnormal Psychology,* 1968, *73,* 84-90.

Davison, G. C. A message from the president. *Association for Advancement of Behavior Therapy Newsletter,* 1974, *1,* 1-3.

Davison, G. C. Homosexuality: The ethical challenge. *Journal of Consulting and Clinical Psychology,* 1976, *44,* 157-162.

Dearborn, C. Behavior therapy of the sexual disorders. *Journal of Sexual Research,* 1967, *3,* 49-61.

Delora, J. S., & Warren, C. A. *Understanding sexual interaction.* Boston: Houghton Mifflin, 1977.

DiScipio, W. Modified progressive desensitization and homosexuality. *British Journal of Medical Psychology,* 1968, *41,* 267-272.

Dix, G. E. Determining and continued dangerousness of psychologically abnormal sex offenders. *Journal of Psychiatry and Law,* 1975, *3,* 327-344.

Dollard, J., & Miller, N. E. *Personality and psychotherapy.* New York: McGraw-Hill, 1950.

Dryer, P. I., & Church, R. W. Reinforcement of shock induced fighting. *Psychonomic Science,* 1970, *18,* 147-148.

East, W. N. Sexual offenders. *Journal of Nervous and Mental Disorders,* 1946, *103,* 626–666.

Edwards, N. B. Case conference: Assertive training in a case of homosexual pedophilia. *Journal of Behavior Therapy and Experimental Psychiatry,* 1972, *3,* 55–63.

Ellis, A. The effectiveness of psychotherapy with individuals who have severe homosexual problems. *Journal of Consulting Psychiatry,* 1958, *20,* 191–195.

Ellis, A., & Brancale, R. *The psychology of sex offenders.* Springfield, Ill.: Charles C Thomas, 1956.

Ellis, A., & Sagarin, E. *Nymphomania: A study of the oversexed woman.* New York: Guilbert Press, 1964.

Ellison, C. Vaginismus. *Medical Aspects of Human Sexuality,* 1972, *6,* 34–54.

Endler, N. S., Hunt, J., & Rosenstein, A. J. An S-R inventory of anxiousness. *Psychological Monographs,* 1962, *76,* 112–118.

Epstein, A. W. Fetishism: A study of its psychopathology with particular reference to a proposed disorder in brain mechanisms as an etiological factor. *Journal of Nervous and Mental Disorders,* 1960, *130,* 107–119.

Epstein, A. W. Relationship of fetishism and transvestism to brain and particularly to temporal lobe dysfunction. *Journal of Nervous and Mental Disease,* 1961, *133,* 247–253.

Evans, D. R. Exhibitionism. In C. G. Costello (Ed.), *Symptoms of Psychopathology.* New York: Wiley, 1970.

Evans, R. B. Sixteen personality factor questionnaire scores of homosexual men. *Journal of Consulting and Clinical Psychology,* 1968, *34,* 212–215.

Eysenck, H. J., & Rachman, S. *The causes and cures of neurosis.* San Diego, Calif.: R. Knapp, 1966.

Feldman, M. P. Aversion therapy for sexual deviations: A critical review. *Psychological Bulletin,* 1966, *65,* 65–79.

Feldman, M. P., & MacCulloch, M. J. The application of anticipatory avoidance learning to the treatment of homosexuality. I. Theory, technique and preliminary results. *Behavior Research and Therapy,* 1965, *2,* 165.

Feldman, M. P., & MacCulloch, M. J. *Homosexual behavior: Therapy and assessment.* Oxford: Pergamon Press, 1971.

Feldman, M., MacCulloch, M. J., Mellor, U., & Pinschoff, J. The application of anticipatory avoidance learning to the treatment of homosexuality: The sexual orientation method. *Behavior Research and Therapy,* 1966, *4,* 289–299.

Fenichel, O. *The psychoanalytic theory of neurosis.* New York: Norton, 1945.

Fenichel, O. The symbolic equation: Girl-phalus. *Psychoanalytic Quarterly,* 1949, *18,* 303–324.

Fesbach, S. Dynamics of morality of violence and aggression: Some psychological considerations. *The American Psychologist,* 1971, *26,* 281–291.

Festinger, L. *A theory of cognitive dissonance.* Stanford, Calif.: Stanford University Press, 1957.

Field, L. H. Benperidol in the treatment of sexual offenders. *Medical Science and Law,* 1973, *13,* 195–196.

Ford, C. S., & Beach, F. A. *Patterns of sexual behavior.* New York: Harper, 1951.

Forgione, A. G. The use of mannequins in the behavioral assessment of child molesters: Two case reports. *Behavior Therapy,* 1976, *7,* 678–685.

Freedman, J. L., Carlsmith, J. M., & Sears, D. O. *Social psychology.* Englewood Cliffs, N. J.: Prentice-Hall, 1974.

Freeman, W., & Mayer, R. G. A behavioral alteration of sexual preferences in the human male. *Behavior Therapy,* 1975, *6,* 206–212.

Freese, A. L. Group therapy with exhibitionists and voyeurs. *Social Work,* March 1972, 44–52.

Freud, S. Some psychological consequences of the anatomical distinction between the sexes. *International Journal of Psychoanalysis,* 1905, *8,* 133–142.

Freud, S. *Letters of Sigmund Freud.* New York: Basic Books, 1910.

Freud, S. Fetishism. *International Journal of Psychoanalysis,* 1928, *9,* 161–166.

Freud, S. Three essays on the theory of sexuality. *Standard Edition,* 1953, *7,* 125–243.

Freund, K. Diagnostika homosexuality u. muzu. *Ceskoslovenska Psychiatrie,* 1957, *53,* 382–393.

Freund, K. A laboratory method of diagnosing predominance of homo- or hetero-erotic interest in the male. *Behavior Research and Therapy,* 1963, *1,* 85–93.

Freund, K. Diagnosing homo- or heterosexuality and erotic age-preference by means of a psychophysiological test. *Behavior Research and Therapy,* 1967, *5,* 209–228.

Freund K. Erotic preferences in pedophiles. *Behavior Research and Therapy,* 1973, *5,* 339–348.

Freund, K., Langevin, R., Cibiri, S., & Zajac, Y. Heterosexual aversion in homosexual males. *British Journal of Psychiatry,* 1973, *122,* 163–169.

Freund, K., Nagler, E., Langevin, R., Zajac, A., & Steiner, B. Measuring feminine gender identity in homosexual males. *Archives of Sexual Behavior,* 1974, *3,* 249–261.

Freund, K., Sedlacek, F., & Knob, K. A single transducer for mechanical plethysmography of the male genitalia. *Journal of the Experimental Analysis of Behavior,* 1970, *8,* 169–170.

Friday, N. *Forbidden flowers.* New York: Pocket Books, 1975.

Friedman, A. *Hermaphrodeity.* New York: Knopf, 1973.

Friedman, D. The treatment of impotence by brevital relaxation therapy. *Behavior Research and Therapy,* 1968, *6,* 257–261.

Fuchs, K., Hoch, Z., Paldi, H., Abramovici, J. M., Brandes, J. R., Timor-Tritsch, I., & Kleinhaus, M. Hypnodesensitization therapy of vaginismus: In-vitro and in-vivo methods. *International Journal of Clinical and Experimental Hypnosis,* 1973, *21,* 144–156.

Gagnon, J. H. Female child victims of sex offenses. *Social Problems,* 1965, 176–192.

Gagnon, J. H., & Simon, W. Sexual deviance in contemporary America. *Annals of the American Academy of Political and Social Science,* 1968, *376,* 106–122.

Gagnon, J. H., & Simon, W. *Sexual conduct: The social resources of human sexuality.* Chicago: Aldine, 1973.

Gallary. Gallary feedback, August 1976, 46.

Gardner, E. *Fundamentals of neurology.* Philadelphia: W. B. Saunders, 1975.

Garfield, Z., McBrearty, J., & Dichter, M. A case of impotence successfully treated with desensitization combined with in-vivo operant training and thought substitution. In R. D. Rubin & C. M. Franks (Eds.), *Advances in behavior therapy.* New York: Academic Press, 1969.

Gaupp, L. A., Stern, R. M., & Ratliff, R. G. The use of aversion-relief procedures in the treatment of a case of voyeurism. *Behavior Therapy*, 1971, *2*, 585–588.

Gebhard, P. G. Factors in marital orgasm. *Journal of Social Issues,* 1966, *22*, 88–95.

Gebhard, P. H., Gagnon, J. H., Pomeroy, W. B., & Christenson, C. V. *Sex offenders: An analysis of types.* New York: Harper & Row, 1965.

Geen, R. G., & Pigg, R. Acquisition of an aggressive response and its generalization to verbal behavior. *Journal of Personality and Social Psychology,* 1970, *15*, 165–170.

Geer, J. H. Direct measurement of genital responding. *American Psychologist,* 1975, *30*, 415–418.

Geer, J. H., Morokoff, P., & Geenwood, P. Sexual arousal in women: The development of a measurement device for vaginal blood flow. *Archives of Sexual Behavior,* 1974, *3*, 359–366.

Geer, J. H., & Quartararo, J. D. Vaginal blood volume response during masturbation. *Archives of Sexual Behavior,* 1976, *5*, 403–413.

Gelder, M. G., & Marks, I. M. Aversion treatment in transvestism and transsexualism. In R. Green & J. Money (Eds.), *Transsexualism and sex reassignment.* Baltimore: Johns Hopkins University Press, 1969.

Glasgow, R., & Arkowitz, H. The behavioral assessment of male and female social competence in dyadic heterosexual interactions. *Behavior Therapy,* 1975, *6*, 488–498.

Glass, S. J., Deuel, H. J., & Wright, C. A. Sex hormone studies in male homosexuality. *Endocrinology,* 1940, *26*, 590–594.

Glaus, A. Zur lebensgeschichte eines transvestiten. *Psychiatry and Neurology,* 1952, *124*, 245–258.

Gold, S. A., & Neufeld, I. L. A learning approach to the treatment of homosexuality. *Behavior Research and Therapy,* 1965, *3*, 201–204.

Goldberg, G. N., Kiesler, C. A., & Collins, B. E. Visual behavior and face-to-face distance during interaction. *Sociometry,* 1969, *32*, 43–53.

Goldfried, M. R., & Linehan, M. M. Basic issues in behavioral assessment. In A. R. Ciminero, K. S. Calhoun, & H. E. Adams (Eds.), *Handbook of behavioral assessment.* New York: Wiley, 1977.

Goldfried, M. R., & Sprafkin, J. N. *Behavioral personality assessment.* Morristown, N. J.: General Learning Press, 1974.

Goldstein, A. Case conference: Conflict in a case of frigidity. *Journal of Behavior Therapy and Experimental Psychiatry,* 1971, *2*, 51–59.

Goldstein, M. Brain research and violent behavior. *Archives of Neurology,* 1975, *30*, 1-35.

Gough, H. G. Identifying psychological femininity. *Educational and Psychological Measurement,* 1952, *12*, 427–439.

Gough, H. G., & Heilbrum, A. B. *The Adjective Checklist Manual.* Palo Alto, Calif.: Consulting Psychologist Press, 1965.

Gould, L. *Such good friends.* New York: Random House, 1970.

Grant, V. W. A case of fetishism. *Journal of Abnormal Social Psychology,* 1953, *48*, 142–149.

Gray, J. J. Case conference: Behavior therapy in a patient with homosexual fantasies and heterosexual anxieties. *Journal of Behavior Therapy and Experimental Psychiatry,* 1970, *1*, 225–232.

Green R. Guidelines to the management of the transsexual patient. *Roche Reports,* 1971, *11,* 3–6.

Green, R. Homosexuality as mental illness. *International Journal of Psychiatry,* 1972, *10,* 77–98.

Greene, R., & Money, J. *Transsexualism and sex reassignment.* Baltimore: Johns Hopkins University Press, 1969.

Greenblatt, R. B., Jungck, E. C., & Blum, H. Endocrinology of sexual behavior. *Medical Aspects of Human Sexuality,* 1972, *6,* 110–131.

Greenson, R. R. *The technique and practice of psychoanalysis.* New York: International Universities Press, 1966.

Greenwald, H. *The call girl.* New York: Ballantine Books, 1970.

Greenwald, H., & Greenwald, R. *The sex-life letters.* New York: Bantam Books, 1973.

Guthrie, E. R. *The psychology of learning.* New York: Harper, 1952.

Guttmacher, M. S. *Sex offenses: The problems, causes and preventions.* New York: Norton, 1951.

Hackett, T. P. The psychotherapy of exhibitionists in a court clinic setting. *Seminar in Psychiatry,* 1971, *3,* 297–306.

Hadden, S. B. Treatment of male homosexuals in groups. *American Journal of Psychiatry,* 1966, *114,* 810–815.

Hamburger, C. The desire for change of sex as shown by personal letters from 465 men and women. *Archives of Endocrinology,* 1953, *14,* 361–375.

Hammer, E. G. A comparison of H, T, P's of rapists and pedophilics. *Journal of Projective Techniques,* 1954, *18,* 346–354.

Harbert, T. L., Barlow, D. H., Hersen, M., & Austin, J. B. Measurement and modification of incestuous behavior: A case study. *Psychological Reports,* 1974, *34,* 79–86.

Harbinson, J. J., Graham, P. J., Quinn, J. T., McAllister, H., & Woodward, R. A. A questionnaire measure of sexual intent. *Archives of Sexual Behavior,* 1974, *3,* 357–366.

Harbinson, J. J., Quinn, J. T., & McAllister, H. An attempt to share human penile response. *Behavior Research and Therapy,* 1970, *9,* 386–390.

Hartman, V. Notes on group therapy with pedophiles. *Canadian Psychiatric Association Journal,* 1965, *10,* 283–288.

Hartman, W. C., & Fithian, M. A. *Treatment of sexual dysfunction.* Long Beach, Calif.: Center for Marital and Sexual Studies, 1971.

Hastings, D. W. *Impotence and frigidity.* Boston: Little, Brown, 1976.

Hayes, S. H., Brownell, K. D., & Barlow, D. H. The use of self-administered covert sensitization in the treatment of exhibitionism and sadism. *Behavior Therapy,* 1978, *9,* 283–289.

Hedblom, J. H. Dimensions of lesbian sexual experience. *Archives of Sexual Behavior,* 1973, *2,* 329–341.

Henry, L. A. *Sexual behavior.* New York: Logan Books, 1948.

Hensen, D. E., & Rubin, H. B. Voluntary control of eroticism. *Journal of Applied Behavior Analysis,* 1971, *4,* 37–44.

Herman, S. H. *An experimental analysis of two methods of increasing heterosexual arousal in homosexuals.* Unpublished doctoral dissertation, University of Mississippi, 1971.

Herman, S. H., Barlow, D. H., & Agras, W. H. Exposure to heterosexual stimuli: An effecfive variable in treating homosexuality? *Proceedings of the 79th Annual Convention of the American Psychological Association,* 1971, 699-700.

Herman, S. H., & Prewitt, M. An experimental analysis of feedback to increase arousal in a case of homosexual and heterosexual impotence: A preliminary report. *Journal of Behavior Therapy and Experimental Psychiatry,* 1974, *5,* 271-274.

Hersen, M., & Bellak, A. S. Social skills training for chronic psychiatric patients: Rationale, research findings, and future directions. *Comprehensive Psychiatry,* 1976, *17,* 559-580.

Hersen, M., & Bellack, A. S. Assessment of social skills. In A. R. Ciminero, K. S. Calhoun, & H. E. Adams (Eds.), *Handbook of behavioral assessment.* New York: Wiley, 1977.

Hersen, M., & Eisler, R. M. Social skills training. In W. E. Craighead, A. E. Kazin, & M. J. Mahoney (Eds.), *Behavior modification: Principles, issues, and applications.* Boston: Houghton Mifflin, 1976.

Hess, E. H., Seltzer, A. L., & Shlien, J. M. Pupil response of hetero- and homosexual males to pictures of men and women: A pilot study. *Journal of Abnormal Psychology,* 1965, *70,* 165-168.

Heston, L., & Shields, J. Homosexuality in twins: A family study and a registry study. *Archives of General Psychiatry,* 1968, *18,* 149-160.

Hill, D., Pond, D. A., Mitchell, W., & Falconer, M. A. Personality changes following temporal lobectomy for epilepsy. *Journal of Mental Science,* 1957, *103,* 18-27.

Hirning, L. C. The sex offender in custody. In R. Linder & R. V. Seliger (Eds.), *Handbook of correction psychology.* New York: Philosophical Library, 1947.

Hirschfield, M. *Sexual anomalies.* New York: Emerson Books, 1956.

Hirschi, T. The professional prostitute. *Berkeley Journal of Sociology,* 1962, *7,* 37-41.

Hogan, D. R. The effectiveness of sex therapy: A review of the literature. In J. LoPiccolo & L. LoPiccolo (Eds.), *Handbook of sex therapy.* New York: Plenum Press, 1978.

Holden, C. Sex therapy: Making it as a science and an industry. *Science,* 1974, *186,* 330-334.

Hollander, X. *The happy hooker.* New York: Dell Books, 1972.

Hoon, E., Hoon, P., & Wincze, J. The SAI: An inventory for the measurement of female sexual arousal. *Archives of Sexual Behavior,* 1976, *10,* 234-240.

Hoon, P. W., Wincze, J. P., & Hoon, E. F. Physiological assessment of sexual arousal in women. *Psychophysiology,* 1976, *13,* 196-204.

Huff, F. W. The desensitization of a homosexual. *Behavior Research and Therapy,* 1970, *8,* 99-102.

Humphrey, L. Tearoom trade: Impersonal sex in public places. *Transaction,* 1970, *3,* 10-25.

Hunt, M. M. *Sexual behavior in the 1970s.* Chicago: Playboy Press, 1974.

Hunter, R., Logue, V., & McMenemy, W. H. Temporal lobe epilepsy supervening on longstanding transvestism and fetishism. *Epilepsia,* 1963, *4,* 60-65.

Husted, J. Desensitization procedures in dealing with women with sexual dysfunction. *The Counseling Psychologist,* 1975, *5,* 30–37.

Hyde, J. S. *Understanding human sexuality.* New York: McGraw-Hill, 1979.

Ince, L. Behavior modification and sexual disorders. *American Journal of Psychotherapy,* 1973, *27,* 446–451.

The International Drug Rx Newsletter, September 1966, *1,* 7.

Jackman, N. R., O'Toole, R., & Geis, G. The self-image of the prostitute. *Sociological Quarterly,* 1963, *4,* 150–161.

Jackson, B. A case of voyeurism treated by counterconditioning. *Behavior Research and Therapy,* 1969, *7,* 133–134.

Jackson, J. Prognosis of disorders of sexual potency in males. *Journal of Psychosexual Research,* 1960, *9,* 195–200.

Jacobsen, E. *Progressive relaxation* (2nd ed.). Chicago: University of Chicago Press, 1939.

Johnson, J. Prognosis of disorders of sexual potency in the male. *Journal of Psychosomatic Research,* 1968, *9,* 195–200.

Johnson, R. D. *Aggression in man and animals.* Philadelphia: W. B. Saunders, 1972.

Johnson, W. *People in quandaries.* New York: Harper & Row, 1964.

Jones, E. E. *Ingratiation: A social psychological analysis.* New York: Appleton-Century-Crofts, 1964.

Jones, W., & Park, P. Treatment of single-partner sexual dysfunction by systematic desensitization. *Obstetrics and Gynecology,* 1972, *39,* 411–417.

Jourard, S. M. *Self-disclosure.* New York: Wiley, 1971.

Kallman, F. J. Twin and sibship study of overt male homosexuality. *American Journal of Human Genetics,* 1953, *4,* 136–146.

Kanfer, F. H. Self-regulation: Research, issues and speculations. In C. Neuringer & J. Michael (Eds.), *Behavior modification in clinical psychology.* New York: Appleton-Century-Crofts, 1970.

Kanfer, J. H., & Phillips, J. S. *Learning foundations of behavior therapy.* New York: Wiley, 1970.

Kanin, E. J. Selected dyadic aspects of male sex aggression. *Journal of Sex Research,* 1969, *5,* 36–42.

Kaplan, H. S. *The new sex therapy.* New York: Brunner/Mazel, 1974.

Karacan, I. Advances in the psychophysiological evaluation of male erectile impotence. *Weekly Psychiatry Update Series,* 1977, *1,* 43.

Karacan I., Williams, R. L., & Guerrero, M. W. Nocturnal penile tumescence and sleep of convicted rapists and other prisoners. *Archives of Sexual Behavior,* 1974, *3,* 19–26.

Karpman, B. *The sexual offender and his offenses.* New York: Julian Press, 1959.

Katchadourian, H. A., & Lunde, D. T. *Fundamentals of human sexuality.* New York: Holt, Reinhart & Winston, 1972.

Kegel, A. Progressive resistance exercise in the functional restoration of the perineal muscles. *American Journal of Obstetrics and Gynecology,* 1948, *56,* 238–248.

Kegel, A. Stress incontinence and genital relaxation. *Ciba Clinical Symposia,* Feb.–

March 1952, *4,* 35–41.

Kegel, A. Early genital relaxation. *Obstetrics and Gynecology,* 1956, *8,* 545–550.

Kenyon, F. E. Studies in female homosexuality: Social and psychiatric aspects. *British Journal of Psychiatry,* 1968, *114,* 1337–1350.

Kercher, G. A., & Walker, C. E. Reactions of convicted rapists to sexually explicit stimuli. *Journal of Abnormal Psychology,* 1973, *81,* 46–50.

Kerchoff, A. Social class differences in sexual attitudes and behavior. *Medical Aspects of Human Sexuality,* 1974, *8,* 10–25.

Kiell, N. *Varieties of sexual experience.* New York: International Universities Press, 1976.

Kilmann, P. R., & Auerbach, R. Treatment of premature ejaculation and psychological impotence: A critical review of the literature. *Archives of Sexual Behavior,* 1979, *8,* 81–100.

Kinsey, A. C., Pomeroy, W. B., & Martin, C. E. *Sexual behavior in the human male.* Philadelphia: W. B. Saunders, 1948.

Kinsey, A. C., Pomeroy, W. B., Martin, C. E., & Gebhard, P. H. *Sexual behavior in the human female.* Philadelphia: W. B. Saunders, 1953.

Kline-Graber, G., & Graber, B. Diagnosis and treatment procedures of pubococcygeal deficiencies in women. In J. LoPiccolo & L. LoPiccolo (Eds.), *Handbook of sex therapy.* New York: Plenum Press, 1978.

Kulver, H., & Bucy, P. C. Preliminary analysis of functions of the temporal lobes in monkeys. *Archives of Neurology and Psychiatry,* 1939, *42,* 979–1000.

Kockett, G., Dittmar, F., & Nusselt, L. Systematic desensitization of erectile impotence. *Archives of Sexual Behavior,* 1975, *4,* 493–500.

Koegler, R. R., & Kline, L. Y. Psychotherapy research: An approach utilizing autonomic response measurement. *American Journal of Psychotherapy,* 1965, *19,* 268–279.

Kohlenberg, R. J. Treatment of a homosexual pedophiliac using in-vivo desensitization. *Journal of Abnormal Psychology,* 1974, *83,* 192–195.

Kolb, L. C. *Noyes' modern clinical psychiatry.* Philadelphia: W. B. Saunders, 1968.

Kolvin, I. Aversion imagery treatment in adolescents. *Behavior Research and Therapy,* 1967, *5,* 245–248.

Kopp, M. E. Surgical treatment as sex crime prevention measures. *Journal of Criminal Law,* 1962, *28,* 692–706.

Krapfl, J. Accountability for behavioral engineers. In W. S. Wood (Ed.), *Issues in evaluating behavior modification.* Champaign, Ill.: Research Press, 1975.

Kronhausen, E., & Kronhausen, P. *The sexually responsive woman.* New York: Ballantine Books, 1965.

Kurland, M. L. Pedophilia erotica. *Journal of Nervous and Mental Disease,* 1960, *131,* 394–403.

Kushner, M. The reduction of a long standing fetish by means of aversive conditioning. In E. P. Ullmann, & L. Krasner (Eds.), *Case histories in behavior modification.* New York: Wiley, 1965, 239–242.

Lacey, J. I., Bateman, D. E., & Van Lehn, R. Autonomic response specificity. *Psychosomatic Medicine,* 1953, *15,* 8–21.

Landsdell, H. C. A general intellectual factor affected by temporal lobe dysfunction. *Journal of Clinical Psychology,* 1971, *27,* 182–184.

Laner, M. R. Prostitution as an illegal vocation: A sociological overview. In C. D. Bryant (Ed.), *Deviant behavior: Occupational and organization basis.* New York: Clover, 1974.

Langley, J. C. Personal communication, March 1979.

Larson, D. E. An adaptation of the Feldman and MacCulloch approach to the treatment of homosexuality by the application of anticipatory avoidance learning. *Behavior Research and Therapy,* 1970, *8,* 209–210.

Lawrence, D. H. *Aaron's rod.* New York: Viking, 1923.

Laws, D., & Rubin, H. Instructional control of an autonomic sexual response. *Journal of Applied Behavior Analysis,* 1969, *2,* 93–100.

Laws, D. R., & Serber, M. Measurement and evaluation of assertive training with sexual offenders. In R. E. Hosford & C. E. Moss (Eds.), *The crumbling walls: Treatment and counseling of prisoners.* Champaign, Ill.: University of Illinois Press, 1975.

Lazarus, A. A. Overcoming sexual inadequacy. In A. A. Lazarus (Ed.), *Behavior therapy and beyond.* New York: McGraw-Hill, 1971.

Lehman, R. E. The disinhibiting effects of visual material in treating orgasmically dysfunctional women. *Behavior Engineering,* 1974, *1,* 1–3.

Levin, S. M., Barry, S. M., Gambaro, S., Wolfinsohn, L., & Smith, A. Variations of covert sensitization in the treatment of pedophilic behavior: A case study. *Journal of Consulting and Clinical Psychology,* 1977, *10,* 896–907.

Lewinsohn, R. *History of sexual customs.* New York: Harper & Row, 1958.

Lindgren, T. N., & Pauly, I. B. A body image scale for evaluating transsexuals. *Archives of Sexual Behavior,* 1975, *4,* 639–656.

Lloyd, C. W., & Weisz, J. Hormones and aggression. In W. S. Fields & W. H. Sweet (Eds.), *Neutral basis of violence and aggression.* St. Louis, Mo.: Warren Green, 1975.

Lobitz, W. C., & LoPiccolo, J. New methods in the behavioral treatment of sexual dysfunction. *Journal of Behavior Therapy and Experimental Psychiatry,* 1973, *3,* 265–272.

London, L. S. *Mental therapy: Studies in fifty cases.* New York: Couici-Friede, 1957.

London, L. S., & Caprio, F. S. *Sexual deviations.* Washington, D. C.: Linacre Press, 1950.

Loney, F. Family dynamics in homosexual women. *Archives of Sexual Behavior,* 1973, *2,* 343–350.

LoPiccolo, J. The professionalism of sex therapy: Issues and problems. *Society,* 1977, *14,* 60–68.

LoPiccolo, J. Direct treatment of sexual dysfunctions. In J. LoPiccolo & L. LoPiccolo (Eds.), *Handbook of sex therapy.* New York: Plenum Press, 1978.

LoPiccolo, J., & Heiman, J. R. Sexual assessment and history interview. In J. LoPiccolo and L. LoPiccolo (Eds.), *Handbook of sex therapy.* New York: Plenum Press, 1978.

LoPiccolo, J., & Lobitz, C. The role of masturbation in the treatment of orgasmic dysfunction. *Archives of Sexual Behavior,* 1972, *2,* 163–171.

LoPiccolo, J., & Steger, J. C. The sexual interaction inventory: A new instrument for assessment of sexual dysfunction. In J. LoPiccolo & L. LoPiccolo (Eds.), *Handbook of sex therapy.* New York: Plenum Press, 1974.

LoPiccolo, J., Stewart, R., & Watkins, B. Treatment of erectile failure and ejaculatory incompetence of homosexual etiology. *Journal of Behavior Therapy and Experimental Psychiatry,* 1972, *3,* 233–236.

Los Angeles Times. Women awarded damages in cable car sex accident. May 3, 1970.

Louys, P. *Aphrodite.* New York: Lancer Publishers, 1894.

Lovingbond, S. H. The mechanism of conditioning treatment of enuresis. *Behavior Research and Therapy,* 1963, *1,* 17–21.

Lowe, J. C., & Mikulus, W. L. Use of written material in learning self-control of premature ejaculation. *Psychological Reports,* 1975, *37,* 295–298.

Lowenstein, L. F. A case of exhibitionism treated by counterconditioning. *Adolescence,* 1973, *8,* 213–218.

Lukianowicz, N. Transvestism. *Journal of Nervous and Mental Disease,* 1959, *128,* 36–64.

Lyndon, S. The politics of orgasm. In N. Garskof (Ed.), *Roles women play.* Monterey, Calif: Brooks/Cole, 1971.

MacCulloch, M. J., Williams C., & Birtles, C. J. The successful application of aversion therapy to an adolescent exhibitionist. *Journal of Behavior Therapy and Experimental Psychiatry,* 1971, *2,* 61–66.

MacDonald, J. M. *Rape offenders and their victims.* Springfield, Ill.: Charles C Thomas, 1971.

MacDougald, D. Aphrodisiacs and anaphrodisiacs. In E. Ellis & A. Abarbanel (Eds.), *The encyclopedia of sexual behavior.* New York: Hawthorn, 1961.

MacNamara, D. E. Sex offenses and sex offenders. *American Academy of Political and Social Science,* 1968, *376,* 148–155.

Maletzky, B. M. "Assisted" covert sensitization in the treatment of exhibitionism. *Journal of Consulting and Clinical Psychology,* 1971, *42,* 34–40.

Maletzky, B. M. "Booster" sessions in aversion therapy: The permanency of treatment. *Behavior Therapy,* 1977, *8,* 460–463.

Maletzky, B. M., & George, F. S. The treatment of homosexuality by "assisted" covert sensitization. *Behavior Research and Therapy,* 1973, *11,* 655–657.

Margolis, H. F., & Rubenstein, P. M. *The group sex tapes.* New York: Paperback Library, 1971.

Marks, I., & Gelder, M. Transvestism and fetishism: Clinical and psychological change during faradic aversion. *British Journal of Psychiatry,* 1967, *113,* 711–729.

Marks, I. M., Rachman, S., & Gelder, M. G. Methods for assessment of aversion treatment in fetishism with masochism. *Behavior Research and Therapy,* 1965, *3,* 253–258.

Marquis, J. N. Orgasmic reconditioning: Changing sexual choice through controlling masturbatory fantasies. *Journal of Behavior Therapy and Experimental Psychiatry,* 1970, *1,* 263–271.

Marshall, W. L. A combined treatment method for certain sexual deviations. *Behavior Research and Therapy,* 1971, *9,* 293–294.

Marshall, W. L. The modification of sexual fantasies: A combined treatment approach to the reduction of deviant sexual behavior. *Behavior Research and Therapy,* 1973, *11,* 557–564.

Marshall, W. L., & Lippins, K. The clinical value of boredom: A procedure for reducing inappropriate sexual interests. *The Journal of Nervous and Mental Disease,* 1977, *165,* 283–287.

Marshall, W. L., & McKnight, R. D. An integrated treatment program for sexual offenders. *Canadian Psychiatric Association Journal,* 1975, *20,* 133–138.

Martinson, F. M. *Infant and child sexuality.* Privately published, 1973.

Martinson, W. D., & Zerface, J. P. Comparison of individual counseling and a social program with mandates. *Journal of Counseling Psychology,* 1970, *17,* 36–40.

Masserman, J. H., & Jacques, M. G. Experimental masochism. *Archives of Neurological Psychiatry,* 1948, *60,* 402–404.

Masters, W. H., & Johnson, V. E. *Human sexual response.* Boston: Little Brown, 1966.

Masters, W. H., & Johnson, V. E. *Human sexual inadequacy.* Boston: Little Brown, 1970.

Masters, W. H., and Johnson, V. E. Current status of the research programs. In J. Zubin, & J. Money (Eds.). *Contemporary sexual behavior: Critical issues of the 1970s.* Baltimore: Johns Hopkins University Press, 1977.

Masters, W. H., & Johnson, V. E. *Issues in homosexuality.* Boston: Little, Brown, 1979.

McBain, E. *Hail to the chief.* New York: Random House, 1973.

McCaghy, C. H. Drinking and deviance disavowal: The case of child molesters. *Social Problems,* 1968, *16,* 43–49.

McCary, J. L. *Human sexuality.* New York: Van Nostrand, 1973.

McConaghy, N. Penile volume changes to moving pictures of male and female nudes in heterosexual and homosexual males. *Behavior Research and Therapy,* 1967, *5,* 43–48.

McConaghy, N. Subjective and penile plethysmograph responses following aversion relief and apomorphive therapy for homosexual impulses. *British Journal of Psychiatry,* 1969, *115,* 723–730.

McConaghy, N. Penile response conditioning and its relationship to aversion therapy in homosexuals. *Behavior Therapy,* 1970, *1,* 213–221.

McConaghy, N. Measurements of change in penile dimensions. *Archives of Sexual Behavior,* 1974, *3,* 381–388.

McCrady, R. E. A forward-fading technique for increasing heterosexual responsiveness in male homosexuals. *Journal of Behavior Therapy and Experimental Psychiatry,* 1973, *4,* 257–261.

McDonald, M. L., Lindquist, C. U., Kramer, J. A., McGrath, R. A., & Rhyne, L. L. Social skills training: The effects of behavior rehearsal in groups on dating skills. *Journal of Counseling Psychology,* 1975, *22,* 224–230.

McGovern, K., Arkowitz, H., & Gilmore, S. Evaluation of social skills training programs for college dating inhibitions. *Journal of Counseling Psychology,* 1975, *22,* 505–512.

McGuire, R. J., Carlisle, J. M., & Young, B. A. Sexual deviation as conditioned behavior: A hypothesis. *Behavior Research and Therapy,* 1965, *2,* 185–190.

McGuire, R. J., & Valance, M. Aversion therapy by electric shock: A simple technique. *British Medical Journal,* 1964, *1,* 151–153.

McMenemy, D. E. Sex offenses and sex offenders. *American Academy of Political and Social Science,* 1963, *376,* 148–155.

Medea, B. R., & Thompson, K. *Against rape.* New York: Farrar, Straus, & Giroux, 1974.

Mees, H. L. Sadistic fantasies modified by aversion conditioning and substitution: A case study. *Behavior Research and Therapy,* 1966, *4,* 317–320.

Melnick, J. A comparison of replication techniques in the modification of minimal dating behavior. *Journal of Abnormal Psychology,* 1973, *81,* 51–59.

Merrill, G. B., & Swanson, D. T. Generalizations on therapeutic gains in the treatment of premature ejaculation. *Behavior Therapy,* 1976, *7,* 355–358.

Miller, W. W. Afrodex in the treatment of impotence: A double-blind cross over study. *Current Therapeutic Research,* 1968, *10,* 354–359.

Mindlin, E. Nymphomania and satyriasis. In C. Wahl (Ed.), *Sexual problems: Diagnosis and treatment in medical practice.* New York: Free Press, 1967.

Mintz, M. H. Psychodiagnostic follow-up of a juvenile sex murderer. *Psychoanalytic Review,* 1966, *50,* 93–113.

Mischel, W. *Personality and assessment.* New York: Wiley, 1968.

Mohr, J. W. The pedophilias: Their clinical, social, and legal implications. *Canadian Psychiatric Association Journal,* 1962, *7,* 255–260.

Mohr, J. W., & Turner, R. E. Sexual deviations Part IV—Pedophilia. *Applied Therapeutics,* 1967, *9,* 362–365.

Mohr, J., Turner, E. R., & Ball, R. B. Exhibitionism and pedophilia. *Corrective Psychiatric Journal of Social Therapy,* 1962, *8,* 172–186.

Mohr, J., Turner, E. R., & Jerry, M. *Pedophilia and exhibitionism.* Toronto: Toronto University Press, 1964.

Money, J. Use of an adrogen-depleting hormone in the treatment of male sex offenders. *Journal of Sex Research,* 1970, *6,* 165–172.

Money, J. Human behavior cytogenics: Review of psychopathology in three syndromes—47, XXY; 47, XYY; and 45, X. *Journal of Sex Research,* 1975, *11,* 181–200.

Money, J., & Brennan, J. G. Sexual dimorphism in the psychology of female transsexuals. *Journal of Nervous and Mental Disease,* 1968, *147,* 487–499.

Money, J., & Ehrhardt, A. *A man and woman, boy and girl.* Baltimore: Johns Hopkins University Press, 1972.

Money, J., & Primrose, C. Sexual dimorphism and dissociation in the psychology of male transsexuals. *Journal of Nervous and Mental Disease,* 1968, *147,* 472–486.

Moore, J. E. Problematic sexual behavior. In C. Broderick & J. Bernard (Eds.), *The individual, sex and society.* Baltimore: Johns Hopkins University Press, 1969.

Montague, J. D., & Coles, E. M. Mechanism and measurement of the galvanic skin response. *Psychological Bulletin,* 1966, *65,* 261–279.

Morales, P. A., Ducrez, J. B., Delgado, J., & Whitehead, E. D. Penile implants after erectile impotence. *Urology,* 1973, *109,* 641–646.

More, J. *The use of videotapes and film in sex therapy.* Paper presented at the 81st

Annual Convention of the American Psychological Association, Montreal, 1973.

Morganstern, K. P., & Pierce, J. Implosive therapy and flooding procedures: A critical review. *Psychological Bulletin,* 1973, *79,* 318–334.

Morganstern, F. S., Pierce, J. F., & Linford-Rees, W. Predicting the outcome of behavior therapy by psychological tests. *Behavior Research and Therapy,* 1965, *3,* 191–200.

Newell, A. G. A case of ejaculatory incompetence tested with a mechanical aid. *Journal of Behavior Therapy and Experimental Psychiatry,* 1976, *7,* 193–194.

New Jersey Commission on the Habitual Sex Offender. New Jersey State Report, 1965.

Newton, E. *Mother Camp: Female impersonators in America.* Englewood Cliffs, N. J.: Prentice-Hall, 1972.

Norman, L. E., Bell, A. J., & Hall, B. A. Transsexualism in adolescence: Problems in evaluation and treatment. *Archives of General Psychiatry,* 1971, *23,* 112–121.

Nunnally, G. C., Knot, P. D., Duchnowski, A., & Parker, R. Pupillary response as a general measure of activation. *Perception and Psychophysics,* 1968, *2,* 149–155.

Obler, M. Systematic desensitization in sexual disorders. *Journal of Behavior Therapy and Experimental Psychiatry,* 1973, *4,* 93–101.

Offir, C. W. Don't take it lying down. *Psychology Today,* January, 1975, 70–76.

Oliver, J. F. *Clinical sexuality.* New York: Lippincott, 1974.

Osborne, C. A., & Pollak, R. H. The effects of two types of erotic literature on physiological and verbal measures of female sexual arousal. *The Journal of Sex Research,* 1977, *13,* 250–256.

Packer, H. L. *The limits of the criminal sanction.* Stanford, Calif.: Stanford University Press, 1968.

Palson, C., & Palson, R. Swinging in wedlock. *Society,* 1972, *4,* 38–43.

Parker, T. *The twisting lane: The hidden world of sex offenders.* London: Hutchinson & Co., 1972.

Paul, G. L. Outcome of systematic desensitization: Background, procedures, and uncontrolled reports of individual treatment. In C. M. Franks (Ed.), *Behavior therapy: Appraisal and status.* New York: McGraw-Hill, 1969.

Pauley, I. B. Male psychosexual inversion: Transsexualism, a review of 100 cases. *Archives of General Psychiatry,* 1965, *13,* 172–181.

Pauley, I. B. The current status of the change of sex operation. *Journal of Nervous and Mental Disease,* 1968, *147,* 460–471.

Paykel, B., & Weissman, M. Marital and sexual dysfunction in depressed women. *Medical Aspects of Human Sexuality,* 1972, *6,* 73–101.

Peabody, G. A., Row, B., & Wall, E. Fetishism and transvestism. *Journal of Nervous and Mental Disease, 118,* 339–350, 1953.

Penthouse. Penthouse forum, October 1977, 102–105.

Peterson, D. R. *The clinical study of social behavior.* New York: Appleton-Century-Crofts, 1968.

Podell, L., & Perkins, J. A Guttman Scale for sexual exposure—a methodological note. *Journal of Abnormal Social Psychology,* 1957, *54,* 420–422.

President's Commission on Law Enforcement and Administration of Justice. *The challenge of crime in a free society.* Washington, D.C.: U. S. Government Printing Office, 1967.

Prince, V., & Bentler, P. M. Survey of 504 cases of transvestism. *Psychological Report,* 1972, *31,* 903–917.

Quinn, J. T., Harbinson, J. J., & McAllister, H. An attempt to shape penile response. *Behavior Research and Therapy,* 1970, *8,* 212–216.

Quinsey, V. L. The assessment and treatment of child molesters: A review. *Canadian Psychological Review,* 1977, *18,* 204–220.

Quinsey, V. L., & Bergersen, S. G. Instructional control of penile circumference. *Behavior Therapy,* 1976, *7,* 489–493.

Quinsey, V. L., Bergersen, S. G., & Steinman, C. M. Changes in physiological and verbal responses of child molesters during aversion therapy. *Canadian Journal of Behavioral Science,* 1976, *8,* 202–212.

Rabban, M. Sex-role identification in young children in two diverse social groups. *Genetic Psychology Monographs,* 1970, *42,* 81–158.

Rachman, S. Sexual fetishism: An experimental analogue. *Psychological Record,* 1966, *16,* 293–296.

Rachman, S. J., & Hodgson, R. J. Experimentally induced sexual fetishism: Replication and development. *Psychological Record,* 1968, *18,* 25–27.

Rachman, S., & Teasdale, J. *Aversion therapy and behaviour disorders: An analysis.* London: Routledge & Kegan Paul, 1969.

Rada, R. T. Classification of a rapist. In R. T. Rada (Ed.), *Clinical aspects of the rapist.* New York: Grune & Stratton, 1978.

Rada, R. T., Laws, D. R., & Kellner, R. Plasma testosterone levels in the rapist. *Psychosomatic Medicine,* 1967, *38,* 257–268.

Radzinowicz, L. *Sexual offenses.* London: MacMillan, 1957.

Raphling, D. L., Carpenter, B. L., & Davis, A. Incest. *Archives of General Psychiatry,* 1967, *16,* 505–511.

Rasmussen, P. K., & Kuhn, L. H. The new masseuse: Play for pay. *Urban Life: Special issue on sexuality: Encounter, identification, and relationships,* October 1976.

Raymond, M. J. Case of fetishism treated by aversion therapy. *British Medical Journal,* 1956, *2,* 854–857.

Raymond, M., & O'Keefe, K. A case of pin-up fetishism treated by aversion conditioning. *British Journal of Psychiatry,* 1965, *111,* 579–581.

Razani, J. Ejaculatory incompetence treated by deconditioning anxiety. *Journal of Behavior Therapy and Experimental Psychiatry,* 1972, *3,* 65–67.

Rechy, J. *City of night.* New York: Grove Press, 1963.

Rechy, J. *Numbers.* New York: Grove Press, 1967.

Reckless, J., & Geiger, N. Impotence as a practical problem. In H. F. Dowling (Ed.), *Disease-a-month.* Chicago: Year Book Medical Publishers, 1975.

Rehm, L. P., & Marston, A. R. Reduction of social anxiety through modification of self reinforcement. *Journal of Consulting and Clinical Psychology,* 1968, *32,* 565–574.

Reitz, W. E., & Keil, W. E. Behavioral treatment of an exhibitionist. *Journal of Behavior Therapy and Experimental Psychiatry*, 1971, *2*, 67–69.

Rekers, G. A. Pathological sex-role development in boys: Behavioral treatment and assessment. *Dissertation Abstracts International*, 1972, *33*, 3321B.

Rekers, G. A. Atypical gender development and psychosocial adjustment. *Journal of Applied Behavior Analysis*, 1977, *6*, 275–277.

Rekers, G. A., Amaro-Plotkin, B., & Low, B. The behavioral treatment of a transsexual preadolescent boy. *Journal of Abnormal Child Psychology*, 1977, *2*, 99–116.

Rekers, G. A., & Lovaas, O. I. Behavioral treatment of deviant sex role behavior in a male child. *Journal of Applied Behavioral Analysis*, 1974, *7*, 173–190.

Rekers, G. A., & Varni, J. W. Self monitoring and self reinforcement processes in a pre-transsexual boy. *Behavior Research and Therapy*, 1977, *16*, 42–50.

Rekers, G. A., & Yates, C. E. Sex-typed play in feminoid boys vs. normal boys and girls. *Journal of Abnormal Child Psychology*, 1976, *4*, 1–8.

Rekers, G. A., Yates, C. E., Willis, T. J. Rosen, A. C., & Taubman, M. Childhood gender identity change: Operant control over sex-typed play and mannerisms. *Journal of Behavior Therapy and Experimental Psychiatry*, 1976, *7*, 51–57.

Renick, J. T. *The use of films and videotapes in the treatment of sexual dysfunctions.* Paper presented at the 81st Annual Convention of the American Psychological Association, Montreal, 1973.

Renshaw, D. C. I'm just not interested in sex, doctor. *Human Sexuality*, May 1978, 37–41.

Reproductive Biology Research Foundation. *Ethical guidelines for sex therapists.* St. Louis, Mo.: Reproductive Biology Research Foundation, 1978.

Revitch, E., & Weiss, R. G. The pedophiliac offender. *Diseases of the Nervous System*, 1962, *23*, 73–78.

Rimm, D., & Somerville, J. W. *Abnormal psychology.* New York: Academic Press, 1977.

Roesler, T., & Deisher, R. W. Youthful male homosexuality. *Journal of the American Medical Association*, 1972, *219*, 1018–1023.

Roessler, R., & Collins, F. *Physiological responses to sexually arousing motion pictures.* Paper presented at the Ninth Annual Meeting of the Society for Psychological Research, Monterey, Calif., 1968.

Romano, K. *Psychophysiological responses to a sexual and an unpleasant motion picture.* Unpublished thesis, University of Manitoba, Canada, 1969.

Rooth, M. Psychiatric aspects of intersexuality. In C. N. Armstrong & A. J. Marshall (Eds.), *Intersexuality of vertebrates including man.* London: Academic Press, 1969.

Rooth, F. G., & Marks, I. M. Persistent exhibitionism: Short-term response to aversion, self-regulation, and relaxation treatment. *Archives of Sexual Behavior*, 1974, *3*, 227–243.

Rose, R. M. Testosterone, aggression, and homosexuality: A review of the literature and implications for future research. In E. J. Sachar (Ed.), *Topics in pseudoendocrinology.* New York: Grune & Stratton, 1975.

Rosen, A. C., & Rehm, L. P. Long-term follow-up in two cases of transvestism treated with aversion therapy. *Journal of Behavior Therapy and Experimental*

Psychiatry, 1977, *8,* 295–300.

Rosen, A. C., Rekers, G. A., & Friar, L. R. Theoretical and diagnostic issues in child gender disturbances. *Journal of Sex Research,* 1977, *4,* 120–128.

Rosen, H. S. *A survey of the sexual attitudes and behavior of mate-swappers in Houston, Texas.* Unpublished thesis, University of Houston, 1971.

Rosenblatt, C., & Pariente, B. J. The prostitution of the criminal law. *American Criminal Law Review,* 1973, *11,* 373–427.

Rossman, P. The pederasts. *Society 10,* 1973, *29,* 22–24.

Roth, M. Electroconvulsive therapy. *Journal of Mental Sciences,* 1952, *98,* 44–45.

Rubenstein, H. S. The effects of testosterone propionate on spermatogenesis in the human. *Journal of Southern Medicine,* 1958, *32,* 499–503.

Ruitenbeek, H. M. *The new sexuality.* New York: New Viewpoints, 1974.

Sacher-Masoch, A. *Confessions de ma vie avec deux portraits.* Paris, 1907.

Sadger, J. *Die lehre von geschlechtsverirrungen.* Vienna: Brezona, 1921.

Sagarin, E. Power to the peephole. *Sexual Behavior,* 1973, *3,* 2–7.

Salter, A. *Conditioned reflex therapy, the direct approach to the reconstruction of personality* (2nd ed.). New York: Creative Press, 1961.

Sandler, M., & Gessa, G. L. *Sexual behavior: Pharmacology and biochemistry.* New York: Raven Books, 1975.

Sayner, R., & Durrell, D. Multiple behavior therapy techniques in the treatment of sexual dysfunctions. *The Counseling Psychologist,* 1975, *5,* 38–41.

Schaefer, H. H. Self injurious behavior: Shaping head banging in monkeys. *Journal of Applied Behavior Analysis,* 1970, *3,* 111–116.

Schatzberg, A. F., Westfall, M. P., Blumetti, A. B., & Birk, C. L. Effeminacy I: A quantitative rating scale. *Archives of Sexual Behavior,* 1975, *4,* 31–41.

Schumacher, S., & Lloyd, C. W. Assessment of sexual dysfunction. In M. Hersen & A. S. Bellack (Eds.), *Behavioral assessment.* Oxford: Pergamon Press, 1976.

Schuster, L. R. Treatment of impotence by behavior modification techniques. *Journal of Sex Research,* 1976, *9,* 226–240.

Scott, L. Sexuality: Changing standards. *Time,* May 1958, 50.

Scott, T. R., Wells, W. H., Wood, D. Z., & Morgan, D. I. Pupillary responses and sexual interest reexamined. *Journal of Clinical Psychology,* 1967, *23,* 433–438.

Selkin, J. Rape. *Psychology Today.* January, 1975.

Semans, J. H. Premature ejaculation: A new approach. *Journal of Southern Medicine,* 1956, *49,* 353–361.

Serber, M. Shame aversion therapy. *Journal of Behavior Therapy and Experimental Psychiatry,* 1970, *1,* 213–215.

Serber, M. Videotape feedback in the treatment of couples with sexual dysfunction. *Archives of Sexual Behavior,* 1974, *3,* 377–380.

Serber, M., & Keith, C. G. The Atascadero Project: Model of a sexual retraining program for incarcerated homosexual pedophiles. *Journal of Homosexuality,* 1974, *1,* 87–97.

Shapiro, A., Cohen, H. D., DiBianco, D., & Rosen, G. Vaginal blood flow changes during sleep and sexual arousal. *Psychophysiology,* 1968, *4,* 394–399.

Shavers, K. G. *An introduction to attribution processes*. Boston: Winthrop Press, 11975.

Sherfey, M. J. *The nature and evolution of female sexuality*. New York: Random House, 1966.

Silverstein, C. *Behavior modification and the gay community*. Paper presented at the meeting of the Association for the Advancement of Behavior Therapy. New York, October 1972.

Simpson, G. M., Blane, J. H., & Amoso, D. Effect of antidepressants on genito-urinary function. *Diseases of the Nervous System*, 1965, *26*, 787–788.

Singer, J., & Singer, I. Types of female orgasms. *Journal of Sex Research*, 1972, *8*, 255–267.

Sintchak, G., & Geer, J. H. A vaginal plethysmograph system. *Psychophysiology*, 1975, *12*, 113–115.

Skinner, B. F. *Walden II*. New York: MacMillan, 1948.

Skinner, B. F. *Science and human behavior*. New York: MacMillan, 1953.

Skipper, J., & McCaghy, C. Stripteasers: The anatomy and career contingencies of a deviant occupation. *Social Problems*, 1969, *17*, 391–405.

Slovenko, R. *Sexual behavior and the law*. Springfield, Ill.: Charles C Thomas, 1965.

Sobotka, J. J. An evaluation of Afrodex in the management of male potency: A double-blind cross over study. *Current Therapeutic Research*, 1969, *11*, 87–94.

Socarides, C. W. Meaning and content of pedophiliac perversion. *Journal of the American Psychoanalytic Association*, 1959, *7*, 84–94.

Socarides, C. W. Theoretical and clinical aspects of overt female homosexuality. *Journal of the American Psychoanalytic Association*, 1962, *10*, 579–592.

Socarides, C. W. A psychoanalytic study of the desire for sexual transformation. *International Journal of Psychoanalysis*, 1977, *51*, 341–349.

Solomon, P., & Patch, V. D. *Handbook of psychiatry*. Los Altos, Calif.: Lange Medical Publications, 1974.

Solyom, L., & Beck, P. R. GSR assessment of aberrant sexual behavior. *International Journal of Neuropsychiatry*, 1967, *3*, 52–59.

Spanier, G. B., & Cole, C. L. Mate swapping: Perceptions, value orientations and participation in a midwestern community. *Archives of Sexual Behavior*, 1975, *4*, 143–159.

Speeling, M. The analysis of an exhibitionist. *International Journal of Psychoanalysis*, 1947, *28*, 32–45.

Stekel, W. *Sadism and masochism*, Vol. I. New York: Liveright, 1953.

Stevenson, I., & Wolfe, J. Recovery from sexual deviations through overcoming nonsexual neurotic responses. *American Journal of Psychiatry*, 1960, *116*, 739–742.

Stroller, R. J. Transvestities' women. *American Journal of Psychiatry*, 1967, *124*, 333–339.

Stroller, R. J. The term "transvestism." *Archives of General Psychiatry*, 1971, *24*, 230–237.

Stroller, R. J. Referenced personal communication in Barlow, D. H. The treatment of sexual deviation: Toward a comprehensive behavior approach. In K. S. Calhoun, H. E. Adams, & K. M. Mitchell (Eds.), *Innovative treatment methods in psychopathology.* New York: Wiley, 1974.

Stroller, R. J. A contribution to the study of gender identity. *International Journal of Psychoanalysis,* 1964, *45,* 220-226.

Stroller, R. J. Passing in the continuum of gender identity. In J. Marmer (Ed.), *Sexual inversion: The multiple roots of homosexuality.* New York: Basic Books, 1965.

Sturgis, E. T., & Adams, H. E. The right to treatment: Issues in the treatment of homosexuality. *Journal of Consulting and Clinical Psychology,* 1978, *46,* 165-169.

Sutherland, S., & Scherl, D. L. Patterns of response among victims of rape. *American Journal of Orthopsychiatry,* 1970, *49,* 503-511.

Sutton-Smith, B., Rosenberg, B. G., & Morgan, E. R. Development of sex differences in play choices during preadolescence. *Child Development,* 1963, *34,* 119-126.

Sviland, M. A. Helping elderly couples become sexually liberated: Psychosocial issues. *The Counseling Psychologist,* 1975, *5,* 67-72.

Swanson, D. W. Adult sexual abuse of children: The man and circumstances. *Diseases of the Nervous System,* 1968, *29,* 677-683.

Synder, A., LoPiccolo, L., & LoPiccolo, J. Secondary orgasmic dysfunction: Case study. *Archives of Sexual Behavior,* 1975, *4,* 277-283.

Tanner, B. A. Avoidance training with and without booster sessions to modify homosexual behavior in males. *Behavior Therapy,* 1975, *6,* 649-653.

Taylor, F. H. Homosexual offenses and their relation to psychotherapy. *British Medical Journal,* 1947, 525-529.

Tennent, G., Bancroft, J., & Cass, J. The control of deviant sexual behavior by drugs: A double blind control study of benperidol, chlorpromazine, and placebo. *Archives of Sexual Behavior,* 1974, *3,* 261-271.

Terman, L. M., & Miles, C. *Sex and personality: Studies in masculinity and femininity.* New York: London, 1936.

Terrance, H. S. Stimulus control. In W. K. Honig (Ed.), *Operant behavior: Areas of research and application.* New York: Appleton-Century-Crofts, 1966.

Thompson, G. N. Electroshock and other therapeutic considerations in sexual psychopathology. *Journal of Nervous and Mental Disorders,* 1949, *109,* 531-539.

Thompson, G. N. Electroshock and other therapeutic considerations in sexual psychopathy. *Journal of Nervous and Mental Diseases,* 1955, *109,* 531-539.

Thorpe, L. P., Katz, B., & Lewis, R. T. *Psychology of abnormal behavior.* New York: Ronald Press, 1961.

Thorpe, J. G., Schmidt, E., Brown, T. T., & Castell, D. Aversion relief therapy: A new method for general application. *Behavior Research and Therapy,* 1964, *2,* 71-82.

Thorpe, J. G., Schmidt, E., & Castell, D. A comparison of positive and negative (aversive) conditioning in the treatment of homosexuality. *Behavior Research and Therapy,* 1963, *1,* 357-362.

Tollison, C. D., Adams, H. E., & Tollison, J. W. *Physiological measurement of sexual arousal in homosexual, bisexual, and heterosexual males.* Unpublished manuscript, University of Georgia, 1977.

Tollison, C. D., Nesbitt, J. G., & Frye, J. D. Comparison of attitudes toward sexual intimacy in prostitutes and college coeds. *Journal of Social Psychology,* 1975, *6,* 316-318.

Twentyman, C. T., & McFall, R. M. Behavioral training of social skills in shy males. *Journal of Consulting and Clinical Psychology,* 1975, *43,* 384-395.

Ullerstam, L. *The erotic minorities.* New York: Grove Press, 1970.

Valenstein, E. S. *Brain control.* New York: Wiley, 1973.

Varnie, C. A. An exploratory study of spouse-swapping. *Pacific Society Review,* 1972, *15,* 507-522.

Vetter, H. J. *Psychology of abnormal behavior.* New York: Ronald Press, 1972.

Vidal, G. *Myra Breckenridge.* Boston: Little Brown, 1968.

Walen, S., Hauserman, N. M., & Lavin, P. J. *Clinical guide to behavior therapy.* Baltimore: Williams & Wilkins, 1977.

Wallender, J. *Transsexualism: A study of 43 cases.* Goteborg, Sweden: Scandinavian University Books, 1965.

Warren, C. A. *Identity and community in the gay world.* New York: Wiley, 1974.

Watson, D., & Friend, R. Measurement of social-evaluative anxiety. *Journal of Consulting and Clinical Psychology,* 1969, *33,* 448-457.

Weinberg, J. Sexuality in later life. *Medical Aspects of Human Sexuality,* 1971, *216,* 226-227.

Wenger, M. A., Averill, J. R., & Smith, D. B. Autonomic activity during sexual arousal. *Psychophysiology,* 1968, *4,* 468-478.

Wickramasekera, I. The application of learning theory to a case of sexual exhibitionism. *Psychotherapy: Theory, research and practice,* 1968, *5,* 108-112.

Wile, I. S. Sex offenders and sex offenses: Classification and treatment. *Journal of Criminal Psychopathology,* 1941, *3,* 11-31.

Williams, M. H. *Individual sex therapy.* Paper presented to the Second Annual Meeting of the Eastern Association for Sex Therapy, Philadelphia, March 1976.

Wilson, C. *Origins of the sexual impulse.* New York: G. P. Putnam, 1963.

Wilson, G. T., & Davison, G. C. Behavior therapy and homosexuality: A critical perspective. *Behavior Therapy,* 1974, *5,* 16-28.

Wincze, J. Sexual deviance and dysfunction. In D. Rimm & J. W. Somerville, (Eds.), *Abnormal psychology.* New York: Academic Press, 1977.

Wincze, J. P., & Caird, W. K. *A comparison of systematic desensitization and video desensitization in the treatment of sexual frigidity.* Paper presented at the Association for the Advancement of Behavior Therapy, Miami, Florida, December 1973.

Winick, C., & Kinsie, P. M. Prostitution. *Sexual behavior,* 1971, *3,* 36-39.

Witzig, J. S. The group treatment of male exhibitionists. *American Journal of Psychiatry,* 1970, *125,* 179-185.

Wolff, C. *Love between women.* New York: Harper & Row, 1971.

Wolpe, J. *Psychotherapy by reciprocal inhibition.* Stanford, Calif.: Stanford University Press, 1958.

Wolpe, J. *The practice of behavior therapy* (2nd ed.). New York: Pergamon Press, 1973.

Wolpe, J., & Lazarus, A. A. *Behavior therapy techniques: A guide to the treatment of neuroses.* New York: Pergamon Press, 1966.

Wood, J. D., & Obrist, R. E. A study of orgasm as a condition of women's enjoyment of coitus in the middle years of marriage. *Human Behavior,* 1968, *35,* 131–139.

Woolston, H. B. *Prostitution in the United States.* Montclair, N.J.: Patterson Smith, 1969.

Wright, B. Membership form. *Better life monthly,* 1975.

Wykert, J. Ethics in sex therapy. *Psychiatric News,* October, 1977, *12,* 38.

Yalom, I., Green, R., & Fisk, N. Prenatal exposure to female hormones: Effect on psychosexual development in boys. *Archives of General Psychiatry,* 1973, *28,* 554–561.

Yates, A. *Behavior therapy.* New York: Wiley, 1970.

Young, W. Prostitution. In J. D. Douglas (Ed.), *Observation of defiance.* New York: Random House, 1970.

Young, W. C., Goy, R. W., & Phoenix, C. H. Hormones and sexual behavior. *Science,* 1964, *143,* 212–218.

Yulis, S. Generalization of therapeutic gain in the treatment of premature ejaculation. *Behavior Therapy,* 1967, *7,* 355–358.

Zajonc, R. B. Attitudinal effects of mere exposure. *Journal of Personality and Social Psychology,* 1968, *8,* Monograph 19, 1–29.

Zeiss, A. M., Rosen, G. M., & Zeiss, R. A. Orgasm during intercourse: A treatment strategy for women. *Journal of Consulting and Clinical Psychology,* 1977, *45,* 891–895.

Zuckerman, M. Physiological measures of sexual arousal in the human. *Psychological Bulletin,* 1971, *75,* 297–329.

Author Index

Subject Index